Marketing in Travel and Tourism

About the principal author

Professor Victor Middleton has some thirty years of international experience of marketing practice. Commencing his career with two international blue chip f.m.c.g. companies and a national tourist board, he has worked directly with The European Commission, Governments in the UK and elsewhere, national and regional tourist offices in many countries and with local authorities. He has extensive experience with visitor attractions, especially in the heritage field, and with hotel and other accommodation interests. His research interests encompass sustainable development, market research, visitor management, cultural strategies and the role of small businesses – within an overall concept of customer orientation and the values of a marketing philosophy.

A full time academic at the University of Surrey for twelve years, he was among the first in Europe to lecture in tourism marketing. A Founder Fellow and former Chairman of the UK Tourism Society, he has been an independent management consultant in tourism since 1984. He combines running his own 'micro-business' with writing books and his Visiting Professorships at Oxford Brookes University and the University of Central Lancashire. Well known on the international conference circuit, his articles, books, contributed chapters and other publications number well over one hundred.

By the same author in recent years

Sustainable Tourism: A marketing perspective (with Rebecca Hawkins) (1998)
Measuring the Local Impact of Tourism (1996)
New Visions for Museums in the 21st Century (1998)
New Visions for Independent Museums in the UK (1989)
Review of Tourism Studies Degree Courses in the UK (1993)

Marketing in Travel and Tourism

Third edition

Victor T. C. Middleton
with Jackie Clarke

OXFORD AUCKLAND BOSTON JOHANNESBURG MELBOURNE NEW DELHI

Butterworth-Heinemann
Linacre House, Jordan Hill, Oxford OX2 8DP
225 Wildwood Avenue, Woburn, MA 01801-2041
A division of Reed Educational and Professional Publishing Ltd

℞ A member of the Reed Elsevier plc group

First published 1988
Reprinted 1988, 1989, 1990, 1992, 1993
Second edition 1994
Reprinted 1995 (twice), 1996, 1997, 1998, 2000
Third edition 2001

British Library Cataloguing in Publication Data
Middleton, Victor T. C.
   Marketing in travel and tourism. – 3rd ed.
   1. Tourist trade – Marketing
   I. Title   II. Clarke, Jackie
   338.4'791'0688

ISBN 0 7506 4471 0

Composition by Genesis Typesetting, Rochester, Kent
Printed and bound in Great Britain by MPG Books Ltd, Bodmin

Contents

Foreword

Marketing is more than ever the primary focus for management in the globally competitive conditions of twenty-first century travel and tourism. It influences the entire business as a corporate response embracing both boardroom and front line staff. It is equally relevant in helping not-for-profit organizations to meet their customer/users' needs.

The third edition of this highly readable text addresses the 'world's largest industry' as an entity in which the whole is greater than the parts. Identifying the different roles of globally branded players as well as millions of micro enterprises in tourism, it defines the coherent role of customer orientation and the strategic and tactical responses of marketing in all its modern aspects. Referring and drawing throughout on contributions of internationally recognized authors, it explains the concepts within a wholly practical and forward-looking framework and a clear focus on revenue generation, cost control and profitability that reflects current industry preoccupations. The book will be relevant internationally to industry practitioners as well as to the thousands of students now entering the field.

I endorse the close attention that the authors pay throughout to explaining the thought processes through which marketing decisions are made. The book's emphasis on the way the Internet is fast changing traditional approaches to marketing in the new century, and its recognition of the need to build sustainability into product development, are timely and appropriate.

Systematic thinking and the collection of appropriate data are the bases for better decision-making in travel and tourism as it is in other industries. But it is a far from perfect process and the big decisions invariably reflect judgement backed by experience. Marketing is very much an evolving body of knowledge, as much art as science, repaying continuous re-evaluation. Above all it is a learning process that daily redefines the leading edge of business practice. This book reflects that re-evaluation process and I am pleased to commend it to readers.

Martin Brackenbury
Director of Airtours, President of
the International Federation of
Tour Operators and Chairman
of the World Tourism Organization
Business Council

Preface

It is now over twelve years since the first edition of this book was published. As every author knows, any book is a leap in the dark. One can hope but one cannot know in advance how readers will receive it. In fact *Marketing in Travel and Tourism* has been sold internationally to tens of thousands of readers, translated into three different languages, endorsed as essential reading on hundreds of courses and reprinted annually (twelve times so far) to meet demand. For the third edition, encouraged by reviews and by many people in several countries, the book has been developed to reflect the global marketing conditions of the twenty-first century. Dr Jackie Clarke of Oxford Brookes University joined the principal author in the preparation of this edition and we share an enthusiasm for the subject of tourism marketing that we hope is transparent.

The information in each chapter has been updated and the content revised. Although the structure of the book remains essentially as before because it clearly works for readers, new material has been added to all chapters, diagrams have been modified and up-to-date illustrations from practice included. In particular, the new edition reflects:

- The rapid growth in volume of more experienced, demanding and sophisticated customers for travel and tourism products whose expectations drive marketing developments.
- The remarkable growth of courses and books on various aspects of tourism marketing that increases the need for a cohesive, holistic understanding of the subject.
- Growing recognition that the full cost of marketing in many sectors of travel and tourism is between 20 and 30 per cent of sales revenue – often the largest target for cost and efficiency savings.
- The growing role of information and communications technology (ICT), especially the Internet, that now influences so many aspects of marketing strategy, planning and the communications mix. Integrated within the text, ICT also has its own chapter (Chapter 10) and is central to the case studies.

- The coming to terms with the environmental implications of travel and tourism growth and what the private sector in particular can and should do about it.

The Epilogue, which offers views on the future for travel and tourism marketing, has been completely rewritten for worldwide travel and tourism in the context of new markets in the new post-industrial economy and the realities of greater competition in the leading tourism countries in the next decade.

Since the 1990s, academic contributions have sought to develop the subject on as many dimensions as there are aspects of travel and tourism marketing. Many adopt a linguistic complexity that is confusing and often impenetrable to practitioners and most students. The authors of this book have no such ambitions. We believe a textbook should aim to explain and illustrate the essential principles in a clear, unambiguous style – simplifying as far as possible and relating the principles within a carefully structured and integrated framework. What is difficult to read is difficult to understand and its utility in the real world is marginalized. We wish this edition to be read and enjoyed by thousands of students and practitioners of tourism marketing all over the world, as its predecessors clearly have been.

Structure and contents

The book is presented in six parts. The structure is designed to follow a logical development of the subject although, as every manager knows, marketing is a circular rather than a linear process with many feedback loops. As far as possible, the parts are designed to be reasonably self-explanatory, with the intention that lecturers and students can fit the chapters into whatever pattern the logic of their courses suggests.

Part One defines travel and tourism and the sectors within the industry that are referred to throughout the book. The subject of marketing is introduced, especially for those who are coming new to the subject, and the characteristics of travel and tourism to which marketing responds are explained. This part of the book also explains the factors in the external business environment that influence demand and customers' purchasing behaviour.

Part Two reviews the four Ps of the standard marketing mix and the seven Ps of services marketing theory in the travel and tourism context, noting their significance for all marketing managers engaged in strategic and tactical decision-making.

Part Three commences with a new Chapter 10 that summarizes the growing use of ICT in tourism, stressing the way it influences all aspects of marketing, not just distribution. This leads into planning for marketing and deals with marketing research, marketing strategy and tactics, and the process for planning and budgeting for marketing campaigns.

Part Four deals with each of the main communication tools or functions used in marketing practice to achieve planned goals and targets. It emphasizes the roles of printed and electronic information, distribution and direct marketing, which are especially important in travel and tourism. The growing significance of distribution as the focus for marketing mix decisions is identified.

Part Five analyses the meaning and application in practice of marketing in the five main sectors of travel and tourism using a broadly common approach.

Part Six contains five new case studies that illustrate the thrust of modern marketing as explained in the book.

The Epilogue draws together the principal trends emerging in the book and identifies seven key influences on marketing in travel and tourism for the coming decade.

Our approach to the subject

We base our approach to travel and tourism as the World Tourism Organization define it – in its full range of day and staying visits for multiple purposes embracing business, social and recreational activity as well as holidays. We aim to be as relevant to domestic as to international tourism. In that broad context we believe that tourism is a structural or core element of modern societies and that the marketing of it is still in the early stages of a development that will influence the industry to an increasing extent in the globally competitive conditions of the twenty-first century. We see marketing as a dominant management philosophy or corporate culture, a systematic thought process and an integrated set of techniques focused on understanding customer needs and aspirations. Combined, the application of the thought process and techniques are used in marketing-orientated organizations to define their strategic options and goals, and guide the way they understand and influence their target markets in a rapidly changing business environment.

Marketing is equally relevant to both private and public sectors of travel and tourism, and to smaller businesses as well as to international corporations. It is a proactive management response to the industry conditions of excess capacity of production and volatile market demand that are commonly found in international travel and tourism. Marketing perishable products in such conditions inevitably produces highly aggressive competition for market share and growth, and it is easy to predict that competition will continue to intensify rather than diminish over the next decade. The rapid growth of tourism demand around the world in the latter part of the twentieth century served to cushion many organizations from the full effects of competition and delayed the full application of marketing in many travel and tourism businesses. But the easy days are over. A combination of ICT, global competition, environmental challenges and marketing professionalism exposes vulnerable and sluggish businesses, many of which will not survive.

Marketing is not viewed, however, as a goal or the only focus of business management. It does not determine the nature of an organization's long-run goal or mission. Throughout the book the requirement of meeting customers' needs is balanced against the growing requirement of organizations to make the most sustainable as well as the most profitable use of existing assets and to achieve integration of management functions around customer-orientated objectives that respect sustainable goals. But marketing techniques are always essential inputs to specifying revenue-earning objectives that are precise, realistic, achievable and measurable in the markets or audiences in which an organization operates. In this sense the adoption of a marketing approach is as relevant to museums responsible to non-profit-making trusts, national parks for which the long-run goal is a sustainable environment and to local government tourist offices, as it is to airlines, hotels or tour operators in the private sector.

Finally, effective marketing can secure the marginal increases in revenue and the cost-effectiveness of promotion and distribution of budgets on which the difference between profit and loss so often depends in the travel and tourism industry. We call it *Marketing the Margin* and it is a vital contribution to travel and tourism businesses.

Links to internationally accepted marketing theory

Marketing as a body of knowledge is international. Like travel and tourism it does not depend on geographical boundaries. While many of the principles and techniques were developed originally in North America and Europe for selling manufactured consumer goods in the first half of the twentieth century, they are now being practised and developed all around the world in the much larger sectors of modern service industries. For reasons that are set out in Chapter 3 we believe it is possible to construct an overall understanding of travel and tourism marketing based on three essential points: first, that the theories of consumer marketing are common to all its forms; second, that service industries display particular characteristics, which do not alter the principles but must be understood before marketing can successfully be applied in practice; third, that there are important common characteristics of travel and tourism service products that require particular forms of marketing response.

It is too much to claim that an internationally agreed theory of travel and tourism marketing yet exists. But the particular generic and common characteristics of travel and tourism services are leading to increasing consistencies of approach in marketing, adapted in the different sectors of travel and tourism to the opportunities and threats they perceive. These common approaches point to a coherent, systematic body of knowledge within the framework of services marketing that will be further developed in the twenty-first century.

The aim of the book and its intended audience

The book has three aims, which are to provide:

- Concepts and principles drawn from international marketing theory, balanced with illustrations of recent practice.

- A necessary companion volume for all concerned with travel and tourism marketing, but not a substitute for the many excellent texts that explain marketing theory in its overall and service product context.
- An easy to read and comprehensive text about what marketing means in the global travel and tourism industry.

On both sides of the Atlantic the better of the standard texts on marketing are now substantial volumes, many of them having developed over several editions. This book makes no attempt to replace them. It is intended, instead, to fit fully within a framework of internationally accepted marketing principles that have stood the test of time, and to develop these concepts in travel and tourism. Suggested readings, indicating chapters in books that are typically recommended to students in the USA and Britain, are noted at the end of each chapter where relevant. Such books have the added advantage of dealing with the important principles in the wider industrial context in which marketing developed. Students in particular will profit from the breadth of understanding this conveys.

For students, the book is written to meet the needs of all on travel and tourism and hospitality courses and related leisure industry programmes. Marketing will be a very important influence in their careers, whether or not they are directly engaged in marketing practice. The contents are judged to be suitable for all those preparing for examinations in further and higher education courses with a travel and tourism component. The material will be relevant to those on other courses in which service industries are an important element.

For those in the industry, the book recognizes that marketing is a very practical subject and it is aimed at the great majority of managers in travel and tourism who have some responsibility for aspects of marketing but who have not formally studied the subject. Much of the contents have also been exposed to the critical reaction of managers in the industry over the years, and modified in the light of their responses. The book contains no *golden rules*. But if people in the industry read the book with care and relate its principles to the particular circumstances their own organizations face, most should perceive useful insights and ways to improve the effectiveness of their marketing decisions. If they do not, the authors will have failed in their purpose.

Victor T.C. Middleton
Jackie Clarke
November 2000

Authors' note

Repeated use of 'he or she' or of 's/he' can be cumbersome in continuous text. For simplicity, therefore, only the male pronoun is used throughout the book. No bias is intended and, wherever 'he' or 'his' appears, it applies equally to 'she' or 'hers'.

Acknowledgements

All errors and omissions are the authors' sole responsibility but we have had much help in the preparation of this edition – so much that it is impossible to list all who influenced the book with their insights, encouragement and sometimes much needed prods to get on with it. The most important group is undoubtedly the students on undergraduate and postgraduate courses in the UK and internationally to whom the contents were exposed. Their reactions to the material and the ideas discussed improved the thought processes more than they knew. We appreciate, too, the views and reactions of many managers on short, post-experience courses around the world to which we have contributed in the last decade; they sharpened our appreciation of international marketing for travel and tourism, and focused attention on the practice that validates theory. The principal author acknowledges the support of Professor Rik Medlik, who first persuaded him to lecture in marketing and write the earlier editions.

For particular contributions to chapters in this book we wish to acknowledge, in alphabetical order: Rebecca Hawkins, co-author with Victor Middleton of *Sustainable Tourism: A Marketing Perspective*; Roger Heape of British Airways Holidays; Mark Phillips of Horwath UK; Ian Mitchell of Oxford Brookes University; Scott Meis of the Canadian Tourism Commission; Linda Richards of Hotel Systems Support Services Ltd; Derek Robbins of Bournemouth University; Grahame Senior of Senior King Communications Group and Synergy Consulting, London.

For providing the case studies in Part Six we wish to acknowledge the authors whose full affiliations are noted at the foot of each case. They are Steve Allen (RCI Europe), Professor Estaban Bardolet (University of the Balearics), Paul Johnson (Longlands at Cartmel), Guy Parsons (Travel Inn) and Peter Varlow and Ian Woodward (British Tourist Authority).

For their faith in the book and patience while we missed a series of deadlines we thank Kathryn Grant and Sally North of Butterworth-Heinemann.

Figures

Tables

Abbreviations

AA	Advertising Association
ACORN	A Classification of Residential Neighbourhoods
ATM	automated teller machine
ALVA	Association of Leading Visitor Attractions
APEX	Advanced Purchase Excursion Fare
arsp	average retail sales price
ATC	air traffic control system
B2B	business to business
B2C	business to consumer
BA	British Airways
BTA	British Tourist Authority
CD	compact disc
CEO	chief executive officer
CPT	cost per thousand
CRM	customer-relationship marketing
CRS	computer reservation system
CTC	Canadian Tourism Commission
CTX	Canadian Tourism Commission's Tourism Exchange
DMO	destination marketing organization
DMS	destination management system
DVD	digital versatile disc
EC	European Community
EU	European Union
GDP	gross domestic product
GDS	global distribution system
GIS	geographical information system
HR	human resources
IATA	International Air Transport Association
ICAO	International Civil Aviation Organization
ICLEI	International Council for Local Environment Initiatives
ICT	information and communications technology
ILG	International Leisure Group
ISDN	integrated services digital network

MINTOUR	Multimedia Information Network for Tourism
MIS	management information system
MRS	Market Research Society
NTA	national tourism administrations
NTO	national tourism organization
OECD	Organization for Economic Co-operation and Development
OTS	opportunities to see
PC	personal computer
POS	point of sale
PR	public relations
SBA	strategic business area
SBU	strategic business unit
SME	small and medium-sized enterprise
SWOT	strengths, weaknesses, opportunities and threats
TGI	Target Group Index
TIC	tourist information centre
TIPS	tourism industry professionals sites
TUI	Touristic Union International
UKTS	United Kingdom Tourism Survey
UN	United Nations
VALS	Values and Lifestyles typology
VAT	value added tax
WAP	wireless application protocol
WTO	World Tourism Organization
YHA	Youth Hostels Association

Part One

The Meaning of Marketing in Travel and Tourism

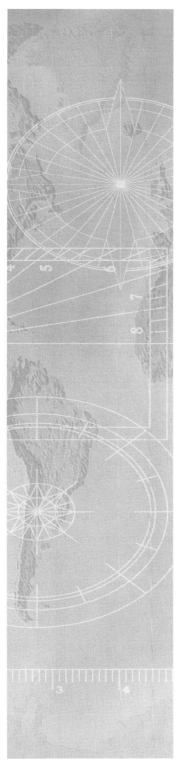

Introducing travel and tourism

Tourism is deemed to include any activity concerned with the temporary short-term movement of people to destinations outside the places where they normally live and work, and their activities during the stay at these destinations. (The Tourism Society, 1979)

This chapter introduces and defines the subject matter of this book. The intention is, first, to identify for practical marketing purposes the nature of travel and tourism and the industry it supports and, second, to indicate the growth potential of the industry in the next decade and its role in post-industrial societies.

Although the niceties of definitions can be debated endlessly, travel and tourism is best understood as a total market reflecting the demand of consumers for a very wide range of travel-related products. It is widely claimed that this total market is now serviced by the *world's largest industry*. At the beginning of the new millennium increasing interest is being shown in many countries in the potential of global travel and tourism as an important contributor to economic development, measured in terms of investment, employment and balance of payments. There is also increasing interest in the potential environmental and cultural contribution of tourism to the social and cultural life of host communities and to the built and natural environment. This is matched by concern about its negative effects in the conspicuous use of energy and water supplies, impact on global warming and damage to marine environments, and on the ecosystems of some destinations developed as major tourism resorts. Tourism is also of interest because of the millions of small and medium-sized enterprises (SMEs) it sustains and its ubiquitous nature – there are now very few regions of the modern world where tourism is not a relevant consideration.

Marketing is a subject of vital concern in travel and tourism because it is the principal management influence that can be brought to bear on the size and behaviour of this major global market.

Within the total market there are many submarkets or segments, and many products designed and provided by a wide range of organizations, which are categorized in Figure 1.1. Defined as a market, travel and tourism is best understood in terms of demand and supply. Marketing is introduced in Chapter 2 as the vital linking mechanism between supply and demand focused on exchange transactions, in which consumers exercise preferences and choices and exchange money in return for the supply of particular travel experiences or products. For reasons discussed subsequently, the principles and practice of marketing are also highly relevant to tourism resources for which no market price is charged, such as national parks and historic towns. Marketing is a vital role for national tourism organizations (NTOs) and other area organizations, most of which are not directly engaged in the sale of products although they are increasingly involved with commercial partners, which are.

The chapter begins with an overview of travel and tourism demand, its international dimensions and main components. A working definition of the subject is provided, with comments on the distinction between *tourism*, and *travel and tourism*, often a source of confusion to students. The components of demand and supply and the linking role of marketing are put together in diagrammatic form (Figure 1.2), which serves also to identify the main categories of supply within the travel and tourism industry.

An overview of travel and tourism demand

In defining travel and tourism for the purposes of this book it is useful to follow the basic classification system, which is used in nearly all countries where measurement exists. This system is discussed in detail in most introductory texts and is based on three overall categories of visitor demand with which any country is concerned; each is a different sector of the total market:

1 *International visitors* who are residents of countries other than that being visited and travel for tourism purposes (see below). Also known as *inbound tourism*.
2 *International visitors*, who are residents of a country visiting other countries and travel for tourism purposes. Also known as *outbound tourism*.
3 *Residents* visiting destinations within their own country's boundaries who travel for tourism purposes. Also known as *domestic tourism*.

Defining travel and tourism is a primary responsibility of the World Tourism Organization (WTO), which undertook a major review of its definitions at an international conference on travel and tourism statistics in Ottawa in 1991. In 1993 revised definitions were adopted by the United Nations (UN) Statistical Commission. The following are the principal terms:

- *Visitors* to describe all travellers who fall within agreed definitions of tourism.
- *Tourists* or staying visitors to describe visitors who stay overnight at a destination.
- *Same-day visitors*, or excursionists, to describe visitors who arrive and depart on the same day. Same-day visitors are mostly people who leave home and return there on the same day, but may be tourists who make day visits to other destinations away from the places where they are staying overnight.

As outlined above, these three categories are easy to understand. In practice the technicalities of achieving statistical precision in measuring visitor numbers are extremely complex and, despite agreed international guidelines, no uniformity yet exists in the measurement methods used around the world. Eurostat, for example, which publishes the statistics for tourism in Europe, issues guidelines for the collection of data but has to rely on the different methodologies used by individual countries to compile their data.

While the definition of travel and tourism outlined in this chapter will be adequate for the working purposes of those involved in marketing, this book does not set out to be a detailed study of the nature of tourism. Readers seeking further elaboration of concepts and measurement issues are referred to the reading suggestions noted at the end of the chapter. Marketing managers will, of course, require their own definitions of the market segments with which they are involved, and these will be far more detailed than the broadly indicative aggregate categories introduced here (see Chapter 7).

International tourism

People who travel to and stay in countries other than their normal country of residence for less than a year, are described as international tourists. They are usually treated by governments as the most important market sector of tourism because, compared with domestic tourists, they typically spend more, stay longer at the destination, use more expensive transport and accommodation, and bring in foreign currency which contributes to a destination country's international balance of payments. International tourism is also easier to measure than domestic tourism and such visitors tend to be more recognizable as tourists at destinations.

Around the world, measured as *arrivals* or *trips*, the numbers of international tourists and their expenditure have grown strongly since the 1950s, notwithstanding temporary fluctuations caused by the three major international energy and economic crises of the early 1970s, 1980s and 1990s. The overall growth pattern is revealed in Tables 1.1 and 1.2, and the reasons for it are discussed in some detail in Chapters 4 and 5. For the purposes of this introduction it is sufficient to note the recent growth and current size of the international market, and to be aware of consistently confident projections that international tourism will continue to grow well into the twenty-first century. Although annual fluctuations in volume reflecting economic and political events are certain, current expectations are for annual growth of the order of some 4 per cent per annum over the period 2000–10 as a whole. The growth in shares of international arrivals projected for the Asia Pacific region (Table 1.2) has major implications for the future of world travel and tourism. (See also WTO, 1997.)

Table 1.1
Recorded and projected growth in worldwide international tourist arrivals, 1950–2010

Year	International arrivals (millions)	Index of growth for each decade
1950	25.3	–
1960	69.3	274
1970	165.8	239
1980	286.3	173
1990	459.2	160
2000(e)	692.0	150
2010(e)	1000.0	144

Notes: These are arrivals as supplied over the years to WTO, plus projections at 1998. Although their accuracy cannot be assured, they provide indicators that are widely used around the world. (e) is a projected figure.
Source. WTO (1997).

Table 1.2
Changes in WTO world regional shares of international tourism arrivals, 1950–2010

Year	Europe	Americas	Asia Pacific
	Shares of total arrivals at end of each decade shown (%)		
1950	66	30	0.8
1960	73	24	1.0
1970	71	23	3.0
1980	66	21	7.0
1990	62	21	11.0
2000(e)	56	19	17.0
2010(e)	55	20	24.0

Notes: These are shares for the three main WTO regions only. The projected growth in the share of Asia Pacific arrivals since 1990 is the most significant trend. (e) is a projected figure.
Source: WTO (1997).

At present, reflecting the proximity of borders in Europe, it is common for well over half the adult population living in Northern Europe to have made one or more international tourist visits during the previous five years, mostly on vacation. Experience of international travel is very much less for Americans, reflecting the size of the USA and the distances most of them have to travel to make international trips. US inter-state tourism, e.g. between the North East and Florida, should perhaps be viewed as similar in principle to tourism between European countries over similar distances, especially as the latter develop the European Union and its common currency, the euro.

Although not shown separately in Tables 1.1 and 1.2, international same-day visits are an important market sector in countries with common land frontiers, such as the USA and Canada, the Netherlands and Germany, and Malaysia and Singapore. Because of the speed and efficiency of cross-Channel ferries and the Channel Tunnel, same-day visits between Britain and France and Britain and Belgium are also important elements of the total market for tourism.

Domestic tourism

People who travel and stay overnight within the boundaries of their own country are classified as domestic tourists. Estimates of the size of this sector of the market vary because in many countries domestic tourism is not adequately measured at present. As an indication, the WTO estimates that domestic tourism around the world outweighs international tourism by a factor of around 10:1 (WTO, 1997). In the USA, where good measurement does exist, Americans take only one trip abroad for every one hundred domestic trips defined as travel to places more than 100 miles distance from home. Even for longer visits of over ten nights' duration, international trips were no more than 3 per cent of the total. For the British, where the statistics are also good and reflecting the shorter distances to travel abroad, there were some four domestic tourism trips (including overnight stays) for every visit abroad in the late 1990s.

Evidence from surveys of the vacation market in Europe and North America in the 1990s indicates that, in most countries, between a half and three-quarters of the adult population took one or more holidays away from home in any twelve-month period of at least one night's duration. This includes international and domestic holidays, although the latter are the largest category. Increasing numbers of people take more than one vacation trip a year, a factor of great importance to marketing managers, for reasons discussed later.

Market research data analysing the complete tourism experience of the same individuals over periods of more than one year are rarely available although they exist, for example, for France and the Netherlands. But, excluding the very old, the sick, the severely disabled and those facing particular financial hardship, recent and frequent experience of some form of staying and same-day tourism now extends to over nine out of ten people in most economically developed countries.

Within the total volume of domestic tourism, same-day visits are the most difficult to quantify. In most developed countries the frequency of day visits is already so great that it is not easily measured by traditional survey techniques, because people find it hard or impossible to remember the number of trips they have taken over a period of months or even weeks. In the early 2000s there is, however, a rough but useful estimate for developed countries that there are at least twice as many domestic day visits for leisure purposes within a country as there are tourist days or nights spent away from home for all purposes. Thus, for example in the UK in 1998 an estimated 100 million domestic tourism visits for all purposes generated 350 million nights away from home. An additional 1250 million same-day visits of at least three hours duration from home for leisure purposes were made by the British in the same year (1998 data). With a population of some 55 million in Britain, this is equivalent to over twenty visitor days per person for leisure purposes over a year. UK estimates of day visits for business and social purposes do not exist, although such visits are obviously a very large market especially for operators of transport, meetings and catering services.

To summarize, the total market for travel and tourism comprises three main elements: international visits inbound to a country; outbound international visits made by a country's residents; and domestic visits including day visits from home. The total market has grown rapidly in recent years and is now very large, encompassing the great majority of the population of economically developed countries. Frequent, repeat purchases of travel and tourism products in a year are already a normal experience for many people. Although the statistics are inevitably open to dispute, travel and tourism is now the largest sector of world trade and in developed countries typically contributes 5–10 per cent of gross domestic product.

As major population countries such as China and India expand and develop their own tourism industries in the coming decades, to take dominant positions as destinations and generating countries in the global market, one may safely predict that marketing will be a subject of growing significance and interest. Adapting and developing in different socioeconomic cultures what are essentially the sophisticated techniques of Western societies will ensure continuing interest in tourism marketing for decades to come.

A working definition of travel and tourism

Before drawing the discussion of the main markets in travel and tourism into a working definition, it may be helpful to clarify one important potential source of confusion. What, if any, are the differences between *tourism* and *travel*, used on their own as single terms, and *travel and tourism* used as a combined term? What can a definition of tourism mean if it does not include travel? This book proceeds in the belief that an acceptable definition of tourism necessarily covers all relevant aspects of travel. In normal usage *tourism* and *travel and tourism* are terms that relate to exactly the same market and they are used interchangeably.

Travel and tourism tends to be the term used most often by managers, especially in North America, because it is convenient, practical and widely understood. Accordingly, this usage is adopted generally throughout the book. Where, for the sake of convenience, *tourism* is used alone, it also means travel and tourism; students should be aware that no conceptual difference is implied between the two expressions in this book.

Although academics have debated conceptual definitions of tourism for several decades, and there were earlier international agreements on statistical definitions, it was not until 1991–2 that the WTO endorsed the following statement, which serves as the working definition of the total market that is used throughout this book. The current WTO definition is very similar to the British one of 1979 noted at the start of this chapter.

Tourism comprises the activities of persons travelling to and staying in places outside their usual environment for not more than one consecutive year for leisure, business and other purposes. (WTO, 1992 – subsequently ratified by the UN Statistical Commission)

The UN definition pulls together the three main elements of travel and tourism:

1 Visitor activity is concerned only with aspects of life outside normal routines of work and social commitments, and outside the location of those routines.
2 The activity necessitates travel and, in nearly every case, some form of transport to the destination.
3 Specific destinations are the focus for a range of activities and a range of facilities required to support those activities. Such activities and facilities have a combination of economic, social and physical environmental impacts that are the basis for tourism policy and visitor management programmes.

Five important points are stressed in relation to the definition:

- There is nothing in it that restricts the total market to overnight stays; it includes same-day visits.
- There is nothing in it that restricts the total market to travel for leisure or pleasure. It includes travel for business, social, religious, educational, sports and most other purposes – provided that the destination of travel is outside the usual routines and places of residence and work.
- All tourism includes an element of travel but all travel is not tourism. The definition excludes all routine commuter travel and purely local travel, such as to neighbourhood shops, schools or hospitals.

- Travel and tourism absorbs large elements of individual leisure time and encompasses many recreational activities, but it is not synonymous with either because the bulk of all leisure and recreation takes place in or around the home.
- All travel and tourism trips are temporary movements; the bulk of the total market comprises trips of no more than a few hours' or nights' duration.

The component sectors of the travel and tourism industry

At the beginning of this chapter travel and tourism was identified from the demand side as a total market comprising three main sectors: international tourism, domestic tourism and same-day visits. This section identifies the sectors of supply that are loosely known as the travel and tourism industry.

A major difficulty in understanding and dealing with travel and tourism as a total market or industry is the sheer number of private and public sector enterprises involved in supplying services and the extent to which so many of them see tourism as only a part of their total business operations. For example, airlines, trains, buses, restaurants and hotels all deal with a wide variety of market segments, many of which do not fall within the internationally agreed definition of travel and tourism. Hotels have local trade for bars and meals, and transport operators carry commuters. Many visitor attractions, such as museums, and most visitor information bureaux also provide services to local residents. This mixture of products designed to serve both tourism and other markets has great significance for marketing decisions; it is discussed in some detail in Part Five of this book, which considers marketing applications in the component sectors of the industry.

comprises the products or outputs of several different industry sectors as these are conventionally defined and measured in most countries' economic statistics. In practice, convenient though the concept is for all working within it, travel and tourism is not an industry that is recognized as such by economists. In assessing the performance of industry sectors it is normal for economists and government statisticians to use standardized classifications of economic activity to measure the outputs of sectors such as transport, hotels and similar accommodation, restaurants and similar outlets, bars, and catering separately. Generally they cannot identify what proportion of each output is generated by visitor spending. Recent work on satellite accounting, pioneered in Canada and taken up by the WTO and the Organization for Economic Co-operation and Development (OECD), provides a methodology for assessing the economic contribution of tourism using a country's national accounts. Fortunately this is not a matter of prime concern for marketing managers and the term *travel and tourism industry* is used throughout this book in the broad sense that it is used and understood without difficulty in practice.

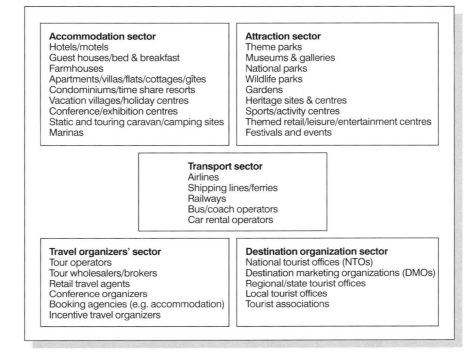

Accommodation sector
Hotels/motels
Guest houses/bed & breakfast
Farmhouses
Apartments/villas/flats/cottages/gîtes
Condominiums/time share resorts
Vacation villages/holiday centres
Conference/exhibition centres
Static and touring caravan/camping sites
Marinas

Attraction sector
Theme parks
Museums & galleries
National parks
Wildlife parks
Gardens
Heritage sites & centres
Sports/activity centres
Themed retail/leisure/entertainment centres
Festivals and events

Transport sector
Airlines
Shipping lines/ferries
Railways
Bus/coach operators
Car rental operators

Travel organizers' sector
Tour operators
Tour wholesalers/brokers
Retail travel agents
Conference organizers
Booking agencies (e.g. accommodation)
Incentive travel organizers

Destination organization sector
National tourist offices (NTOs)
Destination marketing organizations (DMOs)
Regional/state tourist offices
Local tourist offices
Tourist associations

Figure 1.1
The five main
sectors of the
travel and tourism
industry

The five main component sectors of the industry noted in Figure 1.1 are reflected in the chapter headings and case studies included in Parts Five and Six of the book. Each of these comprises several subsectors, all of which are increasingly concerned with marketing activities, both in the design of their products and the management of demand. The authors consider that the linking of sectors in Figure 1.1 as an 'industry' is also justified by the existence within the sectors of certain common, integrating principles that underlie the modern practice of services marketing. Such principles greatly facilitate the understanding of the subject and help to explain the common interests in marketing that practitioners in tourism recognize. Students may find it a useful exercise to extend the list in Figure 1.1, using the same five sector headings and aiming to produce up to fifty subsectors involved altogether in the *travel and tourism industry*.

It can be seen that some of the subsectors are fully commercial and operated for profit, some are operated commercially for purposes other than profit and some are in the public sector and operated mainly on a non-commercial basis. To illustrate, in the first category are most hotels, in the second category many attractions, such as safari parks and heritage sites, and in the third category many state-owned national museums, national parks and most of the operations undertaken by tourist offices. Internationally, growing recognition of the value of marketing in non-commercial operations in the second and third categories has been a remarkable feature of the last decade.

The systematic links between demand and supply and the role of marketing

Figure 1.2 is provided to show vital linkages between demand and supply in travel and tourism that are fundamental to an understanding of the role of marketing. The figure shows the relationship between market demand, generated in the places in which visitors normally live (areas of origin), and product supply, mainly at visited destinations. In particular, it shows how the five main sectors of the industry set out in Figure 1.1 combine to manage visitors' demand through a range of marketing influences. Noted as the *marketing mix*, in the centre of the diagram, this important term is fully explained in Chapter 6.

Readers should note that the linkages in Figure 1.2 focus on visitors in the left-hand box. A detailed knowledge of their customers' characteristics and buying behaviour is central to the activities of marketing managers in all sectors of the industry. Knowledge of the customer, and all that it implies for management decisions, is generally known as *consumer or marketing orientation*; a concept explained in depth in the next chapter. Note also that there are two-way flows of information for each of the links shown.

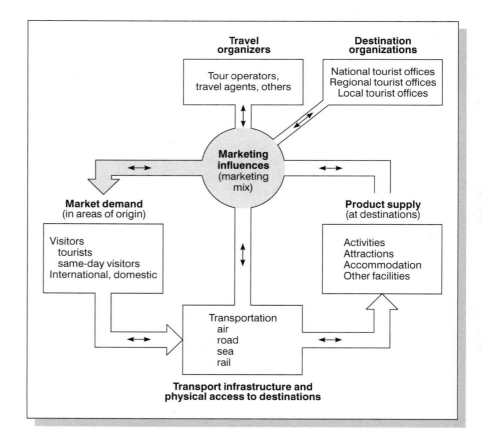

Figure 1.2
The systematic links between demand and supply: the influence of marketing

It should be noted also that not all visits to a destination are influenced by marketing activity. For example, domestic visitors travelling by private car to stay with their friends and relatives may not be influenced by destination marketing in any way at all. On the other hand, first-time buyers of package tours to exotic destinations in the Pacific area may find almost every aspect of their trip is influenced by the marketing decisions of the tour operator they choose. The operator selects the destinations to put into a brochure and selects the messages and images that communicate their attractions. Tour operators choose the accommodation, the range of excursions, the routes, the choice of airline and the prices. Somewhere in between these two examples a traveller on business selects his own destinations according to business requirements but may be influenced as to which hotel he selects. The range of influences, noted as the 'marketing mix', is obviously very wide, and it is varied according to visitors' interests and circumstances.

There are, of course, many other linkages between the five sectors of the travel and tourism industry, for example between national and regional tourist organizations and suppliers at the destination. These additional linkages are not drawn into Figure 1.2, to avoid unnecessary confusion in this introduction. The linkages are, of course, identified subsequently in all parts of the book.

Changing prospects for twenty-first century tourism

Looking back over the last thirty years it is easy to see the key economic and social trends that are transforming the former industrial economies in the developed world into post-industrial societies. On the one hand it is a story of severe economic decline, loss of employment and traditional community disintegration, hastened by the economic crises of the early 1970s, the early 1980s and the early 1990s. On the other hand it is a story of remarkable economic growth as new forms of economic activity, including tourism, have emerged to replace those that have been lost. Developments of information and communications technology (ICT) and of transport technology have unleashed powerful global economic forces, which have simultaneously speeded the decline of traditional industries in countries that developed them for over a century and facilitated the emergence of new forms of employment. It is in this crucible of change that most developed societies are being redefined, and it provides a fertile and volatile context for the trends that are influencing the future of tourism globally. (See also the Epilogue.)

As traditional areas of employment decline in the developed world, many of the industries involved are being re-established in the developing world using the latest technology combined with less costly labour. Such shifts arouse ethical considerations but are expected to promote the economic growth of the developing world and in turn promote further global tourism development.

The main areas of economic decline in developed economies are painfully obvious with hindsight:

- Iron and steel.
- Coal mining.
- Textiles.
- Manufacturing, especially of household goods.
- Shipbuilding.
- Traditional public transport – (with potential recovery to combat congestion and pollution).
- Docks and port facilities.
- Traditional paper-based clerical services.
- Agriculture and fisheries.
- Many small market towns.

The main areas of economic growth are equally clear:

- Information, communications and technology services (see Chapter 10).
- Financial services – banking, insurance, pensions and share trading.
- Media generally, broadcast media in particular, including cable and satellite.
- Retailing – especially as concentrated in out of town/edge-of-town centres or alternatively in large regeneration developments in the centre of cities and towns.
- Education – further and higher education in particular and all forms of training.
- Air transport and associated infrastructure; private cars and motorways; sophisticated road transport systems to service the growth sectors.
- Creative industries such as film, theatre, music and publication.
- The arts and culture generally including music, festivals, museums, libraries and art galleries.
- Leisure, recreation and sport and the products, facilities and infrastructure they support.
- Travel and tourism and its associated sectors of hospitality and catering, conferences, exhibitions, entertainment and visitor attractions – also known as the 'experience economy'.

The forces in society promoting the growth of tourism are developed more analytically in Chapters 4 and 5. This introduction is intended only to underline the fact that world travel and tourism as defined in this chapter has shifted remarkably in a quarter of a century from what the *Economist* in the early 1990s was still assessing as a *Pleasure Principle* (*Economist*, March 1991) to an integral part of modern post-industrial society and a key element of the lifestyle for all with discretionary income that takes them above subsistence level. Students may find it instructive to consider how all forms of tourism, international and domestic, day and stay, are involved in every one of the economic growth trends listed above. Tourism is no longer just the expression of leisure choices for an affluent minority but a core element in modern society, increasingly recognized as a primary economic driver in all countries. This trend also holds good for developing societies that are able effectively to harness some parts of the industrial manufacturing stage and bypass other parts to move straight into post-industrial economic forms as a result of global developments in communications and transport technology.

Changes as profound as those outlined above inevitably had major consequences for the places where millions of people live and work. Most industrial cities and towns suffered economically and environmentally since the 1970s as large sectors of their wealth creation based on traditional industries were rendered uneconomic through international competition, and were closed down. In response, supported in Europe by national governments and international funding through the European Commission, the drive to implement regeneration programmes radically altered the urban structure in Europe in the last two decades with major development schemes focused on the new areas of economic growth. In nearly all these regeneration programmes the process of change embraced aspects of tourism, leisure and recreation, and forged a proactive climate for the arts, heritage and culture that underlies the development of many new tourism facilities in recent years.

The old industrial economies of the twentieth century gave rise to concepts of mass production and mass consumption and hence *mass tourism*. But post-industrial societies everywhere and the new economy reflect the growth of more affluent, more mature, more culturally diverse, more educated, more demanding, more quality conscious, more cynical, more litigious and more sophisticated consumers at the start of the new millennium. Such customers are very far removed from the now outdated notions of 'mass tourism' commonly applied to the 1960s and 1970s, and still widely used in many tourism textbooks.

In post-industrial economies, the arts, heritage and culture are much more than a just vibrant elements of the 'new economy'. They are also vital symbols for place and for a sustainable quality of life including education on which other parts of economic revival can build. The Guggenheim at Bilbao in Spain, the Royal Armouries at Leeds and the Tate Modern in the UK, the Sydney Opera House and Darling Harbour in Australia, Baltimore and Boston in the USA are not just sites for urban regeneration and locations for museums and galleries. They are icons of local pride and phoenix symbols of present determination to regenerate local economies from a lost industrial past into a more prosperous post-industrial future. They provide unique and comprehensible images that are so vital to communication in a modern world overwhelmed by information overload. It augurs well for future tourism that governments around the world are committed to urban and rural regeneration, and that most support the role of culture and heritage within it.

Allowing for business and conference visits, and for day visits for many purposes including non-routine shopping, recreation and entertainment, the thrust of tourism development and the locus for tourism destinations is shifting at the start of the new millennium. Impossible to

15

quantify with available data, the pendulum is swinging away from traditional coastal locations and activities to new urban locations and activities, many on the sites of former traditional industrial activity. New tourism is far more dispersed across virtually every community in developed countries. These changes have important environmental implications, both positive and negative as examined by Middleton and Hawkins (1998). But, overall, we believe they augur well for sustainable growth and an exciting future for the world's largest industry.

Chapter summary

This chapter introduces travel and tourism as a nationally and internationally important market in which the natural focus of management activity is on exchange transactions between visitors (demand side) and the business sectors and destinations that compete to supply their needs (supply side). The overall dimensions of the market are set out and key definitions provided in a form suitable for marketing purposes. The travel and tourism industry is outlined as five main sectors of economic activity, the marketing practices of which subsequently form the subject matter of Part Five of the book. This chapter emphasizes that there are no conceptual differences intended between the use of the terms *tourism*, and *travel and tourism*, and they are used interchangeably throughout the book. All the definitions are based on principles that are valid for all countries, whether they are economically developed or not and whether their tourism industry is mature or just emerging.

The five sectors of the industry are presented in Figure 1.2, which traces the main linkages between supply and demand and, in particular, indicates how marketing influences all aspects of demand and supply. These influences are analysed in depth in later chapters. The final part of the chapter looks at some implications for tourism in the twenty-first century as a key element in post-industrial societies and the 'new' economy.

Students should be aware of a tendency among many authors of travel and tourism books to state or *assume* that tourism is a subset of leisure and recreation, or to treat the subject as exclusively concerned with holiday travel. In fact, as clearly endorsed by the UN Statistical Commission in 1993, tourism encompasses travel for business, social and many other non-holiday purposes. For many hotels, airlines and for most travel agents, business travel is the most important sector for marketing purposes. In terms of revenue, the value of business travel is often much higher than recreation travel and is logically given priority in marketing terms. For many visitor attractions, educational markets and same-day visits from home are more important segments than holiday visitors. It is important for readers to keep firmly in mind this broad and internationally endorsed concept of travel and tourism.

For those who wish to consider the definitions of travel and tourism in greater depth, although this is not necessary for marketing purposes, further readings are suggested.

Further reading

Cooper, C. et al. (1998). *Tourism Principles and Practice*. Chapter 1, 2nd edn, Longman.

Goeldner, C. R. (2000). *Tourism: Principles, Practices, Philosophies*. Chapters 1 and 3, 8th edn, Wiley.

Smith, S. L. J. (1995). *Tourism Analysis: A Handbook*. Chapter 2, 2nd edn, Longman.

Theobold, W. (ed.) (1994). *Global Tourism: The Next Decade*. Chapter 1, Butterworth-Heinemann.

Now dated, the original conceptualization in Burkart and Medlik is still relevant:

Burkart, A. J. and Medlik, S. (1981). *Tourism: Past, Present, and Future*. Chapters 4 and 7, 2nd edn, Heinemann.

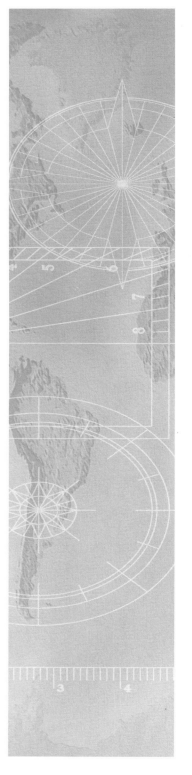

Introducing marketing: the systematic thought process

This chapter explains the meaning of modern marketing as it is applied internationally to goods and services of all types. The intention here is to define the essential characteristics common to all forms of marketing, while Chapter 3 considers the special characteristics of travel and tourism marketing.

To understand marketing it is necessary to distinguish between the familiar word in everyday use and the term as it is used professionally by marketing managers. Popular notions of marketing are probably more of a hindrance than a help to those studying the subject for the first time because, before reading any marketing texts, readers will be aware already of the continuous and competitive process of persuasion and inducements of every kind to which we are all routinely exposed in the conduct of our lives. All of us are daily the targets of massive and sustained marketing activity in a variety of forms, which range from advertising on television and radio, in the press, on posters, on drink mats and on milk bottles, through direct mail and promotional literature of all types, and through special offers and price reductions in retail stores. Many are also exposed to advertising on the Internet. If we pause to think about it, the evidence of marketing activity surrounds us like the air we breathe and take for granted.

However imprecise their initial understanding of marketing, most people approach the subject with the view that it is important both commercially and socially. Many are suspicious about its potential influence on their lives and some have ethical concerns about its negative effects upon society. What consumers see of promotion and persuasion is, however, only the visible tip of an extensive iceberg of marketing management activities, of which most people are completely unaware. Marketing as an approach to the conduct of business developed in the early twentieth century in countries in the Western world with relatively free markets. But the concepts are now found increasingly in less developed countries. In the 1990s, following the remarkable collapse of old-style communist economies in Eastern Europe and the former USSR, there has been a deliberate stimulation of market-based organizations and marketing methods. Although in the short run this shift has led to predatory activities and gangsterism in places, where it succeeds it will promote as powerful a socioeconomic revolution as any we have seen in the twentieth century. For many decades competition, profit and promotional activity were seen in the communist world as wasteful and against the public interest. Now, even in countries such as China, the speed of response to change in the global economy and prospects for greater operational efficiency inherent (but not guaranteed) in marketing principles, are forcing the pace of radical rethinking of the traditional practices of centrally planned economies.

This chapter begins by explaining the essential idea of voluntary exchange between two parties, which underlies all marketing theories of the conduct of business. It proceeds to discuss what marketing orientation means in terms of management attitudes. This leads into formal definitions of marketing, from which five propositions are derived. The most important of these is that marketing is a system comprising a series of stages, which are represented in an important diagram shown in Figure 2.1. The final part of the chapter discusses the combined effect of the five propositions and explains the growing significance of marketing in the new century. While every aspect of this chapter is relevant to travel and tourism marketing, the intention is to introduce the subject as it applies to transactions generally for all types of goods and services.

Marketing means exchanges

Chapter 1 explains that travel and tourism is best understood in terms of demand and supply within a total market. At its simplest, marketing can be explained as the process of achieving voluntary exchanges between two parties:

- Customers who choose to buy or use products.
- Producer organizations, which design, supply and sell the products.

In terms of customers, marketing is concerned with:

- Understanding the needs and desires of existing and prospective buyers (why they buy).
- Which products they choose, when, how much, at what price and how often.

- How they get information about product offers.
- Where they buy products from (direct or through a retail intermediary).
- How they feel after their purchase and consumption of products.

In terms of producers, marketing focuses on:

- Which products to produce and why, especially new products.
- How many products to produce (volume of supply).
- At what price.
- How to communicate their offers, by which media.
- When and where to make them available to buyers.

Not all products are exchanged for money and profit. For example, some visitor attractions such as museums may be available to visitors free of admission charges. Others, such as national parks may charge for admission but are operated on a not-for-profit basis. Provided visitors have choices as to how to spend their time, however, the central notion of exchange remains valid.

From this simple introduction it follows that all marketing involves a *management decision process* for producers, focused on a *customer decision process*, with the two sets of decisions coming together in an exchange transaction – money for products in the case of commercial operators. Assuming that customers have choices between different products, which is nearly always the case in travel and tourism, it is easy to see that producers have the strongest possible motivation to know their customers and prospective customers and to influence them to choose their products rather than those of a competitor.

Throughout this book, especially in dealing with exchange transactions based on services, it is convenient to refer to 'the conduct of business', 'business operations' or 'the management of operations'. In every case, exchange transactions based on the decision processes outlined above are the focus of activity.

Management attitudes and the external business environment

To get below the surface of promotional activity, it is helpful to focus first on the attitudes of managers in producer organizations. The spirit of marketing, its driving force and the reason that its professionals find the subject enormously stimulating, exciting and satisfying, lies in the way in which it is carried out in practice. Important though they are, marketing skills and techniques do not explain what marketing is. Attitudes do. In a few lines it is impossible to communicate the excitement, vitality and sheer energy surrounding successful marketing operations. Most managers will recognize the enthusiasm the subject inspires; students will have to take it on trust, though they should be aware that marketing has to be experienced 'live' before it can be fully understood.

Above all, marketing at a strategic level reflects a particular set of strongly held attitudes and a sense of commitment on the part of directors and senior managers – not just marketing managers – which are found in all marketing-led organizations. Combined, the guiding principles and attitudes that affect the whole of an organization are known as a 'management orientation' or 'corporate culture'. In the particular case of a *marketing orientation*, there are five key elements, as follows:

- A positive, outward looking, innovative and highly competitive attitude towards the conduct of exchange transactions (in commercial and non-commercial organizations).
- Recognition that the conduct of business operations must revolve around the long-run interests and satisfaction of customers rather than on one-off exchanges, and where possible, the selective development of relationships with loyal buyers
- Understanding that the achievement of profits and other organizational goals results from customer satisfaction and customer retention.
- An outward looking, responsive attitude to events and conditions in the external business environment within which an organization operates, especially the actions of competitors.
- An understanding of the strategic balance to be achieved between the need to earn profits from existing assets and the equally important need to adapt an organization to achieve future profits, recognizing social and environmental resource constraints.

With these proactive attitudes integrated as the driving force in a management team, marketing techniques may be implemented with vigour and success, although it is never easy. Without the driving force, the most professional skills are unlikely to succeed because their practitioners will usually lose heart and seek more productive working environments. Management attitudes are partly learned and partly a response to external circumstances, especially the current balance between the capacity of supply and the volume of demand in the markets that an organization serves. The next section considers some important effects of this changing balance or relation between supply and demand. The Epilogue discusses recent developments in the social and environmental constraints to which tourism marketing must respond.

A *marketing orientation* as described above is not the only choice for managers. At the risk of oversimplifying it is possible to comment on two other orientations, which at different times and in different market circumstances guide managers in the conduct of their businesses.

Product and production orientation

This term is often used to summarize the attitudes and responses of businesses whose products are typically in strong and rising demand, and profitable. Because demand does not present problems, there is a natural tendency for managers to focus their main attention on more pressing decisions, such as those concerning production capacity, quality and cost controls, finance for increasing production and maintaining the efficiency and profitability of operations generally. In the short run, where demand is buoyant and growing, an emphasis on production processes and financial controls appears both logical and sensible.

Consider the example of a small town with two hotels and one car rental operator. If the town's business community is prosperous and growing, it is likely that the hotels and the car rental operation will be profitable businesses and they are very likely to be product and production orientated. Such demand conditions are quite commonly found in travel and tourism, even at the beginning of the twenty-first century. Readers should note that the focus of production orientation is *inward looking* towards product decisions and operational needs.

Sales orientation

This term is often used to summarize the attitudes and responses of businesses whose products are no longer enjoying growth in demand, or for which demand may be declining to levels that reduce profitability. Production is not now the main problem; surplus capacity is. The obvious management reaction in these conditions is to shift the focus of attention to securing sales. Increased expenditure on advertising, distribution channels and on sales promotion or price discounts is a logical response in an attempt to secure a higher level of demand for available production capacity.

In the small-town example noted above, suppose a third hotel of similar size and better quality were built. The occupancy of the existing two would probably suffer an initial fall and a sales response from their managers would appear to be logical and sensible. Such changes in demand conditions are frequently met locally in travel and tourism. Readers should note that the focus of sales orientation is still essentially *inward looking* towards the needs of operations and shifting their surplus capacity. In this case additional sales and promotion costs would further erode profit.

Contrast with marketing orientation

As noted above, the focus of marketing orientation is essentially *outward looking*. In the notional small-town example, suppose there were now five hotels of a similar standard for a current demand that will fill only three of them at profitable levels of room occupancy. In these conditions inward-looking concerns with production and operational efficiency will not make much impact on demand, especially if competitors' products are of a similar standard and price. Similarly, a strong sales drive with its emphasis on increased promotional expenditure will not increase demand significantly if competitors quickly follow suit with matching expenditure, and the increased expenditure will further undermine profitability. Reducing prices to increase demand will only cause further losses as competitors will have to follow suit.

In the strongly competitive business conditions noted above, which in fact are typical of those now faced by most businesses in the travel and tourism industry, survival and future success lies in rethinking and adapting the business from the customer's standpoint – in order to secure and sustain an adequate *share* of the available demand and to develop new markets. This always means applying the five strategic principles outlined earlier and, because customers' needs and market conditions are nearly always in a state of constant change, adapting the organization as smoothly as possible and better or faster than competitors. This outward looking approach and process of adaptation lends itself logically to the increasingly important balancing of long-run consumer interests with business interests and the growing twenty-first century concerns with sustainable development.

Defining marketing for the twenty-first century

It would be highly convenient if there were just one standard definition of marketing. But, although the subject has now been studied and taught in academic courses for nearly a century (Bartels, 1976), it is still evolving and most consider it as much an art as a science. There are literally dozens of definitions, although most of them are individual variations within a broad consensus that the marketing concept is both consumer led and profit orientated. It is important to stress that consumer orientation does not always mean giving customers what they want, but it has to mean understanding their needs and wants in order to respond more efficiently in ways that make business sense for organizations – both in the short term of six months to a year, and especially in the long term of several years.

Kotler, the author familiar to most marketing students on both sides of the Atlantic, has traditionally defined the marketing concept as follows: 'The marketing concept holds that the key to achieving organizational goals consists in determining the needs and wants of target markets and delivering the desired satisfactions more effectively and efficiently than competitors' (Kotler, 1991: 16). Recognizing, however, the growing restraints on marketing imposed globally by pressures arising from the social, cultural and natural environment within which businesses must operate, he developed the definition to add the words, *'in a way that preserves or enhances the customers' and the society's well being'* (Kotler, 1991: 26).

The British Chartered Institute of Marketing defines marketing as: 'The management process responsible for identifying, anticipating and satisfying customer requirements profitably, to meet organisational objectives.' Both these definitions hold good for all forms of consumer and industrial product marketing, whether of goods such as soap powders or pianos, or services such as banking, insurance, hotel rooms and airline travel. The Kotler definition is equally relevant to the marketing of people, ideas and places and to any exchange process where target markets and organizational goals exist. It also covers the products of not-for-profit organizations.

While this book is about marketing in travel and tourism, readers must appreciate that tourism marketing is not a separate discipline but an adaptation of basic principles that have been developed and practised for many decades across a wide spectrum of consumer products.

Five marketing propositions

Both definitions noted above provide a basis for five important propositions, which are entirely relevant to travel and tourism marketing but not derived from it:

> 1 Marketing is a management orientation or philosophy.
> 2 Marketing comprises three main elements linked within a system of exchange transactions.
> 3 Marketing is concerned with the long term (strategy) and the short term (tactics).
> 4 Marketing is especially relevant to analysing twenty-first century market conditions and can make a major contribution to sustainable development.
> 5 Marketing facilitates the efficient and effective conduct of business.

1 Management orientation

The first proposition (management orientation) was discussed earlier. Each of the other four is developed below.

2 Three main elements in marketing exchanges

It is implicit in Kotler's and other definitions that marketing comprises the following core elements:

> • The attitudes and decisions of target customers concerning the perceived utility and value of available goods and services, in terms of their needs, wants, interests and ability to pay.
> • The attitudes and decisions of producers concerning production of goods and services for sale, in the context of their long-term business objectives and the wider environment in which they operate.
> • The ways in which producers communicate with consumers before, during and after the point of sale, and distribute or provide access to their products.

In other words, the key elements in any marketing system are the attitudes and thought processes of the two parties – buyers and sellers – in an exchange process or market transaction.

It should be noted that there is no natural or automatic harmony between what consumers want and will pay for and what producers are able or willing to provide. In practice there is usually continuing tension between a producer's need for profit, the need to operate efficiently and sustainably with available assets and resources, and the customer's search for best available value and satisfaction. Marketing managers have to use judgement in balancing between these conflicting needs in the exchange process and to do so with imprecise knowledge about markets, distribution channels and their competitors' decisions. Their judgement is expressed primarily in the third element of the system, distribution and communication of products and prices, on which the bulk of marketing expenditure is spent.

The better the balance between the interests in the exchange process, the smaller the marketing expenditure will need to be as a proportion of sales revenue, and vice versa. For example, if a tour operator has accurately designed, priced and judged the capacity of a programme, sales will be achieved at a relatively low promotional cost. If, for whatever reason, the price is too high, the product design uncompetitive or the capacity excessive for the available demand, only massive promotional expenditure and discounting will bring supply and demand back into balance.

Linked within a marketing system

The three core elements in the marketing system are expressed in more detail in Figure 2.1. This is an important diagram, which in addition to introducing all main processes or stages involved in marketing, also provides a framework for the contents of this book.

In Figure 2.1 the logical flow and linkages between the main processes are shown as an integrated system that is relevant to all forms of service products. The process begins with a detailed analysis of the external business environment, and works through marketing and campaign planning to produce business strategies and operational plans that identify the marketing activities to be undertaken. The research and planning stages of the process incorporate all that an organization knows about its customers and potential customers, their attitudes and buying behaviour. Business strategies express an organization's attitudes and decisions over a specified time period. As the stages proceed, plans are turned into costed action programmes that express how an organization will communicate with and provide access for its potential customers. The marketing process ends with further research into customers' feelings about the satisfaction and value for money they received from the purchases they made and their attitude to further purchases.

To simplify the explanation, the marketing system in Figure 2.1 is shown as a series of logical steps with an obvious beginning and end. In practice, as explained in subsequent chapters, the steps do not proceed in a straight line. They comprise a continuous cycle or rolling programme of decisions, actions and research, incorporating many feedback loops that are under constant management review.

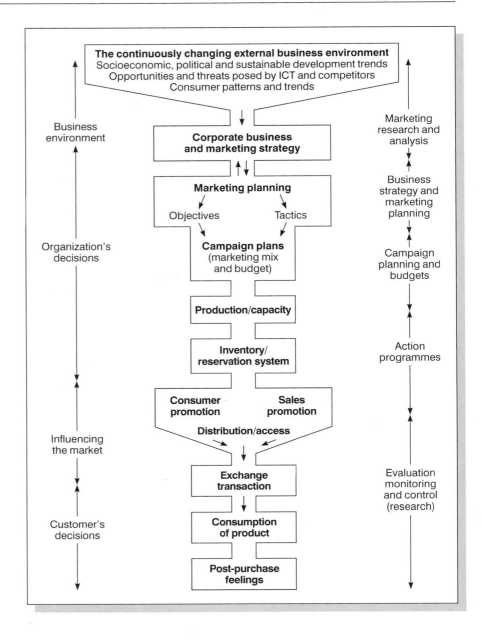

Figure 2.1
The marketing system for service products

Because this book is concerned with services rather than goods, production capacity is shown as being held within an inventory/ reservation system. For an airline this would be a computerized reservations system for seats on flights; for a hotel, a reservation system for beds, and so on. For manufacturers of physical goods all the main stages in the marketing system are essentially the same, but transport, warehousing and related physical distribution systems would be the relevant considerations for inventory.

Process	Description	Main chapter reference
Marketing research and analysis	Continuous, detailed appreciation of the historic and projected trends in the external business environment (including sustainable issues). Includes consumer research and evaluation of previous marketing expenditure and results.	4, 5 and 11
Business strategy and marketing planning	Developing research and analysis into overall business and marketing opportunities and devising strategies and operational plans.	12 and 13
Campaign planning and budgeting	Producing costed operational programmes to integrate the four main elements in the marketing mix – the four Ps.	6 and 14
Action programmes and implementation	Detailed programmes of daily/weekly/monthly activity for all forms of marketing communications.	15 to 19
Evaluation, monitoring and control	Monitoring and evaluating the results of marketing including all forms of market research and use of databases. Taking corrective action as appropriate.	11 and 14

Note: Each of these processes is further illustrated in Parts Five and Six of the book. Each of the case studies is a demonstration of the marketing system at work.

Table 2.1 Summary of the marketing system

A summary of the marketing system is offered in Table 2.1. It should be read in tandem with Figure 2.1 and it notes the main chapters in which each of the stages is explained and discussed in detail.

3 Concerned with the long term and the short term (strategy and tactics)

The meaning of strategy and tactics is discussed in Chapters 12 and 13, but in understanding marketing orientation it is always important to distinguish the timescale within which marketing decisions are taken. The short term (or short run) may be defined as the period of time in which an organization is able to make only marginal alterations to its product specifications, production capacity and published prices. In other words, in the short run an organization has no choice but to offer its goods or services for sale within the limits of a set of operational constraints that were established in part by its own earlier decision process. In the long run, according to its view of future markets and customers' requirements, an organization may decide to alter product specifications, production capacity, introduce new products or phase out old ones, alter its pricing strategy or change its position within a market.

Mergers and business acquisitions or disposals provide other long-run options.

In the short run, organizations frequently find themselves unable to adapt their products quickly enough to meet changes in customers' needs or market circumstances. In order to survive, they have to stimulate the available demand through all the techniques of sales promotion, merchandising and advertising they can command. For example, if a rival airline gains permission to operate a route and reduces its competitor's seat occupancy (load factor) from, say, 64 to 54 per cent in the first six months of a new service, the immediate task for the competitor's marketing is to fight for share and volume using aggressive sales tactics.

What always distinguishes the marketing-led organization in the short run is not the objectives of its tactics, but the speed and the way in which it uses and exploits its deep knowledge of customers to achieve its specified targets, while at the same time holding firm to its longer-term vision and strategy developed around long-run consumer orientation and satisfaction. Readers should note that most marketing definitions (including the Kotler version quoted in this chapter) are relevant primarily to the long run. In practice, however, most marketing decisions are made in the tactical context of the short run. The constraints imposed by marketing highly 'perishable' service products with a fixed capacity on any one day, make short-run marketing decisions especially important in travel and tourism, a point that is explained in the next chapter. They should also focus attention on the strategic vision that underlies the tactical options.

It is not possible to set a precise timescale for either short or long run, because it varies from sector to sector. Suffice it to say that the short run typically means six months to a year ahead, and the focus of decisions is on this year's and next year's operations and marketing campaign. The long run typically means not less than three years ahead, and the focus of decisions is strategic.

In the ideal world of textbooks, products are mostly designed to meet customers' needs and they generate satisfaction and profit. In the real world of travel and tourism marketing, products are mostly less than ideal in one or more respects and marketing managers have to live with the results of decisions that looked right when they were made some months or years previously but which have since been overtaken by unpredicted (and often unpredictable) events. In 1991 the unpredicted and massive impact on international travel and tourism markets of the Gulf War was a classic if extreme illustration of circumstances that faced marketing managers. In 1998 the massive downturn of tourism markets in Hong Kong, Indonesia and Thailand are equally extreme examples of the vulnerability of businesses to unpredicted events. Such circumstances are overwhelming and business failures occur. Skilful marketing performs the only available compensating function for the gaps and mismatches between demand and supply that occur inevitably when markets do not move in the ways predicted by managers.

4 Especially relevant to twenty-first century market conditions

There is really nothing new in a marketing concept based simply on recognizing the need to satisfy customers, understand market trends and exploit demand efficiently. As they are defined in many marketing textbooks, the essential characteristics of marketing have been practised by small businesses throughout history. No one survives long, especially in small service businesses, unless they understand their customers' needs, and provide satisfactory service at competitive prices. What distinguishes markets in the twenty-first century from those in any previous era, is a combination of powerful trends towards:

- A relatively small number of large, still growing, highly competitive businesses with standardized products and brands, and relatively large shares of the markets they serve, operating on a national, international and, increasingly, global scale.
- A massive number of small enterprises (there were at least 2.7 million small tourism firms in Europe at the end of the twentieth century – Middleton, 1998b).
- A revolutionary development of ICT that simultaneously facilitates the growth and management control of large corporations and offers a networking collaborative route for small businesses to compete.
- Capacity of supply considerably in excess of what markets can absorb naturally (without stimulation).
- Growing numbers of consumers in developed countries with sufficient disposable income and leisure time to indulge in non-essential purchases, many of them choosing to engage in frequent travel for leisure purposes.
- Sustainable development requirements epitomized in the post–1992 *AGENDA 21* process that will increasingly have to be embraced and reflected in marketing decisions.

Conditions that favour large-scale operations but not mass tourism

With the exception of the numerical importance of small businesses, these trends are obviously not unique to travel and tourism but they are highly relevant to what is happening in marketing in the industry at the start of the twenty-first century. Large transnational corporations in travel and tourism around the world are increasingly able, through their marketing decisions, to influence customers' expectations of products and prices on the one hand, and to lead the way in the development of marketing skills on the other. In this they are aided by modern ICT, which has greatly facilitated the speed and efficiency with which it is possible to manage and control large, multi-site operations. As for supermarkets and banks, so for large hotels, fast-food restaurants, airlines and tour operators, the conduct of quality controlled standardized operations in many different locations spread over a wide geographical area is already common. In all of these sectors of modern services a greater share of total market turnover is becoming concentrated into fewer large-scale organizations.

The trends have already produced very large, branded organizations in travel and tourism, such as: Bass/Holiday Inn, Accor, Granada, Hyatt, Quality Inns and Sheraton in the hotel sector; American Airlines, Lufthansa and British Airways in the airline sector; Hertz, Avis and Budget in car rental; American Express, Thomas Cook/JMC and Preussag/TUI in travel organizations; and McDonald's, Burger King and Little Chef in fast-food catering. These, of course, are only a few of the internationally recognized corporations competing for shares of travel and tourism markets, and students may find it a worthwhile exercise to expand this list around the industry sectors shown in Figure 1.1 (Chapter 1).

The emergence of large organizations in manufacturing and service industries other than tourism has been well quantified in recent years in the USA, Britain and continental Europe and in the Asia Pacific region. The economic arguments of economies of scale, the search for lower unit costs of production through the operation of larger capacity machines and equipment, and the advantages of international branding are also well covered. Though less well analysed for the travel and tourism industry, the trends to larger scale have been in the same direction for exactly the same main reasons.

A quarter of a century ago large-scale operations generally were still invariably associated with mass-produced products for mass-consumption markets. This is no longer true, however, and in manufacturing as well as in service operations global corporations increasingly have the technology not only to segment and respond to individual customers but also to customize products for them. In the 1980s and 1990s it became commonplace for academic authors to write of *mass tourism* as if it were the dominant form of travel and tourism. Mass tourism is increasingly a myth at the beginning of the twenty-first century. The term may with some justification be levelled with hindsight at the operations of larger international tour operators in the 1970s and 1980s but such operators never had more than a very small share of world tourism. By the end of the century, assisted by ICT, large tour operators have segmented and customized their products. The mass tourism notion is about as much use now in understanding modern travel and tourism as Henry Ford's comment that customers could choose 'any colour as long as it is black' is relevant to understanding the modern motor car industry.

Conditions that also favour competitive small businesses • • •

Paradoxically the trends for the twenty-first century outlined above will also work to the long-run marketing advantage of tens of thousands of competitive SMEs that account for the largest part of travel and tourism supply in most countries (see Chapter 10 and the Epilogue). But the recent emergence and speed of growth of large international organizations justifies the view that their marketing practices will be increasingly influential. They will tend to dominate customer expectations, product design, prices and marketing techniques in all sectors of travel and tourism markets. The emergence of international corporations and their plans for expansion have greatly added to the surplus production capacity available and to the pressures of competition. As Baker noted some twenty years ago for industry as a whole, 'in the modern advanced industrial economy we have arrived at the point where the basic capacity to produce exceeds the basic propensity to consume' (Baker, 1979: 379). The same point, based on the capacity implications of technological innovation and slower growth in more mature markets, is highly relevant to travel and tourism in post-industrial economies now and it will be more so as the new century unfolds.

The authors believe that the trends in this section, underlying the nature of modern international competition and the continuous need to fill thousands of under-utilized beds, seats and other supply components, provide the most powerful motivator now forcing the pace of modern marketing in the travel and tourism industry. There is no equivalent phenomenon on this scale in any previous period of history. These are the driving forces that explain the current and future importance of marketing orientation and the need for improved marketing techniques.

5 Facilitates the efficient and effective conduct of business through monitoring and control

A marketing orientation is not an option for businesses in competitive markets. It is a necessary condition for survival. It is less clear from the definitions of marketing exactly how this orientation leads to the more efficient and effective conduct of business. In practice efficiency emerges from the systematic way that managers undertake the processes set out in Figure 2.1; effectiveness emerges from the business planning and targeting processes. But it is not the processes themselves that are characteristic of marketing orientation. All commercial organizations plan, promote and distribute products, and the processes are common to all larger organizations. What differentiates them is the corporate culture noted earlier and the way that marketing procedures are integrated and co-ordinated with other core business functions, especially the production or operational processes, human resource management and financial controls.

Marketing-orientated businesses are characterized by the systematic organization of their planning processes, their knowledge of the effects of their actions on their customers, the precision with which they state their targets and the speed at which they can act in relation to competitors. Identifying, responding and adapting to market changes ahead of competitors is the essence of the modern marketing approach.

Throughout this book it is stressed that efficiency and effectiveness in marketing is always based upon the specification of precise objectives and action programmes that can be closely monitored and evaluated. Precise marketing objectives also serve in practice as:

- An integrating and co-ordinating mechanism for the operational departments in a business.
- A control system for measuring actual performance against targets, overall and for specific business units.
- A means of evaluating tactical targets against strategic marketing objectives.
- A means of communicating the goals and achievements of the organization to employees and other stakeholders.

Chapter summary

This chapter defines the meaning of modern marketing, first, as a *management orientation*, sometimes referred to as a management philosophy or corporate culture and, second, as a *systematic process* integrating the techniques used by marketing managers to influence demand. To be effective in practice the orientation and the process must be integrated and co-ordinated within the whole management team. Marketing is outward looking and proactive to the changing business environment, and to the needs, expectations and behaviour of customers. While the practice of marketing is most easily understood in commercial operations, the orientation and the processes are increasingly applied in the not-for-profit sectors also.

It is stressed that a marketing approach is a response to business conditions, especially competition, and that such conditions are increasingly common to all producers of consumer goods and services at the start of the twenty-first century. The particular conditions of fierce competition in markets dominated by large-scale, multi-site organizations, often with a considerable surplus of capacity of highly perishable products and seeking to influence available demand, are those that are now found frequently in travel and tourism markets in many parts of the world. The chapter notes the key role of larger international firms because of their influence over modern markets but the numbers and importance of small businesses (SMEs) are also stressed. Competition between large organizations seems certain to leave many gaps and niches, too small to be profitable for big firms with their necessarily standardized operations, but highly profitable for smaller ones practising the same marketing orientation and techniques without competing head-on in large volume markets. Information communications technology can be harnessed to work for the benefit of all sizes of operation.

Figure 2.1 provides a step-by-step diagram of the modern marketing process applicable to all types of organization in the travel and tourism industry. It also serves as a framework for the contents of this book. The diagram is important and should repay careful consideration.

Above all, this chapter stresses that marketing is a proactive approach to business, conducted at best in a marvellously stimulating and positive spirit of competitive enthusiasm that no textbook can convey.

Further reading

Baker, M. J. (1996). *Marketing: An Introductory Text*. Chapter 1, 6th edn, Macmillan.

Brassington, F. and Pettit, S. (2000). *Principles of Marketing*. Chapter 22, 2nd edn, Prentice-Hall.

Davidson, H. (1997). *Even More Offensive Marketing*. Chapters 1 and 2, Penguin.

Jobber, D. (1998). *Principles and Practice of Marketing*. Chapter 1, 2nd edn, McGraw-Hill.

Kotler, P. and Armstrong, G. (1999). *Principles of Marketing*. Chapter 1, 8th edn, Prentice-Hall.

CHAPTER 3

The special characteristics of travel and tourism marketing

Every textbook on marketing should be based upon services with a couple of chapters at the end on the 'special case of goods'. (Bateson, 1995: vii)

Drawing on the contributions of widely recognized authors, Chapters 1 and 2 introduced the essential concepts of travel and tourism as a market, and of marketing as an approach to the conduct of modern business. Organizations in travel and tourism are part of the *services sector* of the global economy, as distinguished by economists internationally from the manufacturing, construction and primary sectors.

This chapter focuses on the special characteristics of the travel and tourism industry as a major provider of services in the 'new economies' of the twenty-first century, highlighting the marketing responses required. Understanding these special characteristics helps to explain the way in which marketing decisions are made in practice in all the industry sectors noted in Chapter 1 and they merit careful consideration. Travel and tourism businesses are by no means unique in marketing terms but they do reflect common structural patterns that determine marketing responses.

This chapter begins by drawing some vital distinctions between the marketing of goods, from which much of the theory of marketing developed, and the marketing of services that now dominate the economies of developed countries. It notes the growth and importance of large-scale service organizations and the contrast with the millions of small businesses that dominate world travel and tourism numerically. It identifies the characteristics common to most forms of service marketing before proceeding to identify the particular characteristics distinguishing travel and tourism services. The responses of marketing managers to these characteristics, and especially the implications for demand management, are noted. The chapter ends by summarizing the basic differences between marketing as a set of principles relevant to all forms of exchange transactions, marketing for services generally and marketing for travel and tourism in particular.

Marketing goods and services

The origins of marketing theory are generally attributed to the USA in the first part of the twentieth century (Bartels, 1976). The early contributions to the study recognized the growing importance of sales and distribution functions for manufacturers of consumer goods. They reflected opportunities provided by rapid improvements in rail and road transport and telephone communication systems, and the consequent growth in the size of markets that businesses could reach with their products. For over fifty years the emerging theories focused almost exclusively on the marketing of physical goods, especially on the marketing of items manufactured on a mass-production basis for mass consumption by the general public.

Until the 1970s the significance of service industries and service marketing generally were largely ignored on both sides of the Atlantic. Or they were discussed in crude simplifications, which lumped together as one broad category personal services such as domestic cleaning and hairdressing, commercial services such as banking, transportation, restaurants and tour operation, professional services such as medical and legal services, and public services such as education and health care. Yet in North America and Northern Europe, for example, countries with highly developed economies, the proportion of the working population employed in all forms of services rose rapidly in the last half of the twentieth century to levels now approaching three-quarters of all employment.

It was the rapid growth in the 1960s and 1970s of large-scale commercial service operations such as banking, insurance and retail distribution, as well as transport, accommodation and catering, which prompted the shift of emphasis in marketing studies towards services. Even so, the first American Marketing Association Conference devoted specifically to service industries took place as recently as 1981, although there has since been a massive output of articles and books on all aspects of service marketing. It is beyond the scope of this book to trace and analyse the growth of service industries and the recognition that the marketing of most goods also involves commitment to the provision of associated services. But the demand for services generally is related to increasing levels of consumers' disposable income, the development of rapid transport communications within and between countries, the growth of telecommunications and the emergence of computerized systems for management information and control purposes. Most importantly, associated with improved communications and management control processes, the recognition of *economies of scale* in service operations, including marketing economies, has triggered much of the recent growth. Developments in franchising and management contracts for services, together with international mergers, acquisitions and alliances, have also facilitated the speed of growth in large commercial organizations in service industries, both nationally and internationally. In the last two decades, accelerated recently by the opportunities inherent in information and communications technology and e-commerce, major international service corporations have helped to shrink the globe with their international brands. McDonald's, Holiday Inn, Accor, Hertz, Disney and American Express are just some examples.

Large-scale service operations dominate travel and tourism marketing

It is not easy to define the point at which a service producer becomes a large-scale operator; it tends to vary in different sectors of industry according to the nature of their operations. Large-scale operations in all parts of the world, however, usually display the following common characteristics, all of which have important implications for marketing:

1 Production and sale of purpose-designed, repeatable, quality controlled products.
2 Typically heavily branded with advertising support and bearing standard prices (with variations by place and time).
3 Products available at many places (multiple outlets).
4 Continuous production and availability throughout the year.
5 Most marketing undertaken by corporate head offices, which control and direct the activities at individual outlets.

These characteristics are common to most retail chains, fast-food chains, post offices, banks, car rental and hotel corporations. They are not restricted to travel and tourism services.

Given the characteristics noted above, it should be appreciated that there are some strong similarities as well as differences between the operating needs of large-scale service organizations and manufacturers of goods produced on a continuous mass-production basis. Levitt, for example, pushed this similarity to its logical conclusion in discussing the need to 'industrialize service production systems'. He explained that this could be achieved by reducing the level of discretion available to service staff through the use of standardized procedures, and the use of what he called *hard*, *soft* and *intermediate* technologies (Levitt, 1981: 37). Levitt cited the McDonald's Corporation as an excellent illustration of the successful blending of industrial processes in food production and distribution, with quality control over every aspect of standardized operations, including the motivation and performance of the staff who provide service in the restaurants. Most airlines, hotel groups, tour operators, retail travel agency chains and the larger tourist attractions, are striving currently to organize, control and deliver their continuous production capacity in equivalent ways, for the same reasons. It is a global marketing issue.

During the last decade considerable interest has been shown by service industries in systematic procedures for defining, regularly monitoring and providing certification for the quality of service products. Using a standards procedure based on auditing tasks, producing manuals that specify all operations and regular assessments by external auditors, the process is known internationally as International Standard (ISO 9000), in Europe (EN 2900) and in the UK as British Standard (BS 5750). Closely related to benchmarking processes for evaluating service quality, such standards were first operated by some hotels, airlines and tour operators in the early 1990s. Quality monitoring poses considerable operational problems for multi-site service businesses but it is a vital development for marketing managers whose product promises have to be based on expectations of satisfactory delivery. Managing standards of service quality will draw marketing managers and operation managers closer together in the next decade, especially in measuring customer satisfaction and value for money.

Not to be confused with mass consumption

The recent developments in modern service industries noted above explain why the concept of services marketing set out in this book is primarily orientated around the marketing of large-scale, widely dis-tributed, quality-controlled products. It has to be stressed, however, that production on a large scale no longer means the mass production of undifferentiated products for mass markets. All the complexities of market segmentation and product differentiation are at least as relevant to service producers as they are to manufacturers of physical goods; there is also ample room for market niches to be filled by the many small entrepreneurial businesses, which are important in travel and tourism in all countries.

A primary reason for the growth of service organizations is the search for lower unit costs of production. From a cost-efficiency standpoint the essential requirement of continuous production on a large scale lies in effective product design and quality control of standardized operations. But once the technical problems of production have been solved, the ability to sustain production at efficient levels of utilization of premises and equipment forces management attention on the systematic promo-tion of continuous consumption. In other words ensuring that there is balance between the volume of demand and the volume of supply. If sufficient demand cannot be generated, massive financial losses are inevitable. Recent examples are the losses sustained internationally by airlines in 1990–2, and by American and European car manufacturers in the same period. The larger the operator, the more important it is to secure and sustain a regular flow of customers to purchase the available capacity. This explains much of the modern focus on the role of marketing by these larger organizations.

It is interesting to speculate that the relative size of businesses is in fact more important in determining marketing responses than whether or not they are goods or services.

> It is the fact of large-scale continuous production of many service products that provides the essential 'like with like' comparison with manufactured products. Of course, this characteristic has little if anything to do with most lawyers, undertakers, cobblers or beauticians. But then neither has it any relevance to basket weavers, jobbing potters, saddle makers or gunsmiths. A dentist and a street corner shoe shiner have more in common (in marketing terms) with each other and with bakers and candlestick makers, than any of them have in common with large scale producers of either goods or services. (Middleton, 1983)

Paradoxically, the vast number of small businesses is also a dominating characteristic of the tourism industry

> *At their best, small businesses reflect most of the features and characteristics that are unique to the tourism destinations in which they operate . . . The sector has vibrancy and originality and can play a vital leading edge role in delivering excellence with personality that big businesses cannot replicate . . .. At worst, however, small businesses make survival decisions that physically degrade the attractions of the local environment, damage the destination image and draw in the lowest spending clientele.* (Middleton, INSIGHTS, 1997)

There is a broad consensus in Europe that small and medium-sized enterprises, commonly known as *SMEs*, play a vital part in the economic, social and environmental life of European Union (EU) member states. Their future role in providing employment and underpinning the economic and social life of local communities, especially in the tourism and recreation context, is well recognized – at least in principle. In practice it is far from clear how best to recognize, measure, appreciate, support and regulate the sector so that it may play its full potential role in achieving national and EU tourism objectives.

Within the SME sector (defined as businesses comprising less than 250 employees) there is growing evidence in tourism that the group representing the smallest employers (less than ten employees) have unique characteristics that merit special attention. Identified as *micro-businesses* to distinguish them within the SME sector, the smallest employers are by far the largest numerically, estimated at more than nine out of ten SMEs. In fact the majority of them employ less than five people and many comprise only the proprietor and immediate family. There were estimated to be over 2.5 million such enterprises actively trading within European tourism at the end of the 1990s, although this may be a significant underestimate (see later in this chapter). Another way to put it is that for every large national or international company operating in travel and tourism, there are at least 1000 micro-businesses.

Individually, micro-businesses are insignificant as players in international and domestic tourism and recreation. In practice they are often ignored in national and regional tourism policy developments. *Collectively*, however, they provide the bulk of the essentially local ambience and quality of visitor experiences at destinations on which the future growth of overseas and domestic visits depends. They also comprise a seed bed of entrepreneurial and enterprise 'culture' that is highly relevant for destination marketing.

Major players in airlines, sea ferries and railways may provide the best of public transport. Global hotel groups may provide the highest standards of branded accommodation. But few tourists are motivated by the joys of transport to a destination, while most hotels and other forms of accommodation are often perceived as just a means to an end. In practice, on the ground, it is mostly small businesses that deliver the bulk of the visitor experiences that define a visitor's perception and enjoyment of a destination. It is likely that nine out of ten domestic and overseas leisure visitors will encounter micro-businesses at some point during their stay in a destination. Those encounters will influence their perception of sense of place, quality and value for money, and their wish to revisit – or recommend friends to visit.

	Europe*	UK(1)	UK(2)
Estimated number of SMEs	2.6 m	72 000	170 000
Estimated jobs generated by SMEs	17.05 m	290 000	500 000

Notes: There are no definitive statistical estimates for these data. However, research undertaken for a European Community (EC) supported conference on SMEs in tourism in 1998 (subsequently published), estimated the volume of SMEs for Europe as a whole and the UK in particular. Using data accepted by the EC as valid for their purposes, UK(1) is an estimate based on data that is broadly comparable across Europe. UK(2) is based on alternative data for the UK from several national sources that provide a more accurate picture – and a volume estimate that is around twice that produced by the EC agreed methodology. *Europe in this context includes Western, Central and Eastern Europe and is a wider definition than the EU.
Source: Middleton (1998b).

Table 3.1
Indicators of the volume and value of tourism SMEs in Europe in 1998

Types of micro-business

Micro-businesses are found in all the industry sectors noted in Chapter 1. Operating in a very local context, many of them are motivated as much, or more, by a mix of personal, quality of life and community goals, as by the economic/commercial rationale that dominates big business. In the UK, for example, there are many semi-retired people who operate small accommodation businesses, not for profit but to support their lifestyle. Numbered in their hundreds of thousands, micro-businesses are unique as individual enterprises and they cannot be standardized – to attempt to do so would destroy their contribution. Unfortunately this makes them amorphous and difficult to measure and 'badge' as a coherent sector. It is often very difficult to influence the sector through any of the existing processes of tourism policy consultation. Many prefer to be left alone and they are not natural 'joiners' of organizations. The sector comprises:

Guesthouses and B&Bs	Self catering in cottages/
Farmhouses	holiday parks
Cafés, inns and restaurants	Museums and other small
Operators of sports activities	attractions
and centres	Coach operators
Taxi drivers	Guides and interpreters
Artists and others involved in	Souvenir shops
cultural provision	Small travel agencies

The importance of micro-businesses

Economically:

- They make up some 95 per cent of all the enterprises providing tourism services. Although the big players dominate tourism expenditure, the smallest players collectively generate perhaps a third of total tourism revenue, and much more locally.
- The money earned by micro-businesses tends to stay in the local community. They typically purchase locally and are part of the fabric of the local money circulation cycle.
- They are a vital part of new job creation – especially in areas of rural and urban regeneration. Even without new job creation they perform an important economic stability role in fragile areas.

In social terms:

- Micro-businesses are part of the lifeblood of local communities – as local residents, neighbours, taxpayers and employers – even where they may be part of the unofficial or 'black' economy. Many micro-business proprietors are also found in local politics.
- To visitors they are often seen as the 'friendly locals'. They may represent all that most visitors will ever experience of real local character, knowledge and individuality at destinations – reflecting the special values of 'place' and 'host encounters'.
- Leading-edge small businesses are entrepreneurial role models of success and may inspire young people in their communities by example.

In environmental terms:

- Micro-businesses typically express the local character of a destination through their operations, and in many ways also help to sustain that character and communicate it to visitors.
- They influence the perceived visual quality of the built and natural landscape by their actions and the buildings they use.
- Their operations impact daily upon local sustainability issues and they are required to implement government requirements for health and safety and environmental good practice, bearing proportionally higher costs than larger businesses.

Some marketing implications

The sheer number of enterprises involved in all countries makes micro-businesses a core, not peripheral part of the experience of almost all tourists. The evidence suggests that such businesses are not scaled down versions of bigger businesses, however, and they cannot be treated in the same terms. At the leading edge, they embody the entrepreneurial spirit and vitality of places, and offer some of the best tourist experiences available anywhere. At the trailing edge, which may be a third or more of the total, many exist on the fringes of the industry damaging the environment of the destinations in which they are located, reducing visitor satisfaction and the perceived quality of the overall visitor experience. Indeed, some of the worst visitor experiences will be found in this sector and they can undermine the other attractions and facilities, reducing the marketing potential of a destination.

Most micro-businesses have no formal management education or training. Most have had little engagement in marketing other than through the medium of print provided by local tourist boards and contacts with their own clients. Only a minority are likely to be involved in some form of co-operative marketing campaigns. Consumer access to the Internet since 1995 is finally changing the opportunities for small businesses, however, and these issues are addressed in Chapters 10 and 18.

Services and their characteristics

The essential difference between goods and services, as noted by Rathmell in one of the earlier contributions to the subject, is that 'Goods are produced. Services are performed' (Rathmell, 1974). Goods are products purchased through an exchange transaction conferring ownership of a physical item that may be used or consumed at the owner's choice of time and place. Services are products purchased through an exchange transaction that does not confer ownership but permits access to and use of a service, usually at a specified time in a specified place. Thus, for example, the buyer of a ready-to-wear suit takes it from the store and wears it when and where he pleases. The producer need have no further involvement unless the article is faulty.

Goods	Services
Are manufactured	Are performed
Made in premises not normally open to customers (separable)	Performed on the producers' premises, often with full customer participation (inseparable)
Goods are delivered to places where customers live	Customers travel to places where the services are delivered
Purchase conveys ownership and right to use at own convenience	Purchase confers temporary right of access at a prearranged place and time
Goods possess tangible form at the point of sale and can be inspected prior to sale	Services are intangible at the point of sale; often cannot be inspected (other than 'virtually')
Stocks of product can be created and held for future sale	Perishable; services can be inventoried but stocks of product cannot be held

Note: These characteristics are those that apply generally to most services and most goods. In practice, most physical goods are marketed with a strong service element attached.

Table 3.2 Generic characteristics distinguishing services from goods

The buyer of a hotel room agrees to arrive on a particular night or nights, and may forfeit a deposit if he fails to appear. Throughout his stay the traveller is closely involved with the hotel and its staff, and may participate directly in aspects of the service product by carrying his own bags, serving himself from a restaurant buffet, making his own tea, and in other ways.

The manufacturer or retailer of suits can put his products into warehouses and shops, and it may not be a vital concern if six months or more elapse between the completion of production and sale to the customer. But, like newspapers, a hotel can perform its services once only on any given day. If customers are not available on that day, products are lost and cannot be held over for sale on the following day.

From this short introduction and the summary of the main generic characteristics that distinguish most goods from most services (see Table 3.2), the principal characteristics of service products may be summarized as:

- Inseparability, sometimes associated with intangibility and heterogeneity/variability.
- Perishability, associated with the inability to hold physical stocks of products for future sale.

Inseparability

This means that the act of production and consumption is simultaneous. The performance of the service requires the active participation of the producer and the consumer *together*. In the context of this book it also means that production and consumption take place on the premises, or in the equipment (such as aircraft or hire cars) of the producer, and not in the consumer's home environment.

It means, too, that most of the staff of service companies have some consumer contact and are seen by the customer to be an inseparable aspect of the service product. Factory workers, managers and many in the distribution chain do not usually meet customers; their attitudes and the way they look and behave in the factory are not necessarily relevant to product performance and customer satisfaction. Physical items can be tested and guaranteed, and precise product performance can be enforced by consumer protection laws. For services, by contrast, a wide range of product performance is determined by employees' attitudes and behaviour for which there can be none of the normal guarantees and no prospect of legal enforcement. Staff cannot be forced to smile at customers, for example. Inseparability of production and consumption is thus a vital concept in the marketing of services and it has special implications for management decisions on the services marketing mix. These decisions are developed in Chapter 6.

Two other characteristics that flow from inseparability are sometimes said to distinguish products based on services from those based on physical goods: one is *heterogeneity or variability* and the other is *intangibility* (see, for example, Stanton, 1981). Taken literally, heterogeneity means that every service performance is unique to each customer. Strictly, because human beings are not machines, this is true; services are intrinsically variable. But in practice it is a somewhat academic concept and it makes no sense to apply it to frequently used convenience service products such as those marketed by banks, transport operators, post offices and other large-scale service operators, all of which are committed to the specification and quality control of service performance. For all practical marketing management purposes frequently used 'convenience' services are no more heterogeneous than convenience goods such as groceries. For larger companies, it is part of marketing controls to minimize the variability element.

Intangibility is an important characteristic of some, mostly the more expensive service products, in the sense that most services cannot easily be measured, touched or evaluated at the point of sale before performance. It follows that many service products are 'ideas' in the minds of prospective buyers. But many physical goods, such as motor cars, perfumes or expensive leisure wear, are also 'ideas' in customers' minds at the point of sale even though they can be inspected and guaranteed. On the other hand, bus services, fast-food restaurants and budget hotels are hardly less tangible to those who use them regularly than Marks & Spencer's socks or a washing powder. Accordingly, although the intangibility of travel and tourism products requires careful understanding by marketing managers and a particular response in the promotion and distribution of more expensive products, it is not a generic difference between goods and services of the same order as inseparability and perishability.

Inseparability, with or without heterogeneity and intangibility does not mean that consumption and purchase cannot be separated. A primary aim of most services marketing is to create ways to distance the act of purchase from the act of consumption. A hotel, for example, which has only 20 per cent of its capacity booked twelve hours before the scheduled performance of its particular services, becomes highly dependent upon passing traffic for last-minute purchases. Customers at the check-in desk may well negotiate prices that are half or less of published tariffs. The same hotel, if it is 85 per cent pre-booked three months before the specified date of service production, is clearly in a much stronger position.

Perishability

It is convenient to treat perishability as a separate characteristic of services, although it follows from the fact of inseparability that service production is typically *fixed in time and space* and has a fixed capacity on any day. This means that if service capacity or products are not sold on a particular day, the potential revenue they represent is lost and cannot be recovered. Service production therefore is better understood as a *capacity to produce*, not a quantity of products. Capacity is utilized only when customers are present on the producers' premises.

To illustrate the point, consider the example of a museum that has an effective visitor capacity (assessed as space in which to move in comfort around the exhibits) of, say, 500 visits per hour. This could mean 2000 visits on a typical busy day, when open from 1000 to 1800, making allowance for peak and slack times of the day. If the museum closes one day per week it has a nominal 'production' capacity of 313 days × 2000 visitors = 626 000 visits over twelve months. In practice such a museum is unlikely to exceed around 150 000 visits per annum but on around ten days it may be overcrowded with 3000 visits per day, whereas on a hundred days in the winter it may never exceed 200 per day. If 10 000 visitors want to visit the museum on a particular day, they cannot do so because the display space cannot be expanded, and the inevitable queues would simply cause most prospective visitors to go elsewhere. A would-be Sunday visitor is unlikely to be impressed by the fact that he could visit on Monday if he is going to be back at work on that day.

Hotels with a fixed number of rooms and transport operators with a fixed number of seats face identical problems of matching perishable supply to the available demand. Perishability is directly linked in the case of travel and tourism services with seasonality, which is discussed later in this chapter.

It follows from the characteristics of perishability that it is not possible for a service producer to create a stock of products to satisfy daily fluctuations in demand. By contrast, manufacturers of Christmas goods, for example, are able to manufacture their products around the year and create stocks, most of which are sold to customers in December. The process of stock creation and physical distribution between factories, warehouses and retailers is expensive, but it does create a relative stability and continuity in the production process that is not available to service producers.

Perishability and the impossibility of physical stockholding does not mean, however, that inventory systems for services cannot be created or that distribution processes are not a vital concern for service producers. On the contrary, one of the most interesting developments in services marketing in the last two decades is the refinement of systems making it possible to retain details of each year's production capacity in a computerized inventory and then treat the inventory in exactly the same ways that physical stocks are treated by producers of physical goods. Thus a hotel may keep an inventory of its 'production capacity' for conferences for two or more years ahead of the actual performance of services and market that capacity through contracts to deliver products at specified times.

Particular characteristics of travel and tourism services

Associated with the basic or generic characteristics common to all services, there are at least three further features that are particularly relevant to marketing travel and tourism services. These are:

- Seasonality and other variations in the pattern of demand.
- The high fixed costs of operations, allied to fixed capacity at any point in time.
- The interdependence of tourism products.

Seasonality: peaks and troughs in demand

It is a characteristic of most leisure tourism markets that demand fluctuates greatly between seasons of the year. Residents of northern Europe and the northern states of the USA tend mostly to take their main holidays of the year in the summer months of June to September, because their winter months of December to March are generally cold and wet and hours of daylight are short. While such climatic variations are not so relevant to many Mediterranean, Middle Eastern, Pacific or Caribbean tourism destinations, their main markets are still accustomed to think of summer and winter months, while schools and many business-year cycles reinforce such traditions. As a result, many tourism businesses dealing with holiday markets fluctuate from peaks of 90 to 100 per cent capacity utilization for sixteen weeks in a year, to troughs of 30 per cent or less for twenty weeks in the year. Seasonal closure of many leisure tourism businesses is still common.

On a weekly basis, city centre restaurants may fluctuate from 80 per cent occupancy on Thursdays to 20 per cent (if they open) at weekends. On a daily basis, seats on a scheduled air flight may be 95 per cent full at 0800 hours, while seats on the following flight at 1000 hours may be only 45 per cent occupied. These demand variations are all the more acute because of the factor of perishability discussed previously and it is always a major preoccupation of marketing managers to generate as much demand to fill the troughs as market conditions permit.

High fixed costs of service operations

When the profit and loss accounts of service businesses in the travel and tourism industry are analysed, it is generally the case that they reveal relatively high fixed costs of operating the available (fixed) level of capacity, and relatively low variable costs. A *fixed cost* is one that has to be paid for in advance in order for a business to be open to receive customers; a *variable cost* is one that is incurred in relation to the number of customers received at any given time. What this means in practice may easily be understood in the case of a visitor attraction which must fund the following main costs in order to be open to receive visitors:

- Premises (capital costs and annual maintenance costs).
- Rents, leases and rates.
- Equipment (including repairs, renewals and servicing).
- Heating, lighting and other energy costs.
- Insurances.
- Wages and salaries and social provision for full time employees.
- Management overheads and administrative costs.
- The bulk of marketing costs.

The point to note is that these fixed costs are mostly committed ahead over a twelve-month period and have to be met whether the attraction draws in fifty visitors, 500 or 5000 on any day. While a significant element of variable cost arises in operating catering and shops and in the numbers of part-time staff employed, the variable cost of admitting one additional visitor at the margin is virtually nil. The same basic fact of operations is true for room sales in hotels, seats in transport operations and all forms of visitor entertainment.

To illustrate the same important point with a transport example, consider an airline that operates a particular flight with either 20 per cent or 80 per cent of seats occupied. Its aircraft maintenance costs are the same, its airport dues are the same, it pays the same wages to cabin and flight-deck staff and to its airport and other personnel, and its fuel charges vary only marginally. In other words, to perform the service at all calls for a high level of fixed cost regardless of how many passengers are carried. Although operating costs are mainly fixed regardless of seat occupancy, the revenue side varies dramatically. For a seat price of say US$200 (average), sales of forty seats produce a basic gross revenue contribution of $8000. If 200 seats are sold, contribution is $40 000. If the fixed costs of operating the flight are $20 000, then forty occupied seats produces a loss of $12 000 and 200 occupied seats produces a surplus of $20 000.

The facts of high fixed costs of operation in combination with seasonality fluctuations focus all service operators' attention on the need to generate extra demand. The need focuses especially on the additional, or marginal sales of which a very high proportion represents 'pure' revenue gain with little or no extra cost.

It is worth stressing that most large-scale businesses are obliged through competition to operate on a very narrow margin between costs and revenue, with costs always under pressure. Plus or minus one percentage point in average load factors for airlines (seat occupancy) or room occupancy for hotels may not sound large, but over a year it may mean the difference between a substantial profit on assets employed or a significant loss. Imagine the atmosphere in boardrooms of Singapore and Hong Kong hotel companies in 1997/8 as they sought to grapple with their marketing budgets in the short-run market downturn that followed the economic crisis in Japan and several Asia Pacific neighbours in 1997. Falls of 25 per cent and more in some markets were recorded in 1998 with the inevitable impact both on room rates and occupancy levels. Such shifts in demand are unusually severe but the history of tourism has many such examples and they impose very daunting tasks for marketing managers as the principal revenue generators.

Interdependence of tourism products

Most tourist visitors expect to combine several products in their travel purchases, not just one. A vacationer chooses attractions at a destination together with the products of accommodation, transport and other facilities such as recreational activity and catering. Tourist accommodation suppliers at a destination are therefore partly influenced by the marketing decisions of tour operators and travel agents, attractions, transport interests and tourist boards, which together or separately promote the destination and its activities and facilities. Over a period of years there is always a relationship underlying the capacity of different travel and tourism products at a destination, and a potential synergy to be achieved in their marketing decisions if the different suppliers can find ways to combine their respective efforts. There will often be opportunities for joint marketing of the types discussed in Part Five of this book.

Interdependence can best be understood when a new resort, e.g. a ski resort, is being planned. The basic capacity for the resort is based on the estimated number of skiers per peak hour who can be accommodated comfortably on the slopes. With an estimate of skiers and non-skiers, and of day and staying visitors, it is possible to determine the optimum capacity of ski lifts, the number of beds needed, the required restaurant facilities, car parks, and so on. Each visitor facility in the resort is functionally related to other facilities and, even if they are separately owned, their fortunes are certainly linked. This vital interdependence was designated *complementarity* by Krippendorf (1971). The same concept appears as 'partnership' in the USA (Morrison, 1989: 175).

The marketing response to the characteristics of service industries

In reviewing the distinctive characteristics of businesses in the services sector generally, and of travel and tourism in particular, this chapter has focused on five very important structural aspects of supply, summarized below. The first two apply to all service businesses; the others have a particular impact in travel and tourism:

- Inseparability and intangibility.
- Perishability based on a fixed capacity in the short run and inability to create stocks of product.
- Seasonality.
- High fixed costs.
- Interdependence.

Simply put, the primary marketing response to these five characteristics is to *manage or manipulate demand* in the short run. The more an organization knows about its customers and prospective customers – their needs and desires, their attitudes and behaviour – the better it will be able to design and implement the marketing efforts required to stimulate their purchasing decisions. The marketing response has strategic, long-run implications reflecting a firm's vision of its future, and also a tactical, short-term role.

To understand the enormous continuous pressure that the five characteristics impose on operators in all sectors of travel and tourism, students in particular will find it helpful to consider operations in terms of daily capacity. To illustrate this point, if the task is to organize marketing for a hotel of, say, 150 rooms, the first step is to express its total capacity over the year. Thus, 150 rooms × 365 days × 2 (average beds per room) ×, say, 65 per cent (target bed occupancy average over a year) = 71 175 bednights to be sold. The marketing task is to break up that total into the estimated number of bookings to be achieved per day of each week, and by the different groups of customers with which the hotel deals, e.g. customers for business, or for conferences and meetings or for leisure products. Repeat customers will be managed differently from first-time customers. Multiply the numbers by, say 100, to get some idea of the corporate marketing problem facing an international hotel chain.

If the task is to market an airline, just one jumbo jet represents, say, 450 seats × 350 days (in operation allowing for routine servicing) × 3.4 (average seat utilization per twenty-four hour period, assuming optimum number of hours in the air) × 70 per cent (target seat occupancy average over a year) = 374 850 seats to be sold. The marketing task is to break up that total by the estimated number of bookings to be achieved on a daily basis, and by the different groups which the airline serves, e.g. first-class, club-class and economy-class passengers, with appropriate consideration for the range of APEX fares and club card deals.

To repeat, it is always a key role of marketing in the travel and tourism industry to manage or manipulate sales, (customer purchasing behaviour) on an orderly, continuous, daily and weekly basis

(a) to utilize the regular daily flow of available, inseparable capacity, and
(b) to generate the extra or marginal sales, which produce revenue at very little extra cost.

The better the product is designed to meet customers' needs and expectations, the easier the task will be. The greater the knowledge of customers, the more effectively the demand management task can be carried out and supported through strategic shifts in supply

Comparing marketing in travel and tourism to other forms of marketing

Students of travel and tourism often find it difficult to be clear about the way marketing in travel and tourism differs from other forms of consumer marketing practice. Standard texts on marketing principles are not much help. Generally speaking, however, it is common ground that the principles of the body of knowledge about marketing and its main theoretical elements hold good for all types of product. In other words the basic or core principles of marketing are relevant to all products, whether they are based on services or manufactured goods. Marketing managers at senior levels of responsibility can, and frequently do, switch between industries with little difficulty. This is only possible because of the integrity of the body of knowledge. In travel and tourism in particular, many marketing managers have been brought in from manufacturing and other service industries to bring their expertise to bear as firms grow faster than the level of expertise available from within their own sector of business.

Against this evidence of common ground, however, experience convinces many in the industry, including the authors of this book, that there are some special characteristics of travel and tourism services that are so dominant in their implications that standard marketing principles must be considerably adapted to ensure success in an operational context. This is clearly a very important consideration and it is based on the belief that marketing in travel and tourism reflects five aspects of demand and supply in the industry, which individually and combined give marketing practice its special approach and style. These special characteristics are developed and illustrated throughout Parts Five and Six of this book.

- The characteristics of demand (see Chapters 4 and 5).
- The characteristics of supply (discussed in this chapter).
- Products and prices, which match the supply to the demand (see Chapters 8 and 9).
- Characteristics of promotion used to influence demand (see Chapters 15 to 17).
- Characteristics of distribution used to facilitate purchase (see Chapters 18 and 19).

On the basis of these five aspects of demand and supply, it is possible to conclude with three propositions about marketing in travel and tourism, that are relevant to all the forms it takes. The full meaning of the propositions and the ways in which they determine and influence marketing decisions at strategic and tactical levels are the subject matter of this book.

1 In the context of opportunities and constraints arising from the business environment of a major global market, products in tourism are designed, adapted and promoted to meet the long-run needs, expectations and interests of prospective customers. This is the common ground with all forms of consumer marketing, and the cornerstone of all marketing theory.

2 Service products generally have particular characteristics of inseparability and perishability, which call for a different application of the traditional marketing mix variables. This is the common ground with the developing theory of services marketing as distinct from marketing goods.

3 Marketing in travel and tourism is shaped and determined by the nature of the demand for tourism and the operating characteristics of supplying industries. The forms of promotion and distribution used for travel and tourism products have their own particular characteristics, which distinguish their use in comparison with other industries. These characteristics form the common ground on which marketing for travel and tourism is based.

Chapter summary

This chapter explains the characteristics of services production that influence marketing generally and notes the polarity between a small number of international and global service businesses at one end of the industry, and thousands of micro-businesses at the other end. The main characteristics of travel and tourism operations are explained and the implications for demand management are stressed. Apart from the sheer volume of micro-businesses, none of the aspects discussed are unique to travel and tourism and it is the combined effect of the characteristics that influences the conduct of marketing in the industry.

Inseparability and perishability are shown to cause inflexibility in the supply of product capacity which, allied to seasonality, make tourism businesses very vulnerable to short-run fluctuations in demand. Marketing managers are therefore unusually preoccupied with the need to manage or manipulate short-run demand around the fixed capacity of supply. The chapter notes that the marketing task is easier if long-run strategic decisions have created products that match customer needs, and especially if marketing managers have detailed knowledge of their customers with which to undertake short-run demand management efficiently.

The high fixed costs of operating most service businesses are highlighted. The fact that additional customers can often be accommodated at the margin at little or no extra cost to the business underlies many of the short-run marketing methods used in travel and tourism, especially the widespread use of price discounting. All the characteristics together help to explain why much of travel and tourism is considered to be a high-risk business, a business in which entrepreneurs with a strong intuitive understanding of rapidly changing marketplace trends and a willingness to make the difficult adjustments in capacity faster than competitors, have so often thrived in the industry with spectacular success. The equally spectacular failures are usually traceable to the effects of high fixed costs and cash flow problems when demand fails in crisis conditions.

Students of marketing will be aware that the core distinctions drawn here between goods and services run some risk of oversimplification because many physical goods require extensive service elements to support their sales and distribution – and vice-versa. For the purposes of this book, however, the distinctions summarized in Table 3.2 should be helpful in clarifying differences that profoundly influence the nature of the marketing responses in travel and tourism. These differences hold good for the thousands of proprietor managed and marketed smaller enterprises that dominate the industry numerically, as well as for larger firms with marketing departments.

Further reading

Brassington, F. and Pettit, S. (2000). *Principles of Marketing*. Chapter 22, 2nd edn, Prentice-Hall.

Kotler, P. and Armstrong, G. (1999) *Principles of Marketing*. Chapter 15, 8th edn, Prentice-Hall.

Lovelock, C. H. and Wright, L. (1998) *Principles of Services Marketing and Management*. Chapters 1 and 2, Prentice-Hall.

Middleton, V. T. C. (1998). SMEs in European tourism: the context and a proposed framework for European action. *Revue de Tourisme*, (4).

Palmer, A. (1998). *Principles of Services Marketing*. Chapter 1, 2nd edn, McGraw-Hill.

Zeithaml, V. A. and Bitner, M. J. (2000). *Services Marketing: Integrating Customer Focus across the Firm*. Chapter 1, McGraw-Hill.

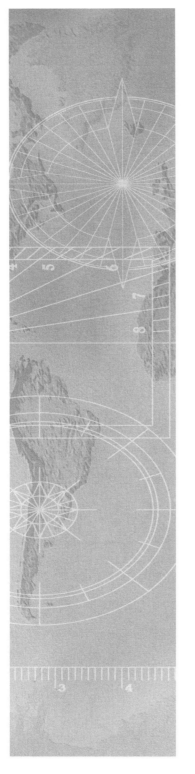

The dynamic business environment: factors influencing demand for tourism

Chapter 2 explains that a marketing orientation is a particular form of business or corporate culture reflecting *outward-looking* management attitudes. Organized around a detailed knowledge of existing and prospective customers, outward looking means being highly responsive and proactive to the constantly changing dynamics of the business environment within which any organization operates. It is widely recognized at the start of the twenty-first century that the pace of change is accelerating around the world as the globalization of economies forces businesses to respond. Figure 2.1, representing the systematic marketing process has, at the start of the process, an appreciation of the external business environment on which all strategy and subsequent marketing decisions are based.

It is the business of marketing managers to understand and seek to influence demand to the maximum extent possible, at the same time adapting their products and operations strategically to take advantage of the dynamics of continuous change. Most marketing managers are not usually concerned directly to measure all the overall factors that influence total market movements, but they are invariably involved with interpreting such movements and deciding how best their organizations should respond. For the purposes of this chapter and the next it is convenient to separate what Burkart and Medlik (1981: 50) identified as 'determinants and motivations'. *Determinants* are the economic, technological, social, cultural and political factors at work in any society that drive and set limits to the volume of a population's demand for travel. *Motivations*, the subject of the next chapter, are the internal factors at work within individuals, expressed as the needs, wants and desires that influence tourism choices.

This chapter commences with a short introduction to the reasons why more demanding consumers are now emerging in most developed countries and notes the determinants influencing the total demand for travel and tourism that are common to all countries. Eight determinants are identified and discussed separately, and combined in Table 4.1. The chapter concludes with a brief note on the implications of the determinants for marketing managers.

The more demanding consumer for travel and tourism – a global development

In all developed countries, reflecting in part a more competitive business climate at the start of the twenty-first century, businesses in travel and tourism are having to respond to more demanding customers for their services. The reasons for this are summarized briefly below and developed in the chapter. Over the last two decades consumers have become, on average:

* More affluent, measured in disposable income per capita, ownership of property and household facilities.
* Better educated and more interested in continuing education.
* More healthy and interested in more active pursuits.
* Older, with a particular shift in the number and attitudes of the more active over-fifties.
* More leisured in terms of hours of work and holiday entitlement, having regard also to earlier retirement – although many at work are also experiencing greater pressure on available leisure time.
* More travelled, for work and business as well as for holidays and leisure, increasing numbers with frequent international travel experience.
* More exposed to the media and information generally.
* More computer literate with ownership of personal computers (PCs) and access to the Internet growing exponentially.
* More heterogeneous and individualistic in their demands and expectations.
* More culturally diverse in terms of ethnic origin as well as in their range of lifestyle choices.

This all adds up to more diverse, more experienced, more demanding, more quality conscious and generally more sophisticated consumers for travel and tourism at the start of the new millennium. It also explains why customers are more likely to complain and take action against firms that do not deliver their promises. It explains the concerns of tourism businesses with staff training and providing ever higher quality standards of furnishings and fittings, in hotels and other forms of accommodation for example, just to keep pace with customers' rising expectations. Better soundproofing, individually adjustable heating and ventilation, bathroom facilities and size of rooms and lighting are other aspects of product provision influenced by relative affluence, to which marketing managers in the travel and tourism industry have to respond with new and modified products.

The main determinants of demand

Fortunately for students and others wishing to understand the nature and potential of demand for travel and tourism, the underlying factors are common to all countries. Although the particular demand patterns generated for a region within any country are unique to that area, the same set of external demand determinants affect individual businesses such as hotels, tour operators, airlines and attractions. The responses marketing managers make as they keep the factors under continuous review and anticipate market shifts, differs according to their understanding and judgement of the factors at any point in time and their view of how best to achieve a competitive edge.

The main determinants of demand for travel and tourism are summarized under eight broad headings:

- Economic factors and comparative prices.
- Demographic, including education.
- Geographic.
- Socio-cultural attitudes to tourism.
- Mobility.
- Government/regulatory.
- Media communications.
- Information and communications technology.

Just as the building of a bridge or a new motorway tends to stimulate demand, tourism markets also respond to changes in the *supply* of products and capacity of supply. For example, the significant volume of demand for leisure travel from the USA and Europe to the Asia/Pacific region in the 1990s could not have been developed until a supply of products was available – based, in this case, on transport technology capable of undertaking the necessary journeys at a speed and cost per passenger that the market could afford. Such products were the result of commercial investment decisions taken by suppliers in the light of their appreciation of demand in countries judged to have high tourism potential. Making supply or product decisions in relation to estimates of changes in demand is a constant theme throughout this book. It is explained in most chapters and for this reason supply based determinants are not discussed separately here.

Economic factors and comparative prices

Wherever travel and tourism markets are studied, the economic variables in the countries or regions in which prospective tourists live are the most important set of factors influencing the volume of demand generated. For international tourism in the late 1990s, thirty major countries of origin continued to account for over 90 per cent of world travel spending. The top ten alone account for some two-thirds of spending and nights. The top thirty includes USA, Japan and West Germany and other developed economies with the highest incomes per capita. By 2010 it is predicted that China will among the top ten, reflecting its economic progress.

The influence of economic variables in supporting tourism growth is especially obvious for leisure and holiday travel but developed and growing economies also sustain large numbers of trips away from home for business purposes of all kinds. Meetings, attendance at conferences and exhibitions, travel on government business and social travel are all important segments of the travel and tourism industry. In 1998, for example, the UK received nearly 26 million overseas visits, of which only 40 per cent were for holiday purposes, accounting for 36 per cent of all expenditure in the country (IPS, 1999).

Using the published statistics of tourist trips and of national economic trends, it is possible to trace the relationship over time between changes in real disposable income (measured in constant prices) and the volume of trips and expenditure away from home. For the bulk of the population in countries with developed economies, notwithstanding the world economic downturns of the early 1980s, early 1990s and the deep Pacific/Asia recession of the late 1990s, an increase in real incomes over the last two decades has led to proportionately higher increases in expenditure on travel and tourism. This relationship between incomes and expenditure on travel and tourism is known as *the income elasticity of demand*. For example, if there is a greater than 1 per cent increase in expenditure on travel and tourism by residents of a country in response to a 1 per cent increase in disposable income, the market is judged to be income elastic. If demand changes less than proportionately to income, the market is judged to be inelastic.

If the other determinants remain relatively unchanged there is a very clear direct relationship between the performance of a country's economy, especially the average disposable income of its population, and the volume of demand that it generates for holidays and leisure trips. For over a quarter of a century up to the 1980s, travel and tourism was generally held to be income elastic. The evidence and projections noted in Chapter 1 indicate that future growth of demand in the relatively mature markets of the main generating countries is now more likely to change only in line with disposable income. Increasingly it is likely that travel and tourism expenditure in such countries will tend to rise and fall in line with the economic cycles of growth and recession that affect all countries. However, in developing countries around the world, such as China and India, tourism markets are currently relatively small but will develop very quickly responding to rapid economic growth. Such markets are likely to remain highly income elastic for many years to come.

Comparative prices

Price, which represents cost to customers in terms of money, time and effort, is relative to their spending power and reflects the economic determinants discussed above. But it is not a simple issue. There is convincing evidence in leisure tourism that, in the short run, the price of a firm's products, or the perceived price of a destination compared with those of competitors, is still the most important single determinant of the volume of demand. For international tourism, price is complicated by the combined effects on holiday prices of comparative exchange rates between countries of origin and countries of destination, and by the comparative level of inflation in the destination area and the area where tourists live. The global price of oil, which is especially important in all forms of air transport, adds a third variable to these price complications and it reflects the current US dollar exchange rate. Add to these the influence of economic growth and recession cycles in generating countries, and it is easy to see why the effects of comparative prices is highly complex in practice and impossible to predict with precision.

The influence on demand of just one of the price factors, the variability of exchange rates, is well illustrated by the following data indicating the relationship of the US dollar and the German Deutsche Mark/euro to the British pound

£1 = US$ £1 = DM
(all rates at year end, except for 2000 which is at approximate mid-year rates)

Year	£1 = US$	£1 = DM
1980	= $2.39	= DM 4.69
1984	= $1.16	= DM 3.65
1985	= $1.45	= DM 3.53
1987	= $1.89	= DM 2.96
1989	= $1.64	= DM 3.08
1990	= $1.93	= DM 2.88
1993	= $1.49	= DM 2.55
1995	= $1.55	= DM 2.22
1996	= $1.69	= DM 2.63
1998	= $1.68	= DM 2.82
2000	= $1.50	= DM 3.00

With these changes affecting the price of travel products, it is hardly surprising that British holiday tourism to the USA fell back year by year to 1985 until it was only 40 per cent of the 1981 level. It recovered strongly in 1986 as a result of the stronger pound and by 1990 the number of British visitors to the USA had more than doubled. In the other direction, for Americans visiting Britain on holiday, 1985 was a record volume year, with the number of trips recorded more than double the 1982 total. In 1986 the number fell by nearly a third and the 1985 figure was not reached again until 1997.

For the British travelling abroad in Europe the most striking event of the 1990s was first the fall in the value of the pound when sterling was driven out of the Exchange Rate Mechanism by speculation in 1995 (£1 = DM 2.22) followed by the bounce back in the late 1990s when £1= DM 3.00 (an apparent appreciation of over a third) with obvious implications for the purchasing power of British holidaymakers. Although to some extent cushioned by the currency purchasing policies of tour operators, the number of inclusive tours taken by the British to Western European destinations fell from 13 million visits in 1994 to 11.4 million in 1996. It then recovered strongly in the last years of the 1990s in line with the value of sterling.

For Hong Kong, one of the few Asia Pacific countries not to have devalued its currency at the end of 1998 following the economic crisis in that region, visits from Japanese tourists fell by some 50 per cent in the period 1997/8 (*Economist*, 28 November 1998).

Demographic factors

The term 'demographic factors' is used here to identify the main population characteristics that influence demand for travel and tourism. Working much more slowly than rapidly changing economic variations, the main characteristics determining tourism markets are ageing populations, social class and household income, household size and composition, divorce and remarriage, and the experience of further and higher education.

In countries with developed economies, one- and two-person households have emerged as the norm over the last two decades, with fewer young children in them and a much greater proportion of women in full- or part-time work. The proportion of households including couples and one or more children in the UK, for example, is now only a quarter of the total and the number of children under the age of fifteen fell by over 2 million between 1971 and 1991. The growing incidence of divorce and the relaxation of traditional sexual attitudes have created many single person, single parent and 'new' families with obligations in more than one household. Such changes have obviously affected the many tourism businesses that targeted traditional family summer holidays, providing products based primarily around the needs and interests of children. Smaller households also mean more households and more reasons to travel to visit family and friends.

At the other end of the age scale the increasing number of active, relatively affluent people over the age of fifty-five who are retired or near retired is a vitally important population trend which will increasingly influence travel and tourism markets in the twenty-first century. In the USA there were some 39 million people over the age of fifty-five in 1970, 46 million in 1980, and over 56 million in 1997. In Western Europe it is estimated that one in four people will be aged fifty-five or over by the year 2000. Apart from the size of the market, these retired and near retired people have very different attitudes from any previous generation of senior citizens in the sense that most of them are far more active, fit and affluent than ever before. By the year 2010 many of them will have been brought up accustomed to high levels of personal mobility and most will have established patterns of leisure activities and holidays that many will be able to afford to continue into their eighties. The prospect that a large and growing proportion of the population will enjoy some thirty years of active travel and activity in retirement opens up marketing opportunities for which there is no historical parallel. Marketing managers around the world are studying ways to develop their shares of this expanding market and there are obvious profit prospects for those who design products that mature markets want to buy – without the stigma of being patronized as old.

The influence of education as an important determinant of travel is not easily separated from associated changes in income, social class and household composition. But it is clear that for business and leisure purposes, the higher the level of education achieved, the greater the amount of travel that is taken. This tendency reflects a greater knowledge of what travel opportunities are available and also the experience of travel and 'gap years' as a normal part of college and university life, especially for those living away from home.

Linked to the economic factors noted in the previous section, especially rising real incomes, socioeconomic groupings have shifted significantly over the last quarter of a century in most developed countries. Traditional industrial labouring employment – skilled and unskilled manual labour in factories, docks, mines and so on – has fallen and been replaced by post-industrial economic activities (see Chapter 1). The members of the traditional 'working class,' are becoming the new white-collar and service-industry employees whose status and attitudes are increasingly identified with what was the 'middle class'.

All these trends led logically in the last decade to greater segmentation and niche marketing of travel products. Examples are youth tour operators (18–30), short breaks marketed at young couples and 'empty nesters,' coach tours for senior citizens, cruising and the separation of holiday village operations to cater for those with children and those without. There has also been an explosion of packaged recreational activity products from golf, to skiing, walking, sailing and an infinite range of cultural options.

Geographic factors

The climate and scenic attractions are undoubtedly two of the principal determinants of travel demand for leisure purposes that explain many destination choices. For example, Spain and other Mediterranean countries offer the most accessible and scenic locations for warmth and sunshine for people living in Northern Europe. Florida provides much the same amenity for many Americans living in the northeastern states of the USA.

and are fostered by the popular media. These attitudes can also be influenced by effective promotion and marketing is always most effective when it works with the grain of changing social attitudes to motivate and stimulate purchase. Associated with economic and demographic factors, socio-cultural attitudes have a powerful influence in the sense that they represent commonly held beliefs and notions with which many people are brought up as children. This section indicates just five such common beliefs in North America and Europe that act as a form of 'received wisdom' for millions of tourists.

First, in northern climates, millions of people hold the belief that there is a therapeutic value in lying on beaches and exposing themselves to the sun. Responding to such beliefs underlies much of the tourism destination capacity provided in Sun Belt areas around the world. Recent concerns about depletion of the global ozone layer and the toxic effects of too much exposure to unfiltered sunlight may shift this deeply held attitude over the next decade, with potentially major effects on future demand for the traditional products of sunshine destinations.

Another common belief is that holidays are 'rights' and necessities for relieving stress rather than luxuries, and that trips abroad for business or pleasure are symbols of economic and social status that serve to indicate an aspirational position in society. Related to this is the belief by many people that hours of work should decrease and the amount of paid holiday entitlement of those in work should increase. Across Europe, at the end of the 1990s, EU social policies reflect and promote such attitudes with the expectation and obligation that employers should pay the costs. World Tourism Organization evidence (1999a) suggests, however, that many employees in most countries are actually working longer rather than shorter hours at the start of the new millennium.

The trend towards longer holiday entitlement in the late twentieth century, associated with rising personal income, has helped to encourage the remarkable development of consumer preference for taking several holidays throughout the year, changing the traditional attitude to holidays as a once-a-year event. Multiple holiday taking has encouraged growth in the supply of 'additional' and short holiday products and made it possible for tourism businesses to extend their traditional summer seasons, confident that there are sufficient people with the necessary holiday entitlement and flexibility in their arrangements to travel outside what were the traditional peak summer months of July and August. The attitude to multiple travel is supported by growing numbers of retired people able to travel when they wish, and the decline in the number of families committed to traditional school holiday periods.

A parallel trend can be seen in North European countries with developed economies, such as the Netherlands, Sweden and Finland, where national attitudes encourage large numbers of people to own second homes, perceiving them as important attributes of a satisfactory lifestyle.

A new attitude, not yet fully developed and currently most evident in Germany and Scandinavia, is the expectation that holiday products should be environmentally sustainable, or at least should observe minimum standards of environmental practice. If, as expected, this attitude hardens in the next decade more consumers will reject polluted, overcrowded resorts and beaches and the influence on the marketing of holiday products will be profound.

Personal mobility factors

The personal mobility provided by cars has become a prime determinant of the volume and types of tourism for many tourism businesses over the last two decades, especially for domestic tourism. In the USA the private car has for years been the dominant holiday transport choice. Between European countries sharing land frontiers the car is also the preferred mode of transport for leisure tourism, and for much of business travel too. Car ownership is highest in the USA (1996 data) with some 600 cars per 1000 population but ownership and access to cars has increased significantly in Europe over the last decade. Italy has 530, and the UK and other Northern European countries between 450 and 500 cars per 1000 population. As older generations of non-drivers die in the new millennium, these figures will rise further.

At the start of the twenty-first century most hotels, nearly all self-catering establishments, most tourist restaurants and the great majority of visitor attractions and entertainments in North America and Europe, are highly dependent on travellers by car for their business. Figures of 90 per cent arrivals by car are common. Looking ahead, however, growing traffic congestion, air pollution and government fiscal and regulatory policies are likely to force some customers to restrict the usage of cars. The historic decision to restrict car access to Yosemite National Park in the USA in 1998 is an indicator of probable developments. But there is currently no reason to anticipate any lessening of the demand for personal mobility and the convenience and comfort it provides. The growing experience of extensive road congestion will, however, cause changes to travel and tourism patterns. Leisure day visits from home at weekends appear to be especially vulnerable to such changes. Traditional arrival and departure days for holidays may no longer favour Saturdays in summer months and the traditional weekend travel pattern of out on Friday evening, back on Sunday evening, is likely to be increasingly unattractive.

The use of surface public transport has declined as car ownership increased. Although rising since the mid-1990s, passenger miles by train were little more than 5 per cent of all passenger miles in Europe at the end of the decade. There remain, however, some important niche segments of the travel and tourism market that use public transport on longer journeys for economic reasons or through preference. Transport operators have developed and marketed a range of products to provide attractively priced choices for target market segments, such as those over sixty, students still in full-time education and special interest groups. Coach and bus operators have found many niches to exploit, for international tourists as well as for the more traditional holidays based on coach tours. Such schemes are likely to develop further as traffic congestion grows and government regulations favour public transport.

Government/regulatory factors

Government and regulatory factors are rather different in kind from the other determinants discussed in this chapter. They are, however, crucially important in understanding the national and international framework within which demand evolves for travel and tourism. Most such laws and regulations are aimed at influencing supply rather than demand but their influence over demand is significant.

Virtually all governments impose laws and regulations to safeguard the health and safety of their populations and to control the use of land and buildings; most impose penalties for non-compliance. Such regulations are important but typically influence all forms of industry and are not referred to in this section, which is specific to travel and tourism. Governments also intervene in markets for four principal reasons that directly influence demand and supply and often have a particular impact on travel and tourism, which marketing managers have to understand:

- The first is to ensure fair competition between suppliers. This is usually intended to prevent the formation of monopolies, cartels or oligopolies, which may otherwise be able to prevent new competition from entering their markets or to control capacity and prices in their favour, and not in their customers' interests.
- The second is to ensure that customers have choices and rights against suppliers that may be enforced by law.
- The third is to influence such market patterns as governments control, for example the timing of school holidays, the issuing (or denial) of visas and advice to their populations as to which countries they should avoid visiting.
- The fourth, which is relatively new but expected to have a particular impact on travel and tourism, is to ensure that proposed project developments and existing business practices do not damage the environment. Rural, coastal and heritage environments will be targeted for special protection. Eco taxes of the kind to be imposed for the first time in the Balearics in 2001 are an illustration of this.

Commencing in the 1980s and reflecting changing political realities and aspirations, there has been a remarkable international shift away from traditional forms of direct intervention and regulation undertaken by or on behalf of governments, especially away from direct ownership of facilities such as airlines and hotels. The trend is to encourage more commercial sector competition but with close supervision by government-appointed regulators, ombudsmen and monitoring bodies, whose duty it is to intervene for one or more of the reasons outlined above. The subject of regulation is vast and the subject of many books in its own right. For the purposes of explanation and illustration in this chapter, four aspects of the regulations are summarized below.

For countries within the EU, in addition to health, safety and environmental regulations it is worth noting the raft of measures under the Social Chapter that is aimed at improving the benefits available to employees. Many believe these measures place a disproportionate burden on the smallest of businesses. Small hotels, guesthouses, cafés, attractions and others are required to implement and administer improvements for pension provision, working hours, disabled access, parental leave rights, equal rights for part-time employees and so on. It is too soon to evaluate the full impact of this regulation but it puts massive pressure on the finances of the tens of thousands of small businesses that characterize the travel and tourism industry.

Transport regulation

For air transport, regulation may determine or influence the routes that can be flown, the airlines that can fly them, the number of flights, the slots available at airports for take-off and landing, the capacity of seats on routes and often the prices that can be charged. Traditionally closely regulated by governments on the basis of bilateral agreements between countries, transport at the beginning of the twenty-first century is still shifting towards more open international competition. Led by the USA in the late 1970s, deregulation and liberalization is being enforced in Europe under EC directives in the 1990s. It is likely to have a major impact on the prices of travel products. For airlines in particular, the charging of airport taxes and flight taxes have become an issue of concern as the charges are inevitably passed on to customers as price increases.

Other forms of transport are also closely regulated, e.g. the influence the UK government exercises over cross-Channel ferries and the nature of the competition they may wage with the Channel Tunnel. The issue of rights to sell 'duty free' items is controlled by governments, and the revenue it generates has influenced the price that customers have to pay for transport. Access to 'duty free' was a strong motivation for choosing to travel by sea rather than by air and operators claimed that routes would be at risk as a result of the European decision to abolish duty free rights between member countries.

Tour operation and hotels

The European Community's Directive on Package Travel, implemented in 1993, is a recent example of direct regulation in the interests of customer protection (see Chapter 24).

The imposition of statutory hotel registration in some countries and the control over classification and grading systems in others, typically influence the type and price of hotel products that are supplied and thereby influence the nature of demand. Other regulatory decisions, such as levels of value added tax (VAT) to be charged and EU law covering the rights and privileges of staff, have a direct influence over price and the levels of service provided.

Computer reservations systems

Around the world, governments are well aware that the large airline owned international computer reservations systems/global distribution systems (CRS/GDS), such as SABRE, WORLDSPAN, GALILEO and AMADEUS (see Chapter 18), can potentially inhibit competition through the way they are set up and operated. Such systems can also work to the disadvantage of small operators. The remarkable expansion of the Internet in the late 1990s significantly undermined the earlier market leverage exerted by the global distribution systems and there are now regulations in North America and Europe as well as international agreements to limit the possible bias inherent in prioritizing the sales of the system owners' products. A wider concern to regulate transactions on the Internet is exercising governments around the world at the start of the new century. See also Chapter 10.

New regulation for the environment

Rapidly expanding, environmental legislation now affects most sectors of the travel and tourism industry. Fully discussed in Middleton and Hawkins (1998), an example is the legal requirement, enforced in North America and by the EC, that all new large projects shall be submitted before planning consent to environmental impact assessments. Such assessments influence the economic viability of locations evaluated for tourism purposes and are certain to become more stringent in the twenty-first century. To date there are no formal requirements for businesses to undertake a detailed environmental audit of their operations, although, since the early 1990s, many larger organizations do. Among leading examples are American Express, British Airways, Inter-Continental Hotels, and TUI the Germany-based international tour operator. The trend to more environmentally responsible businesses is likely to be reinforced as the legislation and regulatory provisions following the Earth Summit Conference at Rio de Janeiro in June 1992 are implemented. The trend is also likely to be strongly supported by the new but growing use of regulation based on the development and regular measurement of environmental indicators to monitor tourism impacts.

Mass-media communications

A major influence over demand for travel and tourism is the massive exposure to colour television and, more recently, the World Wide Web now common to populations in all countries with developed economies. Television-watching emerges as the most popular leisure-time pursuit in many countries, with an estimated thirty-five hours a week per household in the USA and around nineteen hours a week for the average adult in Britain (the figures are not directly comparable). No other leisure activity occupies more time than the number of hours spent at home in front of the TV screen.

Over the last decade cable-TV, space satellite transmitters and the Web have provided instantaneous international images of places and events, as well as a continuous stream of films identifying places and standards of living. They have helped to promote activities such as golf and tennis and patterns of behaviour, lifestyles and access to exotic resorts. The cumulative effect of television over the years in shaping travel and tourism expectations in the major demand-generating countries cannot be overestimated. At the start of the twenty-first century, the digitization of broadcasting is giving better pictures, multiplying by hundreds the number of specialist channels available, while the imminent merging of television sets with broadband Internet access indicates an even more influential role over the next decade.

The cumulative impact of thousands of hours of television-watching, even before the full impact of new access to specialist channels and the Internet, has already had a major influence on travel demand. It influences strongly the social attitudes noted earlier in the chapter. Television is, of course, also a main medium for advertising many products in travel and tourism, and no previous generations ever had such massive, continuous exposure to events, people, places and influences outside their normal places of residence and work.

Not least of the influences exerted by the mass communication media is the effect achieved by regular television travel programmes, which review and expose a wide range of tourism products on offer and provide critical evaluations of their quality and value for money. Such programmes achieve a level of authority and exposure that no individual organization's advertising budget could match. For individual products covered, the programmes have the power to reduce demand for the businesses or destinations that are criticized, or create demand for those that are approved.

At a lower level in terms of overall impact, the exposure of prospective travellers to books, films, newspapers, specialist magazines and radio, also contributes to awareness and attitudes. But the other media cannot reproduce the sense of colour and action conveyed by television, or command the same hours of attention. For specialist activities, digital versatile disc (DVD) and the Internet are already serious rivals for television although the media are likely to be combined as noted above.

The ability of television to expose and draw attention to the things that go wrong for tourists is also part of the effect on demand. It includes, for example, the global coverage given to deaths in airline crashes, the stories of murder, rape and muggings of tourists, and the disasters to ferries that capture the imagination of people around the world. Where the majority of a population participates regularly in travel and tourism, the industry is of great interest to the media and is certain to generate stories the public wish to see and read. The full effect on demand of growing media coverage is still not well understood but there can be no doubt of its importance.

Information and communications technology

Developed later in Chapter 10 and Part Four, this section simply flags up ten of the growing influences over tourism demand exerted by the global revolution in information and communications technology that is still in the relatively early stages of its development. Almost half of all households in the USA and several countries in Europe have Internet access at the turn of the century and within a decade access will be available to virtually all with high propensities to engage in travel and tourism. Based on the ever-growing power and reducing cost of microprocessors, the influences over tourism demand include:

- Increasing promotion and distribution of products on the World Wide Web by both private sector businesses and destination marketing organizations, including online sales and the use of the Internet for vital last minute sales.
- Multimedia information provision in customers' homes enhancing promotional possibilities.
- Linked development of interactive digitized television with broadband Internet access, replacing the traditional PC box for many users.
- Switch to greater use of direct marketing, reducing the traditional role of travel intermediaries such as retail travel agents.
- Customer database development and its role in marketing information systems.
- Power to develop bespoke products for targeted customers.
- Relationship marketing with repeat buyers and other targeted customers/stakeholders.
- Creation of *virtual* enterprises in which ICT provides the linkages – especially networks for micro-businesses.
- Major opportunities both for large corporations to grow larger and small ones to gain access to international markets at low cost.
- *Diagonal marketing* to generate new streams of business from existing customers and linkages with other businesses (as defined by Poon, 1993).

Characteristics associated with high and low demand for tourism

Because the underlying factors determining the volume of demand for tourism are common to all countries, it is possible to summarize the influence of the main determinants in a scale of *propensity* to travel away from home. Propensity is a useful term frequently used in the study of travel and tourism to define the extent of participation in travel activity in a given population. It may be broadly quantified from national tourism surveys of trips taken.

Holiday propensity is a measure of the proportion of a population that takes holidays in a year. Of course some people take one holiday only, while others take three or more. Accordingly, it is useful to distinguish between *gross propensity* and *net propensity*, defined as follows:

- Net propensity is the proportion of a population that takes at least one holiday in a twelve-month period.
- Gross propensity is the total number of holidays taken, expressed as a proportion of a population (proportion taking any holidays multiplied by the average number of holidays taken).

To illustrate, in 1995, 61 per cent of British people aged sixteen or more were estimated to have taken at least one holiday of four or more nights away from home to any destination in Britain or abroad. Net propensity is therefore 61 per cent. On average, those travellers took 1.5 such holidays each, so gross propensity (for four or more night holidays) was $61 \times 1.5 = 91.5$ per cent. Both propensities would be very much higher based on holidays of one or more nights, but such figures are not available in the UK. For countries with highly developed economies, such as Switzerland or Sweden, net propensity already exceeds 75 per cent and gross propensity exceeds 150 per cent, although caution is needed when comparing such figures.

Measured annually over a decade or so, it is possible to assess the extent to which a market for travel and tourism is increasing its size due to increased penetration (more of a population taking trips away from home) or because of increased intensity (the same people taking more trips in a year). Both of these are important measures for marketing managers, especially when related to specific market segments, e.g. to measure the holiday propensity of people aged fifty-five or more, or of a particular social class.

Table 4.1 The scale of propensity to engage in travel and tourism

Low propensity characteristics	High propensity characteristics
Low income per household	High income per household
Single parent household	Two parents (employed) household
Rural-community dweller	Large-city dweller
Educated to minimum age	Degree or other higher education level
Older people (80+)	Young people and 'empty nesters'
No access to private transport	Two or more cars in the household
Three or less weeks' paid holiday	Six or more weeks' paid holiday
No access to Internet	Access at work and at home

Note: In cases where all the determinants combine, such as an 80-year-old retired farm worker living alone without an occupational pension and no access to private transport or the Internet, the propensity to engage in any form of travel and tourism in a year may be near zero. At the other end of the scale, a young professional couple, both working and without children, living in a city apartment with broad-band access to the Internet and owning a weekend cottage, may take fifteen or more holiday and leisure trips in a year. Such a couple may also take as many business trips each in the same year.

Table 4.1 is based on the main determinants of demand discussed in this chapter, especially the socioeconomic aspects. The determinant effects of comparative prices, government/regulatory and communication factors are not separately identified in the table, but each would have the effect of accelerating or retarding the propensities established by the other determinants.

The response of marketing managers

The role of marketing managers in response to the determinants of travel and tourism can be put simply. First, it is their business to monitor and where necessary to research the opportunities arising from external factors in the business environment that influence movements in the particular markets with which they are concerned (see also Chapter 11 on market research). Second, based on this knowledge, it is their business to forecast the direction and speed of change in the determinants and the implications of such forecasts for the travel patterns in their markets, taking action through strategic decisions (Chapter 12) and through the *marketing mix* decisions discussed in Chapter 6.

In both the long and short run, investment and operating decisions in marketing-led organizations will always be based on an understanding of the business environment. This is true in all circumstances, but especially true where markets are no longer growing rapidly, are changing structurally, and are subject to increasing competition.

Chapter summary

This chapter focuses on the marketing implications of eight dynamic, external variables in the economic, political, social, cultural and technological environment within which tourism businesses operate. They are common to all the countries with developed economies that currently generate the bulk of the world's tourism but they are not under the control of any commercial organization and are only partly influenced by government decisions.

Some of the determinants, such as income per capita, geographic factors and population changes, have long-run implications for marketing. Such factors tend to produce fairly stable relationships with consumer demand and they are the basis of most of the forecasting models used to project tourism flows. These long-run determinants are summarized in Table 4.1 in the scale of propensity to engage in travel and tourism. Other determinants, such as exchange rates, regulatory changes and the impact of the mass media, may have a much more immediate, volatile and hard to predict effect on the volume of tourism demand and market patterns.

Socio-cultural factors and the influence of environment issues are mostly not included in econometric forecasting models but their influence may be dominant in shifts of market behaviour. A lesson of the past decade has been the remarkable speed at which social attitudes have changed and more such changes appear certain in the new millennium, fanned by media attention. Changing attitudes in society to watch for in the early twenty-first century are likely to affect:

- The use of cars for international and long-distance travel in an era of congestion and pollution, especially for same-day visits from home.
- The perceived attraction of beach-based sunshine products if further evidence of skin cancers emerges.
- Reaction to environmental deterioration attributed – rightly or wrongly – to overdevelopment for tourism purposes as in Venice, Hawaii, Barrier Reef and other coral areas, or cities such as Oxford and Cambridge.

The importance of understanding determinants underlies the commitment of marketing organizations to marketing information systems, as discussed in Chapter 11.

Further reading

Baker, M. J. (1996). *Marketing: An Introductory Text*. Chapter 2, 6th edn, Macmillan.

Brassington, F. and Pettit, S. (2000). *Principles of Marketing*. 2nd edn, Prentice-Hall.

Jobber, D. (1998). *Principles and Practice of Marketing*. Chapter 5, 2nd edn, McGraw-Hill.

Kotler, P. and Armstrong, G. (1999). *Principles of Marketing*. Chapter 3, 8th edn, Prentice-Hall.

Middleton, V. T. C. and Hawkins, R. (1998). *Sustainable Tourism: A Marketing Perspective*. Chapters 1 to 4, Butterworth-Heinemann.

World Tourism Organization (WTO) (1997). *Tourism: 20:20 Vision*. Executive summary, WTO.

World Tourism Organization (WTO) (1999a). *Changes in Leisure Time*. WTO.

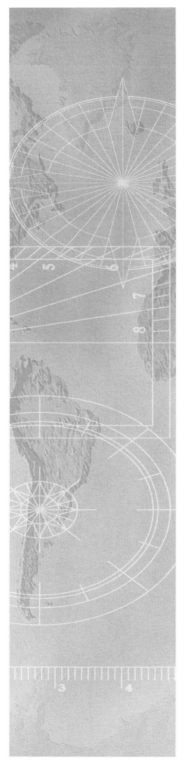

CHAPTER 5

The dynamic business environment: individual motivations and buyer behaviour

The previous chapter discussed the elements of the social, economic and political environment that are essentially external influences on individuals but collectively tend to determine the volume and patterns of travel and tourism generated within any country. The determinants of demand explain why residents of affluent countries such as Germany, the USA and Sweden have high average propensities to participate in travel and tourism, whereas others, such as India, Egypt and much of Africa, currently have low average propensities.

Propensities to participate in travel and tourism explain the overall level of demand generated in different countries but they do not explain the individual product choices that are made by different types of people. A discussion of motivations is required to shed light on why and how consumers make their travel choices. In the context established by the largely external determinants it is necessary for marketing managers to understand also how internal, psychological processes influence individuals to choose between different vacation destinations and particular types of product. That knowledge influences all the subsequent decisions in the marketing process.

The internal, psychological processes are known within marketing as aspects of *buyer behaviour*. Behavioural concepts lie at the heart of marketing theory and have been the subject of extensive literature in recent years. This chapter deals, therefore, with issues that are fundamental to modern marketing and it covers the main issues in three parts. First, the psychological or internal personal influences and motivations affecting buyer behaviour are introduced and summarized in a classification of travel motivations and attitude groupings. Next, a simple input-output model of the buyer behaviour process is explained and illustrated with a diagram shown in Figure 5.1. The chapter concludes with a discussion of the way in which all products can be placed on a spectrum or scale reflecting the complexity of the buying decision seen from the customer's viewpoint. The place a product occupies on the scale greatly influences the way in which it is marketed.

Behaviour influenced by psychological processes

The psychological or internal influences affecting individuals' choices are commonly known as *motivations*. All marketing managers need to have an understanding of why their particular products are preferred or rejected and a working knowledge of the motivations affecting choices will usually be more important than measuring the determinants. Marketing managers expect to influence choices through information, branding, promotion and other marketing mix decisions.

To illustrate the point, consider the vacation decisions of a young, professional, unmarried person, living in a rented apartment in New York and having two vacation weeks to plan. The choice is wide, because disposable income is high, the time is available, distance by air is no problem for a relatively affluent New Yorker and Europe, the Far East or anywhere in North or South America are all easily accessible. This prospective travel buyer has one of the highest propensities to travel.

What motivating factors will influence the choice, for example, between a Club Méditerranée Village in the Caribbean, culture-seeking in Thailand or an adventure holiday in Canada? How far will this prospective traveller make his own decision or be influenced by the preferences of possible companions for the trip? Even more basic, why should, say, US$3000 be spent on a vacation when it could be spent on furnishings or equipment for the apartment? No marketing manager has anything like a full or satisfactory answer to all these questions or their equivalents influencing any form of vacation decision. But the more he finds out about what sort of people choose particular products, what needs they seek to fulfil through each type of vacation and their activity preferences once in a resort, the better he will be able to formulate an appealing product and communicate its benefits and attractions to a target audience of prospective visitors.

Classifying travel motivations

The main broad motives for travel and tourism choices are listed below. These are not motivations in the sense that authors of behavioural marketing texts would express them, but simple groupings of the reasons for different types of travel that share some common characteristics. A more precise discussion of individual motivation has to be related to personal needs and goals, and will be found later in this chapter. The groupings below provide a broad structure within which buyer behaviour operates and may serve a useful function as an introduction to behavioural models.

Many authors of tourism books provide a classification of the basic motivations to be found worldwide in travel and tourism. Variations on such classifications are also widely used in numerous commercial market research studies. The following list draws on contributions by Valene Smith (1977), Murphy (1985) and McIntosh and Goeldner (1990). It is broadly compatible with the overall classification of travel purpose developed by the WTO for use in surveys of travel and tourism internationally.

The main motives for travel and tourism

Business/work-related motives • • •

- Pursuit of private and public sector business, conferences, meetings, exhibitions and short courses.
- Travel away from home for work-related purposes, including airline personnel, truck drivers, service engineers.

Physical/physiological motives • • •

- Participation in indoor sport and active outdoor recreation such as golfing, walking, sailing, skiing.
- Undertaking activities in pursuit of health, fitness, and recuperation.
- Resting/relaxing/generally unwinding from stress of everyday life.
- Finding warmth/sunshine/relaxation on a beach.

Cultural/psychological/personal education motives • • •

- Participation in festivals, theatre, music, museums – as spectator, player, or volunteer.
- Participation in personal interests, including courses and activity involving intellectual, craft and other leisure-time pursuits.
- Visiting destinations for the sake of their cultural and or natural heritage (including ecotourism).

Social/interpersonal and ethnic motives ● ● ●

- Enjoying the company and visiting with friends and relatives.
- Travelling for social duty occasions – from weddings to funerals.
- Accompanying partners travelling for their own reasons, such as business or social duty.
- Visiting the place of one's birth and exploring historical roots.

Entertainment/amusement/pleasure/pastime motives ● ● ●

- Watching sport/other spectator events.
- Visiting theme parks/amusement parks.
- Undertaking non-routine leisure shopping.

Religious motives ● ● ●

- Participating in pilgrimages.
- Undertaking retreats for meditation and study.

Any visit to a large travel agency and a look through the brochures will confirm the wide range of primary motivations for leisure travel and tourism currently catered for by tourism businesses.

Classifying buyers by attitude types

Most large businesses are well aware of the causal links between consumers' attitudes and the products they buy and the implications of attitude shifts on purchasing behaviour. Since the 1970s, in North America, Western Europe and Australia, for example, social psychologists, market researchers and business forecasters have been measuring consumer attitudes and lifestyles. Recognizing that traditional broad classifications of people by age, sex, income, demographics and even stage in the life cycle are of diminishing relevance to marketing decisions, researchers have sought alternative ways to group people and explain their behaviour. Evidence of their work is most obviously seen in the world of advertising, the business of which is to define and communicate images and messages that appeal to targeted customers.

The Stanford Research Institute in the USA pioneered the national measurement of values and lifestyles (VALS) in 1978, dividing the US population into nine segments according to the personal identities and values they seek and implement through marketplace behaviour. This national measurement of values and lifestyles has since been updated and is now based on eight segments that still draw on Maslow's well-known conceptualization of a hierarchy of needs and wants. The measurement has been adapted for use internationally. In the UK, Synergy Consulting has taken over the attitude measurement pioneered by Applied Futures Ltd., which developed a classification of the attitudes of the British population over the last forty years based on regular measurement. Synergy Consulting divide the population into three basic groups that are relevant to many facets of purchasing behaviour including travel and tourism. It is not the same as VALS but the principles are similar.

Sustenance-driven groups

These are people of all ages, mostly in the lower socioeconomic groups, whose attitudes and behaviour patterns are driven by fear for the future and needs for security. Many such people are old and economically disadvantaged, and live in constant fear of losing income, health or what they have managed to achieve of stability and status in their lives. Others are superficially affluent but feel threatened by possible loss of jobs, inability to pay the mortgage, school fees or credit card debt. It is estimated that up to a third of even the most affluent 20 per cent of the population in developed societies are in practice *sustenance-driven*, at least in the short run.

Outer-directed groups

People of all social groups and education levels, with sufficient income and confidence to overcome their security worries, and able to exercise their purchasing preferences and choices according to their perceptions of quality of life. Typically materialistic, ambitious and acquisitive in outlook, and often in their twenties to forties, members of this group tend to organize their purchasing behaviour around the way they look and the expected effect on others of the possessions they own and the holidays they take. Purchasing the 'right' holidays, the 'right' clothes, the 'right' leisure interests (such as golf and boats) – as perceived by the people with whom they associate – provides them with evidence of achievement and belonging to the 'right' group. Fashion motivates this group. Its members are especially open to media persuasion and promotional messages.

Inner-directed groups

In this group, which is projected to double in volume between 1984 and 2023 to cover half the UK adult population, are people of all social categories and income levels. They are mostly educated beyond school leaving age and are usually over forty, having achieved the self-confidence, maturity of personality and tolerance to be able to live easily with themselves and their social contacts. Their criteria for behaviour and purchases lie within themselves and reflect self-reliance, self-expression and self-realization. Such people seek information and control over the quality of their lives and their environment, aim to be responsible for the way they work and live, and intend to achieve the goals they set themselves. Aesthetic, cultural and creative aspirations are strongest in this group.

Since 1973 there has been a consistent and remarkable shift towards the inner directed groups in British society, as Table 5.1 shows. Similar trends appear to be occurring internationally. Each of the three groups noted above may be further subdivided, but the broad divisions will suffice. The groups overlap to some extent and individuals may display divergent rather than cohesive sets of attitudes. They may be inner directed for some activities and purchases and outer directed for others.

	1973 %	1984 %	1989 %	1998 %	2023 %	Trends to 2010
Sustenance-driven	60	52	45	35	20	> falling
Outer directed	20	23	25	30	30	– plateau
Inner directed	20	25	30	35	50	< growing

Note: Although these trends are in the same direction as those presented in the 2nd edition of *Marketing in Travel and Tourism* (1994b), the figures were re-weighted and recalculated by Synergy Consulting in 1998 to take account of changes in attitudes over the years and make realistic projections to 2023. *Source*: Synergy Consulting Ltd, London, 1998 (reproduced here with kind permission).

Table 5.1
The changing composition of attitude groups in the British population

Stimulus and response processes in the buyer behaviour of individuals

The broad groupings of motivations noted in the previous section serve a purpose in pointing to the wide divergence of what motivates people but they do not indicate the reasons why particular individuals have such motivations, nor the processes through which their travel decisions are made. To throw light on this, it is necessary to put the individual, metaphorically, under the microscope and 'de-construct' the purchasing decision into its component parts. Unravelling the purchasing decision makes it possible to model the process involved, drawing on the analysis originally developed in the study of economics and more recently in the behavioural sciences.

Classical economic models of buyer behaviour operate on the well-tested principle that buying decisions (market demand) are primarily governed by price. Other things being equal, the lower the price, the higher the volume of demand, and vice versa. Economic concepts of price response and price elasticity of demand are still highly relevant in travel and tourism markets but they are based essentially on assumptions of rational behaviour. Other, non-rational behavioural influences on individuals are equally important considerations in making marketing mix decisions. As more sophisticated markets continue to divide and it becomes possible to deal with customers as individuals, these other behavioural influences have added importance.

For those considering individual buyer behaviour for the first time it may be helpful to imagine that in some important ways consumers' minds work rather like PCs. Every computer has a given range of functions determined by its designed characteristics and software; every individual has a brain and personality that is partly inherited through genes at birth and partly developed by experience. Computers can perform certain tasks very rapidly through built-in programmes, while other tasks require extensive additional programming in order to produce a required output. Individuals perform some buying decisions very rapidly through habit and with hardly any conscious thought, while other purchases require careful consideration and extensive information gathering and processing.

Both computers and the brains of consumers can only process information that has been fed into their decision systems at the right time, working within the limitations of their design and software (or personality constraints) and memory capacity. If an operator fails to input vital data to a computer, then for that computer the information simply does not exist. Similarly, if an 'ideal' product exists and is available to a prospective purchaser but the purchaser is not aware of it, then for that consumer the product does not exist. In other words, computers and buyers' minds receive information or *stimulus inputs* which they process according in their inbuilt capacities and programmed 'states'. Both produce outputs that are a resolution of all the input variables. Obviously machines are totally predictable and consistent in their outputs, whereas people clearly are not. But the basic systematic principle of inputs (stimulus), information-processing and outputs, is to be found at the heart of all models of buyer behaviour.

Marketing managers aim to supply prospective individual buyers with factual and persuasive inputs of information about specific attributes of particular products. To be effective, it is necessary for marketers to have some understanding of how that information is likely to be received and processed, and how the purchasing decision is made. In the next section a simple input-output model of buyer behaviour is explained.

A buyer behaviour model for travel and tourism

The stimulus-response concept discussed in the previous section is shown diagrammatically in Figure 5.1. The diagram has six interactive processes, with the central components (processes 3 and 4) identified as 'buyer characteristics and decision process', incorporating motivation and perception. The first two processes are the stimulus inputs, key elements of which can be manipulated by marketing managers, while the final two processes represent the purchase output, i.e. the customers' choice and subsequent post-purchase feelings. The six processes within the diagram are explained below. Process 4 is dealt with before process 3 for reasons that will be obvious in the text.

Process 1: Product inputs

Product inputs covers the whole range of products and product mixes that are designed to motivate individuals and are made available to prospective customers. In any developed country there are dozens of tour operators offering holidays abroad to potential vacationers and dozens of domestic destinations and tourism businesses also seeking to attract the travellers' attention. A prospective tourist is faced by an almost infinite variety of choice, amounting to thousands of possibilities. He is only likely ever to be aware of a very few of the options.

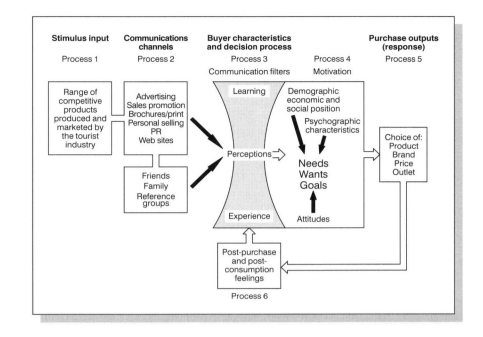

Figure 5.1
A stimulus-
response model of
buyer behaviour

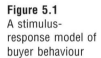

Process 2: Communication channels

These are in two parts. There are the formal communication channels or media aimed at persuading prospective buyers through paid-for advertising, brochures, sales promotion techniques, public relations (PR) activity and the Internet. There is also extensive information accessible to individuals informally through their family, friends and the groups of people with whom they interact at work and socially – known in the jargon as 'reference groups'. In other words the group of people whose approval or otherwise tends to influence large parts of our behaviour. Much research suggests that these informal channels of information, also known as 'word of mouth' and noted in Figure 5.1 as 'friends, and reference groups', are at least as influential on purchase decisions as the formal channels. For the *outer-directed* group described earlier in the chapter, they are especially important.

Process 4: Buyer characteristics, the decision process and motivation

This is the core element of any individual behaviour model and it is convenient to explain process 4 before process 3 since perception is to a large extent determined by an individual's characteristics and attitudes. Grouped around the central focus of needs, wants and goals, there are four main interacting elements, which combine to determine an individual buyer's disposition to act in certain ways. These elements act sometimes to provide or reinforce the motivation and sometimes as constraints upon purchase decisions.

1 Needs, wants, goals (see also Table 5.1) ●   ●   ●

All individuals have a range of needs and aspirations extending, in the well-known hierarchy established by Maslow in 1943, from urgent basic physical needs for food, warmth, shelter and sleep, through safety and social needs for affection and love, to self-esteem and status needs. The most sophisticated level of needs is the inner-directed need for *self-development* (self-actualization in Maslow's terms). Self-development means an individual's striving for personal fulfilment of their potential. Of course, needs for self-development are unlikely to become very important until most if not all the lower order needs are satisfied on a reasonably regular basis. Individuals with a high propensity to participate in travel and tourism, as measured by the determinants discussed in Chapter 4, are those most likely to be in a position to focus on their own self-development and for many of them it is identified with quality of life, as they perceive it – a very strong motivation indeed. The section on attitude groupings earlier in this chapter indicates the growing importance of self-development aspirations or 'inner directedness' that will have an even more significant impact on travel purchase decisions in the next decade.

For centuries travel has been associated with a broadening of awareness and self-development through knowledge and exposure to other cultures and human circumstances. Vacations in particular, and their associations with rest and recreation (in a literal sense of being renewed in mental and physical ways), have always had a stimulating effect upon people's minds and are clearly linked with self-development. The tensions of living at the beginning of the twenty-first century are often associated with a longing to escape for a while into forms of self-indulgence as well as self-development, usually with family or chosen companions whose presence strongly influences personal goals. Personal goals typically include, for example, the respect of friends, the influencing of peer groups, the achievement of a happy domestic life, or achievement and status in employment or voluntary work. Many individuals are prepared to put the satisfaction of others before their own preferences, perceiving the former as their primary goal.

The increasingly frequent links between travel and personal hobbies, culture, sport and other recreational activities may also combine to associate leisure travel and tourism with the fulfilment of self-development and inner-directed needs. It is this powerful association that helps to explain why vacation travel tends to be regarded among those who can afford it as more of a necessity than a luxury. For products catering for self-development goals, it is essential for marketing managers to recognize that their products are valued only to the extent of satisfying underlying needs, wants, and goals, many of which are increasingly sophisticated.

2 Socioeconomic and demographic characteristics ●   ●   ●

These are the easily quantifiable characteristics such as age, income, sex, occupation, region of residence, household size and social class, which were dealt with under determinants in Chapter 4. They are relevant here since they act as constraints or limits within which individuals' motivations and buying behaviour take place. Included in these characteristics is stage in the life cycle, meaning whether a person is a child, young adult living at home, adult married but without children, retired person, and so on. These aspects are further developed in Chapter 7 on segmentation.

3 Psychographic attributes

Also known as personality traits these indicate the type of person an individual is and strongly influence the types of product bought. These attributes also determine the sort of advertising and other communication messages to which buyers respond. Psychologists and marketing researchers measure individuals' psychographic attributes, using dimensions such as confident or diffident, gregarious or loner, conscientious or happy-go-lucky, assertive or submissive, neurotic or well balanced, tense or relaxed, adventurous or unadventurous, risk taker or risk avoider. These dimensions are widely used in product formulation and in promotional messages.

4 Attitudes

All people adopt conscious and unconscious attitudes towards ideas, people and things affecting their lives. An attitude was defined by Allport as 'A mental state of readiness, organized through experience, exerting a directive influence upon the individual's response to all objects and situations with which it is related' (Allport, 1935). Attitudes extend to beliefs and knowledge of products as well as to people and events. Attitudes also cover feelings, such as likes and dislikes aroused, and a disposition to act or not because of such beliefs and feelings. The broad grouping of attitudes into 'lifestyles' was discussed in Chapter 4, and also underlies the categories outlined earlier in this chapter under classifying buyers by attitude types.

It is stressed that there is nothing necessarily right, wrong or rational about attitudes, and also that people do not need to have direct experience of products in order to form an attitude. Consider, for example, Club Mediterranée. There are those who consider the Club offers an ideal holiday for discriminating young people, while others consider the idea of being in close proximity to hundreds of others a daunting and disagreeable prospect. For some people cruise ships are an ideal form of vacation, whereas others prefer walking or fishing in remote rural areas. Some like casinos and gambling, which others find repellent and morally wrong. These attitudes are not income or social class related. They are attributes of individuals.

Modern marketing research methods, especially the power of modern computers to process attitude scaling questionnaires, have made a considerable contribution to the measurement of attitudes and their relationship to product purchasing. While this is still far from an exact science, most large firms in air transport, accommodation, tour operating and national tourist organizations have some experience of attitude measurement in recent years, and the research techniques are improving. The understanding of attitudes is also an essential aspect of product positioning and branding, discussed in Chapter 8.

Motivation, the dynamic driver in the model ◦ ◦ ◦

Motivation stems from the continuous interaction between the four main elements in the buyer decision process outlined above. Psychological theory holds that the continuous churning of largely unconscious feelings of needs, wants and goals generates uncomfortable states of tension within individuals' minds and bodies. Such tension tends to build up and cannot be released until the needs are satisfied. States of tension, including hunger, fatigue and loneliness as well as the drive for self-development are thus the *motivators* that trigger the actions that release tension states. Motivations are the dynamic process in buyer behaviour, bridging the gap between a felt need and the decision to act. Purchase decisions are the action. Most readers will recognize in themselves many less important needs which are not satisfied primarily because the felt motivation is not strong enough to overcome the inertia against decision choices.

A powerful motivator is one that triggers urgent action. In a marketing sense motivation bridges the gap between a general interest in a product, and a decision to go out and buy it. It is in this sense that products can be designed and marketed as solutions to customers' needs (tension states). A marketing manager who has made the effort to understand the needs and attitudes of key groups of customers will clearly be more able to trigger their decisions by adapting both product design and communications in ways that appeal as strongly as possible to their motivating influences.

Process 3: Perception filters in the buying decision process

Perception is the term used to explain the way individuals select and organize the mass of information they are exposed to and perception is a function of attitudes, motivations, experience and learning, especially related to a previous purchase. Perception changes over time with experience and as individuals age and move through a continuous learning process and exposure to reference groups. For all of us, all the information and stimulus inputs, including the informal channels, pass through a perceptual 'sieve' or series of mental filters. These filters serve in practice to suppress much of the available information and to highlight specific parts, often distorting it in the reception process. The message the marketing manager sends is not necessarily the same as the message the prospective buyer receives.

The exact ways in which information is received and processed through perceptual filters remains the most obscure area of all behaviour models. Producers cannot predict how far or how accurately messages will penetrate the filters and stimulate action. While we should be grateful that no advertiser is ever likely to gain the ultimate secrets of perception and be able to manipulate prospective customers against their will, there is obviously scope to make improvements to communications and product design aspects at the margin. Knowledge of an individual's demographic, psychographic and attitudinal characteristics will obviously assist a producer to communicate more effectively in terms suitable to prospective buyers. If consumer research can be used to throw light on the perception and motivation processes, the perceived positive aspects of product design and promotion can be enhanced and any perceived negative aspects can be reduced. More cost-effective marketing expenditure will result.

Process 5: Purchase choices/decisions/outputs

The fifth stage of Figure 5.1 notes the outputs of the decision process that are of most direct concern to producers, including which type of product, what brand, what price, at what time and through what distribution outlet. These decisions are all related to the individual's personal circumstances and are systematically monitored by many large companies through the marketing research procedures discussed in a later chapter. The point to be understood here is that action on purchases is linked directly to motivations, which in turn are linked to the buyers' characteristics defined earlier. Motivations may be influenced through marketing decisions, especially product design and the ways products are presented to prospective purchasers.

Process 6: Post-purchase and post-consumption feelings

Once a customer is sufficiently motivated to buy a product, the experience of consumption will affect all future attitudes towards it. If the product is highly satisfactory, the probability of repeat purchase will be high, the likelihood of good 'word of mouth' will be high and the customer will have 'learned' that satisfaction is associated with that product. Such an experience will lead naturally to good feelings and the prospects of establishing some form of continuing relationship with that customer are high. Such is the basis for the many club and membership schemes operated by businesses in travel and tourism, especially for business users making frequent repeat purchases. If the experience is highly unsatisfactory, the opposite will occur and, depending on the importance of the purchase, the consumer may never buy that product again. Worse by far for marketing managers, such consumers will influence their circle of friends with negative attitudes to that product.

For example, a good experience of an airline, with a punctual flight and friendly service, is highly likely to influence future choices. A long delay, surly service or an overbooked flight can create tensions and frustrations that are observable on any day or night at any large airport. In other words, it is not enough to secure a sale. Good marketing aims to achieve subsequent sales through harnessing product satisfaction as the most powerful means of influencing future buyer behaviour. It achieves this through the learning process that moulds purchasing attitudes and conditions an individual's perceptions.

Personal and situational variables in buyer behaviour

Thus far, travel and tourism buying decisions have been treated as though they all occupied equal significance in the minds of customers. In practice, of course, this is not true. It is necessary to consider a classification that makes it possible to distinguish between a simple purchase, such as routine car rental or a night's motel accommodation for a business user, and a complex purchase such as a world cruise for a newly retired couple.

In marketing texts the basic distinction between convenience and shopping goods, originally drawn in 1923 by Copeland, remains as a standard element of marketing theory. A convenience good is a manufactured item that typically has a relatively low price, is bought frequently, is widely available and satisfies basic routine needs. It is likely to be heavily branded to promote 'instant' recognition. Breakfast cereals, baked beans and batteries are obvious examples. A typical shopping good has a relatively high price, is bought infrequently and it may be necessary to travel some distance and make some effort to buy it. Branding is still very important (as for cars) but may not be essential. Carpets, furniture and cars are shopping goods. Exactly the same distinction can be applied to service products, which may be categorized on a scale or spectrum, with simple convenience items at one end and extensive shopping items at the other. Visits to a bank, post office or petrol station are heavily branded 'convenience services'. Holidays, mortgages, school selection or purchase of a new home are shopping services. The terms *routinized* and *extensive problem-solving* were used by Howard and Sheth in one of the seminal papers on buyer behaviour models in 1967.

Complicating any simple classification of tourism products is the fact that within the total market many customers perform more than one role as buyers. The businessman in the executive suite this month may be a vacationer in two weeks' time using budget accommodation; the hang-gliding expert may also be a regular business-class traveller or a backpacker seeking the cheapest range of accommodation; the hamburger eater at lunchtime may be visiting a top restaurant in the evening, and so on.

Car rental, domestic air flights and city hotel accommodation are essentially convenience products for many American business travellers, who comprise the principal buyers for these products. They involve, therefore, only routinized behaviour and a secretary or a travel agent may make the purchase so that the user has only to collect his key. For European vacationers on the other hand, hotel selection and car rental are often shopping products and a quite different marketing approach is needed.

Figure 5.2 shows a spectrum of buyer behaviour characteristics for both goods and services. The type of products (goods and services) is also

Convenience products	Shopping products
mainly low unit value/price	mainly high unit value/price
mainly perceived necessities	mainly non-essentials
typically heavily branded	branding of growing importance
← - - - - - - - - - - - - - - - - - - -	- →
low problem-solving	high problem-solving
routinized/low information search	extensive/high information search
low customer commitment	high customer commitment
high purchase frequency	low purchase frequency
high brand loyalty	low brand loyalty
fast decision process	slow decision process
high rapidity of consumption	low rapidity of consumption
extensive including online (national) distribution expected	limited distribution expected but Internet of growing significance

This spectrum of behaviour characteristics may be applied equally to goods and services and some examples of both are shown below.

Spectrum of products associated with the spectrum of buyer behaviour

Convenience products	Shopping products
← - - - - - - - - - - - - - - - - -	- - - - - - - - - - - - - - - - - →
urban bus transport	holidays
commuter train transport	hotel accommodation
bank service	air transport
post office services	private education
take-away foods	motor cars
washing powder	freezers
cigarettes	carpets
branded chocolates	antique furniture
beer	

Figure 5.2
Spectrum of buyer behaviour characteristics – goods and services
Source: Middleton (1983).

shown. The principal author summarized the spectrum of behaviour as follows: *'The place a product occupies on the spectrum of buyer behaviour will tend to determine the way in which it is marketed'* (Middleton, 1983). The essential point to note is that it is customer perception that determines where on the spectrum of convenience/shopping a tourism product lies. It is not primarily a characteristic of the product itself.

Chapter summary

This chapter has sought to justify the statement made in Chapter 2 that one of the three key elements in the marketing system 'comprises the attitudes and decisions of consumers concerning the perceived utility and value of available goods and services according to their needs and wants and ability to pay'. An understanding of consumer motivations and behaviour lies at the heart of all modern marketing theory and practice. It underlies the techniques of market segmentation discussed in Chapter 7.

While the behaviour model included in this chapter is descriptive rather than predictive, its practical value lies in focusing attention on the range of variables likely to affect any travel and tourism purchase decision and the linkages between them. The model may serve also as an aide-mémoire in drawing up marketing programmes and as a framework for organizing marketing research. Finally, there is the difference to consider between buyer behaviour that is *routinized*, calling for little conscious decision effort, and that which is *extensive problem-solving*, and may take weeks of careful deliberation and information searching and analysis before a decision is made. Such differences have great significance for the way in which marketing is undertaken. There is, for example, evidence that the World Wide Web is an excellent distribution and sales system for the purchase of convenience services in travel and tourism but much less relevant (except as part of the information search) for shopping services.

If, notwithstanding the attempt to simplify the explanation of buyer behaviour, the reader concludes this chapter somewhat alarmed at the enormous range of the subject, that is no more than a measure of its significance. It is all too easy to say that marketing is about understanding consumers' needs and matching them. Achieving it in practice with limited information is both difficult and uncertain but the rewards to those who achieve even marginal improvements can be great in terms of marketing efficiency and added profitability. Effective marketing in competitive conditions is impossible without some understanding of buyers' motivations and decision processes.

Further reading

Baker, M. J. (1996). *Marketing: An Introductory Text*. Chapter 6, 6th edn, Macmillan.

Brassington, F. and Pettit, S. (2000). *Principles of Marketing*. Chapter 2, 2nd edn, Prentice-Hall.

Chisnall, P. M. (1985). *Marketing: A Behavioural Analysis*. Chapters 2, 3, 4 and 5, 2nd edn, McGraw-Hill.

Jobber, D. (1998). *Principles and Practice of Marketing*. Chapter 3, 2nd edn, McGraw-Hill

Kotler, P. and Armstrong, G. (1999). *Principles of Marketing*. Chapter 5, 8th edn, Prentice-Hall.

Part Two

Understanding the Marketing Mix in Travel and Tourism

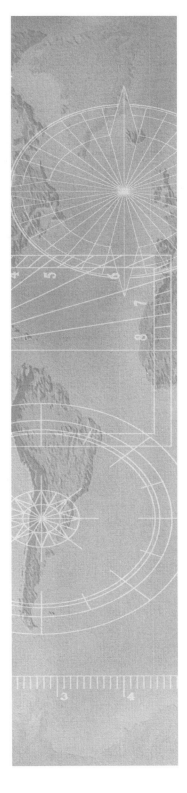

The marketing mix for tourism services

This chapter introduces the four basic variables – widely known as the *four Ps* – about which marketing managers have to make continuous decisions in their efforts to manage consumer demand. Known collectively as the *marketing mix*, these four core variables reflect and express in practical terms the decisions of producers concerning their production of goods and services for sale, in the context of their business environment and long-term strategic objectives. Such decisions were identified in Chapter 2 as the second of the three core elements in the marketing system.

The chapter is in two parts. The first explains the meaning of each of the four core variables in the marketing mix as they were originally conceptualized in the 1960s for the marketing of physical goods. Some typical examples of tourism marketing decisions are provided in Figure 6.1. It is explained how the mix decisions fit within the marketing system for travel and tourism organizations, which is represented diagrammatically in Figure 6.2. The second part explains how the original four variables have been expanded in the last two decades to encompass *people*, *process* and *physical evidence* or design. In services marketing generally there has been extensive consideration of the meaning of 'product' and how the concept should be developed to reflect the modern, post-industrial context of service/experience industries.

In every way, consideration of the marketing mix is central to understanding modern tourism marketing and the key variables discussed in this chapter are subsequently developed and referred to throughout this book. In particular the planning of the marketing mix is discussed in detail in Chapters 13 and 14.

Marketing mix defined: the original four 'P's

The marketing mix may be defined as 'the mixture of controllable marketing variables that the firm uses to pursue the sought level of sales in the target market' (Kotler, 1984: 68).

The concept implies a set of variables akin to levers or controls that can be operated by a marketing manager to achieve a defined goal. By way of illustration the controls may be likened to those of an automobile, which has four main controls. A throttle or accelerator to control engine speed, a brake to reduce speed or stop, a gear shift to match the engine speed to the road speed required, or to reverse direction, and a steering wheel with which to change the direction of travel. As every driver knows, movement of the controls must be synchronized in response to constantly changing road conditions and the actions of others. Effective progress requires continuous manipulation of the four basic controls.

Marketing managers are also 'driving' their products towards chosen destinations. The four controls are *product formulation*, which is a means of adapting the product to the changing needs of the target customer; *pricing*, which in practice tends to be used as a throttle to increase or slow down the volume of sales according to market conditions; *promotion*, which is used to increase the numbers of those in the market who are aware of the product and are favourably disposed towards buying it; and *place*, which determines the number of prospective customers who are able to find convenient places and ways to gain information and convert their buying intentions into purchases. These four controls are manipulated continuously according to the market conditions prevailing, especially with regard to the actions of competitors. The destinations or goals, towards which products are being 'driven' by the four controls, are set by strategic decisions taken by organizations about their desired futures (see Chapter 12).

The central dynamic concept of continuously adjusting and synchronizing the four main controls according to constantly changing market conditions is the important point to grasp about marketing mix decisions. Continuous in this context could mean hourly decisions, especially of pricing, but in practice is more likely to mean weekly adjustments in the light of market intelligence about progress being achieved.

Four Ps and four Cs

As the focus of most marketing management decisions in practice, each of the Ps, *product*, *price*, *promotion* and *place* warrants a separate chapter in this book. Here the object is to introduce and explain them in an integrated way, which also serves as an introduction to market research and planning for marketing strategy and tactics. It will be noted that the four variables all begin with the letter 'p', hence the name *the four Ps* originally used to describe the marketing mix in 1960 by McCarthy (1981: 42). Perceiving that the original McCarthy principles are stated in producer orientated terms, Kotler restated the 'Ps' as 'Cs' to reflect the consumer orientation that is central to modern services marketing thinking in an era of growing competition (Kotler and Armstrong, 1999: 111):

- Product means *customer value* (the perceived benefits provided to meet needs and wants, quality of service received and the value for money delivered assessed against the competition).
- Price means *cost* (price is a supply-side decision, cost is the consumer-focused equivalent also assessed against the competition).
- Promotion means *communication* (embracing all forms of producer/customer dialogue including information and two-way interactive relationship marketing, not just sales persuasion).
- Place means *convenience* (in terms of consumer access to the products they buy).

Product – customer value

Product covers the shape or form of what is offered to prospective customers; in other words, the characteristics of the product as designed by strategic management decisions in response to marketing managers' knowledge of consumer wants, needs and benefits sought. For tourism, product components include:

- Basic design of all the components that are put together as an offer to customers, for example a short-break package marketed by a hotel group.
- Style and ambience of the offer. For service products dealing with customers on the premises where products are delivered, this is mainly a function of design decisions creating the physical environment, and ambience (also known as 'physical evidence') judged appropriate to the product's image and price.
- The service element, including numbers, training, attitudes and appearance of all staff engaged in the processes that 'deliver' the product to the consumer – especially front of house staff.
- Branding, the focus for communications, which identifies particular products with a particular set of values, a unique name, image and expectation of the experience to be delivered.

In current marketing practice, products in travel and tourism are designed for and continuously adapted to match the needs and expectations of target consumers and their ability to pay. Most organizations produce and market not one but several products to match the identified requirements of several segments. For example, tour operators provide a range of products within their brochures and large hotels may have up to a dozen separate products ranging from conferences and business meetings to activity holidays and short break packages.

Price – cost to the consumer

Price denotes the published or negotiated terms of the exchange transaction for a product between a producer aiming to achieve predetermined sales volume and revenue objectives, and prospective customers seeking to maximize their perceptions of value for money in the choices they make between alternative products. Almost invariably in tourism there is a published/regular price for a product and one or more discounted or promotional prices. Promotional prices respond to the requirements of particular market segments or the need to manipulate demand to counter the effects of seasonality or competition resulting from overcapacity. See also Chapter 9.

Promotion – communication

The most visible of the four Ps, promotion includes advertising, direct mailing, sales promotion, merchandising, sales-force activities, brochure production, Internet communication and PR activity. Promotional techniques, explored in detail in Part Four of the book, are used to make prospective customers aware of products, to whet their appetites, stimulate demand and generally provide incentives to purchase, either direct from a producer or through a channel of distribution. A broader view of communication by producers also includes supportive 'relationship' information provided to reinforce awareness and build a positive attitude to products that helps customers, especially repeat purchasers, make their purchasing decisions. Received by customers through perceptual filters explained in Chapter 5, the available range of communication techniques is growing wider and the terms 'communication mix, and 'promotional mix' are frequently used in practice.

It is important for readers to appreciate the relationship between Promotion and the other three Ps to which it is integrally linked in the marketing process. However important and visible it is, promotion or communication is still only one of the levers used to manage demand. It cannot be fully effective unless it is co-ordinated with the other three. See also Chapters 15, 16 and 17.

Place, distribution, access – or convenience

For marketing purposes, place does not just mean the location of a tourist attraction or facility. It means the location of all the points of sale that provide prospective customers with access to tourist products. For example, 'place' for Disney World in the USA is not only Orlando, Florida, but also the numerous travel agents and tour operators located in the north-east of the USA and worldwide who sell products that include admission to Disney World. As a result of marketing decisions, prospective visitors to Florida can obtain promotional information anywhere in the world and buy a range of products that either include Disney World admission or make such visits probable in terms of vacation locations and motivation. Travel agents are of course only one of

Product	Hotel	Scheduled airline	Museum
Designed characteristics/ packaging	Location/building size/ grounds/ design/room size/ facilities in hotel furnishings/decor/ ambience/ lighting/ catering styles	Routes/service frequency Aircraft type/size Seat size/space Decor, meals, style	Building size/ design/facilities Types of collection Size of collection Interior display/ interpretation
Service component	Staff numbers/ uniforms/ attitudes/ customer responsiveness	Staff numbers, uniforms/attitudes/ customer responsiveness	Staff numbers, uniforms/attitudes/ customer responsiveness
Branding	e.g. Holiday Inn, Marriott, Meridien	e.g. American Airlines, British Airways, Virgin Atlantic	e.g. Tate Gallery (London) Metropolitan Museum (New York)
Image/reputation/ position	e.g. upmarket, downmarket	e.g. reliable, exotic food, badly managed	e.g. dull, exciting, modern
Price Normal or regular price Promotional price (for each product offered)	Rack rates Corporate rates Privileged user rates Tour operator discount rate	First class/ business/tourist fares APEX/bulk purchase fares Standby Charter Consolidated fares	(assuming charge made) Adult rate, senior citizen rate Group/party rates Children rate Friends of the museum rate
Promotion (solo and collaborative) Advertising (television/radio/ press/journals/ web sites) Sales promotion/ merchandising Public relations Brochure production and distribution Sales force	Examples not provided since these are generally self-evident and specific to individual organizations (See Parts Four and Five)		
Place Channels of distribution including reservation systems, third party retailers and web sites	Computerized reservation systems (CRS) Other hotels in group Internet Travel agents Tour operators Airlines free telephone lines	Computerized reservation systems (CRS) Internet City offices Airport desks Travel agents Other airlines 800 telephone lines	Other museums Internet Tourist information offices Hotel desks Schools/colleges

Figure 6.1
Examples of the marketing mix in travel and tourism

the ways in which 'place' or convenient access is created for Disney World customers, or indeed for most other products in travel and tourism.

Convenience of place for a self-catering operator, for example, includes direct mail to the homes of prospective buyers, using free-phone numbers and easy access to products via computerized reservation/booking systems. Since the late 1990s, for most travel and tourism businesses, the Internet has literally revolutionized and globalized the concept of convenient access by bringing it directly into millions of homes of prospective tourists. See also Chapters 10 and 18.

The four Ps/Cs, with illustrations drawn from hotels and airlines, are further explained in Figure 6.1. Readers may find it a worthwhile exercise to complete their own illustrations for visitor attractions, tour operators, a cruise ship or a car rental operation.

Marketing mix: cost and revenue considerations

It is important to understand that all the marketing mix decisions represent costs to an organization and have direct implications for pricing and for sales revenue. Moreover, as consideration of Figure 6.1 indicates, three of the Ps require significant expenditure to be to committed in advance of the revenue it is expected to generate. Changes to the product, advertising, sales promotions, brochure production and the organization and servicing of distribution channels, all represent financial commitments made in the expectation of targeted sales. Investment in people, processes and physical evidence also require extensive 'up-front' investment ahead of sales. While pricing decisions do not cost anything in advance of sales, they obviously determine the level of revenue achievable. Any price discounting required to move unsold capacity represents a loss of anticipated revenue.

To illustrate this important point, if a tour operator decides to develop its existing product range by adding new destinations, there will be set-up costs in investigating the options available and contractual obligations to be made months before the first customers make full payment. Advertising and brochure costs will also be committed months ahead of the first sales. To give a different example, the decision by a hotel group to provide improved access for customers through investing in a new, online call centre and Internet-linked reservation system, may have to be made up to three years before the advantages of the new system secure enough additional bookings to pay back the cost and generate extra profit.

Marketing mix in context of the marketing system

Figure 6.2 expresses the marketing system for any organization in three concentric rings. It is an alternative way to represent the marketing process and readers may wish to compare this diagram with Figure 2.1 in Chapter 2. The two diagrams are completely compatible, but illustrate the same process from a different standpoint. Figure 6.2 is designed to

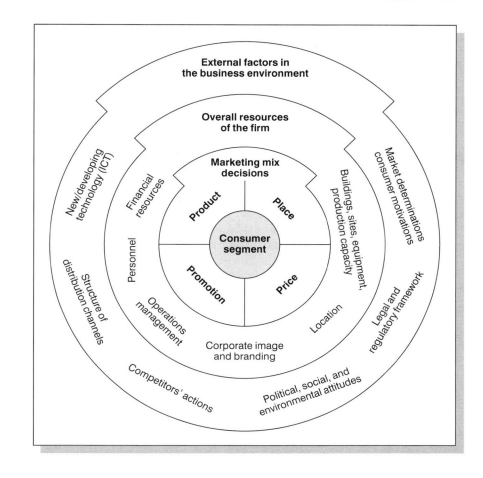

Figure 6.2
The marketing mix in context of the overall marketing system
Source: Adapted from Stanton (1981)

demonstrate how marketing mix decisions, strategic and tactical, operate around the core focus of targeted consumer segments.

As discussed earlier in the chapter, the four Ps in the *inner ring* are under the direct control of marketing managers but they are subject to the other resources and strategic management functions of an organization, shown in the middle ring.

The *middle ring* functions are influenced by and influence marketing decisions but are not usually under the direct control of marketing management. For example, initial choice of location and capacity for a hotel and its general corporate image will be heavily influenced by marketing inputs to the project appraisal process. But thereafter these aspects will be difficult or impossible to change in the short run. The management of personnel and operational systems, e.g. in an airline, will place constraints or limits for manoeuvre on marketing management. Financial resources will govern the size and scope of marketing budgets in all organizations.

In the *outer ring*, summarized under six headings, are the factors external to a business which are not controlled by or even much influenced by marketing managers of any one organization. The powerful effect of these external factors on business decisions has already been made clear in Chapter 4 dealing with market determinants, and in Chapter 5 on buyer behaviour, so they are not repeated here (see also Chapter 12). It is the combined influence of the six external factors in Figure 6.2 that provides the context of opportunities and threats within which strategic and tactical marketing mix decisions have to be made.

People, process and physical evidence: expanding the marketing mix

The second part of this chapter is structured around the expanded marketing mix originally devised by Booms and Bitner in the early 1980s, who added *people* or participants in the service delivery, *process* of delivery and *physical evidence*. The reader will discern overlap between these three additional 'P's' and some justifiably consider them as part-product and part-communications mix. But the extra three-P framework is particularly useful for tourism, which is typically a high contact service (the people component), an extended and complex service (the process component) and a service that can only be evaluated by the consumer as they experience the delivery (incorporates the physical evidence component).

An inclusive tour, for example, involves extensive interaction with the tour operator's employees, with the staff of other organizations such as travel agency, airline, accommodation providers, restaurants, bars and clubs, with other tourists, and with destination residents many of whom do not perceive themselves as part of the tourism industry. The product is rich in human contact and there are plenty of opportunities for error especially if a product is consumed over a lengthy time period, say a week, and involves a number of different service providers. The product is also complex from a process perspective as it is the totality of the many services that make up the overall tourism experience. Some such services may be contracted out by the tour operator, such as airport transfers or excursions, while others are selected by the visitor, such as taxis, bars and cafés or tourist information centres. Third, an inclusive tour is difficult to assess at the point of sale but easy to evaluate during the holiday itself. To assist the prospective buyer and ease the purchase decision, inclusive tour operators need to provide tangible clues about their product offers and to use design or 'physical evidence' to support the service delivery and provide satisfaction with the holiday during consumption. On all three counts, there are benefits accruing to travel and tourism marketers who pay close attention to the extra 'P's' of the expanded marketing mix outlined below.

The people component

It is easy to recognize that most of the variability of the tourism product stems from the substantial human interactions inherent in the experience. It is a useful exercise to categorize the participants for marketing purposes. They are:

- *Visitors*: the individual consumers of the product and the other tourists present at the same time and place. The interaction with other consumers of an inseparable experience will influence the satisfaction or otherwise of the individual.
- *Employees*: the staff of an organization can be subdivided into front-line members with visitor contact and non-contact employees who provide support. Any third party organizations who supply different services to the principal provider will also be represented by front-line and support staff.
- *Host community*: the residents of a destination community who may not regard themselves as part of the tourism business but who, nonetheless, interact with visitors informally and whose friendly or hostile behaviour can make or mar the visitors' experience.

The elements of the marketing mix are traditionally viewed as controllable by the marketer. Clearly, the travel and tourism marketer has greatest control over product design and employees, less over purchasers and very little if any direct control over the host community. Yet marketing activity can still influence behaviour in each of these categories. For example, two-way communication through strong public relations can foster positive attitudes and behaviour amongst destination residents.

Visitors

Holiday tourists are consumers with particular expectations. To deliver satisfaction, travel and tourism marketers need to segment the market by temporal, spatial and other variables to aid compatibility between consumers sharing the same premises (see Chapter 7). The consequences of mis-targeting a communications campaign can be dire in marketing terms because tourists are more than simply purchasers and users. They are also resources, assets and participants in parts of the service delivery whose activities need to be designed into the product offer and the delivery system. Compare the actions of a tourist in an intimate full-service restaurant with those of the same tourist in a self-service restaurant. Some of the activities carried out by consumers in self-service might logically be expected to form part of an employee's job. A no-frills budget airline will include more consumer participation in the product delivery process, reducing staffing and labour costs. For their part, certain tourist segments prefer the greater sense of control that more active participation in the service delivery process creates.

If the product design requires the customer to act in effect as a 'co-producer' in the service delivery, marketing managers must limit the risk and uncertainty for the service provider in three main ways: first, ensuring correct 'recruitment' (i.e. careful segmentation of the tourist market); second, providing imperceptible clues for customers and 'training' (establishing awareness and expectations of the role in the consumer); and, third, encouraging 'motivation' (explaining the benefits of the design to the tourist and harnessing co-operation, just as the organization would be expected to do for a paid employee). The parallels with human resource management are not inappropriate.

Employees and interaction with visitors • • •

For travel and tourism, it is hard to disagree with Zeithaml and Bitner's belief that employees *'physically embody the product and are walking billboards from a promotional standpoint'* (Zeithaml and Bitner, 1996: 304). In other words, staff *are* the organization in the eyes of the consumer. Hoffman and Bateson (1997) refer to front-line personnel as the 'public face' of the service firm. Their physical appearance, behaviour, knowledge and attitude have a powerful impact on the customer's perception of the organization they represent. Logically, one can conclude that employee satisfaction is a prerequisite for obtaining long-term and consistent customer satisfaction. Happy employees give better and more responsive service that, in turn, triggers happy consumers. Placing staff satisfaction before customer satisfaction is the oft-quoted mantra of Bill Marriott, CEO of the Marriott Corporation. Indeed, an inverted view of the traditional organizational pyramid puts front-line contact staff at the top of an organization, with the various layers of management in a facilitating role beneath them.

In practice, many front-line contact staff in travel and tourism would struggle to recognize this portrait of an organization's appreciation of its most valuable resource. Many find themselves performing jobs below the status of the customer in a position that Shamir (1995) refers to as a 'subordinate service role'. This includes most waiters, bar staff, chamber maids, cabin crew, bus and taxi drivers, tourist information staff and so on. The list would be easy to extend. Only a minority of tourist-facing employees, such as airline pilots or instructors in a special interest activity, enjoy professional roles with the measure of control over the service encounter that a higher status affords. For many who serve tourists from a subordinate perspective on low pay, long hours, having little career structure and potentially minimal respect from the tourist, the idea of an inverted pyramid of management support below them would seem absurd. Resentful employees may develop their own methods to 'get even' and overcome perceived inequality between customers and themselves. For instance, the tourist information centre employee who speaks English when dealing with German tourists, despite being able to speak excellent German, is shifting the balance of power to give himself greater control over the situation.

Contact employees who have to reconcile the internal operational requirements of an organization with the expectations and demands of customers are required to show empathy with visitors while obeying the rules and regulations of the organization that employs them. There is often stress associated with these demands that can manifest itself in three types of conflict (Zeithaml and Bitner, 1996).

The first type of conflict may not be apparent to the visitor. It is the struggle between the personal feelings of the contact employee and the role required of them in doing their job. Role demands may grate against self-image. The female air stewardess who experiences lewd comments or physical harassment from male passengers is still expected to behave in role, although had such incidents occurred outside work her reactions would follow her personal feelings. Such conflict is particularly evident in subordinate staff where employees may be subjected to behaviour that lags behind accepted behaviour in society in general. Air stewardesses, for example, have been known to protest against airline advertising campaigns that present them in a sexual light. One might question what, if any, thought was applied to internal marketing in such cases.

The second type of conflict occurs when an employee is pulled between the wishes of the customer and the rules of the organization. The tourist who requests a coach driver to make an unofficial stop or who brings over-sized baggage on to a full flight, or asks for more and more alcohol may initiate this type of conflict. Although the employee may attempt to apply the agreed regulations, given the person-to-person contact stress of the moment they are likely to either side with the tourist against the organization or to show signs of irritability. Frustration will increase if there is no logical explanation for the rule that can be relayed to the consumer. Consumers may interpret employee behaviour as 'bad attitude' even if they do agree to a request; this in turn will have a negative impact on product satisfaction.

The third type of conflict is linked to segment incompatibility. Differing expectations of the experience to be provided and personality differences can create problems between visitors who are sharing the same time and space, a phenomenon well recognized in museums, for example, where adults' interests and those of noisy parties of children may not always be compatible. For destination representatives employed by tour operators, one of the key tasks they are allocated is to facilitate positive interactions between group members in order to enhance satisfaction with a holiday experience. Dealing with conflicts between customers is often stressful for employees, requiring good training and the development of strong interpersonal skills.

The marketing response and internal marketing

In managing employees and harnessing their potential as an element of the marketing mix, there is an obvious requirement for co-operation between the human resources department and marketing management of a firm. Ideally, marketing should have input to the recruitment process, training, motivation and reward systems, which are the classic responsibilities of human resource management. For example, the communications mix should be directed in part at potential job applicants as part of the process of building an organization's reputation as a preferred employer. Reward systems should also recognize and reward qualitative aspects of the work as opposed to being geared only to productivity measures.

Increasingly known as *internal marketing* it is a logical extension of the marketing mix considerations to recognize that the employees of an organization are stakeholders too. Marketing is as applicable to internal audiences within a company as to prospective customers and others outside it, including the host community at a destination. In large organizations market research amongst staff can assess levels of job satisfaction, identify problem areas and discover ideas for product improvement. In small and medium-sized travel and tourism companies, the encouragement of upward communication coupled with an open-door policy may suffice. Use of employees within prestigious advertising campaigns aimed at consumers also targets messages at staff and can be used to reward achieving employees and to motivate others as well as creating a sense of ownership. Communication techniques such as newsletters, in-house magazines, electronic mail, notice boards and open meetings can also be used to transmit internal marketing messages, whilst a clear and credible mission statement can help develop a united sense of purpose amongst staff.

As well as establishing vision and strategy, good corporate leadership nourishes the right cultural environment for the organization and fosters the development of teamwork between employees. The quality of service delivered by contact staff is dependent upon the quality of the process supporting them and each employee in the chain needs to recognize their role in providing the final product and internal as well as customer satisfaction.

Participants, whether they are the visitors themselves, employees or other players in the process, are all operating within a service delivery system, or process. This component of the expanded marketing mix is discussed briefly below.

The service delivery process

The travel and tourism product experience consists of both process and outcome. For customers the outcome is often intangible benefits, such as a sense of well-being, mental and physical recuperation, development of personal interests such as culture, or revived relationships. For individual service providers the outcome is rather more prosaic, for example, arrival at the airport/destination at the specified time. For travel and tourism, perhaps more than for any other service products, the outcome is highly dependent on the quality of service delivery as perceived by the user. A financial investment can be judged by the outcome of monetary return, a degree course by the grade of the award achieved, the advice of a law firm by legal success or failure. Yet travel and tourism only exists through experience of its extended process of production and consumption. It is much harder to separate the outcome from the experience that delivered it.

Given the high contact nature of travel and tourism, staff and consumers form a vital part of the system of service delivery as discussed in the previous section. Consumers move through a series of encounters during the tourism experience. The obvious service encounters are those that involve the consumer interacting with an employee face-to-face on a firm's premises. But encounters may also be remote, by website, automated telephone service or, indeed, with physical evidence or equipment, such as a roadside sign or an automated check-in machine. Some encounters are of greater importance than others and these may be considered as *'critical incidents'*, or (as Carlson of SAS famously remarked) *'moments of truth'*. Critical incidents are also less memorably defined as *'specific interactions between a consumer and service firm employees (or equipment) that are especially satisfying or dissatisfying'* (Bitner, Booms and Tetrealt, 1995: 135).

It is the *'moments of truth'* that stay in the consumer's mind and signify quality and satisfaction. Zeithaml and Bitner (1996), cite Disney Corporation estimates that each visitor to its theme parks experiences around seventy-four 'critical incidents', any one of which, if unsatisfactory, could result in a negative evaluation of the whole visit. A negative, or dissatisfying, critical incident necessitates an attempt at service recovery by the service provider, and this is better conducted at the time of the incident, rather than afterwards. Turning round a negative incident supports both consumer retention and positive recommendation; failure to do so may generate substantial adverse word of mouth and probable customer defection to competitors.

Planned service recovery systems, recognizing marketing as well as operational needs, provide opportunities to convert dissatisfied consumers into satisfied ones. Drawing on work by Bateson (1995) and Zeithaml and Bitner (1996), the following points for service recovery are judged to be particularly relevant to travel and tourism organizations:

- *Measure and track costs of customer retention* in comparison with the costs of attracting new customers. Communication costs, the potential lifetime value of a customer, word of mouth recommendations and the value of familiarity with the service delivery process of customers as co-producers should enter into the cost calculation. It is commonly recognized that the costs of gaining new customers are at least three to five times greater than persuading current consumers to be repeat buyers. A keen commercial appreciation of the long-term value of existing customers is the rationale for implementing successful service recovery following a negative incident.
- *Encourage complaints* and use them as part of a comprehensive service management system that not only addresses consumers' concerns but analyses and rectifies problems. Research suggests that for every complaint made to a company, there may be twenty other dissatisfied customers who refrained from voicing their unhappiness to the company itself. Yet a customer with a complaint typically tells ten other people about it. Thus, one seemingly benign incident drawing a complaint to the company from one consumer could, in practice, reverberate some 200 times through the word-of-mouth network. And this is before consideration of customer defection and loss of lifetime value. Research also suggests that most service companies have ineffective complaint management systems with most companies spending 95 per cent of their service time solving individual complaints and only 5 per cent of their time analysing and correcting the delivery fault that triggered the negative incident in the first place.

Consumer and employee surveys, focus groups, 'mystery shoppers' and suggestion schemes can all play a part in gathering and analysing information useful for service recovery and complaint management.

- *Train employees in service recovery* using, for example, forms of 'empowerment' that simultaneously help employees show empathy for customer problems and understand management's perceptions of what are acceptable and unacceptable responses. Time is of the essence in complaints and swift decision and response is more likely to result in incident turnaround.

Service delivery perceived as scripts ● ● ●

An alternative way to improve the performance of service delivery is to draw analogies with the performance of a play or film. To see a play, for example, is to experience the writer's script in action. The words, movements and props are taken from a script and rehearsed to polished fluency. The notion is relevant in tourism because many services can, in effect, be scripted with the staff playing their roles as actors on a stage. A script is a sequence of actions, equipment and words that enables the service delivery process to run smoothly and seamlessly. At the start of the new millennium only a very few tourism products are formally scripted. For example, the service delivery at Disney Corporation theme parks use written scripts but most scripting in travel and tourism is very informal, although it is often implicit in training schemes for employees.

To be used successfully, of course, it is necessary for all the participants, whether consumers or employees, to be reading from the same script. A much travelled business executive will know the 'script' for airline check-in, embarkation and delays regardless of airport, and would be irritated to be reminded of it. On the other hand, a family taking an infrequent overseas holiday may have no such 'script' in their minds. The service delivery process for airlines has been known to grind to a halt with an influx of first-time flyers unaware of check-in procedures and requiring assistance en masse that had not been designed into the system.

Tourists have to adapt, think and learn new 'scripts', in a tight time frame, which can be a stressful experience. The 'script' for an English pub will not apply to a French bar. Do you wait to be seated? When do you pay? Do you tip? And if so, how much? What behaviour on your part will obtain best service? The journey by bus can be equally daunting. Where do you buy the ticket? On the bus or at a kiosk? What type of kiosk? Does it require punching for validation? And so on. A confused visitor in a foreign country unable to act out the national script for a simple service appears to be stupid. One does not have to think long to remember personal anecdotes where a tourist hovering in uncertainty has irritated employees and other consumers alike. Unfortunately, this lack of understanding by the majority serves to reinforce the classic stereotypes of the ignorant tourist, so often parodied on postcards.

Marketers dealing with the interface between international visitors and developing informal 'scripts' should investigate ways of informing the tourist before and on arrival of expected behaviour. Tools from the communications mix, such as travel guides, brochures, videos, in-flight magazines, post-purchase leaflets, websites and talks by tour representatives, can all serve to facilitate the process. In terms of services delivery processes, marketers should look at system flexibility and train employees to understand and manage customer expectations.

Service blueprinting

Taking Levitt's original conceptualization of the service delivery processes to a logical conclusion some authors have concluded that improvements can be derived from constructing a formal service 'blueprint' or flowchart of the service delivery process (Hoffman and Bateson, 1997). It has also been described as *'a picture or map that accurately portrays the service system so that the different people involved in providing it can understand and deal with it objectively regardless of their roles or their individual points of view'* (Zeithaml and Bitner, 1996: 277).

Much of the work on services blueprinting from a marketing perspective was carried out by Shostack during the 1980s (Shostack, 1994), and the reader is referred to his work for further details. As a graphical representation of a particular service, any blueprint is likely to incorporate:

- All relevant points of contact (or encounters) between the consumer and the service provider.
- A dividing line between activity that is visible to customers and the support activity that is not.
- Activities of participants, both customers and employees, directionally linked in the flow chart.
- Support processes involved in the service delivery.
- Standard length of time for individual activities and any time targets based on consumer expectations. From these, labour costs and hourly or daily throughput can be calculated.
- Bottlenecks, or points in the process where consumers are obliged to wait the longest period of time.
- Points in the process where service failure might occur that is both rated as significant and observed by the consumer.
- Evidence of service that aids positioning and consumer evaluation of quality.

Blueprints are flexible tools. They can be used to examine differences between key consumer segments and investigate differences between employee and consumer expectations. At first glance, the service blueprint looks closely aligned to operations management, rather than to services marketing. There is indeed overlap (for sound marketing practice is an integrated function, not a stand-alone department), but a blueprint from a marketing perspective is derived from research into consumers' and employees' expectations, instead of relying on management opinion.

Managing physical evidence and design

The third additional component of the services marketing mix is that of physical evidence, rooted in the five senses of sight (especially colour and aesthetics), sound, scent, touch and taste. Because tourism products are characterized by inseparability, visitors are present in the production premises and the design of the physical setting for the delivery process is a vital part of the product. Of course, the physical setting is sometimes the *raison d'être* for tourism in the first place but here it refers to the design of the built environment owned and controlled by a tourism organization, for example, a theme park or hotel, or to the efforts of an organization to design a natural or built area to meet particular visitor management objectives. Because tourism products are also characterized by intangibility, physical evidence is used additionally to 'tangibilize' the offer away from the place of consumption, especially at the point of sale, to influence purchasing. It is also used to reduce post-purchase anxiety, although with the notable exception of the brochure and more recently access to websites, the planning of remote physical evidence has often been overlooked.

The uses for physical evidence suggested by Hoffman and Bateson (1997) are relevant to travel and tourism. Physical evidence acts in lieu of the use of 'packaging' for products based on physical goods. It communicates messages about quality, positioning and differentiation, and it helps both to set and meet visitor expectations. Physical evidence can be used to facilitate the service delivery process through, for example, layout and signage that influence customer responses. By creating particular ambiences, physical evidence can help to socialize customers and employees, and facilitate desired emotional states or behaviours. As with any of the marketing mix components, the designing of physical evidence should be organized around stated goals. Skilful use of physical evidence can attract desired segments whilst deterring others, thus aiding demand management. Classical music played in public areas such as car parks or train platforms has been used to deter some groups of people judged undesirable from the premises, thereby enhancing the sense of security and satisfaction with the product enjoyed by targeted groups. For fragile resources such as cave paintings and other historic artefacts, physical evidence may be used as a form of virtual reality to create access while protecting the resource.

The power that the external and internal design of buildings influences over customers and employees is increasingly recognized in all sectors of travel and tourism. Its use in communicating corporate, brand and product values is becoming more important. Design features can influence the beliefs that a customer or an employee holds about an organization (the cognitive element), the emotions aroused in customers or employees (the affective element), the behaviour and actions of customers or employees (the behavioural element) and the physical comfort or otherwise of both parties (the physiological element). Yet the use of physical evidence can be quite subtle, creating the designed effect without alerting the individual to the objective of the service provider.

Ensuring consistency and co-ordination between the different tools of design is an inherent part of planning the physical evidence 'mix'.

Chapter summary

In the first part of this chapter the essential components of the marketing mix are introduced as the four Ps or Cs that have dominated marketing thinking for over forty years. They are discussed as the main levers or controls available to marketing managers in their continuous endeavours to achieve objectives and targets, expressed as sales volume and revenue from identified customer groups. The mix decisions are based on a combination of marketing research, marketing planning procedures and the judgement of individual managers engaged in a strategic battle of wits with their competitors.

This chapter sets the four Ps/Cs in the wider context of non-marketing resources within organizations, and the continuously changing external influences to which marketing managers have to respond. This very important concept of marketing response was succinctly summarized in Stanton's view that:

> *A company's success depends on the ability of its executives to manage its marketing system in relation to its external environment. This means (1) responding to changes in the environment, (2) forecasting the direction and intensity of these changes, and (3) using the internal controllable resources in adapting to the changes in the external environment.* (Stanton, 1981: 32)

In the second part, three additional Ps that are especially appropriate to managing the travel and tourism service delivery – people, process and physical evidence – are defined drawing on current services marketing literature. Much of the thrust for this elaboration of the original four Ps has come from larger international and global businesses in the ceaseless pursuit of a competitive edge in the markets they serve. To achieve and sustain such an edge has to be based on product consistency, quality controls and customer satisfaction, and it has to be managed over multiple sites in different countries and cultures. The same thought processes underlie concepts of Total Quality Management and ISO 14000 and the myriad other charter marks and certification programmes now influencing the industry. The marketing contribution is part of all these processes, especially for identifying the consumer perspective and the interaction between staff and customers in the service delivery process that takes place on producers' premises.

In terms of the physical evidence provided to customers it has been a constant source of surprise over the years that the modern tourist industry, which thrives on the beauty and distinctiveness of place, has created some of the ugliest sites, buildings and infrastructure now to be found in most countries around the world. There has been a general failure in the last half of the twentieth century to understand or apparently to care about the importance of product design and sustainable development. New thinking on the customer impact of design is overdue.

It is interesting to speculate that an understanding of the role of 'physical evidence' is not a modern concept at all. It was perfectly understood in Egyptian, Greek, Roman, Renaissance and Victorian times, albeit for an elite audience. It was also understood in travel and tourism up to the early twentieth century when ships, railway stations and hotels were designed as artefacts of considerable beauty – icons of leading design that clearly had massive customer appeal.

Finally, it is stressed that marketing-mix decisions, including design, mostly imply significant costs that have to be met or committed in advance of the revenue such decisions are expected to achieve. Later chapters will emphasize the need for integration and co-ordination of marketing-mix decisions, in which even small improvements in the effectiveness of marketing expenditure can make a significant difference to bottom-line profitability.

Further reading

Bateson, J. E. G. (ed.) (1995). *Managing Services Marketing: Text and Readings*. 3rd edn, Dryden Press.

Bitner, M. J., Booms, B. H. and Tetrealt, M. S. (1995). 'The service encounter', in J. E. G. Bateson (ed.), *Managing Services Marketing: Text and Readings*. 3rd edn, Dryden Press.

Hoffman, K. D. and Bateson, J. E. G. (1997). *Essentials of Services Marketing*. Dryden Press.

Zeithaml, V. A. and Bitner, M. J. (1996). *Services Marketing*. McGraw-Hill.

Market segmentation for travel and tourism markets

Market segmentation recognizes that people differ in their tastes, needs, attitudes, lifestyles, family size and composition, etc. . . . It is a deliberate policy of maximizing market demand by directing marketing efforts at significant sub-groups of customers or consumers. (Chisnall, 1985: 264)

Chapter 3 stresses that a key role of marketing managers is to influence and, wherever possible, to manage demand: 'The more an organization knows about its customers and prospective customers – their needs and desires, their attitudes and behaviour – the better it will be able to design and implement the marketing efforts required to stimulate their purchasing decisions.' This chapter explains that market segmentation is the process whereby businesses organize their knowledge of current and potential customer groups and select for particular attention those whose needs and wants they are best able to supply with their products, both now and in the future.

In other words, because it is increasingly impossible to deal with all customers on a mass consumption or 'one size fits all basis,' market segmentation is the practical expression in business of the theory of consumer orientation. It is arguably the most important of all the practical marketing techniques available to marketing managers in travel and tourism. It is normally the logical first step in the marketing process involved in developing products to meet customers' needs. Segmentation is also the necessary first stage in the process of setting precise marketing objectives and targets and the basis for effective planning, budgeting and control of marketing activities. It is the basis for positioning, branding and communicating relevant images to targeted users.

In practice, apart from national tourism organizations, no individual business is ever likely to be much concerned with the whole or even many of a country's tourist markets. They will usually be closely concerned with particular subgroups of visitors within the total market or *segments*, which they identify as the most productive targets for their marketing activities. National tourism organizations also find it necessary to segment the total market of potential tourists in order to carry out the specific marketing campaigns they organize, although they may have to provide facilities, such as information services, for all visitors.

This chapter is in three parts. The first part introduces the wide range of segments that typically exist for most producers of travel and tourism products. The second part defines the process of segmentation and outlines the criteria to be applied to any grouping of customers. The third part describes the principal ways used in travel and tourism to divide up markets for marketing purposes.

Multiple segments for producers in travel and tourism

Before considering the techniques used to segment markets we list below an indication of the wide range of subgroups with which businesses in the different sectors of the travel and tourism industry are concerned. The list notes five broad consumer segments for each of the main sectors identified in Chapter 1 (excluding destination organizations that must have regard to all segments):

Hotels
1 Corporate/business clients.
2 Visitors on group package tours.
3 Independent vacationers.
4 Visitors taking weekend/midweek package breaks.
5 Conference delegates.

Tour operators
1 Young people, singles and couples, eighteen to thirty-year-olds.
2 Families with children.
3 Retired /senior citizens/empty nesters.
4 Activity/sports participants.
5 Culture seekers.

Transport operators
1 First-class passengers.
2 Club-class passengers.
3 Standard-class passengers.
4 Charter groups.
5 APEX purchasers.

Destination attractions
1 Local residents in the area.
2 Day visitors from outside local area.
3 Domestic tourists.
4 Foreign tourists.
5 School parties.

The segments listed above are not comprehensive, of course, but simply an illustration of the range of possibilities that exist for each sector. Readers may find it a useful exercise to extend these lists from five to around fifteen segments for each sector, using the analysis discussed later in this chapter.

Even the minimum list above should make clear a very important point: *most businesses deal not with one, but with several segments.* Some segments are largely dictated by the location in which a business operates; other segments may be attracted by products designed and marketed specifically to them.

A marketing and operations view of segmentation

At first sight it may appear obvious that all the managers in a business work closely together to create a range of products and market them to identified customer groups or segments. In practice there is often a real conflict between the needs of operations management and the view of marketing managers. Disputes are not unusual.

From an operational standpoint it is usually most cost-effective and easy to manage if a single, purpose-designed product, such as a standard airline seat or a standard bedroom, can be marketed to all buyers. In that way unit costs can be cut to the minimum, operational controls and training procedures can be standardized and more easily implemented. In such conditions segmentation is still relevant as the basis for separate promotional campaigns but it does not interfere with the smooth operation of production processes. Some marketing-led organizations, most notably McDonald's family restaurants, budget hotels, major theme parks and other attractions, do provide essentially standard products for their customers. But they tend to be the exceptions in the tourism industry rather than the rule. Increasingly around the world, businesses are facing more competitive market conditions in which they are competing for shares of the same markets and aiming their products at the same groups of prospective customers. The need to create and deliver *purpose-adapted* products for each group is becoming more urgent in post-industrial societies with their greater affluence, wider choice and more demanding consumers.

In an ideal world each separate customer would receive special personal service or a custom-built product. They may still do so in travel and tourism if they are able to pay the necessary price, as in penthouse suites in luxury hotels. It is possible also in very small businesses, such as farmhouses taking in a few visitors to stay, in which the level of personal contact between visitor and host is very high and each service delivery unique. In the large-scale marketing of quality-controlled standardized products, however, such individual attention is not possible at the prices most customers are able and willing to pay. There is, therefore, often a considerable level of tension between the interests of marketing managers and the interests of operations managers. The former are committed to offering products designed to meet the needs of subgroups in the market as the best way to secure their custom; the latter are responsible for holding down or reducing unit costs while maintaining the highest possible quality standards of product delivery.

If significant product differentiation is required to meet the needs of different market segments, there are also likely to be management problems in servicing different needs at the same time on the same premises. Segments are often not complementary. To provide an example, a hotel may find it difficult or impossible to satisfy the needs of business people and coach parties of packaged tourists in the same restaurant at the same time; museums have similar problems with noisy school parties and older visitors requiring peace and quiet to achieve their satisfaction with a visit. The problems are very clear in the case of conference halls, which may be separately marketed as the venue for a pop concert one day, a political meeting next day, and a sales conference on the day after. In each case a different segment with different needs is dealt with, but they are not compatible on the same premises at the same time. Considerable strain and careful sequencing and separation requirements are imposed on those who manage such operations. (See also Chapter 6.)

To summarize, the task of marketing management, in close liaison with operations management, is to create and develop compatible products that meet the needs of compatible target segments. This usually has to be achieved on the same premises in a way that permits economies to be achieved in both operational and marketing processes and in ways that generate optimum income from the selected customer and product mix. Such optimization is never easy to achieve in service businesses. It requires compromises and readers should be aware of the conflicting management interests often existing in practice.

Segmentation defined

Segmentation may now be defined as the process of dividing a total market such as all visitors, or a market sector such as holiday travel, into subgroups or segments for marketing management purposes. Its purpose is to facilitate more cost-effective marketing through the formulation, promotion and delivery of purpose-designed products that satisfy the identified needs of target groups. In other words, segmentation is justified on the grounds of achieving greater efficiency in the supply of products to meet identified demand, and increased cost-effectiveness in the marketing process. In most cases travel and tourism businesses will deal with multiple segments and multiple products over a twelve-month period but not necessarily simultaneously.

In the tourism industry most established businesses will often have no practical choice but to target certain segments because of the location and nature of their business. But usually there will be other segments that could be selected as targets if they contribute to a business's needs. For example, as a normal response to monitoring market trends and observing competitors' actions, a tour operator may decide to develop a range of specific products for segments of active people aged fifty-five to seventy-five. If the operator is successful, the over-fifty-fives product may grow from, say 2 per cent to, say, 20 per cent of total turnover over a period of five years. The operator will have changed its segment/product mix as a result of a strategic marketing decision.

Most tourism businesses will have continuous scope and opportunities for altering the mix of revenue generated by the existing structure of segments, through targeting new segments and manipulating the marketing mix. The criteria for choosing new segments for marketing development will stem either from the producer's needs to utilize assets, e.g. to develop off-season business or find users for short-run capacity surpluses revealed by yield management programmes, or from recognizing attractive characteristics of the segments themselves, e.g. high relative expenditure per capita of some groups compared with others.

Actionable market segments

Drawing on the contributions of Kotler and Armstrong (1999), Chisnall (1985) and Middleton and Hawkins (1998) it is possible to focus on five main criteria that must be applied to any segment if it is to be usable or actionable in marketing. Each segment has to be:

- Discrete.
- Measurable.
- Viable.
- Appropriate.
- Sustainable.

Discrete means that the selected subgroups must be separately identifiable by criteria such as purpose of visit, income, location of residence, or motivation, as discussed later in this chapter.

Measurable means that the criteria distinguishing the subgroups must be measurable by available marketing research data, or via such new data as can be obtained at acceptable cost. Research is normally expensive and segmentation must be affordable within available budgets. Segments that cannot be adequately measured on a regular basis cannot be properly targeted. If targeting is not measurably precise, it will be difficult or impossible to evaluate the effectiveness of marketing activities over time. From a marketing standpoint, if a segment cannot be measured, it does not exist, except as wishful thinking. Customer databases have greatly facilitated the segmentation process.

Viable means that the long-run projected revenue generated by a targeted segment exceeds the full cost of designing a marketing mix to achieve it – by a margin that meets the organization's financial objectives.

In the short run it may be necessary to ignore segment viability in order to achieve other strategic organizational objectives. Viability, therefore, is a function of the costs of designing or adapting products for segments, promoting to target groups, and ensuring that prospective customers can find convenient access to such products, once they have been persuaded to buy.

Appropriate, reflects the inseparability of service product delivery (see Chapters 3 and 6) and means it is essential that segments to be serviced on the same premises are mutually compatible and contribute to the image or position in the market adopted by the business. An economy car with a Rolls-Royce label would be absurd, even if the company wished to make it. Similarly, downmarket coach tour business to the Savoy Hotel in London or to Crowne Plaza hotels could only damage those companies' reputations for exclusiveness and luxury at a price that maintains the expected standards. Meeting one segment's needs may sometimes not be achieved without alienating another.

Sustainable, in this context means assessing the extent to which segments contribute positively or negatively to the environmental mission of a business. If a resort business depends for its future on the quality of the coral reefs adjacent to which it is located, for example, it may have to limit the volume of segments shown to cause the greatest damage by their chosen activities. The choice of more sustainable segments and the avoidance of those associated with high impact and damage (and associated segment specific visitor management programmes designed to modify behaviour) are relatively new considerations for marketing. They are expected to become far more significant in the next decade.

To summarize thus far, market segments are identified target groups within a total market that are chosen because they are relevant to an organization's strategic mission statement, interests, skills and particular capabilities. In other words, selected segments have particular needs and profiles a producer feels especially competent to satisfy with relevant products that are both economically and environmentally sustainable into the future.

To be actionable in modern marketing, segments must meet all the five criteria noted in this section, which are as relevant to service organizations as to producers of manufactured goods. The next section discusses the ways or methods through which target groups may be identified and measured.

Methods used to segment markets

There are seven main ways of dividing up markets for segmentation purposes, all of which are used in practice in the travel and tourism industry. They are usually based on some form of database analysis or marketing research and a commitment to segmentation implies a commitment to marketing information systems.

The methods are listed below and subsequently discussed. The sequence in which they appear is not that commonly found in marketing texts but it reflects an order of priority which the authors believe to be most relevant to international travel and tourism markets. The main methods of segmentation are by:

1 Purpose of travel.
2 Buyer needs, motivations, and benefits sought.
3 Buyer behaviour/characteristics of product usage.
4 Demographic, economic, and geographic profile.
5 Psychographic profile.
6 Geodemographic profile
7 Price.

These seven methods are not to be seen as alternative choices for segmentation. They are overlapping and complementary ways by which it is possible to analyse a consumer market in order to appreciate, and select from it, the range of segments it comprises. Many businesses in travel and tourism will use at least three of the methods for any particular segment; all of them could be used if the segment being analysed is important enough to a business. Even if some of the variables are not used to select segments, they may well have a role in building up detailed consumer profiles for the segments that have been selected on other criteria.

Segmentation by purpose of travel

For any tourism business, practical marketing segmentation should always begin with a careful analysis of the purposes for which customers undertake travel and use its and competitors' products. Take, for example, business. Within the broad category of business travel there are many specific aspects of purpose, which determine the nature of the products offered and the promotional approach to be used. Conference markets require different products to those supplied to other business travellers and meetings for groups of different sizes require special provision; some travellers may require secretarial services and business travel ranges from first-class to budget-priced products.

The range of segments noted under the main sectors of travel and tourism earlier in this chapter reflect some of the more obvious purposes. A little thought will indicate a wide range of possibilities. Provided the customer groups associated with any purpose meet the five essential criteria for effective segmentation, a detailed understanding of each purpose of visit will always be useful in practice. For smaller businesses in travel and tourism, segmentation by simple analysis of purpose may be all that is needed for practical or actionable purposes.

For a tour operator, customers' purposes and product needs will differ according to whether they are looking for:

- Main summer holidays.
- Additional holidays and short breaks.
- Winter sun.
- Winter sports.

Within the broad categories of main and additional holidays, typical subsidiary purposes would include sea and beach holidays (with and without children), cultural interests, walking and other activity interests and an interest in exotic destinations. For larger tour operators, the products designed to appeal to such markets usually have a separate brochure or separate sections within a brochure. The provision of different brochures is therefore an obvious sign of segmentation in practice. The flexibility and growing use of Web sites greatly facilitates and extends such segmentation.

For established tour operators and any other successful tourism businesses, the grouping of products currently provided is an accurate reflection of customer purposes served. In other words, and this is an important point, *market segmentation and product formulation are opposite sides of the same coin if they are correctly matched*. The widely used marketing terms *product/market mix* and *product/market portfolio* express this point succinctly.

The other segmentation methods discussed below are ways to refine and develop a clearer, more precise understanding of segments, which already exists in outline through the identification of travel purpose.

Segmentation by buyer needs and benefits sought

Within purpose of travel, and obviously an underlying aspect of it, the next logical consideration for segmentation is to understand the needs, wants and motivations of particular customer groups, as discussed in Chapter 5. For reasons developed in the next chapter on tourism products, it is generally accepted in marketing that customers tend to seek particular benefits when they make their product choices. In the case of the tour operator example, the primary purpose is reflected in the type of holiday chosen; motivations may variously relate to opportunities to meet and mix with particular types of people, indulge in gastronomic pleasures, be highly active or take pleasures sedately, and so on. For organizations dealing with business markets, some business travellers may identify luxury and high levels of personal service as the principal benefits they seek when travelling away from home. Others may identify speed of service and budget prices as their principal benefits. Some business travellers, if they are paid a fixed sum of money for their travel expenses, may seek economy products, especially if they are able to retain the difference between their travel allowance and the actual cost they pay. Some travellers prefer to stay in large, modern, international hotels, while others choose older, more traditional establishments offering a more interesting environment or a more personalized service.

In the case of visitor attractions the benefits sought by family groups may relate to children's interests rather than those of the adults who purchase the admission tickets. In the case of museums, the benefits sought by most visitors are likely to be an hour or two's general interest and 'edutainment', since they have only a limited knowledge of the subject matter's intrinsic merits and depth. Many a museum management team has been misled by its own enthusiasm for its special collection into believing that most visitors are also very interested in the subjects displayed. Usually they are not and their threshold of patience is very easily crossed if the collections are not displayed in ways designed to stimulate general interest.

In many sectors of travel and tourism, the range and perceived importance of the benefits sought by customer segments may not be immediately apparent to marketing managers. Often they can only be discovered through market research among identified target groups, and consumer perceptions change over time. Segmentation by benefits makes it possible for marketing managers to fine tune their products within the broad requirements of purpose noted earlier. Focusing on promoting the benefits sought is a logical objective for brochures and other marketing communications.

Segmentation by buyer behaviour

Within purpose and benefits sought there is ample scope for refining the segmentation process according to the types of behaviour or characteristics of use of products that customers exhibit, including their positive or negative contribution to sustainability. One obvious example is the frequency of usage of products. Business users may be very frequent users of hotels with perhaps twenty or more stays in a year and even more frequent users of airlines and car rental companies.

Frequent users of the same product supplier, a buyer characteristic known as *product or brand loyalty*, may represent only 10 per cent of individual customers in a year but up to 60 per cent of revenue for some hotel groups and airlines. *Loyal* customers are highly attractive to producers for obvious reasons and a combination of high spending, high frequency and high loyalty would be the best of reasons for designing products and promotional campaigns aimed at securing and retaining these most valuable of customers. As such, they are always a key target segment for marketing attention and the benefits they seek are an obvious focus for marketing research.

Visitor expenditure per capita, not necessarily directly associated with levels of income or socioeconomic status, is another dimension of behaviour or user characteristics that is highly relevant to segmentation decisions. For example, many British holidaymakers in Spain outspend German and Swedish visitors, although their per capita income may be less. Other things being equal, high expenditure segments are obviously seen as attractive targets in all sectors of tourism.

A little thought will soon indicate that there is a wide range of characteristics of buyer behaviour use that could be relevant for identifying and targeting particular segments, and developing or adapting products for their specific needs. These characteristics may be divided according to:

- The timing and sequence of buyers' decisions prior to making a booking.
- Decisions made in the booking process.

- Product usage decisions during consumption, including the impact on sustainability.
- Buyer behaviour and decisions after using any travel and tourism product.

Table 7.1 illustrates the range of characteristics in a context relevant to accommodation businesses or tour operators.

The aspects of behaviour noted in Table 7.1 are not fully comprehensive but they cover main aspects that can be adapted to the specific context of most businesses in travel and tourism. Pre-booking characteristics, for example, would be less important to many visitor attractions (but still relevant for group visitors), whereas details of visitor circulation patterns, features visited and rides used, division of time within the attraction during the visit, use of catering, retailing and so on, would be highly significant in product development and product positioning terms. Analysis of behaviour during product usage would indicate the comparative sustainability of one group of users compared with others.

Measuring and monitoring the user characteristics noted in Table 7.1 is the basis of many market research surveys of customers and prospective users (see Chapter 11). In their various forms, user surveys coupled with profile data are the most widely practised type of market research used in all parts of the travel and tourism industry.

By the 1990s the increasing availability and capacity of inexpensive but powerful, networked PCs made it possible for growing numbers of marketing managers in travel and tourism to collect, analyse and retain

Before booking	Booking process	In use/consumption patterns	After use
Previous usage/ experience/expectation loyal/infrequent user	Package/independent arrangements	Utilization of facilities available, positive/ negative impact on environment*	Customer satisfaction level and perceived value for money
Awareness/use of brochures/ use of Internet	Via central reservation office/via Web site	Party size and composition, length of stay	Communication to friends/relatives/ positive or negative 'word of mouth'
Sources of travel information used	Booking direct with producer	Transport mode, accommodation type	
Length of booking time before use	Sale discounts/special offers	Expenditure per head	

Notes: This table indicates some of the variables in each of the four stages in the buying/usage process; the variables are expressed vertically in the columns, not by reading across.
* i.e. an indication of the relative sustainability of the consumption pattern of different segments.

Table 7.1 Buyer behaviour/usage characteristics by sequence of purchase and product usage

information about their customers and their user characteristics in databases. Databases utilizing a unique record number for every buyer (or enquirer) are capable of recording and linking most aspects of customer profile and purchase patterns as they are revealed from telephone, Teletext and Internet enquiries and bookings, booking forms, invoices, etc. Such databases (see also geodemographic segmentation) can now partially replace traditional market research methods based on sample surveys of customers and provide very much faster and cheaper ways to segment markets than was possible previously. The contact with customers on service business premises gives direct access to customer information in travel and tourism that is not generally available to manufacturers of goods using retail distribution systems to reach their customers.

Segmentation by demographic, economic, geographic and life-cycle characteristics

If tourism businesses begin their segmentation process with an analysis of customer needs and benefits sought, within purpose of travel, they will have a clear understanding of the type of products their chosen customer groups want. If that understanding is backed up by information obtained by user surveys of the type noted in the preceding section, and/or database analysis, their knowledge of target groups will already be considerable. For the purposes of efficient promotion and distribution of products, however, especially to prospective new customers rather than to existing ones, they will also need to know the demographic profile and other defining characteristics of their target segments, including potential users.

At the simplest level of analysis, familiar to most readers, customer segments may be defined in terms of basic descriptions of age, sex, occupation, income grouping and place of residence. Known collectively as *customer profiles*, such facts are often easily obtained for existing customers in travel and tourism as a by-product of booking records, registration procedures and regular customer surveys such as the in-flight studies undertaken by airlines and tour operators. Descriptive information about buyers of travel products generally is usually also available in many countries from national tourist offices and commercial surveys of travel and tourism markets. These are commonly available for purchase in countries with developed tourism industries. As noted in Chapter 20, such data is now increasingly to be found on NTO Web sites.

Simple demographic profiles still have their uses in segmentation, for example in deciding which media to choose for advertising purposes. Many smaller businesses in travel and tourism go no further. But on their own, without the prior analysis of purpose, benefits and user characteristics, basic demographic profiles are no longer an adequate basis for organizing effective marketing campaigns. Growing competition is shifting the goal posts and businesses relying solely on such simple data run the risk of being outmanoeuvred in the continuous preoccupation with winning new customers and retaining market share.

At a slightly more complex level of analysing customer profiles it is possible to group together a number of physical characteristics of people to form what is usually termed *life-cycle* analysis. This is based on the stages through which most people progress in life, from infancy, through adolescence and child rearing to different stages of maturity and old age. The travel behaviour of many people aged eighteen to thirty-five may not vary much according to whether they are single or married, but it is likely to vary enormously according to whether or not they have children. Those with young children under the age of four have different travel needs from those with older children between the ages of ten and fifteen. At the other end of the age scale the travel activities of those aged between fifty and seventy will vary enormously according to whether or not they are retired or still at work, and their activity patterns. All developed countries have market research organizations that analyse markets by *life-cycle* categories.

Segmentation by psychographic characteristics and lifestyle

Psychographics is a term used to denote measurement of an individual's mental attitudes and psychological make-up. It is clearly distinguished from demographics, which measures the objective dimensions of age, sex, income and life cycle, noted in the preceding section. Dependent on sophisticated marketing research techniques, psychographics aims to define consumers on attitudinal or psychological rather than physical dimensions. The reason for segmenting buyers on psychological dimensions is the belief that common values among groups of consumers tend to determine their purchasing patterns. For example, some individuals are mentally predisposed to seek adventure, enjoy risks and active vacations. Some seek environmental qualities often represented as ecotourism, while others seek the self-development associated with cultural tourism. (See also VALS in Chapter 5.)

The measurement of consumer attitudes and values is not new. It has been a preoccupation of market researchers on both sides of the Atlantic for decades. The methods of measurement, usually asking consumers to make complex ratings of items included in multiple-choice questions, are now greatly enhanced by the availability of high-power, low-cost computers. Software is readily available to measure the extent and strength of any correlations that exist between people's attitudes and values, and their behaviour patterns as buyers of travel and other products. Such measurements may be further refined by including specific questions about attitudes to, and perceptions of, individual companies in the industry and the products they supply. This type of research underlies the modern concept of product positioning, branding and image projection discussed later in this book.

Related to demographic characteristics and stages in the life cycle, the links between attitudes, perceptions and actual buyer behaviour, combine to determine the *lifestyle* which individuals adopt. An understanding of the lifestyle of target customers has obvious advantages when formulating new products, developing branding or creating messages designed to motivate such people. Among international operators in travel and tourism, American Express and Club Mediterranée, for example, clearly understand and have single-mindedly adopted a lifestyle segmentation approach, as any consideration of their product brochures will confirm.

Lifestyle segmentation reflects an understanding of individuals' needs, benefits sought and motivations. It normally requires significant expenditure on marketing research and it is used within the basic segmentation by purpose of visit noted earlier. Lifestyle-related choices for all kinds of products, including tourism, have become more important at the start of the new millennium, reflecting growing consumer affluence and sophistication.

Geodemographic segmentation

In Britain since the early 1980s, and there are equivalent procedures in most other European countries and North America, a very productive and powerful segmentation tool was developed through combining an analysis of census data with the postal area (zip) codes that identify every group of households in the country. The UK has some 1.6 million postcodes each containing an average of 14.5 households. Allied to the power of modern computers to store and analyse data, the major marketing development was the classification of household/housing types into a total of seventeen groups and fifty-four types in the UK, each with clearly defined characteristics which in turn correlate closely with population characteristics of age, family structure, life cycle and income. The housing types include, for example:

* Wealthy suburbs, large detached houses (2.6 per cent of UK population).
* Affluent working couples with mortgages, new homes (1.3 per cent).
* Council housing areas, high unemployment, lone parents (1.8 per cent).

The UK's ACORN (A Classification of Residential Neighbourhoods) analysis of census data can be readily supplemented by data from major commercial surveys of purchasing patterns, including travel behaviour, which are routinely analysed by ACORN types. In 2000, provided only that a business records the names and addresses of its customers and enquirers (including Internet contacts), it is inexpensive and easy for research companies to pinpoint and map the typical household types in all the areas in which buyers with similar characteristics could be found throughout the country. A detailed consumer profile, including purchasing and media habits, can be provided at the touch of a button to match any selected postcode profiles.

The geographic aspect of geodemographics has been further enhanced in recent years by computerized mapping techniques based on satellite technology. The best-known software system, GIS (Geographical Information System), was developed in the USA. The GIS is expected to develop considerably in all countries and will provide improved linkages between mapping techniques and customer databases generally. This ability to combine mapping software with customer databases provided by census and market research survey data explains the generic title 'geodemographic'. Geodemographic segmentation tools are now capable of targeting individual buyers and households with great precision, and they clearly have 'particular relevance to direct marketing, leaflet distribution, and local media selection' (Chisnall, 1985: 280). Postcode analysis offers great scope for cost-effective direct marketing. (See also Chapter 19.)

To illustrate the usefulness in practice of the demographic, economic, geographic and life-cycle analysis of segments, it is interesting to consider the buyers of weekend and mid-week short-break leisure package holidays in hotels in Britain. Such products are now a core part of the business mix for nearly all hotel groups. The main target group of buyers are typically couples in the age range thirty to sixty, professional people, college educated, affluent and living in cities or suburbs. They either do not have children living at home or are able to leave them with friends or relatives. It is also possible to define the typical distance in miles such couples are prepared to drive to reach their destinations, so that the catchment areas of target customers can be mapped for the location of any hotel with considerable precision drawing on most of the descriptive characteristics referred to in this section. With such information it is easy to develop a broadly relevant promotional campaign and choose the type of media or direct response methods best calculated to reach and motivate the target audience. To refine the segmentation further, market research would be needed to assess customers' reasons for taking breaks and their personal motivations and benefits sought for any particular hotel and its location.

Segmentation by price

In general, buyer behaviour in leisure travel and tourism markets in all countries appears to be highly price-sensitive and many tour operators still act on the assumption that price is the key segmentation variable. In other words, there are segments of customers to be identified and located who respond to different price bands. Strategically this is evidently true when major new tourism developments are planned, such as a new luxury hotel or resort complex. In such cases feasibility studies are required to identify the ability and willingness of sufficient customers to pay the prices that will generate the level of revenue required to pay back investment, cover fixed costs and create targeted profits. One may conclude that this is a form of segmentation by price but it will still rank below purpose, benefits sought and user characteristics in the hierarchy of segmentation modes.

For established businesses in tourism there will nearly always be room for price manoeuvre within broad price ranges in the short run and reducing price is often the major tool for promotional tactics. Yield management programmes for airlines and hotels have proved a fertile and flexible tool for segment targeted tactical pricing in the last decade, although limits are set by the strategic marketing mix decisions and the costs of operating the business and satisfying existing customers. Thus, although there is no doubt that, *other things being equal*, price continues to motivate very large numbers of customers, it is not a segmentation variable of the same kind as the others outlined in this chapter. The 'other things' include maintaining the competitive quality of product delivery needed to satisfy the demands of modern customers.

Chapter summary

This chapter focuses on the role of market segmentation in tourism and the methods or techniques used to implement it in practice. Segmentation enables marketing managers to divide total markets into component parts in order to target and deal with them more effectively and more profitably.

As more consumers seek to express their individuality and reject the values of so-called 'mass markets,' segmentation takes on growing significance. The more that people differ (or perceive themselves to differ) and the greater the level of competition between producers seeking to maintain or increase their shares of the same market, the more that segmentation determines business success. The case for segmentation also increases as markets grow in total volume and subgroups are identified, around whose particular needs it becomes cost-effective (viable) to focus particular marketing activity. For some tourism businesses, for operational reasons, the basic product is essentially the same for all customers. This is usually the case for many visitor attractions. But there are always different ways to promote to subgroups in the market and opportunities to enhance the basic product around a segment's identified needs. The promotion of special group facilities for educational visits to museums and the creation of special facilities for family visitors illustrate this point. The use of museums for functions and events is another form of segmentation.

'There is no single way to segment a market. A marketer has to try different segmentation variables, singly and in combination, hoping to find an insightful way to view the market structure' (Kotler, 1984: 254). This chapter outlines seven variables in the order of importance considered relevant to most businesses in travel and tourism. In particular it emphasizes the importance of segmentation by purpose of travel and of understanding the benefits that different groups of customers seek. The implications for segmentation of researching user characteristics before, during and after purchasing travel products, are also stressed.

Segmentation in a rapidly changing business environment is a dynamic process. New segments emerge as older ones disappear or are no longer viable as a result of market change. At any point in time most organizations in travel and tourism will be dealing with a 'portfolio' of several different segments. All of these are likely to be in a state of continuous change, partly in response to shifts in the external market determinants and partly to changes in customers' needs, attitudes and motivations. In almost every case there will be opportunities for marginal improvements in what a business knows of its customers and, therefore, how best to promote to them and satisfy their product needs marginally better than the competition.

For these reasons, except for the smallest of businesses, segmentation normally justifies a considerable and continuous commitment to marketing intelligence systems and research – an important consideration developed in Chapter 11. For a growing number of larger organizations in the new millennium it also means a commitment to the further development of customer databases for research and marketing purposes.

Further reading

Baker, M. J. (2000). *Marketing Strategy and Management*. Chapter 12, 3rd edn, Macmillan.

Brassington, F. and Pettit, S. (2000). *Principles of Marketing*. 2nd edn, Prentice-Hall.

Davidson, H. (1997). *Even More Offensive Marketing*. Chapter 9, Penguin.

Kotler, P. and Armstrong, G. (1999). *Principles of Marketing*. Chapter 7, 8th edn, Prentice-Hall.

Smith, S. L. J. (1995). *Tourism Analysis: A Handbook*. Chapter 5, 2nd edn, Longman.

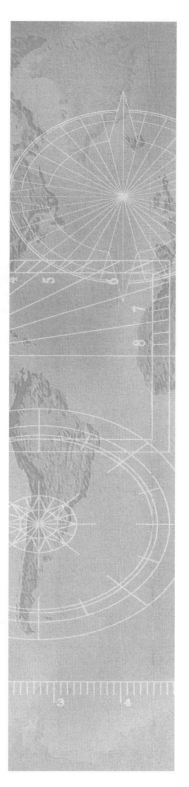

Product formulation in tourism

As far as the tourist is concerned, the product covers the complete experience from the time he leaves home to the time he returns to it. (Medlik and Middleton, 1973)

In response to what they know and forecast of their customers' needs and interests, the ways in which products are put together (product formulation and design) are crucial decisions for marketing managers. Product decisions, with all their implications for the management of service operations and profitability, influence not only the marketing mix but also a firm's long-term growth strategy and policies for investment and human resources. Product specifications largely determine the corporate image and branding an organization is able to create in the minds of its existing and prospective customers.

To a great extent, decisions on the design of products also determine what prices can be charged, what forms of promotion are needed and often what distribution channels are available. For all these reasons, customer-related product decisions are 'the basis of marketing strategy and tactics' (Middleton, 1983: 2). As the most important of the four Ps/Cs in the marketing mix, product formulation requires careful consideration in any branch of marketing. Because of the particular nature and characteristics of travel and tourism services, the subject is especially complex in the tourism industry and the concept of products extends to incorporate people, process and physical evidence as explained in Chapter 6.

This chapter is in three parts. The first part introduces the existence of two different dimensions for understanding tourism products, one of which is the product as perceived by customers and the other is the narrower view of products taken by marketing managers of individual tourism businesses. The second part explains products on each of the two dimensions in terms of their component parts and the benefits they offer to customers. The third part explains the role in product formulation and presentation played by product positioning and branding.

A components view of travel and tourism products – from two standpoints

It follows from the definitions discussed in Chapter 1 that any visit to a tourism destination comprises a mix of several different *components*. These include transport, accommodation, attractions and other facilities, such as catering and entertainments. Sometimes all the components are purchased from one supplier, e.g. when a customer buys an inclusive holiday from a tour operator or asks a travel agent to put the components together for a business trip. Sometimes customers put the separate components together themselves, e.g. when a visitor drives his own car to stay with friends at a destination.

Conveniently known as a 'components view', the conceptualization of travel and tourism products as a group of components or elements brought together in a 'bundle' selected to satisfy needs is a vital requirement for marketing managers. It is central to this view that the components of the bundle may be designed, altered and fitted together in many different ways calculated to match identified customer needs.

The overall tourism product

Developing the components view from the standpoint of the tourist, Medlik and Middleton noted a quarter of a century ago that, 'As far as the tourist is concerned, the product covers the complete experience from the time he leaves home to the time he returns to it'. Thus 'the tourist product is to be considered as an amalgam of three main components of attractions, ... facilities at the destination and accessibility of the destination'. In other words, the tourist product is 'not an airline seat or a hotel bed, or relaxing on a sunny beach ... but rather an amalgam of many components, or a package'. The same article continued, 'Airline seats and hotel beds ... are merely elements or components of a total tourist product which is a composite product' (Medlik and Middleton, 1973). With minor nuances to suit the views of different authors this original basic conceptualization of the product remains valid and has been adopted and used internationally.

The product of individual tourism businesses

Without detracting in any way from the general validity and relevance of the overall view of tourism products noted above, it has to be recognized that airlines, hotels, attractions, car rental and other producer organizations in the industry, generally take a much narrower view of the products they sell. They focus primarily on their own services. Many large hotel groups and transport operators employ product managers in their marketing teams and handle product formulation and development entirely in terms of the operations they control. Hotels refer to 'conference products' for example, or 'leisure products', airlines to 'business-class products', and so on. For this reason, the overall product concept sets the context in which tourism marketing is conducted but it has only limited value in guiding the practical product design decisions that managers of individual producer organizations have to make. A components view of products still holds good, however, because it is in the nature of service products that they can be divided or de-constructed into a series of specific service operations or processes, which combine to make up the particular products that customers buy. Thus for a visitor to a hotel (business or leisure), the hotel product is (or should be) a seamless entity but it is in fact a sophisticated 'bundle' of service delivery experiences, which may be itemized as:

- Initial experience and reactions in selecting from a guidebook, brochure or Web site.
- Experience of the booking process.
- First impression on entering the hotel – design of physical evidence.
- Reception process on arrival – front of house staff contact.
- Standard of room and its range of *en suite* facilities.
- Experience of customer – staff interactions during the stay.
- Provision of meals and any ancillary services.
- Checking out process on leaving.
- Any follow up, such as direct mailing, received subsequently.

This is not a comprehensive list but it builds on the analysis of the services marketing mix set out in Chapter 6 and serves to stress the point that any individual product is composed of a series of elements or processes that combine to satisfy the purchasers' needs. Understanding, unravelling and fine-tuning the elements, provides more than ample scope for marketing managers to increase their knowledge of customers' needs and improve their product presentation and delivery to prospective customers.

It is always highly instructive to analyse any service businesses' operations in terms of the full sequence of contacts and processes between customer and business, from the time that they make initial enquiries (if any), until they have used the product and left the premises. Even for a product such as that provided by a museum, there is ample scope to analyse all the stages of a visit and potential points of contact that occur from the moment the customer is in sight of the entrance until he leaves the building, say two or three hours later. Putting the components view in slightly different terms, individual service producers designing products *'must define the service concept in terms of the bundles of goods and services sold to the consumer and the relative importance of each component to the customer'* (Sasser, Olsen and Wyckoff, 1978: 14). Shostack (1977) used the notion of a molecular product to convey the same idea, while blueprinting and scripting as described in Chapter 6 are further refinements of the service product concept.

To bring the two distinctive aspects of tourist products together – the *overall view* and that of *individual service businesses* – it is possible to consider them as two different dimensions. The overall view is a horizontal dimension in the sense that a series of individual product components are included in it. Customers as individuals, or tour operators acting as manufacturers (see Chapter 24), can make their selection to produce the total experience. By contrast, the service businesses' view is a vertical dimension of specific service delivery operations and processes organized around the identified needs and wants of target segments of customers. Businesses typically have regard for their interactions with other organizations on the horizontal dimension (product collaboration) but their principal concern is with the vertical dimension of their own operations (this point is developed later in the chapter).

A benefits view of products

Before discussing the two dimensions of travel and tourism products in more detail it is important to keep in mind the customers' view of what businesses of all types offer for sale. Levitt's classic statement is succinct: 'People do not buy products, they buy the expectation of benefits. It is the benefits that are the product' (Levitt, 1969). Developing this point, Kotler noted 'the customer is looking for particular utilities. Existing products are only a current way of packaging those utilities. The company must be aware of all the ways in which customers can gain the sought satisfaction. These define the competition' (Kotler, 1976: 25).

The processes of researching targeted customers' perceptions of product benefits and utilities, and designing or adapting products to match their expectations, lie of course at the heart of marketing theory and practice. There is no difference in principle between a benefits view of products applied to travel and tourism or to any other industry producing consumer goods.

Components of the overall tourism product

From the standpoint of a potential customer considering any form of tourist visit, the product may be defined as a bundle or package of tangible and intangible components, based on activity at a destination. The package is perceived by the tourist as an experience, available at a price. There are five main components in the overall product, which are discussed separately below:

- Destination attractions and environment.
- Destination facilities and services.
- Accessibility of the destination.
- Images of the destination.
- Price to the consumer.

Destination attractions and environment – and the visitor activities they generate

These are the component elements within the destination that largely determine consumers' choice and influence prospective buyers' motivations. They include:

- *Natural attractions*: landscape, seascape, beaches, climate, flora and fauna and other geographical features of the destination and its natural resources.
- *Built attractions*: buildings and tourism infrastructure including historic and modern architecture, monuments, promenades, parks and gardens, convention centres, marinas, ski slopes, industrial archaeology, managed visitor attractions generally, golf courses, speciality shops and themed retail areas.
- *Cultural attractions*: history and folklore, religion and art, theatre, music, dance and other entertainment, and museums; some of these may be developed into special events, festivals and pageants.
- *Social attractions*: way of life and customs of resident or host population, language and opportunities for social encounters.

Combined, these aspects of a destination comprise what is generically, if loosely, known as its *environment*. The number of visitors the environment can accommodate in a typical range of activities on a typical busy day without damage to its elements and without undermining its attractiveness to visitors is known as its *capacity*.

Until the 1980s tourism businesses were mostly able to plan their product strategies without much if any regard to either quality of the destination environment or capacity issues. They could take it for granted. This is changing, however, and the development and practice of more environmentally responsible marketing conducted in context of the sustainability of destination environments appears certain to become increasingly important in the twenty-first century. Defining capacity with any accuracy remains a mystery but recognizing tourism damage to the environment is increasingly clear for all to see and marketing decisions are part of both the problem and solution (Middleton and Hawkins, 1998: ch. 9).

Destination facilities and services

These are the component elements located in the destination or linked to it, which make it possible for visitors to stay and in other ways enjoy and participate in the attractions. They include:

- *Accommodation units*: Hotels, holiday villages, apartments, villas, campsites, caravan parks, hostels, condominiums, farms, guesthouses.
- *Restaurants, bars and cafés*: ranging from fast-food through to luxury restaurants.
- *Transport at the destination*: taxis, coaches, car rental, cycle hire (and ski lifts in snow destinations).
- *Sports/interest activity*: ski schools, sailing schools, golf clubs and spectator stadiums; centres for pursuit of arts and crafts and nature studies.
- *Other facilities*: language schools, health clubs.
- *Retail outlets*: shops, travel agents, souvenirs, camping supplies.
- *Other services*: information services, equipment rental, tourism police.

For some of these elements the distinction between attractions and facilities may be blurred. For example, a hotel, skiing piste or a famous golf course may well be perceived as primary attractions in their own right and the reason for selecting a destination. Nevertheless, their primary function of providing facilities and services in the context of the specific attractions and environment of *place* remains clear.

Accessibility of the destination

These are the private and public transport aspects of the product that determine the cost, speed and convenience with which a traveller may leave his place of residence and reach a chosen destination (see Chapter 22). They include:

- *Infrastructure*: of roads, car parking, airports, railways, seaports, inland waterways and marinas.
- *Equipment*: size, speed and range of public transport vehicles.
- *Operational factors*: routes operated, frequency of services, prices charged and road tolls levied.
- *Government regulations*: the range of regulatory controls over transport operations.

Images and perceptions of the destination

For reasons outlined in Chapter 5, the attitudes and images customers have towards products strongly influence their buying decisions. Destination images are not necessarily grounded in experience or facts but they are always powerful motivators in leisure travel and tourism. Images, and the expectations of travel experiences are closely linked in prospective customers' minds.

For example, of the millions of people in North America and Europe who have not so far visited Las Vegas, there will be few who do not carry in their minds some mental picture or image of the experiences that destination provides. Through the media and through hearsay, most people have already decided whether they are attracted or repelled by the Las Vegas image. All destinations have images, often based more on historic rather than current events, and it is an essential objective of destination marketing to sustain, alter or develop images in order to influence prospective buyers' expectations. The images of tourism businesses within destinations, e.g. the hotels in Las Vegas, are often closely related to the destination image. The physical evidence (see Chapter 6) provided by those who market Las Vegas is calculated to create and communicate the chosen image.

Price to the consumer

Any visit to a destination carries a price, which is the sum of what it costs for travel, accommodation and participation in a selected range of facilities and services. Because most destinations offer a range of products and appeal to a range of segments, price in the travel and tourism industry covers a very wide range. Visitors travelling thousands of miles and using luxury hotels, for example, pay a very different price in New York than students sharing campus-style accommodation with friends. Yet the two groups may buy adjacent seats in a Broadway theatre. Price varies by season, by choice of activities and internationally by exchange rates as well as by distance travelled, transport mode and choice of facilities and services.

Some marketing implications of the overall product concept

With a little thought it will be clear that each of the five product components, although they are combined and integrated in the visitor's overall experience, are in fact capable of extensive and more or less independent variation over time. Some of these variations are planned, as in the case of the Disney World developments in previously unused areas around Orlando, Florida, or the purpose-built resorts at Cancun in Mexico. In both those cases massive engineering works have transformed the natural environment and created major tourist destinations. Center Parcs holiday village developments in the UK illustrate recent forms of destination engineering, providing covered, climate-controlled attractions within a central facility, as well as outdoor attractions and capacity-controlled accommodation in carefully landscaped surrounding areas. Center Parcs are planned to protect and in places enhance the environment. *In such cases all five product components are integrated under one management.*

By contrast, in New York, London or Venice, the city environments have not been much altered for travel and tourism purposes, although there have been massive planned changes in the services and facilities available to visitors and all have icon-status buildings designed or adapted for tourism purposes. Many changes in destination environments are not planned, however, they just happen. In Northern Europe the decline in popularity of traditional seaside resorts since the 1960s has been largely the result of changes in the accessibility of competing destinations in the sunnier south of the Continent. Changes in the product components often occur in spite of, and not because of, the wishes of governments and destination planners. They occur because travel and tourism, especially at the international level, is a relatively free market with customers who are able to pursue new attractions as they become available and affordable. Changes in exchange rates, which alter the prices of destinations, are obviously not planned in any way by the tourism industry but have a massive effect on visitor numbers.

It is in the promotional field of images and perceptions that some of the most interesting planned changes occur and these are marketing decisions. The classic example of planned tourism image engineering may be found in the *I Love New York* campaign which, based on extensive preliminary market research, created a significant improvement in the 'Big Apple's appeal in the early 1980s. At a very different level of expenditure, industrial cities in Britain, such as Glasgow, Birmingham and Manchester, are working hard on their image projection to achieve the same type of change in visitors' perceptions and motivations.

The view of the product taken by leisure tourism customers, whether or not they buy an inclusive package from a tour operator or travel wholesaler, is essentially the same view or standpoint as that adopted by tour operators. Tour operators act on behalf of the identified interests of millions of customers and the design of their brochures is a practical illustration of how to blend and communicate the five product components discussed in this section (see also Chapter 24).

The overall view of the product is also the standpoint of national, regional and local tourist organizations, whose responsibilities usually include the co-ordination and presentation of the product components in their areas. This responsibility is an important one even if the destination tourist organizations are engaged only in liaison and joint marketing and not in the sale of specific product offers to travellers.

In considering the overall product we should note that there is no natural or automatic harmony between components, such as attractions and accommodation, and that they are seldom under any one organization's ownership and control. Even within component sectors such as accommodation there will usually be many different organizations, each with different and often conflicting objectives and interests. Indeed it is the diversity or fragmentation of overall control and the relative freedom of producer businesses to act according to their perceived self-interests, at least in the short term, which makes it difficult for national, regional and even local tourist organizations to exert much co-ordinating influence, either in marketing or in planning. Part of this fragmentation occurs simply because most developed destinations offer a wide range of tourism products and deal with a wide range of segments. It also reflects the fact that, for every large business in tourism at national or international level, there are up to a thousand small or micro-businesses, mostly pursuing individual goals. In the long term, however, the future success of a destination must involve co-ordination and recognition of mutual interests between all the components of the overall tourism product. Achieving such co-ordination is the principal rationale for much of the marketing work undertaken by NTOs (see Chapter 20).

Components of specific products – the tourism businesses' view

The overall view of tourism products is highly relevant to the marketing decisions taken by individual businesses in tourism. It determines the interrelationships and scope for co-operation and partnership between suppliers in different sectors of the industry, for example between transport and accommodation. But in designing their product specific offers around their service operations, there are also internal dimensions of products for marketers to consider. These are common to all forms of consumer marketing and part of widely accepted marketing theory. Marketing managers 'need to think about the product on three levels' (Kotler, 1984: 463).

Using Kotler's terminology, which is based on earlier contributions by Levitt, these three levels are:

- The *core product*, which is the essential service or benefit designed to satisfy the identified needs of target customer segments.
- The formal or *tangible product*, which is the specific offer for sale stating what a customer will receive for his money. It is a marketing interpretation that turns the core into a specific offer.
- The *augmented product*, which comprises all the forms of added value producers may build into their formal product offers to make them more attractive than competitors' offers to their intended customers.

Although many regard the labels applied to these three levels of any product as fairly unattractive marketing jargon, the value of the thought process underlying them is potentially very great indeed. The thought process can be applied by businesses in any of the tourism industry sectors and it is equally applicable to large and small businesses. It will repay careful thought and application in particular operations.

The following example of an inclusive weekend break in a hotel will help to explain what the three levels mean in practice. The product offer is a package comprising two nights' accommodation and two breakfasts, which may be taken at any one of a chain of hotels located in several different destinations. Because of the bedroom design and leisure facilities available at the hotels, the package is designed to appeal to professional couples with young children. The product is offered for sale at an inclusive price through a brochure distributed at each of the hotels in the chain, through direct mail and through the World Wide Web. It is in competition with the products of other very similar hotels that are promoting to the same market at similar price levels. Products of this type are now widely available in many parts of North America and Europe and the total market for them grew substantially in the last twenty years.

The example makes it possible to reveal the three product levels inherent in what tourism businesses market.

Core product is intangible, an *idea*, but it always comprises the essential need or benefit as perceived and sought by the customer – expressed in words and pictures designed to motivate purchase. For the weekend break under discussion the core benefit may be defined as relaxation, rest, fun and self-fulfilment in a family context.

It should be noted that the core product reflects the characteristics and needs of the target customer segments, not the hotel. The core product establishes the key message that the hotel aims to communicate. The hotel aims to design and communicate its core product better than its competitors, and to achieve better delivery of the sought benefits. But all its competitors are aiming at the same basic customer needs and offering virtually identical benefits. Customers' core needs usually tend not to change very quickly, although a hotel's ability to identify, communicate and better satisfy such needs can change considerably. Since customer perceptions are never precisely understood, there is ample scope for improvement in this area.

Formal product comprises the formal offer of the product as set out in a brochure or Web site, stating exactly what is to be provided at a specified time at a specified price. In the example under discussion, the tangible product is two nights and two breakfasts at a particular location, using rooms of a defined standard with bathroom, television, telephone, etc. The provision (if any) of elevators, coffee shops, air-conditioning and swimming pool are all within the formal product and the name of the hotel is also included.

In the case of hotel products generally, and certainly in the example cited, there is often very little to choose between competitors' formal product offers. In such conditions, products may be perceived as commodities and price may become the principal reason for choice. Blindfolded and led to any one of, say, twenty competitors' premises, most hotel customers would not easily recognize the identity of their surroundings. The brochure description of the formal product forms the basis for the contract of sale, which would be legally enforceable in most countries. In Chapter 6 the use of design and 'physical evidence' are identified as one of the principal ways to differentiate, make more tangible and communicate the formal product in the minds of prospective buyers.

Augmented product. Both tangible and intangible, augmentation is harder to define with precision. It is driven by the search for competitive advantage and comprises the difference between the contractual essentials of the formal product and the totality of all the benefits and services experienced in relation to the delivery of the product to the customer. It can cover any or all of the stages – from the moment of first contact in considering a booking, to any follow-up contact after delivery and consumption of the product. The augmented product also expresses the idea of *value added* over and above the formal offer. It represents a vital area of opportunity for producers to differentiate their products from those of competitors.

In the example under discussion there may be up to twenty 'add ons' to the formal product – some fairly trivial such as a complimentary box of chocolates or glass of wine on arrival, and some significant, such as entrance tickets to local attractions or entertainments. Some of the added benefits are tangible as indicated, but some are intangible, such as the quality of service provided, the friendliness of staff and the ambience created (see *People* and *Process* and *Physical evidence* in Chapter 6). In the example under discussion all the augmented elements would be purpose-designed and developed around the core product benefits in ways calculated to increase the appeal to the target segment's needs.

The brand image or 'position' that products occupy in customers' minds is always part of augmentation and in the case of a group hotel this will be closely related to the corporate image and branding of the group.

Competitive product formulation

To stay ahead of the competition, proactive marketing managers are constantly looking for product innovation and there are strong advantages in being first with product developments. In order to define the core product, the formal product and to identify the scope for product augmentation with some precision, frequent research into the perceptions and purchasing characteristics of segments is a necessary aspect of consumer orientation in the travel and tourism industry. There is normally considerable scope for creative innovation and for experimentation, especially in the area defined as product augmentation. Much of augmentation, including image, is under a marketing manager's control and it becomes the focus and primary rationale for persuading customers to choose between alternative products.

In the hotel example used to illustrate the three levels of the product it is interesting to note the potential for collaboration between the particular accommodation product discussed (the vertical dimension as it was defined earlier in the chapter) and other components of the overall tourism product (the horizontal dimension). The hotel, for example, may include access to local attractions at the destination as part of the augmented product. Similarly, hotel users may be offered public transport links to the destination with fares included as part of the formal product.

Branding and product positioning

In this chapter, image, typically communicated by branding, is identified as one of five components in the overall tourism product and as a vital element within the augmented product developed and marketed by individual businesses in the industry. In common with most services, the benefits provided by travel and tourism products are essentially intangible and need to be communicated in ways that influence consumers' perceptions. The origins of branding can be traced all the way back to Greek and Roman times, through craftsmen in the Middle Ages, to the branding of cattle on nineteenth-century American ranches. All these early notions of branding provided the core attributes of:

- Statement of ownership.
- Means of identifying a product or service for purchasers and distinguishing it from that of competitors.
- Symbol or shorthand device to which expectations of quality could be attached.

Doyle described a brand as '*a name, symbol, design or some combination, which* <u>*identifies*</u> *the "product" of a particular organisation as having a sustainable* <u>*differential advantage*</u>' (Doyle, 1989: 78; emphasis added).

Doyle's definition is useful but it does not capture the modern concept in its entirety. It reads as if the brand is added to the product. In fact, a strong brand reflects and guides the development of core values throughout the product, staff and organization. The definition also reads from a producer, rather than a consumer perspective. In practice a strong brand has to exist in the minds of consumers as a fusion of readily understood values and benefits and is used by them to achieve their perceived needs and in some cases to make statements about themselves and their personal values.

Figure 8.1, drawn from work by de Chernatony and McDonald (1992), explores the branding concept further. A *commodity* has many substitutes and is compelled to match the prices set by competitors. Many bed and breakfast businesses are perceived as commodities and have difficulty breaking away from a competitive-parity pricing that mirrors the rates set by other accommodation providers in the same location. One step up from the commodity is the *product with a brand identity system* bolted on. The use of a design incorporating a name, logo and slogan that is attached to a product is commonly mistaken for branding. It is arguable that many would-be tourism brands fall into this trap. Davidson (1997) refers to the frequent use of 'labels' attached to 'me too' products, whilst de Chernatony and McDonald (1992) claim that a primary management error in branding is the reliance on the brand name as the differentiating device, rather than the development of genuine competitive advantage. A brand in the modern marketing sense offers the consumer relevant *added values*, a superior proposition that is distinctive from competitors and

Figure 8.1
The concept of branding
Source: After de Chernatony and McDonald (1992).

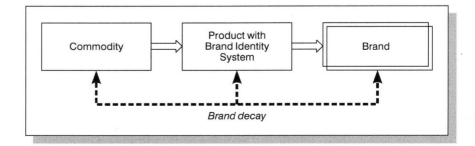

imparts meaning above and beyond the functional aspects. It is also a total entity developed by the integration of the resources, processes and marketing decisions of an organization and much of the effort and input to developing a brand remains invisible to the consumer. As tourism is a chain of service encounters spread over hours for visitor attractions, days for hotels or even weeks for a tour operator, the added values should be integrated into every point of contact with the consumer from pre-purchase through to post-use.

A competitive brand is a live asset, however, not a fixture and its value will depreciate over time if starved of investment and marketing management skill. Brand decay may begin if a brand is over-stretched into new products that damage its essence, or following a merger or takeover. Some writers query, for example, whether the international Virgin brand has been overstretched by the diversification into dozens of products ranging from air transport, rail transport and financial services, to compact discs (CDs), cola and entertainment.

Advantages of branding for travel and tourism

In addition to the initial advantages of branding already mentioned, the characteristics of travel and tourism suggest that other specific benefits may be gained from successful branding:

- Branding helps reduce medium and long-term vulnerability to the unforeseen external events that so beset the tourism industry. Recovery time after a crisis may be shorter, whilst resilience to price wars or occasional hiccups may be improved.
- Branding reduces risk for the consumer at the point of purchase by signalling the expected quality and performance of an intangible product. It offers either an implicit or explicit guarantee to the consumer.
- Branding facilitates accurate marketing segmentation by attracting some and repelling other consumer segments. For an inseparable product, on-site segment compatibility is an important marketing issue. The British tour operator *Club 18–30* attracts certain segments of the youth holiday market while it dissuades others; the resulting mix of clients ensures the clubbing atmosphere of the product experienced.
- Branding provides the focus for the integration of stakeholder effort, especially for the employees of an organization or the individual tourism providers of a destination brand. In popular destinations, reflecting the complexity of the overall tourism product, local residents are also stakeholders in the meaning and values of 'place' even if they consider themselves to be uninvolved in tourism. A strong brand can help provide a common understanding and some unity of purpose for staff, residents and businesses alike.
- Branding is a strategic weapon for long-range planning in tourism, employed by British Airways, for example, in repositioning itself as a global airline, or the repositioning of British Midland from its region of origin (the East Midlands in the UK) towards Europe as 'the airline for

Europe'. Extending or stretching the brand can be a lower risk strategy for product development, market development or diversification. For example, Thomson Holidays and Airtours moved into the cruise ship business as soon as they identified the growth potential of the market.

- Many see clearly recognized international branding is an essential attribute for effective use by businesses of communication and distribution on the Internet. The linking of brands and banner advertising to relevant portals and sites depends on consumer awareness of brands for its effectiveness.

Brand name decisions

Broadly speaking, a tourism business has to decide between choosing one corporate overall brand, for example *Sandals*, or the use of a number of brands to identify separate products, such as individual resorts. The current trend for large international corporations is towards unified corporate brands with an accompanying emphasis on the importance of corporate identity. This trend is supported by consumers wanting to know more about the values of the organizations whose products they use. In time, companies tackling sustainability at corporate level, for example, will succeed in embedding it as a core value of their corporate brand. TUI, for example, based in Germany, already has. (See Middleton and Hawkins, 1998: 193–5.)

Corporate vs destination brands

Leading corporate brands in travel and tourism are household names either nationally or globally; Accor, Disney, Marriott, Cathay Pacific, TUI, Sandals, Thomas Cook, Center Parcs and so on. They are under full management control. Leading destination brands such as London, New York and Singapore have to rely on persuasion and co-operation rather than the full management control enjoyed by individual organizations and it is very much harder to make them effective. Powerful corporate brands, for example, Club Méditerranée and Sandals, can override weaker destination brands of the islands on which they are located. The more local the destination brand, the weaker it is likely to be, not least because of the level of budget available to research and communicate the brand as well as gain local support for it.

Dimensions of function and representation for brands

Basing their research on physical goods products, de Chernatony and McWilliam (1990) examined brands by two dimensions, which they labelled 'functionality' and 'representationality'. The functionality of a brand refers to the functional benefits that the brand delivers to the consumer. It is about what the brand *does* for the person using the brand. For example, McDonald's is packed with benefits – solves hunger, provides convenient locations for easy access, fast and efficient order and delivery system, clean and hygienic surroundings and totally reliable quality. The representationality of a brand refers to its symbolic qualities – to the non-verbal messages that it conveys about the user to other people. Representationality is what the brand *says* about the user, recognizing that we all make use of visibly consumed brands to signal something about ourselves to others. The purchase of clothes with designer labels, status cars such as Mercedes and stays in status hotels such as the Savoy are examples. In this context the brands that we choose may vary by our personality, mood or occasion of use. Conversely, we often use brands to decode meanings and impute values to other people through observance of their brand preferences.

Reference group theory is of particular relevance to the representation dimension (see also Chapter 5), for people make decisions based on their current reference groups, groups they aspire to join or groups they wish to dissociate from. Holiday tourism is a publicly consumed product often undertaken as a group experience. Many visitors select holiday products that reflect their self-concepts and to signal something about themselves to others. Some destinations are 'in' and some are 'out' with particular reference groups. For many, status lies in the use of business-class brands of airlines, and so on.

De Chernatony and McWilliam (1990) showed that brands display different degrees of functionality and representationality to their users and suggested guidelines for appropriate marketing activity. A brand high in the functionality dimension should concentrate on continuing product research and development to thwart 'me too' products, sustain product superiority on relevant attributes, develop strong quality control systems and utilise consumer promotion stressing the functional benefits. A brand high in the representationality dimension should concentrate on qualitative research into consumer lifestyles and the communication of symbolic meaning to users and prospective users, indicating relevant reference group endorsement.

Chapter summary

This chapter stresses the management value of the marketing mix in the vital dimension of product design in the context of market segmentation and customer motivations. Marketing is nothing if not an integrated approach to business and students in particular should note the overlapping structure of the chapters thus far. The chapter emphasizes a components view of travel and tourism products at two separate but related levels. At both levels the components view implies an ability, given adequate marketing research and product knowledge, to 'engineer' or formulate products to match the identified needs of target segments. Because needs are continuously shifting, and competitors' abilities to supply needs are constantly changing, product formulation is a continuous process. This holds good for new, purpose-built products that may be designed years before they are in operation, and for existing products, which may have to be adapted over time through rearranging product components.

Product formulation has two sides, reflecting concerns with demand and supply. In terms of demand, the approach requires market research focused on customer needs, behaviour and perceptions in order to define target segments and to identify strengths and weaknesses of product design and images. In terms of supply, product formulation requires an analysis of product components and elements, and identification of the range of existing and potential products that could be improved or developed profitably to meet customer needs. These demand and supply implications apply equally to tourist destinations and to individual businesses. Matching supply to demand is, of course, the cornerstone of the modern marketing approach and integration between the two levels of the product is often an essential part of the matching process in travel and tourism – communicated using images and brands.

There is always a danger in tourism marketing that the ease with which it is possible to 'engineer' intangible service products on paper and Web sites, and to promise satisfactions in advertising and PR, exceeds a destination's or a business's ability to deliver the satisfaction at the time of consumption. Because tourism products are ideas at the time of purchase, it is relatively easy to oversell them, especially to first-time buyers. Any significant dissatisfaction experienced during consumption may destroy the vital word-of-mouth recommendations and decisions on repeat purchase on which long-term business profit and survival are likely to depend.

The final part of the chapter focuses on the role of branding and image positioning, identified as one of the key components in product formulation. Given the inseparable nature of tourism production and delivery, and the intangibility of the product at the point of purchase, developing and communicating a brand identity is a vital consideration in strategic and operational terms.

Further reading

An understanding of product concepts in travel and tourism is crucial to effective marketing in the industry. Accordingly, the limited space in this book is allocated deliberately to tourism aspects in preference to other important, widely used, standard product concepts, which are fully explained in most textbooks of marketing principles. For an understanding of the concepts of product life cycles, product-mix decisions, branding and product classifications, the following reading is recommended:

Baker, M. J. (1996). *Marketing: An Introductory Text*. Chapter 11, 6th edn, Macmillan.

Brassington, F. and Pettit, S. (2000). *Principles of Marketing*. Chapters 7, 8 and 9, 2nd edn, Prentice-Hall.

Chernatony, L. de and McDonald, M. H. B. (1992). *Creating Powerful Brands*. Butterworth-Heinemann.

Chernatony, L. de and McWilliam, G. (1990). Appreciating brands as assets through using a two-dimensional model. *International Journal of Advertising*, **9**: 111–19.

Davidson, H. (1997). *Even More Offensive Marketing*. Chapters 10 and 11, Penguin.

Doyle, P. (1989). Building successful brands: the strategic options. *Journal of Marketing Management*, **5** (1): 77–95.

Jobber, D. (1998). *Principles and Practices of Marketing*. 2nd edn, McGraw-Hill.

Kotler, P. and Armstrong, G. (1999). *Principles of Marketing*. Chapters 8 and 9, Prentice-Hall.

For the sustainable issues surrounding tourism product formulation see also:

Middleton, V. T. C. and Hawkins, R. (1998). *Sustainable Tourism: A Marketing Perspective*. Chapter 9, Butterworth-Heinemann.

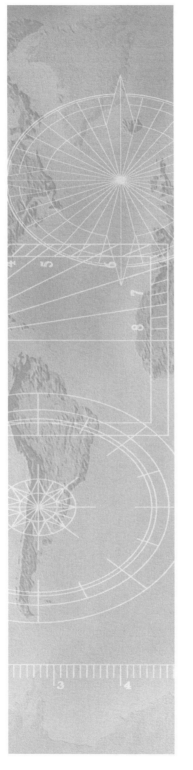

The role of price in the marketing mix

The three most common ways of pricing are cost plus, competitive rates and historical rates adjusted for inflation. Cost plus means you don't know how to price; competitive rates means you don't know how to price but your competitors do; adjusting historical rates means you don't know how to price but someone once did. (Anon.)

Price or cost to the customer is introduced in Chapter 6 as one of the four primary Ps in the marketing mix. For leisure tourism, especially holiday choices, there are many who consider price to be the most important of all the marketing decisions because price fixes the terms of the voluntary exchange transaction between customers willing to buy and producers wishing to sell. Through the agreed terms of exchange, customers are attempting to maximize their perceptions of benefits and value for money as they choose from competing products on offer. Producers are aiming simultaneously to achieve targeted sales volume, sales revenue and market share while optimizing their return on investment. In competitive tourism markets, however, the customers' influence over pricing is ultimately dominant.

This chapter aims to show the significant and complex role that pricing plays in marketing-mix decisions and the growing power of customers over the pricing process. It focuses first on the crucial functional role of price in manipulating demand and therefore sale revenue. The characteristics of travel and tourism that influence pricing decisions are then outlined, followed by a discussion of pricing strategy and tactics. For most businesses in tourism, pricing is still much more art than science and the latter half of the chapter identifies and comments on each of the main influences on pricing decisions.

The chapter concludes with a note on the growing use of computerized yield management programmes which developed rapidly in the 1990s as part of the associated developments in ICT that are revolutionizing distribution methods at the start of the new millennium. Such programmes, initially in the airline industry, are now widely used to assist larger businesses in other forms of transport, accommodation and even larger attractions, to make their tactical marketing segmentation and pricing decisions on a significantly more scientific basis.

Manipulating price in order to manage demand and revenue generation

Getting immediately down to basics, it is easy to appreciate that the volume of products sold × average price paid = sales revenue. It is also easy to see that the potential influence on profit of relatively small changes in price may be massive. For example, if a hotel of 150 bedrooms operates at 70 per cent room occupancy, with an average price across its segments and products of $250 per room night (average room rate achieved), annual room sales revenue = $9 581 250 (150 rooms × 365 nights × 70 per cent × $250). If, by more effective use of marketing techniques within the same marketing budget, the hotel could increase its room rate by an average of 5 per cent to $262.50 without loss of volume, the annual sales revenue would increase to $10 060 313 (150 × 365 × 70 per cent × $262.50. The difference is $479 063 which, if fixed and variable costs were held constant, would certainly represent a significant percentage of gross operating profit earned by this hotel.

Alternatively, if the price were reduced by 5 per cent to $237.50 per room night and the average occupancy rose to 75 per cent, sales revenue now = $9 752 343 (150 × 365 × 75 × $237.50). Thus, in this illustration, reducing the price increases occupancy and overall room sales revenue. Depending on the effect on variable costs of additional occupancy, greater gross profit may lie in price reduction. The role of a marketing manager in reducing average room rates, or raising them through more effective deployment of the marketing mix to stimulate demand, would never be a simple across the board shift in price. It would reflect many separate product decisions spread over the whole year. Continuous judgement would be required as to the price that each of the hotel's segments could bear at any given time.

Many businesses in travel and tourism have to publish their prices months ahead of actual sales, for example in brochures, and many are required by law to display them. But there are usually many opportunities to vary the published price in practice for reasons made clear in this chapter. Over a year's trading, the sales revenue generated in any except very small businesses is a function of many decisions on the optimum price to be charged to the range of segments involved, on a daily or week by week basis. For businesses such as visitor attractions, average prices tend to be relatively stable over a year but for others, such as tour operators and budget airlines, prices may vary widely as managers seek to optimize their short-run revenue. The use of price changes to manage demand is common throughout the industry, and is often a daily or even an hourly concern for many marketing managers. In the era of Internet dealing or e-commerce, the price may vary continuously on-line.

Do businesses or customers set prices?

Traditionally, although they have always had to respond to customer reaction and the actions of competitors, businesses in all sectors of industry have controlled the prices they set. Increasingly in the 1990s and certain to continue on present trends in the new decade, the effective power of customers to determine prices is growing. Partly as a result of globalization of competition and enormously facilitated by modern ICT, especially the use of Internet and interactive television systems, customers can now compare several prices online in ways that were previously impossible in practice. A prospective customer can 'surf' and compare a group of brands that are well known and acceptable to him and select the one available at the lowest price at the time that suits him. The advent of the euro in countries in the EU further facilitates direct price comparisons

As a result, if customers decide that a particular product is overpriced, many of them simply do not buy it. Large companies can now be forced to review and cut their costs in order to reduce prices to the levels that customers will pay. There are no historical parallels for such global price comparisons being available to large numbers of customers.

The evidence suggests, for example, that when nationalized airlines across Europe have been prepared for privatization and loss of state subsidies, the traditional 'cost plus' approach to pricing has been proved to be unworkable. Operating costs have had to be reduced, staff efficiencies introduced with cuts in the payroll and unit costs of operation driven down to a level at which operating profits can be produced at significantly lower prices. Growing price transparency has aided the remarkable growth in low cost/low price airlines such as *Southwest Airlines, easyJet* and *Ryanair. British Airways* could not compete on price using its higher cost network of scheduled flights and launched its own low-cost airline *Go* to compete with its new rivals. *Club Med*, for decades a thriving and profitable company, faltered and posted losses in the mid–1990s in part because its operational structure was driving prices ahead of customer willingness to pay. 'Price cuts of up to 30 per cent, renovated resorts and some new destinations . . . attracted thousands of tourists back to its holiday villages . . . and produced operating profits for 1997/8 of Fr. 386 million compared with a loss of Fr. 104 million in the previous year' (*The Times*, 20 January 1998).

Change is so rapid at present that one can only speculate about a revolution in consumer empowerment in tourism, based on comparisons between available options, that is profoundly affecting traditional approaches to price-setting.

The characteristics of holiday travel and tourism services that influence pricing

While price is a vital decision in the marketing of all types of goods and services, the special characteristics of tourism products explain the industry's particular preoccupation with price. The main characteristics of tourism services that influence pricing are noted below and discussed in this chapter (see also Chapter 3):

- High price elasticity in the discretionary segments of leisure, recreation and vacation travel markets.
- Long lead times in holiday markets between price decisions and product sales. Although such lead times are falling on average, twelve months or more are still not uncommon lead times when prices must be committed to print in brochures distributed months before customer purchases are made.
- No possibility of stockholding for service products, so that retailers do not share with producers the financial burden and risk of unsold stocks and are mostly not responsible for tactical pricing decisions.
- High probability of unpredictable but major short-run fluctuations in cost elements such as currency exchange rates and the price of oil for air travel.
- Near certainty of tactical price-cutting by major competitors whenever supply exceeds demand.
- High possibility of provoking price wars in sectors such as transport, accommodation and tour operation, during which short-run profitability may disappear.
- Effects of official regulation, especially in sectors such as transport, which may include influence over prices.
- Necessity for seasonal pricing to manage demand around a given volume of capacity in the short run.
- High level of customers' psychological involvement, especially with vacation products in which price may be perceived as a symbol of status as well as value.
- The high fixed costs of operation, which encourage and justify massive short-run price cuts in service operations whenever the prospect emerges of unsold capacity of perishable products.
- High level of vulnerability to demand changes reflecting unforeseen international economic and political events.

A major international tour operator such as TUI, for example, has to cope with each of these characteristics in preparing its pricing policies looking up to eighteen months ahead. It has to make its decisions usually without knowledge of its competitors' decisions on the same characteristics.

The role of price in strategy and tactics

Travel and tourism businesses respond to their highly complex pricing circumstances by operating prices at two levels.

The first level, corresponding broadly with marketing strategy, is the price a tourism business has to publish months in advance of production in brochures, guides, on admission tickets and so on. For hotels, this price is the so-called tariff structure or 'rack rate'; for airlines, it is the published fare structure. This strategic price reflects marketing decisions concerning product positioning, value for money, long-run return on investment requirements, operating costs and corporate business objectives such as growth, market share and profit.

The second level, corresponding to marketing operations or tactics, is the price at which an operator is prepared to do business on a weekly, daily or hourly basis. It changes as the date of production or service delivery approaches and in the light of bookings and expectations at the time. This often may be many weeks or months after the published price decisions were made. The tactical price may be widely known, advertised and published, as are the 'sale' offers regularly put out by tour operators as they seek to achieve additional last minute bookings. Alternatively, the price may be a closely guarded commercial secret as happens when tour operators undertake deals with hoteliers facing cash-flow crises or bankruptcy unless they can generate additional revenue from otherwise empty rooms. Unofficial 'dumping' of airline tickets for sale at heavily discounted prices is commonly practised around the world, and frequently criticized but not stopped because discount fares provide a tactical, daily service of great value to the airlines. The Internet now contains dozens of Web sites offering last minute travel prices that are a fraction of the published rates. Members of the public willing to bargain with half-empty hotels in the late evening will often find they can achieve significant reductions from the published room rate.

Travel and tourism businesses are not alone in practising these two-level pricing approaches. Heavy discounting, e.g. of new car sales or computer equipment, is also frequent and undertaken for the same reason – to secure additional sales which it is believed would not otherwise occur. In the case of manufactured goods, discounting is used also to release money tied up in expensive stocks so that the fixed costs of operation can be paid.

Chapters 12 and 13 discuss the meaning of strategic and operational planning. In this chapter it is necessary only to distinguish between the role of price as a management tool designed to achieve strategic business objectives, and as a tactical tool to manipulate short-run demand. In pricing, as with all the other elements of the marketing mix, the tactical or operational decisions have to be made within a strategic framework that steers the business toward its chosen goals.

The main distinctions can be summarized as follows.

Strategic role (regular or published prices)

- Reflects overall corporate strategies such as maximum growth, maximum revenue or new market growth objectives.
- Communicates chosen positioning, image and branding for products among target segments.
- Communicates expectations of product quality, status and value to prospective customers.
- Reflects stage in the product life cycle (newer, increasing share products generally achieve higher unit prices than older falling share products).
- Determines long-run revenue flows and return on investment.
- Determines the level of advance bookings achieved.
- May be used as part of the process for building long-term relationships with customers by offering special price arrangements to frequent repeat buyers.

Strategically, corporate growth objectives in price-sensitive markets are often based on adopting a relatively low or 'budget pricing' strategy in order to make a rapid impact on a large number of potential buyers. Such strategies usually aim for a high volume of sales at low profit margins per unit sold. The life-cycle stage of a product is also very much a strategic consideration as older, mature products will often be more price-sensitive because they are typically likely to be losing share through the competition they face from newer, developing products in rising demand. Because many service products cannot be seen or easily evaluated before purchase, the product's image and associated implications of quality have added significance for prospective first-time buyers. Price is a highly relevant symbol in signalling or communicating what buyers should expect in terms of product quality and value for money.

If the strategic decision of an organization is to operate in the de luxe end of a market rather than the budget end, that decision immediately commits it to a relatively high cost structure that can only be funded by relatively high prices. In this sense the decision to occupy a certain price and status band in the market precedes and determines the other three Ps of the marketing mix. The strategic product/price band decision is therefore also an operational decision that cannot easily be changed. For hotels, restaurants and airlines especially, the chosen price band determines the level of investment required for buildings and equipment. For all these reasons strategic price decisions have implications beyond marketing that necessarily affect the other senior managers of an organization. It is of course the role of marketing managers to research and interpret what price levels are realistic and achievable among the consumer segments whose needs an organization aims to satisfy. The Travel Inn case study in Part Six illustrates this point.

Tactical role (discounted/or promotional prices)

- Manipulates last minute/late booking demand through price incentives, which may be general but are more often restricted to particular segments at particular times.

- Determines short-run cash flows.
- Determines daily revenue yield.
- Matches competition by the quickest available method and sends warning signals of aggressive action.
- Promotes trial for first-time buyers.
- Provides a vital short-run tool for crisis management.

Important as pricing decisions are strategically, they play an even more dominant role tactically. This is because of the inseparable and perishable nature of service production and consumption and the inability of service producers to carry over unsold stocks as a buffer to cope with future demand. Thus, while a hotel with 150 rooms in the budget end of the market has a capacity of 54 750 room nights to sell in a year, the marketing requirement is to organize budget level demand in 'blocks' of 100–150 room buyers every night of the year. Because of the typical seasonal and daily variation in demand for most travel and tourism products, on some nights there may be up to 500 potential room buyers but on others only twenty-five. To deliver the nightly numbers as evenly as possible is no small feat. It requires what amounts to a continuous obsession with demand manipulation in which tactical price changing is usually the most immediate, powerful and often the only available tool. Surplus capacity in any market heightens competition – and an obsession with pricing to deal with it.

The multiple influences on price-setting

From the foregoing discussion it should be clear that there are many influences determining price-setting in practice. Figure 9.1 shows the range of influences relevant to marketing managers in travel and tourism, especially at the strategic level. At the tactical level, discussed above, the considerations focus more narrowly on day-to-day demand management in relation to competitors' actions. The remainder of this chapter comments on each of the influences separately.

It should be noted that there are two rings of influence surrounding pricing decisions. The *inner ring* reflects primary influences:

- Corporate strategy and positioning.
- Marketing objectives for the period over which prices are set.
- Segments with which a business is concerned.
- Operating cost constraints.
- Competitors' actions.

The *outer ring* reflects wider influences of:

- Characteristics of products and capacity.
- Non-price options.
- Legal and regulatory constraints.

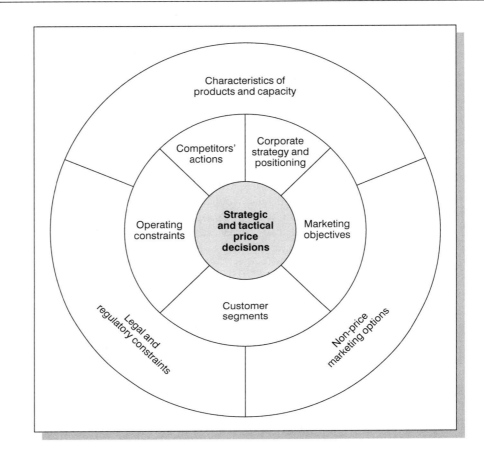

Figure 9.1
The network of
influences on
pricing decisions

Corporate strategy and positioning

The first and dominant influence on product-pricing is that of strategic business decisions concerning image, branding and product positioning, and strategies for growth, market share and return on investment. These decisions set the context for marketing operations over a three- to five-year time span or longer and effectively set realistic upper and lower limits within which product prices are likely to move – other than in crisis conditions.

Marketing objectives

In any modern marketing-led organization, business strategy has to be implemented systematically on a week-by-week basis through operational decisions focused on specific targets for sales volume and revenue. Price, as a highly influential component of the marketing mix, has to be adjusted to meet particular short-run objectives for each product/market segment with which a business is involved. For reasons developed in Chapters 13 and 14, objectives for particular campaigns will be a critical input to price-setting decisions.

Pricing by segments

Since marketing in practice revolves around an understanding of consumer profiles and behaviour patterns, it follows that every pricing decision has to be realistic in the context of the expectations and perceptions of targeted market segments and their capacity and willingness to pay. As noted in Chapter 7, pricing is itself a basic method of segmentation. Through consumer research and experience gained from results of previous price changes, marketing managers are expected to know what price level each segment can bear and to what extent price signifies value for money and product quality. Knowledge of segments also reveals practical ways in which pricing may be made relevant to one group of customers but inaccessible to others. Senior citizen rail cards designed to promote low-cost travel on railways outside commuting times, or hotel weekend prices designed to appeal to non-business segments, are examples. The conditions applied to many APEX airline fares, such as a Saturday night stopover and heavy cancellation charges, are calculated to deter business users. Pricing by segments is developed to maximize yield and minimize the dilution of revenue caused by offering cheaper prices to segments able and willing to pay more.

Operating costs

In order for a business to survive over the long run, the average prices charged must be high enough to generate sufficient revenue to cover all fixed and variable costs and provide an acceptable return on the assets employed. Operating costs, expressed as average costs per unit of production, are therefore a primary input to all pricing decisions and they provide at least a nominal target floor for prices, below which they should not fall. As noted earlier in the chapter, however, if the operating costs are allowed to get out of line with customers' willingness to pay in conditions of growing competition, the business will be quickly forced to reduce its operating costs to competitive levels. Continuous cost-cutting programmes for exactly this reason, especially among airlines, were a remarkable and continuing concern for many travel and tourism businesses throughout the 1990s

Many catering establishments, hotel restaurants and bars still fix prices in traditional ways by adding a mark-up percentage to the basic cost of production per unit sold. The basic idea is to cover return on investment and generate a profit. Unfortunately for most tourism businesses, the so-called 'cost plus' methods are no longer useful in practice. This is partly because most tourism markets are highly competitive and price-sensitive, so that operators are often forced for tactical reasons to accept prevailing market prices regardless of costs and mark-up. It is also because of the influence on their operations of high fixed costs and low variable costs. (See Chapter 3.)

Competitors' actions

It is at the level of tactical marketing that price competition becomes an all-pervasive preoccupation. For example in 1991, after two very difficult trading years, projected summer bookings for UK tour operators failed to materialize in the critical period between January and March. The first quarter of the year roughly coincided with the Gulf War, which, combined with the effects of an unexpectedly severe economic downturn in the UK, totally disrupted normal cash flow for tour operators. Traditional discounting could not influence a crisis of this magnitude and the International Leisure Group (ILG), the UK's second largest operator at that time was driven into liquidation. It was unable to sustain its operational costs and persuade banks to fund the rising cost of its extensive borrowing for a planned expansion of its airline. As a result of the sudden withdrawal of a significant proportion of capacity from the UK package tours market, prices firmed even as survivors bought up released holiday accommodation at 'distress' sale prices. Paradoxically, as a result of the ILG collapse, the survivors achieved large windfall profits in that year.

In the mid–1990s Hong Kong was a favourite destination for high-spending Japanese tourists, with 2.3 million arrivals in 1996. In 1997, following the economic crash in the Asia Pacific region, Japanese arrivals fell by nearly 50 per cent and total tourism income fell by over $2 billion (*Economist*, 28 November 1998) The competitive effect on hotel prices in Hong Kong is obvious, not least because Hong Kong did not devalue its currency and real prices for international tourists were effectively raised. In all countries generating or receiving tourist flows, the travel trade press is likely to contain frequent examples of competitive, tactical pricing decisions. It is a useful exercise for students to select some of these examples for examination and discussion. Students should also consider how far these decisions are planned or are simply forced responses to market circumstances permitting no alternative.

Characteristics of products and capacity

When products have close substitutes and producer organizations have surplus capacity, it is highly likely that price competition will be the dominant consideration in marketing tactics. Many Mediterranean resort hotels find themselves in this position. In Britain, sea ferries operating across the Channel are similarly placed and airlines in de-regulated conditions are also forced into price competition. Across the travel and tourism industry generally the close substitutability of many products, coupled with the need to secure daily customer purchases, heightens the level of marketing dependency on pricing tactics.

Substitutability of products is one of the reasons why leisure products in travel and tourism demonstrate high price elasticity. Other things being equal, especially if both brands are well known and respected, a small increase in the price of one product provokes a considerable shift in demand to other similar products because they are then relatively less expensive. Analyses of price against volume of sales data confirm that many travel and tourism markets do respond in accordance with traditional economic models of *price-elastic* demand and supply.

Most managers are well aware of the effects of price elasticity, although they can rarely predict exactly how any given market segment will respond in a forecast period. Traditionally market responses to changes in price have had to be guessed at by managers relying heavily on judgement and market intelligence to interpret any forecasting models that may be used. Fortunately the developments in software and hardware for yield management programmes noted earlier have begun to resolve these difficulties, at least for businesses such as hotels and airlines with relatively substitutable products that have closely predictable flows of bookings under normal business conditions.

On the other hand, some products, even with large capacity, are able to secure a unique position within the minds of potential customers, which reduces perceived substitutability and lessens their sensitivity to price. The Ritz and Savoy hotels in London, Disney World in Florida and Center Parcs in Northern Europe, have all developed product concepts that for marketing purposes are unique. Marketing managers have a primary responsibility for creating and sustaining such product positions. (See also non-price options below.)

Non-price options

A principal responsibility for marketing managers is to understand all the pricing influences summarized in Figure 9.1. But often, especially as a result of competitors' unanticipated actions, the initiative in pricing may be lost in the short run. Ideally no business aims to be a price follower responding to what the market place dictates but in practice it often happens in many travel and tourism markets and cannot be avoided.

There are, however, other marketing ways in which it is possible to reduce the effects of substitution between products and limit the intensity of price competition. Most of these ways are aspects of adding value to services through careful branding and product augmentation, as described in detail in Chapter 8. Through augmentation it is possible significantly to enhance the benefits that products provide to target segments, especially the all important repeat buyers, and thus develop reasons for choosing according to product attributes rather than lowest price. For example, to meet the needs of frequent business customers, many privileged-user or frequent-user card schemes were developed and promoted by major airlines and hotel groups in the 1990s. Such cards sometimes provide price discounts but almost invariably offer attractive extra services such as rapid check-in/out facilities, credit billing or product up-grades when capacity permits. The expectation is that a holder of a card will use it, in preference to simple price switching to a competitor, for reasons of convenience, familiarity and the status of recognition and special treatment on arrival. Although not without some down sides in the full cost implications, these targeted membership/ loyalty schemes represent an effective marketing method for securing additional sales revenue often at, or very near, the strategically determined price level.

There are also numerous ways of disguising price cuts as consumer benefits. For example offering 'free' spouse accommodation (but not meals) or one 'free' night for every three paid for at the full rate, and so on. The very close link between sales promotion and tactical pricing considerations is a vital one in the tourism industry, and is further discussed in Chapter 16.

For hotels the advantages of a particular location, such as city centres for business persons, may confer a benefit in the minds of users that justifies a premium price. For an airline, the careful cultivation and promotion of a particular image for service and efficiency, or the high standards of their business-class lounges may constitute a benefit for which customers are willing to pay a premium price. For visitor attractions, most of which are already unique in their own intrinsic qualities, the route out of price substitutability lies in enhancing the quality of their sites or the enjoyment benefits conferred by a better presentation of the experiences offered. The Jorvik Viking Exhibition in York, for example, offered a new way to present historic artefacts in the 1980s that initially led to long queues of buyers willing to pay relatively high prices for a short but intense experience. All these are consumer-orientated marketing routes to avoiding head-on price competition between products that may otherwise be seen by customers as close substitutes.

Legal and regulatory constraints

While most pricing is a decision based on commercial calculations, some travel and tourism prices are also subject to government regulation. For various reasons of public health and safety, environmental protection, to ensure competition between suppliers and achieve consumer protection, governments in all countries frequently intervene in, or seek to influence pricing decisions. For example, even under the new liberalization of transport regimes, fares for many international scheduled air routes are still influenced by official agreements between governments and may be subject to investigation to prevent predatory pricing. In some countries, in which accommodation is officially registered and classified, price categories may be fixed annually and can be varied by individual businesses only within given limits. Pricing or new tax regulations designed to protect the environment are still infrequent at the start of the twenty-first century but are expected to grow. The Balearics plan to introduce such a tax in 2001. Other destinations will be watching closely.

In the former communist bloc countries of Eastern Europe, as well as in the developed economies of the Western world, the last decade witnessed massive privatization and restructuring of former state-run enterprises in favour of commercially owned and managed companies. This shift, combined with the development and growing power of national, transnational and global corporations (see Chapter 2), makes it inevitable that regulatory bodies will find it increasingly necessary to intervene in market decisions to protect consumer interests. In all developed countries the law provides for regulators to ensure fair competition and prevent the operation of monopolies or oligopolies against the public interest. As Wheatcroft put it in the context of world airlines, 'There certainly could be abuses of dominant market positions and it is highly desirable that there should be powers, such as those given to the EC under the competition rules, to prevent anti-competitive behaviour' (Wheatcroft, 1992: 19).

Yield management and market segmentation

The use of price to manage tourism demand and revenue tends to be highly complex in practice. First, most travel and tourism businesses deal with several segments at the same time, usually with different prices for different segments. Second, there are usually multiple products with different pricing implications, so that even a medium-sized firm is likely to have a product – market mix in which the range of prices is extensive. Third, there are often unpredictable daily and weekly fluctuations in business requiring a tactical pricing response because in the short run tourism supply is fixed.

In its marketing sense the term *yield management* is increasingly used to describe the process of managing revenue against demand. The implications of this will be clearer in Part Five of the book but in principle any hotel, airline, tour operator, car rental firm or attraction has a *potential revenue* achievable on any given day if all the capacity available is optimally used at the published prices (number of customers × price paid). Yield is the *actual revenue* achieved on that day. For example, two hotels of the same size and equivalent standard and operating with the same published rack rate, may each be 70 per cent full as measured in room occupancy. But hotel A may be discounting heavily to achieve volume through tour operators and hotel B may more successfully be marketing itself direct to customers. In this example, for the same room occupancy, hotel B may achieve an average percentage yield up to 50 per cent higher than hotel A. In the case of an airline a shift of, say, just 5 per cent of passengers from business class to economy class greatly lowers the yield from the same number of passengers. Because some 30 per cent of seat revenue is derived from around 10 per cent of front-end passengers on international flights, any downgrading has a multiplier effect on revenue and profit. For a museum, if two-thirds of all visitors are admitted at less than full adult price (i.e. at special group rates), the yield is much lower than it would be if, say, half the visitors paid full price.

In an era of excess capacity the concept of yield management on a daily and hourly basis is increasingly relevant in all sectors of travel and tourism including large attractions. It is the business of marketing managers to balance the revenue flow from the segments they deal with in ways best calculated to improve yield, not just to increase the number of customers. For businesses that depend on advance bookings weeks or months ahead of service delivery, regular projections of yield are especially important. In the 1990s, developments of low-cost hardware and software for yield management programmes have already revolutionized the sensitivity with which managers can manage databases of seats or bed stock and passenger/guest bookings. Standardized programmes can give early warning with some precision of flights (or nights for hotels) when unsold capacity is highly likely to occur. Some of this early warning is fairly obvious, as with normal seasonal variations and can be handled with special offers, APEX fares and so on that are built into the marketing programme. Other variations occur on a daily basis, often reflecting particular events, and are increasingly responded to by hotels, for example, by varying prices by the hour, with reductions occurring towards evening on the days that capacity remains unsold.

The use of yield management programmes to alert managers to predicted weak sales flows are now common in all large businesses across the tourism industry. They are the basis for organizing tactical responses designed to optimize revenue. The same programmes also provide leading-edge market research and the means to learn through closely monitoring results so that future tactical offers can be refined and better targeted at segments. An interesting recent development has been the growing use of Internet Web sites to make available last minute offers to a potential audience that already runs to millions of customers in most developed countries and is certain to grow in the new millennium.

Although still a minor phenomenon at the end of the 1990s, there are also to be found regular cyber auction sites for travel products in which reservations are sold off to whoever puts in the highest bid. This, perhaps, is the ultimate in buyer driven pricing, at least for tactical purposes. The development of so-called 'intelligent agents' to take customer commands, trawl the Internet at high speed and come up with the best price options is part of that process.

Interestingly, at least up to 2000, easyJet the Internet sales leader amongst British budget airlines, has been able to maintain a bold strategy of cheaper pricing in advance and increasing prices as the last minute approaches. That strategy appears defensible only for as long as demand generally exceeds supply.

Chapter summary

Managing relatively volatile demand on a daily basis around a relatively fixed capacity of highly perishable product supply is identified in previous chapters as one of the principal characteristics of travel and tourism marketing. The use of price as one of the four main levers to be co-ordinated in the marketing mix is particularly important in managing demand and revenue. It is still more of an art than a science but its successful use means reconciling customer interests and operational constraints within a strategic framework of business objectives.

Two levels of pricing – strategic and tactical – are discussed, and these are themes developed later in Chapters 12 and 13. Summarized in Figure 9.1, this chapter identifies and discusses the main influences to be taken into account in setting prices in practice and introduces the concept of yield management. Yield management is used by large international companies to manage prices around predicted daily demand and to optimize the earnings from customer segments. The chapter lays particular stress on the importance of non-price options in tourism markets, the use of which enables marketing managers to reduce the sometimes dominating effects of price-elasticity and product substitution.

Price is an important concern in marketing all types of goods and services. But it is too often an obsession in many travel markets, especially those concerned with closely substitutable products targeted at leisure and vacation segments. It may often be the dominating influence on market demand in the short run, but it is still only one of four levers (or seven if the marketing mix is extended as explained in Chapter 6) to be co-ordinated both strategically and tactically. Examples of strategic and tactical pricing decisions are further developed in Part Five of this book.

Further reading

Baker, M. J. (1996). *Marketing: An Introductory Text*. Chapter 13, 6th edn, Macmillan.

Brassington, F. and Pettit, S. (2000). *Principles of Marketing*. Chapters 10 and 11, 2nd edn, Prentice-Hall.

Davidson, H. (1997). *Even More Offensive Marketing*. Chapter 14, Penguin.

Kotler, P. and Armstong, G. (1999). *Principles of Marketing*. Chapters 10 and 11, 8th edn, Prentice-Hall.

Part Three

Planning Strategy and Tactics for Travel and Tourism Marketing

10

Information and communications technology and tourism marketing

The Internet is turning business upside down and inside out. It is fundamentally changing the way that companies operate. This goes far beyond e-commerce and deep into the process and culture of an enterprise. (Business and the Internet, *Economist*, 26 June 1999: 54.)

Since the second edition of this book was written in 1992/3 (published in 1994), the most profound development in travel and tourism in the last decade has been the impact of change in the capabilities and potential of ICT. It is of course a global revolution, symbolized by access to the World Wide Web, but much more profound in its information management roots and its implications for the future conduct of business. It is a convergence of the information and communications world. In just five years since general consumer access to the Internet was first available through Web browsers serving home PCs, the speed of development has been remarkable. If it is still too soon to be certain to what extent the Internet will dominate tourism marketing, it is at least clear that its impact will be a major influence on nearly every aspect of services marketing. The convergence and 'connectivity' now available through ICT appears to signal one of the historic 'discontinuities' in the way business is conducted that provide massive growth opportunities for the proactive and overwhelm those too slow to adapt.

What is still conjecture at this stage is how fast people in organizations will be able and willing to change the ways in which they work; how as individuals they will adapt to change and to the spate of mergers, alliances and job insecurity that are part of global commerce; how customers will amend their behaviour patterns as seekers of information and buyers; how ever more efficient flows of information will change the culture of enterprises; how governments will react in regulatory endeavours to their loss of influence over global commerce and whether countervailing people-power will generate a different political conscious-ness about the implications of the revolution – as manifested in Vancouver at the World Trade Organization Conference in 1999.

These are not issues of technological competence but of human nature and cultures developed over centuries. There are wider social concerns in the new millennium also for the splits in society between those who are computer literate, employable and well paid, and those who are not – the so-called 'Digital Divide'. Similarly there are millions whose livelihoods in traditional industries in the 'old' economies of the developed world will be lost as the traditional geographical logic for industrial location are overturned and production shifts to low-cost countries.

This chapter sets out the scope of the ICT revolution, stressing that commercial use of the Internet is only possible because of the parallel developments in database technology, which are equally profound in marketing terms. It proceeds to indicate at least the potential influences in ICT on each of the main stages in the marketing mix which are developed in subsequent chapters. Neither of the authors claims to be an ICT expert but nor are the great majority in tourism marketing. It is, however, possible to see at least the direction of opportunities and threats, through observation and analysis of events as they occur. By applying the ideas that emerge to the basic principles of tourism marketing, *which have not changed*, it is possible to form some judgement of the future. This is the aim of the chapter. It is not to pre-empt the chapters that follow but to serve as a useful bridge between the basic concepts of Parts One and Two and the techniques and applications that follow in Parts 3, 4, 5 and 6.

How it used to be

To modern students brought up in the computer age it must seem strange that well into the 1970s and within the lifetime of many now senior managers most travel reservation systems were still manual. Even in the USA, in large as well as small businesses, teams of clerks using telephones toiled like ants around massive pegboards, black-boards, ledgers or charts that filled the whole wall space of large offices. Such charts physically represented production capacity for hotel rooms, campsites and so on, for several months ahead. Although such systems could handle several destinations, the geographical coverage was inevitably limited by administrative difficulties of communication.

Such manual systems were slow, inflexible, liable to failure through human error and very costly in labour employed. They could not cope easily with changes as they occurred, nor identify and suggest alternatives if a particular slot was filled. They required elaborate paperwork support systems and the physical capacity of such manual systems set limits to the volume of transactions that a business could handle. The first use of mainframe computers for reservation systems in the tourism industry started with the airlines in the 1960s and developed quickly into global distribution systems (see Chapter 18). By the mid–1970s, the manual systems had disappeared from large and medium-sized producers, to be replaced by online electronic information systems, operating through each principal's main computer via as many peripheral terminals as the flow of business could justify. Manual systems did not disappear from most small businesses, however; they would have to wait nearly another twenty years before the advent of low-cost, highly efficient, Internet-enabled PCs would make it possible for them to join the information revolution and begin to exploit its opportunities.

The airline industry investment in CRSs to link or connect businesses' inventory directly to intermediaries in the distribution chain was a vital first step in the tourism ICT 'connectivity' process. It paved the way for subsequent change. The level of investment required to set up the new systems was one of the first underlying reasons both forcing and facilitating business growth and the emergence of international/global links, alliances and acquisitions that dominated so much of the tourism industry in the last quarter of a century. The new ICT systems made business growth possible, and the growth in revenues justified the technology and personnel investment required. This 'win-win' cycle has been repeated many times since but it traces its origins to the 1960s and 1970s.

The ICT menu

Five main developments of the 1990s are noted briefly. All of them make possible the more effective and cost-efficient use of marketing techniques in travel and tourism marketing. All of them influence the competitive position of the businesses that employ them:

- Databases.
- The Internet.
- Mobile telephones.
- Call centres.
- Interactive digital televisions.

Databases

Historically 1967 marked a watershed in customer databases when the first 'hole-in-the-wall' credit cards issued by banks became available. They signalled a revolution in marketing opportunities linked with credit facilities that are still the focal element in e-commerce today. The banks obtained access to massive amounts of customer-behaviour data linked to names and addresses and geodemographics that was ahead of its time and exceeded the technology of the 1970s to handle effectively. In travel and tourism a major breakthrough can be seen in the airline, car rental and hotel loyalty membership schemes designed to reward repeat buyers that stemmed from the computer technology of the 1980s. Many of these are now global and are still highly relevant in the twenty-first century (see relationship marketing below). In 1995 another major marketing watershed occurred when leading UK retailers saw the opportunity to develop their own database marketing and e-commerce and TESCO launched its membership card in the UK gaining some 8 million members within a matter of months. Other national retailers followed suit (see Table 10.1).

Database knowledge of customers' profile and behaviour is discussed in Chapter 19 because it is the basis for effective direct marketing. In travel and tourism it is the collection and analysis of data streams that now flow continuously through distribution channels and booking systems, which provide the modern information base for the strategic and operational decisions of large organizations. The rate of technological change as databases connect and interact indicates that the speed and quality of information flows will be further enhanced in the coming decade. There are no parallels for this in the history of travel and tourism and all businesses are entering new territory. Technologically there are few barriers although the investment costs in relevant systems and the human factors noted earlier should not be underestimated.

The Internet

In the first decade of the twenty-first century travel and tourism is one of the world's largest and most refined information based industries. The World Wide Web operates as a global marketplace accessible to the general public twenty-four hours a day, seven days a week (also known as the '24/7' economy). It is a marketplace based entirely on information provision and exchange transactions in which detailed information, for example on prices and availability, is changing every few seconds. It comprises multimedia information to support consumer decision-making; it supports global transactions and bookings, distributes ticketing and invoices, and collects information about customers that are transferred immediately on to databases. Related information flows occur at check-in for transport and registration for accommodation. Other than printed information, some of it via 'downloads', there are no tangible elements in the service delivery process until a customer departs from home and arrives at the destination. Because tourism is an information industry and customer decisions are highly price-sensitive it has become one of the natural lead industries on the Internet.

Table 10.1 is provided as an aide-mémoire for some of the recent developments of the Internet. It cannot possibly be comprehensive and will be quickly out of date but it serves as an indicator of how we got to the present position. It may help to provide at least a handle on events within an overall context that may help to counter some of the wilder exaggerations about the Internet that were occurring daily during the late 1990s.

Business to business (B2B) and intranets • • •

A major development associated with the wider use of the Internet is the way in which it facilitates communications within and between businesses. E-mail and the exchange of information files are the obvious uses, replacing fax and reducing the number of direct telephone conversations. Most large corporations use intranets for their internal communications; a form of closed sector of the Internet that is only accessible to authorized corporate personnel.

By far the most important use of the Internet is the conduct of exchange transactions (marketing) between businesses that are purchasing and businesses that are supplying, also known in the jargon as B2B. As always the estimates vary and the exact total is not known but there is complete consensus that the value of business-to-business transactions far exceeds the value of business to consumer transactions. Although the biggest volume of business is between manufacturers seeking the most competitive international quotes for the components they buy in, B2B also covers the procurement role of leading retailers. In 2000 there is a race to provide procurement services to small businesses through Internet portals that can consolidate multiple small purchases into orders to achieve economies of scale. It is widely predicted that B2B use of the Internet, embracing proactive small businesses, will continue to be its most important commercial role for the next few years.

Mobile telephones

As with database technology, the development of hand-held mobile communications has also had some two decades of development, with the UK's Vodafone celebrating its 500 000th customer in 1989 to become the largest mobile phone company in the world at that time. By mid–2000, having bought the American Air Touch Company and forged links with Germany, it was still the largest mobile telephone company, but with 28 million customers around the world, operations in twenty-three countries across four continents and some 25 000 employees. Such is the speed of progress. In many developing countries it seems probable that mobile telephony will simply bypass the traditional landline systems that established the first telephone systems in the nineteenth century and dominated phone communications until the late 1990s.

In the mid–1990s, mobile phones were heavy to carry, were limited to national boundaries, had very limited battery life and there were large areas where they could not be used. They were expensive to buy and use, required twelve-month service contracts and, however useful, were just alternative telephones used primarily for business purposes. Purchase outlets were very limited and the costs of creating new customers were large and a major factor in pricing. Within just five years mobile telephones had become designer items; pocket/handbag sized, cheap to buy, even for schoolchildren, and were widely available in high street stores so that the costs of finding new buyers fell dramatically. They could provide global coverage and had extended battery life. Usage time costs were reducing, options for pre-payment were very popular for non-business users,

Table 10.1
The Internet and related developments in ICT: a synopsis

> *100 000 computers with Internet connection in 1988; 20 million Internet users in 1995, a projected 300 million worldwide by 2001 . . . Although it is clearly impossible to do justice to the revolutionary developments in ICT in a few words, readers may find it helpful to consider the following short chronology in the context of distribution for travel and tourism. No claims are made for the absolute accuracy of the dates or data. They are indicative of the major developments.*
>
> *The Internet has its origins in the Advanced Research Project Agency set up by the Pentagon in 1957 for military communications. It was first used for academic communications in the late 1960s and e-mail followed in the early 1970s.*

1995	The first practical commercial usage of the *World Wide Web* dates from 1995, following registration of domain names or Internet addresses, and development of Web-browser software and the international TCP/IP standard for international communications. The leading Internet search engines for the Web stem from that date and the first international airlines' Web sites were launched to provide limited information on seat availability and prices, and directions for booking – by e-mail or phone. Several UK travel operators pioneering Web sites also date to 1995, including that of the first British seaside resort (Torbay). British Midland (UK) launched *Cyberseat* at the end of the year, which claimed to be the first airline Internet site to take reservations and payment online.
1995	Around 20 million people were estimated to be Internet users, mostly in the USA.
1995	This was also the launch date for TESCO's membership card, which rapidly gained some 8 million members in its first year, with details retained on a massive consumer database. TESCO was the leading UK supermarket retailer at the end of the 1990s and a leader in the use of ICT. All main rivals quickly followed its lead so that at least two-thirds of all UK households held one or more such retail card within three years of the original launch. Marketed as membership and discount cards, the primary purpose was to collect data about customers for marketing purposes. These cards represent a quantum shift in the commercial sophistication of consumer databases. They also provide a base for strategic developments into new product areas.
1996	The International Air Transport Association (IATA) agreement was reached on a worldwide standard for e-ticketing, facilitating e-commerce in global ticket sales and delivery mechanisms. SABRE launches *Travelocity*, the first Internet version of a global distribution system (travel shop) accepting bookings online. For hotels, Pegasus Corporation attached *Travelweb* to THISCO, the international hotel industry switch company connecting some 25 000 hotels in 180 countries for online hotel bookings
1997	Apart from a relatively small number of early pioneers, 1997 saw the first significant extension of e-commerce in travel and tourism although the numbers were still small. On-line advertising on the Internet (for all purposes) was estimated at $907 million.
1998	Business to business e-commerce (for all purposes) was estimated at $43 billion, compared with around $8 billion for e-commerce transactions from business to consumers. IBM was forecasting that nearly a quarter of its business revenues would derive from e-business sales in 1999. Dell Computers generates an even larger proportion.
1998	Digital television introduced into the UK with estimates that nearly half of all households would have digital sets (with the potential for connecting with the Internet) by 2005. Similar projections were made for Northern European countries. The Internet was estimated to contain some 320 million pages of information (increasing exponentially). Recognition of these developments undoubtedly stimulated a major development and extension phase for e-commerce in tourism dating from 1998/9.

Table 10.1
Continued

1999 Some 40 per cent of US households have Internet access, compared with around 10 per cent in Europe. European figures vary from around 40 per cent access in Finland and Norway to under 1 per cent in Russia. Britain had around 15 per cent of households with PC-based Internet access, and just over 8 million Web site users, rapidly approaching a fifth of the adult population. (Over 30 per cent was claimed in 2000.) Such figures make it practical for entrepreneurial direct marketing budget airlines such as Britain's *easyJet* to target some 60 per cent of sales by Internet by the end of 2000. Its aircraft carry the direct telephone number on one side – and the Web site address on the other.

1999 An almost daily deluge of overoptimistic forecasts that Internet access and e-commerce sales revenue will double internationally every year for the next five were commonplace, with estimates for consumer-related e-commerce ranging from $35 billion to $75 billion by 2002. Such forecasts fuelled extraordinary stock market prices for Internet-related companies in the USA and worldwide. Yahoo!, for example, was capitalized at more than General Motors in mid–1999, not on the basis of profits but extraordinary potential. Travel and tourism along with financial services, music, computer services and books were targeted as prime growth sectors.

1999 Online auctions for perishable or 'distressed' products such as travel were scheduled for major growth as they meet producers' need to move unsold products and consumers' interest in impulse purchase last minute price bargains. The sites are updated hourly, as last minute capacity is made available.

2000 Stock market realities set in USA and countries around the world as doubts concerning the profit potential of most dot.com companies set in. By mid–2000 many of the Internet stocks had plunged in value by over 50 per cent from the earlier part of the year and some of the pioneers had gone bankrupt. More seem certain to follow. Even Amazon, for years a dot.com leader was suffering from concerns about its real profit potential.

2000 Evidence mounted that leading airlines and hotels were now willing to form alliances to invest in developing their own jointly controlled Web sites to undertake the vital last minute booking services thus far cornered by the dot.com infomediaries. Principals can benefit directly from the lower costs and customer knowledge that such involvement provides.

2000 The WTO estimates suggest that China, with around 4 million Internet users in 1999 will have around 27 million by 2001.

2001 Although it was still a year ahead when this book went to print, it was projected that there would be over 300 million Internet users by 2001 (compared with 20 million in 1995). Approaching half would still be in the USA. Belief in such forecasts is encouraged by the fact that millions of people are still accessing the Internet in their daily lives using modems operating at 56 Kbps. At that speed, especially with graphics, the Internet is painfully slow and tedious to surf. New ADSL for telephone lines was becoming available in 1999 over ordinary telephone lines offering speeds of 1.5 Mbps. Broadband access for digital television will also make using the Internet and its multimedia possibilities very much more enjoyable and convenient.

Sources: This section is based on a compilation of press cuttings and research maintained over several years. Main sources include the *Economist*, *Financial Times*, travel trade press and extracts from research by Forrester Research, Merril Lynch, and the Computer Industry Almanac.

avoiding the need for service contracts, and from toddlers to pensioners the mobile phone became a normal accessory for nearly half the population. Mobile phones are part of the infrastructure that supports a twenty-four hour society.

Given the speed of change – the actual life of phones by their users is little over a year – an escalating production process for the manufacturers is assured. So is a major environment problem as millions of used phones are discarded as rubbish even before their first batteries need replacing. With the advent of the so-called third generation of broadband wireless application protocol enabled (WAP) phones, introduced at the end of 1999, Internet access as well as text and messaging services became available. The mobile phone is now operable in most parts of the world and has 'grown down' to become a miniature hand-held computer. It can be used for e-mail, travel and other reservations and bookings, personal banking and for a growing range of entertainment purposes.

Call centres

Use of telephones to service customer enquiries and make reservations and bookings has been widely operational as a traditional distribution channel for over seventy-five years. But around the end of the 1980s a number of trends justified the investment by larger multi-site businesses, such as airlines and budget hotels, to create separate call centres for the more efficient processing of telephone calls. These trends were the increasing volume of telephone use, the demand for services around the clock, growing corporate use of direct response marketing, the growing trend to last minute bookings, the expansion of mobile phone use and, of course, the developments of ICT including satellite relay stations for global communications. It is now possible to establish call centres almost anywhere in the world, certainly in areas far removed from a businesses headquarters, to take advantage of lower wage costs and lower communication costs. A recent illustration can be found in the case study on timeshare in Part Six.

Modern call centres work on shift systems, are fully computerized, linked obviously with customer databases and the Internet (for which they provide a user-friendly alternative to online e-commerce), and have training programmes to maximize efficiency. Shared call centres are common for smaller businesses that cannot justify the full investment. They are just another form of ICT enabled outsourcing for business purposes.

A core part of modern distribution systems and increasingly linked with Web sites, especially for customers who prefer not to engage in e-commerce, call centres are now part of the standard reservation processes for all larger businesses in travel and tourism. It has become a major international development, with India and China especially attractive as locations of choice. Salaries in India, for example, are lower than in the advanced economies, so unit costs per call are lower. Most people in India speak excellent English, the lingua franca of the global tourism world; many people are well educated and the time zone occupied by India often means that communications can take place at cheap phone rates in the countries from which the business flows. Call centre operations and the associated technology lend themselves naturally to undertaking other back office functions such as accounting, data processing and invoicing. British Airways (BA) for example, were employing some 2000 employees in Bombay and Poona by the end of 2000. The operation, producing cost savings of at least a third compared with locations in the UK, initially focused on servicing BA and other contracted airlines. 'But BA has opened talks with companies in the pharmaceuticals, market research, banking and insurance sectors and with charities' (*The Times*, 4 August 2000).

Interactive television

In 2000, there is wide expectation that digital televisions with broadband Internet access will replace the 'traditional' Internet role of home PCs. Estimates that up to half of all homes will be using such sets within a very few years remain to be proven but appear probable at the time of writing. Provided that broadband access is available to speed the process of access and surfing the Web, it appears certain that interactive television will facilitate and speed all of the developments noted in this chapter.

In the UK, although it was not an interactive process at 2000, Teletext information on traditional television screens was estimated to have captured over 10 per cent of inclusive tour sales by the end of the 1990s. A large number of consumers are, therefore, already familiar with the use of television for travel and tourism and will provide an immediate audience for the interactive options when they become available. The use of MINITEL in France will have much the same conditioning effect on prospective users for new, more efficient facilities.

Some of the ways in which ICT is influencing and changing marketing techniques

This section provides notes as a brief overview on some of the main implications of ICT on the principal processes in marketing, each of which is the subject of a separate chapter in this book.

It includes:

- Market research and marketing information systems.
- Strategic planning.
- Campaign planning and budgeting.
- Advertising and public relations.
- Printed or collateral materials.
- Sales promotion and pricing.
- Distribution and access.

Market research and marketing information systems

The second edition of this book noted that 'the inability to measure and forecast travel and tourism adequately in the 1990s is becoming in itself an obstacle to growth and a major barrier to better recognition of the size and importance of the industry' (Middleton, 1994b: 362).

At least for larger businesses the database developments have made massive improvements in the quality of information available to marketing managers. Known in the jargon as 'data-mining,' research can provide detailed knowledge of customer profiles and behaviour together with much better information on the way customers respond to different forms of promotion and distribution. Such information comes at very little additional cost once the databases have been set up, and it makes it possible for service industries with direct access to their customers to discontinue use of previous expensive sample survey techniques

If access to continuous information on customer satisfaction is incorporated (see Chapter 11), databases provide a near perfect tool for marketing managers in travel and tourism to carry out all forms of product formulation, pricing and communications innovations and read the results almost simultaneously. They are able to exploit a service industry asset of having customers on site that has for so long been largely overlooked. It is widely recognized that ICT opens new strategic avenues for businesses to provide new or additional services for existing customers or to enter new service product areas for existing and for new customers (see Chapter 12). The ability conferred by modern database analysis to innovate or test market and read immediate results is part of the ICT contribution to marketing innovation.

Strategic planning

A by-product of the ICT developments is the information flows it provides about the nature of industries and the potential for taking new directions. It makes it possible, for example, for supermarkets to use their customer databases to market financial services and, if they so choose, enter the holiday travel market. It made it possible for AOL to link up with Time Warner (itself linked to CNN) to develop digital in-home and on-the-move entertainment. It makes it possible for BA to operate its call centres in India for its own purposes and at the same time run a profitable data-processing company providing outsourced facilities for other service industries. It made possible the remarkable and rapid shift of Preussag from being the leading German company in the heavy industrial field in the mid-1990s (steel, shipbuilding and coal-mining), to becoming the leading global player in Europe in travel and tourism markets through a planned process of disposal of 'old industry' assets and the acquisition of new ones. Hapag-Lloyd, TUI, Thomas Cook/JMC and Thomson Holidays were all acquired in the space of three years.

The strategic possibilities also exist for creating virtual companies that are branded and exist in cyber space but outsource most of their inputs using B2B methods. The wave of *dot.com* Internet companies that launched themselves in travel in the late 1990s are in many ways virtual marketing companies. They facilitate and provide a platform for the exchange of information and for e-commerce transactions for a wide range of products but they produce no products themselves. They simply provide distribution and marketing services, acting as infomediaries for other service provider businesses.

Campaign planning and budgeting

Direct marketing techniques (Chapter 19) driven by databases developments are increasingly at the leading edge of competitive advantage and provide the continuous flow of information on which campaigns are planned, innovations launched, and their cost effectiveness monitored and evaluated. (See Chapters 13 and 14.)

Advertising and public relations

The Internet already provides a completely new medium for advertising and PR to communicate to targeted customer groups whose profile is identifiable from their access to Web sites. The creative use of corporate Web sites and the creation of links with search engines and with other relevant sites, are already an important part of achieving customer awareness and motivation. Such advertising mostly reaches exactly the customers who are already seeking the products being advertised – these are customers looking for suppliers to match their needs rather than the other way around. When the development of broadband interactive television releases customers from their PCs it will further improve the effectiveness of the Internet's impact as media. It will also set free at least parts of advertising from the now traditional commercial slots that break up commercial television programmes. (See Chapter 15.)

Printed or collateral material

The commercial developments of Web sites in little over three years made the Internet an excellent and relatively low-cost medium for creating customer awareness using multimedia methods that can be supported through the delivery of printed information directed only to prospective buyers who have already shown an interest. At the same time it can replace at least parts of expensive brochures by providing the same, or better, information online with 'download' facilities and the ability to feature the availability of sales promotion offers. As Chapter 17 explains, the cost and wastage of traditional printed brochures has been endemic for decades in travel and tourism and annual print costs for some tour operators in the late 1990s were much greater than their annual net profit.

Sales promotion and pricing

Because of its ability to communicate information right up to the very last minute before service delivery, the Internet is an ideal medium for communicating prices, special offers and late availability of product. Through connectivity between databases and yield management programmes – themselves part of the ICT developments – sales promotions can now be customized to individuals at minimal cost. This is an excellent illustration of the way that computer linkages can simultaneously cut costs, reinvent and improve the efficiency of traditional marketing techniques, and generate profit. (See Chapter 16.)

Distribution and access

As a new pipeline or channel for direct marketing communications between a business and its customers, the Internet is also reinventing distribution as explained in Chapter 18. It provides prospective buyers with access in their own homes to maximize convenience, or wherever they are during the day and night using the latest WAP telephones. Once the investment is made in computer databases and their connectivity with e-commerce facilities, the cost per enquiry and booking can be a small fraction of the costs using traditional distribution intermediaries such as travel agents. An *Economist* survey of airline distribution costs in 1999 estimated:

- $1 e-commerce cost for transacting an airline ticket (average across the USA).
- $8 commission cost for a retail travel agent (for the same average price).

Cost-saving ratios of this magnitude, multiplied by millions of sales, speak for themselves. For some businesses such as budget airlines the attraction of achieving more than two-thirds of sales by Internet are already within grasp.

Given connectivity within the modern spectrum of ICT, however, the Internet is much more than just another distribution channel that delivers business at lower cost per unit sold. It is also a primary channel for interactive targeted marketing and promotional techniques. It is revolutionizing the speed and effectiveness of product innovation and design through the ability to put together the components of the tourism product in apparently bespoke ways to meet customers' interests and wants. By providing a constant stream of marketing data, especially for occupancy projections and consumer response to pricing and sales promotion activity, the Internet drives yield-management programmes and creative revenue generation wherever gaps are identified. Finally, when used in parallel with customer databases and knowledge of repeat customers, modern distribution systems are changing and deepening the knowledge that marketing managers have of their key customer groups.

Customer-relationship marketing (CRM)

Knowing that repeat customers are important is hardly a new marketing insight. It has been understood for centuries. What is new is the ability to recognize repeat buyers instantly and address them individually by name when organizations are dealing with tens of thousands or millions of customers a year. This ability provides the drive behind relationship marketing. Although the cost of gaining a new customer is falling through use of the Internet, global players with large market shares cannot sustain profit unless their repeat levels of business are running at levels of 50 per cent or more for key segments. There are other reasons, too, why a service business wishes to identify, recognize, deal differently and generally form 'relationships' with its repeat buyers or loyal customers. Relationship marketing has been one of the buzzwords of the last decade and it is primarily driven by knowledge gained and communicated by connected customer databases. Apart from the ability to target individuals, databases have a powerful market research value in generating detailed knowledge of repeat buyers and cutting out the cost of undertaking traditional usage and attitude studies among buyers. (See Chapter 11.)

ICT and small businesses in travel and tourism

Chapter 3 explains that one of the defining characteristics of the travel and tourism industry is the marketing paradox implicit in the growth of power and influence of global players in the industry and the parallel growth in the tens of thousands of small businesses that provide so much of the character and 'specialness' of place to be found at destinations. For at least three decades until the mid–1990s, most small businesses were unable to take advantage of the developments in ICT that were increasingly available to the dominant large international players. The investment was too great.

But the position is changing at the start of the twenty-first century. A combination of the opening up of the Internet to search engines and the growth of product/segment specific portals, the remarkably low cost of providing small business Web sites and the growing willingness of customers to surf the Internet for options is helping even the smallest of businesses to go global. The Internet empowers the leading edge of micro-businesses to make the most of their individuality and enterprise. It offers them access to markets and to a supply of lowest cost business necessities that was previously unthinkable. In the last quarter of a century and still in 2000 governments and national tourist boards have paid lip-service to micro-businesses but, in many ways, simply ignored them other than by imposition of regulatory burdens. The developments of ICT and the key role that small businesses can play in environmental terms seems likely to alter that attitude over the coming decade. Information and communications technology will also help SMEs to achieve a collective voice and help them move themselves up the political agenda.

Chapter summary

Given the way in which ICT is now integrated and woven through almost every aspect of marketing, some repetition of the key facts is unavoidable in the chapters dealing with the main techniques. The purpose of this chapter is to create an overview within which the more specific applications in later chapters can be understood.

The 'connectivity' and development of the Internet, access to mobile telephones and to interactive television are the three principal technological developments that are empowering customers and businesses alike to change the way that they conduct the *exchange transactions* that are the core of all marketing (see Chapter 2). It is perhaps the remarkable speed of developments that is providing the greatest challenge. Larger companies especially cannot afford to wait and hope to learn from others' mistakes. Information and communications technology progress distances the leaders from the followers and is a learning process. The failure of a business to act in the short term may mean that it will not have a long term in which to get it right.

From its first edition in 1988, *Marketing in Travel and Tourism* has stressed the significance of a growing role for direct marketing in the industry and the anticipated developments in ICT that would facilitate it. Twelve years on, providing easy and user-friendly customer access for direct marketing is still a major challenge for marketing management and if the costs of investment to make it possible are massive for big businesses, so is the potential for cost saving and achieving a competitive edge.

By the time this book has been available for two or three years, the probable development of the Internet from its current state will be clearer. At mid–2000, e-commerce probably generates no more than 2 to 3 per cent of total international tourism turnover, but for individual businesses, of course, the figures are much higher. 20 to 30 per cent looks achievable for many within five years.

At mid–2000 between a third and half of the populations of many developed countries (probably 80 per cent of international travellers) already have Internet access in their homes and on mobile phones, even before the expected development of broadband online digital television. All schoolchildren in developed countries are now Internet literate and well over half of employees use computers in their work. These are the key facts that provide the driving force for current forecasts and massive investment in the Internet as a primary medium for promotion and distribution.

For a subject that changes as fast as ICT there cannot be a last word. Everyone in marketing is watching the developments outlined in this chapter and the larger players are investing heavily to gain competitive advantage. The process undoubtedly contains as many threats as opportunities and there will be many losers in this struggle.

Further reading

Apart from the Internet itself, newspapers and journals are the best sources for maintaining a grip on changes. Much of the material in this section is derived from articles in the *Economist*, *Financial Times*, *The Times*,

Business Week and through the travel trade press. Two recent reports that cover international developments are significant:

Financial Times (1998). *Distribution Technology in the Travel Industry,* FT Retail and Consumer.

WTO Business Council (1999). *Marketing Tourism Destinations Online: Strategies for the Information Age.* WTO. Although the title focuses on destinations, this report contains much material on the development of the Internet more widely in the tourism industry.

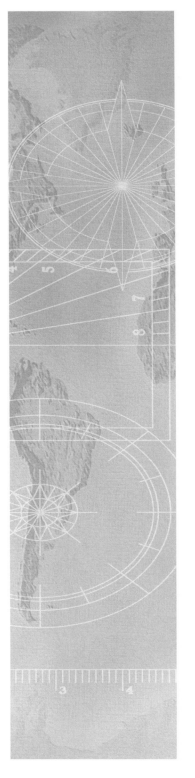

CHAPTER 11

Marketing research: the information base for effective marketing

Imagination, judgement and courage remain important qualities for the successful decision maker. Research is the handmaiden of competent management but never its substitute. (Luck et al., 1970: 8)

What marketing managers know of market trends, consumer segments, buyer behaviour, product performance and consumers' response to all aspects of marketing campaigns, is mostly derived from one or more aspects of marketing research activity. Other than for very small or micro-businesses the planning processes at both strategic and operational levels are research based, as discussed in Chapters 12 and 13. This chapter, therefore, focuses on techniques that are essential in successful marketing practice. The term *marketing research* is used in its broad sense of embracing consumer research and it includes all research-based information used in making marketing decisions, including database analysis and marketing information systems (MIS).

In using computers most readers will be aware of the maxim, 'garbage in, garbage out'. In other words, if the information or data fed into a computer is inaccurate or inadequate, one cannot hope for useful results. There is a marketing research parallel because the whole of marketing strategy and operations are also calculated responses using information input. The lower the quality (or absence) of information used for marketing decisions, the higher the risks of marketing failures, especially in strongly competitive markets.

Commencing with an initial definition, this chapter identifies the six main types of marketing research. It next describes ten kinds of marketing research activity, widely used in travel and tourism, that readers can expect to find in practice. The next section explains a typical 'menu' of marketing research choices available to operators, and illustrates it in a travel and tourism context. The final part of the chapter indicates how to use a market research agency and comments on test marketing and monitoring for travel and tourism products.

Marketing research defined

Marketing research is an organized information process, which 'has to do with the gathering, processing, analysis, storage and dissemination of information to facilitate and improve decision making' (Seibert, 1973: 128). Although dated, this succinct definition serves to stress that the basic role of marketing research has not changed, although the means of gathering, processing, etc., have changed enormously with modern ICT. The value of this definition is that it is sufficiently broad to encompass the whole range of systematic information inputs.

Most marketing decisions require answers as to 'who, what, when, where, how and why'. Marketing research data typically starts with regular analysis of customer databases and flows of 'intelligence' data gathered by a sales force, through trade publications or through cuttings taken from the travel trade press. It includes evaluation of Web site and call centre data; it proceeds with primary research ranging from focus groups to full-scale sample surveys on a local, national or international scale.

Most authors stress that marketing research cannot, as is sometimes supposed, provide solutions to management problems. Research can seldom ensure correct decisions. What it can do, as the quote at the head of the chapter notes, is reduce the amount of uncertainty and risk associated with the results of marketing decisions and focus attention on the probable implications of alternative courses of action.

From observation of the way that travel and tourism businesses are conducted in many countries around the world, it appears to be a distinctive feature of the industry that the use of marketing research is still generally less effective than in other major industries dealing with consumer products. Of course there are exceptions, although they are mainly the very large international corporations in air transport, tour operations, car rental and some hotel groups. The reason for this weakness appears to be rooted in the increasingly irrelevant assumption that research is not needed when producers and customers meet face to face on the producer's premises; and that through such contact, managers 'know' their customers without the need for expensive research. This may still be true for guesthouses, small attractions and neighbourhood travel agencies but it was never true for larger businesses, especially those with multi-site operations and management teams not directly involved in daily service delivery. The presence of customers on the premises is, however, a most important marketing asset to be exploited systematically by producers and this point is developed at the end of the chapter.

Using judgement or research?

In practice it is nearly always the case that managers have to take most decisions with less than adequate information. The cost of obtaining additional information has to be measured in time as well as money and is always related to the prospective gain or loss at risk in the decisions that are made. For example, faced with a decision between two alternative designs for a brochure cover, a marketing manager for a tour operating company has either to exercise judgement or commission research to evaluate target customers' responses to the two designs.

Where millions of brochures are to be printed, a 10 per cent better customer reaction to one of the designs could pay off in thousands of additional bookings. Research in this case would be justified if waiting for results did not delay production and distribution. For smaller operators the expense would rarely be justified by the potential extra business, and close attention to the print design brief (itself research based) would have to suffice, together with experience and judgement gained with other brochures.

By contrast, a strategic decision by a business such as a theme park to restructure its product by making major investment in new facilities would always justify marketing research studies at a cost related to the size of the investment. Such research would be needed to inform decisions about the scope and range of the new facilities, and the design of the new product in terms of identified market needs, behaviour patterns and visitors' capacity to pay. For example, if research indicated that visitors would spend only two hours at a new attraction and not four hours, the implications for car parking, prices, display and content, would be critical. In practice there is always a requirement to balance the need to know against the cost in time and money. But the reasons for using marketing research as well as the techniques available are the same in principle for travel and tourism as for any other form of consumer marketing.

Six main categories of marketing research and their uses

Table 11.1 is capable of almost endless extension and technical detail but an understanding of the six main categories of marketing research noted will be adequate for most marketing decision purposes. The six categories correspond exactly with the information needs required to make efficient decisions for marketing-mix programmes, and the strategic and operational plans within which they are implemented. The categories in Table 11.1 are common to any marketing organization dealing with consumers, although the uses noted are specific to travel and tourism.

Research category	Used in/for	Typical research content and methods
1 Market analysis and forecasting	Marketing planning	Measurement and projections of market volumes, shares and revenue by relevant categories of market segments and product types
2 Consumer research	Segmentation, branding and positioning Motivation research	(a) Quantitative measurement of consumer profiles, awareness, attitudes and purchasing behaviour including consumer audits (b) Qualitative assessments of consumer needs, perceptions and aspirations
3 Products and price studies	Product formulation, presentation, pricing and market assessment	Measurement and consumer testing of amended and new product formulation, and price sensitivity studies
4 Promotions and sales research	Efficiency of communications	Measurement of consumer reaction to alternative advertising concepts and media usage; response to forms of sales promotion, and sales-force effectiveness
5 Distribution research	Efficiency of distribution network/channels	Distributor awareness of products, stocking and display of brochures, and effectiveness of merchandising, including retail audits and occupancy studies Analysis of Web site usage and of call centres
6 Evaluation and performance monitoring studies	Overall control of marketing results and product quality control	Measurement of customer satisfaction overall and by product elements, including measurement through marketing tests and experiments and use of mystery shoppers

Table 11.1 Six main categories of marketing research and their uses

Ten kinds of marketing research commonly used in travel and tourism

Because marketing research has become a large and complex sector of economic activity in its own right, it has inevitably produced its own technical vocabulary. This chapter makes no attempt to cover the full range of technical terms but ten commonly used in practice to denote different research methods will be found helpful and are discussed below. They are:

- Continuous and ad hoc.
- Quantitative and qualitative.
- Primary and secondary.
- Omnibus and syndicated.
- Retail audit and consumer audit.

Continuous and ad hoc

Commercial organizations find it increasingly necessary to measure certain key trend data on a regular or 'continuous' basis. 'Continuous' in this context typically means daily, weekly or monthly, although the growing use of Internet distribution permits literally continuous data review. Data covering enquiries, sales, booking types and patterns, market shares, customer satisfaction and seat or hotel bed occupancy, are typical examples of 'continuous' marketing-research measures in travel and tourism. For reasons developed in Chapter 19, continuous information is increasingly incorporated into databases that provide a fertile source of information for marketing-mix decisions generally.

There are also many specific problems in marketing that require research relevant to a particular circumstance. For example, could a redesigned guidebook for a visitor attraction, with a print life of say three years, produce extra sales revenue? Would the introduction of a buffet-style instead of full-service breakfast reduce customer satisfaction or increase it? Does the market potential warrant investment in a new hotel and, if it does, what size of hotel and what level of service would be justified? To inform such management decisions a specific or ad hoc investigation would be needed.

Most marketing research programmes are a mixture of continuous research involving ongoing investment in the monitoring of trends, and ad hoc surveys when the cost of research is justified to illuminate specific problems or opportunities as they occur.

Quantitative and qualitative

Traditionally, most consumer research studies are based on questions identified in marketing decision making to be asked of random samples of existing or potential customers. For example, a coach tour operator may be aware from national surveys that some 60 per cent of adults take a holiday in a given year, of whom a third travelled abroad, stayed an average of ten nights away from home and spent £400 per person. The operator would need to find out what proportion used coaches and cars, how that proportion varied year by year and by month, the profile of coach clients, their preferred destinations and so on. With due allowance for statistical variation all these are quantifiable dimensions that can be projected into percentages and volume estimates for the coach tour market. Hence quantitative research, meaning studies to which numerical estimates can be attached. Quantitative research is always based on 'structured' questionnaires in which every respondent is asked the same questions. Mostly, because the range of possible answers is also printed on questionnaires drawing on previous experience, variations to suit individual respondents are not possible.

Quantitative methods are often used to give some basic indications of motivations. But generally, research companies cannot predict the ways in which people think about different products and such methods are unsuitable for exploring consumer attitudes, feelings, desires or perceptions. It is always possible to construct hypothetical answers and ask people to agree or disagree, but these may not get at what really matters to prospective buyers.

Qualitative studies commence from the standpoint that there are consumer (or staff) attitudes and motivations to be explored for which the answers cannot be predicted. How customers feel about Brand A compared with Brand B; what attributes and values are perceived as adhering to Brand A and not Brand B; what sort of people are thought most likely to buy Brand A rather than B, and so on. To understand and communicate positioning and branding values, qualitative research is usually essential for larger companies (see, for example, the case study on Travel Inn in Part Six).

Most qualitative studies commence with exploratory or open-ended research in which small samples of targeted individuals are asked to express their views. This may be done on a one-to-one basis or in a focus group where interaction between individuals is part of the research process. The interviewer or focus group leader is typically an experienced researcher, often with some training in social psychology. He is responsible for introducing the subjects for discussion and encouraging views but not imposing any preconceived ideas. What emerges, recorded for analysis on tape, is a discussion in consumers' own words concerning what matters to them. Summarizing an hour-long tape and producing two or three pages on the main attitudes emerging is much harder than it sounds and it involves considerable skills and experience.

By definition, individual and group sessions cannot be quantitative because the ideas are not tied down to structured questionnaires or based on adequate samples of the target group. They can be used to structure subsequent quantitative surveys, or they can be used in their own right to help marketing managers understand the ways in which existing and potential customers think, and what matters to them.

In recent years, given adequate continuous quantification of the main patterns of visitor behaviour and profiles using databases as explained above, qualitative research has been more widely used. It is expensive but relatively quick to implement and especially useful in designing advertising messages and brochure contents in ways best calculated to communicate with prospective customers in their own terms.

Primary and secondary

Primary data, covering both quantitative and qualitative data, is a label applied to marketing research that is specifically commissioned by a business to contribute to its decisions. It requires the gathering of data not available from any other (secondary) source. For example, a survey commissioned by one airline to study the current attitudes of business travellers towards its own and other airlines competing on the same route, would be primary data.

Secondary data is information gathered originally for a purpose not related to the needs of a particular business, but which may be used by it as part of its market information system. All published sources, including government statistics, trade association surveys and commercial publishers' market surveys, represent secondary data.

Common sense dictates that it will always be quicker and cheaper to obtain and use secondary rather than primary data. For any decision requiring research information, initial investigation should always begin at the secondary level before proceeding, if necessary, with primary research. The more efficient a marketing information system is, the less need there may be to commission (and wait for) expensive new data.

Omnibus and syndicated

Not only in travel and tourism, but also in consumer markets generally, there has been a growing tendency for market research companies to operate their own regular (continuous) sample surveys and sell space in them to a range of customers. Such surveys are known technically as 'omnibus' surveys because they are potentially open to all users. Where an organization seeks answers, say, to just four or five key questions, it may be possible to get access to a nationally representative sample of 2000 adults for a tenth of the cost of commissioning its own survey. For the price, a client would not only get answers to his specific questions but also fully cross-tabulated data, using profile characteristics, such as age and readership of media, which are a standard part of any 'omnibus' survey. The United Kingdom Tourism Survey (UKTS) is probably the best-known survey of UK tourism. Up to 2000 it was in fact a series of questions regularly asked on an MAI Research Ltd omnibus survey. There are many other omnibus surveys available, covering not only adults but many segments, such as motorists, doctors, business travellers, frequent users of hotels and so on.

Syndicated surveys serve much the same purpose as omnibus surveys but are usually commissioned by a group of clients on a cost-sharing basis. The regular survey of customer value for money and satisfaction, co-ordinated for its members by the Association of Leading Visitor Attractions (ALVA) in the UK since the late 1990s, is an interesting example. Members not only share costs and receive details for their own attraction; they also gain access to relevant comparisons with competitor sectors in the context of overall trends in the attractions market.

Both omnibus and syndicated studies provide cost-effective forms of research, especially for smaller businesses, for whom the costs of an ad hoc survey would usually be prohibitive. By using such studies, firms can also obtain technical assistance from research agencies with the wording of questions and interpretation of results. The omnibus method is especially suitable for achieving quantified results much faster than would be possible with ad hoc surveys.

Retail and consumer audits

In many sectors of consumer goods marketing other than travel, the most common forms of continuous marketing research are consumer and retail audits. It is no accident that two of the largest international marketing research companies, AGB Ltd and A. C. Nielsen, have built their multinational operations on such audits.

Initiated as long ago as the 1930s for manufacturers of products sold through grocery/chemist retail outlets, retail audits are based on visiting shops and physically checking and analysing product stocks, purchases from wholesalers and consumer sales in a sample of retail outlets selected to represent the national pattern. Such audits, carried out at regular monthly or two-monthly intervals in grocery and chemist outlets, can measure the volume of sales by product type, the average sales price, the volume of stocks and the proportion of outlets with stock on display. Of course, most such data are now audited by computers rather than physical checks. The results collected in the sample of audited outlets can be 'grossed up' to project the estimated sales in the total number (universe) of outlets from which the sample was selected.

In travel and tourism various agencies have audited holiday bookings and brochure display for tour operators, using samples of retail travel agencies. For hotels and other forms of accommodation, room and bed occupancy studies in samples of accommodation units perform the same 'audit' function for the accommodation sector, and have been used reliably for many years.

Consumer audits follow the same basic principles of regular reporting from nationally representative samples, based in this case on panels of consumers who keep specially designed diaries, in which all purchases are recorded. Since the profile of the samples is known in detail through the process of selection and recruitment, recorded purchases can be extensively analysed by segmentation data. The use of diary panels to record travel and tourism behaviour has been used in the Netherlands by the Central Bureau for Statistics since 1980 to measure holidays of four or more nights away from home, and it is satisfied with the reliability of the methodology for that purpose. In France, using a sample of 20 000 adults, national tourism trends for visits of one or more nights a year have also been monitored monthly by diary panel methods since 1990. The Target Group Index (TGI) Survey operated by the British Market Research Bureau is currently the best-known diary panel omnibus style survey operating in the UK. It covers a wide range of consumer purchases of which travel, tourism and recreational activities are only a small part.

A menu of marketing research methods

Drawing together the different categories of marketing research noted earlier and the research methodologies that are commonly used, it is possible to present the wide range of methods available to any business as a 'menu'. This 'menu' or tool kit is a listing of research techniques from which it is possible to make a selection according to need and circumstances. Each technique is available at a price. The menu, in a form relevant to businesses in travel and tourism services, is shown in Table 11.2. The menu concept is developed from papers originally presented on a UK Market Research Society training course. It is important to stress that the menu means prospective users can select items according to their needs and budget. Only large organizations with research staff and budgets in excess of say, £200 000 per annum, are likely to need or be able to use all the items over a period of twelve months.

A	**Desk research (secondary sources)**
1	Sales/bookings/reservations records; daily, weekly, etc. by type of customer, type of product, etc.
2	Visitor information records, e.g. guest registration cards, booking form data, call centre or Web site data.
3	Government publications/trade association data/national tourist office data/abstracts and libraries.
4	Commercial analyses available on subscription or purchase of reports.
5	Previous research studies conducted; internal data bank.
6	Press cuttings of competitor activities, market environment changes.
B	**Qualitative or exploratory research**
1	Organized marketing intelligence, such as staff feedback, sales-force reports, attendance at exhibitions and trade shows.
2	Focus group discussions and individual interviews with targeted customers/non-users – especially to identify the perceptions and attitudes of key users and non-user groups.
3	Observational studies of visitor behaviour, using cameras, electronic beams or trained observers.
4	Marketing experiments with monitored results.
C	**Quantitative research (syndicated)**
1	Omnibus questions to targeted respondents.
2	Syndicated surveys, including audits.
D	**Quantitative research (ad hoc and continuous)**
1	Studies of travel and tourism behaviour and usage/activity patterns.
2	Attitude, image, perception and awareness studies.
3	Advertising and other media response studies.
4	Customer satisfaction, value for money and product monitoring studies.
5	Distribution studies amongst the range of distribution channels being used or investigated for future use.

Table 11.2 The marketing research menu or tool kit

Using the 'menu': a holiday-park operator

To help explain the possible selective use of the menu in travel and tourism practice, consider a holiday-park business with eight parks comprising some 2000 caravans and chalets for let on a weekly or part-weekly basis. A turnover of around £10 million would be realistic for such an operator, with a marketing budget of, say, £750 000 of which, say, £50 000 is allocated for research (all in 1999 prices). Such a budget could be deployed as follows:

A1 A computerized database would show forward bookings for each park on a weekly basis, with analyses of areas from which bookings flow, post codes of bookers, type of caravan/chalet most or least in demand, size of party, repeat business, etc. Many of these data would be collected automatically through the process of keeping business accounts and setting up customer invoices. Profiles of customers accessing a Web site or using a call centre would be part of this process.

A2 On a continuous or a sample basis, customers checking in on arrival could be asked to complete a short form establishing, for example, how they heard of the park, whether the park brochure was seen, distance travelled from home and the number of repeat visits (if any).

A3 Published results of tourist board surveys would throw useful light on trends for the self-catering market nationally and by region. Occasional other inexpensive analyses of the market would be available from time to time (*A4*). Several journals for the holiday parks and caravan industry provide valuable insights into current events and trends in the market (*A6*).

A5 Previous years' records (as in *A1* and *A2*) would provide valuable benchmarks against which to view current patterns on a weekly or monthly basis.

B1 There are numerous trade shows and travel workshops available for the caravan/chalet park operator, as well as national conferences. All provide opportunities to gain market intelligence and to see what others in the industry are doing, especially in terms of park design, accommodation unit design, product presentation in brochures and so on.

Assuming that management time is excluded from the cost, and that business records are a by-product of essential accounting procedures, the cost of information collected up to this point would be measured in hundreds rather than thousands of pounds. To proceed beyond this point calls for more significant expenditure, to be set off against the expected value of results:

B2 Not affordable on an annual basis in this example, the decision to renew the main brochure could repay discussion of alternative covers, contents and formats conducted with small focus groups of prospective clients. Such group discussions would also generate ideas and concepts for advertising. With 2000 units to let, this operator might distribute 300 000 brochures per annum at a cost of say £200 000 (including distribution via retail travel agents), so that up to £20 000 on group discussions could be productive spread over a three-year brochure life span, assessed against sales revenue achievable.

B3   If, for example, the capacity of showers and laundry facilities were judged to be an issue at one or more of the parks, cameras or simple observation of queues and their reactions would be a cheap but effective form of research before any investment is made.

B4   In terms of pricing, different advertising formats, and product developments, e.g. mini-breaks, this holiday park operator is perfectly placed to engage in systematic test marketing and monitoring (see later in this chapter) at low cost.

C2   Park owners of this type may be able to purchase packs of printed, standardized, self-completion questionnaires, organized for them by their trade association and designed by a commercial market research agency. Owners would be responsible for distributing and ensuring completion by samples of visitors, and collecting questionnaires. The price per thousand of these standard questionnaire forms (similar in concept to those used by tour operators to measure customer satisfaction at the end of a holiday) would usually be less than 10 per cent of the cost of conducting surveys with trained interviewers on site. These forms may be designed for electronic scanning to reduce the costs still further.

D4   Of all the research options, D4 would be particularly important for this type of operator. Administered either as part of a syndicated (C2) survey or as a separate entity during, say, six selected weeks of the operating year, measuring satisfaction and value for money would probably account for the largest portion of annual marketing research expenditure in this example. Analysed by type of product, customer segments, time of year and in association with any test marketing initiatives, the value of this research in marketing planning would be considerable. Tracking and analysing the trends in customer reaction over time is essential data for strategic planning.

Commissioning a market research agency

While most marketing managers are expected to be competent in the analysis of marketing research data, relatively few will be also engaged in organizing and conducting surveys. Large organizations such as airlines, tourist boards and major hotel corporations have their own research departments. But most survey work will be commissioned from specialist market research agencies, of which there were over 500 in the UK in the late 1990s to choose from. It is therefore important that marketing managers should be aware of what agencies do and how to get the best response from them.

In the UK the Market Research Society (MRS) is the professional body for all individuals using survey techniques for market, social and economic research. With some 8000 members, the MRS claims to be the largest professional body of its kind in the world (MRS website, 2000) and it has developed and published detailed codes of professional conduct over many years. These codes are designed to protect and enhance the integrity with which research is practised, and to safeguard the interests of the general public and clients as well as the interests of agencies offering research services. Similar codes exist in several other European countries.

In research, as in most of marketing practice, the best way to achieve cost-effective work is to specify the problem with as much precision as possible, setting it in its wider marketing context. Unless a client and an agency have worked together on a regular basis, it is unlikely that agencies asked to quote for surveys will be experts on the client's business. Unless the budget is unusually large in travel and tourism terms, there will not be many hours available for the agency to absorb the key details of the clients' marketing programmes and analysis (expressed as 'diagnosis' and 'prognosis' in Chapter 13 on the use of research data in marketing planning). Time spent learning about the business will be time not available for developing the research approach.

'Problems' in marketing are seldom clear-cut. They are frequently matters of perception and judgement and two managers may well see the same problem in different ways. Time spent systematically analysing the problem, therefore, is seldom wasted. It focuses managers' minds and often changes the way the problem is perceived, or switches attention to a different problem area not at first sight apparent. Part of the process of thinking through the problem is a consideration of how survey results may be used. For example, if a survey of visitors to a visitor attraction is required to reveal ways to achieve higher spending in shops on site, the agency must be given details of current sales policies and trading results before they design their research methodology and the questions to be asked. The expected use of results also determines the nature of the questions to be asked, but surprisingly few research buyers recognize this basic truth when defining the 'problem'.

Problem specification, together with other information noted in Table 11.3, should always be put in writing and filed for future reference. At this stage, with a clearly expressed 'research brief', clients can approach agencies and invite them to tender for the work. Where an agency's work is well known to a client, competitive tendering may be unnecessary. Where it is not, it is usual practice to invite a maximum of three or four agencies to submit tenders, informing them that others have been approached. The commercial market research world is highly competitive and tendering is the usual route to new business.

Preparing tenders is a costly process for agencies; it may take several days' work for larger projects. Unless otherwise agreed the cost of research tenders is not charged but absorbed as a business overhead. In

The client brief

- Identifies the marketing context and perceived problem to be researched.
- Specifies the expected use of results.
- Indicates the time scale for completion.
- States the approximate budget limits.

The agency tender

- Defines or redefines the problem in research terms.
- Proposes a methodology relevant to the problem.
- Specifies a realistic programme for completion, including client liaison.
- Recommends a reporting format and procedure.
- Sets out the terms and conditions of business, including costs and timing of payments.
- Specifies personnel involved, their qualifications and experience, and their respective involvement in the proposed study.
- Indicates agency experience relevant to the problem, including reference to previous studies and other clients whose needs were broadly comparable

Table 11.3 Basic requirements of client and agency in commissioning marketing research

preparing a tender the agency would normally expect at least one meeting to clarify and interpret the way the problem is expressed in the client's brief. Through experience with similar problems, agencies may well be able to restate the problem or illuminate it in ways not obvious to the client. They may also have access to secondary data not known to clients, which can considerably reduce the costs of primary research.

Tenders should cover all the points noted in Table 11.3, and clients will often find broad similarity in the methods and costs proposed by competing agencies. Accordingly, selecting which agency to use will normally be based on the extent to which each one demonstrates comprehension of the problem, and the effectiveness and creativity of the proposed methods of tackling it within stipulated budget limits. A proven track record in travel and tourism research may be helpful but much more important is the quality of the rapport between client and agency. This will be evident from the first meeting and reflected in the tenders. It will always be wise for clients to meet the research executive directly responsible for their job as well as the agency director or senior researcher who is likely to produce and present the tender. If meetings are necessary, visiting the agency's premises will often reveal much more about the nature and quality of its operation than the usual glossy brochure with its predictable claims of all-round excellence and deep expertise.

Successful research depends on trust between client and agency akin to that which develops between advertising agency and client (though on a smaller scale). Reputable agencies will normally reveal names of previous clients and it is quite usual for prospective clients to talk in confidence to previous clients about their experiences with particular agencies.

Customer access: a priceless asset of service businesses

A massive potential research advantage inherent in marketing most service products in travel and tourism is the presence of customers on producers' premises. In the authors' view it is a grossly underestimated advantage.

Anyone who has owned, worked or been brought up in a small business, such as a hotel, travel agency, restaurant, pub or caravan park, will recognize the powerful immediacy of customer contact. They will know the ease with which it is possible to detect (or impossible to avoid) customer needs, behaviour and satisfactions or complaints. Such businesses hardly need market research surveys because, in a very real way, their customer knowledge and 'feedback' are better, more natural and more continuous than any researcher, self-completion questionnaire or database could ever provide.

However, once a business grows large enough to have multiple units, or is run by managers with limited customer contact, direct customer–management communication is lost. The board directors of an airline or large hotel company may not speak at all to customers for months or years and, if they do, may so intimidate them as to negate any research value of the contact. In these management circumstances systematic research is necessary but it can still take advantage of the inherent benefits of customer/product inseparability and the relative ease of communication 'on site' or 'in-house'.

By contrast, manufacturers of most consumer goods usually have either no contact at all with their customers, who purchase anonymously in retail outlets, or at best have access to names and addresses provided for warranty or servicing purposes. Knowledge of who is surfing their Web sites and using call centres is now assisting manufacturers to know more about their final consumers but in travel and tourism all making enquiries and booking services in advance immediately and automatically supply useful marketing information about themselves as part of the process. Visitors using commercial accommodation sign registers and/or enter details on a registration card. Airline customers spend many hours waiting in terminals and in planes for their journeys to start or to end. Visitors to attractions stroll around reception areas and car parks, travel agencies have many opportunities to seek out and record customers' needs and interests, and so on. At the start of the new century it is quite extraordinary, that with the exception of some large tour operators and a very small proportion of other large companies, these easy opportunities for research are for the most part still overlooked and certainly underutilized.

Similarly, all service producers with customers on the premises have a major opportunity to organize internal research both with customers and especially in gaining marketing intelligence feedback from staff with direct customer contact. Researching the knowledge as well as the attitudes of employees provides a valuable stream of marketing decision information that is also often overlooked.

Researching customer satisfaction and value for money

Large tour operators in Britain typically hand out self-completion customer satisfaction questionnaires to all travellers returning from holidays abroad, generally on the flight home. Such questionnaires request rating of all aspects of the holiday, using numeric scales such as 4 = excellent, 3 = good, 2 = fair and 1 = poor, which can also be communicated by words or cartoons. The responses can then be computer-processed to produce numerical ratings or scores. From this information, if plotted on a week-by-week basis, it is possible to detect comparative satisfaction with individual resorts and hotels, check the performance of specific flights, or evaluate customer appreciation of particular aspects of products such as food, excursions or the service provided by resort representatives (see also Chapter 24).

Because 'profile information' is included in the questionnaire, it is possible to analyse satisfaction and value for money by age of respondent, region of origin, postal codes, cost of package and so on. These questionnaires, mostly scanned and processed by computers, provide a vast range of continuous management information. Such information is both a control tool for service operations and a fertile database for marketing mix decisions, such as product formulation and pricing. Airlines use in-flight survey questionnaires in the same way for the same purposes. So do some hotel companies and major attractions. In the UK, Thomson Holidays first used customer satisfaction questionnaires in 1972, well ahead of their competitors. By the mid-1990s they had processed over 12 million forms, using the information systematically to retain their competitive edge as a market leader. Club Mediterranée was processing around 250 000 questionnaires of a similar type in the early 1990s and there is every reason to suppose their use will continue to grow.

Questionnaires to visitors are not welcome in all businesses, however, and the use of so-called *mystery shoppers* is an alternative technique whereby multi-site service providers can evaluate the quality of their delivery. The technique is widely used, especially in the accommodation and restaurant sectors of the tourism industry. Provided they are systematically organized, mystery buyers of meals, nights, users of call centres and front-of-house telephone systems, can provide vital insights in quality terms and expose both the weaknesses and the strengths of service delivery procedures. (See also Chapter 8.)

Opportunities for researching marketing innovations

Especially with multi-site operations, the opportunities for managers to innovate and test market service products are virtually limitless. A hotel corporation might, for example, vary menus and prices, vary the formality of food service, offer new facilities for business or leisure customers, change room furniture and decor or promote a particular type of inclusive weekend-break product. Provided always that the results are measured in enquiries and sales, and that satisfaction is monitored, there are many opportunities to carry out 'live' market research through conducting controlled marketing tests. Through a process crudely but accurately dubbed 'suck it and see', most service producers can test, learn and modify product developments on a limited scale before wider implementation in other sites or premises.

Tour operators can offer new destinations or new product types in the pages of an existing brochure. If the development is popular and sells well, it can often be extended quickly and modified as necessary by evidence gained from customer satisfaction questionnaires. This 'learning' opportunity to set up and read the results of marketing tests at low cost is usually not available to manufacturers of physical goods, especially where powerful retailers control distribution outlets and the shelf space allocated to producers. Test marketing of physical goods is generally a far more costly and time-consuming process than test marketing of services.

If they approach the issue systematically, most businesses in travel and tourism can create opportunities to experiment and monitor. Above all they can build up their marketing knowledge of buyer behaviour by obtaining relatively inexpensive feedback from the customers using their premises. These are powerful opportunities for cost-effective marketing research, which other industries must envy. The recent consumer access to the Internet and corporate Web sites provides a whole new medium for innovation. It makes the process even easier and cheaper to organize, and provides almost instant and continuous feedback from customers.

Chapter summary

This chapter identifies the role of marketing research and its value as the essential information base for making effective marketing decisions. It explains the six main types of marketing research that practitioners in travel and tourism are most likely to encounter and describes ten of the commonly used technical terms applied to research methods. In particular, it draws a distinction between continuous and ad hoc research, 'continuous' implying the creation and use of databases organized as marketing information systems for marketing decision purposes, a very important development explained further in Chapter 19.

A market research menu is offered in Table 11.2, which may serve with Table 11.3 as a useful checklist for those who have to commission research to fulfil particular purposes. In practice each method has strengths and weaknesses that vary according to the company undertaking the research and the particular decisions they have to make. The combined use of several methods is normal, as noted in the holiday-park example.

The remarkable scope in practice that all tourism businesses have for experimentation in the marketing mix is stressed. Combined with detailed monitoring of results, market testing is a particular form of low cost research that is relevant in a strategic as well as a tactical context. Innovation through market testing exploits the advantages of having customers on business premises or sites and it is greatly facilitated by recent ICT developments, especially the Internet. Innovation is now even easier 'off site' by making virtual offers possible in a primary distribution channel that incorporates immediate evaluation of customer response.

The chapter stresses that marketing research is used to throw light on marketing decisions and reduce the level of risk and uncertainty associated with them. But it does not replace the essential quality of judgement from managers. (See also Chapters 12, 13 and 14.)

In the UK, the Millennium Dome was the subject of constant political and media attention in 2000. Developed at great speed that forced the cutting of many management decision corners, the Dome was nevertheless the subject of detailed market research in the two years prior to its opening. A target of 12 million visits was predicted and in late 2000 it appeared that less than 5 million paying visits would be achieved. Subsidy costs incurred for every visit made exceeded £100. Yet research was 'undertaken by the world's leading experts', including 'monthly independent research from 1998 until mid 2000 [showing] that the number of people saying they intended to visit the Dome would result in over 10 million visits' (Former Operations Director for the Dome, *The Times*, 27 September 2000). The Dome experience is a salutary reminder that market research cannot provide all the answers.

Further reading

Baker, M. J. (1996). *Marketing: An Introductory Text*. Chapter 10, 6th edn, Macmillan.

Brassington, F. and Pettit, S. (2000). *Principles of Marketing*. Chapter 6, 2nd edn, Prentice-Hall.

Crouch, S. and Housden, M. (1996). *Marketing Research for Managers*. 2nd edn, Butterworth-Heinemann.

Jobber, D. (1998). *Principles and Practice of Marketing*. Chapter 6, 2nd edn, McGraw-Hill.

Kotler, P. and Armstrong, G. (1999). *Principles of Marketing*. Chapter 4, 8th edn, Prentice-Hall.

Wright, L. T. and Crimp, M. (2000). *The Marketing Research Process*. 5th edn, Financial Times/Prentice-Hall.

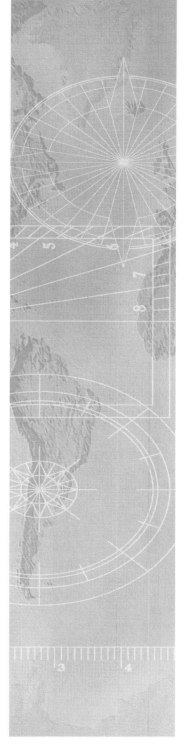

CHAPTER 12

Planning marketing strategy

The future is now. The short term and the long term don't abut one another with a clear line of demarcation five years from now. The short term and the long term are tightly intertwined. (Hamel and Prahalad, 1996: 30)

This chapter and the next focus on the management processes by which organizations decide and communicate the goals and objectives they seek to pursue in the long and short term. The key word here is 'decision' because, at any given time, organizations are faced with a wide range of choices, the implications of which can never be fully clear. Ultimately the strategic objectives that an organization sets for itself and pursues are the most important decisions it makes because these determine survival, prosperity and all subsequent operational decisions.

It is necessary to deal with objectives at two levels. The first level is a strategic level covering the whole of a business over the long term; the second is a tactical level covering specific markets and products in the short term. In practice, as described in this chapter and implicit in the quote above, long- and short-term decisions intermingle but students of marketing must learn to recognize the differences.

By definition, customer orientation in a marketing-led organization will always be a focal concern for senior management and part of the corporate culture. Marketing strategy is a dominant element in corporate strategy because of its focus on balancing delivery of customer satisfaction and value with sales-revenue generation. Marketing is also a vital contribution to corporate vision for the future through its role in interpreting customers needs and market trends in the business environment external to the firm. But marketing decisions will be only one of the core business functions to be developed in an overall corporate strategy.

This chapter deals with marketing at the strategic level, while Chapter 13 develops a step-by-step approach to tactical planning for effective marketing campaigns. As Hussey put it, 'the planning of marketing is really a divided activity. One portion falls squarely under the heading of strategic planning . . . a second portion can easily be seen as the task of the operating manager in planning and developing existing markets' (Hussey, 1979: 159).

The need for strategic planning

To provide vision for the future, leadership and an agreed framework for the conduct of business in an ever more rapidly changing and globally competitive market environment, all organizations are obliged to plan their activities. The larger the business and the more products and markets with which it has to deal, the deeper its commitment to understanding the nature of future change and competition, and the greater the importance of effective planning processes. The more volatile a market is in terms of monthly and annual fluctuations in customer demand, the more important it is to work within a framework of agreed objectives.

At the same time, strategy has a credibility crisis. 'In many companies the very notion of strategy has become devalued . . . what is being rejected is strategy as pedantic planning ritual . . . Strategy as foresight, architecture and intent, and industry redefinition to create new competitive space, is the greatest value added that senior management can contribute' (Hamel and Prahalad, 1994: 308).

In travel and tourism, years of market growth have often tended to obscure and lessen the perceived need for planning, although discontinuities in market trends, unpredicted economic recessions and sudden market decline bring planning issues sharply into focus. The current issues surrounding globalization, mergers, strategic alliances and investment in new developments – or response to business failures – also heighten the focus on strategic decision processes.

In essence, any strategy comprises a statement of goals and objectives, a framework of resources needed and programme of activity intended to achieve the goals. For larger businesses the statement of goals involves market research and analysis and the programmes of activity have to be costed and monitored to work out how well the objectives are actually achieved. All planning is conducted on the assumption that the effort in time and money is essential to produce profitable results and increasing recognition that future growth must be planned and prepared for now and implemented over several years. Strategic thinking is also an essential part of the process by which organizations satisfy their investors and other stakeholders about the directions they seek to pursue.

Managers will recognize how these simple truths tend to disappear in the complexities of planning analysis and techniques, but students should hold on to this simple definition in understanding this chapter.

The twenty-first century context for strategic planning

The subject of corporate marketing strategy and its role in achieving a competitive edge has assumed greater significance in recent years for four important reasons. None of them are particular to travel and tourism but all are relevant to the industry.

The first is the now familiar context of global uncertainty and continuous change that followed from the major international economic crises of 1973, 1979 and 1991–2 and the associated political and environmental upheaval. Over the last two decades the fallout from these events undermined the value of all previous business models based on relative market and industry stability. It rendered pointless many of the long-range econometric forecasting models that developed with computer modelling techniques in the 1980s.

The second reason driving strategic thinking is the remarkable development of ICT in the 1990s that is provoking a revolution in many established corporate practices. 'We are standing on the verge, and for some it will be the precipice, of a revolution as profound as that which gave birth to modern industry' (Hamel and Prahalad, 1994: 29). Among other contributions, ICT has facilitated the globalization of trade through the instant exchange of information so that changes in prices, product offers and international currency rates are now subject to continuous twenty-four hour changes and exposure to customers, competitors and all stakeholders, creating a volatility that changes the whole nature of forecasting.

The third, also driven by the information revolution, is the ability of companies to step across traditional industry boundaries with supermarkets becoming banks, tour operator companies entering the cruise shipping market and dot.com companies entering the field of travel distribution.

The fourth is the continuing growth and expansion in travel and tourism of a small number of large, transnational and global organizations locked in fierce competition for market share and sales revenue. Because of their size and leadership in their markets, their strategies have an important ripple effect in world markets to which smaller operators must make their own strategic responses.

These four reasons are especially powerful in 'information rich', price-sensitive international travel and tourism markets. Without strategies to guide their responses to inevitable changes in the external business environment, organizations can lose sight of their future development goals in the time-consuming and urgent tactical decisions called for in the day-to-day management of demand that all service industries require.

Marketing strategy has to be flexible to cope with change. Old concepts of 'top-down' centralized head office planning departments for large organizations do not work in modern market conditions and new models of delegated planning for separate sectors of a business (known as strategic business units or areas – SBUs or SBAs) have emerged. These new approaches heighten the need for corporate vision, leadership, co-ordination and support, at the same time restricting the direct operational involvement of corporate headquarter staff.

Strategic planning principles

Stripped of its mystery and techniques, all forms of strategic corporate planning attempt to answer four outward looking questions:

- Where are we now in the industry and market spaces we occupy?
- What opportunities are emerging in a changing world, which we could develop and aim to lead?
- Where do we want our organization to be in five or more years' time?
- What decisions do we have to make now to get to where we want to be?

The four questions lead naturally to the idea of a *position*, meaning the 'place' that an organization occupies in an industry sector compared with its competitors and in the minds or perceptions of customers and prospective customers (see later in this chapter). The questions also help to explain three concepts in corporate planning (adapted from Davidson, 1975: 109):

- Vision, goals and objectives (chosen destinations).
- Strategies (chosen routes for achieving goals).
- Plans (action programmes for moving along the route and evaluating achievement against targets).

In these simple terms, although the formality of the process is obviously very different, the strategic planning questions are as relevant to small businesses as to large ones. For marketing purposes, strategic planning may be defined as the process whereby an organization analyses its strengths and weaknesses in its current and prospective markets, identifies its aims and the opportunities it seeks to develop, and defines strategies and costed programmes of activity to achieve its aims.

Strategic decisions are always focused on the longer run, usually defined as three or more years ahead and looking wider than the existing range of products provided for a current group of segments. For larger, global corporations a time vision of up to twenty years may be needed to achieve strategic goals that involve major investment decisions and the development of technology as an essential preliminary to market growth.

A hierarchy of objectives – strategic and tactical

Figure 12.1 shows the two main levels of business objectives and serves also to put marketing strategy into the wider context of future planning for an organization. Corporate strategy defines a vision for an organization as a whole and its place in an industry and markets. It also sets objectives for all the business functions that are needed to get it from where it is at the present time to the position it seeks to occupy at some future date.

For overall corporate objectives, influenced by the external business environment, Figure 12.1 notes seven common elements that are systematically assessed and integrated in most corporate strategies. Although marketing is always a key consideration, it is only one of the seven. It is shown in the centre of the figure with a separate input below it to demonstrate the linkages with tactical or operational marketing planning shown as level 2.

A brief description of the non-marketing elements is provided below with airline illustrations to set a context for the marketing strategy issues, which follow. Other than as context, however, the other elements are not the subject of this chapter and are not referred to further.

While hierarchies of objectives may not appear relevant to small proprietor-run businesses, the thought process and principles discussed in this chapter are fully appropriate to any size of operation. It is often the failure to think strategically, and evaluate and respond proactively to

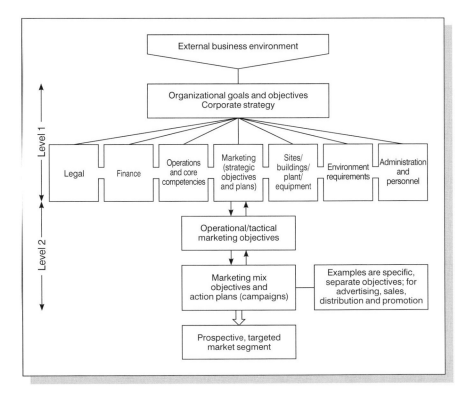

Figure 12.1
Elements involved in a corporate business strategy: the hierarchy of objectives

long-term trends and opportunities, which causes so many smaller businesses to founder.

Corporate strategy in an airline context

In the context of a scheduled airline with an international network of routes, the decisions to be brought together in a strategy can be explained briefly as a series of questions:

- *Legal.* What agreements between countries are required to maintain and develop services on agreed route networks? How far and how fast might deregulation proceed? What are the legal implications of possible alliances, mergers and acquisitions? What action is needed to comply with existing and new legal requirements?
- *Finance.* What asset and loan structure is needed by the airline? What returns on capital are required to service the investment, meet the stakeholders' interests and fund new investment in aircraft, information communications technology and facilities?
- *Operations.* What number, type and size of aircraft are required to perform agreed services, on which routes at what times? How to optimize the scheduling of the fleet? What are the future requirements for the services network looking ten years ahead?
- *Sites, buildings, plant and equipment.* What ground facilities are required at airports and operational bases? What servicing (engineering) facilities are needed for aircraft, etc?
- *Environment.* What changes to aircraft and other operational developments are needed to meet regulations concerning noise, emissions, waste control, night flights and energy consumption? What are the implications for conducting environmental audits and carrying out impact assessments for major new projects? How will future operations be affected by new environmental policies?
- *Administration and human resources (HR).* What core competencies and facilities for management, buildings, equipment and general organization are needed to service the airlines' current operations and assist it to develop in targeted new areas to achieve planned goals and objectives? What competencies, numbers, remuneration levels, qualifications, organization, training and career structure are required for employees, to provide and sustain effective quality assured service delivery across the network?

Marketing strategy

Marketing strategy identifies and is primarily responsible for future sales revenue generation by specifying the segments, products and associated action programmes required to achieve sales and market share against competitors – and deliver customer satisfaction.

Each of the other elements in the corporate strategy requires expenditure out of projected revenue. However vital these elements are to the conduct of the business, they are ultimately conditioned by the organization's ability to persuade sufficient existing and new customers to buy enough of its products to secure a surplus of revenue over costs in the long run. While it is obviously incorrect to conclude that business strategy is only about marketing, it is not difficult to establish that all strategy for commercial organizations has its bottom line in customer satisfaction and sales revenue, and that marketing managers are employed to achieve revenue targets through their specialist knowledge of market needs and circumstances.

To illustrate the point, the decision by an airline to buy new aircraft, such as the new double-deck 550-seater airbus A3XX (a current issue in 2000), rather than additional 'stretched Boeing 747 400s', has strategic implications for each of the seven elements, noted in Figure 12.1. But unless marketing managers can commit to achieving daily seat-occupancy levels (load factors), at average prices (yield) that will exceed average costs, the decision to buy cannot be taken. In practice there is always an element of risk in the decision to buy equipment because the speed and location factors of global market growth cannot be predicted with precision. But the principal risk lies in evaluating and projecting future global customer demand and having the corporate marketing will and competence to envision and then secure the demand against aggressive competition.

The marketing strategy planning process

The key components of marketing strategy are:

- *Goals and objectives*. The position or place in its chosen markets that an organization seeks to occupy in a future period, usually defined broadly in terms of sectors of business, target segments, volume of sales, product range, market shares and profitability. Marketing strategy reflects and at the same time informs corporate vision and leadership. It is related to the external business environment, its view of customer needs and competitors' actions. It is also concerned with the overall values that a business seeks to develop and communicate to customers and stakeholders.
- *Images, positioning and branding*. Where the organization seeks to be in terms of customers' and retailers' perceptions of its products and values. Includes choice of corporate image and branding in relation to competitors.
- *Strategies and programmes*. Broadly what actions, including product development and investment, are required to achieve the goals and objectives?
- *Budget*. What resources, staff and money, are needed to achieve the goals?
- *Review and evaluation*. Systematic appraisal of achievement of goals in the context of competitors' actions and the external environment.

Larger organizations with multiple products in multiple markets, such as hotel chains or international car rental companies, also require strategic planning to achieve effective relationships and allocation of resources between the component parts of their businesses. Strategy in this context is discussed later (see portfolio analysis).

Strategy is essentially proactive in the sense that it defines and wills the future shape of the organization as well as responding to changing industry patterns, technology, market conditions and perceived consumer needs.

The tactical marketing planning process

Tactical decisions are always focused on the short run in which specific marketing campaigns are planned, implemented and evaluated. Short run may be a year, eighteen months, or only weeks. Tactics are responsive to market circumstances and particularly responsive to competitors' actions.

Tactical plans establish the operational details of marketing activity and the key components are:

- *Objectives and targets*. Specified, quantified, volume and sales revenue targets and other specific marketing objectives to be achieved.
- *Mix and budget*. Marketing mix and marketing budget decisions
- *Action programmes*. The implementation of marketing programmes and co-ordination of promotional activity to achieve targets.
- *Monitoring and control*. Monitoring the results of marketing on a regular or continuous basis and applying control systems related to the agreed targets.

The interplay or dialogue between strategy and tactics

Traditionally in all large hierarchical organizations, goals would be drafted by planning departments, debated and set by a board of directors and handed down to managers that were expected to achieve them. But it is increasingly recognized that achievable corporate goals cannot be set without participation by those who have to implement them, especially in service businesses which are so dependent on the knowledge of line management and customer facing staff and the quality of services they are motivated to deliver.

It is increasingly the business of managers, therefore, to work out practical trade-offs through a dialogue between board level aspiration and the operational knowledge and industry expertise of those directly responsible for service delivery. Also known as a 'goals down/plans up process' these trade-offs have both strategic and tactical implications. Resolving the differences between desired, especially long-term goals and achievable, especially short-term, objectives and targets, is a now a key role for management and staff in any large organization. This process brings together and modifies both strategic and operational decision processes and harnesses all the competencies in the organizations around achievable goals. Since strategic goals are also intended to motivate managers and always relate to desired future states, it is normal for there to be some tension and dispute between short-term and long-term planning requirements.

Three key concepts in competitive marketing strategy formulation

Within the limits of this book it is only possible to draw attention to some of the main issues. The sources noted at the end of the chapter must be pursed to achieve further understanding. Students of tourism marketing should, however, be able to distinguish clearly between strategy and tactics. Three strategic concepts in particular, drawn from the extensive literature on business management, will assist in making the important distinctions. These are:

- SBUs and business portfolio analysis.
- Product-market growth models.
- Corporate and product positioning.

SBUs and business portfolio analysis

A very large business, UK-based Whitbread Corporate, had its roots for some 250 years in brewing and supplying a national chain of pubs. The company has diversified enormously in the 1990s and states 'underlying our whole strategy is the simple fact that leisure is playing an ever more important part in people's lives and they're spending a growing part of their incomes in making the most of it. Our job is to match and preferably exceed their expectations and grow our business as a result' (Whitbread Web site). Diversification, which recently included the sale of most of the company's brewing interests, was not because brewing was unprofitable but because greater profit and faster growth was perceived to lie in leisure, broadly defined.

In 2000 the group was providing services to around 10 million customers a week in a combination of some 6000 restaurants, clubs, pubs and hotels. In terms of national brands and major customer databases it included (main brands only) those shown in Table 12.1.

In addition the Whitbread group also included a pizza chain, Café Rouge and other food outlets in 2000.

In terms of the industry sector/market spaces they occupy and the specific products and market segments they serve, these are essentially

Table 12.1
Whitbread main brand databases

Brand	Database (rounded figures)
Brewers Fayre	2 100 000
Beefeater	1 050 000
Marriott Hotels	1 350 000
Travel Inn	350 000
David Lloyd leisure (health and fitness clubs)	275 000

quite separate businesses, each marketed under its own distinctive brand. But they share in common the strength of the corporate entity and its value in delivering strategic alliances, the economies and advantages of bulk purchasing and access to investment finance. All the food buying for the pubs and restaurants is managed in a centralized unit to maximize economies of scale. The same approach is adopted for building contracts, transports, utilities and a corporate marketing division. Whitbread has thus transformed itself in a relatively few years from being a traditional brewer with pub outlets, to an international holding company with a portfolio of businesses or SBUs, each with its own management structure, profit and loss accounts and plans for the future.

The strategic planning process for a large international company requires continuous analysis of its current portfolio of SBUs and a much more difficult set of higher risk decisions on what changes are needed to secure future growth and profit in the light of international market conditions. The latter process is more a visionary than a traditional planning process. For larger companies it involves investment and cultivation of what Hamal and Prahalad (1996: 84) term 'foresight and intellectual leadership', sustained over the long term. 'The end product of the strategic planning process is a *future* best-yield portfolio . . . taking into account risk and short-term versus long-term trade offs' (Boyd and Larreche, 1982: 9).

The strategic shift of Preussag from heavy industry into global tour operating, acquiring TUI, Thomson Holidays and Thomas Cook (although much of the latter must be sold under EU competition rules), reflects a similar approach from an international company based in Germany. The sale of Bass brewers by the Bass Group and that group's diversification into hospitality and leisure by the UK-based company that owns the global Holiday Inn brands is another example of the same strategic realignment process.

Within any portfolio of SBUs, some will be in growing and some in declining markets. Some are more profitable than others. Portfolios are therefore continuously evaluated according to key variables of:

- Shares of current markets held by own and competing companies and trend patterns.
- Perceived market size, growth prospects and product life cycles – including assessment of emerging and predicted markets.
- Cash-flow generation.
- Return on investment compared with other major competitors.
- Strength of competition and probability of others entering markets under consideration.
- Knowledge and core competencies developed within a corporate entity that might be utilized in additional directions.

In any established successful large business it will usually be obvious from analysis that some SBUs in the corporate portfolio have a relatively large share of expanding markets with good profitability. Such products, typically developed as a result of foresight some years earlier, are obvious candidates for strategic support if the general projections remain favourable. Other products, perhaps because the market sector is declining, and not because the product is inadequate, will be in decline and generating little profit, especially if prices are being reduced to maintain volume and market share in the face of aggressive competition.

Corporate portfolios will typically also comprise some relatively new product-market groupings or SBUs with good shares of growth markets ('stars') and some profitable products with well-established shares of mature markets ('cash cows'). In practice portfolios will frequently also contain products with low shares of declining markets and poor profitability ('dogs'), which are candidates for liquidation. The labels (in brackets) are those created by the Boston Consulting Group in the USA, which developed one of the best-known techniques for portfolio analysis.

A portfolio sustainable over the long run will also comprise some longer-term development products for new sectors of the industry or for markets not currently served. Investment in these growth opportunities, including acquisitions, mergers and strategic alliances, are an essential aspect of long-term competition and some of today's development products will become tomorrow's 'stars'. The size and potential overlap of the leisure sector customer databases developed by Whitbread provides a relatively new source of corporate knowledge and a fertile base for cross selling and relationship marketing.

Strategies for product-market growth and development

As noted earlier, the start of the twenty-first century is a time of unprecedented turmoil and change in all industries – not least travel and tourism. No organization can rest on past progress and expect to maintain

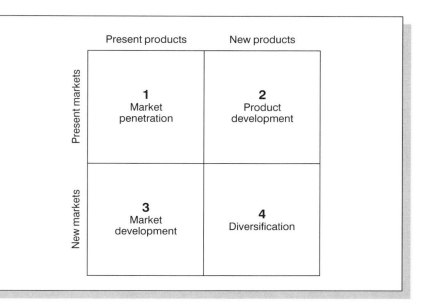

Figure 12.2
Product-market
growth strategies
(four basic options)
Source: Ansoff
(1987: 109).

the structure of existing product-market portfolios and profitability levels, even over a period as short as two years. Profitable product-market portfolios are certain to be targeted by aggressive competitors and businesses also have to respond to other pressures, such as unfavourable exchange-rate movements, changes in regulatory requirement and new technology options.

For competitive businesses the process of reviewing their portfolios is continuous. The options for growth can be neatly summarized in an elegant, four-box model, originally devised by Ansoff and much copied and developed since (see Figure 12.2). Each of the strategies summarized in the four boxes has radically different implications for marketing.

The four numbered boxes in the model may be illustrated with typical travel and tourism examples as follows:

1 The case where a hotel group, already servicing the corporate (business) market as its principal market segments, decides that it is well positioned to expand in this market through aggressive marketing campaigns. With its existing portfolio of products, any expansion above natural market growth would represent an increase in market share, which is also known as increased 'penetration'. This is a relatively low-risk strategy.

2 The case where a European tour operator, already operating a portfolio of inclusive tours to European destinations, decides to expand its operations by developing long-haul tours to destinations in Asia, targeting its existing market segments. This decision represents an addition to the product portfolio and is known as product development (new products for present markets). Its knowledge of and competencies with existing segments will be a valuable platform for expansion.

3 The case where what was originally a Dutch company based in the Netherlands with a largely continental European clientele, first marketed its existing continental villages to the UK market (market development). In the late 1980s Center Parcs was purchased by British owners and developed its holiday village concept in three locations in England. This was an existing (albeit modified) product concept targeted at new markets and it therefore represented market development.

4 Finally, when an airline company (Virgin Atlantic) decided to buy and brand a UK railway operating company (Virgin Rail) through acquisition, it stepped outside its existing product-market portfolio and effectively diversified its business activities with a completely new set of SBUs in a new market sector. In this case, Virgin brought its core passenger-handling competencies to bear on a different form of transport, but this was a relatively high-risk form of diversification.

Each of these choices is a strategic decision usually undertaken on the basis of a detailed analysis of potential revenues and advantages as well as potential costs and disadvantages. They also reflect the strategic vision a company has of the direction in which it wishes to proceed for future profitability.

Corporate and product positioning

Portfolio analysis and assessment of alternative product-market growth strategies focus on securing long-term profitability and competitiveness. The third concept is about securing competitive advantage through a form of perceptual 'ring-fencing' designed to differentiate a company from all its competitors. Positioning underpins product/market growth through creating and sustaining a long-term favorable image or perception among prospective customers and other key stakeholders, such as retailers, on which the future profitability of a business depends.

Linked with branding, the concept of positioning was introduced in Chapter 8. A tourism illustration is that of BA and Air France, and the role the Concorde supersonic plane played in image terms, at least until the crash in Paris in 2000 killed over a hundred passengers and crew, and others on the ground. Concorde was never a profitable aircraft, falling victim to the rising price of fuel and the environmental concerns of noise and pollution before its commercial launch in 1976. Only thirteen planes were in service at the time of the crash, flying on a very restricted route network and they are unlikely to be replaced by a new generation of supersonic passenger plane. Yet, for nearly thirty years, based on 1960s technology, Concorde maintained an almost mystical image and 'state of the art' identity that was globally recognized and envied. It was an icon of twentieth-century style in the skies; a beautiful global symbol of elegance, high standards, premium prices and customer care that had a carry-over branding effect on the airlines which flew them. The fact that by the end of the 1990s the Concorde carried less than 0.5 per cent of BA's passengers in a year did not diminish its flagship image and appeal in any way.

A more recent illustration of corporate and product positioning comes from Travel Inn, a company within the UK-owned Whitbread Group. Targeted for strategic growth, Travel Inn doubled its market share in five years in the 1990s to become the market leader with some 200 properties in a national chain. Budget-priced hotels are very similar in core product and pricing terms, however, and can easily become a 'commodity market'. Moreover the chain was confused with its main competitor (Travel Lodge), even by its own customers. The case study in Part Six of the book explains the research and marketing strategy adopted to assess and define the brand values underpinning the chain and differentiate it from its competitors. Aggressively communicated to users, of whom many are frequent purchasers, the Travel Inn strategy is a good illustration of positioning in the tourism industry.

Chapter summary

This chapter introduces the basic concepts and processes of strategic thinking that are central to the efficient conduct of marketing-led organizations in travel and tourism. It stresses the competitive future orientation of strategy in an era of globalization, constant change and the redrawing of traditional industry sector boundaries facilitated by information technology. It distinguishes between the strategic and operational or tactical levels of planning, making the links between them and between corporate planning as it applies to the whole of an organization's business, and planning for the individual functions of a business.

Marketing strategy and tactics are only one of these functions, however important. 'Corporate planning decisions . . . are decisions that affect the whole structure of a company many years or decades into the future – huge decisions taken in extreme uncertainty about the future' (Argenti, 1980: 14). The quote from Hamel and Prahalad at the head of this chapter brings the thought process up to date, stressing that 'The short term and the long term are tightly intertwined'. They also stress the need for vision and foresight, noting that 'competition for the future is competition for *opportunity share* rather than market share. How can you estimate and compete for shares of markets that do not yet exist?' (Hamel and Prahalad, 1994: 33).

Much has been written by business management authors in the last five years about the failure of strategic planning in the 1990s. What has failed, however, is the traditional approach to top-down planning undertaken by separate planning departments. What has also failed, as only part of the answer, are the management fashions for 'downsizing' 're-engineering', 'de-layering', and endless cost-cutting programmes designed to provide a cure for current ills and yesterday's errors rather than a strategy for tomorrow's growth markets. Creating an organizational sense of strategic direction, putting in place in the short run the investment and organizational requirements for the long-term future product/market portfolio, and involving staff at all levels remain the essentials for corporate survival and growth. These are continuous processes. It is the energy and will to think strategically that matters, not the formal output of annual plans, which will have to be revised and adjusted frequently to cope with unexpected changes.

The chapter focuses on market strategy within corporate strategy as the management function most directly responsible for identifying, interpreting and stimulating current and future customer demand, and converting it into sales revenue. Marketing strategy must define the future mix of products and segments best calculated to meet the organization's long-run goals. It establishes the position that the organization and its products are intended to occupy in the minds of prospective customers. 'Goals down, plans up' is a useful term to describe the strategy dialogue, especially relevant to marketing, which integrates in practice the different levels of strategic thinking in larger organizations. It provides a bridge into the next chapter, in which the main focus is on the process of planning the tactical or operational level of marketing.

Further reading

The issues of strategic planning and strategic management are at the heart of the business policy studies. Not surprisingly these issues have developed a wide literature internationally. The following give a flavour of the field:

Baker, M. J. (1996). *Marketing: An Introductory Text.* Chapters 2 and 3, 6th edn, Macmillan.

Brassington, F. and Pettit, S. (2000). *Principles of Marketing.* Chapter 20, Prentice-Hall.

Davidson, H. (1997). *Even More Offensive Marketing.* Chapters 4, 5 and 6, Penguin.

Hamel, G. and Prahalad, C. K. (1994). *Competing for the Future.* Harvard Business School Press.

Jobber, D. (1998). *Principles and Practice of Marketing.* Chapters 16 and 17, 2nd edn, McGraw-Hill.

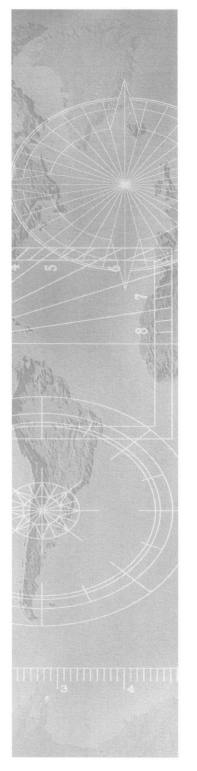

CHAPTER 13

Planning marketing tactics

The problem . . . is not that the philosophy of marketing is not believed; rather it is that most companies . . . have difficulty in making it work. This is largely because of ignorance about the process of planning their marketing activities . . . (McDonald, 1995: viii)

The previous chapter identifies the differences and links between marketing strategy and tactics and the relationship between them in the hierarchy of corporate objectives. This chapter continues the theme with a focus on the planning of marketing tactics to be implemented in the short run through action programmes. Corporate objectives have been described earlier as 'destinations', strategies as 'routes' and plans as 'action programmes' for moving along agreed routes. In other words, strategy sets the framework within which tactics are planned and, in practice, much of the work in marketing departments is concerned with drawing up, implementing and measuring the effects of action plans.

This chapter identifies seven stages of the process common to marketing planning in any industry. It emphasizes that the planning process for strategy and tactics covers the same essential stages, usually drawing on the same research sources and often undertaken by the same people. For strategic purposes, the analysis and forecasting of trends in the external business environment and the implications of demand for the development of future competitive product/market portfolios are the most important parts of planning. For tactical purposes, the setting of precise objectives and targets for the existing product/market portfolio and devising action programmes for six to twelve months ahead are the main focus.

The chapter reviews and explains each of the stages in the planning process, which are summarized in Figure 13.1. It stresses the objectives, resources and tactical budget dialogue that are part of the process of marketing communications within the firm and the means of bringing marketing together with other parts of an organization. Although the process is obviously most relevant to larger organizations, it is ultimately a logical thought process that is just as applicable in principle to small businesses.

The particular significance of marketing plans

In its principles, marketing planning is no more than a logical thought process in which all businesses engage to some extent. It is an application of common sense, as relevant to a small guesthouse or caravan park as it is to an international airline. The scale of planning and its sophistication obviously vary according to the size of the organization concerned but the essential approach is always the same.

Building on the purposes of planning outlined in Chapter 12, it is helpful to emphasize six main reasons why staff time and resources are allocated to marketing planning at the tactical or operational level:

- To identify and focus management attention on the current and targeted costs, revenues and profitability of an organization, in the context of its own and its competitors' products and segments.
- To focus decisions on implementing the strategic objectives of an organization in their market context and identifying competitive short-term action plans relevant to the long-term future.
- To set and communicate specific business targets for managers/SBUs to achieve in agreed time periods.
- To schedule and co-ordinate promotional and other marketing action required to achieve targets and to allocate the resources required as effectively as possible.
- To achieve co-ordination and a sense of joint direction between the different departments of an organization, and to communicate and motivate staff.
- To monitor and evaluate the results of marketing expenditure and adjust the planned activity as required to meet unforeseen circumstances.

Are there alternatives to marketing planning?

The only alternatives to the systematic commonsense planning processes outlined in this chapter are guesswork, hunch, 'gut feel' for the market, simple intuition or vision. Sometimes hunches and intuition are implemented with brilliant success by highly energetic and determined business entrepreneurs. Many of these dismiss systematic planning as bureaucratic, rigid, time-consuming, expensive and often wrong. But hunch and guesswork also have their disadvantages, and the history of travel and tourism reveals many illustrations of brilliant entrepreneurs whose businesses grew rapidly and successfully for some years, only to crash spectacularly in the wake of unpredicted events. Laker Airways, Braniff Airways and International Leisure Group, are just three illustrations that are widely known. There are doubtless thousands more small businesses which fell at the same hurdles but whose names are not known.

In principle, although systematic planning processes and entrepreneurial market flair are usually seen as opposites, they can, and should be mutually supportive. Provided they are not inflexible and the cause of delays, planning procedures may be used to provide a framework of objectives and an information base that support and give a sense of direction or roots in which marketing judgement and flair can grow. 'Entrepreneurial planning' may sound like a contradiction in terms but it is nevertheless a desirable goal to which most modern large businesses aspire (they call it intellectual foresight and vision) and which they seek to build into their internal management procedures. There is very clearly a balance to be struck in marketing management between analytical procedures and creative flair. Both are essential qualities for long-run survival and profitability. Creative flair and vision will always be a vital quality in successful marketing strategies and tactics. Unbridled by agreed strategies and a common sense of direction that commands internal support, such flair can also be self-destructive.

Logical steps in the marketing planning process

There are seven logical steps in a systematic marketing planning process. Each step feeds into the next one with feedback loops built into the process, as noted with arrows in Figure 13.1 and explained in the text that follows.

Explaining marketing planning as a series of logical steps runs the risk of missing the holistic contribution to the decision processes of a business. As Leppard and McDonald put it: 'While the marketing planning process appears on the surface to be just a series of procedural steps, it does in fact embrace a series of underlying values and assumptions' (Leppard and McDonald, 1991: 213). They stress that a marketing-led corporate culture in an organization is a precondition for successful marketing planning in which the process should be an integral part of corporate decisions and communication. The underlying values and assumptions are explicit in the long-term strategy of the business. At worst, if marketing planning is

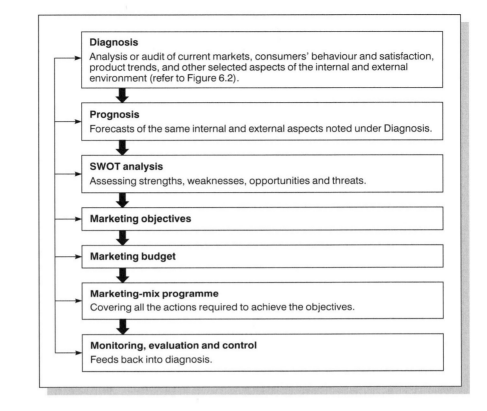

Figure 13.1
The marketing
planning process

no more than a 'bolt-on' procedure, it will scarcely be recognized outside the marketing team and have no real impact on the conduct of a firm in the long or short run.

Diagnosis

Described in some texts as part of a 'marketing audit', the first stage in the planning process is based on the analysis of company databases, supplemented by marketing research as necessary and drawing on available published and unpublished data for analysis of trends under four main headings:

1 Sales volume and revenue trends over at least a five-year period to identify total market movements and market shares for particular segments and for own and competitors' products. A UK tour operator would, for example, compare its own sales data with Civil Aviation Authority data for charter airline passengers and with government and tourist authority survey data for overall travel and tourism volume and value.

2 Consumer profiles for own customers and competitors' customers, including detail of demographics, attitudes and behaviour, as outlined in Chapter 7. This information, including indicators of customer

satisfaction and value for money, usually comes from a combination of business records and through market surveys.

3 Product profiles and price trends for own and competitors' products, identifying product life-cycle movements and in particular noting growing and declining product types. Such information comes from analysing internal business records and through trade press, trade research and other forms of marketing intelligence.

4 Trends in the external environment (as identified in Chapters 4 and 12), such as changing technology, changing regulatory requirements, exchange rate movements or changing distribution structure. This information also derives primarily from government sources, trade press and trade research, although some aspects may justify undertaking marketing research studies.

Under the four headings above, the process of *diagnosis* represents a factual platform, which is the basis for all marketing plans at tactical level. The same platform serves also for strategic appraisals but may need to be supplemented by specially commissioned long-range analyses of trends and opportunities. Since the travel and tourism industry has access to data from many sources, the way in which data are selected, organized and presented for decision purposes is an important marketing management skill.

The level of detail in the diagnosis is a matter for each individual business, reflecting its size and the range of its operations. Diagnosis is likely to extend beyond the products and markets of immediate concern to a business, into adjacent markets. For example, a budget hotel chain would expect to diagnose budget-sector accommodation markets and products in full detail. It might also need to monitor trends in the sectors above and below its chosen market sector in order to assess relative changes in the sectors which could have future strategic implications. Similarly an airline without its own low-cost operator, or links to a low-cost partner operator, would monitor international budget transport market trends to decide whether, when, how and to what extent it might enter that sector in the future.

Prognosis

Summarized in many texts as 'forecasting', the second stage in the planning process is also market-research based but future orientated. It relies on expectations, vision, judgement and forecasting for each of the four headings already covered under 'Diagnosis'. Because the future for travel and tourism products is subject to volatile, unpredictable factors and competitors' decisions, the purpose of prognosis is not accuracy but careful and continuous assessment of probabilities and options with a focus on future choices. It recognizes that most marketing mix expenditure is invested weeks and months ahead of targeted revenue flows. Diversification into other products and markets may require investment years ahead of estimated revenue flows. Since marketing planning is focused on future revenue achievement, it is necessarily dependent upon skill, judgement, foresight and realism in the prognosis process.

Both for diagnosis and prognosis the quality of the management information systems created through the marketing research process (Chapter 11) will make a critical contribution to the effectiveness of the processes of evaluation. A key part of marketing management skills lies also in the way that the essential information is presented so that other managers are able to use data and future scenarios and respond to them in their own strategic and operational decisions.

SWOT analysis

Equipped with relevant information through the process of diagnosis, and the best indications of developing trends through prognosis, the next task is to assess what the information means for marketing strategy and tactics. A framework for this assessment is contained in the traditional but still useful acronym SWOT, which stands for strengths, weaknesses, opportunities and threats.

Strengths are normally expressed as inherent current advantages, whether by earlier strategic decisions or historic good fortune. Strengths may exist in an organization's market/product portfolio and its operations in relation to competitors. Products with increasing shares of markets predicted to grow are obviously strengths. Dominance of market share among key market segments is another strength while strategic alliances with other companies may have achieved a particular set of competencies and value-added that customers are willing to pay premium prices for. For hotels and visitor attractions, location may be a major strength. Strength may lie in historic artefacts or architectural style and it may reflect a particularly favourable consumer image. Strength may lie in the professional skills of a marketing team or a distribution system, or in the future orientated competencies of key staff, or in customer service staff with a recognized reputation for being especially helpful and friendly.

It is impossible to indicate all the possible dimensions of an organization's strengths, but such dimensions are always identifiable and recognizable characteristics that an organization has more of, or does better, than its competitors. Once identified, strengths are the basis of corporate positions (see Chapter 12) and can be promoted to potential customers, enhanced through product augmentation, or developed within a strategic framework.

Weaknesses, ranging from ageing products in declining markets to surly customer contact staff, must also be clearly identified. Once identified, they may be subject to management action designed to minimize their impact or to remove them where possible. Weaknesses and strengths are often matters of perception rather than 'fact', and may often be identified only through consumer research.

If, for example, a historic hotel in a market town is perceived by many of its customers as an attractive building but old-fashioned, noisy and uncomfortable for its users, it may be possible to highlight its strengths by repositioning the hotel to stress old-world charm, convenience of location and atmosphere. Such a repositioning may necessitate extensive refurbishment, including double glazing and refurnishing, but it could provide a strategic route to turn a weakness into strength. If a modern competitor hotel were to be built on the outskirts of the market town, the historic hotel would probably lose some of its non-leisure clients and might be forced to reposition its products and develop new leisure market segments in order to survive.

To enhance their own foresight and bring to bear an independent, fresh vision, it is common practice in large marketing-orientated businesses for managers to commission consultants to carry out regular audits of all aspects of their business, including SWOT analyses.

Opportunities in a marketing context may arise from elements of the business under direct control, such as a particular product or process, or a particular set of staff competencies. They may also arise from shifts in the external environment, which a firm may exploit. Club Méditerranée, for example, strongly exploiting the consumer strengths of its concepts of freedom and activities in enclosed resort destinations, extended its operations throughout the world during the 1970s and 1980s. The external market trends were right for it to seize the opportunity to develop its particular holiday concepts with a powerful image in a way no other operator matched at that time.

A different type of opportunity arose for Australia when the USA was defeated in the America's Cup and it was agreed to stage the 1987 event at Fremantle, near Perth, Western Australia. With four years' notice, Perth did everything possible to use the opportunity to develop a modern tourist industry around this major event, which was the focus of the world's attention for several months. Perth and Australia were assured of film, television, radio and press coverage beyond the dreams of any conceivable advertising budget. It is a classic example of opportunistic marketing, appropriate to its time. The Sydney Olympics of 2000 provided a stimulus for future tourism of even greater power. Throughout Europe in the 1990s, heritage and culture have represented opportunities that have been turned into strengths in cities such as Bruges in Belgium, Prague in the Czech Republic and Bilbao in Spain.

Threats may also be presented by internal elements within the business's control or by external events such as exchange rate changes, rising oil prices or acts of international terrorism. In Britain, traditional seaside resorts offering beach-based summer holidays have been under heavy threat for three decades from seaside resorts along the Mediterranean coastline. They have also suffered from a form of management inertia implicit in the traditional public sector structures that are responsible for their futures. The competition has severely eroded their customary markets and, some would say twenty years too late for many, is finally forcing a strategic reappraisal of their futures in the twenty-first century.

Although it is not easy to justify the point theoretically, practical experience of marketing proves that the time and effort spent in a systematic, wide-ranging and creative SWOT analysis is invariably productive. It is much more than routine analysis of market statistics. There is ample scope for creative interpretation, judgement and lateral thinking, both at the strategic and tactical levels of planning. There is also good reason and ample scope for marketing managers to bring other managers into this process and also to involve the staff of an organization in the process, to draw out their expertise and perceptions of a business and its customers.

Because information is never perfect and the future is always unknown, there is never one right conclusion to be drawn from the evidence gathered in the SWOT process. Best guesses are required. Managers change and their memories are often faulty so, whenever strategy and tactics are reviewed, it is essential for larger businesses to record the assumptions made and conclusions drawn. Establishing a formal record, however succinct, is equally valuable for small businesses.

Marketing objectives and targets

Marketing objectives and targets at tactical level derive logically from the previous stages of the planning process. Targets express what managers believe can be achieved from a business over a specified time period.

To be effective and actionable in practice, tactical marketing objectives must be:

- Integrated with long-run corporate goals and strategy.
- Precise and quantified in terms of sales volume, sales revenue and, if possible, market share.
- Specific in terms of what products, which segments.
- Specific in terms of the time period in which they are to be achieved.
- Realistic and aggressive in terms of market trends (revealed by prognosis and SWOT) and in relation to budgets available.
- Agreed and endorsed by the managers responsible for the programmes of activity designed to achieve results.
- Measurable directly or indirectly.

If these seven criteria are not fully reflected, the objectives will be less than adequate for achieving the success of the business and the marketing programmes will be harder to specify and evaluate. The more thorough the diagnosis, prognosis, and SWOT, the easier the task of specifying precise objectives.

To give an example, consider the case of a medium-sized European tour operator with a capacity of say 500 000 packages sold to European destinations in the previous year and a five-year strategy to grow through a combination of market penetration and product development. Assuming that favourable market circumstances are revealed by diagnosis and prognosis, and starting from a good competitive position, the operator might look for a 15 per cent increase in volume in the following year, e.g. to achieve sales of 575 000 tours over the next twelve months.

Even if revenue targets and market share were added to this statement, it could not be considered fully actionable in marketing terms. To meet the seven criteria previously noted, and drawing on a notional analysis of the operator's business for the sake of the example, the same objective would have to be developed as follows.

To achieve sales of 575 000 tours in targeted European destinations between April and September, at average 95 per cent occupancy, to achieve a gross contribution of £7 million, with an overall market share of 3 per cent:

(a) *by sales of 355 000 summer sun tours (+2 per cent on previous year)*
(b) *by sales of 115 000 lakes and mountains tours (+ 15 per cent on previous year)*
(c) *by sales of 30 000 coach tours (+ 5 per cent on previous year)*
(d) *by sales of 75 000 city breaks (+25 per cent on previous year).*

The figures in brackets represent target increases on previous years' sales, reflecting the prognosis stage of planning as well as a particular growth strategy, in this case to extend penetration in the city breaks market and develop new products in that sector of the market.

This level of precision would be the basis for planning weekly capacity for airports of origin, resort destinations, flight and bed capacity and contracting for the necessary seats and rooms. In tour-operating practice the process of targeting numbers is built up on the basis of aircraft flight capacity and schedules, so that the operational implications of targeted increases for contracting purposes are immediately apparent to managers (see Chapter 24).

From these quantified capacity targets, the promotional and other marketing tasks in achieving the targeted volumes can be drawn up and costed for budget purposes. Subsequently, the marketing effort can be evaluated in terms of bookings against target sales on a weekly basis.

It should be apparent, even from this brief consideration of setting objectives, that precision of this kind cannot be achieved without prior analysis in some depth (diagnosis and prognosis) and evaluation of SWOT. In every case, except for very small operators with one product and one segment, it will be found necessary to disaggregate the objectives into specific products and segments. Once this is achieved, the specification and costing of marketing-mix tasks immediately becomes easier.

Marketing budget: a dialogue

The marketing budget (discussed further in Chapter 14) determines the amount of money that has to be spent in advance of bookings, reservations and purchases in order to secure targeted sales volume and revenue. In the tour operator example noted above, costs of brochure production, distribution and of advertising would be committed months before the full payments or even most of the deposits were received from customers.

The budget represents the sum of the costs of individual marketing-mix elements judged necessary by marketing managers to achieve specified objectives and targets. There can never be total precision between costs and results for reasons discussed in Chapter 14 but this does not alter the principle of allocating money to specific tasks in order to achieve targeted results.

Because the budget is required to achieve volume and revenue objectives through expenditure on a marketing-mix programme, there is a vital feedback or 'dialogue' loop between target setting and marketing management agreement on what can realistically be achieved with affordable budgets (see Figure 13.2).

Figure 13.2 demonstrates the essential systematic interaction that takes place in marketing planning between goals, objectives, budgets and programmes. The proposed objectives reflect business goals and strategy, as previously described. The marketing resources include the numbers, competencies and skills of staff to undertake programmes. Also in resources are the size, structure and costs to service of the distribution channels available to the business, its links with advertising agencies, etc.

For each marketing objective there will normally be a range of options as to how it will be achieved – more or less advertising, more or less price discounting and so on. Marketing managers are required to consider these options and the associated costs using judgement, experience and analysis of previous results. If an evaluation of objectives and the cost of marketing tasks demonstrates that planned resources are inadequate, then additional budgets will be needed or the objectives must be amended.

Over the space of several days or weeks, each of the interlocking elements in Figure 13.2 will be modified until an agreed marketing mix programme is finalized for implementation. In describing targeting for the Thomas Cook Group, Davies commented, 'The essential features of

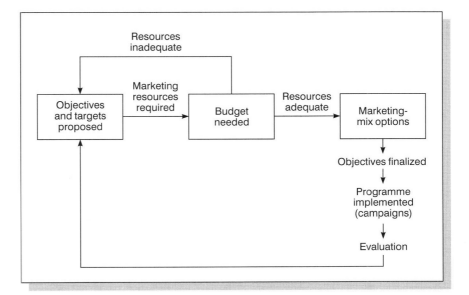

Figure 13.2
Co-ordinating tactical marketing objectives, budgets and programmes

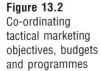

targets are that they should be meaningful and that they should be acceptable to those responsible for striving to achieve them' (Davies, 1990: 213).

Marketing-mix programmes

Action programmes comprise the mix of promotion, distribution and other marketing activities that are undertaken to influence and motivate buyers to choose targeted volumes of particular products. These include:

- Advertising.
- Direct marketing.
- Sales promotion and merchandising.
- Personal selling.
- Promotional literature and electronic information provision.
- Public relations.
- Distribution plans, Internet provision and sales-force deployment.
- Planned price discounts.
- Commissions to retailers.

A marketing-mix programme or marketing campaign (see next chapter) expresses exactly what activities will take place in support of each identified product/market subgroup on a week-by-week basis. Since brochure production, distribution, advertising and merchandising in retail travel agencies have different timescales, there is a considerable management art necessary in scheduling programmes of work to make the best use of the marketing department staff's time.

Monitoring, evaluation and control

In Chapter 12 we posed three key strategic questions of: where are we now? Where do we want to be? How do we get there? Implicit in that is another question, how do we know if we arrived? Perhaps the most important reason for insisting on precision in setting objectives is to make it possible to measure results. In the case of the tour operator business discussed above under 'marketing objectives and targets', it would be possible to monitor results for each market/product sector under at least seven headings, most of them at least weekly:

- Flow of bookings against planned capacity.
- Enquiry and sales response related to any advertising.
- Customer awareness of advertising messages measured by research surveys.
- Sales response to any price discounts and sales promotions.
- Sales response to any merchandising efforts by travel agents.
- Consumer use of Web sites and flow of bookings achieved.
- Customer satisfaction with product quality measured by customer satisfaction questionnaires.

Evaluation and control is a complex subject, further discussed in Chapter 14. It is sufficient here to stress that efficient evaluation is also a vital input to the diagnosis process and that it is impossible to have efficient evaluation without first establishing precise targets against which to measure results.

The corporate communication role of marketing plans

Involving as many staff contributions as possible in the process of setting objectives and drawing up plans that communicate well is an important aspect of motivating staff at all levels and securing enthusiastic participation in the implementation process. It is a subject of increasing attention in many travel and tourism organizations; it is especially important for service businesses in which so many staff have direct contact with customers on the premises (see Chapter 6). It is usually possible to time the stages in marketing planning so that managers and as many staff as possible in all departments can take some part in initiating and/or commenting on draft objectives and plans. It is common sense that those who have to carry out plans should identify themselves with their success and not see them as impositions laid down by senior managers who may not have recent practical experience of what can be achieved within known constraints. Where target setting and evaluation are linked with some form of performance incentives, the motivation of staff is likely to be easier to secure.

Many managers will be aware of the damaging effect on staff morale of working within an organization where the objectives appear to change according to management whim, or where directives are issued by planning departments and there is no opportunity to debate their practicality in operation. While marketing planning is conducted primarily to achieve more efficient business decisions, its secondary benefit is to provide a means of internal participation and communication, vital in creating and sustaining a high level of organizational morale.

Marketing plans are also important in communicating to stakeholders outside the company. An approach to banks or other investors, for example in tourism projects funded by EU sources, invariably requires a business plan in which marketing is a primary component. Where money is granted, evidence of results will be required through a formal evaluation process.

Distinguishing between marketing planning for strategy and tactics

Earlier in the chapter it was noted that the seven-stage process for drawing up marketing plans is the same in principle for both strategy and tactics. Strategic planning usually focuses mainly on diagnosis, prognosis and the SWOT analysis, and is likely to look backwards over the trends of several years as well as forward to the extent that projections are sensible. As explained in Chapter 12, strategic planning is much broader in its approach than tactical planning, and strategic goals are normally not expressed in quantifiable terms. Strategic goals state where an organization wishes to be with regard to its markets, expressed in broad terms and evaluation of opportunities that can be turned subsequently into short-term operational plans.

For example, BA's decision to establish its own low cost airline *Go* in the late 1990s to compete with *easyJet* and other budget airlines was driven by strategic considerations not to be cut out of a growth sector of the market and not to miss out on the direct marketing scope opened up for low-cost airlines by the Internet. Strategic goals may be expressed in terms of projected growth and profit, organizational structure or in relation to competitors. Strategies may be expressed in terms of the four main Ps of the marketing mix or any other aspect influenced by marketing managers and ultimately measurable in customer attitudes and purchase behaviour. For any large organization they will be concerned with the way a company does business looking at least five years ahead.

Effective marketing strategies always require considerable organizational commitment and effort. 'Strong, offensive strategies do not come easily. They are usually the result of prolonged and painstaking analysis of the market, competitors and the trend of change' (Davidson, 1975: 115).

Tactical marketing planning is a 'practical exercise in deciding what a business is to achieve through marketing activity in the year ahead. It is a logical thought process and an application of common sense. It provides a basis of objectives around which marketing tasks are set, budgets drawn up and results measured' (Middleton, 1980: 26). Tactical plans express in precise, quantifiable, short-run terms what an organization is seeking to achieve for its portfolio of products and segments within the context of an established long-run strategy.

Chapter summary

At the start of the twenty-first century virtually all medium to large organizations in travel and tourism undertake some form of marketing planning. Unless they need to approach banks or other investors, most smaller ones still rely on 'feel for the market' to guide their decisions on objectives and the ways in which they intend to achieve them. In the authors' experience, only very large organizations have established systematic planning processes comparable to those in manufacturing and leading service industries such as the retail and financial sectors. For most organizations there is great scope for significant improvement in the time, effort and expertise that is employed to undertake what is perhaps the most important single aspect of conducting any business. Compared with the constant preoccupation in most companies with cutting current costs, more time spent on the processes that will generate future revenue would be well spent. The process offers the best available route to increasing performance at the margin.

Understood as the systematic process whereby objectives, strategies and plans are devised and adapted to changing circumstances, marketing planning – for strategy and tactics – is the essential basis for effective marketing action. Planning does not replace flair and judgement but it does provides a fertile base of information and broad strategic direction within which imagination, flair and vision can be harnessed to produce their best results.

Organizations vary as to the headings and labels used in their marketing plans; they may not be same as those used in this chapter. Readers should note that it is not the words that matter, but the logical stages and thought processes which they describe.

In all cases the current marketing plan represents the sum of the knowledge and judgement an organization has built up over time about its products, markets, its competitive strengths and weaknesses, and its future direction. Students should not be surprised if commercial organizations are unwilling to provide access to such plans.

Further reading

Brassington, F. and Pettit, S. (2000). *Principles of Marketing*. Chapter 20, 2nd edn, Prentice-Hall.

Davidson, H. (1997). *Even More Offensive Marketing*. Chapter 8, Penguin.

Kotler, P. and Armstrong, G. (1999). *Principles of Marketing*. Chapter 2, 8th edn, Prentice-Hall.

McDonald, M. H. B. (1995). *Marketing Plans*. Chapters 2 to 5, 3rd edn, Butterworth-Heinemann.

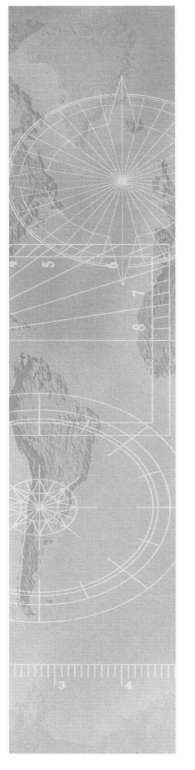

CHAPTER 14

Planning marketing campaigns: budgeting and measuring performance

This chapter draws the other chapters of Part Three together in a practical focus on the meaning and nature of marketing campaigns. The broad, unifying concept of campaigns is explained here and developed subsequently throughout Parts Four and Five of the book. 'Campaign' is not a term widely used in marketing texts except in the specific contexts of advertising or public relations. For all forms of travel and tourism, however, production operations, service delivery and marketing are very closely interlinked. The marketing campaign concept is especially valuable for the practical insights it provides into organizing and controlling marketing tactics and programmes and the term is strongly recommended to readers.

The word *campaign,* with its connotations of military action, is well suited to the activities of marketing managers aggressively promoting their organizations' interests and aiming to defeat their competitors. Marketing managers, or product managers responsible for undertaking campaigns, have been aptly described as the 'storm troopers of marketing' (Davidson, 1975: 95).

The chapter begins with definitions relevant to the whole of Part Four. It identifies the techniques that marketing managers deploy in their campaigns to influence consumer demand and generate sales revenue. It proceeds with an outline of basic methods used for budgeting in marketing and explains them by working through typical campaign budgets. The final part of the chapter defines the approaches used to measure performance and includes practical ways to monitor results.

Marketing campaigns are action programmes

Marketing campaign describes any co-ordinated programme of marketing activities in the general field of product design, pricing, promotion, communication and distribution that is designed to influence and mould customers' behaviour. In marketing practice and in texts the term is often used only in a restricted sense of advertising, sales promotion or public relations. In fact the term is not used by Kotler, but Stanton defined a campaign as 'a co-ordinated series of promotional efforts built around a single theme or idea and designed to reach a predetermined goal . . . we should apply the campaign concept to the entire promotional programme' (Stanton, 1981: 391).

Without challenging the principle underlying Stanton's definition, the authors believe it makes sense to broaden it further and to tie it specifically into the implementation phase of the marketing planning process. Thus:

> A marketing campaign is a planned, integrated action programme designed to achieve specific marketing objectives and targets, through the deployment of a budget on the promotion and distribution of products over a specified time period.
>
> Campaigns may be aimed directly at consumers, or indirectly through a distribution network, or both. The focus of a marketing campaign is a short-run action programme and several campaigns would normally be necessary to achieve particular strategic objectives.

The menu for marketing campaigns in travel and tourism

The full range of marketing techniques to be woven into campaigns is set out in Table 14.1 as a *menu*. Each technique has its own methods, skills and implications for action, which are explained in subsequent chapters. The implications for campaigns are generally perceived to lie in the promotional aspects of the marketing mix but price is included in its discounted sense, product augmentation is included where it overlaps with sales promotion, and distribution is both a target for campaigns and increasingly a part of the promotional process. The menu represents choices from which marketing managers will select according to their particular targets and market circumstances.

Activity	Notes
Paid for media advertising	Includes television, press, radio and outdoor. Also includes tourist board and other travel guides, books and brochures.
Internet	Web sites/banner advertising and links to other sites.
Direct mail/door to door	Includes sales literature and print items specially designed for distribution for this purpose.
Public relations	All media exposure achieved as editorial matter. Also other forms of influence achieved over target groups – customers and stakeholders.
Sponsorship	An alternative form of media to reach specified target groups.
Exhibitions/shows/workshops	Important alternative forms of distribution and display for reaching retail, wholesale and consumer target groups.
Personal selling	Via meetings, telephones, e-mail and workshops. Primarily aimed at distributors and intermediaries purchasing on behalf of groups of consumers.
Sales literature (print)	Expecially promotional brochures and other print used in a servicing/facilitation role.
Sales promotion	Short-term incentives offered as inducements to purchase, Including temporary product augmentation. Covers sales force and distribution network as well as consumers.
Price discounting	A common form of sales promotion. Includes Internet offers and extra commission and bonuses for retailers.
Point of sale displays and merchandising	Posters, window dressing, displays of brochures and other materials both of a regular and temporary incentive kind.
Familiarization trips and educationals	Ways to motivate and facilitate distributor networks through product sampling. Also used to reach and influence journalists.
Distribution networks and commission	Organized systems or channels through which prospective customers achieve access to products. Includes CRSs and the Internet.

Table 14.1 The principal marketing campaign techniques used in travel and tourism

Marketing campaigns in travel and tourism have two main dimensions:

1 Promotional techniques designed to motivate and move prospective customers towards a point of sale and also to provide incentives to purchase (includes promotion to distributors).
2 Facilitation of access techniques designed to make it as easy as possible for motivated people to achieve their intended purchase, especially at the point of sale (access is defined in Chapter 6).

Marketing texts, even when dealing with service products, generally exclude access facilitation from discussions of campaigns and focus only on aspects of promotion. In the context of travel and tourism products, especially in the light of rapid Internet developments in the late 1990s, this is myopic. Where products are normally purchased ahead of consumption, as is the case, for example in accommodation, transportation, tour operation or car rental, it always makes sense to programme and include the full cost of access facilitation in the total campaign budget. Where multiple distribution channels exist and are diversifying rapidly, as again is the case for much of travel and tourism, creation of consumer access for products is getting much closer to what is conventionally discussed as promotion than it is to what is conventionally described as distribution.

Access to the Internet as a marketing tool since the mid-1990s provides a wholly new means of bringing the two dimensions together by integrating promotion and access. The power of Web sites is that they can simultaneously advertise, inform, display, promote special offers, make a sale and provide instant booking and confirmation – in customers' homes or while they are on the move (see Chapters 18 and 19).

In summary, marketing campaigns include all four variables of the marketing mix (four Ps), where their use is designed in the short term to influence and facilitate buyer behaviour to achieve targeted campaign objectives. To focus only on promotion is seriously to underestimate the cost of marketing. The campaign menu in Table 14.1 is provided as an indication of what lies within the spectrum of choice for marketing managers. The main techniques are all discussed separately in Part Four of the book.

Marketing campaign budgets

The marketing budget may be defined as *the sum of the costs of the campaign action programme judged necessary to achieve the specified objectives and targets set out in the marketing plan.*

In practice the most difficult decisions in a marketing manager's year lie in estimating and agreeing the budget. The budget, usually drawn up on an annual campaign basis for each major product/market in an organization's portfolio, represents money that has to be spent 'up front' or ahead of the targeted volume and sales revenue it is expected to generate. Every $1000 spent on campaign action programmes has to be paid for out of reserves, current cash flows or by borrowing. It is money that can only be recovered at some future point from the projected surplus of income over operating expenditure, i.e. gross operating profit. On the other hand, as marketing managers are expected to demonstrate, if the money is *not* spent, revenue targets will not be achieved. Perhaps the hardest decision to justify is that of borrowing thousands or millions of pounds to spend on promotional campaigns, not to secure a projected operating surplus, but to reduce the probable size of an expected loss. Such decisions have had to be taken by most airlines and many hotels in the international economic crises of the early 1990s, and again in the Asia Pacific region in the wake of the massive downturn in 1997 of the Asian 'Tiger' economies.

In practice, setting campaign budgets depends on finding answers to three fundamental questions.

- How much money must be spent *in total* on a marketing campaign, in order to achieve objectives? This amount will usually be expressed as a percentage of total sales revenue or as a ratio. Thus a £50 000 marketing budget on a sales turnover of £1 million will be 5 per cent or a ratio of 1:20.
- How will the total be *split between the products and segments* included in the campaign? In practice it is essential to divide a total budget between the specific sets of targets it is expected to achieve. The process for analysing product/market groupings, discussed in Chapters 12 and 13, provides a logical basis for such division. Naturally, if an international organization such as an airline is marketing itself in several countries, then the budget also has to be divided between the targeted countries. In larger organizations each SBU as well as each product/market grouping will have a separate campaign budget.
- How will the total be *divided between the component parts* of the action programme? The component parts of the action programme are the marketing tools or techniques shown in Table 14.1. The choices and the costs will be different for each of the targets within a campaign and for each of the countries included in a campaign.

With a few moments' thought, it should be clear that the apparently simple tasks implied in the three fundamental budget questions become very complicated in practice for large businesses marketing their portfolio of products to a range of segments in different countries.

Budgeting methods

Kotler (1984: 621) noted four common methods of setting both the total budget and any sub-division of it:

- Affordable method.
- Percentage of sales revenue method.
- Competitive parity method (matching competitors' spending).
- Objective and task method.

The first three of these methods are, in fact, quite closely related and rely primarily on historic information (previous budgeting levels), marketing intelligence about competitors' actions and received wisdom about 'industry norms'. In essence, they are all 'rule of thumb' or 'gut feel' methods, which commence with a fairly broad notion of an appropriate marketing expenditure considered affordable, expressed as a proportion of targeted sales revenue or turnover, such as 5 per cent. Over time such aggregate percentages often become a 'norm', which sets an expenditure ceiling not to be exceeded unless a company is forced to do so to match the competition, or to respond to other unforeseen events. Although they are still widely used in practice, especially by small businesses, these are aggregate or top-downwards methods that shed no light on how total expenditure *should be* allocated between product-market groupings or divided between campaign elements, two of the three basic questions posed earlier.

The objective and task method is quite different. It begins with a specification of what is to be achieved (objective) and proceeds by stating and costing the techniques (tasks) required to achieve it. This method, which is closely related to so-called zero-budgeting methods, is obviously the one most closely associated with the systematic marketing planning approaches discussed in this book. If there are precise objectives for each product/market grouping, the objective and task method can be used to construct a budget from the bottom upwards through specification of tasks, so that all three budget questions posed earlier are answered. Objective and task methods are, however, time-consuming and the procedures for costing are often dependent on marketing judgement. The tidy logic of the textbook may not be easily implemented in practice, especially for organizations with multiple objectives and several product/market groupings.

The next section explains and illustrates how these methods work in practice.

Affordable and percentage of sales revenue methods

An illustration of a notional British tour operator's budget is shown in Figure 14.1 to indicate how budgeting methods often operate in practice. The example assumes sales are achieved at targeted load factors (typically over 90 per cent) and the items, representing a typical trading, profit and loss account, have simplified headings for the sake of presentation. The budget is based on hypothetical figures but it broadly represents British tour operator cost structures of the late 1990s, before the impact of the Internet on tour operators' distribution costs. Figure 14.1 can be altered as necessary and adapted to suit the circumstances of most businesses and is offered as a useful model for examining budgeting issues. See also the explanatory notes accompanying Figure 14.1.

While the percentages noted in the budget would fluctuate from year to year and from one firm to another, the broad orders of magnitude hold good over time and the following points can be made:

- Of the total sales revenue, some 80 per cent is absorbed in contracted product component costs and a further 4.5 per cent is committed in fixed costs of operation and investment in systems. Of the remainder, the brochure commitment is inescapable, and so also is the retail agency support system to achieve the given volume of sales. In other words, a total approaching 90 per cent of sales revenue is, to all intents and purposes, committed in advance of any revenue received.
- In Figure 14.1 advertising, sales promotion and other discretionary campaign costs to be decided by the marketing manager, represent just 1 per cent of total turnover. Since it is most unlikely that in practice such costs would be either halved or doubled in any one year, the real level of budget discretion is remarkably small, probably under 0.5 per cent of sales turnover.

Budget summary	Year (000s)	%
Total turnover @ £500 (arsp)[1] on 1,000,000 tours sold	£500,000	
Less cost of contracting tour components[2], say	– 400,000	80
= gross trading surplus	100,000	
Less targeted operating profit before tax @ say 3% of turnover	– 15,000	3
= maximum sum to cover all administration and marketing costs	85,000	17
Specific costs of administration, operations and marketing		
Committed costs of operation (fixed)	7,000	
Reservation system and overheads[3]	6,500	
Non marketing administration costs[4]	4,000	4.5
Marketing staff and overheads (UK)	5,000	
Overseas support costs	22,500	
Marketing campaign costs (fixed and variable)		
Advertising	3,000	
Sales promotion	1,500	
Brochure and distribution	8,000	11.3
Other[5]	1,000	
Sales commission to retail agencies (@ average 10%)[6]	43,000	
Contingency reserve[7]	6,000	1.2
	85,000	

Notes
1. arsp = average retail sales price, per package tour sold. Total rounded to simplify the calculations
2. Accommodation, transport, transfers.
3. Includes Internet investment, computer systems, staff and all communication costs and depreciation.
4. Office expenses, rates, staff equipment etc., including general administration.
5. Workshops, PR, familiarization visits etc.
6. Assumes 90 per cent of all sales commissionable, others booked direct.
7. Held in reserve especially for tactical discounts to promote unsold capacity.

Figure 14.1
Model marketing budget calculations for a British tour operator
Source: Adapted from Middleton (1980), updated in 1992 and 1999 with advice from a leading tour operator.

- In this example the contingency reserve for tactical discounts at £6 million is already 50 per cent of the itemized discretionary expenditure, although it represents only £6 per tour package. In practice, if bookings fell seriously below targeted levels, the contingency reserve would be increased by a factor of two or more but the money could only come from the £15 million targeted gross operating profit. In the late 1990s no large UK tour operator averaged anything near 5 per cent gross profit on trading operations, because of fierce competition and the need to spend contingency money on marketing, especially tactical price discounting. Figure 14.1 is based on 3 per cent.
- There is no common agreement as to exactly what items should be included or excluded from a marketing budget. There is a strong case for including retail commission, since it is part of the money paid out to ensure effective distribution and sales of products, the fourth 'P' of the marketing mix.
- With brochure-related and commission costs exceeding 10 per cent, which is over three times the size of the targeted operating profit, much attention is being focused on the alternative costs associated with investing in systems that use the Internet. At 2000, although widely expected to grow, the use of the Internet as a percentage of tour

operator sales was still very small (under 5 per cent) and the specific costs of such business are absorbed in the model as 'other' and not shown separately.

From Figure 14.1, it should be clear that the so-called affordable and percentage of turnover methods of budgeting are at least relevant and practical. Apart from establishing upper limits to expenditure, however, such methods do not provide any guidance whatever as to how best to apportion the affordable sums. For that, it is necessary to use the objective and task method discussed next.

The objective and task method

To illustrate this method, consider the hypothetical but realistic case of a hotel consortium comprising one hundred individually owned hotels with a combined capacity of 6000 rooms. Assume that, through careful diagnosis and prognosis, the consortium has set itself a marketing objective to sell 45 per cent of its aggregate capacity (equivalent to 2700 rooms) as weekend packages over twenty selected weekends between October and April. For ease of calculation, assume that each package lasts for two nights and covers two people. Also for ease of calculation, assume the average price, published in the consortium's brochure, is £100 per person/package, which includes breakfast and dinner for the two nights – but not additional expenditure in the hotels.

The sales revenue target is, therefore:

2700 (rooms) × 20 (weekends) × 2 persons
× £100 per person
= total weekend package sales revenue   = £10 800 000

2700 (rooms) × 20 (weekends) × 2 persons × 2 (days)
× £12 per day
= additional revenue spent in bars, etc.   = £2 592 000

Total sales revenue   = £13 392 000

Because the fixed costs of hotel operation are already committed, the hotel consortium stands to achieve a gross contribution (additional revenue over variable costs) of around 45 per cent on this business, say £6 million.

The question to resolve is how much should the consortium spend on marketing in order to achieve the £6 million additional revenue? By applying conventional ratio methods, it is easy to calculate (using rounded figures) that:

5 per cent of total sales revenue
(including additional spending is)   £670 000

10 per cent of total sales revenue
(including additional spending is)   £1 340 000

20 per cent of total sales revenue
(including additional spending is)   £2 680 000

Even beyond the 20 per cent level of expenditure on marketing, the consortium would still find it advantageous to invest assuming that without marketing effort, at least a half of the potential £6 million gross contribution would not be achieved.

With clear objectives set, which in practice would be split by area of the country and the projected profile of target buyers, the next step is to itemize and cost the tasks in an effective marketing campaign.

Task-based campaign budget

The following costs are indicative of what would be spent in practice (2000 prices) by the consortium to meet the objectives noted in the preceding section:

Cost of producing say, 500 000 brochures (allows for agency distribution)	£150 000
Direct mail, say 100 000 pieces (via hotels' own lists and coupon response)	£80 000
Advertising in consumer media and trade press	£200 000
Advertising in tourist board guides etc.	£3 000
Point of sale material (retail agents and hotels)	£35 000
PR campaign costs	£15 000
Retail travel agency commission (assuming 35 per cent bookings via this route and 10 per cent of package price)	£380 000
Other, including costs to service retailers and Web site	£50 000
Total	*£913 000*

The following points can be made:

1 Selecting the itemized tasks and estimating the expenditure required are based on a mixture of *fact* (postal costs, brochure costs, retail commission), *experience* (knowledge of which activities are most relevant for selling weekend packages and the costs and quantities of any previous campaigns) and *judgement* (especially in relation to media expenditure but drawing on advertising agency knowledge and expertise).

2 There can be no absolute certainty that £913 000 will produce the targeted bookings for the consortium. There is, however, a systematic method and framework for making decisions, within which it is possible to focus facts, experience and judgement. Given adequate evaluation of the campaign's results (see later), the systematic framework would also serve as a learning mechanism to refine the decision process for any subsequent campaigns.

3 If the sales target is achieved, £913 000 happens to be 8.5 per cent of £10 800 000 (the sales revenue from selling the product packages), 6.8 per cent of the total sales revenue and 15 per cent of the gross contribution of £6 million. The advertising (paid space in the media) is 2 per cent of the package sales revenue. In the end these ratios have little meaning except to establish that the bottom line return is worth the investment. The cost of the campaign can be seen as the price for achieving the targeted business, and at that point the ratios are only of interest for control and evaluation purposes – they were not used to determine the size of the marketing budget.

4 In practice, in monitoring and evaluating a campaign of this sort, the hotel group would wish to analyse the proportion of its bookings which came from previous customers. It may be possible to adapt the components of the campaign to achieve a higher proportion of sales from repeat bookers, thereby lowering marketing costs. The group would also wish to evaluate the relative cost and revenue generation of sales via retail outlets vs sales over the Internet. Commission on just over a third of the sales amounts to the largest single element in the marketing budget.

5 The functional relationship between marketing expenditure and targeted revenue should be clear.

Performance measurement: evaluation, monitoring and control

Kotler states that 'marketing control is the natural sequel to marketing planning, organization and implementation' (Kotler, 1984: 773). All marketing texts stress the importance of measuring the results achieved by action programmes against the planned targets. But, given the importance of the subject, it is surprising how little space most books offer on measurement and there are no recognized guidelines for travel and tourism. The subject is too often seen, as in most hotel groups, as the responsibility of accountants and financial controllers. It is far too important for that.

Performance measurement provides the vital information for marketing managers to:

- Respond quickly and effectively if actual sales and other indicators vary significantly from targets.
- Learn from current experience in ways that will make the subsequent year's campaign targets and budgets more cost-efficient.
- Adjust strategic objectives in the light of current results.
- Integrate marketing decisions with those of other key business functions, especially accounting and finance and operations management.
- Make the vital marginal adjustments to campaigns, which in high fixed-cost businesses will always have a major impact on profit or loss.

It is not too much to claim that the effectiveness and efficiency of marketing is actually determined by the quality of the performance measurement techniques used. It is also worth repeating that it is impossible for marketing managers to respond effectively to aggregate measures of the total volume or revenue. In other words, the number of airline passengers carried over a year is a useless measure in practice, except perhaps for annual reports and PR purposes; the total number of room nights sold by a hotel, or total bed occupancy, is just an academic statistic of no marketing management value. What matters is how many first-class passenger bookings were received against monthly targets, and which of the routes flown were up or down, or how conference bookings for events for over a hundred persons responded to the action programmes targeted at conference organizers.

The all-important linkage between targeting, budgeting and measuring performance *disaggregated by product/market groupings* is a constant theme throughout this book. It is reflected in the hotel example used in this chapter and further illustrated in Part Five. As Kotler put it 'market-share analysis, like sales analysis, increases in value when the data is disaggregated along various dimensions. The company might watch the progress of its market share by product line, customer type, region, or other breakdowns' (Kotler, 1984: 748).

In travel and tourism it will be found helpful to distinguish between three aspects of performance measurement that are the responsibility of marketing managers. There is a fourth related form of measurement outlined below under innovation, experimentation and test marketing:

1 *Evaluation* – defined as the systematic periodic evaluation of achievement of stated objectives. Evaluation is usually an annual process and often a focal part of regular marketing audits carried out as part of the strategic planning process described in Chapter 13.
2 *Monitoring* – the systematic measurement of performance on a daily, weekly or monthly basis, which assesses actual results against targeted sales. The results of monitoring are typically collated through a marketing information system, used immediately for marketing control and also fed into the annual evaluation process.

For effective evaluation and monitoring, it is essential that the practicalities of measurement are included in the process by which marketing targets are drawn up. It is a central criterion of the planning process described in Chapter 13 that no target is accepted unless the method of measuring it is defined in advance. In this sense performance monitoring is more than a 'sequel of marketing planning, organization and implementation', it is an integral part of the targeting and objective setting process. If objectives cannot be monitored and assessed by affordable methods, they should not be selected.

3 *Marketing control* – means tactical marketing management actions taken continuously in response to the information provided by monitoring. Generally this action will be funded out of contingency sums in marketing budgets, although in crisis conditions additional funding will be required. Such actions normally focus on tactical pricing, sales promotion and advertising, and last minute sales on the Internet.

Innovation, experimentation and test marketing

Not normally seen as part of performance measurement, the opportunities for systematic innovation and testing represent a massive and underutilized asset to most marketing managers in travel and tourism. It can and certainly should be used regularly as a highly cost-effective form of both testing and measuring the effectiveness of marketing programmes for travel and tourism products, as well as in the more traditional role of product testing and evaluation.

The opportunities arise in two ways. The first is because customer contact on premises or sites is a normal part of service delivery operations and the feedback can be virtually instantaneous. Where an organization such as an airline or hotel group operates multiple sites, it is possible to test market innovations and compare responses between outlets, often very quickly. The change may be to room design, new staff procedures, uniforms or any of the many components that make up the formal and augmented product outlined in Chapter 8. The second way reflects the fact that much of travel and tourism is booked in advance on the basis of information provided. A tour operator can offer a small number of new products or a new destination and monitor the response; any firm can experiment with their Web sites as promotional tools and, again, monitor the response; a hotel can collaborate with local heritage attractions and build them into a product offer, and so on. There are countless ways in which forms of test marketing are easier in travel and tourism than in most other industries.

Campaign plan monitoring: sales variance

In several parts of this book, reference is made to 'marketing the margin'. Because of the effects of operating on high fixed costs, it means concentrating marketing effort on the incremental percentage occupancy, load factor or visitor numbers that in travel and tourism usually generate additional revenue at very little or no additional variable cost. If a business loses sales at the margin – sales falling below targets – the margin typically represents a significant loss. In the case of a rail operating company, for example, an additional 1 per cent extra seats sold on a train with available capacity represents 'pure' profit at zero additional cost. One per cent fewer sales reflect a complete loss. Performance measurement must be designed to highlight those margins and the effectiveness of marketing programmes in influencing them.

The more that operational marketing objectives are made precise in terms of volume and revenue targets, time periods, and specific products and segments (discussed in Chapter 13), the easier it is to measure results. Airlines, for example, forecast their passenger volume over a long-run period, by product type, e.g. first class, business class and by types of economy fare offered, and by route, making projections on a daily basis. With modern yield management programmes they are able to read advance bookings and current sales on an online basis for every flight on

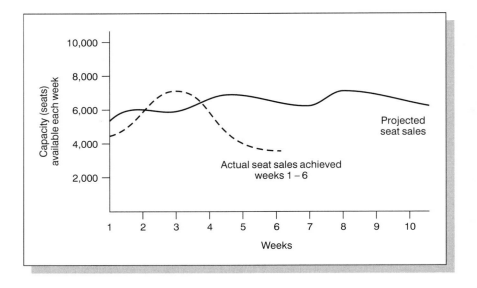

Figure 14.2
Variance of sales
against targets for
an airline

every route. The information is used to drive the tactical pricing responses described in Chapter 9.

In Figure 14.2 projected sales represent weekly planning targets, based partly on previous years' operations and partly on diagnosis, prognosis and SWOT analyses. Airline capacity and operations are scheduled on such projections, timetables are published, seats are made available through CRSs and on Web sites, and marketing campaigns are carried out ahead of sales. In weeks 4 to 6 the graph showing 'actual sales' achieved drops significantly below projected sales. As soon as the fall is detected marketing managers must establish the cause of the drop and consider action to generate more sales, employing contingency reserves if necessary. This type of monitoring is known as variance analysis and, in forms suitable to the products in question, it is the cornerstone of most marketing control. A visitor attraction would target its weekly sales by key segments such as school groups, holiday visitors, day visitors and coach parties, and monitor actual sales against those targets. The management would separately plot actual shop and catering sales against their targets to measure variance, and so on.

Sometimes sales may move far enough ahead of target to make it possible to reduce marketing budgets. When Center Parcs opened their first enclosed resorts in the UK they were able to cut back on national advertising because of the initial volume of response. This does not often happen in travel and tourism.

Market share variance

In consumer goods marketing, market share analysis and variance over time is a second basic aspect of marketing monitoring. Own sales analysis, without knowledge other than general marketing intelligence of competitors' sales, can of course provide misleading information. There is no satisfaction in knowing that a business has created a 5 per cent increase in its sales revenue, for example, if its two main rivals have increased by 10 and 15 per cent respectively in the same period. In much of travel and tourism, however, apart from transport and tour operations that are legally required to register capacity and carryings, share data is often not known at all, or has to be estimated months afterwards, too late to trigger a variance response.

Customer satisfaction variance

The third principal element in variance analysis can be achieved by regularly monitoring customer satisfaction, both overall and by product components. As described in Chapter 11, providers of travel and tourism service products are particularly well placed to exploit opportunities to measure customer satisfaction on a regular basis and to read any shifts from average scores. Figure 14.3 illustrates the point in the context of a tour operator monitoring the performance of one of the resort hotels included in its programme.

In Figure 14.3, based on data collected and analysed over many months, normal customer satisfaction ratings for hotels overall typically vary between 4.8 and 5.5. In that band hotels are generating good satisfaction in the judgement of customers using them. In weeks 1 to 4 satisfaction is normal. In week 5 it plunges and stays down. Why? Analysis of other scores may reveal a particular problem with food or service, and management action can be taken to rectify the problem and return scores to the average band. To be useful, such variance must be known within hours of its occurrence. Modern computer technology is of increasing value in making such rapid response possible. In this case

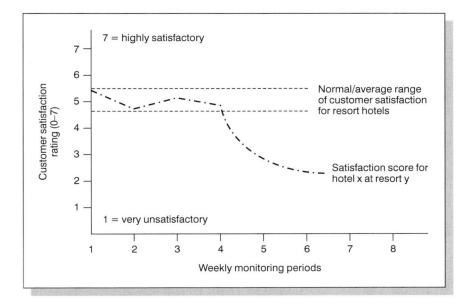

Figure 14.3
Variance of satisfaction against sales for a tour operator

marketing research methods to monitor satisfaction also operate as management control mechanisms.

The growing importance of retaining repeat or loyal customers means that particular attention is likely to be paid to their satisfaction. Any downward variation in this group is a matter of immediate concern and their responses should be separately analysed in all types of tourism business.

Ratio variance

Once the marketing campaign budget is agreed it is possible to calculate a series of financial comparisons between marketing expenditure and revenue targets, and they can subsequently be reviewed against actual revenue achieved. Provided that an organization divides its total portfolio of product-markets into logical groupings or profit centres for management purposes, it is possible to establish the costs and revenues attributable to each grouping and then calculate for each:

- Ratio of total marketing expenditure: total sales revenue.
- Ratio of total marketing expenditure: gross contribution.
- Ratio of total marketing expenditure: net profit.
- Ratio of total marketing expenditure: unit cost of production.

The comparisons of current and historic ratios and of ratios between product/market groupings in the total portfolio, yields very useful evaluation data. It helps to establish growth and decline trends in product life cycles and revenue generation. Total marketing expenditure can also be divided into the main component parts noted in Table 14.1 to establish separate ratios for each of the main techniques used.

As with other variance measures, the purpose is to alert managers to any deviations from normal that may require marketing action, both within the campaign period and strategically in the longer run.

Chapter summary

This chapter defines marketing campaigns as 'integrated action programmes designed to achieve specific marketing objectives through the deployment of a budget . . . over a specified time period'. Within the deliberately broad definition adopted in this chapter, campaigns can be seen as the final stage in an interlinked framework of business goals, strategies and plans, introduced in Chapter 12 (see Figure 12.1).

Effective action programmes must be carefully researched and costed before implementation, and this requires marketing managers to find answers to three vital questions concerning the budget: how much to spend in total, how the total should be split between the products and segments in an organization's total product portfolio, and how it should be allocated among the wide range of promotional and other marketing-mix techniques presented as a menu in Table 14.1.

The chapter works through two different tourism-related marketing budget models to explain the process and methods of budget setting, and especially to explain the important *objective and task* method. This is the budgeting process that most closely meets the needs of modern marketing-led organizations. It is relevant in its principles to all sectors of the travel and tourism industry, both commercial and non-commercial. In particular this method is the only one that directly facilitates the systematic processes for performance measurement and control defined in the chapter. The form and main aspects of performance measurement are noted and their role in *marketing the margin* is highlighted. Stress is laid on the size of the opportunity and the potential value of continuous innovation and test marketing for travel and tourism businesses.

Finally, this chapter serves as a bridge between Part Three, which explains the meaning and processes of strategy and tactics and the role of marketing managers, and Part Four, which reviews each of the main promotional techniques, and the way they are implemented effectively in practice. The marketing campaign is the co-ordinating framework for all the marketing mix techniques included in action programmes.

Further reading

Brassington, F. and Pettit, S. (2000). *Principles of Marketing*. Chapter 21, 2nd edn, Prentice-Hall.

Kotler, P. (1991). *Marketing Analysis: Planning, Implementation and Control*. Chapter 26, 7th edn, Prentice-Hall.

Kotler, P. and Armstrong, G. (1999). *Principles of Marketing*. Chapter 2, 8th edn, Prentice-Hall.

Part Four

Using the Principal Marketing Tools in Travel and Tourism

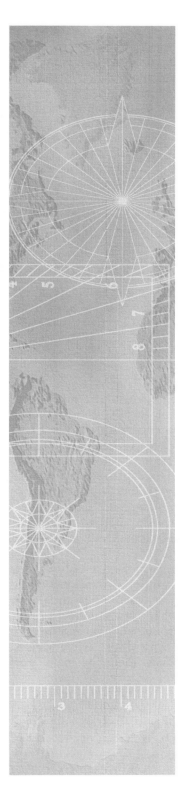

Advertising and public relations

People can't believe you if they don't know what you are saying, and they can't know what you are saying if they don't listen to you, and they won't listen to you if you're not interesting. (Bill Bernbach of Doyle Dane Bernbach)

Advertising and public relations are two of the classic communications tools used by marketing managers as part of marketing campaigns to develop awareness, understanding, interest and motivation amongst a targeted audience. Of particular importance in tourism, the wider communications mix also includes sales promotions, point of sale and merchandising, personal selling, direct marketing, and printed and electronic information – aspects that are covered in separate chapters. It was emphasized in Chapter 8 that training, the conduct of employees and the design of 'physical evidence' must also feature in the total communications effort for service products.

In marketing practice, tourism organizations are constantly communicating, whether intentionally or unintentionally, through each personal and non-personal interaction with the public. The role of marketing is to co-ordinate all the elements under the control of the organization in order to deliver consistent messages that enhance the chosen positioning. Although it is not under the immediate control of marketing management, taking steps to influence positive 'word of mouth' by satisfied customers is an additional important aspect of communications activity for service businesses.

Of the directly controllable elements, advertising and public relations with their use of press, television and other mass media, are popularly perceived as the glamorous side of marketing. For some sectors they are the most costly part of a total campaign budget and planned integration of such expensive tools is essential to ensure maximum effectiveness. Integration means achieving mutual support in the communications process, for example using public relations to raise the profile of an advertising campaign, using advertising and printed communications to create awareness of a Web site, or using information from a direct response advertisement for sales promotions. The communications mix itself must be integrated with the rest of the marketing mix. It is the job of marketing to review the consistency of marketing mix decisions with communications messages and to develop particular promotional themes through time as well as across the different communications tools available.

This chapter begins by examining the scale of advertising and public relations before exploring basic concepts about the communications process. Definitions are given for both advertising and public relations, along with a table of common terminology. The functions of advertising and public relations are then explored in turn, with particular reference to the processes involved.

The scale of advertising and public relations

The British Advertising Association (AA) estimates that advertising expenditure in the UK totalled over £13 billion in 1997, the sum being equivalent to 2.6 per cent of all consumer expenditure. This figure includes all press, television, direct mail, outdoor posters and transport, radio and cinema advertising. Press advertising, currently still the dominant medium in the UK, can be divided into display advertising and the small line entries known as classified advertising. A compilation of figures taken from AC Nielsen-MEAL analysis suggests that the travel and tourism industry spent approximately £425 million on display advertising in 1997, around 11 per cent of total expenditure on this form of advertising in the UK.

As explained in Chapter 14, marketing managers usually evaluate advertising and other communications expenditure as a percentage or ratio of sales revenue; such percentages are used as comparative indicators of performance. Research suggests that the advertising/sales ratios typically lie between 0.5 and 4 per cent for most travel and tourism businesses. But this is a very low average expenditure when viewed alongside the 20 per cent or more that is typical for many major fast-moving consumer goods. Indeed, although the service sector was well represented in the top fifty British advertisers spending league for 1997, excluding the breweries there was only one advertiser in the list (McDonald's Restaurants) that could be considered even relevant to the travel and tourism industry. These are overall percentages, of course, and a particular advertising campaign for specific segments may merit an exceptional 10 or 20 per cent of sales revenue spend to achieve the set objectives. Visitor attractions are among the higher spenders on advertising in the tourism industry, generally needing to spend 10 per cent or more of admissions revenue, partially reflecting the heavy reliance on spontaneous decisions to visit.

There is a trend towards an increase in public relations expenditure relative to advertising expenditure as organizations recognize the merits of a formal PR programme. The British Institute of Public Relations estimated that some 50 000 people now work in PR in the UK, giving a total PR turnover of approximately £1 billion per year. A breakdown of figures relating to travel and tourism is not available but the larger players in the industry appear to be following the general trend with a greater appreciation of PR reflected in the proportion of budget allocated to its activities.

The basic purpose of advertising and PR

Although both advertising and public relations are highly technical subjects in implementation, their essential functions are easy to grasp. They are primary means of manipulating demand and influencing buyer behaviour. Simply stated, they enable businesses to *reach* people in their homes or other places away from the places of production and delivery, and to *communicate* to them *messages* intended to influence their *purchasing behaviour*.

Tourism purchasing behaviour is often a complex process, however, comprising a web of personal roles, such as the idea initiator, the information finder, the influencer, the decider and the purchaser as well as the actual final user. Typically, many leisure tourism purchases are often seen as 'high risk' and they offer a 'group', not an individual experience that involves a pattern of joint decision-making within a larger decision-making unit, such as a family. Thus other people are concerned in the purchase and use decision as well as the actual buyers, and they need to be identified and reached with relevant messages.

Once an advertiser has identified the audience he hopes to influence, the *reach* part of the process is relatively straightforward. It is also the most expensive part, requiring money to buy space in advertising media. Driven by the accelerating cost of popular advertising space and increasing media fragmentation, there now exists substantial professional expertise in media planning, scheduling and buying, into which advertisers can tap. The primary problem for marketing managers, therefore, tends to focus on the choice of design and communication options in devising *messages* in a form most likely to communicate with the desired audience. The messages may be received, but if they are not understood or lack memorability, effective communication will fail to take place and the communications budget will be wasted.

Not surprisingly given their importance, decades of research have been conducted into the process of creation and interpretation of messages. Linear models examine all the steps of information processing from initial stages of product awareness through to trial purchase. Some linear models include opinion leaders who act as informal reference sources in endorsing the message. Semiotic studies interpret the meaning attached to advertising signs and symbols. Many communication campaigns are based upon the need to move prospects through the consecutive stages of attention, interest, desire to purchase and actual purchase (AIDA and similar models), while semiotics provides a rich source for message pre-testing and improvement. Such research is important but the exact ways in which both advertising and PR work on buyers' minds and influence their behaviour are still not fully understood. The communication process is highly complex and remains something of a 'black box'.

The complex communication process and the barriers to overcome

For reasons introduced in Chapter 5, all of us have barriers and filters in our minds. These barriers and filters, themselves products of our personalities, experiences and attitudes to life, condition our perception of the world around us. Bombarded by a continuous background 'noise' of up to 2000 advertising messages a day in developed countries, we use these barriers and filters to select the messages of interest to us. In other words, we only see what we want to see. It requires a combination of good understanding of the target audience, coupled with creatively pertinent message design, for tourism marketing managers to break through the clutter of background noise.

The basic 'reach and communicate' process is represented in Figure 15.1 in a linear model form. To understand it, consider the example of a national hotel group with a 10 per cent share of the market for sales conferences. The group uses its sales team to motivate key conference buyers in prospective client companies and it also targets business people who have attended a residential sales conference at least once in the last three years. The hotel group has decided to use press advertising to reach and gain an increased share of this target audience. Using data that would be derived in practice from consumer research, Figure 15.1 shows how the original message works through several stages to the purchase decision. Illustrating the barriers that diminish the impact of advertising, Figure 15.1 serves as a timely reminder of the necessity to integrate the different communication tools to drive the consumer through the process.

Column A represents 100 per cent of the potential target market of people who attend sales conferences; their profiles would be detailed in the marketing plan. With a realistic budget, the hotel group might hope to reach and expose its message to, say, 75 per cent of this total. This entails buying media space in magazines and other press that three-quarters of the target are known to look at, at least once during the campaign period.

Column B indicates that, in this case, 30 per cent of the target audience are able to recall seeing the hotel group's advertising. The remaining 45 per cent may not have glanced at the right page or have simply ignored it as irrelevant or uninteresting to them. In practice, the size of the

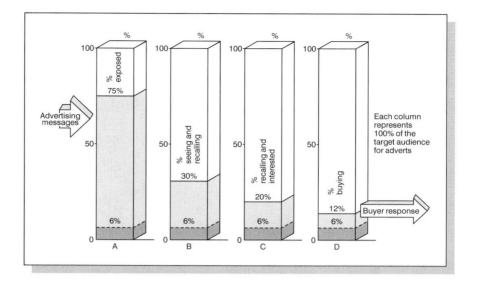

Figure 15.1
Filters in awareness
and interest that
obscure the
communication
process

advertisement, the frequency of insertion and the creative execution all influence the level of recall. Measurement of recall, either prompted or unprompted, is a commonly used method of advertising evaluation.

Column C reflects the proportion of the target audience (20 per cent) who remember the advertising and were additionally sufficiently interested to consider using the hotel at some time. This suggests a potentially positive attitude (recall alone may be for negative reasons!).

Column D represents the final stage of actual use and shows the 12 per cent of the target audience that attended a sales conference at one of the group's hotels in the twelve months duration of the campaign. The dotted line in all four columns shows the 6 per cent of existing buyers, for whom the advertising may have served to reinforce their intentions, but who would have purchased anyway – they are satisfied, repeat buyers. The additional 6 per cent represents first-time buyers, or lapsed buyers. The total 12 per cent market share is 2 percentage points higher than the original 10 per cent. Assuming that the objective was to raise market share to 12 per cent over twelve months, the advertising can be judged as successful. Its costs can be evaluated against the additional revenue gained.

Figure 15.1 makes it easy to appreciate the expertise required at each stage of the communication process to minimize wastage from one stage to the next. It explains why businesses have to monitor conversion rates between the stages to help measure and develop the effectiveness of their communications campaigns. The expertise implicit in Figure 15.1 includes:

- Media purchase decisions best calculated to reach the target cost-effectively (percentage of A).
- Design of appealing messages and symbols best calculated to arrest and capture attention (percentage of B).

- Communicating memorably the key points that matter to buyers (percentage of C).
- Motivating prospective buyers and turning interest into purchase (percentage of D).

Defining advertising and public relations

The American Marketing Association defines advertising as *'any paid form of non-personal presentation and promotion of ideas, goods or services [to a targeted] audience by an identified sponsor'*. The words in brackets are inserted by the authors to convey the fact that segmentation and targeting always precede advertising. Several points help to unwrap the definition. First, 'non-personal' implies the use of media to access a large audience, as distinct from individually targeted forms of communication using a name and address (direct marketing). Second, an 'identified sponsor' means that the advertiser's name or brand is clearly evident in the communication.

The advertiser has full control over the message content and, depending on the budget size, can choose advertisement size, position and insertion frequency.

These decisions are, however, subject to legally imposed regulations and voluntary codes of practice. The British Code of Advertising Practice states that all advertisements should be 'legal, decent, honest and truthful', show 'responsibility to the consumer and to society' and obey the 'business principles of fair competition'. Other countries have similar codes to regulate advertisers' conduct in what are judged to be consumers' best interests.

Most travel and tourism advertising is product focused and targeted either at the public or the travel trade. But large organizations, such as airlines and hotel groups, also buy media space to communicate with shareholders, politicians or the financial sector. Here, the emphasis is on corporate name and image.

Public relations operate at the corporate level as well as within marketing communications. Indeed, within a large organization the two are treated quite separately, with corporate PR funded from corporate resources as opposed to a marketing budget allocation. The British Institute of Public Relations defines PR as *'the planned and sustained effort to establish and maintain goodwill and mutual understanding between an organization and its publics'*. Public relations may be personal or non-personal, for it uses an array of techniques. It does not, however, involve the purchase of media space. This fact limits the control of message content, although it may enhance perceived credibility with the audience.

Two points from the definition need clarification. First, professional PR is about building 'mutual understanding' or trust between the organization and its publics; it is about two-way communication and is strongly rooted in the idea of developing credibility ahead of raising visibility. Second, the range of 'publics' or target audiences is typically much wider than for advertising. In travel and tourism, publics such as local residents and businesses, other industry sectors, environmental pressure groups, politicians and suppliers of service components, all spring readily to mind as particularly important in developing 'mutual understanding'.

Although fully planned in its direction, PR is also more opportunistic than advertising, exploiting events as they occur and managing negative incidents. An extreme example of negative incidents requiring an orchestrated response was the crash of the Concorde in Paris in 2000.

Terms commonly used in advertising practice

Being technical subjects, advertising and public relations are accompanied by their own terminology. Eighteen commonly used terms are presented in annotated form in Table 15.1. They are intended to serve as an aide-mémoire.

A small note on the distinction between 'above' and 'below' the line expenditure is included here rather than within the table as its usage is now largely historic. Advertising was traditionally referred to as 'above the line' expenditure because agencies used to earn commission from the purchase of media space, whereas other activities were conducted on a fee-paying basis, hence the term ' below-the-line' expenditure. With the shift towards alternative approaches to agency remuneration, the advent of the Internet and the increased expenditure on so-called 'below-the-line' activities such as direct marketing and sales promotions, these original distinctions are less helpful in today's environment.

Stages in the advertising process

The six main stages in the advertising process are noted below and explained in the pages that follow. Fuller explanations can be found in the recommended texts at the end of the chapter.

- Advertising objectives.
- Target audience identification.
- Creative planning.
- Media planning.
- Media costs.
- Measuring the results.

Advertising objectives

Any advertising campaign needs clearly stated objectives about what it is setting out to achieve, related to the processes expected to take place in target segments' minds, such as awareness, interest and positive feelings.

Audience	Often used generically to describe readers, viewers, listeners exposed to all forms of media. 'Target audience' describes the segments identified for communication purposes.
Copy	The words included in an advertisement, normally having three components: a 'headline' to attract attention; 'body copy' to convey information; 'strap line' to conclude or sign off.
Coverage	The proportion of the target audience that is reached by the advertisement.
CPT	'Cost per thousand' of the target group to whom any advertisement is exposed. Cost per thousand is a basic cost figure used in buying media space. As it suggests, it refers to the average cost of reaching 1000 of the target audience, and is useful for comparison across different media types and vehicles.
Creative execution	The choice of appealing themes, ideas, pictures, situations, symbols and words chosen to communicate the desired message.
Direct response	Advertising from which the intended audience response is a direct contact with the producer by telephone, letter, coupon or Internet, without going through a distribution channel such as a travel agent.
Editorial matter	The content of the media, other than advertising, controlled by editorial policies.
Fees and commission	Traditionally, advertising agencies earned their income through commission paid on purchase of media space. Today, payment structures vary, using fee-based activities and/or results achieved alongside commission-based payments.
Frequency	The number of times an advertisement is placed or inserted in a specific time period. A 'burst' strategy concentrates the advertisements in a short period of time, and a 'drip' strategy shows advertisements steadily over a longer period of time.
Insertion	One appearance of an advertisement. Media buyers usually purchase a series of insertions, rather than a single insertion.
Media	Newspapers, television, radio and all other mass circulation means of communicating either paid or unpaid messages to people. Advertising media are those that sell space to advertisers as a commercial transaction.
Media vehicle	Individual media titles, e.g. *The Times*, *Newsweek*, *Vogue*, etc.
OTS	'Opportunities to see' or opportunities by the target audience to see any particular advertisement. It is a function of coverage and frequency (coverage × frequency).
Position	The place where the advertisement is shown, e.g. front cover, inside front/back cover, left/right pages, top/bottom, etc. Media costs vary with the quality of position.
Proposition	The single-minded clear message of an advertisement, usually focused on the reason to purchase the product i.e. the key benefit.
Rate cards	The published prices for advertising space produced by the media vehicle concerned. Agencies receive discounts on the published prices, which was part of the commission-based system.
Share of voice	Compares an organization's advertising spend to the total market spend on advertising. In the UK, domestic tourism and inbound tourism have a small share of voice compared to outbound tourism.
USP	'Unique selling proposition' – a particular product or organization characteristic that distinguishes it from competitors and is a main reason to buy.

Table 15.1 Advertising and PR terms in common use

Classically, advertising is best at creating awareness, informing, persuading and reminding. Thus, the objective might be to *inform* the audience of product benefits, a new product launch or a revised pricing structure; to *persuade* them by changing attitudes towards the brand, building product preference or altering product positioning; or to *remind* the consumer after purchase to reduce post-purchase anxiety, trigger word-of-mouth recommendation or keep a brand name front-of-mind for future purchases. Objectives must be fixed to a specified time period and be amenable to measurement. For example, 'to raise awareness of business-class upgrade in a target audience from 30 per cent in January 2000 to 60 per cent by April 2000' is specific enough to be evaluated.

Some advertising in travel and tourism is designed to stimulate 'immediate' action. Direct response advertisements with a Web site address or free-phone telephone number may seek to increase brochure request rates and generate enquiries or bookings. Similarly, classified advertisements are often linked to late deals and price cuts. But, generally speaking, advertising is chiefly about consumer or travel trade awareness of and interest in the brand and, like all marketing mix objectives, relates back to the marketing objectives and strategies that drive management decisions.

Target audience identification

The target audience needs to be profiled in detail, including the media habits that will facilitate *reach*. Although the target audience may be the intended purchaser and user, other members of the decision-making unit must not be ignored. Opinion leaders and the travel trade are also potential audiences.

Creative planning

The aim is to produce a creative execution using pictures, symbols and words that capture the message in a way judged best able to penetrate the barriers and filters of the target audience. Memorable examples of creative executions in travel and tourism include:

- 'The World's favourite airline' (British Airways).
- 'I love New York' (New York State).
- 'We try harder' (Avis).
- 'Everything under the sun', and subsequent campaigns such as 'Passion for Life' (Spain).
- 'Mind Body Spirit' (Champneys).

Because of the expense surrounding creative execution, concepts are often tested as they are developed. For example, storyboards and key frames may be used as visual stimulation to gain the reaction of audiences, using focus groups. Advertising agencies often require clients to 'sign off' at key stages in creative planning to avoid backtracking that can undermine the whole process.

Over the years, many businesses in the travel and tourism industry have been damaged by a reputation for over-promising in advertising, creating expectations among buyers that cannot be matched by the reality of the experience. The intangible nature of leisure tourism in particular makes such behaviour tempting and hotels, destinations, airlines and attractions have all succumbed. But such practice runs contrary to the fundamental principles of marketing centred on delivering tourist satisfaction; it creates bad word of mouth as well as negative media interest and may damage or destroy the prospect of creating repeat business.

As Morgan and Pritchard put it, 'tour operator advertising has frequently proved to be a fertile breeding ground for clichéd and even bad ads as operators have focused on sun, sand and sex clichés or value for money concepts. Originality has tended to play a very minor role' (Morgan and Pritchard, 2000: 34).

Media planning

Concurrent with creative planning is media planning. It is concerned with programming the ways in which advertisements will be seen and heard through media selection, scheduling and buying. The choice of *media type* is wide for travel and tourism, as indicated in the list below. Approximate numbers for selected media types are given in italics and serve to illustrate the complexity of the marketplace. The figures are taken from the British Advertising Association 1996 estimates for the UK.

- Television (terrestrial and non-terrestrial) – including Teletext.
- National press (daily and Sunday newspapers and magazine supplements. *Eleven daily titles and eleven Sunday titles*).
- Banners on Internet search engines and Web sites.
- Regional and local press and free sheets (daily and weekly. *Around 570, excluding free sheets*).
- Consumer magazines and special interest magazines (*over 2100*).
- Business and professional magazines (e.g. travel trade press. *Over 4000*).
- Directories and *Yellow Pages*.
- Tourist board brochures, guides and directories.
- In-house magazines (airline and hotel magazines selling space to other operators).
- Radio (national and local stations. *Over 170 commercial stations*).
- Outdoor and transport poster sites.
- Cinema (*around 2000 screens*).
- Direct mail (using purchased address lists).
- Miscellaneous 'space' for sale or so-called 'ambient media' (e.g. airport trolleys, towed aerial banners, balloon displays, bus tickets, petrol pumps, airline ticket wallets and visitor attraction tickets).

Modern media planners use sophisticated software to aid decision-making in media selection, buying and scheduling. The fundamental principles, however, rest on two basic requirements:

1 That the target audience can be identified and profiled with some precision, using key demographic, socioeconomic and psychographic variables (see Chapter 7)

2 That media owners can provide reader/viewer numbers and characteristics with considerable precision. Because revenue from advertising generally far exceeds revenue from sales to readers/viewers, the media have a vested interest in providing such analysis.

According to Smith (1998), media planners need to resolve a number of issues relevant to buying advertising space:

- Audience size, type and profile.
- Advertising objectives; allocated budget and cost per thousand (as discussed elsewhere in this chapter).
- Creative scope of the different media in terms of colour, contrast, sound and movement.
- Lead-in times for booking space. Some press are suited to topical messages relating to events, while planning other media may require a long lead-in time.
- Compatibility of media type and vehicle with product positioning, hence the old adage 'the medium is the message'. The image of the media vehicle itself should 'rub off' on the product to positive effect.
- Anticipated activity of competitors to advertising; will they aim to copy, or counter it?
- Audience state of mind or receptivity at the time of receiving the message. It is no accident that holidays feature heavily in Sunday newspapers when the recipient is in a relaxed frame of mind.
- Regulations and restrictions in operation, including clearance procedures (varies with media type).
- Amount of space sought; the frequency, timing and mix of media types available.

Some authors refer to the creation of a 'personal media network', where the aim is to wrap the messages around the target audience throughout the day. Target X wakes in the morning to the message on his local commercial radio station, looks at the advertisement in a newspaper over breakfast, drives to and from work past the poster advertisements, and relaxes in the evening to the cinema or television advertisement. It may also flash up at intervals on e-mail and on his mobile phone.

Media costs

The critical issue for media planners is juggling *media costs*. As much as travel and tourism companies wish to screen television advertisements, at roughly £110 000 in the UK for national ITV broadcasting of a single thirty-second advertisement, national television coverage is prohibitively expensive for most. All commercial media publish rate cards showing their regular prices for advertising spaces. These prices reflect the size of an advertisement and the numbers of readers/viewers that the media vehicle reaches. The standard in the industry is the CPT reached. If a full page colour advertisement in the *Sunday Times* magazine is seen by 4 million adults and costs £60 000, the CPT for that media vehicle is £15.00. The CPT for other media may only be £4.50, but there is more to media buying than CPT. Some British media, such as *TV Times* and *Radio Times*, have traditionally been known to be especially effective in travel and tourism around December and January time. Accordingly their CPT rates are higher, but may still represent good value for money calculated in responses and subsequent bookings per £1000 spent.

As with any perishable product, the rate card prices are indicative only. They change as the time of production approaches and agencies are highly skilled at bargaining and negotiating discounts. Few agencies pay anything like the nominal rate card prices. As the number of media opportunities escalates, including the Internet, the expertise available to advertisers for cost effective media purchasing is becoming an ever more important criterion in agency selection.

Measuring the results of advertising

Mainly because advertising and PR expenditure are only two of the ways used to influence sales in the tourism industry, and often only a small percentage of the total marketing budget, it is seldom possible to isolate the sales effect of such expenditure with any precision. Price cuts, competitor activity, sales promotions, political events and even the weather can all distort the relationship between advertising and outcomes. Yet advertisers are increasingly demanding accountability for the results of their advertising and, without measurement, there is no way of knowing how effective communications expenditure has been and no evidence on which to justify a budget allocation in the next year.

Standard techniques available to large firms include:

- *Response measurement* – where advertising is designed to produce a certain action, such as an enquiry, brochure request or booking, it is common practice to code advertisements with letters or numbers that identify the media used and the date of insertion. Replies can then be assessed against the original expenditure. The use of coupons to generate responses is common in travel and tourism and monitoring telephone calls and Web site hits are also relevant. Ratios of enquiries/bookings etc. to advertising expenditure can be calculated and used for comparative purposes across media, as can the average advertising cost per enquiry etc. With such data, even the simplest advertising programmes can be fine-tuned year-on-year.
- *Market research measures of the communication effect* – before and after sample surveys of the target audience can be used to quantify changes in awareness, interest, attitudes and preferences. Many advertising agencies conduct recall tests, either unprompted where no stimulus is given, or prompted where the respondent is shown a

card naming or illustrating recent advertising campaigns and asked to indicate which he remembers seeing.

- *Pre-testing of communication effects* – to help generate a more successful creative execution prior to full implementation of a large campaign, focus groups of the target audience are a popular method. Many travel and tourism organizations have the advantage of multisite operations, where 'live' tests can be carried on a small scale before a campaign is taken nationwide. Equipment in laboratory settings can be used to measure eye movement, pupil dilation and other physiological responses to images shown.

The role of advertising agencies

Only very small businesses, such as guesthouses or local visitor attractions, are likely to undertake their own advertising without professional help. At the very least, as noted earlier, advertising agencies can assist with the purchase of advertising space at discounted rates. Even small to medium-sized clients with about £20 000 to spend on media may find it advantageous to approach regional or local advertising agencies. Large organizations prefer multinational agencies whose offices or networks reflect their patterns of business. Most advertising agencies enjoy working on travel and tourism accounts as intrinsically interesting products and may welcome the account as a stimulating break from their usual subject matter.

Typically, advertising agencies today are leaner than they were during the 1980s. Many have responded to the growth in so-called 'below-the-line' communications activities by adding such services to their armoury. Such agencies can, therefore, take responsibility for an integrated communications campaign. As well as full participation in the marketing planning process, advertising agencies typically provide:

- Creative planning and execution, including developing original concepts and ideas, design of all visual material and copy, and any pre-launch research.
- Media planning, scheduling and buying, and negotiating discounted rates.
- Advertising production services and implementation of agreed campaign elements and materials.
- Monitoring and evaluation of advertising performance.

Advertising agencies are usually selected through competitive tender and, once selected, seek to build up long-term relationships with their clients. The relationship between agency and client is handled by an account director or executive, who ensures that creative and media briefs are adhered to and liaises between the agency team and the client. In addition to the creative and media team, 'traffic control' staff are needed to ensure that advertisements get to the right place at the right time and that deadlines are met.

Public relations in travel and tourism

Public relations programmes are usually thought of as complementary to media advertising. They are, but it is missing an important contribution to perceive PR only its narrow role of generating non-paid-for media coverage. Good practice indicates that effective PR starts with developing credibility across an organization as a whole before seeking to raise its visibility through media relations and other techniques. With the increasing emphasis on PR activity, two points are stressed in relation to travel and tourism. First, much of tourism is inherently interesting, capable of catching media attention more easily than most physical goods. This is not to say that achieving media attention is uncompetitive, however. Of the 125 million press releases distributed in the UK every year, around 121 million are estimated to be thrown by editors into the waste bin (Smith, 1998). Nonetheless, with professional handling, most travel and tourism organizations should be able to exploit a wide range of creative subjects. Second, as 'ethics and social responsibility have traditionally been the bastion of public relations' (Smith, 1998: 361), PR is expected to continue its growth in importance as environmental issues and the implementation of sustainable tourism rise up the political and business agenda in the twenty-first century.

In common with all other forms of marketing communications, successful PR needs a planned and budgeted programme incorporating objectives and publics to be targeted, activities to be carried out and research and evaluation to assess performance against the objectives set. The remainder of this chapter briefly reviews these processes.

PR objectives

Public relations objectives may relate to the product/market needs level or to the corporate level (or both). They can also be divided into internal corporate PR objectives, such as building loyalty among staff or more effective employee relations, and external corporate PR objectives, such as developing better community relations, altering public images and attitudes, correcting a public misunderstanding or keeping influential groups informed of changes. All objectives stem from a desire to instil trust of the organization among its publics and its employees and PR executives are paid to defend and promote their company's reputation. They are, therefore, required to look internally at the organization to ensure credibility before, say, seeking to raise awareness externally of the organization's environmental performance or safety procedures.

Target audience identification

It is worth repeating that PR deals with a much wider range of target audiences than advertising. Potential audiences or publics include existing and potential buyers, suppliers and distributors in the travel trade, present and future employees, the media and opinion leaders, local and central government, planning and regulatory bodies relevant to tourism, investors and the financial sector, local communities and businesses, industries whose activities impinge on tourism, trade

associations and pressure groups. Some public relations agencies special-
ise in targeting particular publics, for example, the financial community,
employees or government.

Public relation activities

The public relations activities included as part of PR programmes are
noted in Table 15.2. Some are more suited to corporate PR than they are

Writing and editing	Press releases and feature articles for busy editors, annual reports, shareholder reports, newsletters and in-house magazines, film and video scripts, press packs.
Building press relations	Mailing lists and databases of media contacts, liaising with media.
Public speaking	Meetings, presentations, platform participation, after dinner speaking, seminar papers, television and radio interviews, community events.
Training, briefing and counselling executives	In handling media interviews for all types of media.
Press launches and press conferences	Announcing new products, changes or improvements, brochure or advertising campaign launches, annual report publications.
Photography	Studio and location photographic shoots, maintaining photographic library, photo calls.
Lobbying and persuading	Regulatory bodies and government at local, national and international level, e.g. over abolition of duty free, tourist taxes, visa controls, unfavourable policies or laws. Sometimes manoeuvring against competitors, sometimes in collaboration for the greater good of the industry.
Event management	Staged events around which a story of media interest is woven, award events based on employee motivation schemes or environmental programmes, celebrations such as millennium or jubilee, personality appearances, stage-managed product launches.
Product visits	Open days for general public, familiarization trips for distributors, product visits for journalists.
Exhibitions and trade fairs	Planning and running exhibitions, attending trade fairs and conferences
Corporate identity	Including corporate graphic identity from business cards to on-site signage, logo design.
Sponsorship programmes	Producing packages to attract potential sponsors plus formation of own sponsorship programme.
Product placement	Getting the organization or destination into films, television, and video footage
Crisis management	Development of possible crisis scenarios and relevant skills training. Handling negative events as they occur.

Table 15.2 Types of public relations activity in travel and tourism

Product defects	Outdated lifts in older hotels, brochure inaccuracies.
Product disaster	Aircraft crash, ferry or cruise ship sinkings, hotel building collapse.
Industrial action	Strikes in airlines or hospitality industry, picket lines.
Service delivery system breakdown	Failure of computer reservation system, aircraft fault to remedy.
Takeovers and corporate raids	Hostile bids for an organization.
Customer/employee accidents	Injury or death. Vehicle collisions and crashes, death from natural causes in old age, drink or recreational drug-related injuries and deaths.
Crime against tourists	Pick pockets, vandalism, car theft, muggings, knife attacks, danger of paedophilia in attractions targeted at children.
Collapse of supplier	Airline or tour operator bankruptcy.
Environmental pollution incidents	Fuel spillage, algal blooms, beach and bathing water pollution from sewage.
Health scares	Food poisoning, water contamination, outbreaks of viruses, epidemics.
Tourist/employee kidnapping	Taken hostage for political or financial reasons.
Terrorism and threat of terrorism	Shooting of tourists, bombs in aircraft or hijacking incidents, product sabotage, also threats of terrorism and sabotage. Tourism seen as good way of gaining publicity for a cause, making tourism vulnerable to terrorism.
Conflict or war	International and civil conflict, armed protest, riots, military coups.
Severe weather	Droughts, heat waves, lack of snow fall for skiing holidays, flooding, storms, hurricanes and cyclones.
Natural disasters	Earthquakes, volcanic eruptions, hurricanes, landslides, avalanches, tidal waves, fire.

Table 15.3 Potential negative events requiring crisis management in travel and tourism

to marketing but many of these tools are flexible and can be adapted. The spectrum of options is wide-ranging and each may be considered a specialization in its own right. Indeed some, for example exhibitions and sponsorship, are treated separately from public relations in large organizations. Five of the activities of particular relevance in travel and tourism are pulled out of Table 15.2 for further comment below.

- *Media relations* are still the backbone of PR activity. Media relations are about obtaining non-paid-for media coverage and activity includes writing press releases, feature articles, scripts, preparing press packs, obtaining interviews, holding press conferences and photo calls, and creating an up-to-date database of media contacts. Media relations requires day-to-day maintenance for smooth operation.

- *Crisis management* is especially important in tourism organizations. Given the inseparability of production and consumption and product perishability, the vulnerability of the industry to external events is considerable. The potential for damage to corporate image and reputation incurred by negative incidents requires skills training and professional management to be in place to deal with events that are bound to occur at some time. Problems are exacerbated if customers are in unfamiliar environments. Table 15.3 illustrates the extensive range of negative events that could befall any tourism organization or destination at any time. Some are controllable to an extent, for example those relating to product quality. But most are uncontrollable and even unpredictable. Whether caused by natural events or human errors, some of these negative events may be localized in their impact but many are likely to have far-reaching consequences. Destinations, unaffected directly, may still be damaged by events, such as tidal waves, flooding and hurricanes if they occur in a neighbouring area. Most people's geographic perceptions are hazy and it is widely recognized that the Gulf War affected USA visits to Europe, although the conflict was almost as far from Northern Europe as it was from the east coast of America. Recovery time from any negative event will vary with incident severity, crisis management handling and the strength of the tourism brand concerned. PR professionals plan activity for at least twelve months after a major incident and journalists often revisit a particular incident to see what changes have been made one year later.

- *Product placement* is another form of PR and part of a $100 million industry where particular products are 'placed' in films and documentaries. There are no rate cards for this activity; deals are negotiated on a fee and/or promotion basis, and there are product placement agencies that specialise in this field. Just as fast cars can be 'placed' in James Bond films, so can airlines, restaurants, hotels, car rental agencies and destinations. Apparent endorsement by a film's star will be more influential than a simple shot of a background logo. Destination tourism officers encourage filming in their locations as successful television or film productions can boost visitor numbers at a fraction of the cost of an advertising campaign. Paul Hogan (*Crocodile Dundee*) for Australia, Steve McQueen for San Francisco, *Inspector Morse* for Oxford, and *Bergerac* for Jersey in the Channel Islands have all served to raise awareness and interest in destinations, increasing tourism. Three recent films featuring Scotland, *Braveheart*, *Rob Roy*, and *Loch Ness* are estimated to have generated £7–15 million additional visitor spending in the Scottish economy (Morgan and Pritchard, 2000). Product placement is increasingly a matter for actively pursuing potential opportunities. Of course, if a product placement agreement facilitates integration with the rest of the communications mix, sales promotions and advertising can enhance the effect of the original product placement. The role of PR is to exploit the potential of the opportunity with press releases, feature articles, media interviews, Web sites and so on.

- *Sponsorship* is also big business. According to the British Association for Business Sponsorship of the Arts, theatres, museums, opera, festivals and music each enjoy a greater than 10 per cent slice of a total £72 million spend by corporate sponsors in the UK. Travel and tourism possesses plenty of potential to attract such sponsorship from business. The job of packaging benefits, identifying and negotiating with possible sponsors and carrying out agreed programmes often falls within the remit of PR. Larger firms need to plan which events, causes or activities they might approach to support and enhance their own image and achieve corporate objectives. For example, a residential sports activity centre might sponsor local athletes and achieve increased business through improved awareness that PR coverage brings.

- Typically *exhibitions and travel fairs* may be dealt with by a PR department if they are not managed as part of the sales function. Participation in exhibitions and travel fairs has to be planned, monitored and evaluated in parallel with other communications techniques, to meet specific budgeted objectives through a programme of events. Exhibitions and travel fairs often prove fruitful for competitive intelligence work as well as for generating new product ideas and providing opportunities to talk with the public and the travel trade. For smaller businesses there is a trend towards shared or 'umbrella' stands where they may achieve their objectives under a collective banner provided, for example, by a destination marketing organization.

Table 15.2 indicates the breadth and depth of activity involved in professional PR programmes. Even a small tourism organization with a small budget will find a well-planned 'do-it-yourself' PR programme beneficial in achieving communication objectives, and often more effective than a low-cost attempt to influence target audiences using media advertising. Only large organizations are likely to employ a public relations agency.

Measuring the results of PR

As in all marketing activities, evaluation of PR results should be against the objectives set for the programme. Measuring the outcomes of PR is not an exact science, but usually includes:

- Media content analysis using word counts or, more popularly, column centimetres of media coverage obtained. Column centimetres can be converted to currency equivalents by calculating how much the same space would have cost if purchased at rate card prices for advertising purposes. Key word counts monitor the number of times the organization's name or brands are mentioned.

- A more qualitative approach to media content analysis can assess whether comments were favourable, neutral or unfavourable, note the inclusion of photographs and headlines, and the position of the material on the page (top, middle, bottom, which column, etc.), as well as the type of page itself (editorial, front cover, inside back cover, left, right of page, etc.).
- For larger PR campaigns, attitude or awareness market research studies carried out before and after the programme can be used to monitor any changes in consumer and other publics' perceptions of an organization.

Most large businesses use a press-cutting bureau to carry out a continuous media content analysis. In addition to their control function, press cuttings can also provide material for product endorsement to be used in direct marketing print, exhibition stands, press releases and Web sites.

Chapter summary

This chapter presents advertising and public relations as two of the most important and sometimes the most expensive choices to be made by marketing managers when planning communications campaigns. As communications tools, they have different but complementary roles to play and it is vital to integrate them with the rest of the communications mix and the marketing mix as a planned whole. Both advertising and public relations are primarily used to communicate messages designed to influence attitude, feelings and understanding in target audiences away from the places where tourism products are delivered and sold. The communications process is complex, comprising multiple filters and barriers to overcome. Any message that breaks through must be relevant to the audience and creatively encoded; to paraphrase an old Levi's slogan, *it must zag in a world that zigs.*

The main stages in advertising revolve around objective setting, target audience identification, creative and media planning, budget agreement and measurement. This process is broadly mirrored for public relations. It is worth stressing three points that are particular to tourism services. The first is accurate targeting of the audience because errors in the communications mix that attract the wrong segments can cause on-site tourist incompatibility and dissatisfaction with the experience delivered. The second is that employees and destination residents form a secondary audience for many communication messages. If consumer campaigns serve to raise the morale and motivation of internal stakeholders this is a valuable effect. But it can be wholly damaging if ill-considered messages create resentment and upset. Flight attendants may be riled by airline advertising portraying them as sex symbols, residents by destination advertising of a native paradise, and so on. Such feelings in those entrusted with the delivery of the service will, in turn, damage visitor satisfaction. The third point, reflecting the fact that much of tourism is a business of 'selling dreams', is the constant danger of over promising and the negative impact on visitors of perceived failure to deliver.

In travel and tourism the ancient nonsense that 'half of my advertising is wasted but I don't know which half' is still being peddled. It should be rejected. Planned as outlined in this chapter, advertising and public relations are demonstrably effective ways of linking products to markets and organizations to their publics. Sometimes, when times are really hard and sales are falling, the only way to succeed is to increase budgets. For an identifiable cost, both advertising and PR provide opportunities for organizations to reach and communicate their chosen messages to selected audiences. It is worth noting that there are no willing advertisers in the world, only operators who invest in advertising and PR because they do not know of any more economical way of achieving their aims.

Further reading

Brassington, F. and Pettit, S. (2000). *Principles of Marketing*. Chapters 15 and 19, 2nd edn, Prentice-Hall.

Jobber, D. (1998). *Principles and Practice of Marketing*. Chapters 11 and 14, 2nd edn, McGraw-Hill.

Kotler, P. and Armstong, G. (1999). *Principles of Marketing*. Chapter 15, 8th edn, Prentice-Hall.

Morgan, N. and Pritchard, A. (2000). *Marketing Communications: An Integrated Approach*. Chapters 2, 3 and 4, Butterworth-Heinemann.

Smith, P. R. (1998). *Marketing Communications: An Integrated Approach*. Chapters 3, 7, 11, 14, 15 and 16, 2nd edn, Kogan Page.

CHAPTER 16

Sales promotion, merchandising and personal selling

In general, the purpose of advertising is to improve attitudes towards a brand [product], while the objective of promotion is to translate favourable attitudes into actual purchase. Advertising cannot close a sale because its impact is too far from the point of purchase, but promotion can and does. (Davidson, 1975: 190)

The previous chapter explained how advertising and PR messages are used to communicate with prospective buyers away from the places of production, consumption and purchase of products. The main object of that communication is to move people towards purchase decisions at the point of sale, with good awareness of product offers and with their attitudes favourably disposed.

This chapter explains how a different range of mainly tactical promotional techniques are used to communicate special incentives designed to motivate prospective buyers, especially at the point of sale. The main object of this communication is to convert initial awareness and interest in products into actual sales.

The 'perishability' of tourism products means that marketing managers are constantly preoccupied with the necessity to manipulate demand in response to unforeseen events as well as the normal daily, weekly or seasonal fluctuations. Sales promotion and merchandising methods are especially suitable for such short-run demand adjustments and they are vital weapons in the marketing armoury of most travel and tourism businesses.

The chapter begins with the reasons for using sales promotion and merchandising. It proceeds with definitions, the meaning of 'point of sale' and the role of display. The three targets for sales promotion are identified, followed by a review of the marketing objectives attainable by sales promotion and the range of techniques available. The chapter outlines the process of planning for sales promotions, budgeting and evaluating results, and ends with a review of the role of personal selling in the tourism industry.

Reasons for using sales promotion and merchandising

At the stage when the sales promotion elements of a marketing campaign are planned most of the elements of the marketing mix for established products have already been largely determined by previous strategic decisions. For example, in the case of a hotel chain planning a marketing campaign for the next six months, its products exist, the price range is broadly fixed and the normal channels of distribution are established. In practice even some key promotional elements, such as advertising, brochures, exhibitions and use of a sales force are largely committed, with only limited scope for significant changes unless a crisis in demand occurs.

Against this background marketing managers are well aware that, for predictable and unpredictable reasons, daily demand for their products will be subject to surges and fluctuations. Occasionally demand will exceed supply but more often it will not and demand manipulation is a primary requirement of tactical marketing. For example, predictable shortfalls in demand for city hotels occur from Friday to Sunday and at certain times of the year. Other shortfalls in leisure tourism demand also occur, often as a result of unfavourable political, economic or social events and, sometimes, the weather. Such events affect demand and require rapid tactical promotional responses. Some events are positive, such as favourable exchange rate movements, and these represent opportunities to be exploited with equally rapid tactical responses.

Sales promotion and merchandising defined

Adapting the American Marketing Association definition, the essential characteristics of sales promotion and merchandising are:

Sales promotion and merchandising are parts of marketing communications other than advertising, PR, personal selling, and sales literature. They are techniques primarily designed to stimulate consumer purchasing and dealer and sales-force effectiveness in the short-term, through temporary incentives and displays. Traditionally such techniques have been known as 'below-the-line' marketing.

The definition stresses the short-term, non-regular, incentive nature of sales promotion and the fact that it extends beyond consumers to distribution networks and the sales force. Much of sales promotion in practice takes place at points of sale, and the term *merchandising* is often used specifically to mean sales promotion at the point of sale.

Points of sale

Having stressed the important distinction between forms of marketing communication that take place away from the 'point of sale' and other forms that focus on it, it is necessary to consider what this means in practice. At its simplest, a point of sale (POS) is any location at which a purchase transaction takes place.

Chapter 18 deals with distribution networks created to provide access or points of sale to products at places away from the producers' premises. But in travel and tourism 'point of sale' means much more than distribution networks. It covers three very different kinds of location, each with very different marketing requirements:

External POS	e.g. retail travel agency (for most products), ticket/booking office or desk (for transport and car rental) or tourist information centre (TIC – especially if bookings are taken).
Internal, 'in-house' (or 'on-site')	e.g. reception desk (hotels and attractions); a reception desk may also operate a referral system linked with other outlets in the same organization. Locations within an operator's premises such as bars, restaurants, retail sales points (souvenirs and other items), duty-free POS shops, etc.
Customer's home as POS	Individual customers making enquiries or bookings, responding to direct mail and promotional offers by television, radio, promotional mail, Internet or telephone calls.

Since 1995, and especially by the turn of the twenty-first century, Internet Web sites have become a major new development in the array of points of sale that tourism businesses can choose to provide. The Internet acts primarily as a new personal POS within customers' homes. For some operators, such as budget airlines and hotels, the combination of Internet and call centres, now provide the principal POS for the business, acting in lieu of traditional distribution systems. (See Chapter 18.)

All readers will be familiar with sales promotions in traditional shops and other external points of sale. Because the production and consumption of tourism service products on a producer's own premises are simultaneous, however, a considerable amount of internal sales promotion also occurs 'on-site' or 'in-house'. Service businesses have full control

257

of their premises and continuous opportunities for on-site promotion in ways that are not available to manufacturers of most physical goods. For tour operators, for example, their destination representative are typically trained to act as an 'on-site' points of sale for excursions, events, etc., persuading 'captive' customers to buy specific products and generally to spend more once they have arrived at their destination. Airlines use cabin crew to promote in-flight sales of a range of goods. Banks, supermarkets and post offices provide other service industry illustrations of growing awareness of the value of 'in-house' promotion.

In travel and tourism, apart from tour operators and airlines, most businesses achieve the bulk of their annual sales by dealing directly with their customers through a combination of guides and brochures, or in direct response to advertising and the Internet. Each of these techniques conveys opportunities for sales promotion in customers' homes that, if not unique to travel and tourism, are certainly a hallmark of the industry. The buyer's home is increasingly the primary target for tourism promotion.

The three main targets for sales promotion

Tactical techniques designed to stimulate sales to customers have three main targets:

- Individual buyers or customer segments in their homes or place of work.
- Distribution networks (points of sale), including 'in-house'.
- Sales force.

Individual buyers

All sales promotion is designed to achieve *additional* short-run purchases by customers that a business believes would not occur without specific marketing action. Aimed directly at buyers, the objective is to provide specific incentives or inducements to buy particular products at particular times. Much of sales promotion is restricted to chosen segments to avoid the dilution of total sales revenue that occurs if unnecessary incentives are offered to all customers, many of whom intended to purchase without the added incentive.

Distribution networks

If an organization receives a large proportion of its sales revenue through third party distributors, such as travel agents, achieving customer sales objectives will require their active participation. Distributors are bombarded daily by operators wishing them to provide extra display space for their products and other forms of support. Any special effort therefore usually requires special incentives and if they are not provided, sales targets are unlikely to be achieved.

Sales force

For larger organizations, sales forces are generally required to service and motivate corporate customers and distribution networks. Being human, any additional effort on top of continuous routine sales efforts often requires some additional forms of incentive or reward. See later in this chapter.

For larger organizations, sales promotions typically include all three targets. They must be integrated to maximize effectiveness and be co-ordinated with the other communication tools covered in Chapter 15.

Marketing objectives attainable by sales promotion

The types of tactical marketing objectives attainable through sales promotion efforts are summarized in Figure 16.1. In practice the objectives stem from response to a combination of factors that may vary on a weekly basis, including:

- Sales volume targets and variance analysis (see Chapter 14).
- Problems of over- or under-capacity of production.
- Competitors' actions.
- Other business environment factors representing unforeseen threats or opportunities.
- Problems with the coverage, stocking and/or display of brochures in distribution networks.

Both for distributors and for sales forces, sales promotion objectives tend to be implemented through display techniques. 'Display' denotes the availability, visibility and accessibility of products in distribution outlets

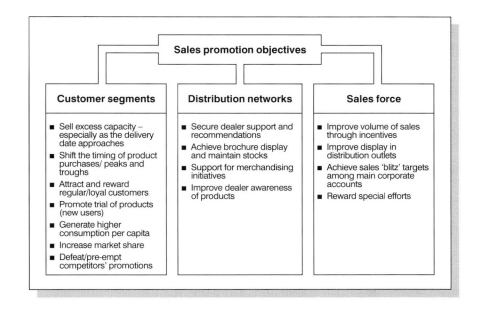

Figure 16.1
Marketing objectives attainable by sales promotion

or points of sale. Every metre of counter, shelf or rack space performs a selling role for products in a retail travel agency or other outlet. Other things being equal, more space in more accessible parts of a shop will sell more product because more people's attention will be attracted by the higher visibility of display. In much the same way a double-page spread advertisement in a magazine has more chance of being seen and read than a quarter-page one, mixed with others. If eye-catching window displays, video films and 'special offer' leaflets are added to a competitive product's display space, there is a high probability that more sales will result. In self-service outlets, where customers browse, compare and select brochures, the amount and position of display is crucial to achieving sales volume.

Display space in retail outlets is always in short supply and it is usually allocated, very roughly, according to a producer's market share. In other words, if tour operator 'A' has 20 per cent of a market and tour operator 'B' has 10 per cent, 'A' will normally be given around twice the available display space. One of the usual objects of sales promotion is to change these relative space allocations but it can only be achieved tactically for short periods. At any time, but especially in the main booking weeks, the competition to achieve prime display space for holiday products is enormous and the costs of sales promotion incentives to distributors rise proportionately.

The objectives noted under 'distribution network' relate to the broader issues of distribution discussed in Chapter 18.

Sales promotion techniques used in travel and tourism

Figure 16.2 summarizes the main promotional techniques on which marketing managers can draw. Advertising agencies and specialist sales promotion agencies are available to assist larger companies in the choice and design of techniques. Smaller firms will have no choice but to use their judgement, basing it on previous experience of the tools that are effective in their field, and to undertake their own research into the range of promotions on offer by competitors. For students, perusing the travel trade press and marketing journals provides continuous information about current promotional campaigns in all sectors of travel and tourism.

It can be seen that the incentives noted for consumers and distribution networks in Figure 16.2 have three common elements:

- A featured offer (or 'special deal' outside the normal terms of trade).
- A tangible advantage (adding value not inherent in the normal product formulation).
- Intention to achieve marketing objectives.

These three elements fit precisely with the overall definition of sales promotion noted earlier.

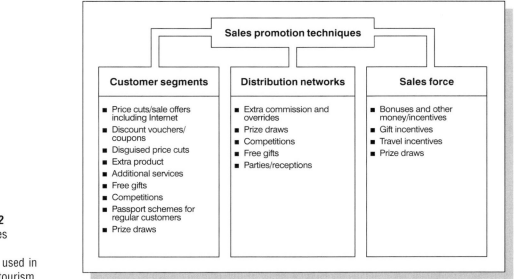

Figure 16.2
Typical sales promotion techniques used in travel and tourism

Some examples of customer sales promotion incentives

Price cuts for all categories of goods and services are commonly recognized as the most powerful of all consumer incentives. Linked with yield management programmes, they are almost universally used by airlines, hotels and tour operators to sell off unsold capacity. 'Sale' boards are a common feature in travel agents' windows, with last minute offers of large discounts on specific tours notified by the operators.

Discount vouchers offering, say, 15 per cent off admission prices or a money equivalent coupon such as '£1.00 off', are commonly used by tourist attractions on the basis that most coupons are allowable on one adult admission only and a typical party size is nearer three persons. '£1.00 off' in the context of a high fixed price operation with spare capacity does not undermine a very real gain in net profit terms, even before any additional on-site spending occurs.

Disguised price cuts are a popular way to maintain the regular price structure while offering added value to customers and an incentive to buy. Hotels with space to sell often offer double-room occupancy for single-occupancy rack rates, but expect to generate added revenue through meals and spending in bars. The rather coy 'spouse travels free' promotions, often used on long-haul routes to motivate business travellers to switch brands, are another example of disguised price cuts.

Extra product (more of the same) may be offered as a value added incentive to purchase, e.g. four nights for the price of three, 'free' wine with meals at specified times, additional features offered 'free' by visitor attractions at times of the year when they are not crowded, or additional sightseeing excursions may be added by tour operators.

Additional services may include chauffeur driven cars from airport to town centre offered by airlines to first-class and some business-class passengers, or the welcome receptions and vouchers for beauty salons offered in some hotels to weekend visitors.

Free gifts range from tour operators' travel bags and passport wallets to badges or pens offered to children at some attractions.

Competitions are a commonly used travel incentive to motivate consumers (and gain their names and addresses for databases) and distribution networks.

'Passport' and other 'club' membership schemes designed to reward and promote loyalty and frequency of purchase by identified repeat customers. Greatly assisted by the power of customer databases; the history of special passport-type deals goes back to the early 1980s. At that time the now defunct airline Pan Am first offered 'reward points' for journeys undertaken at normal prices in the USA that could subsequently be redeemed for free air travel with the company. The more journeys, the more points and the greater the reward built up. Aimed primarily at frequent business travellers paying full fares through their companies, some of these schemes got out of hand in the late 1980s through over-generous provision. Miscalculations are, however, just that. They do not alter the logic of providing incentives for repeat customers.

In 2000 most car rental firms, accommodation chains, airlines and other transport companies are offering some form of membership club, privilege card or passport scheme to reward their core of identified regular, especially business customers. The logic is clear. The marketing cost of attracting a new, first-time customer through advertising and other communications far exceeds the cost of persuading an existing known customer to 'come again' or make additional purchases. In due course some such schemes can become a regular part of product augmentation or products in their own right, for example British Airways' *Air Miles*. Air Miles had become a strategic business in its own right with over 6 million account holders on its database in mid–2000 and was part of the sales promotion methods for other non-travel purchases via banks, petrol and other retail partners. But the principal aim of all such schemes is to build relationships with and encourage repeat travellers, typically by means of personalized direct marketing methods (see Chapter 19). Names and addresses of regular buyers are invariably used for targeting short-run promotions within the scope of the definition offered at the beginning of this chapter.

From this brief review it should be clear that the range of possible incentives is both extremely wide and very creative. There is constant rivalry between competitors to innovate and achieve a lead in incentives and gain market share. Sales promotions may be greatly improved by test marketing as defined in Chapter 11 and most service companies have virtually limitless opportunities for such testing. Large sales promotions may also generate sufficient media interest to gain additional unpaid coverage, supported by skilful PR activity and other techniques in the communication mix.

Examples of sales promotion incentives for distributors and sales forces

Although separately designed to appeal to managers and/or counter staff, many of the incentives used to motivate distributors are the same as those offered to customers, including gifts, prize draws and competitions. In addition, to achieve the objectives of a major promotion, it is likely that additional commission will be paid on extra sales. Additional commission payments, known in the retail travel trade as 'overrides', may be paid also for all sales above an agreed level. Because of the nature of the product, it is normal in travel and tourism for distributor incentives to include some form of free travel or 'educational' to sample the promoted items.

For sales forces, incentives are also designed to appeal to the individuals concerned and mostly they are available in the form of money bonuses, and gifts available on achieving specified additional sales targets. There is also a large sales incentive industry, especially in the USA, which specializes in designing and supplying incentives for sales forces and distributors in all sectors of industry. Within the range of incentives offered by specialist agencies, travel products to exotic destinations are frequently found to be powerful motivators.

How long is 'temporary' for incentives?

By definition, all sales promotion inducements, incentives and rewards are tactical responses of a temporary, short-term nature. If they are sustained for too long, they become perceived as part of the standard product, price or terms of trade. They erode profitability as well as lose their effectiveness to secure vital additional sales. Kotler suggested that 'probably there is risk in putting a well-known brand on promotion more than 30 per cent of the time' (Kotler, 1984; 662). He also draws attention to the dangers of subsidizing existing users by over-frequent promotions. There are no precise rules and everything turns upon the state of the market. For international airlines responding to the international travel market from the USA during and after the Gulf War of 1991, the overriding necessity was to stem massive daily losses as fixed costs far outweighed available revenue. In such conditions sales promotion is not an academic concept but a principal means of continuous competition and route to survival that actually works faster than cutting operating costs. Fortunately for service businesses, they can usually be far more segment and product specific in their promotions than manufacturers of physical goods. They also enjoy more influence over much of the distribution networks in which most of their sales promotions are featured.

Without contradicting the limit on how long any one promotion may be sustained, it should be noted that there are often strong reasons for linking individual promotions within an overall theme. Themes must be relevant to the organizations and products being promoted, and can be used strategically over time both as a form of branding and to create a sense of continuity in customers' minds. McDonald's Restaurants use the character Ronald McDonald with many of their specific promotions, and so on. Some sales promotions feature collectable items, which together form sets of linked items, as another way to build themes and continuity into sales promotions. It is also possible to build a series of merchandising initiatives into recognizable themes, especially when they are used 'in-house'.

Good examples of segmented promotions with a clear strategic dimension can be seen in the marketing work of the privatized British railway operating companies. Any railway company has a major interest in promoting travel frequency outside peak times and the companies have effectively created a series of 'passport' holders through, for example, special identity cards now held by hundreds of thousands of students and senior citizens. Profile information on holders of these cards is retained on databases and holders can be reached directly and cost-effectively to promote travel offers. Using yield management programmes (although these were still being developed for rail use in 2000), other promotional offers can be made, restricted to specified times of travel that are calculated to contribute to fixed costs but not to dilute normal revenue flows.

Pricing down or adding value/packaging up?

Not confined to travel and tourism, there has been a debate in marketing for years as to which of two strategies is most likely to achieve targeted sales volume. One is a strategy for low prices relative to competition, supported by additional promotional price discounting; the other is adding value to products (also known as packaging up) to achieve targeted volume by promoting product enhancement. Packaging up means adding short-term value into one or more of the bundle of components of which travel and tourism products are comprised. Adding value has implications for product design, as noted in Chapter 8 under the heading 'Product augmentation'.

There is no doubt that price discounting is the easier option to implement. It works faster and is usually highly popular with customers. But there is also no doubt that price cuts are easily matched and can degenerate very quickly into price wars that leave all producers worse off. They may have an unintended strategic result in eroding product quality. To some extent producers cannot stand aside if they are losing sales volume to an undercutting competitor. But, wherever possible, especially with key segments such as repeat customers, the marketing advantages of adding value are clear and should always be explored first. Provided that a product is competitive and generating good satisfaction levels at existing prices, there is every reason to limit price-cutting unless it becomes essential for survival. A commitment to product enhancement, a clear communication strategy and knowledge of customer segments offers the only long-term route out of price-cutting wars, in which products become commodities and price becomes the primary reason for customer choice.

The choice of options has dominated the tourism industry for decades and Greene concluded some twenty years ago that 'the hotel and airline sector have tended too often to use price reductions as the first tactic for obtaining more business when other choices could be more profitably employed' (Greene, 1982: 62–7). But the debate goes on and the strategic decision in 1999 of British Airways to invest more in premium fare business, and less in the heavily discounted economy end of the airline market, is a recent illustration of it. It seems probable that growing concern with the environmental impact of tourism will force future attention more on adding – and justifying – value, than on traditional price-cutting.

Planning and evaluating effective sales promotions

The process of planning and implementing successful sales promotions can be represented as six logical steps. The steps are based on the marketing planning process outlined in Chapter 13, and are undertaken in practice as part of planning campaigns (Chapter 14):

1 Using yield management programmes, calculate the volume targets and the pattern of sales that sales promotion activity is expected to achieve over a defined promotion period. For a hotel group, for example, this would be expressed in bookings per hotel over a specified number of nights. For airlines it would be seat sales by route, by period of time. For a visitor attraction it would be visitor numbers on specified days, and so on. The procedure is the same, whether the objective is to gain *additional* business above previously targeted levels, or *reduce* the level of an expected loss resulting from some unpredictable external event.
2 Calculate the potential revenue gain that would arise if the sales promotion volume targets were achieved in full (targeted volume × average price of nights, seats or admission). This establishes the limits within which a budget must be set.
3 Specify the consumer profile of the segments to be targeted for sales promotion drawing on details available from marketing research. Customer-database mining is the obvious source of such information.
4 Choose the incentives best calculated to appeal to the target segments and cost them in relation to budget limits.
5 Draw up and implement an action programme co-ordinated with other promotional elements in the campaign, especially advertising, PR, personal selling, Internet and distribution arrangements.
6 Monitor and evaluate the results achieved.

Budgeting and evaluating results

By their nature, all forms of sales promotion and merchandising are task-orientated techniques. The tasks relate to identified shortfalls or opportunities, which can be expressed precisely in volume terms of bednights, seats, admissions, etc. and in the amount of sales revenue that is at risk, or achievable. It follows that *objective and task* methods are the only efficient way to calculate sales promotion budgets (see Chapter 14).

Again, because sales-promotion methods are so specifically targeted, results can be measured in sales or bookings achieved during the promotional period. Inevitably it will not be possible fully to separate the sales promotion effects from other marketing decisions such as current advertising campaigns or recent product enhancement. But short-run promotional efforts provide the best opportunity most marketing managers have to measure the results of their marketing expenditure with some precision.

Personal selling

Defined as direct contact between buyer and seller, face to face, by telephone or through video-conferencing, personal selling is another of the core marketing communication tools. Personal selling includes individual front-line staff activities, for example when a hotel waiter recommends a more expensive wine, and group sales transactions, for example when an airline sales person negotiates a bulk contract to supply 100 000 seats to a tour operator. Personal selling has both a strategic and tactical role and is directly associated with sales promotion and merchandising techniques.

Because of the high level of personal 'front-of-house' staff contact in the delivery of most tourism services (see Chapter 6), personal selling in travel and tourism divides between the sales activity of a few professional sales staff and the day-to-day selling activity by all staff with customer contact whose job involves sales potential. Only large firms will have dedicated sales teams but the nature of the business means that most staff in most businesses have almost infinite opportunities for personal selling.

Personal selling must be integrated within the overall communications mix so that it may be supported by advertising and PR that creates awareness, knowledge and liking for the organization and its products; printed and electronic information that provides product detail; sales promotions that create incentives to buy; and merchandising and point of sale material reinforcing the message at the point of sale.

Traditionally, personal selling focused on securing targeted sales transactions – 'doing the business'. Today, it is more about securing not only the transaction in hand but also the potential future stream of transactions that a sale may create. The focus is on customer retention, building relationships and solution-driven selling, rather than one-off sales transactions. The rapid development of ICT (see Chapter 10), especially the Internet, is undoubtedly changing the role of personal selling in the twenty-first century, especially in the business-to-business area and in undermining the traditional role of retail distributors in tourism. It will not, however, affect the special role of personal selling by front-of-house staff in the service delivery process that is so characteristic of the tourism industry.

Personal selling functions

The functions can be summarized as persuasion to purchase under four headings:

1 *Persuasion to purchase additional goods and service during the service delivery process*. Often linked with sales promotions, most tourism employees are engaged in this type of activity, whether they recognize it or not. Waiters recommend 'specials,' ask diners to choose from the dessert trolley or suggest wine; receptionists recommend a hotel's health care facilities; and travel agency staff recommend insurance. Few travel and tourism organizations formally recognize the opportunity of such continuous selling or provide training in selling techniques plus motivation and reward schemes to support it.

2 *Business-to-business purchases*. Although the fashion for employing a sales team changes quite frequently, most airlines and hotel chains use sales teams to sell seats and beds to tour operators, corporate travel buyers and conference organizers; attractions sell facilities to events organizers and sell educational trips and workshops to schools and colleges; ground handling companies sell excursions and services to inbound tour operators, and so on.

3 *Big value purchases*. In all the business-to-business purchases noted in 2, one sales transaction typically has to generate a large enough volume of revenue to justify the cost of the sales team. If a consumer purchase is big enough, as with most new houses and cars, for example, personal selling at that level may also be justified. In a tourism context, timeshare property developers use personal selling to great effect with the individual consumer, employing a mix of telesales and face-to-face communication.

4 *Motivating purchases through distribution channels*. Where third party distributors such as travel agents are used for the sale of tourism products (see Chapter 18), the business of servicing the channels with information and motivating their front-line staff to sell is a core role for a sales force. Tour operators, cruise ship operators and other principals, for example, may deploy a sales force and offer product familiarization trips to their key distributors in order to motivate the latter's staff to operate as an extension of their own sales team. Because travel agents take commission or a fee on sales but do not actually purchase the principals' stock, the role of a sales force has to be focused more on partnership motivation than transactions.

The first of these four types of selling is undertaken by front-line staff, although they may well be trained and motivated by a sales team. The other three types employ sales professionals engaged primarily for that purpose.

Typical tasks for sales forces and sales management in travel and tourism

The time that a sales force spends actually making sales may vary between only 5 and 20 per cent of their working hours. Typical tasks include:

- Planning sales call programmes in collaboration with the marketing team.
- Developing new business-to-business partnerships and presenting the features and benefits of both new and existing products as part of building trading relationships – including attendance at trade exhibitions.
- Negotiating for big purchase contracts and closing the sale.
- Servicing existing customers as part of relationship marketing, handling problems and complaints and assessing future needs. Entertaining customers as appropriate.
- Travelling from one location to the next for meetings with customers.
- Searching for new customers using desk research and verbal leads, and grading such prospects according to attractiveness before making contact.
- Attending training courses on selling skills and product or company knowledge
- Carrying out administrative backup work such as letter writing, telephone calls, sales reports and forecasts. Much of this is now done by portable computers and the Internet.
- Intelligence gathering for marketing purposes as the 'eyes and ears' of the organization on new product initiatives and competitors' activities.

A successful sales person requires excellent time management, personality, negotiation and organizational skills to carry out the job. As they are representing a company and its brand values they also need in-depth company and product knowledge.

Typical tasks for sales managers

The management of sales teams can be summarized under five headings:

- *Sales team structure and organization needs*. A sales force, for example for an airline, may be structured by territory (such as by country or region), by product (business class and economy class), by market (corporate buyers, travel agents or tour operators) or by some combination. Decisions on the size of the sales force will relate to the frequency of visits judged necessary, the number of contacts to be serviced and the revenue potential the team can generate. A small in-house sales team may be boosted at busy times by contracting work out to a field marketing team from a specialist agency, for example to help a tour operator with brochure drops at travel agents following the launch of a summer programme.

- *Sales team recruitment*, which tends to be an ongoing process involving close liaison with the human resources department in drawing up job analyses, job descriptions and devising ideal personal profiles. Recruiting, induction and training are expensive processes that merit careful attention.
- *Motivation and reward systems*, which are critical in motivating the sales force and in reducing staff turnover. Financial reward may be based on salary only, commission only, basic salary plus commission, or bonus packages. Good sales people are goal orientated and clearly communicated sales targets can be motivational as well as linked to reward schemes. Award and recognition programmes add psychological value through a sense of achievement and overseas trips, in themselves a sector of the tourism industry, are often considered more motivating than their monetary equivalent. Training and development courses also have a role in motivating participants.
- *Support activities*, including the production of visual sales aids, computer software and training packages, telephone sales backup, point of sale material for the travel trade, distributor newsletters and mail shots, and product knowledge and skills training for sales personnel. Back up support may also be provided online and through a call centre help line.
- *Evaluation and control* is an essential part of successful selling. Fortunately the process lends itself naturally to targeting and individual goals can be set for activity by product, region or market sector, allowing weekly (or, indeed, daily) monitoring. For example, the number of calls made, ratio of new to existing customers, conversion rates from enquiries to customers and the average size of sales agreed, can all be tracked precisely. Sales managers may accompany individuals on visits to assess the qualitative aspects of performance. Measures of client satisfaction and retention should be included in the appraisal of sales team performance.

Chapter summary

This chapter defines sales promotions and merchandising in their primary tactical role of managing the short-run variations in customer demand for products that occur in all forms of tourism business. Both techniques are aspects of marketing communications that operate by providing additional incentives at the point of sale. Advertising and PR have different objectives. They are used away from the point of sale and serve to bring in customers whose attitudes and interest in products are already favourably preconditioned. Sales promotion and advertising are complementary techniques, not alternatives – the left and right co-ordinated 'punch' for the 'storm troopers' of marketing.

Reflecting the perishable nature of travel and tourism products and the operational implications of high fixed costs, the use of sales promotion and merchandising in managing demand is more important in the tourism industry than in industries marketing physical goods. The full costs of so-called below the line techniques will often exceed the cost of advertising. At the least, sales promotion and merchandising warrant equal attention with advertising in campaign planning. The strategic choice in sales promotions between *pricing down* and *packaging up* is addressed and the advantages of the latter approach are identified.

The existence of three different kinds of point of sale is noted, with particular stress on the merchandising opportunities conveyed by having customers 'in-house', on the businesses' own premises. Although the desired effect of sales promotion is on purchases by targeted customer segments, sales promotion techniques are also designed separately for distributors and sales forces in order to maximize the short-run effects at chosen points of sale. The planning for sales promotion and merchandising follows systematic procedures, which will be familiar by now to readers of this book, and which are integrated in the vital marketing and campaign planning stages discussed in Chapters 13 and 14.

Finally, the role of personal selling and sales forces is explained in the latter part of the chapter. Sales forces are only relevant to larger organizations but they have an important role to play in business-to-business relationship marketing as well as in support of sales promotion and merchandising objectives.

Further reading

Brassington, F. and Pettit, S. (2000). *Principles of Marketing*. Chapters 16 and 17, 2nd edn, Prentice-Hall.

Jobber, D. (1998). *Principles and Practice of Marketing*. Chapter 12, 2nd edn, McGraw-Hill.

Kotler, P. and Armstong, G. (1999). *Principles of Marketing*. Chapters 15 and 16, 8th edn, Prentice-Hall.

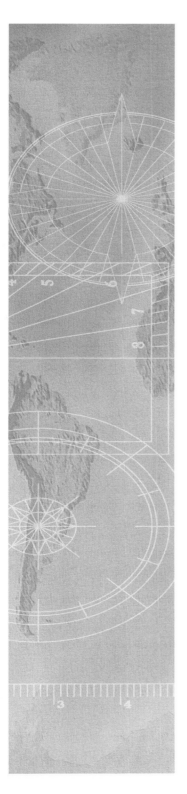

CHAPTER 17

Brochures, other print and electronic information

If a tour operator prints ten brochures, only one will generate a sale and of that brochure 98 per cent is wasted . . . interactive digital TV will destroy brochures by 2010. (Travel Trade Gazette report of proceedings of an Institute of Travel and Tourism conference at Las Vegas, June 2000.)

Improbable though predictions such as that noted above are, it serves to highlight the waste implicit in most forms of brochures, sales literature generally and other forms of printed communications paid for out of marketing budgets. Known in the USA as *collateral materials*, print and its modern Web site equivalents represents the third distinctive group of marketing communications to be planned in marketing campaigns, in addition to advertising and PR, sales promotion and merchandising.

For over a century the nature of service products, especially those that are relatively expensive and infrequently bought, has conferred a special significance on printed communications as an integral part of the marketing process that has had no parallel in marketing physical goods. Whereas all producers of consumer products use advertising and PR, sales promotion, merchandising and personal selling, few producers of physical goods have used print to anything like the extent found in tourism. The design, distribution and large volume use of printed items has been and remains a major distinguishing feature of travel marketing.

The fundamental customer demand for information and the rationale for its provision covered in this chapter will not change in the next decade. But, as the quote at the head of this chapter indicates, the means of supplying it is undergoing revolutionary technological change in 2000. The future points to information provision, at least for tour operators, becoming predominantly a matter for interactive digital television. This is a revolution driven equally by the search for waste reduction, cost savings, consumer demand for continuous access to information twenty-four hours a day, and the need to adapt to the more fluid pricing and tactical discounting regime of the early twenty-first century.

For those happy with the technology, Web sites and the so-called e-brochures that became available at the end of the 1990s, are more flexible, more convenient and in some ways more user-friendly forms of information provision than print. The Internet is challenging the world of printed information and, writing in 2000, the main issue is how fast and to what extent the electronic medium will replace paper. Tour operators are, however, something of a special case (see Chapter 24) and, while ICT options will certainly shift the balance markedly from print to electronic access, we do not believe it will remove the marketing role of collateral material substantially for most tourism businesses over the next decade. Printed materials and electronic information will coexist and be mutually reinforcing.

Where a large proportion of sales turnover is achieved by direct communication between producer and consumer, with no intervention of third party distributors, the role of sales literature has traditionally been at its strongest. This, of course, is the case for the bulk of all international and domestic travel and tourism products. It is also the context in which Internet access has most to offer. While many tour operators have not thus far engaged significantly in direct marketing, they have had other important marketing reasons for focusing their efforts on brochures in retail outlets. For some public sector organizations such as tourist boards at national, regional and local level, the design, production and distribution of printed materials takes up the bulk of the time of marketing staff although here, too, the shift to electronic provision is rapid at the turn of the century (see Chapter 20).

This chapter begins by explaining why printed information materials are such an important part of marketing communications in travel and tourism. It provides a definition in the context of marketing campaigns. The types of printed materials used and their multiple roles in marketing travel and tourism are identified, followed by a step-by-step explanation of the process of producing effective print, both 'in-house', and through external agencies. The key issue of achieving distribution to the user is discussed, including reference to electronic information issues, followed by brief notes on evaluating the results of expenditure on information provision.

Print production and wastage on an heroic scale

The sheer volume of traditional printed items associated with travel and tourism products is staggering. At the turn of the new century the travel world is awash with brochures and other print items paid for out of marketing budgets. The environmental cost in trees destroyed for printmaking, the costs of road haulage and the cost of waste disposal is vast. In the UK alone, there are estimated to be over 150 000 organizations and establishments wholly or partially concerned with aspects of tourism. Nearly all of these are generating pieces of printed information, ranging from the millions of brochures distributed by large tour operators, down to farmhouses designing and distributing a few hundred leaflets for their prospective customers. There are over 750 tourist information centres acting as a major outlet and some 7000 retail travel outlets. In the USA, although the calculation is on a much narrower basis than that noted above for the UK, the US Travel Data Center identified just under 500 000 'total firms' in the USA travel industry in 1990, including over 30 000 travel agency locations (excluding satellite ticket printer locations).

In the early 1990s just one distribution contractor was distributing 150 million brochures a year, weighing some 20 000 tonnes, to UK travel agency outlets. Around the developed world travel and tourism firms are producing billions of printed items for the purposes defined in this chapter. Chapter 15 noted the filters at work to prevent much marketing communication from influencing the targeted customer. In the case of printed items it is obvious that much of the material does not even reach the first stage of 'opportunity to see', and the level of wastage is widely acknowledged to be prodigious. Surveys in the USA have estimated that fewer than six out of every ten agents opened all the brochure packs they received and much of the total is simply dumped. A study carried out for the European Travel Commission confirmed the same massive wastage of national tourist organization printed materials.

In the UK, the leading tour operators distributing through travel agents in the 1990s were typically producing between six and ten brochures per person booking a holiday in their main summer programmes; smaller operators would have to produce comparatively more per customer achieved. Developments in print technology and international sourcing policies have tended to keep the cost of production down compared with other marketing costs. Even so, the cost of a large summer brochure of 200 or more pages (some run to over 500 pages), assuming over a million were produced, averaged out at around £1.00 per brochure in 1999 prices. Smaller operators, with much smaller programmes to communicate, would be spending less but with smaller print runs their unit cost would be around £0.75p or more. Bottomley Renshaw noted for UK coach tour operators that 'through agencies they convert only about one in every forty brochures into a sale' (Bottomley Renshaw, 1992: 90).

Thus the print cost of a booking for two persons, assuming ten brochures are needed at £1.00 = £10.00, or £5.00 per person. At the end of the 1990s a typical seven-night package to a Mediterranean resort might cost around £400 per person (published price) and tour operators would consider it a good year if they achieved an average of 3 per cent gross profit on that price = £12.00. Allowing for brochure distribution costs as well as production costs (but not retail commission), it is obvious that print and distribution cost alone could be the equivalent of over half the gross operating profit on a tour package. In a bad year the print and distribution costs will far exceed profit per holiday sold. What is clear is that the cost of print as a proportion of marketing expenditure, is a major 'up front' cost item to be paid for out of the tour operator's earnings. What is also clear is that half and often much more of that cost represents waste. The importance of achieving even marginal improvements in the effectiveness of brochures and thus reducing print wastage, is obvious. The massive attraction of the Internet in this context is clear on the base of cost alone, although there are many other advantages too, covered in Chapters 10, 18 and 19.

Defining information materials

Information materials are part of marketing communications. They may be defined as comprising:

> Any form of printed or electronic information materials, paid for out of marketing budgets and designed to create awareness among existing and prospective customers, stimulate interest in and demand for specified products, and/or facilitate their purchase, use and enjoyment.
>
> This definition covers not only the familiar promotional use of information, but also an important 'facilitation' use covering the ways in which many tourism businesses producers assist customers to decide between and to purchase particular products, and achieve full benefit and enjoyment from using them. Leaflets provided on admission to visitor attractions, to inform and 'orientate' visitors to the experience they will receive, are one illustration of print designed to facilitate use and enjoyment.

While travel and tourism is a market of obvious interest to a wide range of commercial publishers, the definition above includes only information that is part of a communications mix intended to achieve marketing objectives. Excluded from the definition, therefore, are all commercial publications, such as directories, maps, guidebooks, timetables and CDs, which are sold through bookshops and other outlets, and for which the object of production is to achieve profit for the publisher through the cover price, and/or advertising revenue. While maps, for example, may be elements of promotional print for tourist boards, the criterion for inclusion in the definition is whether or not their production is geared to marketing objectives. Occasionally, printed items within the definition may also be sold at a cover price. But if so, it is always seen as a contribution towards marketing costs and not a main reason for production. Similarly, in the UK it is normal for the production and distribution costs of some tourist board brochures at national and regional level to be fully covered by advertising revenue received from businesses buying advertising space. Some tourist boards achieve a surplus on their brochure production costs but, since the surplus is typically set against marketing budgets, such brochures are included within the definition.

The bulk of all information materials are aimed at consumers but they are also produced to achieve promotional and facilitation objectives targeted at a distribution network. Trade directories and promotional materials, plus their modern B2B Web site equivalents are important elements in a marketing budget that uses intermediaries to reach customers and provide booking access. For consumers, information may be designed for use in any of the three types of 'points of sale' noted in Chapter 16 and the cost of information provision is often the largest single element in the overall marketing communications budget of travel and tourism businesses.

Types of printed material used in marketing travel and tourism

From the previous discussion it will be obvious that the range of printed information materials is immense. The lists below summarize typical items used in practice to influence individual consumers.

Promotional print

- Tour operators' brochures.
- Hotel, holiday centre, caravan park, campsite, and other accommodation brochures.
- Conference centre brochures.
- Specific product brochures (e.g. activity holidays, theatre weekends).
- Attraction leaflets (theme parks, museums, amusement parks).
- Car rental brochures.
- Sales promotion leaflets (specific incentive offers).
- Posters/show cards for window and other displays in distribution networks.
- Tourist office brochures (general and product-specific).
- Printed letters/inserts for direct mail.

Facilitation and information print

- Orientation leaflets/guides (attractions).
- Maps (mostly provided free out of marketing budgets).
- 'In-house' guides and magazines (accommodation and transport).
- Menus/tent cards/show cards/folders, used 'in-house'.

- Hotel group (and equivalent) directories.
- 'What's on' leaflets (such as those provided out of destination marketing budgets).
- Timetables produced by transport operators.

The marketing role of information materials and their multiple purposes

Drawing on reasons first outlined in Chapter 3, it is possible to restate briefly the characteristics of travel and tourism products that underlie the need for information materials and explain their importance in the conduct of marketing campaigns. We wish to stress that these characteristics and the discussion of multiple purposes that follows apply equally to printed and electronically provided information (especially if the latter can be selectively downloaded).

- Products are produced and consumed on producers' own premises and cannot be inspected and assessed directly at points of sale away from the place of production. There are no physical stocks of tourist products as there are for manufactured goods. *Information materials are used as product substitutes.*
- While service production and consumption are simultaneous, the production process is often separated by weeks or months from the act of purchase. Inevitably, many products are ideas and expectations only at the point of sale. *Information materials provide reassurance and a tangible focus for expectations.*
- Especially where infrequently purchased expensive products, such as holidays, are concerned, most customers seek full information and consider several options before making choices. Retailers of holidays are well aware that every minute spent answering questions costs money. *There is a powerful incentive to distribute information materials that reduce customer contact time.*
- There are many marketing reasons for communicating with customers during the production/consumption process, partly to 'facilitate' the experience and inform, and partly to generate a greater level of 'in-house' expenditure. *Information materials serve both facilitation and sales promotion and merchandising roles.*

The multiple purposes

It is obvious from the definition and the range of items included, that information materials perform a wide range of functions in travel and tourism. Printed information performs all the roles; electronic media perform most of them. They are summarized here in bullet form and explained below:

- Creating awareness.
- Promotional (messages/symbols).
- Promotional (display/merchandising).

- Promotional (incentives/special offers).
- Product substitute role.
- Access/purchasing mechanism.
- 'Proof' of purchase/reassurance.
- Facilitation of product use and information.
- Providing education.

Creating awareness

Some prospective first-time customers will become aware of products through advertising, PR and through the Internet (see Chapter 15). Many others in travel and tourism will gain initial awareness through marketing print first seen in a hotel, at an airport, in a travel agency or passed on by friends. The battle for awareness is fierce and continuous, and the design appearance of all marketing items is a matter of immense importance. The role of front-cover designs for print can be compared with the role of the packaging of products in a supermarket designed to attract the attention of people passing along the aisles. Web site design follows the same principle of attention getting and retaining.

Promotion

Brochures such as those provided by tour operators are designed to stimulate customers and motivate them to buy. They identify needs, demonstrate in pictures and words the image and positioning of products and organizations, and carry the key messages. In this role they act in the same way as advertising. They also perform a vital display function in the racks of distribution outlets, such as retail travel agents, where they serve in lieu of physical products. In the typical self-service shops run by most travel and tourism retailers the display role, and the customer appeal of brochure covers and contents, are vital to marketing success. Supplementary brochures and purpose-designed leaflets are also typically used to communicate and promote special offers and the other sales promotion incentives discussed in Chapter 16.

Web sites perform the same promotional role in a different medium. Given adequate receiver technology in the home, the multimedia options and the ability to change prices continuously as market circumstances alter, give greater flexibility and visual advantages to 'e-brochures' that printed items lack. On the other hand, the feel and smell and the sheer tangibility of a well-produced brochure are not easily replaced.

Access/purchasing mechanism/marketing research

Many product brochures contain booking forms to facilitate purchase and these contain the basis of the contract to provide services. Some of these forms may be overstamped and filled in by travel agents but all are designed to specify the purchase details. What is primarily designed as a purchasing mechanism, however, is increasingly also used for marketing research purposes. Booking form information can be transferred electronically into databases and used by businesses as a source of valuable customer profile data, such as area of origin, party size and type. The addresses can be analysed by ACORN methods to provide a detailed profile of typical buyers. Web sites perform the same role. Whether booking facilities are direct online, or via e-mail or call centres, the Internet is an access/purchasing mechanism providing simultaneous data capture and analysis.

Product substitute role

Above all, for travel and tourism operators whose business depends on bookings or decisions made away from the place of production, brochures perform a tangible product substitute role, the marketing importance of which it is impossible to overemphasize. The brochure *is* the product at the point of purchase, especially for first-time customers. It establishes expectations of quality, value for money, product image and status that must be matched when the product is delivered. Theoretically the Internet can match much of this role, certainly for lower-cost items and for heavily branded products such as an overnight in a hotel or a flight. But the quality of downloads and the need to change consumer behaviour established over centuries leaves a major question mark in 2000 as to the speed at which the majority of purchasers will use e-brochures for more expensive and first-time purchases. Some clearly will. But will it be 10 per cent, 25 per cent or over 50 per cent within a decade? Marketing managers have a major task in test marketing their investment in electronic access modes and evaluating customer response. The shift from print to electronic information is inevitable but it will vary from business to business and there are no industry 'norms'.

Proof of purchase/reassurance

Traditional brochures also act as a substitute for the product in the period between purchase and consumption, which in the case of vacations may extend to several months. It becomes a document to be read several times as a reminder, to stimulate expectations and to show to friends and relatives. It helps to reduce any post purchase anxiety through reassurance. In Europe, under the terms of the 1993 EC Package Travel Directive, the contents of brochures are covered by precise regulations setting minimum standards. Dissatisfied customers are given rights to claim compensation and failure to provide required information may be a criminal offence for operators. Electronic media can deliver proof of purchase but its effectiveness in the role of product substitute for high-expense items is open to question.

Facilitation of product use and information

Once customers arrive on a tourism organization's premises, it is normal for them to be provided with a wide range of printed materials. Some may be found in rooms (hotels) or seat backs (airlines), at information desks (attractions) or on tables (restaurants and bars). The literature is designed to explain and promote what is available:

- To promote awareness and use of ancillary services/products.
- To assist customers to get the most value out of their purchase and enhance satisfaction.
- To feature special offers (sales promotion).
- To provide basic information which may be useful.
- To influence customer behaviour.

Producers can and do train their staff to communicate some of these options, but staff are usually busy and may not have time to cover the full range. Television screens, videos and interactive options in hotel rooms can also provide some of this information but printed items remain the main way to provide user-friendly messages to all travellers in exactly the same way. The fact that customers are often 'co-producers in the service delivery process' (see Chapter 6) provides a further role for information that is intended to influence and guide buyer behaviour.

Carefully designed print can do much to create a sense of welcome from an establishment to its customers. It can communicate the message that an organization understands and cares about customer needs and interests. An illustration is the choice that visitor attractions have, either to provide a simple admission ticket or a leaflet of welcome and user advice. The orientation process at Disneyland and other USA theme parks uses print to guide and support the enjoyment of visitors in ways that are still exceptions in much of Europe.

Providing education ● ● ●

The role of education is certainly not yet widely associated with marketing, except perhaps at more enlightened museums and galleries, but there is every reason to consider it an important and growing role for the new millennium. The impact of tourism, for example, on the social, cultural as well as physical environment is already an important issue in destinations such as national parks in developed and developing countries. Tourism businesses have a vested interest and a powerful motivation to create customer awareness and provide 'orientation' and understanding of the issues. It is in their long-run interest to help create and sustain an attractive and healthy environment, recognizing that destination capacity may depend more on *how* customers use a destination than on the number of visitors.

Education is not confined solely to leisure tourism. Many hotel chains around the world have developed sophisticated programmes to contribute to the environment and they need to tell all their customers, many of whom are on business. Of course, the word 'education' will not be found in marketing print or on tourism Web sites. But education it is, and education is a communication business. The professional skills of marketing managers have a potentially important educational role for the future and printed communications will be its primary focus where it matters most – on tourism business premises, in transit and in consumers' homes.

Stages in producing effective information material

The seven stages noted below are presented in a logical decision sequence judged relevant to all managers responsible for producing printed or electronic information materials for marketing purposes. Although the distribution of printed materials has special considerations (see later in the chapter), the other stages are similar to those used for designing any form of marketing communication. For larger organizations they are based on marketing research. Planning the provision of information is normally carried out as one of the elements in the campaign plan and it draws on data used for planning marketing strategy and objectives. The budget required for print production is best calculated by the 'objective and task' methods outlined in Chapter 14.

1 *Determining the size, profile and needs of the target audience.* Information about target customers is derived through market segmentation and print volume is related to the quantified objectives in the marketing plan. The target profile for advertising (media selection), sales promotion and for print production will normally be identical. Electronic media that is linked to booking systems and e-mails generates its own profile data as prospective customers respond – one of its primary advantages for marketing organizations.

2 *Marketing strategy, branding and positioning.* Here also advertising, print and Web sites are likely to be planned together, with co-ordinated messages, images and positioning. If print is the larger part of the budget, it may take the leading role in expressing product images. It will certainly take a leading role in communicating specific brand and product messages to the target audience.

3 *Paper quality, choice of colours, density of copy, graphics,* and the style and density of photography are varied in practice to match chosen images to selected target audiences. Up-market target groups respond better to heavier quality paper, lower density per page, pastel colours and thematic photographs. Down-market target groups are more influenced by bold colours, direct and straightforward copy and are not put off by greater density per page. Web site and multimedia design decisions are similar in principle having regard to the possibilities of the new medium rather than print.

4 *Specifying brochure/Web site objectives.* The essential task is to clarify and state concisely what the brochure or web site is expected to achieve in the campaign, especially in terms of the specific products it covers. A list of specific messages, rank ordered according to perceived customer priorities, should be drawn up within the context of the agreed marketing objectives. These statements will be crucial in briefing designers.

5 *Deciding the method of distribution.* The distribution of print to its intended recipients is perhaps the most vital of the six stages, because

communication can only work if sufficient numbers of prospective customers receive it. The cost of distribution per unit of print may easily exceed the unit cost of its production and most producers in travel and tourism will have to choose between several distribution options. This vital decision is discussed later in this chapter. For Web sites on the Internet, of course, the medium is distribution, information, promotion and booking access all in one. Its cost advantages are covered in Chapter 19.

6 *Creative execution.* As for advertising, the way in which product concepts and images are presented in print and Web sites will strongly influence the way in which consumers receive and respond to messages. For printed items, the appearance and appeal of the front cover, especially of items to be displayed in self-service racks, will be crucial in establishing eye contact and initial visual interest – in comparison with many other brochures aiming to appeal to much the same customers. Without the initial appeal, a leaflet or brochure is unlikely to be picked up and looked through. As Maas noted two decades ago, 'the cover of a brochure is just like the headline of a print advertisement: four out of five people never get beyond it. For these readers, you must get your selling message across on that page (or waste 80 per cent of your money)' (Maas, 1980: 23). That judgement is still appropriate and it applies equally to the visual appeal and user-friendliness of Web sites, especially the opening page.

While creative execution will usually be the business of designers (see below), marketing managers must accept full responsibility for the designer's brief and any marketing research associated with it.

7 *Timing.* Most travel and tourism print is required to fulfil its role at particular times. Tour operators and other producers, for example, must have their material available for distribution when customers are making their travel decisions. Print production and advertising normally require carefully co-ordinated phasing. Since it usually takes several weeks from an initial brief to final production of print, it is vital that print requirements are carefully programmed and that agreed timings are adhered to. If photographs are required, they have to be taken at the right time of the year. Many a hotel and visitor attraction has started to plan its brochure in September for production in January, only to find that the key photographs it needs should have been taken in July.

While this may seem obvious, experience demonstrates repeatedly that the bulk of all print is commissioned too late; that most brochure work is rushed, often involving mistakes and penalties of cost; and that important deadlines are missed with consequent loss of revenue. Marketing managers have only limited influence over creative execution but they should exercise total control over timing. The scope for marginal improvements in better timing alone may have a considerable impact on revenue. This is one of the ways in marketing to achieve marginal revenue gains and marginal budget savings at the same time.

Yet another of the advantages of Web sites is that they can be changed, modified and updated online at any time and with minimum cost. For tour operators in a 'fluid pricing' market context, the problems of publishing real prices in print are becoming increasingly difficult and forcing reprints of brochures at extra expense.

Using agencies to produce information materials

In large organizations the creative aspects of print and electronic media design may be handled within the organization itself and through advertising and other specialist agencies. Where print production runs are involved the business is usually outsourced to firms specialising in such services.

Smaller businesses are more likely to outsource both the creative and production processes, obtaining quotes from two or three specialist firms, many of which have access to designers, photographers and copywriters. It is interesting to note that, provided they are computer literate and have some basic training, very small businesses employing fewer than five people are now able to design and create much of their own print. They can also design their own small Web sites for as little as, say, $300.

Specialist firms will normally undertake whatever aspects of the total information design and production process clients specify. Most will be willing to provide professional and technical assistance with all or most of the following decisions.

Creative execution of the client's product concepts

- Most effective structure, layout, content and size of brochure or Web site.
- Design theme, and image presentation, especially of the front cover/first page.
- Use of colours and 'atmosphere' – and multimedia options for Web sites.
- Artwork and use of photographs/video clips (with due allowance for the delays these may cause in downloading on to most household PCs).
- Captions, graphics, copy and choice of typefaces.

For print production and distribution

- Choice of paper weight (affects production and postal costs and indicates quality).
- Packing (bulk and individual copies).
- Distribution.

To get good work from any agency, especially to get the best assistance in aspects of design and layout, it is essential for the client to supply a detailed written brief. The brief should refer to all the stages in producing effective information materials noted in the previous section and include extracts of the marketing plan and the size of the budget available. While agencies may not always be concerned with the distribution of materials, distribution considerations (see later in this chapter) must be clearly explained, as they will heavily influence the creative execution, especially for relatively heavy printed items.

In practice many smaller organizations fail to produce adequate briefs for agencies, and worse, they change their minds after the initial design, layout and artwork have been produced. Although Web sites are a much more forgiving and flexible medium than print, design changes are certain to add to cost, cause delays and produce a less than satisfactory result. Where external agencies are used, the process of agreeing print production usually calls for detailed liaison at the following points:

- Agreement and interpretation of initial design brief, production schedule and costs.
- Preliminary ('rough') artwork sketches, headlines, format and content, colours and typeface.
- Photography (if necessary), finished artwork and copy.
- Printer's proofs for correction.

Distributing information to target audiences

In the enthusiasm for creating an attractive leaflet or brochure it is easy to focus all attention on the design, photographs, images and copy. In practice the most important consideration for any information is how it will reach its intended target audience. If the answer is direct mail, there is an immediate design concern related to the cost of envelopes and postage. It is not unusual for the cost of packaging and postage to exceed the print design and production costs. If the intention is to distribute through travel agencies, it must first be ascertained how many travel agents are willing to handle the item. For every brochure currently displayed in travel agency racks there are probably at least twenty others seeking space. Again, if travel agents are an agreed distribution source, the size of their standard display spaces will tend to dictate brochure size and page layout. These may appear obvious considerations but experience suggests that distribution problems often come last and not first in the print decision process.

The distribution options for getting printed items into prospective buyers' hands were always very wide. They just became wider when Web sites were made accessible to home PCs in the late 1990s. Where brochures or leaflets are displayed and given out 'in house' or 'on site', the distribution process and costs can be fully controlled by the producer. Where a larger company, such as an airline, hotel group or car-rental company controls multi-site outlets, the literature distribution process at those sites is also easily controlled and costed.

For distribution away from owned premises, there are at least ten main options for getting print into the hands of prospective buyers. These are summarized below:

- Advertisements carrying coupons to be completed by those requiring information.
- Cards or other inserts into press and magazine media, which are an alternative form of media space.

- Direct mail to loyalty club members and other previous customers, using own databases and names and addresses bought for the purpose from a list broker.
- Direct distribution on a door-to-door basis in targeted residential areas.
- Direct distribution at exhibitions and shows open to the public, e.g. camping and caravan exhibitions, and travel trade fairs.
- Distribution via retail travel agencies.
- Distribution via tourist information centres and public libraries.
- Distribution via relevant third parties. For example, American Express, and many clubs and societies will, for a fee, include printed leaflets with their regular mailings to members; alternatively via hotel reception desks and similar relevant outlets (suitable for attractions, entertainments, car rental).
- Collaborative distribution via marketing consortia and trade associations (this is a variation of distribution via multi-site operation under one owner).
- Distribution via Web sites that offer e-mail addresses or call centre numbers as the means to access printed materials.

Beyond these common choices, there will usually be many other places, such as airports, railway station concourses, bus station waiting rooms, supermarkets and petrol/gas stations, at which relevant opportunities to distribute information may occur. Any controlled place that attracts a sufficient throughput of targeted prospects may be used for information distribution purposes. The scope is very wide indeed.

For an established business the choice of distribution outlets will normally be based on experience of what has worked in previous years for the same or similar products. But the scope for innovation and test marketing with new forms of distribution is wide and global in its scope, especially with the new electronic options. Innovation in information distribution is an essential method of learning how to improve the effectiveness of distribution at the margin.

Evaluating the results of information distribution

Assessing the cost-effectiveness of producing and distributing information will be hard to separate with any precision from the combined effects of advertising, PR, sales promotion and merchandising. Bookings and sales revenue result from the marketing mix as a whole. Through marketing research, however, it is possible to reach some conclusions, and studies may be carried out:

- To choose between the customer appeal of alternative cover designs and content, using evidence of qualitative discussions with target groups of potential customers (see Chapter 11).
- To measure the results of 'split-runs', in which two different brochure formats are distributed to matched samples of target recipients and the volume of bookings compared. Using direct mail to distribute print makes this a relatively easy option for many producers.

- To measure customer recall, use and evaluation of brochures through ad hoc telephone or postal surveys of brochure recipients identified, for example, from completed coupons included in advertisements.
- To measure customer recall, use and evaluation of brochures in brief surveys conducted, for example, at reception desks when customers arrive on a producer's premises or site.

In every case where printed materials are part of the marketing mix it is common sense to identify all items with code numbers or letters, which identify as appropriate:

- Through what media the print was requested.
- By what distribution methods print reached the customer (assuming more than one method).

Provided that consumer responses are analysed by the codes assigned, the use of printed materials and the associated distribution methods normally provide many opportunities for innovation and testing responses. Use of Web sites can be measured directly, unequivocally and at low cost by recording the number of customers that open a site and explore its pages as well as by use of e-commerce, e-mail or call centre numbers/references unique to the Internet. The Internet is an excellent low-cost tool for marketing innovation and experimentation and this is an important part of its attraction in services marketing.

Electronic alternatives to print

Since the early 1990s, and rapidly since the late 1990s, the global infrastructure for the communication of electronic information has developed exponentially, facilitating and lowering the cost of using digital multimedia information technology, Web sites, CDs, video films, computerized images, video text and Internet enabled mobile phones. As a result, online communications between a principal's stock of products and a consumer's home television, are confidently predicted to replace much of the role traditionally performed in tourism by printed materials. In the frequent repeat purchase of convenience travel items such as hotel stays, car hire, air and rail travel for business people, this is already happening for a quarter and more of the market served. For budget airlines, estimates of 60 per cent of bookings by Internet are cited in the travel trade press.

But if much of the promotional and access roles of information can be more cost-effectively handled by electronic media, the facilitation role is harder to replicate. Moreover, the physical value and qualities of attractively produced print; the ability to touch it, hold it and show it to others; its appeal to humanity down the centuries and its ability to inspire images and dreams, appear to be critical in much of travel and tourism. The death of books has been confidently predicted for over forty years but more books than ever are being produced and sold, and there is a powerful human attachment to the simplicity, reliability, user-friendliness and great convenience of portable print. The authors do not believe that print is likely to be replaced by electronic communications in the near future.

Electronic information has both a powerful leading *and* complementary role to play, however, and clearly can be used effectively to reduce costs by substantially reducing the existing levels of wastage in retail outlets and in the traditional methods for direct response marketing.

Chapter summary

Travel and tourism are information-rich industries. From the initial idea of a visit, through all the stages of decision, booking, payment and anticipation through to arrival and the experience, the process is one of information provision. This chapter identifies the vital part that information materials play in marketing travel and tourism products within the context of communications paid for out of marketing budgets. It notes the massive volume and wastage of printed items traditionally produced in the industry, especially in tour operating, and the range of functions they perform, distinguishing between promotion and facilitation.

The different purposes for which information is used in marketing are discussed and the six main stages in producing effective information are explained with reference to the roles of specialist agencies available to assist in design, production and distribution.

The chapter emphasizes a particular need for organizations to analyse the problems of securing effective distribution for printed materials to targeted readers and notes the choices available to tourism businesses, recently enormously facilitated by direct customer access to the Internet. The *objective and task* method of budgeting for information provision requirements (introduced in Chapter 14) is recommended because it makes it easier in practice for managers to measure the results of their expenditure.

In summary, it is interesting to reflect that, at least for commercial businesses in the travel and tourism industry, the information they distribute physically in print or virtually via the Internet embodies and communicates all aspects of the marketing mix to the extent that they:

- State and physically represent the product in consumer terms.
- State the price and other details as the basis of a legally enforceable contract.
- Are a principal medium of communication.
- Are part of the distribution process that represents 'place' for customers.
- Facilitate the customer experience and sense of enjoyment and value for money.
- Facilitate the relationship that businesses seek to develop with their repeat customers.

Given the nature of service products in general, and travel and tourism products in particular, the communication of information is often the most important (and expensive) single element within co-ordinated marketing campaigns. Growing use of the Internet offers significant opportunities for cost savings in traditional print budgets, but the Internet and printed communications still perform complementary rather than alternative roles for the great majority of consumers.

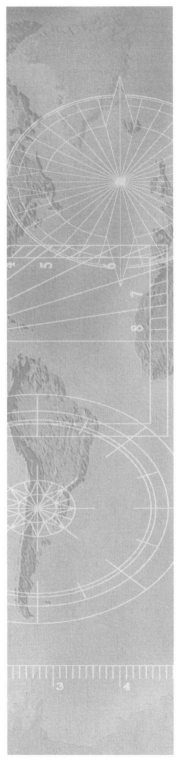

CHAPTER 18

Distribution channels in travel and tourism: creating access

The ultimate winner is the consumer, the purchaser of travel, who will only adopt technologies and shopping habits with which he or she is comfortable. If advances in electronic travel distribution catalyse a shakeout of the travel industry, it is because the consumer wants it that way. (Financial Times, 1998: 3)

This chapter considers the last of the basic four Ps in the marketing mix, *place* or distribution as it was introduced in Chapter 6. Distribution comprises 'access', points of sale and convenience for customers. In revising this chapter for the third edition the principal author has obviously reflected on the extent and speed of changes in digital ICT that are producing a revolution in the way that many firms in the industry are able to do their business and create convenient access for their customers – while at the same time reducing marketing costs. See also Chapter 10.

The Internet and e-commerce systems that are now accessible to consumers were not available when the last edition of this book was written in 1993. In little over three years in the late 1990s these systems have came to dominate the strategic thinking of the entire industry, even though the actual proportion of sales via e-commerce was still minimal for all but a handful of businesses as we reached the new millennium.

This chapter stresses the continuing need to provide access for consumers at multiple points of sale away from the places of service production. Definitions of distribution channels, also known as 'pipe-lines', are discussed and key terms defined. The marketing functions performed by distribution outlets are assessed and reservation systems discussed, including a note on the current state of play of the leading global GDSs. The costs of distribution, often underestimated in the industry, are highlighted and an approach to calculating distribution costs is shown, although the primary issue of costs is dealt with in Chapter 19.

Because of the traditional importance of travel agents as a leading and influential sector in the transport and tour operating sectors of tourism, most texts on travel and tourism marketing deal with the distribution function from the standpoint of the retailer. This book recognizes the importance of retail travel agencies but stresses that they are not the most important channel for most businesses in tourism. In the USA and in Europe, the majority of travellers (domestic and international tourism combined as defined in Chapter 1) do not and did not use travel agents, and the majority of businesses in the industry use more than one form of distribution channel. Smaller businesses, which are numerically the largest part of the industry in all developed countries, are effectively excluded from retail distribution channels because individually they are too small.

On current evidence travel agents are still very important in specific sectors of the industry. But their influence within the overall distribution pattern is declining rather than gaining in importance at the start of the new century as all businesses are forced by competition and ICT to evaluate their current distribution costs and future options.

Issues underlying the changes in tourism distribution

Four underlying points help explain the 'revolutionary' speed of change in tourism distribution channels:

1 The nature of distribution systems is one of the main ways in which the marketing of 'intangible' service products has always differed from the marketing of goods.
2 While the digital revolution and the Internet are certainly changing the way that businesses are conducted and opening up alliances based on a depth of knowledge of customers that was previously unthinkable, the new ICT options are still only business tools and they do not change the *principles* underlying the consumer need for distribution channels or the trend to direct marketing explained in Chapter 19. What ICT does is greatly increase the speed and convenience of purchasing for customers, and significantly reduce the cost at which access can be provided by businesses. The Internet in particular is attractive as a very fast, low-cost new channel of immediate value and immense potential. Concepts of access have

always revolved around speed, convenience and cost, however, and the new channel will replace some of the existing ones, just as electricity replaced gas for lighting purposes and telephones replaced letters around a century earlier.

3 The compatible, low-cost hardware and software systems comprising the digital infrastructure that supports the Internet and e-commerce, did not just emerge in the mid-1990s. It was developed globally over the last two decades of the twentieth century. E-commerce in its business-to-business form was pioneered by the airlines' global distribution systems. Such development reached a point around 1997/8 where there was a sufficient quantum mass of online businesses and customers, suggesting very rapid progress in the first years of the new century. Technical feasibility, now supported by practical availability and backed by massive industry investment, fully came together only at the end of the 1990s.

4 Travel and tourism is one of the few 'pure' global information industries. Intangibility at the point of sale places great weight on the role of information provision and the industry is especially well placed to profit from the new developments in ICT. From exposure to advertising messages, through the selection of information and evaluation of options and prices; from the placing of a booking, payment and receipt of confirmation and tickets, right up to the point of departure on a visit, all the processes are conducted by exchanges of information. Currently, and increasingly, the exchanges take place between computers that also finalize the settlement of bills and store information about customers on databases.

Overall, the real distribution 'revolution' lies in the speed of the new processes and the lower costs that are now attainable by businesses that invest in the necessary infrastructure. Exchanges of information can be, and historically were conducted by letters, telephones and faxes, albeit slowly and at a far lower volume of transactions than big businesses require in the new millennium. Many such exchanges traditionally also involved intermediaries or 'middlemen,' such as retailers, because they added value to the basic processes, providing convenience and access at what was formerly an acceptable cost.

Right up to the 1990s a widespread myth persisted in marketing theory that, because services cannot be inventoried on shelves and in warehouses, distribution systems or 'channels' were actually less important in service industries than in others. Paradoxically, the inability in travel and tourism to create physical stocks of products is exactly the reason why the distribution process has now become so significant in the information age. It creates innovative opportunities and a flexibility that manufacturers must envy. Creating and manipulating the distribution systems that provide access for consumers is one of the principal ways to manage demand for highly perishable products, and distribution has become the primary area for seeking competitive advantage in both cost reduction and service improvement.

The importance of location and access

Location, location, location was the traditional mantra for profitable tourism businesses. For most small or micro-businesses with only one 'production unit', such as proprietor-owned guesthouses, small visitor attractions, equipment hire operators or indeed independent travel agents, the choice of location is still likely to be the most important business decision. A well-located small business can expect a good flow of customers to its area and past its doors. Product formulation, promotion and above all pricing have always been vital marketing considerations for small businesses, but not distribution. Traditionally, location is both place of production and the primary point of sale. As noted later, however, even the established distribution certainties of the smallest business are increasingly challenged and undermined by a combination of excess capacity in mature markets and the new opportunities provided by the Internet.

The fundamental requirement for well-located sites remains vital for large tourism businesses also. The more or less continuous search in the 1990s by international hotel companies for suitable development sites in the major cities of Europe provides some illustration of its importance. But location of production units is seldom, if ever, a *sufficient* source of sales volume for bigger businesses; one or more distribution channels are required to provide supplementary points of sale away from the locations of service production and consumption. Apart from the opportunities opened up by the World Wide Web, the factors that focus increasing attention on developing distribution channels are:

- The growing size of businesses (greater production capacity has to be matched with more points of sale to generate the required volume of enquiries and bookings).
- The increasing number of units within a group or chain (under one ownership, or linked in strategic marketing alliances and co-operatives) that opens up distribution options.
- The greater distances that customers are willing to travel, especially international travel, and the need to provide reassurance through reservations that suitable accommodation and other facilities are available.
- The importance of reaching and drawing in more first-time visitors in order to make a business grow.
- The even greater need to provide the most convenient forms of access for repeat or 'loyal' customers.
- Growing competition for shares of markets where there is excess capacity in a destination.
- The need to sell capacity ahead of production to optimize business cash flow and operational planning.
- The need to make maximum use of the sales promotion and tactical pricing opportunities afforded by modern distribution channels, especially in response to yield management programmes that identify periods where bookings are weak.

These eight factors, separately and combined, focus attention on the need to develop more efficient and cost-effective distribution systems that move the purchase decision away from the location of production towards places that prospective customers find more convenient, especially their own homes and offices.

As this chapter will indicate there are other good marketing reasons for developing distribution or access systems, especially cost reduction and control, protecting market share and matching competitors. But the overriding reason is usually to generate sales revenue additional to that which may be sustained solely by a good location. While, to some extent, additional expenditure on advertising or other communications is an alternative to developing points of sale, in practice there is a balance to be achieved between promotion and place. A massive demand generated by advertising would be lost, for example, if convenient points of access were not available to turn demand into sales. As modern distribution systems increasingly embrace both advertising and sales promotion functions, the balance has tilted strongly toward investment in distribution in the last decade.

Defining distribution or access systems: the notion of pipelines

Whether applied to travel agents or to Web sites the following definition of distribution is proposed for travel and tourism:

'A distribution channel is any organized and serviced system, paid for out of marketing budgets and created or utilized to provide convenient points of sale and/or access to consumers, away from the location of production and consumption' (Middleton, 1994a: 202).

The essence of this deliberately broad definition is that channels are carefully planned by marketing managers and serviced regularly through a combination of online access, call centres, sales visits, sales literature, multimedia options and in other ways. Each channel, once established, organized and serviced at a cost to be paid for out of marketing budgets, becomes in effect a 'pipeline'. Through each pipeline flows a targeted volume of sales and revenue over a marketing campaign period.

For most travel and tourism businesses the cost of distribution is by far the largest element in the marketing budget and the logical target for continuous innovation and investment to reduce unit costs.

The definition noted above excludes the activities of sales representatives employed to negotiate individual contracts with corporate clients to deliver a specified number of products, over a specified period of time, at a specified price. The essence of any pipeline is that it is a non-personal system, set up in advance to facilitate targeted sales volume but the actual flow of sales achieved over the period of a campaign cannot be known in advance. The rate of flow may be strongly influenced, however, by marketing activities in the pipeline such as sales promotions and price reductions, or external to it, such as advertising.

Key terms in the distribution of tourism products

Because of the special nature of distribution in travel and tourism, confusion is often experienced over the way in which terms are used. Drawing on the views of the principal American and British contributors, the definitions below appear to represent common ground:

Distribution process	The systematic process of creating access for potential customers in one or more places convenient for them, including their homes and offices but away from the place and time of delivery of products being bought.
Location	The geographical location of a site, or premises at which service products are delivered to customers.
Service delivery	The physical process of producing or performing the service product simultaneously with consumption, at a location.
Distribution channel or pipeline	Any organized and serviced system, created or utilized to provide convenient points of sale and/or access to consumers, away from the location of delivery.
CRS	All modern large businesses operate computerized reservation systems for processing enquiries and bookings and maintaining a consumer database. They play a core role in the distribution process. See also call centres, below.
GDS	The airline owned global computerized distribution systems originally created in the 1970s and 1980s prior to the emergence of Windows software and the Internet, primarily to provide e-commerce access for trained intermediaries to airline fares and booking systems around the world.
Intermediary	Any corporate third party or organization between producer and final consumer that facilitates purchases, the transfer of title to the buyer and sales revenue to the producer.
Disintermediation	The process of taking third party intermediaries out of a distribution chain, for example travel agents, when businesses deal directly with their final consumers by call centres or the Internet.
Call centres	Sophisticated 'call direct' telephone information and booking systems, often employing dozens or hundreds of people in places where property prices and staff costs are relatively low. India has become a key destination for such centres that can provide services

	all around the world. Call centres are used to deal with enquires and bookings directly from consumers and are the core response mechanism for advertising campaigns offering direct access via phone numbers. Increasingly linked with Web sites to process information requests and e-commerce, call centres are also used to create and manage consumer databases.
Web site	A site created on the Internet by a business to provide motivating information and possibly e-commerce facilities for customers. Each Web site has a unique address that may be accessed direct or by 'search engines.' A Web site is a distribution channel within the definition of this chapter.
The Internet	Global communications network, not directly owned by any organization, which is accessible by personal computers with modems (and via digital television sets with modems to provide interaction).
Infomediaries	A term attributed to Hagel of McKinsey, 'infomediaries' are globally branded 'virtual businesses' on the Internet that collect and sell information about a specific sector of a market and create a convenient platform (Web site/cyber marketplace) on which buyers and sellers can gain information and do business. They are a form of intermediary in cyberspace, operating at a fraction of the cost per transaction of traditional intermediaries. Many are the dot.com Internet companies that took the American and European stock markets by storm in the late 1990s.
E-commerce	Electronic trading and retailing on the Internet. Buying and selling online using credit cards and enabling customers to search for best prices and other options and then make, pay for and confirm bookings.
Intranets	Secure networks that operate via the Internet but which are open only to authorized users. Most large businesses operate intranets for internal communications, to manage their businesses and for B2B transactions.

Distribution – the largest cost in the marketing budget

Addressed more specifically later in this chapter, the core point needs to be stressed here that the fixed and variable costs of distribution are typically by far the largest element in the marketing budget of any large travel and tourism business. Seldom less than 15 per cent and usually far higher than advertising expenditure, in some circumstances the costs amount to between a quarter and a third of turnover. Remarkably, this fundamental truth was largely ignored by most travel and tourism businesses throughout the great expansion of international tourism markets over the thirty years to the mid-1990s. Exposure and comparison of the full costs, which have been possible only since the mid-1990s, helps to explain the current massive interest and investment in the Internet.

For example, for airlines, the IATA Director-General stated in 1995 'distribution costs, including commission and overheads, accounted for approximately 25 per cent of the global industry's operating costs' (*Travel Trade Gazette*, 28 October 1995). But it was only in 1995 that Delta Airlines, grappling with a relatively high-cost operation in the USA, was the first to put a cap on commission and overrides paid to travel agents which then handled over 80 per cent of ticket sales. American Airlines and others immediately followed suit and commission rates almost halved in the next five years with a massive impact on the bottom line. It has been estimated that airlines saved some $3 billion in costs between 1995 and 1998 as a result of commission capping alone (*Financial Times*, 1998: 90). For hotels it was estimated in 1998 that for a standard $100 hotel booking, the cost of using the basic pipelines specified below could be around $27.50 (*Financial Times*, 1998). The sum comprised:

Credit card charge	$ 3.00
Hotel CRS charge	$10.00–12.00
Ultra Switch	$ 0.50
GDS charge	$ 3.50–$4.00
Travel agent's percentage	$10.00
Total	$27.50

For hotels contracting with tour operators that also use travel agents, the real cost of the marketing and distribution function can be higher still, especially on discounted or 'distressed' sales.

Principals, customers and intermediaries

In the traditional terms used to discuss distribution in travel and tourism, businesses with products to sell, such as airlines, hotels and attractions, are often identified as 'principals'. For all practical purposes it is convenient to include tour operators as principals within this definition, although most of the larger operators are now linked by ownership or alliance with retail travel agency chains. Principals have a basic choice whether to sell direct to the customer or to achieve sales through one or more third parties, known as agents or intermediaries. Drawing on the definitions used by Kotler (1984: 542) the five main choices open to any principal are presented in Figure 18.1.

From the examples provided, it will be clear that distribution channels vary according to size and types of organization and that larger principals use more than one form of distribution channel, generally including retail travel agents. Thus a car rental business may establish its own corporate desks at airports to service travellers arriving and departing by air; it will

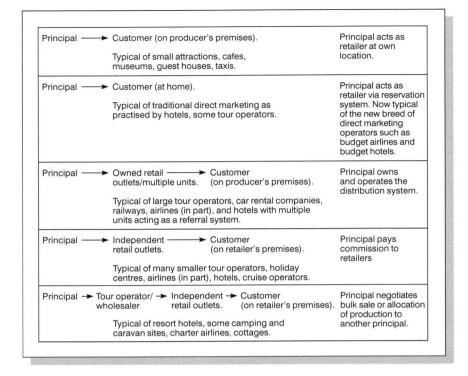

Figure 18.1
Distribution channels in travel and tourism marketing
Source: Adapted from Kotler (1984: 542).

provide direct 'pipelines' for its frequent 'loyal' users; it will usually offer commissions on sales made by travel agents and provide allocations of cars to tour operators that include car rental in their holiday packages. The same company will create and maintain Web sites including details of products and prices and how to book, with or without an e-commerce option. By contrast, a guesthouse or a small tourist attraction usually dealt only directly with customers and tourism information centres as a channel for display and bookings. By the turn of the twentieth century, however, leading small business entrepreneurs were creating their own Web sites to provide low cost information and booking services and extend their access globally. For small businesses, the Internet is a revolution indeed.

Multiple channel options for a hotel chain

The essential point arising from Figure 18.1 is that most producers or principals dealing with advance bookings have several distribution options to choose from. Common sense suggests that business strategy should be to use as many channels as are economic in order to optimize the demand for products. The difficulty in practice is to evaluate the costs and revenues arising from a spread of channels given the speed at which the options are changing in the new millennium. This is an important issue of investment in systems, costs to service and commission payable,

Each of the channels meets the definition of a distribution channel* and can provide all the main distribution functions outlined in the chapter.

1   Multi site outlets (for chains, alliances and individual hotels linked in co-operatives), in which each individual unit promotes and distributes the other's products.

2   Call centres, linked to central reservation systems, responding to promotional communications.

3   Hotel representative companies.

4   Tour operators and their equivalents such as branded short break operators.

5   Retail travel agents.

6   Business travel agents and conference brokers.

7   Arrangements for a specified number of corporate clients with whom the hotel group deals direct, for example with airlines for the accommodation of aircrew and with a government office or local businesses with regular accommodation needs.

8   Privileged user cards provided to stimulate repeat purchase from regular customers.

9   Tourist information networks (assuming they can make bookings).

10 Third party deals (for example with automobile clubs, which may provide discount vouchers as part of their own benefits for members).

11 Web sites, with direct access for final consumers and increasingly for other intermediaries to use.

12 Allocations to Internet companies specializing in travel, including cyber auction/distressed sales Web sites.

Note: * As defined in this chapter, 'any organized and serviced system, created or utilized to provide convenient points of sale and/or access to consumers in one or more places convenient for them, including their homes, but away from the place and time of delivery of products being bought'.

Table 18.1 Typical distribution channels for a large hotel chain

discussed later in the chapter. To illustrate the flexibility inherent in travel and tourism distribution systems, Table 18.1 summarizes the main distribution channels that could be used by a hotel chain.

Each channel is a specific system set up to receive a targeted but unknown volume of business over a specified period such as a year. Some of the channels, for example call centres and Web sites, may work in conjunction with other channels or may be used individually as parts of a comprehensive distribution service. Privilege cards for loyal users are included because they represent an organized system, which has to be serviced and supported, and their use may be targeted but sales volume cannot be known in advance. The third party channels in this context are not service contracts for a specified volume (such as a conference), but relatively open-ended commitments to a targeted volume of business over a specified period of time. Each of the channels listed is capable of providing users with all the ten functions listed later for a full distribution service.

The introduction of the Internet into the distribution pattern makes a fundamental difference since it both adds a flexible new low cost channel of almost limitless capacity and joins up seamlessly what previously were essentially discrete operations. Principals that dealt exclusively in the past with tour operators/wholesalers may open their own Web site and deal with some customers direct. The Internet and call centres will be the linked routes for privileged cardholders. Travel agents may make their bookings through global distribution systems or directly to an Internet site, or some combination of the two and so on.

Flexibility in alternative, informal points of access

The extensive use of information to communicate the nature and availability of most products in travel and tourism means that provision of access to information and promotion, if not points of sale, can be easily created wherever sufficient numbers of prospective customers congregate. At a tourist destination, for example, product information may be provided in tourist information centres, via porter's desks in hotels and in reception areas of visitor attractions. There is also obvious scope for using petrol filling stations, roadside restaurants, newsagents and post offices, all of which provide places to communicate with potential visitors. In the sense that all these points of access are permanent locations that have to be regularly maintained and serviced by producers, they are, in effect, alternative distribution channels.

For many smaller tourism businesses with no access to travel retailers, such flexible and low-cost informal channels provide valuable opportunities to display and distribute information and sales promotion materials, and to sell their products to prospective customers away from their location of production. Some of the channels may also provide informal word-of-mouth advice to prospective customers.

Other forms of travel and tourism distribution channels targeted at user groups

Further reflecting the flexibility conveyed by the intangible nature of travel and tourism products another group of targeted pipelines exists that are increasingly used by large businesses such as airlines, hotels, car rentals, restaurants and some attractions. These are not normally referred to as part of a distribution process yet they meet the essential criteria included in the definitions noted earlier in this chapter and can be used to fulfil all the distribution functions noted below. They are also strongly associated with sales promotion and direct marketing, and restricted to specific users or segments. Two examples are:

- Secretaries' clubs (created and serviced by some hotels and airlines).
- Special links with other bodies such as schools, clubs, societies, trade associations (created and serviced by many visitor attractions as well as hotels).

Two main roles of a distribution system – the key focus on advance bookings

As previously indicated, the primary function of any distribution system is to extend the number of points of sale or access, away from the location at which services are performed or delivered. In this sense at least, the function of distribution is the same for tourism products as it is for physical goods.

An important secondary function in services distribution is to facilitate the purchase of products in advance of their production. 'Advance' could be anything from two to three hours (for transport bookings) and up to two or three years or even longer (for major conventions or exhibition venues). It is a basic law of service production that the greater the volatility of daily demand, the greater the imperative to sell forward if possible. Obviously, for an airline running shuttle services on busy routes, the daily and hourly demand is closely predictable to within a very narrow margin. For a seasonal resort hotel, daily or weekly demand is open to very wide fluctuation and some bookings are made months ahead of delivery. The logical marketing response is to focus maximum effort on advance sales and organize reservations systems to that end.

In practice, products in travel and tourism are split between those for which reservation or pre-booking are both normal and a focal point of marketing effort, and others in which the capacity of supply normally exceeds demand so that pre-booking is not necessary. In the first category, which is by far the largest in travel and tourism, are most hotels and other accommodation suppliers, airlines, inclusive tour operators, car rental companies, coaches, long-distance trains, car ferries, theatres and shows. In these cases advance bookings are typical and managing demand by price and promotion is a marketing response to the volume of bookings achieved. In such cases several distribution channels are normal, with points of sale mostly away from the producer's location. In the second category are museums, other managed attractions, touring camp sites, pubs, popular catering, taxis, country parks and so on. Where reservations are not made, the point of sale is usually the reception desk at the producer's location. Pipelines may still be needed to reach and service particular customer segments, such as tour operators and schools and to provide points of information and display (such as in TICs).

By 2000 the sophistication of customer and inventory databases, plus online accessibility via the Internet, makes possible 'last minute' bookings literally up to a few minutes before a flight in the case of an airline. Instant access is highly valued by customers and an immensely valuable opportunity for producers to gain sales and revenue from otherwise unsold 'perishable' service products. The posting of last minute deals on Web sites and the use of cyber auctions have become popular in the USA for airline seats and hotel rooms that would otherwise be empty.

Ten functions of full-service distribution outlets

Distribution outlets that provide the full range of services to tourism industry producers carry out the following ten functions. For hotels, such outlets (see Table 18.1) include other units in the same ownership (or collaborating), airport, rail or coach terminal booking offices, hotel reservation companies, TICs if they include booking facilities, and retail travel agents. Since the late 1990s the Internet has become a primary channel for many businesses and has considerable scope for further development. All channels provide:

1 Points of sale and convenient customer access, either for immediate purchase or for booking in advance.
2 Display and distribution of product information such as brochures and leaflets – or multi media information that may be accessed and down-loaded via the Internet (providing choice for customers).
3 Sales promotion and merchandising opportunities, especially special deals on prices responding to yield management programmes.
4 Advice and purchase assistance, e.g. itinerary planning, suggestion of options and helpful product knowledge.
5 Arranging transfer of title to a product through ticketing and travel documentation, or provision of a unique reference number that can be presented at the point of delivery.
6 Receiving and transmitting sales revenue to principals.
7 Possible provision of ancillary services, e.g. insurance, advice on inoculations, passport assistance.
8 Sources of marketing intelligence for producers, often including building up consumer databases.
9 May be used as part of a principal's advertising and PR campaigns.
10 A route for receiving and assisting with complaints from customers, or directing them to another source.

With two fundamental differences the ten functions listed are identical to those carried out by the distributors of physical goods. The obvious difference is that there are no physical stocks to move about and maintain – the tangible evidence is primarily printed brochures. The other is that travel and tourism intermediaries do not purchase products in bulk and do not, therefore, share with principals in the financial risks of production. By contrast retail distributors of physical goods purchase their stocks, take responsibility for selling them to customers and risk losing money on unsold goods. This process of sharing risk has led to the search for economies of scale by buying in bulk and given crucial impetus to the growth of large, nationally branded, multi-site retail chains for physical goods in the last three decades. Wal-Mart in the USA and its links with ASDA in the UK is a recent example in the supermarket sector.

Branding has given such retailers great power over manufacturers. It has also led to the larger supermarkets using their 'own brand' labels to sell products they have bought in bulk at factory prices. Some distributors have integrated their operations backwards by buying producer organizations to service their needs and increase their profitability. Retailers in this context have massive power over suppliers and are, in effect, 'principals' rather than intermediaries in the process. Retailers have also been able to generate massive customer databases that they are able to use as a platform for developing new streams of business.

In travel and tourism by contrast, the prime responsibility for generating and managing demand has always remained in the hands of producers and principals. It is they who control product design in the industry, bear the bulk of the marketing costs, fix prices and are generally responsible for the volume of sales their products achieve. In the UK the leading retail travel chains account for over two-thirds of all package tour sales but they are actually owned by tour operators and have never achieved the sort of power that is common in the retailing of manufactured products. As a result, tourism businesses are effectively free to organize as many distribution channels as the economics of the business dictate. No such freedom and flexibility exists for most manufacturers of physical goods.

Calculating the costs of distribution channels in the tourism industry

For the reasons explained in this chapter, businesses in travel and tourism enjoy a greater flexibility in the use of multiple distribution channels than in other major consumer industries. At least in theory, the only limit to creating additional channels is the marginal point at which the unit costs of providing and managing each multiple access point exceeds the marginal unit profits of bookings using that access. Up to that limit, more profit is achieved by creating more access points. There are both fixed and variable costs in distribution.

Fixed costs

Some of the costs of maintaining and supporting distribution systems or pipelines are fixed in advance for the duration of any marketing campaign. *Fixed costs* in this sense include:

- Investment, capital and write off costs of installing and maintaining the hardware and software of reservation systems (CRS), call centres and the full annual revenue costs of employing staff required to deal with enquiries and monitor the bookings through each separate pipeline.
- Costs of brochure production, distribution and maintaining supplies of up-to-date information at all the points of sale, for businesses using intermediaries. For businesses using the Internet and e-commerce, creating and maintaining Web sites and servicing website visitors are the equivalent costs.
- Costs of sales promotion incentives designed to motivate intermediaries and any other points of sale.

301

- The costs of maintaining and motivating a sales force (if any) to negotiate agreements with intermediaries, in order to maintain brochure distribution and display.
- The costs of support visits to distribution intermediaries, including any costs of merchandising efforts and display materials that may be used at points of sale.
- Costs of staff training and any education, trade fairs and workshops organized to inform, motivate and support the distributor systems.

Variable costs

Variable costs in travel distribution may be very substantial, as measured in commission and overrides to intermediaries, or minor as in other costs associated with individual direct bookings such as costs of phone calls and postage. Although they are paid only when sales are achieved, it is the size of the variable costs and the proportion they absorb of the final price of many products that matters. Such costs are concentrating marketing management minds and focusing on the potential role of the Internet and direct marketing (Chapter 19).

Some comparative cost examples

EGG is a brand name of one of the larger British insurance and banking companies, Prudential, which was launched in autumn 1998 and attracted over £6 billion in customer accounts in less than a year by offering highly competitive interest rates. EGG accounts were initially available only by telephone and Internet, and within a year they were to be available exclusively by Internet, which was then the brand's only distribution channel. Its success is based on savings it makes in transaction costs. It was estimated in 1999 that charges for staff to deal with each customer transaction involving a visit to a branch office were £1.20, for a phone call taken by a call centre the charge per transaction was £0.40 and for an Internet transaction, £0.10, which was also significantly cheaper than a transaction at an automated teller machine (ATM) (*Economist* survey, 26 June 1999). The same survey indicates that it cost an average of around $1.00 to process an airline ticket on the Internet compared with an average commission of $8.00 via a travel agent. Costs savings of this magnitude (excluding the unit costs of investing in the corporate information technology infrastructure) are so massive that they are certain to challenge the use of most existing distribution channels.

A distribution cost illustration for a hotel

In practice, although database technology is making it much easier to trace the costs and the revenue of individual channels, the exact margins are often too difficult to measure. But producers have to monitor and endeavour to balance the costs of distribution as the following example shows. Assume a small hotel group, with three hotels and 500 double occupancy rooms, which is analysing the results of its previous years' marketing budget. Assume it has targeted 25 per cent of sleeper nights to be achieved over the next twelve months through three specified channels other than referral between units and direct bookings arising from its locations and repeat customers. For the sake of simplicity it is assumed that all bookings have the same unit value (e.g. £50 per person-night):

500 rooms × 2 persons × 365 nights × 25 per cent distribution via channels = a target of 91 250 sleeper nights to be achieved through three channels. When the results are evaluated:

- Channel A is estimated to have cost £100 000 to service and generated 50 000 sleeper nights. The average unit cost of distribution per night = £2.00 (not including commission).
- Channel B is estimated to have cost £30 000 to service and generated 25 000 sleeper-nights. The average unit cost of distribution per night = £1.20 (not including commission).
- Channel C is estimated to have cost £97 500 to service and generated 16 250 sleeper-nights. The average unit cost of distribution per night = £6.00 (not including commission).

'Cost to service' is the calculated cost of staff, and reservation system overheads, which had to be spent to sustain each channel in achieving its targeted level of business turnover. It also includes brochure costs and expenditure on incentives required to secure distributor support. In this example it does not include the cost of any commission on sales, which is assumed to be standard for all three channels. If commission levels were variable in practice, it would be sensible to include them in the cost to service, since it would alter the average unit cost of distribution.

The logic on this evidence for setting targets for the next year's budget is clear. Spend more on Channel B and less on Channel C. In practice, of course, the average yield produced by bookings may be greater in Channel C or more useful in creating low-season or last minute bookings, but these complications should not obscure the basic need to assess and compare the unit costs of providing customer access in each pipeline. Such annual calculations are inputs to decisions about which existing channels to develop and are essential for assessing the actual value of any new channels that might be opened up. Such an approach also facilitates innovation and monitoring. Provided that a hotel group or other principal apportions the costs of servicing and commission for each channel, the costs of creating pipelines for customer access can be budgeted with some precision, using the objective and task methods described in Chapter 14.

Global distribution systems: for tourism

Although computers have been used for individual airline inventory management since the early 1970s, database management of inventories made massive strides in the late 1980s through the development of international airline-developed CRS systems, some of which now span

System name	Countries of origin	Airline origins[1]	Agency installations in total and by world area	
AMADEUS established 1987	France, Germany, Spain, Sweden	Air France, Lufthansa, Iberia, SAS	Approx. 48,000 agency installations	c.30,000 installations in Europe, 6000 in N. America, 6000 in Caribbean/Latin America, and 4000 in Far East/Australia
GALILEO (APOLLO) established 1987	USA, UK, Netherlands, Italy, Switzerland, Greece, Belgium, Portugal	United Airlines, US Air, Air Canada, BA, KLM, Swissair, Olympic Airways, TAP	Approx. 40,000 agency installations	c.14,000 installations in Europe, 15,000 in N. America, 1600 in Caribbean/Latin America, and 6000 in Far East/Australia
SABRE established 1976	USA	American Airlines (ABACUS Group of Asian Airlines joined in 1998)	Approx. 48,000 agency installations	c.18,000 installations in N. America, 6000 in Europe, 5000 in Caribbean/Latin America and 18,000 in Far East/Australia
WORLDSPAN established 1990	USA and Far East	Delta, TWA, North West Airlines	Approx. 18,500 agency installations	c.9000 in N. America, 7000 in Europe and 100 in Far East/Australia

Source: Data compiled with the support of Hotel Systems Support Services Ltd based on Travel Distribution Report vol. 7, no 20 (2000) via Hotel Electronic Distribution Network (HEDNA).

Note: Although GDSs originated with airlines, under competition rules they are not permitted to favour particular companies and are essentially open to all airlines on the same terms and conditions.

Table 18.2 The four leading global distribution systems in 1999

the globe and are known as GDSs – global distribution systems. Led initially by American Airline's SABRE system, the GDSs were designed primarily as a distribution channel or pipeline for the use of business and retail travel agency intermediaries that were generating over 80 per cent of ticket sales in the early 1990s. The systems became independent of airline control in the 1990s and they are important 'information society' pioneers in exploiting global developments in information communications technology.

Table 18.2 provides brief information on the four main GDSs operating around the world at the end of the twentieth century. At that time it was estimated that over 300 000 users – travel agents and other travel professionals – were linked into GDSs.

Accessible globally via PCs, GDSs developed as professional systems that undoubtedly facilitated the rapid expansion of international travel over the last two decades. Their dominant concern, reflecting the airline owners' interests, was to service business travel and they were never significantly involved in leisure tourism and packaged tours using charter airlines. They have been the primary distribution system for booking scheduled airline tickets for nearly two decades and their use for worldwide hotel bookings has grown remarkably from 10 million reservations in 1991 to some 45 million in 1999. At the turn of the new century, GDSs handled nearly 90 per cent of all Business-to-Consumer (B2C) electronic reservation transactions in travel – including Web site bookings – and they appear to have largely resolved five major difficulties they faced during the 1990s.

1 The four major systems were originally developed some years before Windows software was widely available and rapidly became almost standard on the world's PCs. They used a form of computer language based on complicated *alphanumeric* codes that can only be used with training. In practice their use has been largely restricted to the travel agents for which they were designed. The codes worked well for airlines but did not so easily translate into other sectors such as hotels, car rental and events and festivals.

2 The systems require massive capital investment to build and update, and are expensive to operate and maintain. Costs per transaction to the businesses that use them are estimated to have doubled in the first half of the 1990s. At around $4+ (in 1999), the cost is at least as large as credit card charges and several times larger than the same transaction (where it is possible) via the Internet.

3 Much of the initial competition gain to the owning airlines has been lost as international regulatory provisions were brought in to prevent any form of preferential programming giving priority to particular airlines. The four main systems now operate as independent corporations.

4 Especially for non-airline products, GDSs were challenged in the late 1990s by new competition from Internet developments, which have particular advantages both for large and many small businesses in servicing 'loyal' or repeat consumers in their own their homes. In response, all the main GDSs now have linkages with major Internet players, such as *Travelocity* (SABRE) and *Expedia* (WORLDSPAN).

5 As communications technology opens up new strategic business options for owners of multimillion consumer databases such as supermarkets, banks and insurance providers, involvement in *e-commerce* for travel becomes a feasible option. But access to cost-effective global inventory management systems capable of continuous updating is still the vital part of all forms of distribution management. As long as GDSs provide such access cost-effectively for airlines and other travel services, their use is likely to grow as strongly through servicing direct marketing via the Internet and call centres as it did through travel agencies.

Thus the global developments of the GDSs were the essential forerunners to the subsequent developments of the use of the Internet for travel bookings. For airlines now using the Web to reach customers directly, GDSs are fully integrated into the information and e-commerce options, albeit using new forms of user-friendly Windows-based 'front-end' software. When interactive digital television is more widely available with high-speed, broadband modems to access the Internet, the consumer use of PCs for travel information and bookings will become less important. It is widely expected that travel agents' share of total airline bookings will fall for reasons of cost and convenience but, on current evidence, the GDSs will remain an essential management and control tool for the online sale of airline, accommodation and car rental products via the whole range of intermediaries noted in this chapter.

Some key aspects of the pioneering developments associated with GDS distribution systems are that:

- They developed 'intelligent,' online PC systems to link with travel agents rather than the earlier 'dumb' Viewdata terminals, so that other software programmes could be added and linked to CRS inventory-management software. These included automatic ticketing and invoicing of course, but also accounting and other office management systems, including word-processing and capability to link with customer databases.
- They were 'hard wired,' mostly using dedicated cable systems rather than dialling through the public telephone service. This improved the speed of connections to databases and increased the volume of traffic the systems could handle. It was needed when one considers that a system such as SABRE was already handling over 1 million bookings a day in the early 1990s.
- The subsequent rapid development in the 1990s of digital telephone systems (plus integrated services digital network – ISDN) enhanced the capacity of information processing networks and made it possible for the GDSs to communicate acceptable visual material for the first time, which is especially helpful to hotels.
- They provided leading-edge competitive advantages to system owners and major airlines and travel intermediaries in capturing the vital marginal business that has such a massive gearing to profit. In fact they were so good at this that GDSs were early targets for competition policy to prevent undue bias in the use of systems to favour the owners. In the 1990s, in the USA and EC, competition policy regulations were implemented to limit unfair competition.
- They broke the traditional mould of distribution models by providing rapid online access to international travel in the 1980s and 1990s that paved the way for the subsequent Internet developments.

At the start of the new century, GDSs remain the primary automated reservation-handling and management systems that drive e-commerce in travel and tourism. The development of new user-friendly 'front end' connections has greatly increased their flexibility and they are firmly locked into Internet distribution systems, including their links with leading travel infomediaries. The deregulation of traditional state telephone monopolies in Europe and the parallel development of the latest WAP mobile telephones has accelerated the development of personal, twenty-four hours a day access to the Internet, giving a further boost to its development and value to both buyers and sellers.

Chapter summary

At the beginning of the twenty-first century, although the signs appear very positive, it is still impossible to predict the extent to which the Internet will replace traditional B2C distribution channels and achieve the claims of its protagonists plus the profit expectations of its investors. It is, as the opening quote for the chapter indicates, a powerful business tool available to all competitors but its take-up depends more on its perceived value to customers than on its technical capabilities. Regardless of its level of penetration as a primary channel for tourism marketing and distribution over the next decade, however, there can be no doubt whatever that some twenty years' development of digital communications technology and software have put in place an infrastructure for travel marketing which is revolutionary in its global implications.

Connected PCs, satellite and terrestrial communications, sophisticated and connected consumer databases, call centres and the growth of interactive digital television provide a combined impetus for change, for which there is no historic parallel. The 'consumer infrastructure' is also in place in 2000 with growing proportions of the populations in developed countries and well over half of frequent travellers already experienced users of the new technology. All children in developed countries have the opportunity to be computer literate now and are experienced Internet users from their education at primary school all the way through to higher education.

While the ICT infrastructure was obviously not provided for travel purposes, tourism is an important user of it and the industry is singularly well placed to benefit because of its special characteristics. From the evidence summarized in this chapter we believe that distribution, traditionally the last of the famous four Ps in the marketing mix, has moved to the forefront of modern marketing. Direct marketing (see the next chapter) has also come of age as distribution processes can now address consumers as individuals or small groups, making irrelevant the traditional concepts of so-called 'mass marketing'.

Distribution channels (Internet and other direct forms) are the new forums for product innovation and development; they establish the parameters for pricing against competitors and are becoming the most important tool for sales promotion, merchandising and other forms of promotional communication. In addition to these benefits, the new technology can dramatically reduce the cost of marketing and distribution, making significant inroads into the 20–30 per cent of turnover it traditionally cost to make a sale. It can also deliver the vital last minute sales that have always been a problem for most tourism businesses.

With all these powerful advantages it is small wonder that distribution has become the key issue in tourism marketing. The new channels are clearly not for the faint-hearted, however. They are the cyber cockpits for competition in which there will be many losers as well as winners.

Further reading

Brassington, F. and Pettit, S. (2000). *Principles of Marketing*. Chapter 12, 2nd edn, Prentice-Hall.

Davidson, H. (1997). *Even More Offensive Marketing*. Chapter 15, Penguin.

Kotler, P. and Armstong, G. (1999). *Principles of Marketing*. Chapter 12, 8th edn, Prentice-Hall.

O'Connor, P. (1999). *Electronic Information Distribution in Tourism and Hospitality*. CAB International.

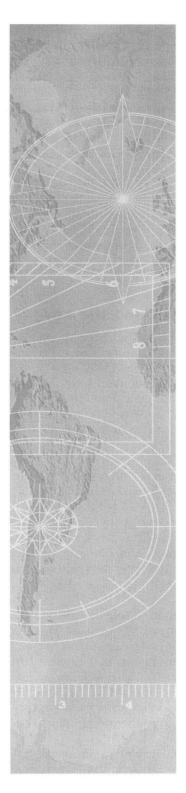

Direct marketing

We at easyJet have a simple and straightforward relationship with travel agents. They hate us, we hate them and that's it. (Stelios Haji-Ioannou, owner of easyJet, addressing an IATA conference in California, April, 2000.)

This chapter discusses the basic strategic choice and 'bottom-line' implications of marketing on a *direct* or an *indirect* basis. Direct means that a business promotes to and deals directly with the customer. Indirect means that sales are achieved through third party distribution channels created and maintained for that purpose as described in Chapter 18. The choice is seldom clear-cut, and the balance of advantage shifts continuously as new ICT emerges and influences decisions. A combination of both strategies for achieving sales response is common in the travel and tourism industry and this chapter argues that the choice is the most important decision that has to be made in current marketing practice.

Reflecting the flexibility in distribution channels for service products generally, the strategic choice between direct or indirect marketing has always been much more important in travel and tourism than for most manufactured products. Recent ICT developments for identifying individual customers by their addresses, profiles and purchasing behaviour, together with the ability to 'mine the data' for marketing advantage, are altering the strategic choices facing many operators in the new millennium. It now appears certain that this new technology, combined with the use of the Internet as a primary distribution channel, will shift the emphasis in marketing further towards direct-response strategies for all types of product, whether physical goods or services.

This chapter begins by viewing travel sales from the customers' standpoint in the practical context of enquiries, reservations and bookings. This is followed by key definitions and a review of the strategic options for generating sales, using a diagram representing the marketing flows in the producer/distributor/customer triangle (Figure 19.1). The chapter reviews traditional and new methods available to businesses engaged in direct marketing and summarizes the potential benefits achievable by those who use such methods in conjunction with new forms of customer databases and reservation systems. The chapter concludes with a discussion of the balance to be achieved in travel and tourism between direct and indirect marketing methods having regard to the growing opportunities for e-commerce.

The characteristics of sales in travel and tourism and the key strategic choice

The purchase decision process, introduced in Chapter 5, is especially complex in much of leisure tourism because of the relatively high cost of many products and the relatively high level of customers' psychological involvement with what they buy. Holidays are good examples of what are described in marketing texts as 'shopping' or 'speciality products', in the purchase of which many buyers are willing to invest considerable time and effort.

Because of the nature of holiday products, many buyers make enquiries of several producers and evaluate the choices according to their perceptions of what is offered, their interests and needs, and their ability to pay. At the same time, the growth of multiple holiday taking in a year and the success of corporate branding means that many customers are now willing to make relatively 'instant' impulse decisions about travel – if they have access to key information when they decide they want it. The way in which travel brochures and customer Web sites are laid out is an obvious illustration of producers' response to this purchasing behaviour.

Accordingly, because all businesses seek to create the maximum possible awareness of their products and convert it into sales, much of marketing effort is aimed first at promotion to generate interest and motivation, and second at distribution or access to optimize the convenience with which purchases can be made. As noted throughout Part Four of this book, the flexibility and versatility of multiple communication and access possibilities in modern travel and tourism means that it is increasingly difficult to identify where promotion ends and distribution starts – and vice versa.

This means that marketing managers have to review continuously the vital strategic questions. Is it better – more cost-effective – to create interest and awareness by communicating directly with their customers? Or to communicate indirectly through distribution channels? Or to communicate via a combination of the two main options? For larger businesses the implications for investment, costs and profitability are considerable.

Defining marketing methods of achieving sales

This section sets out the key definitions relevant to this chapter. It deserves careful reading because the loose usage in practice of terms such as 'sales', 'selling', 'personal selling', 'direct selling', 'direct marketing', 'direct-response marketing' and 'database marketing', is the source of great confusion to students. To judge from the travel trade press this confusion is just as deep among practitioners and it reflects the speed of change in the travel and tourism industry. It is worth the effort to use the main terms with some precision. Three important clarifications can be made at the outset:

- Distinguishing reservations or bookings from in-house sales.
- Distinguishing bookings by the general public from bulk or group sales.
- Distinguishing marketing methods from those that are sales orientated.

The first clarification is to stress that this chapter is concerned only with advance bookings or reservations made by customers either from their homes, their mobile phones or through a more formal distribution channel. It is not concerned with any of the aspects of in-house or on-site selling described in Chapter 16.

The second is to note that this chapter is about the methods used to generate bookings from the general public and is not concerned with the techniques of using a sales force to generate corporate sales. The use of a sales team to generate corporate and group bookings is of course very important in the travel and tourism industry and widely known as *personal selling* (see Chapter 16) because it usually comprises a form of person-to-person negotiation between buyer and seller.

The third clarification is to draw a distinction between traditional direct selling methods aimed at the general public and modern ICT focused direct marketing. The use of cut-out coupons, free phone numbers with advertising to generate enquiries and the regular mailing of brochures and leaflets direct to previous customers to encourage repeat purchases, are all techniques of considerable vintage. Modern direct marketing still employs many of these traditional methods but there are fundamental differences in the way they are used, outlined below.

Direct selling or direct marketing?

In their traditional form, simple direct communication links between businesses and prospective customers are known under the generic title of *direct selling*. Direct selling means the 'selling of goods and services, which involves direct communication between the producer and customers, without the use of retail outlets, distributors, wholesalers or any other type of middleman' (Medlik, 1993). In the 1960s and 1970s direct selling was the norm for most businesses in tourism other than tour operators and transport companies and practised also by businesses in sectors other than tourism, typically using direct-mail colour catalogues, often targeted at housewives. Names and addresses of prospective buyers were obtained by advertising with coupons to complete or telephone numbers to ring, and were added to lists of previous customers. List brokers could be used to purchase new addresses. This form of selling, a forerunner of modern methods, was always more significant in the USA than in Europe but it was effectively used as a way to shift products more cheaply than using alternative third party forms of distribution.

Modern, customer-focused approaches to direct marketing are founded on databases and iterative learning procedures incorporating detailed information, building two-way *relationships* between customers and businesses and continuously adapting products around the identified needs of targeted segments. In travel and tourism the shift from direct selling to direct marketing began in the 1980s. It reflects five important changes in the business environment:

- The growing need to know more about customers' profiles for targeting purposes; to customize products, and to work harder at retaining the loyalty of repeat customers.
- The need continuously to review and cut distribution costs to gain competitive advantage in pricing.
- The development of low-cost database technology capable of collecting, storing, retrieving and analysing data on hundreds of thousands of individuals – and linking databases for marketing purposes.
- The need to create competitive advantage in marketing methods, for which a review of traditional distribution systems offered some of the best potential returns.
- The new potential offered by the Internet for communicating directly with customers, available since the mid-1990s.

In the UK, ACORN and other geodemographic analysis systems available since the 1980s revolutionized the ability of producers to obtain and exploit a detailed knowledge of their customer segments. The subsequent development of Web sites that can be used to collect information about individuals who visit the sites has taken the process forward in the same direction, but by a quantum leap. As this chapter explains, the new technology opens routes to more cost-effective generation of enquiries; it leads to better conversion of enquiries into bookings and it is rapidly developing user-friendly multimedia communications and e-commerce options that are especially well suited to the requirements of businesses in travel and tourism.

The essence of the direct marketing approach was expressed succinctly by Gater, who used the term *database marketing*, which he defined as 'the building of a continuous relationship between principal and customer. That means not always selling when a communication is made and not always demanding a response . . . It means . . . obtaining loyalty through customer service and care, by building a relationship centred around the customer rather than the product' (Gater, 1986: 41).

What distinguishes the modern marketing approach from traditional direct selling is first the systematic way it develops a detailed knowledge of customers, and second how it uses the information gained to hone the effectiveness of the response process (including e-commerce) and convert awareness into sales. Direct marketing is also a highly cost-effective tool for market research, segmentation, market innovation and test marketing, as well as a means of reaching customers, making sales and monitoring sales revenue. As an approach to business it embraces and integrates every aspect of the marketing mix around chosen distribution or access systems under the direct control of marketing management.

Key definitions

Five important, frequently used, terms are defined below to assist communication:

Personal selling (group sales)	Achieving group or bulk sales through direct negotiation, normally face to face between a tourism business's sales personnel and buyers on behalf of groups.
Direct selling	Selling to the general public using direct communication between a producer and its customers. Direct mail, and telephone selling are included in this definition. Direct selling is characteristic of traditional sales-orientated businesses.
Direct marketing	Direct marketing links producers with their customers in a two-way communication, using individually addressable media (such as mail, telephone and e-commerce). Interaction is organized through a database recording unique details of actual and prospective customers, including their geodemographic profile, product purchasing behaviour and their responses to different communications media.
	The primary objective of direct marketing is to achieve more cost-effective use of marketing budgets based on a deep and evolving knowledge of customers and their behaviour, and direct communication with them. It is this objective which distinguishes direct marketing from traditional forms of direct selling.

The development and use of customer databases facilitates the selection, budgeting and specification of advertising communications media such as television,

313

Web sites, radio, press, post and door-to-door distribution because individual responses to each medium may be recorded against bookings.

Analysing databases also facilitates marketing research and marketing innovation as well as being an integral part of measuring marketing results. Linking different individual organizations' customer databases with their Web sites and with other national and international databases, such as the databases of mobile telephone companies, will open up new routes to achieving more cost-effective marketing in the next decade. As Fletcher et al., put it, database marketing 'is a customer orientated approach . . . and its special power lies in the techniques it uses to harness the capabilities of computer and telecommunications technology' (Fletcher et al., 1990: 7).

Response-fulfilment package   Marketing term for the traditional promotional package of envelopes, letters, leaflets, brochures, gifts and other printed materials, such as prize draw announcements, which are distributed in response to enquiries generated by direct-response marketing methods. In Web sites and e-commerce the response fulfilment is typically the multimedia graphics and information that can be accessed and downloaded for future reference but it may incorporate printed materials within the response.

Relationship marketing (CRM)   Usually identified as customer-relationship marketing, this is a term much used since the early 1990s to denote the frequent communication that goes on in direct marketing between producers and their repeat customers/loyal buyers. The use of loyalty/club cards is commonplace in travel and tourism and these cards are a special form of direct distribution and promotion channel. Relationship marketing aims to identify all the points at which customers are in contact with a business in buying and using a product and improving the efficiency and satisfaction that product purchase involves.

The marketing triangle for producers, distributors and customers

Figure 19.1 is used to represent the main transactions and flows of information in marketing that take place between producers (or 'principals'), distributors and customers. The diagram is valid for the marketing of all types of travel and tourism companies, whether in accommodation, transport, attractions, or tour operation. The shape of the triangle reveals the two basic options:

- Two-way direct response between producer and prospective customer.
- Indirect response, with distribution channels as third parties.

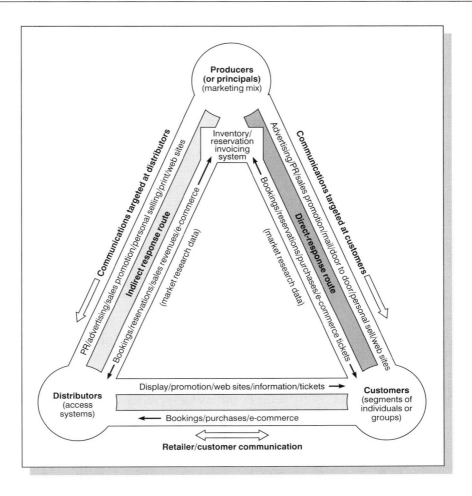

Within the triangle, there are three types of transaction:

1 On the right-hand outer leg of the triangle, outwards from producers, is the whole of the communications mix targeted at existing and prospective customers. It includes media advertising, PR, and sales promotions as well as any direct mail and telephone marketing. Since the mid–1990s it also includes Internet communications via PCs, mobile phones and interactive digital televisions.

  If businesses choose to market direct to customers, their bookings and money transactions flow inwards on the right-hand inner leg of the triangle to be serviced via e-commerce, e-mail, call centres and direct mail, operating through an inventory management system (CRS). The tickets/confirmations flow back along the same routes. This process is a rich information source for businesses and a very important feeder for customer databases that are also a source of marketing research. Databases may be used to identify responses from different forms of promotional techniques, such as bookings from advertising in different media, and response to specific sales promotions. The information, including names and all the information that flows from addresses (see Chapter 11), is a by-product of modern reservation systems and it costs very little to collect once the inventory/database system has been set up to record and analyse the flows of routine data within a management information system.

2 On the left-hand outer leg of the triangle, outwards from producers, is the communications mix targeted at the distribution system (all the third party pipelines identified in Chapter 18). It includes online communications and intranets accessible only to distributors.

If customers purchase through distributors, bookings and money transactions flow inwards on the left-hand inner leg to an inventory management system, and tickets/confirmations flow outwards on the same leg.

3 The base leg of the triangle represents the two-way flow of transactions between customers and distribution channels where the customer has no direct contact with the producer at the point of sale. Distributors include travel retailers and other pipelines that offer display space and access to products, and pass title on behalf of principals in return for a commission on sales. Distributors deal directly with customers in providing information, displays and promotional materials; they take money and supply tickets and other services. On the base leg, businesses have no access to their final customers – or the flow of continuous market research information they represent.

Direct or indirect, except for very small businesses, all inward flows of bookings and revenue are managed within an inventory or reservation system. These are linked to call centres that are themselves increasingly linked to Web sites. Such systems are typically set up to handle the provision of options if the customer's first choice is not available, as well as confirmations, ticketing and invoicing.

The strategic choice and its implications: the changing perspective

The triangular concept of flows makes it easier to understand the importance of the strategic question raised earlier in the chapter – whether, and to what extent, producers should distribute and promote their products direct to the customer or organize sales through third party channels of distribution. With few exceptions, there is rarely a simple answer to this question and the answer varies over time and for different products within the same principal's portfolio. Thus it may be advantageous for a hotel to market most of its domestic business travel direct to corporate clients, but to market the bulk of its international business and weekend packages through retail travel agents.

At any point in time a principal has to make a judgement on the marginal revenue and the marginal costs implied by the balance between direct and indirect sales. The judgement is made according to the ever-shifting circumstances and costs influenced by external and internal constraints, especially developments in ICT. The decision is mainly a financial one, reflecting the fact that any use of retailers has traditionally cost a minimum of 10 per cent of the sales revenue generated, usually deducted at source. Commission may be as high as 15 per cent and there are additional costs of servicing retailers with brochures and online connections, promoting to them and possibly employing a sales force to maintain product awareness and levels of display. On the other hand, commission is a variable cost that is not paid until sales are made and the principal's cash flow is not affected ahead of the sale. In most countries, travel agents' commissions have been cut significantly since 1995 following rate capping imposed by airlines in the global drive to cut costs.

The traditional approach – up to the 1990s

Traditionally, as the principal author noted in 1980 in the first systematic analysis of direct marketing in British travel and tourism, most businesses before the 1960s developed their businesses through direct communication with their clients. Direct selling was the industry norm for all but a few principals, such as scheduled shipping lines and their ticket agents. (Middleton, 1980). This norm never changed for small businesses, as previously noted. The rapid expansion in the numbers of retail travel agents, mainly to service airline passengers, inclusive tour customers and business travellers, occurred mainly in the 1960s, 1970s and 1980s. By the 1990s a national network of some 7000 retail travel outlets existed in the UK. Similar trends in the USA, biased more towards domestic business travel and the US internal airline and car rental markets, produced over 33 000 retail outlets. As a result, massive networks of retail travel outlets were conveniently situated to provide easy access for the bulk of the urban populations in both countries. Parallel developments have produced similar situations in most European countries, too, although travel agency usage has been typically lower in most continental European countries than in the UK.

If they were large enough to secure display space for their brochures and able to give retailers efficient online access to their reservation systems, it was entirely logical that airlines and hotels as well as tour operators should adapt and use these large distribution networks to sell their products. In Britain traditional direct marketing organizations, such as Butlins, Haven, and Hoseasons Holidays, made great efforts in the 1980s to adapt their marketing to travel retailers and achieve a greater proportion of their sales indirectly. Other domestic businesses followed this lead, notably hotel groups seeking maximum distribution for their weekend breaks to achieve vital marginal, last minute revenue. Again it was an entirely logical and cost efficient response to the availability of retailers, the state of information technology and the business economics of the time.

In the 1980s and early 1990s, with the support of principals investing in online access systems, efficient travel agency chains – increasingly linked with tour operators through vertical integration – were able to achieve economies of scale and much greater operational efficiency through the rapid introduction of newly available computer technology. Their largely automated offices could handle very large volumes of bookings, cancellations, surcharges and invoicing, and their computer networks had direct 'instant' access to the larger principals' systems and to GDSs, reducing the costly time spent in satisfying their customers' requirements. As a result, in the UK, the balance of advantage in producing the most cost-effective sales was seen to shift at that time in favour of the indirect or retail system of travel distribution.

The new approach for the twenty-first century

Some tour operators in the UK, such as Portland and the older established operators such as SAGA, retained their single-minded focus on direct marketing. Newer operators, such as Center Parcs, with attractive products in high demand, found that direct marketing was more efficient and cost-effective than retailing. Interestingly, the developments in information technology that enabled retailers to achieve greater operational efficiency in the 1980s and deliver the vital last minute sales, shifted again in the 1990s and are now assisting direct marketers to improve the efficiency and reduce the costs of their own marketing efforts. By the late 1990s, when many tourism Web sites were firmly established, it became certain that the future of travel and tourism sales lies more with direct marketing in the continuous competitive struggle to achieve marginal sales at least cost. Along with the twenty-four hours a day convenience of access to customers, the last minute direct sales opportunities provided by the Internet are crucial in the shifting balance of competitive advantage.

Looking back, by using modern direct marketing techniques, many tourism businesses have been able for years to achieve the bulk of their bookings at a much lower average cost per unit sold than was available through channel intermediaries. Looking ahead, the Internet and e-commerce offers many more businesses new opportunities to achieve a growing proportion of their sales at an even lower average cost per unit sold. (See comparative costs in Chapter 18.) But to do this a business has to invest large sums in direct promotion and computerization ahead of any sales achieved (see Table 19.1). Cash flow is obviously affected and there is no guarantee that the investment will succeed.

Of course, at the turn of the new century the Internet is not just *one* distribution channel. It comprises a number of direct pipelines or 'portals' designed to give customers convenient and user-friendly access to products. There will clearly be a major marketing battle for market share among the leading search engines and increasingly among the travel 'infomediaries' providing the branded Web sites that give customers confidence to deal in e-commerce. There will be an even more important battle as principals engage more directly in e-commerce and fight for channel share against the pioneering dot.com companies, many of whom seem likely to lose their early lead and may not survive.

Leading infomediaries in 1999 included *BargainHolidays*, *Expedia*, *E-Bay*, *Preview Travel*, *Priceline*, *Travelocity* and *Travelselect*. Such sites are the virtual equivalent of third party pipelines and they can readily connect (at much lower cost than retailers) with all the main producers in the industry. By mid–2000, however, it was clear that leading airlines and hotel groups, alone and through their strategic linkages, were investing in developing their own heavily branded Web sites to provide last minute booking and other valuable services direct to the customer.

An issue of channel power and politics

Prior to the availability of the Internet, if the initial expenditure on direct marketing did not produce all the required sales, further expenditure was needed to influence last minute sales. In that case, direct marketing costs per sale achieved rose very steeply and the techniques were not cost-efficient in generating the marginal sales that make all the difference between profit and loss in most tourism businesses. In the difficult trading years that are all too frequent in tourism, the marketing costs were just too great. This fact of life for service providers put power into the hands of retailers in the 1970s and 1980s. Since 1995, the economics changed dramatically with the benefits held out by cyber auctions and other low-cost means of targeting last minute sales via the Internet, as the date of production and delivery approaches.

The Internet, with its combination of owned Web sites and the many dot.com *infomediaries* available in travel, now provides the most efficient means to achieve last minute sales, creating near ideal conditions for what classical economists termed the 'market clearing price'. Although expectations that the Internet will perform this last minute role more efficiently than traditional distribution channels are very high among larger businesses, it has to be stressed that the volume of e-commerce business at the start of the new millennium was still tiny and developments have to be watched very carefully. E-commerce volume will vary greatly between familiar branded budget airlines and hotels where repeat usage is already high, and the more exotic end of holiday products for which Internet sales are still very low.

Although the direct/indirect choice is ultimately one of cost and revenue equations there are other implications, such as being seen to be supportive of retail travel agents. Where retail distribution chains deliver a significant share of a business's total sales, it will not be possible for a principal to exercise his direct marketing options without risking the goodwill of distributors that he needs for other parts of his business. Sometimes known as 'channel politics', the travel trade press in developed countries provides endless illustrations of the struggles between principals and distributors, of which the commission rate-capping saga is a prime example. Many caravan-park operators, for example, would be glad to use travel agents to sell their spare capacity in April, May and October, while marketing the easier and more profitable peak-season weeks direct. But this is not a practical option as the majority of retailers would understandably refuse to handle the off-peak weeks unless they had a main season allocation, which is easier to sell and generates more revenue and commission through higher prices.

Because travel retailers do not take risks by purchasing the products they sell, it appears most unlikely that they will ever dominate travel producers in the way that supermarkets have been able to do with the manufacturers of fast-moving consumer goods. The speed with which airlines collectively reduced agency commission rates since 1995 is an eloquent illustration of channel power. The blunt views of easyJet noted in the introductory quote for this chapter will infuriate travel agents but they are a succinct statement of *real politik* – for budget airlines.

For small businesses, there has traditionally been no alternative to direct marketing because the amount of revenue they can generate is too small to interest retailers and too costly to handle. Few small businesses could provide online access to third party distributors. Their telephone response systems were too slow and inefficient and their brochures would take up too much valuable display space. Smaller firms that group together to form co-operatives with a single joint brochure and reservation system are a different proposition and collective representation may offer an effective route to achieving retail distribution.

At the end of the 1990s, however, the Internet has totally changed the access options for innovative smaller businesses and opened up opportunities for national, international and global reach. At low cost the smallest of businesses can create a Web site to reach and provide direct access to customers anywhere in the world. Many leading small businesses have done so with remarkable results. Some are already achieving a third or more of their sales in this way. The Internet offers international direct marketing opportunities at low cost, high speed and flexibility in a way that was impossible only a decade earlier. Web sites are liberating proactive smaller operators from the traditional distribution shackles imposed by their size and location. See the case study in Part Six.

Direct marketing methods

Table 19.1 shows the range of direct-response marketing methods available to producers aiming at target segments of prospective customers. The techniques were outlined as elements in the marketing campaign planning process covered in Chapter 14 and need only brief additional comments here. Any direct marketing campaign is likely to use a combination of these methods rather than any individual one.

In terms of direct mail the collaborative use that many hotels and airlines make, for example, of American Express or credit card company membership databases, illustrates the value of third party address lists. Such lists can usually be accessed at a cost per thousand names and, although the names are not released to the businesses that pay to use them, such lists can be targeted (for example by post codes) and printed items can be distributed at low cost. An example of a joint mailing with a partner would be a country hotel group joining with, say, a manufacturer of conservatories, so that two non-competing leaflets, appealing to the same group of prospective customers, could share the cost of envelopes, administration and postage.

Direct mail	• to previous customers • to purchased lists of targeted prospects • via lists owned by third parties • in response to enquiries/returned coupons from advertising • via joint mailing with relevant partners • to targeted households selected because they have characteristics matching those of known purchasers
Telephone/telemarketing (via call centres)	• to targeted-customer lists • in response to enquiries
Door-to-door distribution	• to homes in targeted blocks of residential streets/roads
Travel related exhibitions	• to enquirers at stands, e.g. boat shows, travel exhibitions, and caravan and camping shows
Media advertising	• with coupons • with response telephone numbers, or 0800 lines
Web sites and e-mail	• Internet access via PCs and interactive television in customers' homes and offices

Table 19.1 Direct marketing methods to reach individual consumers

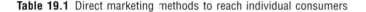

Telephone marketing or telemarketing has developed massively in the 1990s through a combination of technology led development of consumer databases, telephone communications and the creation of call centres. Many specific products, especially in financial services and insurance, have been developed for the purpose of dealing with customers on a direct contact only basis. Some are available only via the Internet and more will follow. As indicated in Table 19.1, call centres may be reactive to enquiries and proactive to target customers. In the last years of the twentieth century call centres have linked with Web sites and e-commerce as a highly cost effective combined response mechanism for dealing with direct bookings from the public and these forms of communication are certain to play a larger part in overall travel distribution in the next decade.

Door-to-door distribution costs of printed materials can be much cheaper per household than postal costs, and the ability to utilize this method more accurately using geodemographic targeting supported by database analysis has refined another of the important traditional direct marketing techniques.

Media advertising covers the whole spectrum of choice covered in Chapter 15. Interactive television for use by the general public in their own homes was developed in France using the Minitel system and in the UK using Teletext but, although the companies may survive in a different media, these are now yesterday's technology and latest estimates indicate that well over half of all homes in the main travel-generating countries will have direct access to the Internet via digital television within a decade. At that point the Internet is expected to be the primary channel for direct marketing.

Summarizing the potential benefits of direct marketing

The five benefits discussed below are potential in the sense that they cannot be achieved without considerable prior investment in hardware and software and in marketing planning. They require the co-ordinated use of consumer databases for accurate segmentation and targeting, detailed attention to product presentation on Web sites, in advertising and in print. They also require linked investment in call centres and efficient reservation systems to provide a competitive quality of customer service and a rapid response to enquiries and bookings. With those provisos, the following benefits are achievable and available to even the smallest of businesses willing to invest in a personal computer and modem:

- Detailed knowledge of customers, not only name and address, but neighbourhood type (ACORN) and purchasing behaviour. Telephone, e-commerce and coupon-response mechanisms provide other valuable streams of market research information, such as identifying new or repeat customers, frequent users and how they heard of the product. Such systems are the technology foundation for building effective CRM.
- Lower costs per transaction coupled with the ability to analyse the cost-effectiveness of generating enquiries, including the number of respon-ses by each form of media used, type of advertisement, type of leaflet and responses according to timing of advertisements. Such responses can be analysed by market segments, market areas and product variations offered. Cost per enquiry can be monitored with precision and the cost per booking can be quantified if the database is programmed to match bookings with enquiries. E-commerce results are obviously included in these analyses and can be compared directly with alternative forms of communication and distribution.
- Ability to measure the effectiveness of alternative response fulfilment packages sent out to enquirers, in terms of converting enquiries into sales.
- A framework for marketing innovations, whereby relatively small-scale test marketing with new or adapted products, new segments, alternative forms of media, alternative sales promotion options or different response fulfilment packages, can be systematically evaluated at low cost.
- Ability via the Internet to offer remaindered or 'distressed' products for last minute sales via specialist Web sites and cyber auctions aimed at customers seeking bargain offers, especially for branded products that secure instant recognition.

These five groups of direct marketing benefits are fundamental in their implications for achieving more cost-effective marketing. They are especially useful to businesses that are too small to engage in large-scale advertising or to achieve cost-effective access through retail distribution channels. Once again it is worth stressing that these benefits derive from the use of new information technology not available to any earlier generation of marketing managers. The scope for pioneer users to achieve competitive advantage is considerable.

Bearing in mind that most large tourism businesses, such as hotels, car rental companies and scheduled airlines, have a large proportion of frequent repeat customers that are vital to their profitability, the balance of advantage must now lie with direct marketing. It is no accident that hotel groups and airlines have been competing ever more strenuously in recent years to bind their 'loyal' customers to them with a wide variety of membership or club schemes, frequent traveller awards and other 'special relationship' arrangements for their key accounts.

The flexibility conferred by the range of direct marketing mechanisms is also important. Third party distribution networks require careful planning and organization, plus continuous motivation and servicing (Chapter 18). By contrast, product and sales promotion options on Web sites can be set up and modified in a matter of days or hours or continuously online, as the need arises.

And the major disadvantage, overcome in the 1990s

For years, although direct marketing was always cost-efficient at generating advance bookings, its biggest disadvantage lay in its limited capacity to secure vital last minute sales. For tour operators and many carriers, a national distribution system of retailers provided the only available mechanism for notifying and promoting their unsold capacity in the vital two to four weeks before the departure dates in their programmes and schedules. In that period all sales are likely to be marginal and their effect on profitability is high. Using online links with a principal's inventory, agents could provide a national top-up bookings service with a speed and flexibility that direct marketing could not match. It gave them power over principals for many years.

But now, through the Internet and especially through Web sites and 'infomediaries' specializing in last minute sales, a twenty-four hour virtual global marketplace exists that is accessible from homes and mobile phones. It conveys opportunities to promote and change prices continuously as the deadlines approach. Such business was growing rapidly at the start of the century and seems certain to expand in line with the development of interactive broadband television access.

Chapter summary

This chapter deals with the fundamental strategic marketing choice concerning the methods and costs involved in creating awareness of products and achieving sales that has to be made by all sizes and types of business in the tourism industry. It is a choice that vitally affects their competitive position and the cost-effectiveness of marketing. The use of direct marketing techniques embracing the Internet is advocated because it is especially suited to the common travel marketing tasks of generating enquiries, converting them into bookings, securing repeat business and maintaining customer relationships. It is vital too for the majority of businesses that are too small to use retail distribution channels, and the many others that market themselves partly direct and partly indirectly and are reviewing the balance.

In all countries, the number of travel and tourism companies that sell *only* through retail travel agents is very small indeed and, although powerful in their sectors of the industry, they appear to be a special case and provide no general rule. The evidence suggests that direct marketing is actually the norm in travel and tourism and that the remarkable rise in the number of travel agents was a temporary phenomenon in the second half of the twentieth century. It reflected a particular stage in consumer demand (mass marketing for mass produced service products) and a particular stage in the development of information and communications technology that is now being supplanted by newer technology that empowers customers and businesses alike in the exchange process that lies at the heart of marketing.

The balance to be struck between direct and indirect marketing is based first and foremost on the business economics of unit costs per transaction achieved. Second, it is a matter of adjusting to the opportunities and threats associated with rapidly changing information technology, which are continuously altering the relative costs of achieving distribution and making sales. Third, the balance is an issue of travel trade politics reflecting the relative power of principals and retailers within the distribution process.

Finally, this chapter stresses the point that over and above the core decision on the relative costs of doing business, direct marketing using modern ICT delivers additional information benefits that make the case for their maximum use overwhelming. These include knowledge about customers, a mechanism for relationship marketing, information about media costs per booking, a framework for innovation and a means of achieving last minute sales for unsold products. The combination of advantages points powerfully in the direction of direct marketing in the first decade of the twenty-first century. The advantages are especially valuable to the thousands of innovative smaller operators now able to provide instant low-cost national and global access for prospective customers for the first time.

Further reading

Brassington, F. and Pettit, S. (2000). *Principles of Marketing*. Chapter 18, 2nd edn, Prentice-Hall.

Jobber, D. (1998). *Principles and Practice of Marketing*. Chapter 13, 2nd edn, McGraw-Hill.

Kotler, P. and Armstong, G. (1999). *Principles of Marketing*. Chapter 17, 8th edn, Prentice-Hall.

Poon, A. (1993). *Tourism Technology and Competitive Strategies*. CAB International.

Part Five

Applying Marketing in the Travel and Tourism Industry

Marketing countries as tourism destinations

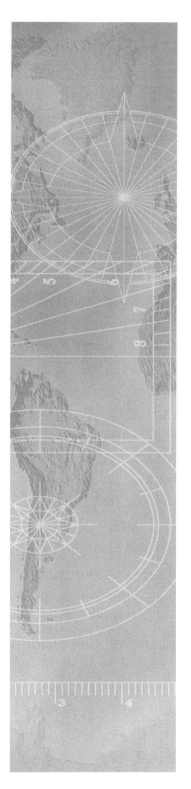

Imagine a time when Destination Marketing Organizations (DMOs) no longer need a network of national tourist offices within the major outbound markets of the world. All that is needed is a centralized organization that is online to the world. (WTO Business Council, 1999: 137)

This chapter is about the marketing role of national tourism organizations, also known as destination marketing organizations and sometimes as national tourism administrations (NTAs). The terms tend to be used interchangeably although a DMO is always the marketing side of an NTO/NTA, responsible for the overall marketing of countries as tourist destinations. Concern with them shifts the focus from the marketing practice of private sector organizations to what are commonly government organizations or public sector agencies that receive all or part of their funding from government.

The majority of NTOs/DMOs are not producers or operators. They generally do not sell products directly to visitors and they are not directly responsible for the quality of services delivered, although most aim to influence it. In developed countries they are typically responsible for only a small proportion, however important it may be, of all the travel and tourism marketing programmes carried out on behalf of their country. The principles and practice of a DMO approach to marketing outlined in this chapter are essentially the same as those adopted by regional, state or local tourism offices although the scale of operations is obviously different.

The chapter begins with a definition of NTOs/DMOs and the scale of their marketing operations internationally. The factors influencing NTO marketing are summarized and the nature of marketing strategy is discussed, distinguishing between what NTOs can achieve by spending their budgets mainly on promotion and what they can achieve through various forms of *facilitation*. Facilitation means providing assistance to the component sectors of the travel and tourism industry within a country and in other countries from which visitors are drawn. Because the marketing process for a DMO is different from that for providers of accommodation, transport or attractions, the process is outlined in some detail. The term *facilitation* is explained in general and with specific reference to the growing influence of the Internet in destination marketing.

NTOs defined: some international dimensions of destination marketing

A tourist organization, as Medlik and Burkart explained it, 'is defined by reference to the interests of a geographical area as a tourist destination, which may be a country, region or an individual town' (Burkart and Medlik, 1981: 255). Within this context, 'the term NTO is used to designate the organization entrusted by the state with responsibility for tourism matters at the national level. It may be a fully-fledged ministry, a directorate general, a department, or corporation or board' (a neat definition adopted by McIntosh, 1972: 86). The principle of government support through official recognition and usually some funding is normal even in cases where the NTO is not part of the state administration.

Around the world there are estimated to be some 200 NTOs of different sizes and organizational patterns, supporting altogether some 1000 foreign branch offices (Millington and Cleverdon, 1999). Around two-thirds of the world's tourism offices are estimated to be government ministries or departments and the other third are separate legal entities.

Nearly all of them are engaged in one or more aspects of destination promotion although relatively few are practising the systematic approach to marketing developed in this book. Most of the promotional effort organized by these NTOs is aimed at international markets but in recent years many have also been spending considerable sums on the promotion of domestic tourism by residents within their own countries. Larger branch networks, such as those supported by Britain, France or Greece, comprise over thirty offices in the main countries from which they draw their visitors. Most developing countries can afford to maintain only a very few offices in key markets.

The best, although still limited source of data about the activities of NTOs, is the WTO based in Madrid. The WTO is an intergovernmental organization to which most but not all countries belong. From time to time it undertakes surveys of the activities of NTOs via self-completion questionnaires that include reference to promotion. Unfortunately, the quality of the responses and the sheer difficulty of establishing the exact size of marketing and promotional expenditure mean that the results must be treated with great care. For example, should 'marketing' include costs of staff and premises as well as promotional budgets? Should it include research and product investment? Should it be presented as gross expenditure or net after allowance for sales of advertising space in brochures and contributions to campaigns and Web sites by commercial sector partners? Is it possible to separate marketing for international tourism from domestic tourism? Countries tend to answer these questions differently according to their own accounting conventions. The estimates provided to the WTO are then converted into US dollars for international comparisons, using rates of exchange that may have altered radically by the time the results are used.

Notwithstanding these important caveats, at least it is possible to use WTO data for broad indicative purposes and compare declared marketing expenditure with declared international arrivals and receipts from international tourism. Relevant data for five European countries is shown in Table 20.1.

Table 20.1 indicates that NTO marketing expenditure in leading European countries as a percentage of gross receipts from international tourism (excluding air and other fare payments) is typically less than 0.5 per cent (column d). This evidence supports earlier WTO surveys noted in the 2nd edition of this book. European spending is relatively high by international comparisons and, assuming an average of say just 0.3 per cent of the US $5000 billion estimated by WTO to have been spent on world-wide international tourism in the late 1990s, the annual global expenditure on destination promotion could be of the order of $1.5 billion.

Country	(a) International tourism arrivals (million)	(b) International tourism receipts (US$ million)	(c) Marketing budget (US$ million)	(d) (c) as % of (b) budget as % of receipts	(e) (c) / (a) budget per visitor (US$)
Spain	43.4	26 595	72	0.3	1.7
Netherlands	6.7	6 597	43	1.1	6.5
UK	26.0	20 569	84	0.4	3.2
France	66.9	28 316	57	0.2	0.9
Austria	16.6	12 393	58	0.5	3.5

Source: World Tourism Organization data.

Table 20.1 The indicative size of NTO marketing expenditure for international tourism in 1997 (Europe)

Interestingly, although tourism arrivals increased in the 1990s, expenditure by NTOs on marketing did not. A recent WTO comment notes, 'total NTO budgets reported have tended to decline ... by nearly 20 per cent from 1993 to 1997. Promotional budgets were only just maintained' (Shackleford, 1999). These estimates are no more than orders of magnitude but they illustrate the scale and importance of modern destination marketing, still largely funded by governments. Expenditure aimed at domestic tourists would be additional to this figure but it is quite impossible to estimate it at the present time.

Another useful indicator of the importance of NTO marketing is the evidence, also from WTO data, that expenditure on marketing typically accounts for between one-half and two-thirds of the total budgets of NTOs.

It appears reasonable to conclude for all practical purposes, therefore, although the figures provide no guidance as to what *should* be spent, that an annual expenditure on marketing international tourism of between 0.3 and 1.0 per cent of international visitor receipts, covers the range represented by current budgets of most NTOs for mature market destinations around the world. Larger proportions will have to be spent by governments in small destinations and by developing destinations that do not have a well-established tourism industry to participate in the cost of reaching and persuading international travellers to visit their destination.

NTO marketing has influence, but limited control

The influence of the marketing activity undertaken by NTOs/DMOs differs from commercial marketing: first, because much of the travel between developed countries is for business and other non-leisure purposes, such as visits to friends and relatives, and these segments are not significantly influenced by the promotional expenditure of a DMO. Second, especially for developed destinations, it is obvious that a large proportion of leisure visits would continue to be made without DMO expenditure because they are influenced by previous visits, recommendations of friends and, of course, the private sector marketing efforts of the tourism industry as a whole. Great care must be taken, therefore, in using the average percentages noted in the previous section as any sort of guide.

In practice, NTO/DMO marketing budgets are not aimed at all tourism but targeted at specific market segments. If DMOs published information relating marketing expenditure to the receipts attributable to particular target segments, the NTO marketing percentages would reveal figures equivalent not to 1 or 3 per cent, but to 10 per cent or even more of some targeted customer spending. The statistics of tourism demand are very seldom adequate to identify tourism expenditure by segments, however, and most DMOs have a vested interest in the notion that their budgets can somehow be related to the whole of tourism receipts.

In common with many other sectors of the expanding tourism industry, the development of professionalism in marketing around the world is still relatively recent in NTOs. It appears certain to become more important over the next decade as markets mature, technology challenges multiply, competition between countries for shares of markets increases and governments put ever greater pressure on the agencies they fund to set targets and demonstrate value for money. On the broad evidence of the data above, notwithstanding the lack of precision in the available statistics, it is reasonable to expect that the application of systematic marketing techniques by NTOs could make a major contribution to cost-effectiveness measured in dollars spent per targeted tourist arrival.

Ideally, all governments would like their DMOs to prove that for every 1000 dollars spent on marketing there is a response that can be measured in the number of visits and expenditure achieved over a given period of time. If such proof were possible, governments would be able accurately to allocate larger or smaller budgets to tourism according to their policies for growth, maintenance or other priorities discussed later. For all countries, however, apart from the size of their marketing budgets and the quality of the marketing activities in which DMOs engage, there are three main underlying factors outside their control that are continuously at work in determining the actual volume and expenditure of tourism generated between markets of origin and countries of destination. These factors, discussed separately below, distort the measurement of expenditure and response in all countries:

- Expenditure on marketing is only one of the influences that determine tourism volumes and expenditure to any country.
- The marketing effort of DMOs is only a part of the total tourism and travel trade marketing effort made on behalf of a country.
- Very few DMOs sell products to prospective visitors directly. Even where they take responsibility for operating, say, hotels or transport, these activities are typically only a part of the total product supply.

Marketing is only one of the influences

Chapters 4 and 5 set out the economic, social and behavioural factors at work in societies that collectively determine the volume and types of travel and tourism generated by any particular country. These so-called 'determinants and motivations' of tourism include disposable income per capita, amount of leisure time available, personal mobility, availability of transport systems, the price of travel and exchange rates. The importance of understanding the external business environment as the basis for marketing strategy has been stressed throughout this book and needs no further emphasis here.

Therefore, NTO/DMO marketing must aim to understand and respond to these external factors but it cannot influence and change them directly. For example, Britain derives about a quarter of its international tourism revenue from American travellers who are its most important market. But neither the British government nor the British Tourist Authority (BTA) has any influence over the level of US incomes, the international value of the dollar or the state of the US economy – the factors that ultimately drive US international tourism. Effective NTO marketing begins with an understanding of the determinants influencing its main markets; it aims to work with the opportunities created by favourable events and to limit the impact of unfavourable ones. For example, when the so-called 'Tiger' economies of Asia Pacific suffered a severe economic downturn in the late 1990s, the tourism marketing efforts of countries such as Singapore, Hong Kong and Thailand were simply overwhelmed by events from which they took some years to recover. This point in no way denies the value of destination marketing, but does set it in the wider context of national and international events over which NTOs have no control or influence.

NTO marketing is only part of the total marketing expenditure for a country

Although the evidence is now very dated the Irish Tourist Board (Bord Failte) in the mid-1970s, calculated that the marketing expenditure contributed by the board amounted to about 15 per cent of all tourism marketing expenditure being undertaken for the Republic of Ireland in the USA (Heneghan, 1976). It is difficult to calculate such figures because mostly records do not exist. But the proportion looks realistic having regard to what is spent by airlines, shipping companies, tour operators, accommodation interests and others based in Ireland, and the travel trade in the USA. For most developed countries judgement suggests that a DMO's expenditure on marketing to international visitors is seldom more than around 10 per cent of the total marketing expenditure. It follows that, if the bulk of all tourism marketing expenditure is not controlled by a DMO but by independent third parties, it is impossible for a national organization either to claim all the credit or to be blamed for failure in the fluctuations in visitor arrivals occurring over any given period of time. For countries where tour operators dominate the marketing process, the DMO influence is likely to be especially weak.

Since the mid-1990s, the BTA has formally acknowledged this important fact, stating that for 1994/5 'our [marketing] activities were responsible for some 7.5 per cent of the total inbound tourism spend' (BTA Annual Report). In other words, although they were carefully targeting the expenditure for which they claimed responsibility, and could still have influence over non-targeted visitors, they were not responsible for over 90 per cent of inbound tourism expenditure. Similar proportions certainly apply to other mature destinations.

Limited influence over the supply of products.

In developed tourist destination countries there are thousands of commercial firms and hundreds of public sector organizations engaged in providing and marketing international tourism products and services. Of these, only a small minority have any formal relationship with an NTO through membership of state, regional or area tourist boards. Thus a large number of businesses generate a very wide range of tourism products, most of which are beyond the marketing influence of an NTO with regard to volume, design, price and promotion decisions.

Summarizing the marketing role of NTOs/DMOs

One may conclude from this consideration of the three external factors that the marketing effort of an NTO/DMO, measured against international tourism flows to a destination, will always be:

- Partial or even marginal in terms of the range of segments it covers and the products it influences.
- Submerged to a large extent in the greater impact of the determinants and motivations affecting markets of origin.
- Outweighed by the marketing effort of private sector partner interests in tourism.

Paradoxically, the NTOs of developing tourist destination countries have a far greater *potential* influence over their countries' tourism. They are potentially better able to evaluate the success of their marketing efforts. In practice, however, they mostly have very restricted budgets, lack the professional management skills to exploit their advantages and are often dominated by powerful tour operator influences.

These conclusions are not intended to imply that NTO marketing expenditure is necessarily ineffective or wasted. They do mean that most DMOs are not in direct control of the tourism products they promote or the results that are achieved as measured in annual visitor numbers and expenditure to or within a country. It is therefore helpful to explain the role of NTO marketing from a perspective of targeted margins and influence rather than control, a very different perspective from that used to explain commercial practice.

On the other hand, NTOs/DMOs have an influence over tourism marketing that extends well beyond the small proportion of tourism for which they claim direct responsibility. The influencing role is, of course, a two-way or partnership process. There are many different models and they have to be tailored to suit different countries. In the UK the influence comes through collaboration between BTA (for international marketing), other tourist boards and commercial partners, which contributed some 50 per cent of international marketing budgets in the late 1990s.

In other developed countries, such as Canada and Australia, powerful public/private sector organizations have been formed to act as lobbies and provide a forum within which NTOs and the travel and tourism industry collaborate. There are equivalent associations in some European countries but not in the UK, although the government that took office in 1997 did set up a consultative forum in which it retained control over appointments and agenda. In Canada, 'Tourism Canada' was a 100 per cent government-funded NTO until 1995 when it was replaced by the Canadian Tourism Commission (CTC). The CTC is a partnership organization between the federal and provincial/territorial governments and private sector partners. This successful partnership combined to increase funding for tourism marketing from C$15 million in 1995 to over C$100 million in 1998/9. The private sector contributed just over 50 per cent of this total.

Destination promotion role for NTOs or marketing facilitation?

From the previous discussion it can be concluded that there are two levels to consider in marketing a country as a destination. The first level, concerned with the destination as a whole, is the primary focus of what NTOs/DMOs do. The second level covers the marketing activity of the mainly private sector operators promoting their individual products. In the first level of marketing, DMOs have to choose between two alternative strategies. One of these is reaching prospective visitors via expenditure on a promotional mix intended to achieve destination awareness and influence prospective customers' attitudes and purchasing behaviour; the other is concerned with exercising a facilitating influence over the tourism industry. The following two sections deal with each strategy in turn.

A promotional strategy

The promotional strategy means devising and implementing promotional programmes to communicate destination images and key messages to targeted segments of potential visitors. The objectives are typically to make customers aware, motivate their interest, encourage them to surf the Web, send for product brochures, call direct or go to travel agents in their area. Using a metaphor that has been widely quoted, Burkart and Medlik summarized this strategic choice as creating an 'umbrella campaign' under which the various individual providers of tourist services can market their own components of the overall tourism product.

Destination marketing organization promotions may thus cover the full range of communication and distribution tools, providing a context in which 'airlines and other transport operators, hotel groups and tour operators can market their individual services to a market of potential buyers already aware of and predisposed to the destination . . .' (Burkart and Medlik, 1981: 197).

The decision to invest the greater part of their budgets in promoting destination awareness and images appears to be an obvious and convincing strategy. Certainly it was still the chosen route for most national and regional DMOs around the world at the end of the 1990s. Following the logic of the strategy, the bulk of NTO marketing expenditure and its organizational structure should reflect promotional campaign priorities and be invested in advertising, publicity and promotional materials. In selecting this strategy, however, it has to be assumed that the budget an NTO has to spend is large enough in practice to implement effectively the promotional campaigns its market segmentation studies identify as necessary. To be effective, such campaigns must be of sufficient weight and impact to reach and motivate the necessary numbers of potential buyers who are aware of and predisposed to the destination. But if budgets are not adequate for the task, expenditure on an image-creating strategy may in practice be a complete waste of money – on perfectly logical and desirable objectives that cannot be achieved.

With NTO budgets for marketing purposes equivalent to an average of 0.5 per cent or less of tourism expenditure, and the fact that most DMOs cannot influence more than around 10 per cent of all prospective visitors, the question of how effective many DMO marketing campaigns are in practice is valid. As discussed in Part Five of this book, the typical commercial operator investment in marketing lies between 15 per cent and 30 per cent if the full costs are counted.

A facilitation strategy

Fortunately there is an alternative strategy, relevant to all NTOs/DMOs. This is the strategy of *marketing facilitation*, as it is defined in this chapter. Facilitation creates marketing collaboration bridges between a DMO and individual operators in the travel and tourism industry, and between the 'umbrella' campaigns and industry marketing expenditure. The case for marketing facilitation is based on five considerations that are commonly found around the world:

1 That governments have policy objectives for wishing to promote tourism. Typically these are now expressed in economic, social and environmental terms that can be interpreted and defined as marketing goals.
2 That budgets granted to NTOs will usually be much less than adequate to undertake all the marketing tasks identified, so that selection of priorities is always required.
3 That the destination country possesses a range of tourist areas, products and segments, some growing and some declining, to which it attaches differing priorities and which have different marketing implications for achieving government policy objectives.
4 That DMO goals cannot be achieved without private sector support, collaboration and contributions to the cost of campaigns.
5 Although most DMOs can reach no more than 10 per cent of visitors through promotional campaigns, they can aim to reach virtually 100 per cent through one or more forms of facilitation.

These are powerful considerations. The most cost-effective marketing role for a DMO lies in focusing on the contributions that it can best make. These are:

- Research to establish and communicate to its industry partners, promotional priorities for targeted markets and segments. Defining destination images and branding are part of this process.
- Liaising with and influencing private sector partners to achieve the priorities.
- Co-ordinating elements of tourism products (such as tourist information and destination Web sites) not provided by the private sector.
- Providing investment and marketing support for new or growth products relevant to policy goals.

- Creating marketing facilities and co-operative campaigns accessible especially for the thousands of small businesses that would otherwise be unable to participate in marketing on a national or international scale.
- Providing advice and leadership based on its information sources, including intranets to support businesses.

These marketing processes, co-ordinated often with a planning and regulatory role, amount to a *facilitation strategy* that has important implications for NTO/DMO marketing organization and personnel. Such a strategy requires extensive co-operation and joint decision-making with private sector partners. It also requires a substantial commitment to market research and intelligence, and to performance evaluation. Facilitation decisions bring into sharp focus the very difficult task, which all NTOs face, of allocating less than adequate budgets between competing marketing priorities.

The strategy a DMO adopts in practice should vary according to the stage of development a country's tourism has reached. Where destinations are largely unknown in the markets they seek to promote, where existing tourism flows are small and where the tourism industry within the country is mainly weak and fragmented, the NTO will have no choice but to take the leading role in putting its destination on the international map. It will have to play a major role in promoting its destination's products. Even in these circumstances the available budgets will normally not be adequate to engage effectively in image campaigns in several markets and the marketing support of international operators such as airlines, hotel chains and tour operators will be essential for success.

For better known, well-established destinations such as Spain, Australia, the UK and the USA, where the tourism industry has forged its own international links, it should increasingly be possible for the DMO to commit more of its expenditure to the strategy of support and facilitation; more on image definition and branding and less on buying media space for general image advertising.

Destination positioning themes, branding, images and concepts

Whatever the main thrust of strategy, be it promotion or facilitation, NTOs always have a vital function to perform for their destinations in choosing the single-minded communication propositions (messages and symbols) that serve to identify and position or 'brand' their countries in the minds of prospective visitors, and differentiate them from all others.

I love New York, Canada's *The World Next Door,* and BTA's Heritage themes all serve to brand and identify their destinations with unique labels. To be successful in practice (see also Chapter 8), such labels must:

- Be based on genuine product values and attributes that can be delivered and that visitors recognize as authentic, not fake.

- Be readily understood by customers at the point of purchase.
- Involve at least the leading players in the commercial sector.
- Be incorporated into the promotional efforts of a country's regions and resorts.
- Be sustained over several years if they are to overcome the communication inertia and barriers referred to in Chapter 16.
- Be systematically exploited in a range of sales-promotion and customer-servicing techniques designed to reach visitors on arrival at the destination as well as prospective visitors in countries of origin.

Developing successful images and implementing them effectively requires detailed consumer research and creative flair in relation to a destination's intrinsic attractiveness to visitors. This is usually a role that only an NTO can fulfil, and only an NTO/DMO can take on the task of communicating the chosen positioning to the tourism industry. But it does not follow that DMOs should have to spend the bulk of their own scarce resources in promoting the image to the general public in markets of origin.

It will often be possible for DMOs to develop co-operative promotional efforts arising directly out of the facilitation and positioning strategy. They can use the processes of collaboration to draw on the financial support of the tourism industry to mount any advertising and publicity campaigns judged necessary to support or enhance the destination image. Working within a strategy of facilitation, an NTO will often play a tactical role with its PR campaigns, e.g. to correct the short-run effects of negative attitudes in markets of origin arising from news stories about prices or personal security.

The marketing role for NTOs/DMOs: the process

Figure 20.1 illustrates the marketing process for NTOs/DMOs (on the left of the diagram), side by side with the same process for individual businesses in the travel and tourism industry (on the right). The figure reveals both the similarities in marketing and the important differences that exist. Readers may wish to refer back to Figure 2.1 in Chapter 2 with which Figure 20.1 is fully compatible. The main difference occurs at the budget-decision stage where DMOs have the choice of apportioning funds between the two routes shown as direct control of the promotional mix on the left and marketing facilitation in the middle of the diagram. Facilitation forms the important bridge between NTO and the component sectors of the industry, while the promotion strategy reflects the more traditional approach to destination marketing.

The important liaison and co-ordination linkages between a DMO and private sector partners are shown in the diagram at the policy level, at the budget decision level (industry financial participation in DMO expenditure and vice versa) and between marketing facilitation and the individual marketing decisions of businesses in the tourism industry. Each of the main stages in Figure 20.1 is discussed briefly below, followed by a more detailed explanation of the less familiar methods of marketing facilitation.

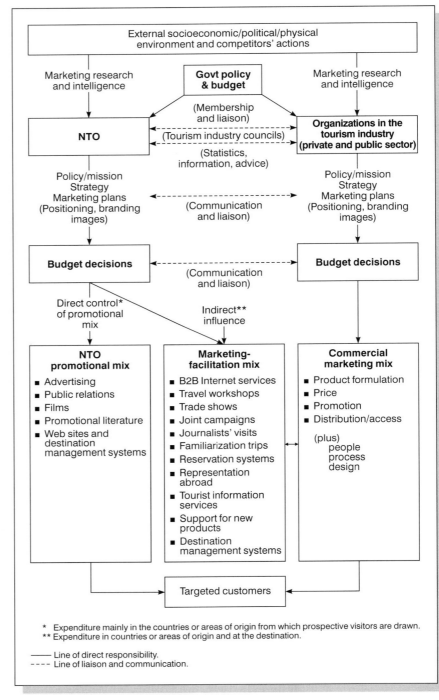

Figure 20.1
The destination marketing process for NTOs

Researching the external business environment

As in all marketing, the process begins with researching current and potential customers and the external environment. Only a few larger operators, such as airlines and hotel chains, will have the resources to undertake their own large-scale marketing research, especially into international markets. National tourism organizations have a unique role to play, therefore, in gathering and communicating market analysis and trend data, not only for their own marketing purposes but also for the tourism industry as a whole. Most NTOs publish research facts, but few appear to perform the task in a way that is easily accessible and understandable to the majority of smaller businesses. Provision of usable market information is the most important single basis for effective facilitation. Failure to communicate data effectively means that the most potentially valuable method of influencing the decisions of suppliers is lost. (See the Canada and BTA case material in Part Six.)

Government policy and tourism strategy

Where governments provide the bulk of an NTO's funding, marketing objectives are naturally required to serve government policy. Most governments do not normally go into tourism marketing objectives in any detail, but lay down the broader strategic goals that DMOs are expected to pursue. These goals, in principle, are much the same all over the world, requiring that tourism revenue should generate employment and foreign exchange earnings in accordance with national economic policy and environmental objectives. Government policies relevant to tourism marketing strategy may be summarized as:

- To generate increased tourism revenue.
- To channel demand by season and by area of the country.
- To protect consumers' interests and enhance the quality of the product and the destination environment.
- To secure sustainable development, often termed 'wise growth'.

The first two of these policies tend to be common to most countries. The second two, discussed later under facilitation, are less well developed.

The representation of the private sector and other organizations on various committees and boards of DMOs is also a common feature of NTO operation. It is intended to create a productive dialogue between the main organizations in the travel and tourism industry and the direction of government and NTO policy. Marketing strategy is an important aspect of this dialogue and the liaison stages are noted in Figure 20.1.

Marketing planning

As noted earlier, the limitations of a DMO's budget focus attention on selecting priorities and turning these into strategies and specific targets for products and segments – to be achieved through facilitation and/or promotional campaigns. The marketing planning process for an NTO is no different in principle from any other marketing organization; the techniques are the same. Unfortunately, however, long experience confirms that the travel and tourism industry in most countries is still notorious for the paucity of its research information base compared with what is commonly available for most other manufacturing and service industries. It is a criticism of most NTOs that they have been willing to spend millions of dollars on advertising campaigns and representation at international trade fairs, while expenditure on basic marketing research into visitor interests, behaviour and attitudes, necessary to achieve the most effective use of the money, has been very limited. One of the most far sighted marketing planning decisions in destination marketing can still be seen in the now classic *I love New York* campaign which commenced with a massive investment in research before any promotional decisions were taken. That was thirty years ago. In the twenty-first century such wisdom is still rare.

Marketing objectives and targets

The most important output of the marketing planning process for a DMO is identification of market/product strategies to match market trends and the product resource base and the selection of specific, broadly quantified targets for allocating marketing budgets. Figure 20.2 sets out in a format that can be adapted for use in any destination, a simplified model of a market/product planning matrix comprising a number of cells, each of

Market areas (visitor origin) — Product types (destination)	Country A	Country B	Country C	Country D	Other market areas/ segments
	Segments 1, 2 and 3	Segments 4 and 5	Segment 6	Segments 7 and 8	Segments 9+
Resort-based holidays	volume: value: impact	volume: value: impact	volume: value: impact	volume: value: impact	volume: value: impact
Touring holidays by car					
City short break holidays					
Business and conferences					
Other products					

Notes:
1 A developed destination country with domestic tourism and visits from several countries of origin may identify and target as many as fifty or more relevant segments.
2 The products in the matrix are those identified by marketing research, or by analysis of supply. A developed destination country may easily identify over twenty-five principal products that it seeks to promote or facilitate, allowing for area and seasonal variations.
3 Where research is available, it will obviously be used to complete the cells of the matrix; where it is not, the matrix model may still be useful as a tool for summarizing managers' judgements. The process of completing the model may also serve to identify aspects of products and markets requiring new, or additional market research.

Figure 20.2
A market/product matrix model for NTO marketing planning

which represents the volume and value of target segments and products.

Deciding which segments and products should be included in the matrix is determined by marketing analysis and planning in collaboration with the travel and tourism industry. Research (and judgement) is used to estimate the volume and revenue figures to be inserted. The matrix may be used for historic data or as a framework for forecasting. With appropriate supporting statements, the model may also play a useful part in summarizing strategy and communicating it to the tourism industry. For the UK, a matrix of this type has been used and continuously developed over many years (see for example, Jefferson and Lickorish, 1991: 140–9). Since the end of the 1990s, a refined form of the model is accessible for registered users on BTA's professional Web site under the title Market Product Fit (PROFIT). (See the case study in Part Six.)

Budget decisions

Politicians decide the amount of money that NTOs receive. Whatever the budget, as stressed in Chapter 14, marketing tasks must relate to objectives and the cost of undertaking specified tasks should act as a primary constraint on the choice of objectives. Exactly the same principles apply to DMOs in apportioning budgets between promotional and/or facilitation tasks. Very few countries, however, have successfully developed a systematic method of relating the size of budget required to the achievement of specific objectives. Precedent (what was done last year) and broad comparisons with other precedent-based budgets for public expenditure are still the general rule in budget allocation for NTOs, adjusted – more or less – by annual levels of inflation in a country's economy. Research-based specification of tasks is the only logical basis for budget allocation and for the newer public sector disciplines of targeting, performance monitoring and evaluation.

Marketing facilitation strategies for an NTO

Because marketing facilitation is so important we outline below twelve of the most important facilitation processes used by NTOs around the world. Each of these processes was included in the 2nd edition of this book in 1994 but they were based then on traditional methods of communication and distribution. It is instructive to note how every one of the processes has been influenced since or overtaken by ICT developments, especially the role of the Internet, in the space of little more than five years. In the sections below, drawing on the BTA and Canada case study material in Part Six, the emerging Internet role is noted for each process to illustrate the speed of change and depth of influence over NTO marketing of the new technology.

The old technologies are not dead and will continue to be used in tandem with the new methods for many years. But the balance of emphasis is changing daily in the first years of the new millennium. The new technology not only makes the facilitation role cheaper, it dramatically extends its potential influence over the whole tourism industry. To stress the point, the ICT influence is indicated in italics at the end of each section.

1 Flow of research data and marketing intelligence

By providing a regular, user-friendly flow of research data to large and small businesses in the tourism industry, through digests of statistics, short reports on market trends and help with research enquiries, an NTO may make valuable inputs to the marketing planning processes of individual businesses in all sectors. Co-operative and syndicated research surveys also provide cost-effective ways in which an NTO can stimulate the flow of relevant data. The regular distribution of research summaries is a practical way of developing contacts with the industry and exercising influence over marketing strategy at the same time. *The development of B2B Web sites and intranets for this purpose is already the logical and most cost-effective way to provide access.*

2 Representation in markets of origin

By establishing a network of offices in foreign countries generating the bulk of its international visitor flows, an NTO can create and maintain vital travel trade contacts while acting also as a point of information and distribution for the destination's range of tourism products. The network of offices may also generate flows of vital marketing intelligence, to be fed into the NTO's information system and used in marketing planning. *At least in theory (see quote at the head of this chapter) it is already possible to replace much of the representation role by Web sites and operate a 'virtual tourist office'. In practice it is not, but the scope for utilizing the Internet for many of the traditional information, contact and distribution functions is clearly an attractive and cost saving route to develop.*

3 Organization of workshops and trade shows

Since the 1960s NTOs have been making arrangements whereby groups of suppliers of tourist products may meet with groups of prospective buyers, such as tour operators, travel agents and other travel organizers, at relatively low cost. Either in the market of origin or at the destination, individual hoteliers, attractions, suppliers of conference facilities or businesses offering youth products can make contact and discuss business in one or two days of intensive meetings. By selecting the theme of workshops, such as self-catering, coach tours or attractions, issuing the invitations and possibly subsidizing the costs of accommodation and travel, an NTO can make a powerful contribution to its objectives. It may, of course, use the workshops as an opportunity to gain marketing intelligence as well as to convey information and other messages designed to promote its aims. *There will always be needs for 'pressing the flesh' in personal meetings but much of what occurs at workshops and trade shows can now be done more easily, quickly and more cost-effectively using dedicated B2B Web sites, video-conferencing and e-mail.*

4 Familiarization trips

By arranging for parties of selected foreign travel agents, journalists and tour operators to visit the destination and sample the products available, NTOs can influence the effectiveness with which the travel trade in markets of origin acts in support of the destination and its products. Such trips are part of the sales-promotion process discussed in Chapter 16; they are also a method of improving the advice and information available to customers at key retail outlets and gaining better display space at points of sale. The trips also serve an important PR role and offer many opportunities for communicating key messages to influential people in distribution and media channels. *Although Web sites cannot replace the actual experience they can back up such trips with much improved multimedia information and extend the reach to a second tier of those who cannot gain a place on the trips available.*

5 Travel trade manuals

With a wide variety of products provided by hundreds of businesses in many destinations, it is usually impossible for all foreign travel agents and tour operators to be serviced individually by a DMO. It is therefore customary for NTOs to produce one or more printed trade manuals, which serve as references and guides for use by the travel trade. A conference users' manual, for example, lists the details of all conference facilities, probably classified by area, particular facilities available, prices – including commission available – and how to make bookings. A different trade manual would be required for activity holidays and so on. For smaller businesses such manuals provide access to foreign markets at low cost. *Multimedia information on B2B Web sites can now replace traditional manuals and provide much better and more up-to-date information as well as direct online contact.*

6 Support with literature production and distribution

Most NTOs sell advertising space in the range of printed brochures that they promote and distribute internationally. The object is to provide cost-effective advertising and distribution opportunities, especially for smaller businesses, and many brochures produce a surplus of revenue over costs. National tourism organizations may also offer direct-mail distribution services for tourist industry printed material or produce *brochure shells* for use by small businesses. These are normally full-colour leaflets containing themed photography and areas of blank space that may be overprinted by a businesses logo and product messages. *Shells* suitable for a range of purposes, such as activity holidays or weekend breaks, may be bought at standard prices per thousand as required, and then overprinted in one colour to produce a professional leaflet at a cost well below the price of commissioning a purpose-designed colour brochure in small numbers from a printer. Low cost desktop publishing software for leaflets and small brochures now offer a better alternative to many small businesses.

Although claims that the Internet will simply replace printed brochures appear exaggerated, at least for the next decade, well-planned DMO sites with the capability to put pages on a virtual clipboard for downloading are already a vital source of information in travel and tourism. The immediacy and convenience of the contact and response, including online booking options, is powerful. The ability to maintain up to date information on prices and use Web sites simultaneously for information, promotion, distribution, relationship marketing and marketing research is a massive marketing advantage even before the cost savings over conventional methods are considered. It is less obvious to what extent NTOs will be able to generate income from their sites but these are still early days.

7 Participation in joint marketing schemes or ventures

Joint schemes or joint ventures are specific marketing projects that an NTO may be willing to support on a joint participation basis of, say, $100 for every $300 contributed by a partner(s). Participation in such schemes normally requires formal application procedures and criteria are applied, e.g. whether or not the products concerned are likely to proceed without some financial support for their marketing or whether they contribute to stated national marketing objectives. Equally important, participants in an adopted scheme may draw on the professional expertise of an NTO's marketing department and the other facilities available for production of print, overseas representation, research advice and so on.

By managing the criteria for selection an NTO can use joint schemes to influence operators in the tourism industry along lines indicated in its strategic planning process. By monitoring the performance of such schemes it also develops its research knowledge of particular products, segments and markets. *Dedicated B2B sites, developed in conjunction with destination management systems (DMS) and databases, will be part of the communication process and also the primary means of delivering the expertise and linking a business to other DMO facilities.*

8 Information and reservation systems

Using CRS technology linked to a DMS, NTOs are now able to assist small businesses in their tourism industry to distribute their product offers and achieve bookings. Such systems were traditionally very limited in reach, managed by costly telephones and faxes and were often designed to facilitate commissionable bookings by travel agents.

Modern DMSs clearly facilitate the process by providing direct access to customers around the world using the Internet and call centres and cutting out the costs of intermediaries. For the first time ever, small businesses can access global markets using DMSs as their gateway or portal. With their detailed databases of products and availability and online links with suppliers, DMSs simultaneously service and drive the TICs provided for visitors and are the basis for proactive DMO marketing campaigns.

9 Support for new products

Through selective proactive marketing support, using criteria established through marketing planning, NTOs can help innovative new products to emerge and establish themselves in their markets in the initial two to three years after their launch. Smaller businesses are usually unable to afford the start-up costs of national and international marketing; they need access to some form of 'pump priming' as this form of support is often called. It is a well-established technique by which NTOs may contribute to their long-term policy goals. This form of assistance overlaps with the investment and development support programmes that many NTOs also operate, increasingly using marketing orientated criteria. *The Internet and access to markets via a DMS database and gateway provide the lowest cost means for implementing this form of marketing support.*

10 Trade consortia

Another interesting illustration of the facilitation role for NTOs exists in the support they may offer to private sector consortia of small businesses, formed for the purposes of more efficient marketing. Aided by NTO marketing expertise and some funding support for promotional activities, groups of hire-boat owners, museums, caravan parks, hotels and other facilities may be assisted. *As with joint marketing schemes and support for new products, a B2B Web site offers the most cost-effective means of communication for members and a DMO Web site offers the most cost-effective means for communication and distribution to visitors.*

11 Consumer assistance and protection

It is well recognized that the marketing task for service products extends into concern for customer satisfaction with the service delivery. In tourism this task includes information services provided to enable visitors to become aware of and gain access to the full range of available products, about which many would otherwise have no knowledge. By creating and subsidizing a network of TICs in destination areas an NTO can extend its influence and communicate messages direct to a far wider 'audience' of its visitors than it can hope to reach with available budgets through promotional efforts in countries of origin. A DMO may not influence more than say one in ten visitors at most in their country of origin but it may reach two out of three at TICs. By their choice of emphasis in the information provided, DMOs can exert considerable promotional influence over visitor movement in destinations and their expenditure patterns. Market research indicates that many visitors to tourism destinations, especially foreign and first-time visitors, are open to suggestion and persuasion from all sources of information, especially those having the official endorsement and authority of an NTO and its regional bodies.

Associated with this concern for customer satisfaction are forms of consumer protection, such as the requirement that tourism prices should be clearly notified and the operation of tourism complaint procedures, supplemented in some countries with tourism police. Finally, there is a growing concern in many countries to protect and enhance the quality of tourism products through schemes of quality assurance, such as classification and grading of accommodation and recognition of environmental good practice. Not normally considered a part of NTO marketing, such schemes make no sense unless they are firmly marketing-led and designed around the identified needs of the customers an NTO seeks to promote.

A typical example is *Qualmark*, an independent body established by the New Zealand Tourist Board and the New Zealand Automobile Association in 1994 to provide a classification and grading system for New Zealand's hotel, motel and holiday park accommodation. Usually negotiated with private sector partners, once quality standards have been agreed, DMOs may limit inclusion in their brochures and display in tourism information centres to operators who comply. In this context facilitation becomes a quality control tool for marketing purposes. *Here, too, the roles already defined for DMSs and DMO Web sites can be adapted to recognize and support the quality control process and communication to customers.*

12 General advisory services for the industry

Although the provision of advice to businesses is traditionally a time-consuming process that could never reach more than a fraction of the tourism industry, access to information can make a very important contribution to the marketing decisions of suppliers with limited market contacts and budgets too small to commit more than a minimum sum to market research. There are many ways in which expensive person-to-person advice can be extended. An NTO may, for example, organize seminars and conferences on marketing topics and disseminate the contributions as widely as possible through its publications. *The development of interactive B2B Web sites offers the most cost-effective means of providing advice, with appropriate back up systems for dealing with more detailed enquires and for charging for the services provided. Provision of marketing research data via dedicated Web sites is just one of the ways that advisory services are being streamlined and improved. See also the case material in Part Six.*

Chapter summary

This chapter explains the scope and extent of NTO marketing worldwide, drawing attention to the large sums of money that are spent annually on persuading international visitors to choose particular destinations. It discusses three principal reasons why NTOs or DMOs, especially in developed destination countries, are not likely to achieve more than an important but marginal influence over total tourism volume and expenditure. It outlines two levels of destination marketing, distinguishing between the role of NTOs and the suppliers of particular products.

The strategic choices facing NTOs in deciding how best to deploy their limited budgets are discussed in some detail.

The chapter outlines the stages in the marketing process for NTOs, paying particular attention to the facilitation strategy. Facilitation is defined as the unique marketing role for an NTO – unique in the sense that if the NTO does not fulfil it, it is unlikely that obviously important tasks will be undertaken at all. Twelve facilitation tasks are described; they serve to co-ordinate the tourism industry as a whole, recognizing and strengthening industry linkages in the products that destinations provide, and devising themes and images to integrate promotional efforts. By its nature, facilitation is task orientated and, in terms of securing value for money from promotional expenditure, it is usually easier to prove success through this strategy than through expenditure on image campaigns. The links between marketing and product formulation, which emerge naturally through the facilitation process, help to ensure that tourism development in a country is market led.

Although facilitation as a process is not new, the availability since the late 1990s of the Internet and cheap connectivity for businesses of every size, as well as access for at least half the experienced travelling population in mature markets, is still new in 2000. It is revolutionizing the traditional facilitation processes for NTOs, making them far more efficient and cost-effective as well as opening up new opportunities. It suggests a continuing switch in the use of NTO resources to facilitation processes using a co-ordinated range of Internet enabled techniques to achieve and promote more professional marketing in the sector.

The principles set out in this chapter are broadly applicable to regional and area tourist boards, which have much the same co-ordinating role and strategic choices in using their resources as NTOs do. Area boards work mainly on domestic tourism and deal with smaller, mainly local operators, but they are in many ways microcosms of their larger national organizations. They are equally able to use and benefit from the use of the new information age technology. In particular they can profit from the destination management databases that provide the ideal backup platform for Internet support for small businesses.

Further reading

Jefferson, A. and Lickorish, L. (1991). *Marketing Tourism: A Practical Guide.* Chapter 10, 2nd edn, Longman.

Millington, K. and Cleverdon, R. (1999). National tourist offices: their budgets and performance. *Insights*, September, English Tourist Council.

WTO Business Council (1999). *Marketing Tourism Destinations Online: Strategies for the Information Age.* WTO.

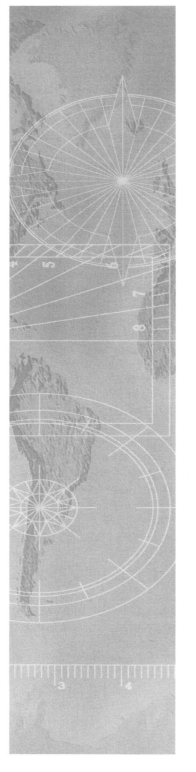

CHAPTER 21

Marketing visitor attractions

Growth in supply is outstripping growth in demand. This results in lower profitability, lack of investment and hence less good value for visitors. (English Tourist Board report, 1997)

Museums will stand or fall not only by their competence to care for collections but also by their ability to care for people. In other words, they need to be market-orientated if they are to survive . . . (Cossons, 1985: 44)

Visitor attractions that command the attention of media and politicians in most countries are the large national museums and galleries in capital cities, and commercial operators such as the Disney Corporation (USA); Madame Tussauds, Alton Towers and Legoland Windsor (UK). All of these draw over 1 million visits a year, and the largest over 10 million. But, as with the other sectors of the tourism industry, attractions are increasingly polarized between a few large attractions and thousands of small and micro-sized enterprises. Most managed visitor attractions in the UK and in many other countries receive less than 30 000 visits per annum and less than £50 000 earned revenue. Most are based on a single location. Many are owned and managed within the public sector or by trusts and are not operated as businesses for profit.

This chapter aims to show that the principles of marketing are fully applicable, even in a sector of the tourism industry not generally distinguished by a customer-orientated culture or by its business management skills. It focuses on *managed attractions* based on a wide range of natural, cultural or built resources that, either naturally or after development, have the power to draw or motivate visitors to their locations. The term 'visitor attractions' rather than 'tourist attractions' is used, partly to reflect industry practice and partly because many attractions are visited as much by the residents of an area as by tourists.

The chapter begins by reviewing changes in developed societies that are accelerating the growth in supply of attractions, increasing competition and necessitating the adoption of management and marketing techniques. It offers a definition of 'managed attractions', categorizes the types of attraction to which systematic marketing techniques are increasingly applied and reviews their common characteristics. The nature of the product that attractions offer and the customer segments on which they typically draw are indicated and marketing management responses are summarized under the headings of strategic and operational tasks and constraints. The chapter ends by reviewing the growing role for developing better linkages between attractions and with the publics and other users they serve.

Traditional and modern concepts of attractions management and marketing

Functionally, visitor attractions play an essential role in tourism as 'elements within the destination's environment that largely determine consumers' choices and influence prospective buyers' motivation' (Chapter 8). In fact, as much of transport and accommodation services are increasingly globally branded and marketed, visitor attractions have a particularly important role to play in both representing and delivering the particular sense of *place* that provides the basis for competition between destinations. Many natural, cultural and built attractions are created specifically to conserve and celebrate the unique characteristics of places and the local features and character that make them worth a visit.

Traditionally, many visitor attractions did not need to practice marketing. They were slow adopters, sometimes because they were operating with public sector subsidies and were not expected to charge for admission, and sometimes because their owners, trustees and managers were imbued with vision and passion for the resources they were responsible for, making them inward looking (or product orientated) rather than outward looking to customer requirements. Until the last decade, with the exception of the largest attractions, the ideas of marketing management had not reached the majority of the sector.

In recent years, however, the global growth of travel and tourism and the impact of unrestricted public access to natural, cultural and built resources in their unmanaged state has led to growing recognition of the need for *visitor management*. The overused cliché that 'visitors tend to destroy the very things they travel to see' has its applications in most popular destinations and underlies the growing use of visitor management techniques, especially marketing.

Many visitor attractions are located in environmentally sensitive areas. In some places the promotion of public access may be secondary to the principal requirement to conserve a resource for its own intrinsic value. There are cases, for example sustaining wetlands for the sake of the wildlife, where the objective is to inhibit rather than provide for visitor use and where environmental objectives will take precedence. Allowing for this important caveat, the admission of visitors – especially the revenue they generate to contribute to environmental objectives – is generally a key element in resource conservation schemes. What is new is a growing awareness and sense of urgency that environmental resources generally have a finite capacity in places attractive for tourism, and that visitor management techniques along with resource management techniques must be improved.

Within the range of visitor management techniques available to attractions, marketing is increasingly seen as fundamental to success. It is recognized as the best way to generate revenue to contribute to the costs of operation and maintenance of the resource base, develop and sustain satisfying products, create value for money and influence the volume and seasonality patterns of site visits. But it can only be practised effectively when focused on sites or areas that are enclosed or have controlled access. Large museums and commercial attractions are the obvious examples but the principle of controlling access for management purposes applies also to parts of national parks, country parks, lakes and heritage coastal areas.

What principally distinguishes the present from the past is the polarization between large and small attractions in the public and private sector, the remarkable growth of supply in provision of all forms of attractions, competition for visitors' time and money and the reduction of annual subsidies by the public sector. These changes increasingly require the exercise of sophisticated management techniques that may be used simultaneously to protect the resource, to enhance the visitor experience, to promote a site and to generate revenue for it in a competitive market.

The concept of applying systematic modern business management techniques at visitor attractions as diverse as museums and national parks is still not yet fully accepted in all countries. The idea of charging for access to the primary assets of national heritage is even less widely accepted, although charging is now common in most new purpose-designed attractions. Some of the most rapid changes in approach could be witnessed in Eastern European countries where, freed from decades of central planning, the ideas of marketing were forced upon surviving attractions by the withdrawal of state subsidies and the need to attract tourist spending. Change was injected into the most traditional of management cultures in the 1990s by brutal necessities that few attractions in the West could imagine.

The evidence suggests that the rate of change in management and marketing awareness at visitor attractions was rapid in the 1990s. This change is supported by the expanding higher educational provision internationally for travel, tourism and recreation managers, and one may confidently predict a far wider extension of modern management techniques early in the new century.

Modern management underpins the development of new attractions

As the developed world shifts into the post-industrial era, the role in society of arts, heritage, culture, hospitality and entertainment take on greater economic importance and tourism makes an integral contribution as a growth market within the 'new economy'.

This role is fully recognized commercially and is driving massive investment at the turn of the century in new retail-based facilities that are marketed as day visitor attractions. Typically comprising a themed mix of entertainment and hospitality as well as retail, these are located close to motorway access within easy reach of city centres. Originating in the USA and Canada as enclosed shopping mall developments, they crossed the Atlantic to Northern Europe in the mid to late 1990s. The largest of these in the UK (of which there are around eight major players) are attracting over 30 million visits a year each, year round, up to twenty-four hours a day. The new attractions are managed and marketed with the best professional teams and are designed to appeal to modern consumers with their one-stop, undercover facilities for all age groups. Their potential competitive impact on traditional visitor attractions can be gauged by the fact that some 2500 museums generate just over 70 million visits a year between them.

Associated with the development of management and marketing is a growing understanding of the ways in which visitor attractions can be developed out of resources and structures not originally thought to be of any interest to visitors, or where none existed previously. Early examples are the construction of Disney World and EPCOT in Florida, which began with the purchase of some 27 400 acres in the mid-1960s of low-lying swamp and agricultural land of no obvious attraction except to mosquitoes. More recent examples of creative development of attractions can be seen in the development of canal-basin warehouses at Wigan Pier in the North of England in the mid-1980s; the redevelopment of former industrial cities such as Liverpool, Manchester and Birmingham, using cultural visitor attractions as a lead sector in economic regeneration; and the modern art gallery movement, epitomized by the Guggenheim at Bilbao and the Tate Modern in London, that has extended over much of Europe in the last five years.

It is noteworthy in England that over half of all the visitor attractions available at the end of the 1990s had been developed in the previous two decades. New attractions, typically more dependent on admission income rather than public sector subsidies for their survival, tend to be user orientated in their ethos from the outset, in contrast with more traditional sites. They are also mostly larger and employ professional managers. In the late 1990s, as countries and communities prepared to celebrate the new millennium, there was a natural focus on creating new and refurbished attractions. In the UK the largest of these was the Millennium Dome targeting some 12 million visits for a year at a cost of over £800 million. Size and government support does not guarantee success, however, and by mid-year 2000 the likely volume of paying visits was estimated at little over 6 million, with an effective public sector subsidy of over £100 per visitor achieved.

The characteristics of managed visitor attractions

Managed visitor attractions as discussed in this chapter may now be defined as: designated permanent resources that are controlled and managed for their own sake and for the enjoyment, entertainment and education of the visiting public.

Designated means that the resource has been formally committed to the types of use and activity outlined in the definition. Designation may be either a commercial decision within the normal statutory planning regulations that apply to land and structures, a decision by a public sector body acting on behalf of community interests, or the decision of a trust acting on behalf of trust objectives and stakeholders. In all cases effective management requires that the boundaries of a resource or site must be clearly specified – even for wilderness areas such as the upper slopes of mountains – and normally attractions are enclosed or controlled to reduce or prevent public access except at established points of admission.

Permanent is used to exclude from the definition the marketing of festivals, carnivals, pageants, temporary entertainments, concerts, travelling fairs and shows, and any other form of visitor attractions not based on a fixed site or building. Temporary attractions ranging from international sports events to village fairs have their own different forms of marketing, which are not discussed in this chapter. Many permanent sites are, however, used as the venue for such temporary attractions, promoted as part of an annual programme of events designed to promote multiple uses and draw in different audiences.

Within the definition it will be obvious that there is a wide range of different types of attraction. To illustrate the range, ten different categories of permanent managed attractions are listed in Table 21.1. The marketing principles outlined in this chapter will be found applicable to all of them. The definition is not restricted to attractions that have an admission price, although the attractions listed in Table 21.1 mostly do charge and the trend is in this direction rather than for free provision. The charge for using the attraction may be made at a ticket office, barrier or a car park, or for the use of parts of the site; it may be obligatory or operated on a voluntary basis. Prices may be intended to cover the full cost of operating an attraction, to cover its current (not capital)

1	Ancient monuments	Typically protected and preserved sites such as fortifications, burial mounds and buildings dating up to the end of the Roman Empire
2	Historic buildings	Castles, houses, palaces, cathedrals, churches, town centres, villages, commonly termed heritage sites
3	Designated areas, parks and gardens	National parks, country parks, long-distance paths, gardens (excluding urban recreation spaces), including sites of particular scenic and resource quality
4	Theme parks	Mostly engineered as artefacts, such as Disney World, but may be associated with historic sites such as Colonial Williamsburg in the USA, or with Gardens as at Alton Towers in Britain
5	Wildlife attractions	Zoos, aquaria, aviaries, wildfowl parks, game parks and safaris, farms open to visitors
6	Museums	The range is enormous; it includes *subject*-specific museums, such as science and science centres, transport, farms and ships; *site*-specific museums, such as Colonial Williamsburg (USA) or Ironbridge Gorge (Great Britain); or *area*-based museums, with either national, regional or local collections
7	Art galleries	Most traditional galleries with collections built up over many decades. Includes the new wave of modern art galleries in striking new buildings
8	Industrial archeology sites	Mostly sites and structures identified with specific industrial and manufacturing processes, such as mining, textiles, railways, docks or canals, and mostly relevant to the period post-1750
9	Themed retail sites	Mostly former commercial premises, such as covered market halls, commodity exchanges or warehouses, used as speciality retail shopping malls, often themed. Includes modern, purpose-built, multi-purpose sites.
10	Amusement and leisure parks	Parks constructed primarily for 'white knuckle' rides, such as roller coasters, log flumes, dodgem cars and associated stalls and amusements

Table 21.1 Ten main types of managed attractions open to the public

expenditure or simply to make some contribution to costs that are otherwise funded by a grant from another source.

Polarity between small and large attractions

In all countries the visitor attractions shown in Table 21.1 are mostly small in terms of the number of visitors and the revenue they receive. Their lack of marketing knowledge and their small marketing budgets limit what they can achieve in practice to improve their revenue performance. In the terms introduced in Chapter 2, most visitor attractions do not have an outward-looking, proactive corporate culture to guide their decisions and many are still in the cottage industry stage.

Historically, most small attractions were formed and are directed by dedicated enthusiasts and scholars. These enthusiasts have generally always been short of funds and have had to overcome great difficulties in defeating the forces of inertia to establish their sites. As a result, many attractions are located in structures and sites that are barely adequate for the purpose and have only limited facilities for display and interpretation to the general public. At the same time, the management structure of individuals, trusts, local-authority recreation departments and government agencies that control many attractions is not noted for its marketing expertise.

In the UK the tourist boards had records of just over 6000 attractions open to the public in 1998 for which they had actual or estimated visitor numbers. Over twelve months in 1998 those attractions recorded a total of some 400 million visits. Compared with a UK population of just over 57 million, plus some 25 million overseas visitors a year, the importance of attractions is clear. But only 7 per cent of them attracted more than 200 000 visits a year and just seventeen sites making an admission charge exceeded a million visits, of which twelve were in or near London, drawing on the large number of overseas visitors. Eight out of ten known attractions were recording less than 50 000 visits a year and at that level they cannot afford to employ professional marketing managers although marketing is clearly vital to all of them. The principal author's experience suggests that attractions achieving less than around 250 000 visits per annum are unlikely to be able to generate the revenue needed to operate competitively in marketing terms. Even then they will not generate sufficient revenue to cover all their operating costs *and* a surplus for capital renewals and refurbishment.

Knowledge of the sector suggests that the typical manager of an attraction with less than 100 000 visits is responsible for one site location only, has very limited links with other attractions, has never undertaken any form of market research, has had no formal management and marketing training, and has a marketing budget of under £5000 per annum. Such a manager is likely to be more concerned with the daily problems of financial survival than with expansion and development through marketing initiatives. Through public sector subsidies, grants from national agencies, bequests and the actions of hundreds of thousands of volunteers, smaller attractions continue to perform a vital role in destinations. But for many, survival and development lies in collaboration with others and finding synergy partners to support their operations and marketing programmes. (See later in the chapter.)

While collaboration, branding and joint marketing of individually owned businesses are common in accommodation and transport, there are only a few multiples established in the attractions field. The National Trust in the UK, the largest non-government conservation organization in Europe, is an interesting exception. Its massive property portfolio includes 19 castles, 165 historic houses, 47 industrial monuments and mills and 150 gardens. Some 200 of these properties attract more than 10 000 visits each a year. With over 11 million visits a year, and 2.6 million individual members in 1999, the National Trust is a remarkable example of an organization that manages and markets individual attractions under a unified brand image and under central and regional management control. There are some much smaller equivalents and branded voluntary groupings are a logical development in the marketing of attractions, for promotion and distribution purposes and to communicate to customers their commitments to product quality.

At the other end of the spectrum there are the large branded players, such as Disney World, Disney Land and the other major operators in the USA, Disneyland Paris, Legoland, De Efteling, Port Aventura, Madame Tussauds and Alton Towers in Europe. All of these exceed 1 million visits a year and the largest have more than 10 million. Although many national museums achieve more than a million visits, many do not charge for admission and in the UK all of them receive annual government subsidies of several million pounds each. Judgement suggests a million visits is the bare minimum at which most visitor attractions are likely to approach commercial viability and even then they will need a very favourable site location to succeed.

The attractions product: marketing the experience

As noted in the introduction, most visitor attractions provide or contribute to an important part of the reason for travel. Many heritage attractions are part of the local character and specialities of *place* that lie at the core of the overall travel and tourism product. Some owe their original existence to celebrating and communicating local characteristics (natural and built) and their attractiveness to visitors depends on the intrinsic quality of their resources or collections.

Because the product for many attractions, for example museums and galleries, is first a function of the resource and only second a function of marketing strategy, it is appropriate to consider first the nature of attractions products and the basic segments or audiences they draw on.

Important as the resource is for most attractions, it is not the resource or collection that is the product; it is the *visitor experience* that the resources provide. The attractions product cannot be effectively marketed unless this key point is understood. Theme parks, for example, develop their whole product offering around the experience provided. Attractions based on the natural environment also need to communicate and facilitate access to their resource 'products' interpreted as visitor experiences.

The range of experiences provided by attractions is very wide and in each case reflects the resource that the site provides and its interaction with the interests and personality of each visitor. It ranges from aesthetic pleasure and interest, as in gardens, through 'white-knuckle' thrills and excitement of amusement parks, fantasy as at some of the Tussauds exhibitions, to learning, awareness and self-development associated with many museum and art gallery displays and interpretation.

In practice what a particular experience provides to visitors can usually be established only through consumer research among key market segments, not through management guesswork. But at all managed sites, the experience provided is a matter of continuous concern with design and product formulation, which can be influenced or controlled by management decisions.

The product components

The visitor experience at managed attractions begins with anticipation. It may be stimulated by effective promotion, especially printed materials and electronic information, and by personal recommendation. It begins in earnest at the entrance to the site. From the moment of arrival, well exemplified by the sense of scale and quality conveyed by Disney World's astonishing motorway-style entrance route and the row of parking direction booths spread across the traffic lanes, every aspect of the experience visitors undergo is potentially under direct management control. To some extent this is also true of transport and accommodation operations but more so for attractions because the purpose of being on site is not usually functional but to derive satisfaction in an awareness and enjoyment of the experience. In some historic buildings and sites the degree of management control may be limited by planning and policy restrictions, but the essential components of the product are internationally the same and may be summarized as follows:

- Quality of the advertising material, promotional literature and Web site information, which establishes a 'promise' and influences initial expectations of a visit.
- Effectiveness and appeal of signage that guides first-time visitors to a site/building.
- First visual impression of the appearance of a site and the interest it arouses in prospective visitors – related to a pre-visit expectation. Efficiency of car/coach-parking arrangements and ease of access to the entrance.
- Physical appearance, ambience and motivating appeal of the entrance to an attraction.
- Appearance, friendliness and effectiveness of staff in the reception/ payment area where most visitors make first contact, and elsewhere on site.
- Efficiency of receiving visitors at the entrance or in a reception area including processes of ticketing, information provision and initial orientation at the point of sale/admission.
- Effectiveness of visitor circulation patterns around the site/building, managed through the logical layout of the resource elements, paths, signposting, leaflets and personal guides.
- Displays, presentation and interpretation of the main elements of the resource, including any audio-visual materials and any events or activities provided.
- Location, layout and quality of any subsidiary attractions on the site.
- Location, layout and quality of facilities such as toilets, cafés, and shops.

- Facilities to assist visitors with disabilities to have access and enjoy the experiences available.

Part of the marketing process for attractions is to audit and assess these product elements, both separately and within the overall experience, as part of a 'bundle' or package of components (see also Chapter 8). All parts of the 'package' may be varied by management decisions. Since one of the prime objects of attractions management is to motivate visitors, the processes they adopt for monitoring customer satisfaction and value for money (see Chapter 11) will be crucial to success.

Market segments for visitor attractions

Experience with researching attractions both in Britain and in other countries indicates that market segmentation is always the practical basis for marketing orientation. Interestingly, in varying proportions, all attractions tend to draw their customers from the same basic range of segments. Differences between sites in the proportions of segments attracted are likely to be explained either by the size and motivating pull of the attraction and its particular features or by locational factors such as proximity to holiday destinations.

For most attractions the influence of locational factors (proximity to main markets) will be at least as strong as the 'pull' of the resource base. The reason is that, apart from specialist visitors with knowledge of the subjects covered by the resource, most first-time visitors to any attraction will have little or no knowledge of the resource when they decide to make a visit. For example, visitors to parks and gardens may well include a few botanists with a deep knowledge of plants and horticulture but they will be a very small proportion of all visitors. Railway museums will draw a few engineers but there will not be many of them and most attractions have to appeal to generalists rather than specialists.

Internationally known attractions, such as Disneyland Paris in France or Shakespeare's birthplace in Stratford-on-Avon, are strong enough and sufficiently well known to break through the normal locational limitations that govern visitor flows but they are the exception, not the rule.

Practical segmentation of the visiting public begins with user types and only then proceeds to the demographic and other segmentation factors, which are covered in Chapter 7. Within most developed countries in Europe, the following seven segments will normally apply:

1 Local residents living within approximately half an hour's drive from the attraction's location.
2 Regional residents making day visits away from home and drawn, depending on the motivating power of the site, from a distance of up to two hours' driving or more in the case of sites of national significance.
3 Visitors staying with friends and relatives within about an hour's drive from the site.

4 Visitors on holiday staying in hotels, caravan parks and other forms of commercial accommodation within about an hour's drive from the site.
5 Group visits, usually arranged in association with coach companies or organized by direct-marketing contact between groups and the attractions' management.
6 School visits and other educational groups.
7 Corporate and other users of facilities such as conference and seminar rooms, and uses of buildings for receptions, weddings and other functions.

Table 21.2 provides a practical illustration of a segmentation model developed by the principal author for a large heritage attraction just outside London and easily accessible by train. The characteristics of each segment were derived by market research and became the basis for devising marketing strategy and marketing campaigns, and for forecasting and evaluating the results achieved.

Because of the nature of attractions, their fixed locations, spare capacity on most days and the need to draw in as many visitors as possible, it is always logical to target campaigns on selected segments but it is very rarely practical to approach the marketing task by concentrating only on one or two of the possible segments. Where attractions charge for admission, the need to generate revenue will make it even more important to appeal to as many visitor groups as possible.

For the accommodation and transport sectors of travel and tourism, selecting segments is always an essential first step in product design and adaptation. Segmentation for attractions, however, is more important for targeting promotion and distribution than it is for product formulation. For example, if it appears for a particular attraction that holiday visitors will be especially important in its visitor mix, the implication is not so much to design the product for holiday visitors but to focus most promotional and distribution efforts on them. The marketing approach to local residents will be quite different from that aimed at tourists but the product experience they enjoy is essentially the same for most.

Such product flexibility as exists comes mainly from organizing the components and interpretation to meet the needs of particular user groups. Marketing attractions to corporate users for function and meetings, for example, is not based on the 'product' marketed to the visiting public and it obviously depends on the quality of the facilities available for such purposes. Where such use is feasible, it adds a potential stream of non-seasonal revenue, often outside normal public visiting hours and may also provide valuable integrating links with a local community.

Marketing strategy for attractions

Commencing from a basic appreciation of products and segments noted above, the primary task for marketing managers is to monitor and

Visitor characteristics	Core location/categories for promotion	First time/ repeat visitors	Transport used for visit	Timing (months)	Current visitor numbers	5-year target numbers
a. Residents in local area and day visitors	Approx 3- to 5-mile radius of site	90% repeat	60–65% Car	Year round but mostly weekends except July/ August	12% 66 000	10% 85 000
b. Residents of Greater London, Home Counties, S. East – day visitors (excluding a.)	1 hr travel time of site (effectively 25-mile radius)	55–60% repeat	55–60% Car	Mostly weekends and July/August	30% 165 000	27% 230 000
c. UK tourists staying with friends/relatives (VFR)	1 hr travel time of site (effectively 25-mile radius)	60% first time	50–55% Car	Mostly March–June, September–December	8% 44 000	6% 52 000
d. Overseas tourists staying with friends/relatives (VFR)	1 hr travel time of site (effectively 25-mile radius)	65% first time	55–60% Car	Mostly April–October	12% 66 000	14% 120 000
e. UK tourists to London (not VFR)	Central London, mostly on short breaks in hotels	70% first time	80% public transport	Mostly February–May, September–November	3% 16 500	2.5% 23 000
f. Overseas tourists to London (not VFR)	Central London mostly on 1 week visits staying in hotels	80% first time	90% coach	Mostly April–October	19% 104 000	20% 170 000
g. Overseas tourists in groups (additional to d. and f.)	Central London mostly on 1 week visits staying in hotels	85% first time	90% coach	Mostly February–May, September–November	9% 49 500	12% 105 000
h. British visitors in groups (day visitor groups and staying visitor groups (additional to c. and e.)	1 hr travel time of site (effectively 25-mile radius) Central London mostly on short breaks in hotels	75% first time	90% coach	Mostly February–May, September–November	3% 17 000	4% 35 000
i. School/educational parties	5-mile radius of site 1 hr travel time of site (effectively 25-mile radius)	90% repeat (i.e. same schools)	80% coach	September–December and April–May	4% 22 000	3.5% 30 000
				Totals	550 000	850 000

Table 21.2 A segmentation planning model for a large visitor attraction, approximately 10 miles from London

interpret the factors in the changing external environment that influence strategy. Four main issues are:

1 *Actions of competitors.* As more places look to tourism and recreation to generate employment lost from primary and manufacturing industry, competition in the same market catchment area for the same visitor segments seems certain to increase over the next decade. Much of the new competition will be purpose designed or adapted to attract and satisfy visitors. Some of it will be subsidized by government and its agencies. In this more competitive environment some older attractions are likely to disappear or have to merge with others, no longer able to attract sufficient customers or adequate funding from other sources to cover their operating expenses and fund the refurbishment needed to remain competitive.

2 *Customer sophistication.* For attractions, as for other service industries, visitors' expectations and their perceptions of satisfaction and value for money are in a continual state of change and development. 'Yesterday's products' quickly lose their appeal if suppliers fail to keep pace with current requirements. All successful attractions pursue a product quality strategy of continual enhancement while increasing visitors' perceived value for money – the best measure of being competitive. The leading edge rapidly becomes the standard against which others are judged.

3 *ICT developments.* Information and communications technology is changing traditional approaches to market research, promotion and distribution as explained in Chapters 10, 18 and 19. It has also opened up opportunities that many attractions can utilize in the display and interpretation of their resource base, including lighting, sound, film, lasers, IMAX (very wide screen effects for film displays), and new materials such as carbon fibre, Kevlar and fibre optics. For some attractions, such as museums and galleries, digital technology creates income earning possibilities through the communication of objects to audiences away from the sites in which they are located.

4 *More sustainable approaches to managing resources.* In common with all tourism enterprises in the new millennium, visitor attractions have to respond to global needs to review and develop more sustainable practice in their consumption of energy and water, use of chemicals, production and disposal of waste and integration with local community partners for supplies. More importantly, because so many visitor attractions are part of or directly associated with the conservation of built and natural environment resources at destinations, they will also play a much wider role in communicating sustainable issues to the visiting public. Table 21.3 (adapted from Middleton and Hawkins, 1998: 169) summarizes the potential role of attractions in sustainability, from a marketing perspective. Looking ahead, the effective performance of this role in destination sustainability may give some attractions an added justification for the continuance of operational subsidies.

By the nature of their operations resource-based visitor attractions are key players in sustainable development from a marketing perspective. Their marketing decisions strongly influence and in some cases directly control:

- The specific customers targeted for promotion and distribution (from among those staying at a destination and others within easy day-travelling distance).
- Overall design and quality of the experience which the attraction provides.
- The most direct 'hands on' experience of environmental resources accessible to most visitors.
- Communication of information explaining and interpreting the nature of the attraction/resource and its significance.
- The specific presentation of objects, stories and themes, and all the forms of display provided for visitors.
- Opportunities for visitors and residents to meet on equal terms; qualified local guides and interpreters can perform a key role in this process.
- Prices at which visitors are admitted including any promotional and discounted offers.
- Product offers put together with other destination partners such as accommodation and local public transport operators.
- Evaluation of customer profiles and satisfaction through customer research.
- Customer profiles held on databases for analysis and future marketing.
- Marketing objectives, visitor volume targets, budgets and programmes.

This combination of influences, all of them part of the modern process of marketing for visitor attractions, is especially important where the attraction being managed is a core part of the environmental quality and appeal of a destination, for example a castle, a cathedral, a museum or a national park. Non-commercial attractions such as museums have a special role to play because of the authority and extra credibility often attached to their communications.

Source: Adapted from Middleton and Hawkins (1998: 169).

Table 21.3 Sustainability: a marketing perspective for resource-based visitor attractions

Strategic marketing plans

Responding to the external factors, the strategic task for attractions revolves around the process of refining the segmentation of the total market (as noted in Table 21.2) and targeting the potential volume of demand from each group. Segmentation is the base for:

- Market research and monitoring the nature of the experiences that the resource base is capable of sustaining for each of the main groups in the audience market.
- Product formulation and augmentation to enhance customer satisfaction through development and improved presentation, display and information techniques.
- Pricing and forecasting revenue flows that directly affect both capital and operating revenue decisions.
- Developing effective targeted campaigns for promotion and distribution.
- Evaluating the seasonality and sustainable implications of different groups.

- Analysing the options to develop new segments; new user groups may also identify new uses, such as opening museums in the evenings for functions and receptions.

For image and promotional purposes, it will usually be necessary to identify one principal underlying theme, idea and image, which encapsulates and communicates the experiences the attraction offers. The theme may develop from the research required to appreciate visitors' perceptions of the experience and it will be the basis for positioning the attraction and the benefits it offers, in all marketing communications.

Strategy may often require the search for effective promotional and distribution linkages and alliances between the attraction and other sites of the same type, or of different types in the same location. Such links, supported by intranets and B2B Web sites, may be achieved with the support of tourist boards, or directly between co-operating attractions. (See later in this chapter.)

Operating constraints on marketing

There are three main operating constraints that influence the marketing of attractions.

The first reflects the familiar concern with the implications of high fixed costs and low variable costs of operation. This affects many attractions even more than it affects transport and accommodation suppliers because of the second main constraint of seasonality. The combination of high fixed costs and seasonality acts as a powerful constraint to which marketing has to respond. A seasonal attraction may experience maximum demand on only about twenty days in the year, which may generate up to a quarter of the year's admissions. For example, a busy summer day at an attraction drawing some half a million visitors a year in a seasonal location will see over 7500 visitors through the turnstiles. By contrast, a day in February may produce only 150 people. Yet, if the quality of the visitor experience is to be maintained, the fixed costs of operating in February are much the same as in July. Any savings in the numbers of part-time staff are offset by the increased costs of heating and lighting. Closure may not be an option if it leads to staff losses and other costs.

Obviously, on a simple pro rata basis, attractions may operate at a loss in February and at other times of the year, so the role of marketing is to influence demand to generate marginal extra admission income outside the limited number of peak days and maximize throughput on the main revenue earning days. Seasonality also forces the evaluation of alternative audiences such as schools and a range of corporate users that are not geared to normal seasonal patterns.

A third constraint affecting many attractions is the extent to which repeat visits to any one site in any one year are usually a minority of all visits. Some attractions have the kind of resource that encourages repeat visits, but many in popular tourist destinations are designed for one visit only. With the competition now facing most attractions, reviewing the product experience and finding new ways to encourage repeat visits as well as first-time visits is therefore a primary concern for most attractions.

This fact also helps to explain why the successful large attractions find it necessary to spend 10 per cent or more of their admission revenue on promotion and distribution.

Unlike profitable businesses in other sectors of travel and tourism, it appears to be characteristic and normal for most smaller visitor attractions to survive from year to year on a financial knife-edge. Rising costs of operation tend to overtake any rise in available sources of revenue. Certainly this is true of those in the heritage sector, which usually exist to achieve non-profit-related goals. Costs rise at least in line with inflation and the potential demands of the resource for optimum conservation and refurbishment are usually far in excess of available income. Times of economic recession of the depth experienced in many countries between 1991 and 1993 and in the Pacific area in 1997–9 reduce income from visitors and play havoc with budget forecasts. With high fixed costs committed in advance, a 10 per cent downturn in earned revenue over a year can usually only be tackled by severe cost-cutting for the year following. It is, however, all too easy for attractions to cut costs (including marketing budgets) to the extent that the visit experience becomes tired and worn, and further falls in revenue result as customers turn elsewhere.

The size of the marketing budget

Experience suggests that allocating around 10 per cent of admissions revenue for marketing purposes is a realistic guideline for most visitor attractions. There may well be a convincing argument for spending more than this, however, especially to promote awareness of new facilities and on seasonal sales promotion efforts if the evidence achieved through visitor research indicates that the promotional efforts are paying off in admission revenue.

The objective and task approaches to budgeting, outlined in Chapter 14, are particularly appropriate for visitor attractions and the segmentation model set out in Table 21.2 provides an appropriate structure for budget allocation and monitoring.

Developing new marketing and management linkages

Given the average small size of attractions, there is typically only one or at most two managers/owners at most visitor attractions. They have to provide all the management skills needed to compete in a more sophisticated visitor market against the major operators with their large management teams. In common with developments in other sectors of the economy, the only logical response to small scale is to join with others to share the management skills that cannot be achieved individually. Such a response has strategic and tactical dimensions but it is not easy for small operators, and the process typically needs a catalyst organization, such as a tourist board, or professional body, to lead the process.

The evidence of the 1990s indicates that all proactive attractions, and most if not all new developments, are seeking a future based on forging business synergy links and collaboration with partners. On the one hand these are intended to help them secure audiences and revenue, and on the other hand to provide mutual management support systems. Based on extensive research into UK museums in 1998, and clear evidence of some of the new linkages being developed, it was recommended that all museums should undertake a formal audit of their existing and potential links with other organizations, working to national and regional guidelines (Middleton, 1998a).The options include:

- Collocation with partner organizations, especially for new attractions and those faced with closure.
- Development of catering and related facilities to act as stand alone revenue earning entities rather than just a facility for the visiting public.
- Links with universities and other colleges of further and higher education in the co-production of courses and education for life.
- Links with local businesses for the provision of meeting spaces, functions and training seminars.
- Links with other attractions that are not competing directly for the same audiences and users.
- Links with other attractions to share management expertise.
- Links with other companies, especially for museums and galleries, that may be interested to market aspects of their collections using the new digital communication technology.

Many attractions can benefit from a systematic review of public and corporate uses of their facilities and many have developed 'friends' and similar groups to support their objectives. Cathedrals in popular destinations in the UK, for example, apart from the normal congregations for worship, appeal mostly to first-time visitors. But their prime locations in the centre of cities and towns can also support a combination of events such as concerts and the development of high-quality catering facilities. Such provision can develop and sustain a substantial level of repeat visits (and revenue contribution) from a resident community. They are not just revenue-earning opportunities, they are also ways to integrate visitor facilities functionally within their communities.

Another aspect of this search for linkages may be the arrangements for promotion and distribution that can be made with transport and accommodation interests seeking to provide extra interest and motivation in their own product offers. An obvious link is with coach tour operators, but hotels offering weekend breaks may be interested to feature admission to attractions as part of an inclusive price. In this context attractions become a part of the augmentation of an accommodation product, which in turn serves as a form of distribution channel for the attraction. Looking ahead, developing synergy between different groups of public and corporate users will be a key requirement for the survival and prosperity of smaller attractions.

Chapter summary

Stressing the important role of attractions as one of the core elements in the overall tourism product that motivates leisure travellers, this chapter identifies the common characteristics that influence the way that attractions are marketed. Ten categories of managed attractions are noted, all of which are controlled and managed, sometimes to protect and conserve precious heritage resources but mostly to provide access, enjoyment, entertainment and education for the visiting public.

The sector divides into larger attractions that usually charge for admission and increasingly these are professionally managed and marketed. Very few are commercial. Traditional heritage and theme park attractions are facing major new competition from retail-based complexes that are a purpose-designed mix of themed hospitality, leisure and entertainment as well as retail – marketed as leisure day out experiences.

The great majority of all attractions are still remarkably small in visitor numbers and revenue. Few were purpose-built for modern tourism and they are inherently product or resource orientated. Most are stand alone operations and have low levels of visitor management and marketing skills. The 'corporate culture' and the profile of this latter group, many of which are subsidized and provide their facilities 'free' or at low admission charges, are obviously not conducive to the development and application of the systematic marketing procedures recommended in this book. For reasons discussed, the pressures of competition and the need to generate revenue are forcing changes in professional management throughout the sector.

The definition of products as 'experiences' and the use of research to assess the components of the experience for product formulation are important to successful marketing. Product formulation has to be based on identified segments and this also means market research among visitors. Owners of attractions, in common with other producers of travel and tourism services, always have a 'captive audience' on their premises, providing opportunities for cost-effective research that should always be exploited as the first step in the marketing process.

The strategic marketing tasks for attractions reflect the high fixed costs of operation, the seasonality of visitor flows that many experience and the constant need to sustain repeat visits as well as motivate first-time visits. Marketing strategy focuses on segmentation, product formulation and positioning, and the need to ensure that the benefits offered by the attraction are clearly understood by targeted prospective visitors.

In their essential need for marketing, managed attractions are not different in principle from most other travel and tourism producers. The small scale of most of them puts a particular emphasis on reviewing their traditional stand-alone operations for the visiting public and developing collaborative linkages for management and operational purposes, and for revenue earning purposes. The opportunities for more effective mutual collaboration are changing the agenda for many attractions in the new millennium.

Further reading

Middleton, V. T. C. (1998). *New Visions for Museums in 21st Century.* AIM.
Swarbrooke, J. (1999). *The Development and Management of Visitor Attractions.* Butterworth-Heinemann.

Marketing passenger transport

Airline profit margins have been well below average compared with firms in other industries, and in some years there have been some very heavy losses indeed.
(Hanlon, 1999: 1)

The forms of transport available at any period of time and the ways in which they are marketed have a direct, functional influence on the costs and patterns of tourism flows and on the types of product that travellers purchase.

Historically, transport design and development reflect the need to move goods and mail, the need to administer countries and empires, the need to move armies and military equipment, the development of new weapons of war and the need to facilitate the movement of people efficiently in the conduct of business and in their daily lives. Even now, most public transport systems are still primarily geared to business, administrative and social requirements, and draw the bulk of their revenue from non-leisure related traffic.

In the latter part of the twentieth century, however, transport operators developed their systems increasingly to service leisure and recreation travel. The shift reflected market opportunities to develop into new and growing markets and to utilize surplus capacity, both overall and especially at times of otherwise slack demand. For some, such as charter and budget airlines and cruise ships, expanding leisure markets provided opportunities to create new products and methods of doing business, overturning traditional industry structures.

This chapter traces briefly the historical links between transport supply and tourism demand, and the increasing orientation of transport systems to travel for leisure and recreation purposes. It proceeds by defining the nature of transport systems and their products, identifying the powerfully binding constraints that exist on their marketing decisions. Passenger transport marketing decisions, more than any other in travel and tourism sectors, are unusually dominated by factors in the external and internal operating environment. The sector's marketing costs are also generally much higher as a proportion of revenue earned than those in other sectors, and it is the combination of pressures in the business environment and from marketing costs that explains the strategic and tactical marketing tasks for passenger transport operators that are covered in the second half of the chapter.

Historical links between transport supply and tourism demand

Chapter 8, transport is the physical means of access whereby travellers can reach their chosen destinations. As such, it is not difficult to trace the ways in which the growth of tourism around the world has been directly influenced by developments in transport. There are three main phases of development. The first covers the pre-industrial period up to the early nineteenth century, when leisure travel was very small in volume and confined to a wealthy elite. The second spans the next hundred years or so to the Second World War, which witnessed the development of mass transport by rail and sea and latterly by road, for mass tourism. The third covers the post-war period of large-volume tourism since 1945 and covers the growth of air transport underlying modern international tourism and the segmentation of demand for most forms of transport operations.

In the third phase access to cars rapidly increased to approaching two-thirds or more of the population in Europe, with higher levels in North America. Aircraft development received a massive impetus through the technological developments associated with war and continuing East–West confrontation, and aircraft quickly took over from ships as the main means of long-distance transportation. A growing volume of travel became international and on many routes vacation traffic (but not revenue) came to match and often greatly exceed other purposes of travel. Tour operation emerged on a large scale, stimulating the development of charter airlines, which in the 1990s carried more traffic than scheduled airlines on many European routes. Since the early 1990s, however, the distinctions between scheduled, charter and budget airlines are being reduced under more liberal competition policies introduced by EC rules that follow American precedents. Similar de-regulation has altered rail and bus transport in the UK, changing the rules under which marketing is conducted.

The ways in which tourist destinations developed are obviously closely linked to changes in the means of transport. In the nineteenth century, for example, seaside resorts in Northern Europe could not have developed as they did without the building of railway links to provide access for the markets emerging in the growing industrial cities and towns. Across the Atlantic, the state of Florida could not have developed as a major vacation destination in the 1970s for domestic and international tourists without its national and international air links, and the corresponding development of the state road system for cars and buses. In the South Pacific, tourism destinations are almost entirely dependent on the availability, speed and cost of air transport, all of which are improved by new technology.

The nature of transport systems

Table 22.1 summarizes the wide range of modern transport systems, the marketing of which affects all tourism destinations to some extent. Most destinations are simultaneously influenced by several of these systems. Although this chapter does not deal with private transport, it is included in Table 22.1 because in many countries it is the principal form of competition for public transport to which marketing managers have to respond. For domestic tourism and for much of international tourism in Europe, private cars were used by up to 90 per cent of all visitors in 2000.

At first sight it is easy to suppose that each of the forms of transport is so different in kind that comparisons, and the development of common principles for marketing, are impossible. In fact all the systems share some common characteristics, which have important implications for marketing practice. As Burkart and Medlik expressed it: 'A transport system can be analysed in three parts: the track, the vehicle, and the terminal' (Burkart and Medlik, 1981: 111).

- Tracks: controlled air routes/corridors, sea routes, canals, permanent ways (railways), roads, trunk routes and motorways.
- Vehicles: aircraft, ships, trains, buses and coaches, private vehicles.
- Terminals: airports, seaports, stations, garages, and off-street parking.

In considering the external threats and opportunities in the transport marketing business environment that influence marketing managers decisions, one should note that the three basic elements outlined above are typically owned and controlled by different parties. For example, in the case of air transport, the vehicles are owned and operated by airlines, (which in turn may be privately owned or run by state-owned corporations); the routes are effectively owned by governments that allocate and regulate the use of air space, although control may be outsourced to agencies that include private sector funding; and the terminals are owned for the most part by national, regional or local governments and their appointed agencies. At the terminals too, there is a mix of private and public ownership. Ownership and control of sea ferries and buses are similarly divided. In most of Europe, the tracks,

Air transport	**Long-haul scheduled airlines** operate strongly branded scheduled services around the world carrying business, VFR, leisure and holiday travellers. Product differentiation is achieved by separate cabins for first, business and economy class and it extends to check-in and lounge facilities at terminals. Segmentation is reflected in an extensive range of promotional fares, especially for economy class, with consolidated fares widely available through specialist agencies and the Internet. Since the 1990s, long-haul airlines operating with a comparatively high cost base have faced growing competition from charter airlines on profitable leisure routes such as UK–Australia and N. Europe to the Caribbean.
	Medium/short-haul scheduled airlines operate networks mostly within and between developed countries but they also perform a vital role in developing countries in which alternative modes of transport may not be viable. They operate as long-haul carriers do with product differentiation, segmentation, strong branding and promotional fares, and they are often part of the same companies. Medium/short-haul carriers on popular routes have faced strongly growing competition under deregulation from rivals with lower cost bases, such as budget airlines and charter airlines in Europe.
	Charter airlines primarily operate short/medium haul routes for leisure/holiday travellers. Developed in the 1960s and 1970s for inclusive tour holiday companies (with which most are integrated and often branded), charter airlines dominated most short-haul leisure routes in Europe in 2000. The shift to deregulation of air transport regulation in the 1990s and the growing popularity of short city breaks made it possible for charter airlines to operate scheduled services, develop 'seat-only' sales and extend their operations onto popular long-haul routes. Charter airlines face strong and rapidly growing competition from budget airlines in the twenty-first century in the markets for inter-city leisure and business travel segments.
	Budget or 'no frills' airlines developed in a deregulated air transport regime to provide short/medium inter-city services in the USA in the 1980s, mostly using leased airplanes and secondary rather than primary (high cost) airports. Strongly branded and copied in Europe in the 1990s from the successful model of Southwest Airlines, budget airlines mostly fly cherry picked popular city routes using secondary airports to keep costs down. Avoiding product differentiation and segmentation; providing no additional services; using direct marketing via the Internet and providing no commission for agencies, budget airlines compete aggressively on price for all purposes of travel. They provide competition for scheduled and charter airlines.
Sea transport	**Ferries**, initially mostly developed by railway companies, now operate strongly branded scheduled services on short sea routes that serve as extensions of the road network. By 2000, most are roll-on, roll-off ships designed to carry a balance of cars and their passengers for all purposes, and freight. Seasonality of traffic flows sustains an extensive range of promotional fares to promote use. Most ferries have developed strong marketing links with other businesses to increase their traffic. On highly popular routes where the revenue flows justify it, ferries may face fixed link competition from tunnels (Channel Tunnel between England and France) and bridges (Sweden and Denmark).
	Cruise ships. At one time (early 1980s) thought to be a dying industry, strongly branded cruise ships acting as floating inclusive resorts, have had a remarkable resurgence in the 1990s to become one of the fastest growing sectors of the global holiday industry. Although still only a small segment of the inclusive tour market, the newer ships being built are bigger than the former transatlantic liners of the 1930s and have become a popular alternative to traditional package tours in the USA and Europe. Twenty-first century cruising is facilitated by low cost flight access (fly-cruise deals) to ports such as Miami and Barcelona.
Rail	**Scheduled rail services** (excluding commuter trains) mostly operate on short-haul city routes for journeys of up to around four hours' duration although fast trains in Europe cover longer journeys and provide competition for air and road traffic. Trains serve all purposes of travel although holidays are now only a small part of the mix and business related revenue is targeted as a vital segment. Product differentiation and segmentation by class of travel is reinforced through a wide range of promotional fares to combat seasonality and draw in traffic at less popular times and days of the week. Rail marketing is becoming more sophisticated in the UK following privatization (mid 1990s) and traffic congestion encourages rail travel for all purposes.
Bus and coach	**Bus services** (excluding local and commuter buses) divide into scheduled express services providing inter-city competition for rail for non-business users, coach tours and excursions, and private hire. Buses play a significant role in the budget price end of the inclusive tour market and excursions for segments such as schools and the over 60s. They can provide support services such as couriers and a social ambience that niche markets value. Buses also link places that rail may not serve and perform key services such as transfers for other forms of transport by air and sea. Private hire for groups, clubs and associations is an important part of modern tourism and may increase as traffic congestion difficulties impede the use of private transport.
Private transport	At the start of the twenty-first century, cars are the dominant form of transport in developed countries for most domestic tourism, leisure day visits and recreational purposes. In Continental Europe cars are also the preferred mode of travel for tourism between countries. The sheer convenience, flexibility, relevance to modern lifestyles and what often appears to be the low marginal cost of using a car, especially for two or more people, provides private transport with massive competitive advantages. Since the 1990s, however, internationally growing environmental concerns with traffic congestion at destinations, pollution and global warming are likely to tilt the currently favourable regulatory framework against cars. A combination of subsidy, regulation, taxation and promotion is expected to achieve a move toward public transport in the twenty-first century. Car rental at destinations, supporting the use of public transport for the main journey, is likely to grow in popularity.

Table 22.1 Principal passenger transport systems used in travel and tourism (with acknowledgement to Derek Robbins)

vehicles and terminals of rail transport are still in state ownership although not in the UK where ownership was separated in the late 1990s as for air and sea transport.

Without permission to fly to specific airports, or with permission to fly but only for a specified capacity of certain types of product (such as scheduled rather than charter flights), airlines do not enjoy full scope for responding to the market forces they perceive. Similarly, if the external agencies controlling the routes or the terminal facilities cannot cope with the added volume, marketing decisions to develop new routes or products have a very restricted meaning. Marketing constraints arose in the 1990s through airport congestion in much of Europe and America, and because public sector air traffic control systems have not been developed fast enough to cope with increases in demand.

In private transport, individuals own the vehicles but the routes they use are typically developed, owned and controlled by government and its agencies. On some routes and in some cities, tolls are applied to control use and generate income. At tourism destinations the bulk of the terminal or public parking facilities available for private transport are often provided by local government or otherwise controlled through parking regulations and planning controls. Government policies are increasingly in place in many countries to try to shift tourism from private to public transport systems.

In other words, passenger-marketing strategies have to take account of changes and interactions between the capacity, routes and terminals of both public and private transport. They have to reflect a changing pattern of public and private sector ownership. Such strategies are usually a key element also in the external business environment of all other destination businesses in the tourism industry.

In summarizing the common characteristics of transport systems influencing marketing decisions, it should be noted that:

- All passenger transport systems operate through more or less closely controlled and regulated vehicle movements along controlled networks which link points of origin and destination. When capacity is approached or exceeded, the regulatory role becomes predominant.
- The operation of all passenger transport systems requires continuous concern with the utilization of available capacity, whether of vehicles, routes or terminals.
- All passenger transport systems display typical characteristics of peaks and troughs in demand, whether by month, week, day or hour.
- Most transport systems need massive investment in infrastructure, vehicles, track and control systems. This in turn requires efficient marketing both to justify and to pay back the expenditure.
- Most systems move freight as well as passengers and freight requirements may take precedence.
- Most transport systems are only partly concerned with leisure travel.
- All transport systems put pressure on the physical environment, especially that of host communities at popular destinations.

Supply increasingly leads demand for transport products

In most industries, supply is led by demand. Historically, transport services have generally developed in response to demand arising from economic growth and rising incomes. But, especially in leisure travel, the availability of affordable supply clearly facilitates and generates demand. When the Channel Tunnel opened between England and France in the mid-1990s it immediately generated new traffic. New bridges and new roads often have the same effect. Much of modern tourism for leisure purposes can be persuaded through effective marketing, pricing and promotion to switch its choices to alternative destinations. There is in Britain, for example, a huge potential demand for holidays in the USA. Whenever the dollar/pound exchange rate has been favourable to the British, the traffic has surged and vice versa. The greatest obstacle to growth is the cost of travel across the Atlantic and the sheer range of promotional fares on the route proves the point. If the cost of transport could be significantly reduced through new economies of scale, or through some technological, cost-saving breakthrough, there can be little doubt that demand would be led by the supply of cheaper transport.

The powerful leading effect of supply of transport in international tourism markets is especially obvious in the case of islands, such as those in the Pacific area, where the development of new routes acts almost like a tap for new demand. The important point in travel and tourism is that supply and demand is essentially interactive. It is an interaction that can be exploited to good effect by transport marketing managers.

A strictly functional role for transport in the tourist product

Although a core part of all tourism products, modern transport is no longer a part of the motivation or attraction of a destination visit. There are some exceptions to this, such as steam railways, the Orient Express or cruise ships, although the latter are better understood as floating hotels or resorts than as forms of transport. The transport element, as Holloway (1985: 23) described it, is only an 'enabling condition', i.e. a functional element essential to the existence and growth of tourism but not of itself a sufficient reason for travel.

The role of transport in leisure travel was not always so functional. In the pioneering days of both public and private transport, journeys of all kinds, especially those by air and sea, could be presented as exciting, glamorous and romantic. In those circumstances the journey was an adventure and an important part of travel motivation. By the 1980s, however, except possibly for children and first-time travellers by air and sea, the journey had lost most if not all of its earlier magic. Experienced travellers, especially those on business trips, increasingly see the journey element as a necessary but unpleasant part of the trip to be endured, not enjoyed.

Journeys by public transport have to be paid for not only in money terms but also in the stress and strain of heavily congested access routes, queuing in crowded terminals, delays, missed connections, harassed staff and risk to personal safety. With private transport, the strain of driving along congested trunk routes and not finding convenient parking space at the destination has removed most of what was once the glamour of the open road. 'Today, Heathrow is regarded by millions of travellers as a noisy, polluting, necessary evil where we suffer an interlude of hell in order to reach business or holiday destinations' (*Evening Standard*, 10 September 1997) – a journalist's purple prose, for sure, but a view now shared by many. Marketing for business travel focuses rather more on alleviating the misery than on selling the pleasures.

The nature of the transport product

For charter airlines, cruise ships and most long-distance coach tours, the transport element is usually no more than one component within the overall tourism product, the marketing of which is not normally the responsibility of transport operators. Indeed, the physical transport element may be subcontracted or 'outsourced'. By contrast, although they may also provide linkages with accommodation and destination interests for their customers, scheduled transport operators have full responsibility to design and market specific products based on their vehicles, networks and services.

As defined in Chapter 8, any specific service product offered to customers represents a combination or *bundle* of components available at a specified price. The main components in the passenger transport bundle are:

- Service availability and convenience (reflecting routes offered, schedules and capacity).
- Cost in comparison with competitors on the same routes.
- The design and performance of the vehicle (comfort and speed).
- Comfort, seating, ambience and any services offered during the journey.
- Passenger handling at terminals and car parks.
- Convenience of booking and ticketing arrangements.
- Contact with staff and their roles in contact with customers.
- Image and positioning of each operator.

Viewed from the customer's standpoint, the core products offered by operators of the same type of transport, such as airlines or sea ferries, tend to be remarkably undifferentiated in comparison with the products offered in other sectors of the tourism industry. Perceived 'sameness' of product is an obvious problem for marketing managers and it is interesting to note the reasons for it. In what was traditionally a closely regulated transport environment, a combination of formal and informal agreements between governments, other regulatory bodies and other transport operators, served to produce virtual uniformity in the basic components of the formal product (see Chapter 8). In the case of international air transport until the 1980s almost every aspect of the product was covered by agreements, from price down to the smallest detail of in-flight services. The products were commonly offered in identical aircraft with the same cabin layouts.

Even in the more liberal or deregulated transport climate of the new century, the use of the same type of equipment, shared terminals and fierce price competition still produced virtual uniformity in the core product. As a result, most airline marketing focused on product augmentation, corporate images and the quality of service provided by staff. Apart from obvious distinctions between first-class, business-class and economy-class products, and with limited but important exceptions such as Concorde, the traditional approach to marketing airline products was rather sterile and unimaginative. Seats on transport are just commodities in the eyes of most consumers.

The dominance over marketing of the external business environment

Before identifying the strategic and tactical marketing tasks in passenger transport it is first necessary to appreciate the extent to which marketing is constrained by factors in the external and operational environment. Part One of the book illustrates how the business environment dominates tourism-marketing decisions generally. Passenger transport marketing responds to seven specific external factors over most of which the operators have only very limited control and not much influence. These factors are listed and four of them are briefly discussed below:

- Vehicle technology (major innovations).
- Information and communications technology.
- Regulatory framework.
- Price of fuel.
- Economic growth or decline (national and international economy).
- Exchange-rate fluctuations.
- Environmental issues.

Vehicle technology

It is competition among manufacturers such as Boeing and Airbus that develops the capabilities of vehicles in terms of their size, seat capacity, speed, range, fuel efficiency, noise and passenger comfort. Such developments affect the potential seat/mile costs achievable and thus the profitability of operations. They also influence customer choice, especially as to which destinations can be reached within acceptable time and cost constraints. The development of wide-bodied long-haul jets, for example, made possible the rapid expansion of leisure tourism between continents during the 1980s and 1990s.

While the implications of developing vehicle technology for tourism markets are most obviously seen in public transport, the extension of car ownership and the increasing comfort, reliability and efficiency of motor vehicles, is equally vital to the market growth of many forms of tourism. Most short weekend breaks, self-catering accommodation and day visits to attractions are primarily dependent on car travel.

Information and communications technology

Information and communications technology developments (covered in Chapters 10 and 19) have made it possible for passenger transport operators to deal efficiently with the increasing volume of business. Led by airlines, the processes for dealing with enquiries, reservations, cancellations, ticketing, invoicing and options on routes and fares are now handled seamlessly by computers. These processes simultaneously generate a wealth of research data on the characteristics of customers of great value in the marketing planning process. Information and communications technology developments are also transforming the distribution process for travel and tourism generally, driving down costs and prices and greatly facilitating last minute sales. Many of the developments have been led by transport operators in search of greater cost-efficiency in the conduct of routine operations and, equally important, in the conduct and control of their marketing operations. New strategic marketing linkages between product elements are greatly facilitated by the creation of interactive online computer networks, connecting the reservation systems of transport operators with those of hotels, car rental organizations and destination marketing organizations.

Regulatory framework

For most of the twentieth century, the operations of international and national passenger transport systems were closely controlled and regulated in all countries, both for domestic and international movements. In air transport, permission to fly into airports, between countries and through national air spaces, derived from an extraordinary patchwork of treaty agreements between governments. These covered which airlines would be permitted, over what routes, with what capacity and with what price ranges and options. The government agencies that control these decisions were, in effect, participating directly on behalf of governments in crucial areas of marketing decisions and acting in lieu of market forces. If an agency controls product capacity (supply of seats), and determines or influences price, it exerts a greater influence over demand than any amount of advertising and sales promotion.

The idea of non-commercial agencies and governments acting in lieu of market forces, however, is increasingly seen as inefficient. Originating with legislation in 1978 covering USA domestic airlines, there has been a widespread international shift towards removing regulatory controls over transport. There are strong arguments that the forces of supply and demand and relatively unfettered competition between operators are a better way to determine air-transport markets than regulation. The same arguments have been applied to other forms of transport. The full, long-term effects of deregulation in the USA are still far from clear at the time of writing and, with the notable exception of the mould-breaking Southwest Airlines, dozens of new entrants to the airline industry failed and the evidence points to market dominance by four or five very large corporations.

In the 1990s the pace of change in air transport deregulation was dramatic. 'The airline industry throughout the world is in the process of profound change. Fresh news about deregulation, privatization, mergers, alliances, foreign ownership and other developments appears in the press almost every week' (Wheatcroft, 1992: 5). Wheatcroft predicted that around the turn of the century there would be no more than around a dozen very large/global airlines with four based in the USA, four in Europe, and four in the Far East. Although governments still control the all-important bilateral treaties that cover major routes, such as the Atlantic, liberalization represents a major revolution and a quantum leap in competition. It has profound marketing implications, especially as subsidies are removed from former state-owned airlines.

In Europe, where the control of transport policy and competition rules has passed to the EC, a phased process of dismantling key elements of existing airline regulation took place as part of the process of clearing barriers to the Single Market, which came into force in 1993. The scope of these changes is too complex for analysis in this chapter but they influence the evolving framework within which transport marketing takes place. Free-market arguments for transport are not without critics, but the shift to de-regulation in the 1990s and the privatizing of formerly state-owned airlines appears unstoppable in most parts of the world.

The combination of liberalization and ICT opens strategic opportunities for new market-led developments, such as budget airlines that now handle around 25 per cent of scheduled passengers in the USA and are increasing remarkably in Europe.

Environmental issues

There are five main areas of environmental concern for transport operators. They are noise, emissions, use of energy, congestion, and waste production and disposal. Up to the 1990s these issues had only minor implications for the conduct of marketing. But they were all subjects for growing regulatory control in the 1990s and these regulations seem certain to affect future costs and the types of transport products that can be marketed. Car journeys are being actively discouraged in Europe and short-haul journeys by air are likely to be discouraged in favour of rail travel. Not all these issues are new, however, and airlines in particular have been active for over two decades, at least in reducing the noise impact around airports and increasing fuel efficiency.

Aircraft are subject to noise certification standards established by the International Civil Aviation Organization (ICAO). Emissions of carbon dioxide – produced by all forms of transportation using fossil fuels – are also under regulatory influence as carbon dioxide is the principal global warming gas. Aircraft emissions of carbon dioxide are estimated at 1 to 1.5 per cent of global warming, and are small in comparison with those of motor vehicles, although large measured in emissions per passenger carried.

Congestion of transport systems, e.g. at airports, on motorways and in cities, is a major contributor to environmental costs, as it leads to delays, extra fuel usage and increased emissions. In Europe air traffic control systems (ATCs) are an important cause of congestion. Europe still had thirty-one different ATCs and thirty-three different computer languages to control its air traffic, as recently as 1992. In the USA at the end of the 1990s, shortage of slots and air traffic congestion had become a major issue for US airlines and airports.

Responding to the 1992 'Earth Summit' at Rio de Janeiro, most leading airlines set up environmental departments and introduced environmental management programmes. British Airways is a leader in this field and aims to integrate environmental considerations into all the airline's normal business practices. In 2000, however, bearing in mind that they are one of the principal determinants of future international leisure travel there is little evidence that airlines yet recognize the importance to them of sustaining the quality of the natural and built environment of the destinations they fly to. It is perhaps ironic that, as the traditional regulation of routes, capacity and prices is being lifted from transport operators, new forms of regulation for environmental purposes are being introduced. They appear certain to influence future marketing.

Other external factors

External economic factors generally are discussed in Part One of this book and in Chapter 9 on pricing. Economic growth or recession and the changing price of oil obviously have a major influence on the market volume carried by transport operators for business and leisure purposes, with the latter especially price elastic. The massive power of economic and political factors over market demand has been highly visible in the 1990s, in the economic recession of 1990–2, at the time of the Gulf War and again in the crash of the Asian Tiger economies in the late 1990s.

Two operational constraints on public transport marketing

This section focuses on two important constraints that arise from the nature of operating a passenger-transport system.

Capital investment and fixed costs

A principal characteristic of most modern passenger transport operations is the high level of capital investment and fixed costs that is required in terms of purchasing and maintaining vehicles and equipment, setting up and maintaining route networks, funding modern reservation and other marketing systems and employing staff. The level of investment is especially high for international airlines, with modern long-haul 'jumbo jets' costing up to £100 million each at 1999 prices. But, relative to the size of their revenues, heavy capital investment applies equally to shipping lines, railway systems and to bus and coach operations. In each case expensive new equipment, often associated with increased seating capacity per vehicle, is usually justified on the grounds that through more efficient operation it will lower the operating cost per passenger seat/mile and thus permit potentially lower fares to be charged, or more profit to be made at the existing prices. A vital proviso in this argument is that the potentially lower costs can only produce real savings, if enough of the seats on offer are sold.

A related dominant characteristic acting as a constraint on marketing decisions is that the committed costs, or 'fixed' costs, of operating any service are high and the variable costs are low. For airlines, strictly speaking, fuel costs and landing charges are variable costs since they are not incurred if a flight does not take place. In practical terms, once the decision is taken to fly a particular route at a particular time and the service is marketed, all the main costs become effectively 'fixed' and they have to be paid regardless of the number of seats sold. While full aircraft use more fuel than empty ones, the difference measured on a per seat/mile basis is very small. From a marketing standpoint, it concentrates the mind to recognize that any seat sales achieved after the decision is made to operate a service, and that may be weeks before it is performed, represent over 90 per cent revenue contribution. Up to the break-even load factor this contribution covers fixed costs and, once the break-even load factor is reached, it represents gross profit.

Load factor, yield management and fleet utilization

Because of the investment and high fixed cost implications of passenger transport operations, there are three key measures of operational efficiency that are especially relevant to marketing managers. The most critical measures for marketing are seat occupancy and yield. Seat occupancy is also known technically as the load factor. Yield is a revenue calculation defined as load factor × *average* seat price paid, and seat occupancy and yield are related. For example, a load factor of 55 per cent for a flight in which half the passengers were paying business fares, and the others full economy fare, would yield very much more revenue than a load factor of 60 per cent if only a quarter of the passengers were paying business fares and the others were travelling on heavily discounted promotional fares. Yield may be divided by kilometres flown to provide a comparative measure across different routes.

The third key measure is fleet utilization. As in any form of production based on expensive plant, the more intensively a piece of equipment is used, the better the performance in terms of revenue achieved against the fixed costs incurred. If, for example, an expensive aircraft (on long-haul routes) can be kept in the air and flying with more than a break-even load of passengers, for an average of some sixteen hours in every twenty-four around the year (with allowance for routine inspections and servicing), it can obviously generate more revenue to cover its fixed costs than the same aircraft flying for an average of only twelve hours a day. Utilization is partly a function of efficient maintenance and scheduling the network to achieve the shortest possible turnaround of vehicles; but it is much more a function of generating sufficient demand to justify keeping the vehicles moving.

377

Ferries, trains and buses typically have a more limited utilization profile over twenty-four hours than long-haul aircraft.

The role of marketing in passenger transport is not confined solely to achieving higher load factors and increased yield and utilization at the margin. Nevertheless, the imperative need to maintain the level of seat occupancy on each service performed, while achieving high utilization rates throughout the year, dominates all passenger transport marketing. Typically, for scheduled airlines, average load factors and yield exceed the break-even level by little more than two percentage points and in poor years carriers fail to cover their operating costs.

The real impact of these operational constraints was neatly summarized by Harvey Elliot in the context of American Airlines:

> 'If one less passenger flew on each of American Airline's flights (in 1991), its annual revenue would fall by $114 million. The calculation is simple. Each passenger carried on the airline's 854,461 departures last year paid, on average, $134 for a ticket. Remove one passenger per flight and, with costs fixed, the missing $114 million carried through directly to the bottom line.' In fact American Airlines, the world's largest carrier, posted a $240 million loss in that year. (*The Times*, 22 February 1992)

Defining the marketing task for passenger transport operators

The marketing process set out in Chapter 2 (Figure 2.1) is as applicable to transport operators as to any other producer of consumer products. The marketing tasks in passenger transport derive logically from the characteristics of operations and the strength of the internal and external environment in which they are conducted, as noted above. The main tasks are summarized below under the headings of strategic and tactical marketing, which apply to all forms of public transport operators, whether by rail, road, air, or sea.

It is not easy to get a precise understanding of the level of expenditure on marketing by transport operators. The full marketing cost includes not just advertising and sales promotion but the major investment in providing CRS systems, securing distribution channels and paying commissions. The evidence suggests that the real cost of achieving an average booking for traditional scheduled airlines on international routes is still around 25–30 per cent of sales revenue. It is interesting to compare that with the net profit generated by international airlines expressed as a percentage of sales revenue. According to Doganis (1991), it reached 5 per cent only once in the last twenty-five years he reviewed and for several years there were massive losses, with the years 1990 to 1992 being the worst that international airlines have experienced to date.

Scheduled airlines have the highest pro rata marketing costs, which helps in part to explain the success of both charter and budget airlines whose costs are lower. But competition between forms of passenger transport ensures that the full costs of marketing are normally of the order of 20 per cent or more of sales revenue if the full costs of marketing and overheads, including price discounting from published fares to fill empty seats, are allowed for. (Chapter 23 explains the process of estimating discounted sales as part of a marketing budget for hotels and the principles are the same for transport.)

Strategic marketing

The strategic marketing task has five main elements:

- Forecasting demand.
- Finding ways to reduce marketing costs
- Building corporate product and brand strengths.
- Relationship marketing.
- Strategic linkages.

Forecasting demand

Through extensive use of marketing-research techniques and continuous passenger monitoring, all passenger transport operators develop marketing information systems to provide forecasts of market potential. Continuously reviewed, these are the basis on which future operational networks, schedules and the associated investment can be planned. Because fleet leasing or purchases along with other investment needs are geared to revenue forecasts (volume of customers × the average seat kilometre prices they will pay), the ability of marketing managers to provide realistic inputs to demand forecasting is crucial to the profitable development of any transport business. Estimates of traffic flows have to be built up route by route, separately for each main market segment. In practice, while forecasting models are normally the responsibility of transport economists and statisticians, the quality of the marketing research inputs relating to segments, products, customer satisfaction and willingness to pay, is a vital contribution.

At the time of writing, a high profile demonstration of this strategic task is being fought out on a grand scale between Boeing, which did not initially identify a big market for aircraft larger than the 420-seater 747, and Airbus, which did. Investment in the 550-seater Airbus A3XX is predicated on the airlines' need for larger aircraft on key routes to help overcome the shortage of landing and take-off 'slots' available at busy airports. With development costs for the big plane estimated at around $15 billion and a cost per aircraft of around $200 million, understanding how to fill the new vehicles and keep them in the air around the clock is vital to airlines' decisions to purchase. Such understanding means the strategic ability to forecast and deliver competitively priced attractive products to their targeted segments.

Inevitably, estimates of future traffic flows will always be surrounded by risk because of the unpredictable nature of the business environment. But the better the operator's knowledge of customer profile and behaviour, the better the chance of reducing the risk.

Finding ways to reduce operating costs through more effective marketing • • •

As noted earlier, transport operators' marketing costs are high, at around 20 to 30 per cent of the seat price. Traditionally costs include travel agent commission, commission on credit card usage, GDS costs and the associated heavy investment in computer facilities to service booking systems. It is the analysis of these costs and finding ways of forcing them down which has driven much of strategic marketing in the 1990s. It was not until 1995 that Delta Airlines was the first to break with traditional high levels of commission payment, rapidly followed by competitors around the world. More radical solutions, building on the pioneering career of Southwest Airlines and taking advantage of the European air traffic liberalization process, have been developed by budget airlines in Europe, which either do not use travel agents at all, or require them to charge service fees.

The combination of using secondary (low-cost) airports, cherry-picking high volume linear routes, controlling operational costs (no frills) and slashing distribution costs, has proved a highly successful formula in an era of congested hub airports and rising demand. It effectively halves the operating costs faced by major scheduled carriers. In a very few years, Ryanair, easyJet, Go and others have demonstrated their value to target markets. They achieved a 50 per cent growth in passenger numbers in 1999 serving more than fifty cities. Avoiding the use of travel agents altogether, easyJet claimed over 60 per cent of its sales in 2000 were made direct via the Internet on a ticketless basis, with the remainder of sales using call centres.

In rail transport, drawing heavily on its airline experience in developing advance bookings, Virgin Trains invested £50 million in the late 1990s in an online rail booking company formed initially in 1997 as a telephone sales booking system. Known as WWW.TheTrainLine.Com, the system was handling some 64 million combinations of routes and fares in 2000 for all of Britain's train companies. Such systems are wholly new for UK rail transport but are essential for achieving maximum utilization of the expensive new trains due in service from 2001. For almost 150 years nearly all train tickets were sold on a turn up, pay and travel on the same day basis. The system will facilitate product innovation with airline style capacity and yield management as the basis for marketing advanced sales. Some 90 per cent of all mainline service tickets are likely to be pre-sold within a very few years. The opportunities of privatization, ICT and constraints on road traffic through congestion have revolutionized rail transport marketing strategy in Britain in little over two years.

Building corporate product and brand strengths • • •

The third element in marketing strategy lies in the way in which operators seek to gain competitive edge over their competitors in the continuous struggle for market share. In an increasingly deregulated market environment, strategy focuses on identifying operators' strengths from a customer standpoint. These strengths may be developed into the product offer, for example by designing segment specific product 'benefits' for business users, such as business lounges, 'free' drinks, express check-ins, larger reclining seats and limousine services. All of these are forms of product enhancement in ways that alleviate the actual pain of the transport experience – for those that can afford it.

Also part of strategy are the corporate images, branding and 'positioning', that are built into the customer appeal of products and communicated through advertising to targeted segments. At the highly sensitive margin of business either side of the break-even load factor, assuming they have a choice between more than one operator, uncommitted potential customers may have their choice influenced by positive or negative images of different companies. Recognition of the power of such images explains the considerable commitment of operators to both corporate and product advertising. Interestingly, the budget airlines seem able through their modern approaches to appeal as much or more to customers through 'personality' as the scheduled airlines do spending far more per capita on advertising.

Relationship marketing

The fourth common element in strategic marketing lies in the effort all operators now tend to put into creating and retaining regular, repeat buyers of their services. Mostly business travellers, a small number of frequent users typically provide a very high proportion of total revenue. For example, 20 per cent of customers could easily generate 75 per cent of all revenue on some routes because of the fares they pay and the frequency with which they travel. Such customers are identified in great detail in modern customer databases. They justify careful cultivation and it is logical to create schemes that reward and incentivize such people. Most leading scheduled airlines make arrangements with 'in house' travel agents located in the offices of their major corporate clients.

Traditional season tickets have been available for many years on rail and road commuter routes, but competition between airlines is generating new forms of frequent flyer loyalty programmes, which are likely to develop further as the databases of transport operators become more sophisticated and direct marketing gains importance (see also Chapters 16 and 19). In mid-2000, for example, the Danish airline Maersk Air were using the Internet to develop their customer database with an appeal to existing customers to log on to their Web site and 'create your own personal profile and win two return tickets . . . All new profiles will be entered automatically into our competition held every month until the end of 2000'. This combines database-building, relationship marketing with individual buyers, and cost-cutting in a neat, low-cost form of sales promotion.

Strategic linkages and alliances

The fifth element in marketing strategy has two aspects. The first aspect lies in the formation of strategic links and alliances between international airlines in the post-regulatory era of market liberalization that has been one of the most striking transport marketing developments of the last decade. It seems set to continue. Such alliances make it possible to exploit and facilitate global computerization and reservation system linkages, service customers through code-sharing and develop dominant marketing positions. They provide a means to integrate marketing and operations to achieve vital marginal increments in seat occupancy and yield, and gain a competitive edge over rivals in a fiercely competitive marketplace.

Alliances offer a form of 'virtual' corporate consolidation without the full cross-border mergers that most governments have refused thus far to countenance. They provide a way around the regulation of routes imposed by the patchwork quilt of bilateral treaties that still govern international airline operations. In 2000 the leading major alliances were Star Alliance (including Lufthansa, United, Air Canada, BM, SIA and others), and One World (American, British Airways, Qantas and Canadian Airlines, Iberia, etc.). The alliances are fluid and change continuously for the reasons noted above. Since Europe followed America's internal liberalization in the mid-1990s there have been more than forty deals between the USA and countries in Europe, Asia and South America to get around government controls on routes and fares – although not in 2000 on the prized route, between London and the East Coast of the USA.

A second aspect of linkages is the way in which some transport operators shift their focus outwards, away from the performance of their traditional roles as operators of vehicles, routes and terminals, towards linkages with other elements of the overall travel and tourism product. In other words, the extent to which providers of transport seek strategic marketing links with destination interests and with the distribution networks of other travel products. The scope for these links is already wide and immensely facilitated by Internet accessibility. It ranges from relatively limited links with car rental operators, accommodation providers and attractions, all the way up to full integration with marketing organizations such as tour operators or wholesalers. From the earliest days of railways, links with hotels were seen as necessary to the efficient development of transport businesses. A century later some airlines formed similar links with hotel groups for exactly the same reasons. In leisure travel the logical extreme of the linkage strategy is seen most clearly in the charter airlines that are integrated with tour operators in Britain, such as Britannia (Thomson Holidays), and Airtours International (Airtours). In this latter context the charter fleets provide a vital but essentially functional role within a wider product, of which the marketing is undertaken by the principal and not by the transport operator.

Closer linkages between transport and the other elements of the product, especially with destination interests, appear probable in the new century. In the case of the Channel crossing between England and France, most sea ferry companies have already formed functional links with accommodation interests such as the 8000 holiday cottages (gîtes) in France and campsite operators, and most offer short-break packages in which the transport is just a component of the overall product. This appears to be more than product augmentation and a real shift into packaging of the kind discussed in Chapter 24.

Tactical marketing

In generating demand for unsold seats and achieving additional hours of profitable utilization for expensive vehicles, the contribution of tactical marketing is to mould demand within the already established constraints and to cope with unforeseen fluctuations in demand. Using the wide range of promotional tools set out in Chapter 16, the object is to manipulate customer behaviour to buy more of the available supply of 'perishable' service products than would occur without such expenditure. This section notes four of the main dimensions:

- Marketing the margin.
- Segment specific promotions.
- Tactical pricing and yield management.
- Managing crises.

Marketing the margin

Overall, especially around the break-even level of seat occupancy, the focus of tactical marketing decisions is to secure on a daily basis the vital marginal increment in customer purchases that makes a major difference to profit or loss in the high fixed cost operations of passenger transport systems. Of course some routes on some days at some times of the year are likely to be fully booked. But for the bulk of any transport operator's planned services, extra demand at the margin is a vital contribution to annual profitability. Scheduled operators face much greater problems of this sort than the budget airlines which carefully 'cherry pick' growth routes calculated to produce the best seat occupancy.

Segment specific promotions

The success of promotion is directly related to the knowledge that marketing managers achieve of the profile, needs and the probable behaviour of the customer segments with which they deal. Chapter 14 stressed that commitment to knowing the customer is a necessary prerequisite for the planning and execution of all forms of effective promotion. The more that promotion is segment and product specific, the greater the need for a detailed understanding of target customers. Data-mining of customer databases provides the necessary market analysis and, in addition to loyalty schemes for regular buyers, most transport operators can develop specific offers, often with third parties such as organizers of events, sports fixtures and festivals that appeal to the targeted group but do not dilute forecast revenue.

Tactical pricing and yield management • • •

For transport operators, most tactical pricing is also segment specific. For example, railways usually do not reduce the fares paid by commuters because their services are overcrowded at commuter times. Similarly they do not reduce the fares paid by first-class travellers because most of them are travelling on business and their demand is proven to be relatively inelastic to changes in price. On the other hand, operators have every incentive to use price, with or without a special product offer, to promote use of the network outside peak periods. A common response is to devise segment-specific fares with conditions designed to prevent the 'dilution of revenue', as it is known, if passengers switch from higher fares they otherwise would have paid.

The whole concept of segment-specific fares, often accompanied with the presentation of services as 'special products', is found internationally under a multitude of different names. Advanced Purchase Excursion Fares (APEX), which are widely used in Europe and North America, are obvious examples of segment-specific fares and products. They usually depend on advance booking, minimum lengths of stay at a destination and restricted times of travel to reduce the possibility of revenue dilution. The object is to generate the marginal revenue on specific journeys that yield management programmes indicate would otherwise be performed with empty seats. Where it is possible to provide group fares for pre-booked parties, operators will invariably allow a very significant price reduction; in this context groups are just another illustration of segment-specific promotional activity.

An interesting combination of marketing strategy and tactics is used by easyJet to promote advance booking. Their cheapest fares are bookable well in advance of the service to encourage early reservations that facilitate planning. As the time of the flight approaches the cost rises. Many other operators in tourism operate on the reverse principle and reduce price as the date of a service approaches. EasyJet succeed because their routes are carefully selected and so far they have not had to handle a major crisis of falling demand.

Managing crises • • •

Reflecting the many unpredictable variations in the external business environment, there is always a strong element of contingency and crisis planning in marketing tactics for transport operators. Each year brings its own examples. In 2000, leading examples were the need to respond tactically to the rising cost of oil (from around US$10 to $35 in twelve months and, for Europeans, the decline in the value of the euro currency (around 25 per cent from launch), affecting travel from European countries and exacerbating the effect of oil costs that have to be paid in US dollars. Earlier unforeseen events such as the dramatic late 1990s downturn in the Asian economies caused market falls of 50 per cent or more against forecast.

Crisis conditions may require massive promotional response, far in excess of any planned budget. The tactics are employed, however, as the only known way to combat unexpected trading losses and to invest in a rapid return to normal trading conditions.

Chapter summary

This chapter stresses the functional links between the development and capacity of transport operations and the demand for travel and tourism products. Although transport is only one of the five elements of the overall product and performs an enabling rather than a motivating role, accessibility is a fundamental condition for the development and growth of any destination, especially for international travel. The extent to which transport marketing is constrained by constantly changing factors in the external business environment and by the pressures of operational constraints, is explained. The continuous preoccupation with achieving revenue above the break-even level is emphasized. The contrast between the overall tourism products that ultimately determine travel flows and the specific transport products that are the focus of transport marketing campaigns is discussed. The route to product augmentation through a detailed and carefully researched knowledge of consumer segments is stressed.

Throughout, although this chapter tends to use airline examples, it seeks to define and illuminate the characteristics of marketing strategy and tactics practised in all forms of transport rather than focus on the specifics of particular modes. Undoubtedly there are aspects of marketing which are particular to individual forms of transport but they are derived from the general principles outlined here and they do not alter the conclusions drawn.

The chapter does not deal specifically with charter airlines because these are referred to later in Chapter 24. In practice most charter airlines adopt a form of industrial marketing in which they negotiate their routes, products and capacity, with a relatively small number of major clients. Major charter operators are now owned or linked financially with tour operating companies and usually they do not market their products directly to individual customers. In these circumstances charter airlines provide a vital operational function for tour operators, but it is the latter that take on the responsibility for marketing to the public.

Further reading

Hanlon, P. (1999). *Global Airlines: Competition in a Transnational Industry.* 2nd edn, Butterworth-Heinemann.

Shaw, S. (1999). *Air Transport: A Marketing Perspective.* 4th edn, Pitman.

Marketing accommodation

Businesses are now being challenged as never before to improve their marketing capabilities worldwide. (Lewis, Chambers and Chacko, 1995: xvi)

The case for hotel marketing is seldom powerfully advocated in the boardroom because most of the heads of marketing aren't even in the boardroom. (D. Michels, CEO Stakis PLC, 1997)

With the obvious exception of same-day visits from home, all other forms of tourism involve overnight accommodation. Accommodation is, therefore, one of the five integral components of the travel and tourism product defined in Chapter 8. The many different forms of accommodation and the ways in which they are marketed have a massive influence on visitor choices, behaviour and the types of product they buy.

As with transport, the early development of accommodation for travellers was not concerned with leisure but with the needs of commerce and industry and the administration of countries and empires. The development of accommodation for travellers has always been inextricably associated with the growing and changing needs of transport systems. Inns and taverns and, later, the forerunners of modern hotels were located logically in cities and ports and along the routes that linked them, for much the same reasons that many modern hotels are located along motorways and at airports.

Chapter 22 noted that transport systems are still vitally concerned with non-tourism services, such as journeys to work and the carriage of goods. Accommodation services also have important dimensions unconnected with travel and tourism, such as institutional and welfare provision in sectors as diverse as schools, prisons, hospitals, the armed services and the care of the elderly. In all these other areas of hospitality the influence of marketing is being felt but this chapter is, of course, only concerned with tourism products. Thus, when considering the meaning of marketing for the accommodation sector, it must be recognized that tourism contributes only part of total turnover. Many hotels, depending obviously on their locations, also provide food, drink and meeting facilities for residents in their surrounding local communities.

In the new millennium, most national and international hotel groups are still orientated primarily to the needs of business travellers and the expenditure they generate. In the last quarter of a century, however, in the sunshine resorts of the USA, Europe and the Pacific area, thousands of resort hotels have been built specifically to cater for the needs of the leisure market. Similar developments in timeshare resorts also owe their origins to leisure travel. In all such cases developments have exploited the market potential made possible by increasing disposable income in developed countries and modern transport systems.

This chapter begins by defining the constituent parts of the serviced and non-serviced sectors of accommodation and their role in the tourism product. It considers accommodation products as service experiences and discusses the business characteristics common to all forms of commercial accommodation operations. The marketing tasks for accommodation suppliers are considered under the headings of strategy and tactics and, in particular, the implications for the size of marketing budgets in the sector are reviewed. Expenditure on marketing is very much greater than the received wisdom in the sector believes.

Defining tourist accommodation

For the purposes of this chapter, tourist accommodation is deemed to include all establishments offering overnight accommodation on a commercial or 'quasi-commercial' basis to all categories of visitor. The definition does not cover the use of privately owned accommodation for weekends and holidays, such as second homes, caravans, chalets, boats and wholly owned apartments in condominiums – unless they are commercially rented through a marketing agency. Timeshare resort marketing is referred to briefly in this chapter but there is a case in Part Six of the book that deals with this important sector of the tourist accommodation market.

'Quasi-commercial' refers to the many tourist accommodation products outside the commercial sector, for which a charge is made to contribute to costs (even if a subsidy is involved).

For example, the British Youth Hostels Association (YHA) is a membership organization that provides a national network of hostels in the UK, mostly for young people willing to use inexpensive and sometimes shared accommodation. The YHA is a non-profit-making body but, in the context of its corporate objectives, it operates increasingly on commercial principles to secure the revenue needed for its refurbishment and development programmes. Other forms of quasi-commercial accommodation products may be found in colleges and universities, many of which now market their accommodation capacity for conferences and for holidays at times when students are not in residence. Such operations are increasingly required not only to cover their direct operating costs but also to make a contribution towards the overhead costs of the providing institutions.

Serviced and non-serviced accommodation

An important distinction in accommodation for visitors is the split between serviced and non-serviced types. Serviced means that staff are available on the premises to provide some services such as cleaning, meals and bars, and room service. The availability of such services, even if they are not in fact used, is included in the price charged. Non-serviced means that the sleeping accommodation is provided furnished on a rental basis, normally for a unit comprising several beds, such as a cottage, an apartment or caravan. While services for the provision of meals, bars and shops may be available on a separate commercial basis, as in a holiday village, they are not included in the price charged for the accommodation.

The serviced sector ranges from first-class and luxury hotels providing full service on a twenty-four hours a day basis at relatively high cost, all the way down to homely bed and breakfast establishments, which may only operate informally for a few weeks in the year. The non-serviced sector, which is known in Britain under the unattractive label of 'self-catering accommodation', comprises a wide range of different units, including villas, apartments, chalets, cottages and caravans. These units are rented on a fully furnished and equipped basis but with no personal services included in the published price. Some of these units, e.g. in converted historic buildings, may be furnished with antiques and may cost more per person night than four-star serviced accommodation. The bulk of self-catering units, however, still cater for a budget-priced market and the cost per person per night is very much less than could be obtained in the serviced sector.

At the start of the new century there are so many variations of serviced and non-serviced accommodation products that the distinction is often blurred in practice, although it remains useful for the purposes of analysis and discussion of marketing implications. Styles and types of accommodation also vary according to the traditions of different countries. The accommodation in many holiday villages and timeshare resorts is marketed as 'self-catering' units, for example, but within the village or resort there is often extensive provision of bars, restaurants, coffee shops and a wide range of other services available for purchase, although not paid for in the initial holiday price. In these circumstances the real difference between serviced and non-serviced accommodation appears increasingly irrelevant. In the customer's perception and from a

Figure 23.1
Principal serviced
and non-serviced
types of
accommodation
used in tourism, by
market segment

Market segment \ Sector	Serviced sector		Non-serviced sector (self-catering)	
	Destination	Routes	Destination	Routes
Business and other non-leisure	City/town hotels (Monday–Friday) Budget hotels Resort hotels for conferences, exhibitions Educational establishments	Motels Inns Airport hotels Budget hotels	Apartments	Not applicable
Leisure and holiday	Resort hotels Guesthouse/pensions Farmhouses City/town hotels (Friday–Sunday) Budget hotels Some educational establishments	Motels Bed and breakfast Inns Budget hotels	Apart hotels Condominia/timeshare Holiday villages Holiday centres/camps Caravan/chalet parks Gites Cottages Villas Apartments/flats Some motels	Touring pitches for caravans, tents, recreation vehicles YHA Some motels and budget hotels

marketing standpoint, however, the difference is clear. The endeavour by accommodation interests and tour operators to keep down published holiday prices explains much of the growth in non-serviced tourist accommodation in recent years.

Using the serviced/non-serviced split, discussed above, the types of accommodation referred to in this chapter are summarized in Figure 23.1. The boxes in the diagram divide each of the two accommodation sectors by destination and by routes because this fundamentally influences the nature of the accommodation products that are offered and the type of marketing required. It further distinguishes segments of users for business and other non-leisure purposes. Non-leisure purposes include stays away from home on family business such as school visits, funerals and weddings, or stays in an area while seeking a new house or apartment, and so on.

The role of accommodation in the overall tourism product

For business and other non-leisure visits, it is obvious that accommodation is not normally a part of the trip motivation or part of the destination's attraction. Rooms, serviced or otherwise, provide a necessary facility that makes it possible, convenient and comfortable to engage in the primary reason for travel. In marketing terms, locational convenience, high standards of comfort and efficiency and value for money are, therefore, the primary features or core product to be communicated. Within their price band, the extent to which the primary elements are perceived to be delivered is the basis for customer choice. Accommodation plays a functional role.

For holiday and leisure purposes, however, accommodation plays a very different role in the tourism product. While a destination's attractions are likely to remain the dominant motivation for most visitors, destination choices are also influenced by perceptions and expectations of the accommodation available. Sometimes, as with repeat trips to stay at the same hotel or caravan park, the image and quality of the accommodation may be strong enough to make it a primary rather than a secondary aspect of destination choice. More often, though, especially for packaged tours, the destination's appeal is the more important element in motivation and choice of destination.

Leisure visitors are also likely to spend many hours of a stay in their accommodation, especially if the weather is poor. Serviced or non-serviced, their trip and destination enjoyment will be highly geared to perceived value provided and satisfaction experienced with the bedrooms, bathrooms and any other rooms and facilities such as swimming pools and health clubs that may be provided. This holds good in relative terms for tented pitches in camping sites as well as for bedrooms in five-star resort hotels.

In other words, for leisure purposes, accommodation is integrally related to the attractions of a destination as well as part of the facilities. While transport in the late twentieth century appears to be losing much of its former glamour and appeal as part of the attractions of a trip, it appears probable that accommodation is moving in the opposite direction and enhancing its appeal. Current marketing trends to shorter stays suggest that destination and accommodation marketing are likely to come even closer together in a logical partnership of mutual interests.

The accommodation product as a service experience

It is worth restating that accommodation products of all types are perceived by customers as 'experiences.' The experience is organized and orchestrated to meet the identified needs and benefits sought by customer segments, as described in Chapters 7 and 8, and it comprises a series of service operations. For larger organizations, these operations correspond with operating departments, of which the most important are:

- *Booking services* – handling enquiries and bookings, including Internet, telephone, mail and reservation systems.
- *Reception/checkout services* – registering arrivals and departures, checking bookings and allocating rooms, possibly associated with support services, such as baggage handling – includes invoicing and settling accounts.
- *Rooms/site services* – delivering rooms or self-catering units cleaned, checked and ready to occupy.
- *Food and beverage* – (if provided) including restaurants, bars and coffee shops.
- *Other services* – (if provided) including room service, shops, leisure, entertainment and health facilities, secretarial, dry-cleaning, and all other services.

As noted in Chapters 6 and 8, product experiences are complex. They are influenced by physical elements (such as buildings and provision of food and drink), sensual benefits (experienced through sight, sound, touch and smell, and conveyed by the quality of buildings and their furnishings) and psychological benefits experienced as mental states of well-being, status and satisfaction. For resort visitors, the perceived benefits of the accommodation product are likely to be closely associated with the benefits associated with the destination's attractions. In other words, a successful destination may provide a 'halo' effect that supports the available accommodation, while an unattractive destination experience will have the opposite effect.

In Chapter 8 a weekend break in a hotel is used to illustrate recommended product formulation methods for tourism, organized around an analysis of target customer segment's needs and benefits sought. The basic components of core formal and augmented products were described, and the roles of process, people and physical evidence or design are covered in Chapter 6. They are not repeated here although they are especially relevant to this chapter.

The nature of the accommodation business

This section focuses on five particular characteristics of any accommodation business, serviced or non-serviced, which strongly influence the way in which marketing is conducted at the strategic and tactical level. Of particular relevance are:

- Choice of location.
- Existence of peaks and troughs in demand.
- Influence of room sales on profits.
- Low variable costs of operation, especially at the margin.
- Focus on 'bookers', not occupancy levels.

Location

Location tends to dominate all accommodation operations. It initially determines the customer mix the business can achieve and, therefore, the direction of marketing strategy and tactics. Location is also a major influence on the profitability of an operation. Where feasibility studies are undertaken to investigate the value of alternative sites prior to investment in new facilities, the inherent demand potential for each location under investigation is always the primary consideration. Of course, once an accommodation unit is established, location of operations becomes fixed for the lifetime of the asset. Whereas airlines and tour operators can move their operations around the world to serve alternative destinations in response to changes in demand, hotels and holiday villages are an immovable fixture. They have to use skills in marketing to overcome any difficulties that may emerge after the initial location is determined.

Many of the problems faced in accommodation marketing are in fact difficulties stemming from external environment shifts that have affected the market potential of the locations in which they are established. For example, seaside resort hotels in Britain, which relied on the traditional summer holiday market, were in considerable difficulty at the end of the twentieth century because their locations were no longer able to attract the volume or type of holiday demand for which they were originally built. Similar problems face Bulgarian resorts around the Black Sea that were built under communist regimes for a market that largely disappeared in the 1990s. For different reasons, modern, successful hotels in Hong Kong and Singapore faced very difficult times in the late 1990s because too much capacity was available to accommodate a demand that dwindled as a result of external political and economic shifts.

Greater commitment to sales and marketing is the only option for tackling the impact on location of unforeseen shifts in the external business environment. Marketing cannot cure all problems, of course, and in some circumstances accommodation businesses have no choice but to operate at a loss for as long as their resources allow or until the market expands. The only alternative is to sell properties, which in a buyer's market, usually means a massive capital loss. Forced sales are a common phenomenon in the accommodation industry, especially among smaller businesses with limited financial resources.

Less obviously, the type and architectural style of accommodation provision influences the places in which they are located. In vacation destinations certainly, the physical appearance of hotels, apartments and other accommodation buildings becomes part of the image as well as part of the physical environment of a destination. The attractions of the new island destinations on the Great Barrier Reef in Australia are in fact identified with the physical appearance of the accommodation structures built upon them; the image and attractions of Austrian ski resorts are highly dependent on the traditional wooden chalet style of hotel building, which gives them a distinctive appeal and position in prospective customers' minds; the appearance, style and ambience of up-market safari lodges in South Africa such as Londelozei and Mala Mala are an important part of the safari experience.

In Britain Brighton's current image and appeal is strongly associated with the fine Victorian architecture of its promenade hotels, while in Singapore the appeal of the refurbished Raffles Hotel is an important element in the destination's image. Around the Mediterranean and in Honolulu, for example, there is now ample evidence that the over-dense construction of functional but remarkably ugly high-rise buildings of no architectural distinction creates negative images in the minds of prospective customers. The Balearics case study in Part Six illustrates a current approach to what is being done in that context.

Business peaks and troughs

By weeks in the year and days in the week, nearly all forms of accommodation are vulnerable to highly variable demand patterns, just as transport operators are. The patterns reflect the nature of the market demand a location sustains. Thus hotels in many towns and cities in northern Europe can normally expect high occupancy from business travellers from Mondays to Thursdays, and the peak of their occupancy in the autumn and spring. Their business trade falls at weekends and in the July–August period. Most self-catering units by the seaside in Northern Europe can anticipate full demand for a period of little over sixteen weeks, and many still close completely for around five months of the year. The existence of peaks and troughs in demand is certainly not unique to accommodation businesses but it is a common characteristic to which marketing managers are required to respond.

Marketing efforts cannot reverse the natural locational rhythms of demand but product development and campaigns can be targeted around both existing and new segments to lessen the impact and to generate increased business at the margin.

Profit is driven by room-night sales

Although sales of room-nights, especially in the serviced hotels sector, seldom contribute more than around 50 per cent of total sales revenue, the average contribution of room sales to profitability is very much greater. According to BDO Hospitality Consulting the gross profit on room sales averaged 75 per cent for London hotels in 1998 (defined as room sales less room operating costs), while the gross profit on food and beverage sales was in the region of 30 per cent. The effect of high fixed costs means that the profitability of *additional or marginal* room sales may be closer to 90 per cent, while the marginal profitability of food and beverage sales tends to remain fairly constant.

Accordingly, the main focus and effort of accommodation marketing has to be on room-night sales. In practice, because nine out of ten people typically make reservations in advance as distinct from impulse purchases by walking in off the street, this means targeting bookings that are made ahead of a customer's arrival. The focus on accommodation sales and on advance bookings is even more important for self-catering businesses. Obviously the level of room occupancy achieved directly affects the sale of food and beverages, and effective merchandising to customers once they are 'in-house' is a logical marketing approach to increase total turnover.

Targeting *bookers*, not room or bed occupancy

There is a common misunderstanding that accommodation marketing focuses primarily on room or bed occupancy. The preoccupation with occupancy is certainly understandable for reasons already discussed, but marketing targets cannot sensibly be expressed as occupancy levels. Occupancy levels are a *result* of marketing effort; they are at best a retrospective statistical measure of marketing success or failure. Marketing targets are always prospective customers and, to use an unattractive but useful word, not just customers but 'bookers'.

A 'booker' is a customer or an agent of the customer, who makes a reservation for one or more persons, for one or more nights, in any form of accommodation. Thus, a person making a family booking for two rooms over seven nights for four people (fourteen room-nights and twenty-eight bednights), is a proper target for marketing strategy and tactics. A secretary who makes regular hotel reservations for one or more members of a company may never see a hotel or meet its staff, but he or she is a 'booker'. The secretary of a national association, responsible for organizing an annual conference for members, may be seeking several hundred room-nights in more than one hotel and is also a booker, and so on.

In the holiday parks sector of accommodation, offering caravans and chalets for holiday rent, marketing is traditionally considered in terms of 'unit sales' or 'unit rentals'. These terms are no more than trade jargon and accountants data. The marketing task in this sector, as in the others, is to identify, persuade, sell to and satisfy targeted groups of those who make the bookings.

High fixed costs of operation

The marketing implications for service businesses operating with high fixed costs and low variable costs are discussed in several parts of this book and require little further comment here. Suffice it to note that, once the fixed costs of operation have been covered at the break-even level of occupancy, the marginal costs of filling an additional, otherwise empty room are negligible in all sectors of accommodation. Beyond the break-even level the contribution to gross profit of additional room sales is very high, especially for self-catering operations, where the marginal costs are even lower than in the serviced sector.

Because the marginal cost of supplying an additional product is low, accommodation suppliers are very often tempted to reduce prices in an attempt to achieve sales, especially last minute sales before unsold capacity is lost forever. The higher the proportion of fixed costs to total costs, the wider the range of price discretion. But there is a counter-argument as the confident strategy of easyJet reveals. Their circumstances are not the norm for services marketing, but their commitment is to reduce the price of advance sales and increase prices as the service delivery time approaches. (See Chapter 22.)

Strategic marketing tasks for accommodation businesses

In the 1980s, a former president of Holiday Inns succinctly summarized the accommodation-marketing task, as follows. It remains the same today for all forms of accommodation:

> All segments of our travel and tourism business have become more competitive. A growing number of competitors offer their products to the same customer groups . . . travellers have a wider range of choices than ever before for matching a hotel to their particular travel needs. Those needs change according to the travel purpose. Unless a company can understand those changing needs and deliver a quality product and services appropriately targeted to specific customers needs, wants, and expectations, that business cannot survive. (Travel and Tourism Research Association (TTRA) Annual Conference Proceedings, 1986.)

There are six main elements in the strategic marketing response that accommodation suppliers make to their external business environment and the operational characteristics noted in the first part of the chapter. These are:

- Evaluating strategic opportunities for growth.
- Planning the most profitable business mix of segments, products and price ranges having regard to yield rather than volume.
- Deciding the position, brand or image each accommodation unit (or chain of units) should occupy.
- Encouraging and rewarding frequent users (relationship marketing).
- Developing marketing integration between units in common owner-ship (chains) or units in individual ownership (voluntary co-operatives).
- Exploiting the cost savings and other benefits deriving from the direct marketing potential inherent in the new ICT.

Evaluating strategic opportunities for growth

In an age of global expansion and development, and the opportunities created by information and communications technology, marketing management plays a vital and growing role in identifying strategic market opportunities. The remarkable development of budget hotels in the UK, building on models earlier developed in the USA, is one of the more dramatic illustrations of strategic marketing in the accommodation sector. The case of Travel Inn is illustrated in Part Six of the book, along with the case of RCI, illustrating marketing strategy in the timeshare market for holiday accommodation.

Strategic growth through mergers, alliances, acquisitions, and other deals with third parties that optimize the value that can be delivered to (and extracted from) existing and targeted groups of customers, is another form of strategic opportunity based on market evaluations as outlined in Chapters 10 and 12 and not further developed here.

Planning the business mix

In the context of the demand potential inherent in each location the basic strategic decision for accommodation businesses is to determine the optimum or most profitable mix of segments, for whose needs specific products may be created and promoted. For example, a city centre hotel will obviously target clients travelling for business and meeting pur-poses, a resort will draw a higher proportion of leisure visitors, and so on. Table 23.1 provides a fairly typical illustration of a customer mix that has important implications for the conduct of marketing. The same table, with additional calculations (Table 23.3), is used later in the chapter to illustrate an important point about marketing budgets.

Table 23.1 is based on a coastal resort hotel within a large urban location that supports a significant element of business visits within its chosen mix of segments. The hotel has two basic customer types (business and leisure) which permit of six primary segments, each representing a

Coastal hotel located near to a business centre generating visitors for conferences and general commercial purposes as well as holiday visitors.

120 twin rooms, with 65 per cent annual room occupancy = 28 470 room-nights' capacity over a year (120 × 365 × 65 per cent).

Rack rate £150 (twin/double) per room night, including breakfast; £100 (single occupancy).

Customer mix	% of room sales (per annum)	Volume of room sales (per annum)	Tariff type
1 Business (individuals)	20	5 695	Rack rate
2 Business (corporate clients)	30	8 540	Corporate rate
3 Vacation (individuals)	10	2 847	Weekly rate
4 Coach tour clients	10	2 848	Inclusive group rate
5 Holiday breaks (i)	15	4 270	Inclusive price
6 Holiday breaks (ii)	15	4 270	Wholesale rate
Totals	100	28 470	

Notes:
(i) Marketed directly by the hotel to customers.
(ii) Rooms allocated to tour operators; and packages marketed by the operator.

Table 23.1 A typical market/product mix for an urban coastal hotel

strategic marketing choice and requiring separate marketing campaigns. For convenience of illustration, the business/leisure ratio in Table 23.1 is 50:50. But it could vary from, say, 70:30 to 30:70, according to the strategy the hotel's owners choose, based on their judgement of marketing potential and what they seek to achieve for the hotel in its location.

The optimum customer mix for most businesses will usually comprise several segments, targeted to maximize achievable revenue yield and minimize the effects of seasonality and other normal business fluctuations.

While the serviced sector may appear to have more scope to plan a co-ordinated customer mix, exactly the same principle operates for self-catering operators in the non-serviced sector. For example, holiday-park owners who market units such as caravans and chalets for holiday lets, may plan a segmentation strategy that separately targets adults aged over fifty travelling in pairs, from families with children of school age who are largely tied to school holiday periods. They can differentiate between visitors who purchase traditional one or two weeks' stays, and others who are interested in weekends and shorter stays.

Devising the optimum mix for any accommodation business usually requires some form of marketing research or at the least an analysis of a customer database or guest-registration records to analyse the volume and revenue of current customers in each location and estimate the potential. Very few operators in the commercial accommodation sector cannot achieve at least a four-way customer split, or business mix, as the basis for a more efficient marketing strategy.

Deciding the position, brand or image

Relevant always to selected target segments, the next and obviously related strategic consideration for accommodation suppliers is to determine the 'position' each unit or group of units should aim to occupy in the minds of its targeted customers. Increasingly, where competitors offer closely similar products to the same group of customers at very similar prices, it becomes necessary for operators to differentiate and brand their products with particular values and identities that can be communicated. Identities, known in marketing jargon as 'positions', are perceptions in the minds of customers. They may be based on specific associations with a company name, such as Four Seasons or Dorchester, or on the strengths of a building and its location. They may be based on management design decisions about the specifics of products on offer, the quality of the staff and service provided, the design and quality of rooms and furnishings, or any combination of these characteristics.

Encouraging and rewarding frequent customers

The fourth element in strategic marketing responses for accommodation suppliers is to find ways to encourage and reward their regular or 'loyal' customers. The level of repeat customers in larger hotels in Britain in the late 1990s is running at over 40 per cent. Since most of these are business travellers their total yield contribution will be higher. Not surprisingly, for exactly the same strategic reason as airlines, most hotel groups developed their membership clubs and other frequent user schemes during the 1990s, often supplying privileged user cards designed around the interests of their regular customers. The process is greatly facilitated by the sophistication of customer databases and techniques for data-mining, as well as the ability to use Web sites to identify customers' profiles. Some of these schemes offered credit facilities in addition to the normal range of benefits, such as rapid check-in and check-out, and upgrades of rooms if availability allows. Some also offered awards through which frequent travellers could earn points for each stay, leading to attractive benefits according to the number of points collected over a given period.

Regular customers represent an important strategic marketing asset for any accommodation business, not only in terms of their own decisions but because they provide a very cost-effective route through which it is possible to reach their friends and others like them, using carefully designed and targeted direct marketing. Customer loyalty strategies in this context are an essential consideration for all accommodation businesses.

While the strategic objective of rewarding repeat visitors is very clear, not all the schemes currently in use are immediately or fully successful. In part this is because they are difficult and often expensive to administer, and partly because they may also serve, unintentionally, to reduce the average room rate to some customers who were prepared to pay a higher price.

Integrating marketing across several units

The fifth strategic consideration reflects a growing dimension in accommodation marketing that is relevant to the other four elements and focuses on the level of co-ordination that individual units can achieve in marketing their products. The strategic advantages of marketing co-ordination lie in economies of scale and may be summarized as:

Distribution	Referrals of business between units, central reservations services and call centres. Web site presence and linkages with other sites. Better access to retail distribution networks.
Promotion	Corporate positioning and branding. Joint advertising and PR opportunities. Use of professional marketing and sales teams. Access to group brochures and leaflets. Group representation at trade fairs and shows.
Product and pricing	Design and harmonization of products and group quality assurance schemes designed to build up customer satisfaction. Use of yield management programmes to develop and promote price options. Group loyalty schemes for frequent users. Access to group market research.

Obviously, co-ordination is most easily secured through ownership and mergers and is part of the process whereby large, multi-unit accommodation chains have emerged over the last twenty years and expanded the scale of their operations. However, modern ICT greatly facilitates the formation and management of strategic alliances and a range of franchising and leasing operations. As a result, branded multi-unit chains are now found in all parts of the world. Many of the chains are global and international in their scope, and there was no indication that this level of growth had reached its limits at the end of the 1990s.

Collaborative alliances of smaller businesses, of which one of the best known is the Best Western chain, provide a competitive response route for individually owned hotels. The search for the marketing advantages of Internet facilitated co-operation is spreading into the small businesses sector of both serviced and non-serviced units. The marketing of gîtes in France and holiday cottages in the UK are examples.

The direct marketing potential of new information communications technology for hotels

Table 23.2, based on a Horwath World Wide Hotel Study of 1998 and reproduced here with kind permission of Horwath UK, provides a valuable snap shot of the marketing distribution processes used world wide, mainly in four- and five-star hotels at the end of the 1990s before e-commerce was a significant element in bookings. The strategic

	Europe (%)		N. America (%)		Australia/NZ (%)	
Direct contact with the hotels[1]	38.8		29.5		38.8	
Via intermediaries:	61.2		70.5		61.2	
Own reservation system		10.8**		23.6**		12.7**
Independent reservation system[2]		5.8		4.1		5.4
Travel agents[3]		18.7		17.3		20.9
Tour operators[4]		19.0		16.9		14.6
Hotel representative companies[5]		3.7		7.0		4.2
Transport companies[6]		1.7		0.7		2.9
Web site/Internet companies[7]		1.5**		0.9**		0.4**
		100		100		100
Total 'direct' allowing for items marked **		51.1		54.0		51.9

Notes:
1 Via phone, letter, fax and 'walk ins'.
2 Pegasus/THISCO and destination management systems.
3 Direct or via GDS or Pegasus Systems.
4 Contracts.
5 Such as UTELL.
6 Especially airlines for staff accommodation.
7 Own Web sites and via other dot.coms such as Travelocity.
Source: Based on a Horwath World Wide Hotel Study, 1998. Reproduced with kind permission of Horwath UK.

Table 23.2 Distribution channels used by hotels worldwide in 1998

relevance of the data lies in adding the direct contact with hotels percentage to the other direct elements that are marked **. If the Web site proportion grows as expected, the total business achieved through direct marketing may well exceed two thirds of all bookings within a decade.

Tactical marketing

Strategic decisions are calculated to establish a profitable mix of bookings and room occupancy through the production and distribution of appropriately priced, distinctive products that match the needs of identified customer segments. In other words, for accommodation operators in all sectors, three of the traditional four Ps of the marketing mix are strategic decisions, and even the fourth, promotion, must be planned within boundaries set by the positioning strategy.

Tactically, as for passenger transport marketing, the main contribution of marketing is to secure additional marginal sales from targeted buyers at times when rooms are predictably likely to be operating at less than optimum occupancy, usually reflecting normal seasonal variations. Its other contribution is to cope with the sudden and often dramatic losses of anticipated business that happen all too often as a result of unpredictable economic or political events.

Occasionally, in certain destinations at certain times, room occupancies in hotels may exceed 80 per cent on an annual basis, as they did in London in the late 1980s and late 1990s. At this level, most hotels are full for most of the time and the owners enjoy a rise in prices and profitability. Such circumstances are not the norm, however, and usually are not achieved by marketing alone but by a combination of favourable circumstances in the external business environment. It is more common for accommodation businesses to operate somewhere between 55 and 65 per cent of room occupancy over the months in which they are open for business. In extremes, as in the depths of the 1991/2 economic recession, they may drop to 40 per cent or less.

As in other sectors of travel and tourism, reflecting the highly perishable nature of the products, marketing managers are required to manage demand by stimulating additional bookings on a daily and weekly basis. The high fixed costs and low variable costs of operating accommodation give extensive scope for providing short-term incentives to buyers. Tactical marketing for accommodation businesses requires choosing from the range of sales promotion tools discussed in some detail in Chapter 16. See, for example, Figure 16.2.

Specifically, sales promotion tactics for accommodation businesses include:

1 Short-term price discounting used especially to sell unsold capacity in unanticipated circumstances (see also Chapter 9). Sales promotions, adding temporary value to products in order to attract targeted customer segments, are often used to attract business at times of predicted seasonal troughs in demand.
2 Partnership deals with complementary partners such as transport operators to achieve mutual objectives.
3 Sales promotions, often using commission incentives, designed to motivate a retail distribution system (where applicable) and achieve added influence at points of sale, including improved display for brochures.
4 Sales promotions, invariably using deep price discounts, designed to motivate and conclude deals with third parties such as tour operators, coach tour operators and other agents making bulk contracts for the supply of accommodation. (This form of selling capacity may have strategic as well as tactical implications.)
5 Use of a sales force (where applicable) to generate additional sales, both from the range of normal buyers and from others targeted for short-run sales initiatives.
6 Tactical use of advertising and Web sites, usually in association with items 1, 2, and 3, in order to achieve better communication of promotional offers.

While the use of these tactical techniques is clearly sales orientated, their efficient use depends on the detailed knowledge marketing managers have of the profile, needs and probable behaviour of target segments in responding to promotional incentives. As with transport, the accommodation sector is frequently subject to unpredictable external factors and it is always necessary for businesses to allocate contingency funds for use in influencing short-run demand. Since the late 1990s the Internet has become increasingly used to promote and sell last minute availability on corporate Web sites, on a range of other sites specializing in last minute travel sales and using virtual auctions and other e-commerce means to secure sales.

The size of accommodation marketing budgets: challenging received wisdom

With an understanding of the nature and size of the task of implementing strategy and tactics in accommodation marketing, it is appropriate to consider some implications for the size of budgets. The cost of achieving marketing objectives is usually a relatively high proportion of sales revenue in the accommodation sector and the budget allocation is rightly seen as a high-risk decision.

A systematic procedure for allocating money to marketing campaigns in order to achieve planned volume and revenue targets is set out in Chapter 14; the principles in that chapter apply fully to all sectors of commercial accommodation. But this section sets out to challenge what continues to be a widespread belief in the industry in a norm, or rule of thumb, that it is appropriate to spend between 2 and 5 per cent of total sales revenue on 'marketing'. According to Surveys of British hotels by BDO and Horwath in the late 1990s, expenditure on marketing equates respectively to 2.4 and 2.6 per cent of sales revenue – see later in the chapter.

In fact, although this may be a contentious statement, the real proportion of sales revenue devoted to marketing by most successful organizations in the accommodation business is probably ten times higher than the hotel consultancy figures indicate. Properly calculated, and based on the view of marketing expressed in this book, the real average proportion of sales revenue devoted to marketing activities by accommodation businesses of all types is probably over 20 per cent in most countries. Calculations for the argument will be found in Table 23.3 and it is justified as follows:

1 In analysing the annual accounts of an accommodation business, room sales revenue should always be calculated in two ways. First, the sum of actual receipts for a year from accommodation sales should be calculated (this figure, divided by the number of room-nights sold, provides the *average* room rate achieved over a year). Second, room sales revenue should be calculated as the sum of theoretical sales revenue achievable if rooms were sold at the published rack rates (with due allowance for planned discount rates for targeted segments, as noted in Table 23.1).

2 Marketing expenditure should then be calculated as the sum of the costs of all the decisions businesses make to secure the business they

actually achieve (not just the expenditure on advertising and sales promotion). The total expenditure should be expressed as a percentage of room-sales revenue and total sales revenue achieved over a campaign period.

In practice, hotels around the world continue to produce their accounts according to the agreed conventions in the US originated Uniform System of Hotel Accounts. As a result of an accounting, not a marketing derived process, highly valuable marketing insights are lost. It is recommended that the full costs of marketing can be gained only if separate calculations are undertaken by marketing managers for their own purposes. Table 23.3 provides a method.

In an ideal world a hotel with an excellent product range and a good location will set its rack rates, corporate rates and other group rates for the year ahead. It will complete the trading period without unpredicted events preventing it from achieving the targeted mix of bookings that best matches its capacity. No one in this ideal position accepts group bookings at a discount if they are confident of filling their rooms with rack-rate business that raises their yield towards the theoretical maximum. No one offers special rates for leisure-break business if they can fill their rooms at higher rates.

In the real world, of course, hotels and other accommodation businesses must pay their contracted fixed costs out of daily cash flow while contemplating unsold rooms and beds and consequent loss of potential revenue. In these circumstances most discount their rack rates in order to manipulate short-run demand. Putting the point bluntly, they reduce prices in order to 'buy' business from whatever sources they can find at whatever price they think is better than the alternative of lost sales. The high fixed cost of accommodation operations makes business at almost any price appear worthwhile in the short run. Of course, over time, price discounting may be counter-productive because it damages the brand positioning and upsets regular customers' goodwill. But businesses in serious cash-flow crises may not have a long run and they will aim to survive by any possible means.

The foregoing explanation is designed to make the point that marketing expenditure should always be calculated as the full cost of all the expenditure actually incurred in achieving their annual turnover. Marketing costs therefore include expenditure defined in the Uniform System of Accounts for Hotels, on:

- Advertising, PR, and other media.
- Sales promotion and merchandising print.
- Production and distribution of information (including direct mail).
- Marketing research.
- Consortia fees (marketing proportion only) or group marketing levy imposed by chains.
- Staff costs, expenses and share of overheads for all undertaking the above work.

It should (but does not under the uniform system) include the full costs incurred in:

- Negotiating with, servicing and paying commission to travel agents, wholesalers, THISCO, credit card companies and any other distributors who receive commission.
- Negotiating and agreeing discounts for tour operators, coach tour companies and any other group sales.
- Negotiating discounts to secure other forms of group business, such as conferences or airlines.
- Share of costs of central reservation systems and links with GDSs – the vital tools of efficient marketing operations, which must be organized around marketing requirements.
- Investment in Web sites and connectivity with call centres and CRSs.

It has to be stressed that several key cost elements noted above, which account for the bulk of all the marketing costs of securing business otherwise judged to be at risk or lost, are not in practice included as marketing costs in the Uniform System of Accounts for Hotels. This is not a criticism of the uniform system, because it was not conceived around marketing principles but to facilitate industry comparisons using standard definitions for accountants.

The uniform system does the hotel industry no service by perpetuating the myth that marketing costs are of the order of 2–3 per cent of room sales revenue. If an accommodation supplier wishes to understand costs and revenues and make his marketing more efficient, he must count all the costs noted above.

The marketing budget for a resort hotel: a model approach

This section, with the illustrations in Table 23.2, provides a practical model for analysing a hotel's annual room-sales revenue by segments and products – the basis in practice for drawing up a marketing campaign. Although hotel based, the model could be easily adapted for use in marketing non-serviced accommodation. The model is as simple as the authors can make it and, although it is still not an easy read, we believe it will repay careful consideration.

The text explains why the actual revenue achieved is almost always less than the theoretical revenue targeted by managers at the start of a budget year. To set the section and the model in a broadly practical context, the example chosen is a medium-sized, four-star resort hotel in Northern Europe, part of a national chain. Its location in a coastal resort, which is also a large urban centre, generates a mix of business, and justifies an average bed and breakfast rack rate per *room night* of £150 (assuming double occupancy). The hotel has 120 twin rooms and is targeted to achieve 65 per cent room occupancy over twelve months.

Originally built for non-business customers seventy-five years ago, changing market patterns have caused the hotel to shift its focus and upgrade its facilities to appeal to a business market. The hotel does not

Resort hotel located near to a business centre generating visitors for conferences, general commercial purposes as well as holiday visitors.

120 twin rooms, with 65 per cent annual room occupancy = 28 470 room nights capacity over a year (120 × 365 × 65 per cent).

Rack rate £150 (twin/double) per *room* night including breakfast; £100 (single occupancy)

Customer mix	(a) % of room sales (per annum)	Volume of room sales (per annum)	Tariff type	(b) Published room rates (in brochure)	(c)* Actual room rate achieved	(d) Theoretical revenue (a × b)	(e) Actual room revenue achieved (a × c)
1 Business (individuals)	20	5 695	Rack rate	£150	£115	£854 250	£654 925
2 Business (corporate clients)	30	8 540	Corporate rate	£125	£100	£1 067 500	£854 000
3 Vacation (individuals)	10	2 847	Weekly rate (per night)	£90	£80	£256 230	£227 760
4 Coach tour clients	10	2 848	Inclusive group rate (per night)	£90†	£65	£256 320	£185 120
5 Holiday breaks (i)	15	4 270	Inclusive price	£100	£85	£427 000	£362 950
6 Holiday breaks (ii)	15	4 270	Wholesale rate	£100	£70	£427 000	£298 900
Totals	100	28 470				£3 288 300	£2 583 655

*Includes allowance for corporate/group rates; single occupancy of rooms; and retailer commissions for segments 4 and 6 of the customer mix.
† Not published.
(i) Sold directly by the hotel to customers.
(ii) Rooms allocated to tour operators; and packaged and marketed by the operator.

Table 23.3 Calculating the full marketing cost, including discounts and sales commission, as a proportion of *potential* hotel revenue

have its own conference facilities but it is located near a conference centre from which it draws a significant part of its total visitors for business purposes. Short-break holiday business, to fill the weekends when business visits are not available, is now its principal involvement in the leisure market.

The business mix and tariff types

Following normal marketing logic, the total annual business is divided into segments. It is necessary to organize different products, prices, promotion and distribution for each of these segments. As set out in Table 23.3, there are two types of customers (business and vacation visitors) but they generate six viable segments. All other types of customer are excluded from the table to avoid complicating the example. The rationale for the segmentation strategy is simple. The location cannot generate its target occupancy at rack rates, and the hotel has to organize marketing initiatives (in this case with its parent company) to secure the targeted level of sales at discounted prices.

Of the six visitor segments shown in Table 23.3, only the first group pays the full rack rate, comprising only 20 per cent by volume of the hotel's business. The second segment is composed of business visitors paying a corporate rate that is 15 per cent below the rack rate; some of them are conference visitors, who also receive an average discount of 15 per cent off the rack rate.

Of the vacationer groups, it would not be possible to achieve targeted levels of business at the full rack rate. Accordingly most hotels of this type offer a special rate for leisure products, usually built into a product with a minimum length of stay and perhaps meals and other services to reduce the possibility that this tariff will be used by business visitors. If the individual vacation business is projected on the evidence of recent years to leave many rooms unoccupied, the hotelier will normally have no alternative but to approach tour operators, in this case coach operators (segment 4 in Table 23.3). Such operators will, if the hotel suits their own product range, take allocations of rooms. If they do, it will normally be at a large discount in order to cover their own costs of administration and marketing, including distribution. The discount, which must also cover the tour operator's profit, will be calculated on the hotel's published tariff for that type of business (in this case an average per room night of £60).

The two final vacation segments are short breaks of two to three nights offered as an inclusive product. For segment 5, the product is sold from a brochure put together by hotel marketing executives at group level and there is no discount from the target tariff of £70 per room night. Because this hotel still has spare capacity at weekends, it also makes an allocation of rooms to another wholesaler or tour operator, which includes the hotel in a brochure comprising a range of products marketed under a brand name. In Britain several such brochures are currently branded and marketed by national groups such as *Superbreaks* . As with the coach-tour operators, marketing through a group has to be paid for, and discounts of around 30 per cent are common, to cover wholesaler costs, marketing and profit margins.

Revenue calculations in Table 23.3

Column (a) shows the volume of room-night sales per annum for each segment, as targeted at the beginning of the year in the hotel's marketing plan. The total of 28 470 is the sum of 120 rooms × 365 days × 65 per cent occupancy. Column (b) lists the published room rates per night designed to attract each of the segments. Column (c) converts these into actual room rates achieved. The column (c) figures would in practice be calculated by the hotel accountants and they allow for the fact that some of the rooms are let to only one person at less than double occupancy rate, that group discount must be deducted from some segments and that travel agency commission is payable on some sales. Where reception staff are instructed to accept last minute bookings with even bigger discounts, this would also be accounted for in column (c).

Column (d) shows the maximum revenue potentially achievable if all rooms could be sold at target published prices for each segment. The reason for making this calculation is to demonstrate that there is always a cost, represented as potential revenue forgone, in accepting business at less than the optimum target rate. In fact, not all target prices are published to the public but are commercial negotiating rates established in a marketing plan.

Column (e) shows actual revenue received over the year (a × c). By comparing the actual and theoretical revenue totals, it can be seen that the sum of column (e) is 79 per cent of column (d). By dividing the total revenue (e) by total room sales (28 470), the average room rate achieved can be calculated at £90.75 over the year.

To summarize, almost every accommodation business will operate at average room rates significantly below the theoretical maximum. The difference between actual and potential reflects the composition of its segment/product mix and the level of discounting and commission required to achieve business in each segment. Measured over periods of time and between different hotels in a group, the size of the gap between theoretical and actual revenue provides a valid measure of a hotel's marketing efficiency.

Conclusions on the cost of marketing

In Table 23.3 part of the costs of achieving sales in some segments is reflected in the discounts and commission payable. Additional costs (*not* included in the table) are advertising, sales promotion, Web sites, print and any other expenditure on marketing judged necessary to secure the targeted 65 per cent occupancy. In the example discussed part of this marketing expenditure will be paid by the hotel direct, and part through the group to which it belongs, usually through a group marketing levy amounting to around 3 per cent of the hotel's annual turnover.

Whichever way the marketing budget is calculated, it is obvious that the true cost of marketing reflected in Table 23.3, will be a very far cry from the meaningless industry 'norm' of 2–5 per cent usually quoted.

Chapter summary

This chapter seeks to explain and illustrate the characteristics of operations and marketing practice that are common to all sectors of serviced and non-serviced accommodation. It is not restricted to a particular sector or only to large operators in the industry. As with transport, some aspects of marketing are peculiar to individual sectors but the common aspects are more important than the differences. The principles outlined are broadly relevant to all sectors of serviced and non-serviced accommodation defined at the outset.

As in other chapters dealing with key elements of the overall tourism product, this chapter stresses the growing importance of linkages between sectors in the tourism industry for marketing in the future. Other important marketing linkages are currently occurring within sectors, such as those found in accommodation consortia formed by serviced and non-serviced operators. Individual producers, especially those owning small units, see consortia as a logical route to achieving branding and the economies of scale in marketing that are vital to successful competition against the growing power of the large chains. The development of destination marketing systems with access to online marketing and booking (see Chapter 20) is another collaborative route for smaller businesses with clear potential for growth.

In particular, this chapter reviews the full costs of marketing accommodation in some detail using a model approach that is based on current practice. It sets out to challenge the conventional wisdom concerning the cost of marketing that continues to inhibit recognition in the industry of the importance of marketing. The quote by David Michels at the head of this chapter, now chief executive officer (CEO) of a leading UK hotel chain and formerly a sales and marketing manager in the industry, is an instructive insight into the real level of understanding of hotel marketing at the end of the 1990s.

Further reading

Lewis, D., Chambers, R. E. and Chacko, H. E. (1995). *Marketing Leadership in Hospitality*. 2nd edn, Van Nostrand Reinhold.

Medlik, S. (1999). *The Business of Hotels*. 4th edn, Butterworth-Heinemann.

Morrison, A. M. (1989). *Hospitality and Travel Marketing*. Delmar.

CHAPTER 24

Marketing inclusive tours and product packages

Research shows customers want more choice . . . We have been stuck in a one-size-fits-all model of working. (Thomson Holidays announcing in 1999 its first 'product customization' programme for the year 2000 – *Travel Trade Gazette*, 26 July 1999)

This chapter focuses on the commercial operators that assemble the components of tourism products and market them as *packages* to the final consumer. A package is essentially a selected combination of individual elements of the travel and tourism product, marketed under a particular product or brand label and sold at an inclusive price. Most such products are aimed at leisure and holiday markets although business incentive travel and many conferences are packaged in similar ways.

International tour operators, such as Touristic Union International (TUI) in Germany, and Thomson Holidays and Airtours in the UK, take millions of customers abroad every year and are the best-known and most obvious illustrations of modern tour operation. But independent tour operators are by no means the only businesses marketing travel packages and, increasingly, such packages are part of the marketing armoury of the leading branded suppliers of accommodation, transport, cruise ships and other businesses that were traditionally involved in providing only one of the total product components.

This chapter begins with a brief historical review of the development of travel organization and tour operation, followed by definitions presenting a broad view of packages. It proceeds to consider the role of tour operators in the overall travel and tourism product and the nature of the tour-operating business that determines the marketing response. This is followed by an assessment of the marketing task for tour operators and the implications for strategy and tactics.

Historical development of tour operating

Modern, risk-taking tour operators and others with interests in packaging aspects of transport, accommodation and attractions, have a history of continuous development over the last century. The origins of travel organization and tour operation are usually traced back to 1841, the year in which Thomas Cook organized one of the earliest whole-train charters, for a day excursion to a temperance meeting. The excursion was a sell-out, achieving 100 per cent seat load factor! By 1845 Cook was operating longer, overnight tours in Britain on a commercial basis and in 1871 he organized the first round the world tour (Swinglehurst, 1982: 9).

Before the Second World War, international tour operating developed through contracting with railway companies, hotels and ocean liners, and there were well-patronized circuits around Europe, especially to Switzerland and the South of France. Skiing tours owed their origins and early popularity to another Briton, Sir Henry Lunn, in the 1880s. The pioneer coach tour operators established themselves after the First World War and began to run excursions and longer tours in the 1930s, adding a new dimension to the possibilities for packaging. Commercial air travel dates back to the 1920s but its early days were very much for a small elite group of wealthy travellers.

It was the Second World War that provided the necessary quantum shift in air transport technology, especially through the development of powerful long-distance aircraft originally designed to carry a large payload of bombs. Entrepreneurs quickly recognized the speed, distance and low seat/mile costs that post-war aircraft could deliver and these characteristics underpinned the early growth of packaged tourism. In fact Thomas Cook claim to have pioneered the first air-inclusive charter holiday to the South of France, planned for 1939. But the advent of war put back the development to 1950 when Vladimir Raitz of Horizon chartered 300 seats for his first year's operation to Corsica.

Out of such modest beginnings the modern European tour operating industry developed. The British market for international tours to all destinations abroad (air and sea), still the largest in Europe, was measured at just over 1 million packages in 1962, when formal measurement began, 12 million by 1989, 15 million in 1994 and just over 17 million in 1998. By the mid-1990s, the British market had matured and the leading tour operators took on an international dimension in the search for market growth.

From mass market tourism toward product customization

From a tiny minority of the British that had ever travelled abroad on holiday in the 1960s, the late 1990s estimates are that around three-quarters of British adults have travelled abroad at some time in their lives, and the proportion is higher among the more affluent socio-economic groups. Multiple visits abroad in a year are now common and packaging has extended from its main summer holidays origin to every aspect of the modern tourism market. While Britain's island situation and climate have been particularly conducive to the market growth for inclusive tours, similar trends may be observed throughout Northern Europe and the Asia Pacific region. Many believe that market sophistication and market maturity moved rather faster than the operators' product response so that many were trapped in the 1990s in a mass-marketing mode that was no longer relevant to a growing proportion of prospective consumers.

Distinguished more by the quick thinking short-term entrepreneurial flair of individuals than by strategic marketing models of business management in the last quarter century, the nature of packaging is changing at the turn of the new century. In the 1960s to the 1980s international tours were primarily a business of handling a booming demand by combining the product elements at the lowest possible price into standardized 'one size fits all' programmes – the Model T Ford production-line approach to holidays. Packaging of that type was ideally suited to the 'pile it high and sell it cheap' mentality of mass marketing. By the 1990s more experienced, more demanding consumers and the flexibility conveyed by the new information and communications technology were changing the business model. Tour operation is now increasingly dominated by international corporations and mass, undifferentiated commodity marketing is finally giving way to extensive segmentation, customized products, use of scheduled as well as charter airlines and growing attention to environmental issues. Packaging was far more sophisticated at the end of the 1990s than it had been a decade earlier and the customization trend is certain to develop further.

Although appearing much later than the packages to international destinations, the production of domestic holiday packages has also enjoyed remarkable growth over the last two decades. Depending on definitions used, for there are no accurate statistics in this sector, the volume of British domestic holiday packages, for example, is probably of a similar volume to holiday packages abroad although fragmented and very much smaller in value.

Defining inclusive tour and product packages

In Chapter 8, the overall tourism product was identified as a package and defined in terms of five main components, comprising destination attractions, destination facilities and services, accessibility of the destination (including transport), images, brands and perceptions, and price to the customer. Drawing on Burkart and Medlik's succinct view, an inclusive tour operator is 'the manufacturer of a true tourist product; he buys the components of the package . . . from the suppliers of the individual tourist services and packages and brands them into a single entity' (Burkart and Medlik, 1981: 216).

This chapter takes a deliberately broad view of packages comprising three distinctive types of business model:

- The first type always includes transport as well as accommodation in the package and acts primarily as an independent contractor doing deals with other businesses on a contractual basis. These contractors are the traditional tour operators that put together programmes for sale, months in advance of product delivery. The largest of them now have global links and are structurally integrated with airlines and retail chains under the same ownership. Tour operators are also known as wholesalers in some countries but the tour operator label is more common in Europe. Smaller contractors include inbound travel agents and the many niche operators providing packages for every type of recreation and leisure activity.
- The second type always includes accommodation in the package but may or may not include transport. This group of packages is put together by hotels and other accommodation and the larger visitor attractions that find it profitable to develop and market their own packages both directly to the consumer and indirectly through travel intermediaries. For many in this group, packages are a form of sales promotion designed to combat the effects of high fixed costs and seasonality. Some airlines and sea ferries develop and operate their own packages for the same reason.
- The third type is a hybrid that emerged as a direct result of recent advances in ICT, the disenchantment of many consumers with undifferentiated mass marketing and their demand for products that meet their own specification. These are the so-called modular packages, which can be put together at short notice by travel agents or smaller tour operators using the low-cost online options available through consolidated fares and budget airlines plus discounted branded accommodation. This is a new form of product customization in packaging that seems set to grow as familiarity with and access to the new technology increases.

So many commercial and non-commercial organizations in the travel and tourism industry are now marketing packages that it is important to be as precise as possible in definitions. There are two main considerations in this, reflecting:

- The nature of the package provided for sale and the business relationship between operator and owners of the main product components.
- The dominant method of distribution to the customer.

411

The nature of the product and the business relationships involved

Product packages are:

> Quality assured, repeatable offers comprising two or more elements of transport, accommodation, food, destination attractions, other facilities and related services (such as travel insurance). Product packages are marketed to the general public, described in print or electronic media, and offered for sale to prospective customers at a published, inclusive price, in which the costs of the product components cannot be separately identified.

The definition *excludes* special packages put together for a closed group of users. For example, many conference products in hotels have standard elements and are often referred to as packages. But they are generally put together to meet the needs of specified members of particular organizations and are 'one-off' packages specially adapted for each group purchaser. While important, such packages are not marketed according to the principles outlined in this chapter.

The terms 'quality assured' and 'repeatable' no longer imply mass production of one or two types of identical product. It means that products offered for sale will be delivered in a consistent or quality-assured way, with quality judged by targeted customers (through market research). In practice, quality assured means operating product control processes to ensure the delivery of product consistency of a standard that matches or exceeds the needs and expectations of consumer segments.

As part of a European Community approach to securing and enforcing customer protection, including requirements for financial arrangements to compensate clients in the event of claims, the EC Package Holiday Directive was drawn up for implementation in all EC countries from 1993. It states:

> Package means the pre-arranged combination of not fewer than two of the following when sold or offered for sale at an inclusive price and when the service covers a period of more than 24 hours or includes overnight accommodation: transport, accommodation, other tourist services not ancillary to transport or accommodation and accounting for a significant proportion of the package. (EC Directive)

To summarize, packages may be standardized or bespoke, 'manufactured' by contractors or assembled by accommodation and other tourism businesses providing part of the total offer. In every case the packages that operators assemble are drawn from the five basic elements of the overall tourism product, plus whatever added value of their own operations is built in, such as price guarantees, convenience, accessibility to the customer, image and branding, high standards and sense of security in dealing with a reputable company.

The business relationship is either one of contractual arrangements by independent firms in which the identity of the component elements is normally subsumed within the operator's brand, or contractual arrangements between one component collaborating with targeted partners to produces packages that are branded and marketed under the name of the leading component. Branded hotel packages, for example, are in the latter category, of which many are in domestic rather than international travel. There are probably as many packages now in the second category as in the first.

Distribution method

The second consideration relates to the form of marketing used to sell the packages. All organizations' marketing packages have the basic choice between a strategy based on direct marketing or marketing through third party distribution networks as explained in Chapters 18 and 19. The development of the Internet and e-commerce is rapidly shifting the traditional distribution patterns used for inclusive tours and packages, and opening the route to strategies that are partly direct and partly through retail intermediaries. Information and communications technology greatly facilitates the process of searching, finding and comparing the options available in ways that were not practical before the late 1990s. Its power is especially important in an information-rich area such as holiday decisions and it also facilitates the modular approach to packaging noted earlier. Distribution has become the key strategic issue in packaging and is further discussed later in the chapter.

The functional role of inclusive tours and packages

Around the world, firms providing international tours and product packages would not have survived and grown as they have unless the services they provided were firmly rooted in the needs of both buyers and sellers. Price and convenience are the dominant characteristics but it is possible to identify five main reasons that explain the significance of packaging:

- Delivering price advantages that most customers are usually unable to achieve for themselves.
- Providing convenience and both psychological and financial security in a 'single purchase' transaction that facilitates and simplifies an otherwise complex process of choice and booking, especially for travel abroad.
- Providing product quality assurance in a branded context and 'guaranteeing' delivery of the promise.
- Backing up the quality assurance promise with legal liability for delivery and obligation to compensate if the contract is not delivered.
- Overcoming the inherent inefficiencies in the supply and demand for leisure travel and tourism, especially for international travel.

First, in a market notorious for its price elasticity, the prices charged to individuals attempting to put together for themselves the components of their chosen packages will be relatively high. This is because individuals cannot obtain the volume discounts available to any large buyer in competitive conditions and (although the Internet is now changing the traditional business models) they are unlikely to gain access to the B2B yield management programmes of different component producers which often provide the best available deals. Delivering low prices has always been a primary basis for competition in major consumer markets and many observers see this as the tour operator's most important function in the travel and tourism industry.

Although the search and compare capability of the Internet can now match tour operator prices, at least for last minute deals, it cannot provide the advance booking offers and security of provision that most customers need and many consumers put a value on their own time that they have to spend in searching for the options. E- commerce is still psychologically unattractive to many consumers and the rate of its take-up for holiday products may be slower than many advocates believe. Tour operators are likely to put more of their own last minute offers on to Web sites in the coming decade, using the new medium for their own sales promotion purposes.

Second, from the customer's point of view, attempting to define options and choose the elements of an overall product separately, especially for the first time in an unknown destination, is often a very hit and miss and time-consuming process. It is fraught with the risk of making an expensive mistake as well as experiencing a personal sense of failure if things go wrong. For travel abroad, with its added complications of language, currency and distance from home, the problems and inconvenience for inexperienced travellers acting on their own account may be too daunting and too time-consuming, even if the cost is not a problem.

The provision of high street access through travel agents still provides the convenience that most consumers value. Internet access in the home and on mobile phones provides even greater convenience and its use is expected to grow most rapidly for repeat purchases with which customers are already familiar, such as branded weekend breaks and deals that give access to branded budget airline prices.

Third, through their contracting procedures, specification of the product in brochures, strategic use of branding and use of representatives at destinations as well as through close monitoring of customer satisfaction, tour operators can sustain and develop the product quality standards needed to reassure many buyers at the point of sale.

Fourth, modern competition increasingly focuses on product quality promises and, through the EC Package Travel Directive in European countries and through self-regulatory mechanisms, operators must accept legal liability for the products they offer. Consumers can expect virtual guarantees of acceptable product delivery and the right to redress if they have a reasonable complaint.

Finally, with a few exceptions at certain periods and in certain locations, the matching of tourism supply with demand is a remarkably inefficient process for most businesses in travel and tourism, especially in leisure markets. On the supply side, producers of accommodation and attractions typically operate in a single fixed location, aiming to attract infrequent buyers, many of them buying for the first time and on a once-only basis. Moreover, prospective buyers are usually drawn from a very wide catchment area. For example, over the space of three months in the summer, a hotel in Scotland may draw its customers from up to six overseas countries and up to half of all the regions in the UK. A resort hotel in Greece or Turkey may draw most of its customers from only four or five countries, yet their addresses may be geographically spread across half the landmass of Europe and the Middle East.

Effective marketing on a national and international basis needed to secure exposure and promotion of their product offers to target customers is not an option for independent hoteliers and other small businesses. While advertising in national tourist office guides is as sensible for the Greek and Turkish hotelier as for the one in Scotland, it is seldom a certain or sufficient process to secure the sale of otherwise unsold capacity on a daily basis. Such businesses have no choice but to look to other sources to supply business they are not able to achieve through their own direct marketing efforts. Until the practical advent of the Internet 'other sources' usually means tour operators seeking room allocations for their programmes. It is marketplace inefficiency that explains the prime function of inclusive tours and product packages for component suppliers, and why it is possible for operators to secure such favourable bulk contract prices for product allocations.

A combination of the Internet for direct marketing and access to destination marketing databases operated by national tourist organizations is beginning to provide alternative sources of business for small operators previously dependent on third party contractors (see Chapter 20). But for most, it is still only part of the solution to market inefficiency and the contractors' role is still dominant for many.

To summarize, the core value of inclusive tours and product packages is to provide a well-honed marketing mechanism that simultaneously solves producers' needs to sell their capacity and customers' needs for convenience and security at advantageous, affordable prices. At a profit to the companies that do it, packaging solves the natural inefficiency that is inherent in matching demand and supply in most leisure sectors of travel and tourism. That vital role explains its importance in the industry and, notwithstanding growing consumer interest in independent travel, it will be new forms of customized and modular packages – a far cry from the mass-market commodity products of the 1970s – that will provide it. There appear to be no reasons why these five fundamental marketing contributions will diminish significantly in importance over the next decade, although the Internet will become the growth distribution channel of choice for many.

The process of constructing an inclusive tour programme

All those engaged in marketing packages assemble product elements into what are known as *programmes*. A programme is held on a database and communicated in brochures (and Web sites), which usually contain a range of product choices in several destinations. To explain how programmes are constructed, this section focuses on air-inclusive tours as the most developed sector of packaging, but the principles are the same in constructing any programme.

A tour operator offering international tours by air has a choice of using bulk fare rates on scheduled and other airlines or bulk fares available from their own airline. The cost per seat naturally varies according to volume bought and whether the operator charters the whole flight or only a number of seats. All the largest international tour operators now have their own subsidiary airlines to transport the bulk of their programmes and are thus able to secure the lowest possible seat cost available. For example, Britannia Airways, owned by the International Thomson Organization, carried over 5 million passengers in the mid–1990s, and is a bigger and more cost-efficient airline than many of the scheduled carriers in Europe.

A large air international tours programme out of Britain at the turn of the twentieth century uses up to twenty airports of departure, up to a hundred resorts and cities in a dozen or more countries, and a range of products based on accommodation types from luxury hotels through villas to simple self-catering apartments. Putting a large programme such as this together depends on translating estimates of market demand into production capacity, and matching aircraft seats with beds in batches that add up to full aeroplanes flying between pairs of airports. The skill lies in matching estimated demand with contracted supply, to achieve optimum aircraft utilization, optimum average load factors for flights and maximum occupancy of contracted beds.

The process of putting a programme together is shown in Figure 24.1, in a diagram adapted by the author from an original version produced by Roger Heape, Managing Director of British Airways Holidays. The diagram reflects the initial planning dialogue, common in all marketing, between marketing research and forecasting, corporate strategy and marketing implementation. The hardest decision in programme planning always focuses on what volume of products will be offered in the year ahead. Planning may start eighteen months before the first customers travel, and product volume has to be turned into numbers of seats and beds in order to see how flight schedules and bed capacity in resorts can best be matched. This process identifies capacity objectives for the staff that negotiate for beds and seats. Optimizing the best match between flight schedules and blocks of beds to achieve the most cost-efficient utilization of aircraft and hotels is, of course, a computer process and the finalized programmes become inventory systems and communication tools. It is an interactive process, strongly affected by the hotel prices being contracted.

With a draft programme worked out to meet projected demand, the next stage is to draft the all-important price and departure panels, which will appear in the brochure and on Web sites, stating the price of each inclusive tour product according to the date of departure and number of nights. (See Chapter 9 for a discussion of pricing.) Normally included on

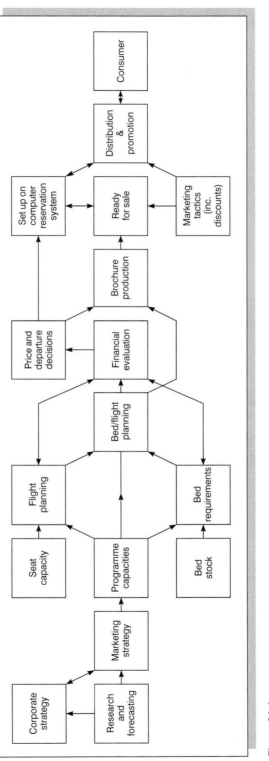

Figure 24.1
The logical sequence of putting together and marketing an air-inclusive tour programme

each product page of the brochure below the description of the accommodation, price and departure panels are increasingly produced separately in loose-leaf format to facilitate tactical price changes without reprinting the whole brochure. Up to this stage there is ample room for change in all aspects of the programme, and there are numerous feedback loops in the process, although not all are shown in Figure 24.1, to avoid clutter. Product prices and capacity are not in practice finalized until the last possible moment, about ten weeks before the brochure is distributed and customer purchases begin. Even then, as noted later under 'tactics', both may have to be changed more than once after publication.

Until the 1990s, most customers would book months ahead of product delivery and the January/February booking period for summer holidays is still the most important time. The consumer trend in all countries to ever-later booking upsets the old certainties, however, and a combination of fluid pricing and repackaging of programmes to meet shifts in last minute demand is not easy for tour operators to handle. The use of the Internet and Teletext facilitates the process and provides another reason for greater use of the Internet for distribution and promotion.

As soon as the programme is on sale, the capacity is sold through computerized reservation systems, as discussed in Chapter 18. In the case of larger tour operators, view data was still the predominant method of distribution via travel agents but newer forms of direct online access to their programme capacity via B2B intranets are being developed, along with direct access through call centres and Web sites.

Strategic issues for contracting tour operators

Although this book is concerned with marketing issues rather than overall strategic business decisions, it is nevertheless overall business strategy linked to modern marketing capability that is driving international developments in tour operating. In the UK and Northern Europe, the traditional independent tour-operating models based on firms operating within national boundaries have been overtaken by the processes of globalization. The 1980s and 1990s saw significant developments in horizontal and vertical integration whereby major operators purchased or merged with airlines and retail agencies, and merged with rival operators adding brands within an overall corporate envelope as the opportunity occurred. The purchase of airlines and travel agency chains gave a measure of control and cost containment in the dominant transport and distribution channels although at a cost in future flexibility that may become a major issue in the future.

The 1990s, especially the latter half have witnessed a remarkable worldwide expansion of takeovers, buy-ups and mergers reflecting business response to a combination of factors:

- Need to match competitors and grow to maintain shares of market – made possible for large players by funding investment through market capitalization on leading stock markets. The 1990s growth in the market for sea cruises and the involvement of leading tour operators, for example, required major investment funded by capitalization.

- Opportunities and threats provided by information and communications technology, especially the improved knowledge derived from customer databases and the greater efficiency with which large organizations can now be managed.
- Ever greater pressure on costs to maintain price competition, especially distribution and transport costs, and the perceived options of larger size to achieve economies of scale and secure efficient control of sales through retail outlets.
- Need for existing large players to continue to grow – if only to avoid being taken over by competitors – and recognition that such growth in mature markets means expansion into other countries, usually through the purchase of, or mergers with, relevant companies.
- Need to respond to growing customer sophistication and expectations of service excellence.
- Need to respond to the opportunities provided by international branding and developing customer loyalty.

Response to these factors has seen the emergence of a small number of very large companies in Europe. Preussag, TUI, Hapag and Thomas Cook had some 10 million customers worldwide; Airtours PLC a similar number and Thomson Holidays some 7 million. The Preussag purchase of Thomson Holidays as this book goes to print provides another turn of the merger wheel. The future ownership of Airtours was uncertain. In the UK holiday market, the four leading operators had over 70 per cent of the air inclusive tour market between them at the end of the 1990s. Table 24.1 indicates the position at that time.

Marketing strategy for tour operators

For tour operators, as for other producers in the travel and tourism industry, it is appropriate to divide the discussion of the marketing task between strategic and tactical considerations. In practice, as any reading of the travel trade press will confirm, the nature of tour operation and the relatively long lead time between planning, promotion and final delivery generates a seemingly continuous atmosphere of 'boom and bust'. This hothouse environment puts great emphasis on the short-run tactics required to survive in a fiercely competitive marketplace. The strategic dimensions are nevertheless vital and become more so as the main generating markets in developed countries reach maturity and international rather than national competition intensifies for the reasons noted above.

Five elements are noted in this section:

- Interpreting the strength and direction of change in the external environment.
- Strategic decisions on volume and pricing.
- Choice of product/customer portfolio.
- Positioning and image.
- Choice and maintenance of distribution systems/preferred marketing method.

419

(This is a fast-changing environment with takeovers, mergers and buy-outs occurring continuously – it provides only an indicative appreciation of the multiple links common in the industry at the turn of the century.)

Operator	UK capacity[1]	Airline	Retail links	UK market share[2] (%)	International alliances
Thomson Holidays	4.4 million pax	Britannia	Lunn Poly; c. 950 outlets	27	Purchased by Preussag in 2000; operations in Germany, Scandinavia and Ireland
Airtours PLC	3.4 million pax	Airtours International; 37 aircraft	Going Places/ Advantage Travel; c. 1000 outlets	17	17 countries in Europe and North America
First Choice	3.1 million pax	Air 2000; 25 aircraft	Various brands; c. 650 outlets	14	Ireland and Canada; 10% owned by Preussag
Thomas Cook/ JMC/Carlson	2.5 million pax	Caledonian Flying Colours; 34 aircraft	Thomas Cook; c. 1400 outlets	17	51% owned by Preussag; links with Carlson Leisure (UK)

[1] Capacity registered with the CAA for 1998/9.
[2] Indicative market shares of licensed air tours capacity at end 1999.

Notes:
1. Each of these operators has multiple brands although they were being rationalized at the turn of the twentieth century. In early 1999, for example, Airtours had some forty different brands in its portfolio and Thomson over twenty-five. Each had strategic links with sea cruise companies, including ownership of several ships. Thomas Cook was planning a brand rationalization under the new JMC brand for 2000.
2. Each of these operators owns direct response marketing companies such as Portland, Freestyle and Country cottages (Thomson), Direct Holidays, Go Direct and Late Escapes (Airtours). Each is establishing Direct Call Centre operations with Internet links for e-commerce for the year 2000.
3. The number of retail outlets is approximate as each of the companies has a range of connections with smaller retail chains.

Table 24.1 Indicative strategic linkages for major UK tour operators in 1999/2000

The external environment

External influences are especially powerful in their implications for tour operation, reflecting both the 'non-essential' character of most leisure products (consumer decisions are easily changed and postponed), fierce competition and the international nature of much of the business. Although lead times are shortening, the susceptibility of operators to changes in the external environment is of course heightened by the advance planning needs. Specifically the demand for inclusive tours demonstrates large annual fluctuations triggered by:

- *Economic events,* such as growth and decline in the economic cycle affecting consumers' real income and confidence, and the impact of international exchange-rate movements on prices.
- *Political events and disasters,* as in Indonesia, the former Yugoslavia and the 1999 earthquakes in Turkey.
- *Information and communications technology,* for reasons explained in Chapters 10, 18 and 19.
- *Sustainable development requirements* stemming from changing business and consumer attitudes in the 1990s following the Earth Summit of 1992. At the turn of the century, the leading international tour operator TUI, was in the vanguard of the major tour operators' response to more sustainable development (Middleton and Hawkins, 1998: 193). Most tour operators have been slow to recognize the opportunities this presents but the first decade of the new millennium will see significant change. Global developments in Local Agenda 21 Initiatives fostered by the International Council for Local Environment Initiatives (ICLEI) are gathering strength in destinations around the world and the importance such initiatives place on public and private sector partnerships suggests marketing will become increasingly central to the agenda and action programmes for more sustainable tourism at destinations. Tour operators will have to become more involved.

Strategic decisions on volume and pricing

For hotels, visitor attractions and transport operators, annual decisions on capacity and price levels tend to be essentially tactical decisions implementing previous strategic judgements and fixed investment in buildings and equipment. Not so for tour operators. A combination of the lead times in programme planning, the unpredictable external business environment and the flexibility options of contracting additional capacity, means that annual decisions on volume and price are strategic rather than tactical issues. Volume and price are of course closely related because of the influences on pricing policy of what the market will bear at any point in time.

In recent years in the UK, massive discounting in January/February of 25 per cent and more have been part of the marketing strategy to move the available stock and gain or defend market share. If the initial guesstimates of capacity and pricing are proved wrong by events and overcapacity results, the whole of marketing tactics revolve around attempts to retrieve the situation in the face of fierce competition. It takes strong entrepreneurial flair and very strong nerves to hold to decisions or change them boldly as events occur. Figure 14.1 (Chapter 14) provides ample evidence of the narrowness of the margins at stake in the crucial volume and price decisions.

Product/market portfolios

The third, related strategic consideration for operators is concerned with the content and balance of the product portfolio, as represented in their programmes. The volume and price aspects noted earlier are not independent variables but reflect the chosen product portfolio's mix of destinations, accommodation types, and range of other elements included in the product, such as excursions. For example, tour operators that had targeted growth in long-haul destinations in the Asia Pacific region for 1998/9 were strategically wrong-footed when the devaluation of the Thai Baht in July 1997 was the trigger for a massive international economic crisis in the region and consumer concern. Relative prices of destinations also drive portfolio choices and visits to Greece from the UK fell by nearly a third between 1994 and 1996 while visits to Turkey rose by nearly 50 per cent. Where profit or loss is balanced on just a few marginal percentage points above break-even load factors, it becomes vital to offer the range of products most in demand.

Segmentation of tour operator products developed strongly in the 1990s facilitated by the growing use of consumer databases and it is reflected in the way in which brochures, still the main marketing tool for operators, are put together. There is a strategic balance to be struck between the need for separate brochures to appeal to different market segments, and the even more powerful current need to reduce the number of brochures because of the cost and limitations of rack space in retail outlets. There is an uneasy balance at present in which segmentation often occurs within the brochure, but this is not necessarily a cost-effective or consumer-appealing procedure, and strategic changes may be expected in the next few years. Well-designed Web sites may offer greater flexibility and efficiency.

Positioning, branding and image

Historically, reflecting the strong demand that low prices stimulated in a highly price-elastic market, competition between tour operators tended to focus primarily on price and on product portfolios. Image and positioning, although not ignored, very clearly took second place to price competition. As markets mature, however, the focus of competition is finally switching to branding and images at the turn of the century. The larger the operators grow, the more they depend on repeat customers and have to switch the competitive focus to communicating brand values reflected in product quality and value for money. In June 1999, for example, the UK operator Airtours announced it would refocus its business by establishing a set of customer orientated values and training its entire staff in value delivery (*Travel Trade Gazette*, 28 June 1999). Airlines and hotel chains have moved in this direction over the past decade and tour operators are following exactly the same path for the same business reasons. Strong branding is also recognized as essential for effective direct marketing on the Internet and all the main players are now developing their options.

Choice of distribution options

Providing access for customers and its implications for costs, flexibility in pricing, promotion and last minute sales is the primary strategic issue in packaging and the way ahead is far from clear as we enter the new millennium. For tour operators, as noted in Figure 14.1 (Chapter 14), the cost of distribution is by far the largest item of their total marketing expenditure. Apart from the basic variable costs of commission paid on sales, there are heavy, essentially fixed costs incurred in distribution, including the printing and distribution of brochures, investment in information and communications technology to develop and maintain computer links with retail outlets and via the Internet and call centres, regular sales promotion and merchandising efforts to retail outlets to maintain display space, and educationals. A sales force may also be required in the continuous process of motivating distributors in competitive conditions.

Chapter 19 addresses the core strategic choice to be made between marketing direct to customers or achieving sales through travel retailers and the basic economics and marketing rationale of the choices made. At the end of the 1990s the major tour operators in Britain (Table 24.1) still sell the bulk of their programmes through travel retailers (especially the chains in their ownership). The travel agents' share of total sales is falling, however, and the first decade of the new millennium is likely to see this balance shift further as leading tour operators establish call centres to deal with direct and e-commerce sales. First Choice, for example, announced it expects to take up to half of all bookings through its new direct-sales centre including Internet sales within five years (*Travel Trade Gazette*, 16 August 1999).

The scope for creating completely new distribution channels outlets by linking strategically with the customer databases of large retailers, banks and credit card companies will further undermine the share of sales handled through traditional retail travel outlets.

Tactical marketing

As noted in the previous section, strategic decisions determine the product/market portfolio, the product branding and positioning, the capacity of the programme to be offered, the price range in the brochures and the structure of the distribution system to be used. In other words, for tour operators, all the four main Ps are essentially strategic decisions and the principal role for marketing tactics is to secure a continuous flow of bookings for the programme from the day it is offered for sale. The flow of bookings is of course related to the target load factors for seats and beds and the rate at which bookings and deposits are achieved also determines the weekly cash flow required to meet fixed costs and contractual obligations to the component suppliers.

Because of the lead times in getting a programme from initial planning to the point of sale, and especially because competitors' prices and the capacity of their programmes cannot be known in advance, it is almost inevitable that every year operators will find themselves with too much or too little capacity in relation to the available demand. Most years they will also be forced into a discounting war to achieve their monthly share targets. This is not incompetence, it is the nature of the business described earlier in the chapter. If sales are slow (see Figure 24.3) demand will have to be stimulated through sales promotion techniques including price discounting.

Figures 24.2 and 24.3 illustrate the key point that tactical responses are a function of the rate at which bookings are achieved over the selling period for each programme. Any programme that has been on the market for a year or more will have established a sales pattern, which can be represented as a graph with percentage load factor on the vertical axis, and weeks during which the product is on sale on the horizontal axis. For new products, the pattern will have to be estimated drawing on previous experience with comparable products. With modern computer technology linked to reservation systems, it is easy to monitor actual bookings against target on a daily basis.

If bookings for a summer product follow the predicted 'normal' sales pattern, the operator's strategy is working as planned, and tactical

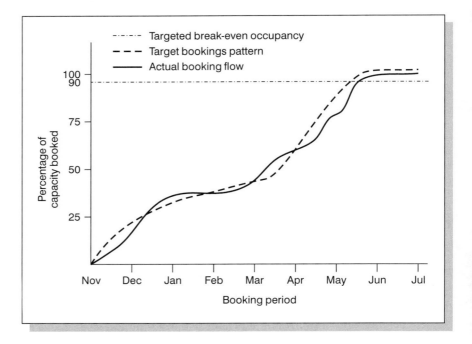

Figure 24.2
Targeted vs actual bookings achieved in a normal year for a tour operator

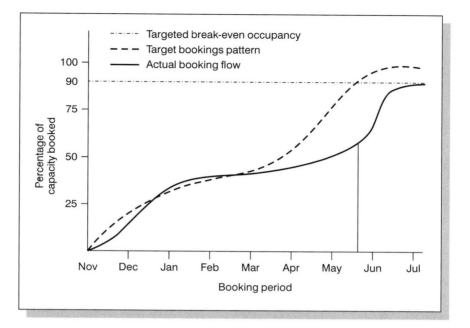

Figure 24.3
Targeted vs actual bookings achieved in a problem year for a tour operator

promotional intervention will be minimal with no need to commit contingency funds. Some last minute intervention may still be necessary in the four weeks before departure, but otherwise Figure 24.2 represents the implementation of a successful strategy in a good year. If bookings move significantly ahead of prediction and are sustained at a high level over some weeks, provided that the market indications remain favourable, the tactical response will be to look for additional product capacity.

If, as in Figure 24.3, bookings for a summer product fall significantly below the targeted level during February and March, decisive, aggressive tactical action becomes essential to reach the targeted break-even occupancy level represented in the figure at around the 90 per cent load factor level. For every booking below the 90 per cent level, the operator loses money; for every booking above it up to maximum occupancy, he generates a significant addition to profit. The incentive to engage in active tactical promotion will be obvious.

Although modern revenue yield programmes help the decision process, it is still very much a matter of judgement as to when any additional promotional activity should be committed. Assuming that operators' prices and products are broadly competitive, if one operator identifies a bookings problem ahead in the trend noted in Figure 24.3, it is probable that all operators in the same product field will see the same problem at about the same time. They will all have to react, but how quickly and by how much will be closely guarded commercial secrets, reflecting their view of the influences at work in the external environment.

For tour operators, discounting has always been the first and most powerful tool but other choices for tactical promotion are:

- Increased advertising weight, especially through daily newspaper offers.
- Sales promotions aimed at consumers, such as competitions, free childrens' places (assuming these are not part of the original product), and special discounts for bookings received by a certain date.
- Sales promotion aimed at retailers.
- Since the late 1990s, action via the Internet (see below).

In Figure 24.3 the tactical action taken in mid-April is shown to push the rate of bookings back up towards target, although only to the break-even level. Traditionally, if tactical effort did not succeed in stimulating demand, the operator would have no choice but to consolidate its programmes by cancelling some departures. Consolidation is increasingly not an option for large companies that depend on the reputation of their brands for quality of delivery and reliability, while consumer protection legislation acts to further reduce this option.

Again traditionally, operators' online links with retailers have been the main focus for notifying and selling last minute discounted offers. The merchandising power of a national retailer distribution system to secure last minute sales, often in the days before departure, has been perhaps the retailers' most powerful advantage to operators. Until the advent of e-commerce on the Internet, in practical terms not until 1998/9, no other form of marketing in the industry worked as fast and cost-effectively as the combined operator and retailer promotion focused on price. Since 1998 there has been an explosion of travel Web sites dedicated to last minute sales, including cyber auctions, which appear likely to achieve the same result at less cost and will therefore grow in popularity. Leading operators will, obviously, create and use their own sites for this purpose and tactical marketing will take on new dimensions as a result.

Chapter summary

This chapter sets out a deliberately broad view of marketing inclusive tours and product packages. It notes that, as accommodation businesses, transport companies and the larger managed attractions grow in size and international reach, they are increasingly likely to assemble and market their own packages to improve utilization of their high fixed cost assets and gain cost advantages in marketing.

All packages are intended to solve the natural inefficiencies inherent in matching demand and supply, especially in the leisure sector of tourism. All are designed to optimize customer convenience and choice and intended to optimize utilization rates for available capacity that would not otherwise be sold.

The chapter stresses the strategic advantages of packaging in the travel and tourism industry. These advantages are likely to become more significant over the next decade, especially as the major tourism markets mature and the emphasis of competition shifts from price to product customization, branding, quality and better access. It stresses also that in marketing terms the four Ps for marketing inclusive tours are essentially strategic decisions although the day-to-day pressure on marketing managers to sell their programmes is enormous and puts great emphasis on the tactical sales management of demand.

Finally, it is interesting to consider that a tour operator's brochure and Web site pages demonstrate all an operator knows about the aspirations and needs of his targeted customers. What is presented, therefore, represents the state of the marketing art as it is understood by operators at any point in time. Few other 'manufacturers' have to wear their marketing knowledge quite so obviously 'on their sleeves', as tour operators must. Content analysis of brochures and Web sites is a good exercise for students and competitors.

Part Six

Case Studies of Marketing Practice in Travel and Tourism

Case studies

This section contains five case studies:

- *Travel Inn*: strategy for market development, market leadership and branding in the budget hotel sector.
- *Longlands at Cartmel*: an innovative Internet marketing strategy for a pioneering micro-business.
- *RCI Europe*: marketing strategy for a timeshare exchange company.
- *The Balearic Islands of Spain*: strategy for more sustainable tourism development.
- *British Tourist Authority and Canadian Tourism Commission*: ICT and the role of the Internet in NTO strategies for marketing and facilitation.

In its own way, each of these cases illustrates the practical implementation of many of the key processes outlined in this book. All of them have analysed and are responding to the opportunities in the external business environment and are at the leading edge of utilizing ICT. All are redefining the services they offer to their users/consumers, all are 'new consumer' focused (see the Epilogue), all are competitive and all are committed to product quality and the search for higher standards. Most

are responding to, or could easily adapt their processes for, the need to achieve more sustainable tourism at the destination. In particular they illustrate aspects of:

- *Market research for marketing planning*: Travel Inn and RCI for their own commercial purposes. The BTA and CTC for new forms of dissemination of data to the tourism industry. Balearics to develop a sustainable destination management strategy.
- *Specific use of consumer databases to derive and monitor the success of strategy*: all are utilizing databases for data-mining and research as well as for connectivity with other ICT systems.
- *Utilizing ITC and the Internet to drive new forms of marketing, especially cost-efficient direct marketing*: the BTA and CTC, Travel Inn and RCI Europe, Longlands at Cartmel.
- *Branding and positioning, and communicating brand values*: the Balearic Islands, RCI, Travel Inn, BTA and Longlands at Cartmel.
- *Repeat business focus*: Travel Inn, RCI Europe, Longlands at Cartmel, and the BTA.
- *Public/private sector collaboration in marketing*: the BTA and CTC, and the Balearic Islands.
- *Relevance to small and micro-businesses*: Longlands at Cartmel (directly); The Balearic Islands and the BTA and CTC, indirectly.

Case 1
Travel Inn: a strategy for marketing development, market leadership and branding in the budget hotel sector

Travel Inn like most hotel chains was a successful product – not a brand. (Guy Parsons, Marketing Director, 1999)

Branded chains of budget hotels in the UK owe their inspiration to the USA budget motel market, which has had some thirty years of development since the 1960s. In Europe the first branded chains date from the success of the one- and two-star hotel groups in France, such as Campanile, Ibis and Formule 1. But significant British market growth dates back only to the mid 1980s when there was recognition by the *Little Chef* roadside catering chain that dozens of their sites either had or could purchase inexpensive development land for building hotels adjacent to restaurants located on main trunk routes (initially not motorways) in all parts of the UK.

Planning permissions were generally not a problem in the 1980s and 1990s and the concepts of low-cost formula built hotels, with standardized bathrooms and room furniture manufactured off site and installed on location, were well developed. *Little Chef* was part of the Forte Hotel Group at the time and it was a logical development for the company to pioneer the *Travelodge* brand, which quickly dominated the UK market and remained market leader until the early 1990s. From the beginning, the concept of branded budget hotels in convenient locations adjacent to profitable restaurants providing optional catering found an enthusiastic market response. High annual occupancy rates combined with low maintenance and staffing costs ensured profitability, and the development opportunities soon motivated competitors. One of these, the Whitbread Group, seeking a growth strategy to diversify out of a declining core market of brewing and pubs, had a logical route to follow in locating around or associating with its own nationally branded catering chains, *Brewers Fayre* and *Beefeater*. The *Travel Inn* chain, essentially a 'me too' product at that time, was formed in 1987 when

there were some 3000 to 4000 branded budget hotel rooms, more than half of them in *Travelodges*.

In 1993/4 the *Travel Inn* brand was brought within Whitbread's expanding hotel division, providing an impetus for the subsequent developments. By the late 1990s, although there were at least ten branded budget hotel chains operating in the UK, the market was dominated by two main players. *Travel Inn* doubled its share of market between 1992 and 1997 – taking market share from *Travelodge* – accommodating over 5 million guest nights a year. *Travel Inn*, with a network of almost 200 hotels, had made itself the market leader with some 40 per cent of rooms in the sector, driving *Travelodge* into second place with 27 per cent of rooms. Other brands (all under 10 per cent of rooms) included *Campanile, Ibis, Etap, Formule 1* and *Express Holiday Inn*.

Strategic issues to resolve

By 1997, *Travel Inn* had grown very successfully over a decade as a corporate chain. A new inn was opening every ten days or so and market demand was growing at 30 per cent a year. The chain had gained market leadership with a 40 per cent share, had high occupancy rates and excellent repeat business. But, paradoxically, research also showed that brand awareness and recognition were surprising low while recognition of the main competitor, *Travelodge*, was remarkably high. Both chains were offering the same core product and making similar quality claims, and both looked similar in locations and architectural terms and choice of logos for external signs. So strong was the original brand name that most customers thought *Travelodge* was market leader long after it was overtaken by *Travel Inn*, which was hampered by weak branding and poor logo communication. In short, the customer–brand relationship was weak and customers did not perceive the chain as the brand of choice. A crucial marketing handicap that had to be tackled by a determined market leader competing for future growth. As the marketing director put it 'Travel Inn like most hotel chains was a successful product – not a brand'.

Five interrelated strategic issues explain the Travel Inn market development decisions:

- The first was the need to understand the brand and its customers to provide a secure base for future investment. Commencing in 1998 some 5500 qualitative and quantitative interviews were conducted, customers profiled and development patterns in the USA studied. The research provided vital evidence of the distinctive values already possessed by the chain on which it was possible to build. In particular it guided the choice of a new image and logo style.
- The second, in the context of bullish growth expectations for the budget sector, was to analyse and forecast market growth against which to make major investment decisions to grow the brand and protect its position as market leader.
- The third issue was how to differentiate the Travel Inn brand from competitors, highlighting and building on its known strengths and values. Customers can switch easily between rival operators in the same or adjacent locations and there is, therefore, a powerful need to establish and maximize differentiation between brands.
- The fourth was to develop the vital product quality and consistency of delivery that underpins the brand promise and provides value for money in a highly competitive market.
- The fifth was to secure the most cost-effective marketing, especially promotion and distribution for a hotel chain in which the essentials of room product and price are similar to those of competitors.

A note on UK market size projections

It is estimated that the volume of UK budget rooms doubled from around 4000 (1992) to 10 000 (1996) and volume was set to double again in the next five years with capacity in the UK growing at 17.5 to 20 per cent a year. Average annual budget room occupancy rose by some twenty percentage points from a low in 1991 to approaching 75 per cent in the late 1990s, with Travel Inn exceeding 85 per cent. Compared with the USA, budget rooms per thousand population was estimated in the mid-1990s at 0.37 (UK) against a figure of 2.39 per thousand in

USA, and the UK had a much smaller proportion of bedstock in the budget sector compared with other categories. Budget hotels provide competition for and draw market share both downwards from the three-star category and upwards from the small hotel sector. They compete very strongly on value for money, pricing per room rather than per person night.

Some indication of the industry's belief in growth in this sector can be judged when in July 1999 alone, after the launch of Travel Inn's new strategy, two new players announced significant budget sector development plans for the UK market. Premier Hotels, which holds the master franchise in the UK for Days Inn and Howard Johnson Hotels, announced plans to build forty Days Inns in the next three years. Accor announced a target of fifty new Ibis budget hotels to be built by 2003 and expansion for its Formule 1 and Etap brands. A month after that Friendly Hotels, the European master franchisee for Choice Hotels International announced plans for thirty-five new budget properties branded Sleep Inns.

The strategy adopted and launched in 1999

1 Expanding the property portfolio and network of hotels

Following the detailed research, analysis and planning that identified the prospects of investing in a profitable growth market, the corporate decision was taken that Travel Inn would adopt a strategy of retaining market leadership. This decision meant that the portfolio of Travel Inn properties would be doubled in size over a five-year period in line with the forecasts noted earlier, and an investment programme of some £300 million was committed. The decision was underpinned by the close corporate and customer links with associated hospitality companies in the Whitbread Group, some of which act as franchisees in the development and management process for new hotels. In the late 1990s the Travel Inn estate comprised some 200 inns at, on or near to major motor routes across the UK. But doubling the network and adding some 10 000 rooms necessitated a subdivision of the overall brand to reflect new locations and associated price bands. It was agreed to differentiate between the core property portfolio of roadside inns and the new properties targeted at growth areas in London and the major urban centres of the UK, while retaining the overall recognition of the brand. A start had been made on *Travel Inn* Capital hotels of which the first opened in London in 1998 and the planned development focused on three sectors of the brand:

- *Travel Inn* – (the core estate of some 200 properties) priced at £39.95 per room in 1999.
- *Travel Inn Metro* – to develop in suitable locations in a target of thirty regional cities and towns, plus others located at leading regional airports. Their price was at £44.95 in 1999.
- *Travel Inn Capital* at £59.95 in the centre of London; at least ten will be built in the main boroughs which comprise Central London.

2 Defining and marketing the values of the Travel Inn brand as the platform for expansion and a more competitive offer

As the core marketing contribution to the growth and market leadership strategy, a clearly focused differentiation strategy was drawn up, derived through extensive consumer research and based on the brand statement that Travel Inns are 'The UK's favourite place to stay'. The statement, was designed to encapsulate and communicate to customers a strong and confident proposition and corporate image. It is backed up by new integrated logostyles and bold colours for each of the three main divisions within the Travel Inn brand. The statement incorporates a series of key values or promises associated with the brands that are to be communicated and delivered to customers, especially by the front line staff. Based on research, they include:

- Fairness: ensuring that customers feel confident of the way they will be treated by staff if they have a problem to resolve.
- Accommodating: ensuring helpfulness in meeting customer-booking requirements.
- Straightforward: tone of voice, body language and friendliness.
- Easement: ensuring that the whole product experience delivers the promises.

The new image and logo styles were introduced in April 1999 and were core elements in the major national advertising to improve awareness and recognition that commenced in January 2000, supported by national distribution systems. (See below.)

3 Enhancing the quality of the product and the consistency of the delivery systems – especially for repeat visitors

In the budget hotel market sector, prices are set by the market leader and fierce competition ensures that prices are kept within a fairly narrow band with relatively little room to manoeuvre except for special promotions. The costs of operation and the ratios of property maintenance, staff costs, distribution costs and overheads are also very similar in buildings that follow similar design and costing policies. To retain market leadership and achieve profit targets in this market is, therefore, highly dependent on the last 5 per cent of annual occupancy levels and this depends on satisfying customers and retaining customer loyalty over as many repeat purchases as possible. The research conducted indicated that, in spite of its weak brand recognition, some 75 per cent of all customers stayed more than one night in a year at *Travel Inns*, 36 per cent stayed over twenty-one nights and a remarkably loyal 1.6 per cent stayed for over 200 nights in a year. There was a good base from which to develop a convincing quality message and reach a loyal customer base.

The branding and growth strategy has to be delivered in the hotels through a combination of product quality, customer satisfaction and value for money that must be better, however marginally, than the competition. In particular the delivery requires full, wholehearted commitment by all employees. *Travel Inn* was an early adopter of *Investors in People* (a UK quality mark to signify high standards of staff training). To support the new image and communication of the brand and to explain its values, a major campaign was undertaken with *Travel Inn* staff including road shows to introduce the planned developments, a new informal uniform or 'wardrobe' for staff that is designed to reflect the core values of the brand and provide a warm, unintimidating welcome for customers. Over a period of six months, every member of staff was involved in the initial awareness campaign that has been followed up by regular communications.

To monitor the quality of delivery, *Travel Inn* developed a research programme that includes quarterly tracking studies of consumer awareness and understanding of the brand and how it is rated against competitors. Other research includes mystery customers to test the delivery standards. See also 'Database developments', below.

Segments targeted

Although budget hotels are popularly associated with the leisure market, the bulk of their revenue – some 66 per cent – is derived from the travelling business market, especially from Monday to Friday. The primary market is male and ABC1 with a higher than average income. One in four customers was a woman in the late 1990s, however, and the *Travel Inn* brand and staff training is designed to cater for their interests, such as security at reception and in rooms, and full equality of treatment in restaurants and bars. The weekend market is, of course, leisure related but typically the same or similar customers, mostly travelling without children.

In common with other branded hotels that draw their core market from business users, repeat visits are vital to maintain occupancy and provide a platform for growth, and also because the marketing costs of dealing with satisfied regular customers over a whole year are a fraction of the cost of finding, communicating with, and persuading new customers to spend their first night. *Travel Inn* has not invested in a loyalty club or similar award scheme used by many of its competitors, preferring instead to operate a customer recognition and welcome programme for its repeat visitors.

Database developments

With its operations established for over a decade, *Travel Inn* was initially slow to develop a dedicated consumer database. In 1999 the company was developing a system to link all its front offices and connect these also with the databases of the group's restaurant companies associated with hotels. With the goal of achieving greater corporate synergy through a cross-fertilization of customers, the company has built up a database of well over 1 million customers who are, or might be, regular buyers. It retains the usual detail of profile and purchasing habits which can be mined for targeting and promotional purposes, while the databases are logically linked into management information systems and especially into the operation of a national call centre to facilitate plans for the development of e-commerce.

Communication and distribution

In 1999 *Travel Inn* operated a one-price system for all the hotels in each of its three categories and had a policy of not varying price by location by day of the week or season. With product design and pricing essentially established by the characteristics of the marketplace and corporate decision, the efficiency and effectiveness of communications and especially distribution processes are primary targets for marketing.

Advertising and PR

The new image was the subject of a major advertising campaign launched in January 2000. A total of £20 million above the line expenditure was committed over a four-year period as essential to support the growth plans and communicate a strong market leader image in the face of extensive activity by competitors.

Distribution channels

Supported by a sophisticated customer database, the principal distribution channels for *Travel Inn* are direct via the 200+ locations themselves which market themselves to repeat customers and local businesses, and the national *Travel Inn* CRS which links with the call centre established to deal with the flow of enquiries and bookings generated by consumer promotions and business to business marketing.

Travel Inn opened its first Web site in 1997 and was planning to accept e-commerce transactions in 1999. Linked with the national call centre, the Web site was achieving some 20 000 hits a day by 1999 and use was growing at 20 per cent a year. It was targeted to be a principal method of booking within the development period with up to 25 per cent of business being achieved by e-commerce early in the new century.

Access is, of course, open to travel agents of which the principal users are business travel agents making bookings on behalf of the companies they service. Such was the strength of the 'in-house' booking systems (and the narrowness of margins) that *Travel Inn* did not pay commission to travel agents.

Summary

This case reveals the thoroughness of the planning needed to commit the capital investment involved in doubling the size of the market leader in the UK budget hotels sector over a five-year period. It indicates how a market leader developed a strategy to be more competitive by differentiating its offer and delivering product quality, value for money and satisfaction ratings ahead of its rivals, recognizing that they are seeking to exploit exactly the same marketing opportunity. The need to turn a good product into a market-leading brand underlies the approach adopted, backed up by a major advertising campaign and a cost-effective distribution system that utilizes modern ICT developments and incorporates the synergy available from a large network. The case illustrates all the principles of modern services marketing including the value of marketing synergy between related companies operating within the same corporate group. At the time of writing the success of the strategy is not known and it will be at least three years before the investment decisions can be evaluated in terms of budget hotel market developments.

Acknowledgement

The material used in this case was kindly supplied by Guy Parsons, Marketing Director for *Travel Inn* who also read, corrected and much improved the original draft. His support and advice is gratefully acknowledged.

Case 2

Longlands at Cartmel: an innovative Internet marketing strategy for a pioneering micro business

Longlands at Cartmel, purchased in 1987, was developed to high quality standards as a small up-market cottage/gîte-style self-catering business marketed to domestic and international visitors. Sold in 1999 this is a case study of a micro-business that was among the UK's Web site pioneers in 1993/4. Within four years it was deriving over 40 per cent of its business via the Internet at a time before the majority of micro-operators in tourism had got as far as buying a computer with Internet access. Serendipity played a part, as it does with any successful pioneer, in that the owners' son was extensively involved in computer use in undertaking his PhD. Longlands at Cartmel could, therefore, tap into 'home-grown' expertise at exactly the right time. This is a case study of a micro-business with entrepreneurial drive that saw its future prosperity linked to Internet access ahead of nearly all its rivals, large and small, in the North of England. As always, to be good at one function in the marketing process – in this case Internet promotion and distribution – usually means being good at all the others too, and so it was for Longlands at Cartmel.

The business established and marketed itself in the 1990s as a top-of-the-market small operator of self-catering cottages. It was open year round and located on the edge of (but within) the Lake District National Park in England, just outside the small Lakeland village of Cartmel. The village, which has its own priory and traces its visible history to monastic times in the twelfth century, is widely recognized as one of the most attractive villages in the southern half of the Lake District and draws scores of day and staying visitors for the quality of its environment. The name, Longlands at Cartmel, was chosen at the beginning as part of the branding process and to help ensure that prospective visitors would know where it was located. Cartmel is approximately twenty minutes drive time from the M6 motorway that links England and Scotland, and provides easy access to most parts of the national park. In 1999 Longlands at Cartmel had nine cottages with a total capacity for twenty-seven guests located around a courtyard attached to a Georgian house that dates from the eighteenth century and looks today essentially as it did then. The house is set in four acres of attractive wood and parkland and had a walled garden for visitor use.

The business was run by the two proprietors and, latterly, their son (as a part-time contributor) and five part-time staff. It fits neatly within the concept of a micro-business or micro-enterprise.

The characteristics of the business and product considerations

Five cottages were available in 1999 for two persons: one for three people; two for four persons and one for six. Three of the cottages could accommodate small families. All were let on a weekly or (in winter months) a Monday–Friday/ Friday–Monday basis. With nine cottages and fifty-two weeks of the year, there is a theoretical marketing job to do in achieving annual sales of 9×52 = around 450 bookings. In practice, because not all weeks are sold and there is a combination of both one-week and longer and shorter stays, the real target for sales in the late 1990s was around 400 bookings. Prices of units range according to size of unit and the time of the year, with August commanding roughly twice the price of February. Self-catering in the North of England has traditionally been a very seasonal business with many operators still having a 'season' of little more than twenty-six weeks of which only around eight would approach 100 per cent occupancy. With careful design, full central heating, double glazing and 'living flame' gas fires, however, the Longlands cottages are attractive places to relax and 'get away from it all' at any time of the year and weather is less of an issue than for many other self-caterers in England.

Traditional self-catering has also been very much a family-orientated operation in England, which tended to exacerbate the seasonality problem as most family holidays are geared to school holidays. Longlands identified and targeted couples as its primary market, not only the 'empty nesters' and early-retired group but also the affluent under thirty-fives and people with young families. The later accommodation provided on the site is aimed at couples.

A restaurant was operated in the main Longlands house to serve evening meals to those staying on the site. As befits the operation this provided first-class cuisine and was deliberately up-market with the traditional ambience of an English country house hotel. Working to sustainable principles, the restaurant used local ingredients and produce.

The attention to product quality, supported by the necessary investment, was part of the owners' vision from the outset. Quality was required to achieve both the pricing and seasonality pattern that would justify such investment. Reflecting their success in this, Longlands at Cartmel cottages were the first in England to be awarded the highest grading provided by the national tourist board. In 1993 they were winners in the national board's 'Self-Catering Holiday of the Year' category of the *England for Excellence* Award Scheme. This recognition gave the business access to national television coverage in 1995 when the leading British television holiday programme featured a stay at Longlands. In addition to providing a great publicity story to build into all promotional material, that programme alone produced some 3500 enquiries – roughly ten times the amount of bookings that could be handled in any year. In 1998 and again in 1999 Longlands at Cartmel went on to win a *Cumbria Award for Excellence*, the Regional Tourist Board's accolade for best practice in the sector.

Less obviously, but at exactly the time when environmental quality issues were rising up the customers' expectations list at the upper end of the market, the owners were also committed to preserving and enhancing the quality of the fabric and environment which was always a hallmark of their product. Listed building status was applied for and secured. The refurbishment of the courtyard cottages was designed to respect the original structures and local building materials were used. Extensive landscaping of the grounds was undertaken and literature is provided for all guests to communicate the 'specialness' of the place and its unique characteristics.

The evidence of quality can also be judged by the fact that some 40 per cent of business was repeat business by the mid-1990s. Bearing in mind that these cottages draw on international as well as domestic visitors from all over Britain, this is a very high level of repeats for this type of operation. In common with all small tourism businesses in which the owners deal personally with guests, Longlands at Cartmel has a large file of correspondence, comments and 'thank you' e-mails and letters, which leave no doubt as to the highly positive customer perceptions of enjoyment and value for money.

Promotion and access issues

Reflecting the quality of the accommodation provided and levels of visitor satisfaction achieved, the first obvious task was to work on existing customers to generate repeat visits and encourage referrals. But the key issue for the owners was how to achieve greater awareness and promote interest among the targeted group of potential *new* customers that they needed to attract each year. The related issue was how to provide easy and rapid access for people seeking more information and wishing to book. The Lake District, blessed with the powerful international images associated with poets such as Wordsworth and authors such as Beatrix Potter as well as its National Park status, has attracted international as well as national visitors for over 200 years. Importantly, Longlands sought to bring their product to the attention of international visitors, especially North Americans, Japanese and Europeans.

Spending on national, let alone international promotion and distribution, in order to gain new first-time bookings to add to the existing levels of repeat business, was not possible in the mid-1990s on the level of budget that could be sustained from some 200 week's bookings a year. National advertising and use of travel agents was either impossibly expensive or simply not feasible since the volume of sales was far too small to attract retailers. Providing access via wholesalers/tour operators was an option, but an expensive one at a price per booking equivalent to around a third of the brochure price allowing for marketing and the wholesaler's margin. Regional tourism brochures were affordable and used to promote Longlands, plus local area tourism brochures produced by a public/private sector marketing consortium that was chaired by one of the proprietors. This consortium was able to gain European funding because of the economic status of this largely rural area.

The answer to the issues for Longlands at Cartmel was to experiment with a Web site, the global technology for which became available for the first time in 1994, although at that time the speed of its development and the willingness of consumers to use it could not be predicted.

The Web site

In 1993/4, at least a year before the first global operators in travel and tourism opened their first tentative Web sites anywhere in the world, Longlands at Cartmel recognized the opportunities and *longlands@cartmel.com* was the logical name for the e-mail address. Not quite the first in the Lake District the site was nevertheless among the first dozen tourism businesses and gained enormously from the press and other coverage that this pioneering initiative created. By mid-2000 there were probably over 1500 tourism businesses in Cumbria with some form of Web site access. In common with all such sites they were initially for information

only with access to phone and fax for bookings, later adding e-mail. By January 1999 a secure server was added to the site to make online bookings feasible.

The Web site's success is partly a matter of its design but also online promotion, including search engine submissions, appropriate newsgroup advertising, competitions and securing links with other relevant travel sites.

All advertising, brochures and marketing material for Longlands at Cartmel carries the Web site address and features it as an excellent way to find out more and to book. The site itself has won awards for its design and ease of use for customers.

Results

The most obvious measure is the number of Web site visitors a week.[1]

Year	Visitors a week (annual averages that vary strongly by month)
1994	0
1995	150
1996	220
1997	350
1998	450
1999	600 (estimated)

Translated into bookings received there were few in the first year but from 1996 the speed of development was quite dramatic. By 1999 the Web site accounted for approximately 40 per cent of all bookings. As repeat business accounted for another 40 per cent, just two sources generated 80 per cent of all business. Most importantly, both sources were under the total control of the owners, a massive advantage in marketing.

Access via the Internet has also strongly increased the volume of overseas guests. From very few in 1993/4 the proportion in 1999 had grown to around the 20 per cent level. Once again this is a very high level for this type of business in a relatively remote area off the normal tourism 'hot spots' track.

Summary

The early adoption of the Web site produced six powerful advantages for the owners:

- 'Pole position' for access to the first customers who initially had relatively few sites to choose from.

- Securing site and e-mail names that are explicit and logical for the property – easy for browsers and easy to link with other sites via search engines.
- Providing access to international markets and all parts of the UK market.
- An early learning curve that enabled the site to keep ahead of its competitors.
- All the advantages of low-cost promotion and distribution – less than 1 per cent of sales revenue – for the bulk of all business, leading to bottom line profit and ability to invest in product quality.
- Significant reduction of expenditure on traditional advertising media.
- A form of continuous market research in measuring the level of interest in the site and monitoring enquiries.

These advantages, together with the owners' undoubted personality, entrepreneurial flair and focus on quality delivery, made Longlands at Cartmel a very successful business in the 1990s. This was a micro-business at the leading edge of using ICT for marketing purposes, well ahead of its slower moving, larger rivals. The son who joined the business formally in 1996 after completion of his PhD has gone on to found his own internet travel promotion and facilitation company – The Dedicated Partnership, <www.dedicate.co.uk> which operates globally from its Cumbria base.

Acknowledgements

The information used in constructing this case study was supplied and checked by the former owners of Longlands at Cartmel, Judy and Bob Johnson, and their son Dr Paul Johnson. Their help and advice in improving my drafts is gratefully acknowledged.

Note

1 A visitor in this context means a 'distinct host' which provides the best approximation for the number of actual visitors to a site. This is not the same as a 'hit' which reflects the way visitors to a site move around within it. For this site, there are around ten 'hits' for every 'distinct host'.

Case 3

RCI Europe: marketing for a timeshare exchange company

The concept of timeshare, also known as vacation ownership or holiday ownership, offers purchasers the right to use a specified resort based apartment, villa, chalet or other accommodation facility for a specified number of days at the same time of year, every year. Buyers usually purchase their time slots in modules of a week and keep the right to use their days – or exchange the right for the use of accommodation in another resort – for a specified number of years or in perpetuity. Annual maintenance charges are payable and ownership rights can be sold and, in some circumstances may appreciate in value. Although resorts vary in size and sophistication, most modern timeshare accommodation is provided in secure enclosed resorts that contain a range of associated facilities that make them largely self-contained. Resorts are located around the world in attractive environments with shops, restaurants, bars, clubs and a wide variety of health and sports and recreation facilities normally provided as important elements in the overall product offer. In other words, the purchase by individuals of an ownership right to use accommodation is the basis for developing sophisticated and highly efficient leisure, retailing and catering complexes at the leading edge of tourism accommodation development and marketing around the world.

Timeshare as a means of achieving sales revenue for vacation properties has its origins in France in the mid-1960s. But the concept caught on rapidly when it was dramatically expanded in the early 1970s in the USA by the urgent need to find revenue streams for blocks of condominiums in California and Florida, which had been built but could not be sold as whole units in the immediate aftermath of the 1970s international oil crisis. The combination of energy crisis and the associated global economic downturn hit the leisure/vacation property market badly and timeshare was an excellent short-term solution that developed over the next twenty years into a major vacation marketing strategy. RCI's full name – Resort Condominiums International – illustrates the point. The success in North America turned timeshare into the internationally successful phenomenon it is today.

Market growth around the world over the 1990s has been estimated at a remarkably high compound rate of approaching 15 per cent per annum – much faster than any vacation product of equivalent global size, with the possible exception of parts of the cruise market. Over a decade, this translated into a 260 per cent increase in the number of owner families and a 230 per cent increase in timeshare sales, while the number of resorts more than doubled.

At the turn of the millennium timeshare resorts were located in over eighty countries around the world with more than 4.0 million households in 175 countries owning timeshare units in some 5000 holiday resorts. Since a family typically averages around three persons, the timeshare market is now dealing with over 12 million customers with every prospect of further major growth because the economics are right for the developers, the resort operators and their marketing agencies. In particular the product is attractive to prospective customers reflecting the continuing growth of independent rather than package tour holidays and the recent introduction of stronger consumer protection legislation, notably the implementation from 1997 of the European Timeshare Directive.

Timeshare components – the role of timeshare exchange companies

The overall timeshare market effectively divides three ways between developers who put up the finance to construct the new resorts and market the units, operating companies for the resorts, and

companies that operate on a membership or club basis to facilitate and market the travel options for owners who wish to swap or exchange the use of their own accommodation rights for the use of accommodation in other resorts. Every timeshare ownership is identified by a number of factors (depending on time of year, size of accommodation, location, etc.) and carries an exchange value relative to other timeshare units, which may be used for exchange purposes. Exchange has become a vital part of what motivates the initial purchase decision and has driven growth in the timeshare market. There are two major timeshare exchange companies operating worldwide:

- Resort Condominiums International (RCI).
- Interval International (II).

Of the exchange marketing companies, RCI was significantly the largest by the end of the 1990s with around two-thirds of the market. Each of the resorts affiliated to the company is audited regularly and carries a quality rating that is used by individual owner members wishing to make exchanges. The exchange system works rather like a bank. Owners of holiday weeks at RCI-affiliated resorts, each of which is allocated an exchange value, deposit their weeks in the RCI 'bank'. They then select the weeks they require from the same 'bank', from any of the thousands of resorts in the RCI's global exchange network. If owners prefer to use their own units they may still buy the travel and other arrangements from RCI especially if their resort is located in a country abroad. RCI provide a range of travel products that facilitates owner/members to use or exchange their purchase in the ways that suit them best, acting in effect as the members' travel agent. RCI is able to use its size to negotiate good deals with airlines, tour operators, car rental companies and travel insurance providers.

RCI became a subsidiary of the Cendant Corporation in 1996, headquartered in New York and one of the world's foremost providers of consumer and business services with some 35 000 staff in over a hundred countries. Cendant has four operating divisions; travel-related services, real-estate related services, alliance-marketing related services and other business and consumer services. The travel-related division is the leading franchiser of hotels and car rental agencies worldwide and, with alliance marketing, provides access to travel and related products to more than 73 million memberships worldwide across more than twenty consumer service programmes. RCI has a powerful network of related companies or 'synergy partners' on which to draw.

Marketing issues for timeshare exchange companies

At one level it would be easy to confuse timeshare exchange companies with tour operators which they superficially resemble. It would be wrong, however. RCI's core business is to organize, market and develop a membership organization or club dedicated to facilitating exchanges for its members and providing associated travel products. Globally, timeshare owners are not 'just' 12 million potential customers a year, they are a locked-in 'captive audience' of 12 million members with a common interest in a particular form of vacation travel. In marketing terms they are a group of extraordinarily loyal, repeat customers for travel and tourism with a built-in relationship with a supplier who has the opportunity to deliver a range of products – and the means to ensure that they match consumer expectations and needs.

At the end of the 1990s the RCI worldwide database is estimated to include some 2.5 million timeshare-owning households, with 220 000 in the UK alone. The company sent more than 6.5 million people on a timeshare holiday in 1999. In addition to exchanges, the company offers seats (scheduled and charter), car hire, travel insurance and other travel offers such as cruises, short breaks and packaged holidays. It has broadened its product range for members beyond timeshare by forging new relations with small specialist operators of products likely to be of interest to its membership.

Compared with traditional tour operators dealing primarily via travel agents as their major source of distribution, or traditional resort hotels competing within a destination to market their bedspaces, mostly to new customers every year, timeshare exchange companies have powerful and vital marketing advantages for the next millennium:

- Most resorts get as close to year-round occupancy (over 90 per cent) as is possible, partly because of their design and location but primarily because of the nature of the ownership structure and the exchange options.
- Maximum cost and operating efficiency in the resorts is achievable and year-round occupancy delivers optimum pricing for given product

quality standards and makes maintenance and continuous refurbishment viable.

- RCI and its competitors can control quality by trading only with resorts that meet their criteria for affiliation. As the largest operator with the capacity to deliver business, almost like turning on or off a tap, RCI has obvious leverage to exercise over its affiliate resorts. Dis-affiliation is an effective threat if resorts fall below customer satisfaction targets.
- Customer satisfaction is relatively easy to measure for every aspect of the business, bearing in mind that RCI is dealing with frequent, repeat users who are also club members in a clear relationship with the company.
- The timeshare purchase process delivers a loyal client base for RCI, with a frequent repeat purchase and communication potential which most tour operators can only dream about.
- Relationship marketing is highly efficient as the comprehensive details of members and enquirers are all on corporate databases. There is virtually 'total' information on geodemographics, lifestyle, holiday purchase preferences and patterns, number of years of ownership, expenditure on site, time of year chosen, type of resort preferred. Individual customer satisfaction ratings are also incorporated into the database.
- The exchange company 'mines' and analyses its customer database continuously and practises highly sophisticated segmentation of its membership base, developing new products it can measure as having synergy with its target segments. There is obvious scope also to engage in cross-selling and for doing deals with third party companies which work to the same brand values as the timeshare company. Included in this are arrangements with the Cendant Corporation companies in the same ownership.
- The nature of the direct marketing practised by RCI provides as near total control over the costs and measured efficiency of promotion and distribution methods as any travel and tourism business is likely to get as we enter the new millennium. It also provides an ideal means of innovation and test marketing to hone such efficiency, for example by introducing and measuring the results of new forms of media, new products, or changing distribution methods to include delivery through the Internet.

RCI defines the principal focus areas in its late 1990s business plan as:

- Customer intimacy.
- Product leadership.
- Operational excellence.

'Captive' customers and database marketing, combined with modern information technology, provide the means for achieving these goals and measuring company achievement in unlocking the potential expenditure from customers. Information systems provide early warning of resorts and/or product types that are losing customer appeal and identifies others that are growing in popularity.

Overall, the timeshare and exchange system provides a near perfect captive audience for marketing targeting and monitoring purposes and as good a vehicle for modern communications as one finds in travel and tourism. In comparison with other sectors of service industries, RCI and the timeshare systems probably come closest to the customer knowledge and marketing sophistication practised at the start of the new millennium by leading-edge retailers such as TESCO or financial companies dealing exclusively by phone and on the Internet.

Distribution issues

Direct response mechanisms: call centres

Distribution decisions for RCI stem directly from the marketing process identified above. Within the travel and tourism industry RCI is unusual in that it has very narrow distribution channels because it is a membership club. Members write or more usually telephone RCI direct and RCI products have not been available through retail travel agents. Accordingly, RCI operates primarily by telephone call centres, which still handled over 99 per cent of its travel sales at the end of the 1990s.

Up to 1997 it is estimated that more than 95 per cent of member contacts have been organized through call centres established in local markets wherever there was a viable membership base. In early 1998 there were fifteen call centres in operation throughout Europe serving between 10 000 and 200 000 members each. Across Europe RCI employed more than 1100 people, of which some 45 per cent were in the call centres with another 15 per cent providing call centre support. Clearly this represents the major distribution cost, which has recently been under scrutiny.

A strategic review revealed that the level of service delivery and call centre management practices have diverged over time as offices have tended to create their own identity and modus operandi.

Quality and timeliness of information provided by the call centres was judged to be variable leading to difficulties in ensuring an acceptable level of consistency in quality and efficiency of the service being provided – clearly this inhibits the delivery of the corporate strategy set out above.

A consolidated pan-European call centre strategy for the late 1990s

As part of its globalization ambitions, the company decided in late 1997 that it would be more effective to shift the responsibility for call centres from its national centres into key locations only. It announced the consolidation of nine of the current call centres into a major international centre based in the Republic of Ireland with a £25 million investment that became fully operational by end 1999. Using the latest 'intelligent' telecommunications technology and local call rates, the call centre delivers higher levels of efficiency and employs around 500 holiday and travel consultants speaking some seventeen different languages.

This consolidation strategy is possible today owing to advances in the telecommunications industry together with the availability of skilled multilingual staff. Three years earlier such a strategy would not have been feasible. To members ringing for information and making bookings it does not matter, of course, where the call centre is located – provided that the cost of the call is at local rates, the staff can deal in the relevant language and the necessary quality of response is provided. To the company the evidence points to efficiency gains and improvements in quality and consistency – at less cost on average per call where call centres are consolidated and located in the same place. The linkage of the call centre to e-commerce developments is a logical development.

For the same reasons, companies such as Hertz, American Airlines and Delta Airlines have shifted to consolidation and advances in the telecommunications market look set to support the strategy into the foreseeable future.

Use of the Internet

RCI in North America started to encourage its members to undertake transactions via its Internet site in April 1997. By early 1998 the RCI site was receiving about 6000 hits a day from North American members who had been provided with an acceptably secure means to make their bookings on the system. A further 5000 hits a day were being received from members who were not able to make bookings on the system but could browse the Web pages for information. At that time the proportion of e-commerce bookings was tiny (probably less than 2 per cent) but the cost per enquiry and booking was much lower than for telephone servicing at call centres and the growth potential of the system was obvious.

RCI in Europe developed its first Internet strategy in 1997 and the first phase, with e-mail and telephone directions for specified customer actions, was running in 1998. Within five years RCI was projecting that up to 15 per cent of bookings could be Internet generated and was investing accordingly in its systems and links with the call centres. Full transactional capability (online e-commerce) was planned for introduction in 2000. As at least half of all timeshare owners either are or will be Internet users on PCs or interactive televisions at the turn of the millennium, an e-commerce strategy is logical. Its use will further reinforce the company's knowledge of consumers and enhance the efficiency of the timeshare exchange business model.

Estimated costs of distribution

The major costs of distribution for RCI are the staff employed to handle the enquiries for exchange, make reservations and bookings, and deliver tickets and associated products in connection with the purchase.

- Staff costs typically represent over 50 per cent of the total cost base of RCI.
- Call centres represent over 43 per cent of the total staff costs, so allowing for the associated telecommunications costs and direct marketing costs, distribution can be said to equate to around a third of operating costs.
- Investment in technology associated with the call centres is estimated to be of the order of 6 per cent of revenue.
- Direct sales and marketing costs represent 7–8 per cent of sales revenue.
- Sales literature costs, which primarily reflect the production of an annual directory for members together with regular member and developer publications and mailshots, account for 4 per

cent of sales revenue. Online directory access is an obvious development to cut cost and simultaneously add value to customer service.

These costs have to be compared with those of traditional tour operators who have far higher brochure costs, higher marketing costs (because they have to bring in at least 50 per cent 'new' or lapsed customers each year) have a similar level of cost for operating a CRS, spend less on call centres but have to maintain online computer links with several thousand travel agency outlets and, of course, pay commission of over 10 per cent on approaching 90 per cent of their sales. In addition, most tour operators in most years are obliged to take part in discount price wars to shift their last minute unsold capacity which should also be added back into the full cost of marketing. Vertical integration with airlines and travel agency chains has changed the traditional tour operator business model and helped the largest tour operators to reap significant cost benefits in the 1990s but the timeshare exchange business model is developing its own direct marketing efficiency gains as noted in this case.

Although the situation is changing rapidly with the opportunities now delivered by ICT, traditional tour operators do not have customer databases which are anywhere near as sophisticated as those operated by RCI and its partner companies, primarily because retail travel agents have had a vested interest in preventing customer details reaching the operators and thus encouraging them to market more of their capacity direct. Leading players such as Thomson, Airtours and TUI do have access to databases because they are merged with their own large retailer chains and have struck alliances and ownership deals with other companies that deliver such information. Even so, the advantage lies with the *modus operandi* of membership or club operators.

Summary

RCI's business goals are clearly identified as 'customer intimacy' 'product leadership' and 'operational excellence'. Logically exploiting its status as a membership organization, RCI has developed a highly targeted and cost-efficient global marketing operation based on database marketing and direct distribution and promotion backed up by effective controls over day-to-day product delivery. It has developed a business model in travel and tourism with powerful global branding and marketing advantages that put the company into a leading-edge position to further develop the timeshare market. The company is especially well placed to exploit developments in ICT – and understand customer reaction to them – as they emerge over the next decade.

Acknowledgement

This case is based on material supplied by Steve Allen, Executive Director of Marketing for RCI Europe in 2000, located in Kettering (UK). His many helpful comments in developing, correcting and enhancing the case for publication are much appreciated.

Case 4

The Balearic Islands of Spain: strategy for more sustainable tourism development

The main, recent Balearic tourism regulations have the common objectives of quality of life (through territorial planning) and tourism sustainability (through excellence for money and competitiveness).
(Bardolet, 1998)

The four main Balearic Islands in the Mediterranean Sea, of which Mallorca or Majorca is by far the largest, lie some 250 kms off the coast of Spain, south of Barcelona. Strategically, with three international airports, the islands are ideally located to meet the holiday demand of much of the EU population. As the new millennium dawns, they generate some 10 million visits a year (20 per cent of all international arrivals to Spain) but only 1 million of these are residents of Spain. The visits are accommodated in some half a million tourist beds (registered and unregistered). Tourism generates some 60 per cent of the islands' economy (gross domestic product – GDP) compared with just 2 per cent for agriculture. Through tourism, the Balearics have achieved an income per capita for residents of around 130 per cent compared with the average for Spain and 110 per cent compared with the average for the EU and they are dependent on tourism for their future prosperity. In 1999 there were some 750 000 residents of the islands, including at least 70 000 foreign nationals, especially Germans in recent years, buying property for use as second homes and investment purposes.

Professor Bardolet, Professor of Marketing at the University of the Balearics, identifies two clear-cut historical periods in the islands' tourism. The first is the *milch cow* era of the 1950s, 1960s and 1970s before the Autonomous Government of the Balearics was established in 1983 under Spain's democratic constitution of 1978. The second is the era of developing *controls and management* of the 1980s and 1990s. Prior to 1983 market forces effectively determined development and individual municipalities provided only minimal controls. Tourism grew from 100 000 arrivals in 1950 to nearly 4 million in 1981. Even before 1983, however, when visitor arrivals were still under 5 million there was growing concern for what would happen in the long term unless capacity limits and quality controls could be developed and imposed jointly between public and private sectors.

This case summarizes the processes, especially since 1983, which have brought together the public and private sector in the Balearics into a pioneering role for more sustainable tourism in the new millennium. The islands, together with the Costa Brava, were in the first wave of sun-and-beach tourism in the Mediterranean from the early years of the twentieth century and the Mallorca Tourism Board was founded in 1905. It was, however, the process of unchecked success of popular tourism destinations, accelerating after the Second World War with the developments of air transport, that led to the critical issues of managing excessive urbanization of the coastline, water depletion and population increases. These are problems that are now also common in most of the Mediterranean resorts, but especially in small islands. The simultaneous need to combine planning and marketing techniques to maintain high levels of visitor demand in a mature and increasingly competitive European market while tackling seasonality, make this a highly relevant case for all students of destination marketing in the new millennium.

The strategic issues of tourism in the Balearics

The Balearic Islands possess natural advantages of climate, scenery, beaches and inland areas that have attracted foreign visitors in ever increasing numbers for over fifty years. The islands were both fortunate and unfortunate in that the period of the most rapid growth (from 1 million in 1965 to almost 7 million in 1987) occurred in an era prior to effective planning and before the issues of sustainability were recognized. Fortunate in the sense that they achieved economic advantages which revolutionized the income and associated benefits of residents well ahead of much of Spain. But unfortunate in that the largely unplanned developments brought with them exploitation of building densities, development and architectural practices and a general unconcern for environmental quality that has marred so many coastal zones in tourism attractive areas in the Mediterranean and elsewhere.

In the late 1990s Balearic tourism still bore many of the hallmarks of 1970s-style mass holiday tourism. Some 97 per cent of all arrivals on the islands came by air; 87 per cent of them were packaged by tour operators with the German and British market contributing some 70 per cent of all visits. Seasonality was the most important strategic issue in the capacity debate as only 18 per cent of all visits took place between November and April and less than a third of all tourist beds were open for business at that time. Annual bed occupancy was not much over 50 per cent in the late 1990s. (The 18 per cent is an average figure for the islands, ranging from 22 per cent of all visits to Mallorca to only 5 per cent for Menorca and Eivissa.)

Although it is commonly assumed that the Balearics have been heavily overdeveloped for tourism it is worth noting that only 9 per cent of the islands' land area is classified as urbanized, of which less than half is urbanized for tourism

purposes. Some 75 per cent of the area has been protected by law either for nature conservation (35 per cent) or as rural land (40 per cent). By being among the first significant traditional tourism destinations to tackle the management issues with a growing appreciation of sustainable development, the islands are well placed to restore and maintain their appeal to the more discriminating customers of the new century, using modern marketing methods to achieve overall community goals.

The five key issues identified for Balearic tourism at the start of the twenty-first century and the responses developed over the last twenty years are:

• Promoting the acceptability in the islands of the idea of controlling market-led growth within concepts of capacity that do not alienate either residents or the tourism industry, including extensive zoning schemes to control where and how future development can take place.
• Overall commitment to quality enhancement, especially by renovating existing accommodation capacity where possible and demolishing substandard capacity where renewal is not feasible. The upgrading of the physical product is to be accompanied by a dedicated education and training programme to improve service standards for visitors and job satisfaction for employees.
• Developing and marketing new products that are related to year-round open air sports and recreation activities, and at the same time provide a climatic and social quality of life (based on second homes) that will appeal to and retain more discriminating visitors.
• Extending the season through a combination of product development and marketing.
• Supporting small businesses, including a Multimedia Information Network for Tourism (MINTOUR).

Overall the strategic issue for the Balearics is long-term investment in forms of sustainable tourism development that maintain and enhance the economy, the quality of life of the islands' residents and their environment. It is to be achieved by a combination of marketing and planning influences and controls in public and private sector hands, supported by a major investment programme and commitment to education and training.

The planning and investment chronology summarized

For other destinations contemplating management action for tourism, it is important to note that it took around twenty years to develop the Balearics tourism management controls and get them accepted and implemented. The main stages are noted below:

1983 The Balearics became the seventeenth Autonomous Regional Government of Spain with responsibility for its own tourism policy.

1984 First protective land planning decree was issued to begin to limit uncontrolled tourism development and protect natural resources. The decree linked the development of beds to land requirements (first 30 sq m and later (in 1987) 60 sq m per tourist bed to be built) but was still dependent on the willingness of municipalities to co-operate with the regional government for the islands

1987 First Law on territorial planning controls published and elements of it incorporated in the first Regulatory Tourism Supply Plan (POOT) noted below, but the full implementation would not take place until 1999 (DOT) and it needed the impetus of the subsequent developments noted below.

1994 Participation in the EU funded ECOMOST project provided an important rationale and defence for the new legislation dealing with capacity issues and calling for better local government control and links with tour operators.

1995 The Tourism Supply Plan (POOT Decree) transferred the approval of all new tourism buildings to the Ministry, away from the previous control by municipalities. It also limited the bed capacity of Mallorca's coastal zones, thus tightening the earlier limits set by the 1984/7 regulation but only for accommodation units.

1995 As part of Spain's overall commitments to quality, (*Futures Plan*) the municipality of Calvia in Mallorca adopted a local Agenda 21 Programme – displayed as an exemplar at the UN Commission for Sustainable Development meeting in New York in 1998.

1998 Moratorium placed on any increases in tourism capacity pending the implementation of a new tourism law and a comprehensive law on the use of land – *Ordinance Territorial Plans* – known as DOTs.

1999 The government of the Balearics approved a new Tourism Law that pulled together previous legislation and froze tourism bed capacity for the whole of the Balearics (thus confirming the requirement to exchange one obsolete bed for every new one already set by the 1995 POOT legislation. Another new law passed was the implementation of the 1987 law by the DOTs, which identify the tourism use of virtually every hectare of land available. It also puts a limit to further development of urban land (except in sites already approved for building on plots of land inside the city/town boundaries). The new limit is set at 1 per cent increase a year for the next ten years. Last, but not least, the new law forbids any construction closer than 500 metres to the seashore (the 1988 Spanish State Law had set a previous limit of 100 metres).

2000 The new government elected in late 1999 proposes an ecotax at one euro per day to be collected from 2001 by registered accommodation and from holiday homes.

Investment underpinning the sustainable objectives

The achievements in the Balearics have required extensive public and private sector investment. In a programme that many destinations must envy, the equivalent of over US$1.5 billion has been invested in little over a decade as follows:

1989–97 US$200 million implementing a 'Global Sanitation Plan', building sewage plants to prevent raw sewage discharge into the sea. As a result, the Balearics had some fifty Blue Flag beaches in the late 1990s.

1990–4 US$100 million invested in the 'Plan to Embellish Tourism Resorts' including seafront promenades, demolition of obsolete or unaesthetic units, and new lighting schemes.

1990– US$800 million invested by the private
continues sector under the legally imposed 'Hotel Accommodation Modernization Plan' imposed on all units built before 1984. Under this plan all hotels are inspected

and must meet modern quality standards; approval for any new beds is linked to the removal of substandard bedstock.

1995   The Balearics' 'Tourism Supply Quality Plan' focuses and integrates the quality programmes for island tourism and fosters tourism planning resources and education and training.

1996–continues   'Law on Modernization of Complementary Tourism Supply' covering the catering sector (cafés, bars, etc.), involving some US $20 million by 1999.

1992–9   The Spanish government's 'Futures Plan' embraced the islands within its 'Excellence and Dynamization' quality development plans and generated a further US$20 million. It was under this plan that the Municipality of Calvia was a pilot project and famously demolished five of its old seafront hotels, replacing them with landscaped areas.

1997–continues   'Pla Mirral' (Mirror Plan) designed to restore the architectural qualities of the island towns. Over two years 1998–2000, some US$280 will be invested, including EU funding.

1997–continues   A voluntary 'ECOTUR' programme was approved by the Balearic government to co-ordinate and regulate the award of quality ecolabels for tourism suppliers, including small enterprises.

1997–continues   'D Plan' (for off-peak tourism) is launched with the co-operation of local Chambers of Commerce.

Marketing issues summarized

To sustain the economic contribution of tourism in an increasingly competitive international market, the Balearics have an absolute need to achieve some 10 to 12 million visits (or a target of 100 million nights a year because the average length of stay is falling). At the same time the islands must tackle the major issue of seasonality and achieve their needs in ways that meet long-term sustainable objectives. It is very clear that these aims will not be achieved for the Balearics without a determined and co-ordinated marketing effort. Six specific aspects of destination marketing are noted below.

Research and marketing planning

Ongoing research is the vital foundation for effective tourism destination marketing. Through the upgrading of the tourism (1987) and hospitality (1997) schools at the University of the Balearics, and the foundation in 1998 of the Centre of Tourism Research and Technology, the islands now have better access to market research than most equivalent destinations. Better research was an urgent priority as tour operators had in effect controlled and monopolized research data between the 1950s and 1980s, which they did not share with the government. Marketing research was undertaken by professors of the islands' university acting as consultants for the Balearics government. A White Paper on tourism, prepared by the university in 1987 and based on research, set the key strategies subsequently developed by the government. In 1991 and 1996 the University of the Balearics prepared the first and second Tourism Marketing Plans for the Balearics, focusing on product quality enhancement and off-peak marketing as noted earlier.

Product quality development

As noted under planning and investment decisions, there has been a determined campaign across Spain (the Futures Plan) to improve product quality as the basis for more effective marketing. In the Balearics, tourism businesses realized since the mid-1980s that when Spain joined the EU, its traditional low-cost base would steadily get closer to the higher average level of the EU. The only option available to compete with emerging lower-cost non-EU destinations in the Mediterranean was to focus on product and service quality and value for money rather than on low price. The legal requirement to link the demolition and upgrading of old bedstock as a condition for developing new accommodation is especially important.

Off-peak tourism

An 'Off-Peak Tourism Season Plan' ('D Plan') was launched in 1997. It focuses on developing products other than the traditional sun/sea/beach mass tourism products still associated with summer months. New products include facilities for retirement age customers, rural, heritage and cultural tourism and a range of specific all-season activities such as walking, cycling, golf and sailing. The off-peak tourism marketing strategy had become the clear priority at the end of the 1990s as the only option given the agreed capacity limits at peak season.

Public/private sector collaboration in marketing (and planning)

Collaboration throughout the islands has been developed over the last decade. It has been facilitated by new information communication technology and is generally ensured by a regular flow of information. At the end of the 1990s there was:

- Broad social and political consensus on the main marketing strategies for tourism (although strong opposition from hoteliers on new tax proposals of 2000).
- Privately managed tourist boards (with public sector representation) established on each of the main islands.
- A tourism council responsible to the Balearics Ministry of Tourism, providing a forum for the islands' tourist boards, plus the main private sector tourism businesses, and representatives from other public bodies such as the airports, harbours and planning authorities.

The strength of the collaborative system is that it is voluntary, embraces the principal public and private sector players and has been able to achieve consensus for the broad thrust of marketing strategy, quality enhancement and advertising communications. There are, however, some weaknesses in implementing and monitoring agreed targets. Particular strengths include links with tour operators and support for small businesses.

Links with tour operators

Traditionally the Balearics left their tourism marketing and distribution in the hands of tour operators (mainly British and German). This was still largely true at the end of the 1990s and the success of tourism over the decades can only be fully explained through the participation of those operators. Through consultation following the conclusions of the tour-operator led and EU-funded ECOMOST project (published in 1994), the leading tour operators, especially those based in Germany where green consumer issues are more important than in most other parts of Europe, responded in product presentation in ways that promote and highlight more sustainable tourism and provide

better information for their clients. Often seen as predatory companies with no vested interest in specific destinations, the leading tour operators have responded to the sustainable aims of the Balearics and are collaborating in the agreed strategies for product quality enhancement and off-peak marketing.

Support for small businesses

As in nearly all established destinations, SMEs account for over 90 per cent of tourism employment. Their specific interests are recognized in the Balearics ECOTUR programme (co-ordination of quality and ecolabels) and the EU programme MINTOUR intended to become the embryo of a future pan-European network to be used by private and public sector operators in tourism. The Balearics are also part of the EU programme INTOUR-ISME designed to provide information and marketing tools for tourism SMEs. All these systems link also with the Hotel Association's CRS developments to provide alternative distribution channels to traditional tour operator contracts.

Summary

The process of moving from pioneers of mass tourism since the 1950s into pioneers of more sustainable, higher-quality and segmented tourism in the new millennium is still in progress in the Balearics. It is a painfully slow and sometimes rough process but it has been socially and politically accepted thus far. The tourism resort islands have a vulnerable natural and social environment and limited territorial space that put tight constraints on the scope for future tourism development. But what is logical and obvious on paper is not always economically feasible in practice. Only when islands such as the Balearics reach such a high level of income per capita, low unemployment, good public sector infrastructure and a consolidated share of key tourism markets, can some form of 'de-marketing' be economically tolerated and become the basis for government decisions in collaboration with the private sector.

Since the 1990s the Balearic Islands agreed to put strict limits on further capacity growth in the peak season and to focus all marketing efforts on new products for year-round tourism. Parallel policies to improve the quality of the product offer and the levels of service are in place. So, too, are support mechanisms for SMEs and collaboration by tour operators in the destination objectives. The regulatory process was facilitated when in 1999, after sixteen years of right-wing dominance, the regional elections produced a new government formed by a coalition comprising nationalist, socialist and green party interests. This government, although with only a small majority, is inclined to impose a 'hard stop' policy for tourism growth to protect the environment and the cultural identity of the islands. Thus, after ten years of delays and political disputes, agreed regulation was imposed to control future growth. Its focus on territorial planning and building constraints is calculated to influence tourism demand patterns as well as the supply of tourist accommodation capacity. At the end of 2000 the new government was planning to impose an ecotax on tourism to be collected by registered hotels, in addition to the airport tax already in place. If it is implemented as planned it may strain the current public/private sector consensus and its impact on demand will be closely watched.

On the islands, while the ultimate aim is sustainable tourism, it is accepted that competitiveness is a fundamental requirement for achieving it. Marketing techniques provide the essential means to be competitive. But competitiveness outside the framework set by sustainable goals may lead to disasters for residents' welfare (quality of life) and the natural environment (ecology). The equilibrium point has to be found, not only by balancing economic needs against judgements of environmental carrying capacity, but also by understanding residents' socio-cultural carrying capacity. This is art rather than science and the Balearic Islands do not claim to have found a perfect solution to this equilibrium. Compared with the situation less than a decade ago, and having regard also the Agenda 21 developments in the leading Mallorca resort of Calvia, the progress has been remarkable.

Acknowledgements

This case is based on material supplied by Professor Esteban Bardolet, Professor of Marketing at the University of the Balearics, Member of the Mallorca Tourist Board and Tourism Consultant to the Government of the Balearics, who has been closely involved in the development of tourism marketing and planning in the Balearics for over twenty years. He has published widely on the issues covered and his support in commenting on and improving this case summary is warmly acknowledged.

Case 5

British Tourist Authority and Canadian Tourism Commission: ICT and the role of the Internet in NTO strategies for marketing and facilitation

A – British Tourist Authority: <www.visitbritain.com>

The British Tourist Authority, first established as the British Travel Association in 1929, has been at the forefront of NTO marketing for many decades. It is one of the five largest NTOs in the world, with twenty-seven 'full service' offices in countries from which the UK draws its visitors plus 'information-only' operations in a further eleven markets where the BTA is represented by the British Council. The BTA has won many international accolades for the quality of its promotion and information services over the years and pioneered some of the marketing developments now common in many destination marketing organizations around the world.

The BTA has also been very successful in developing marketing partnerships with some of the large players in the UK tourism industry, including financial contributions to its promotional campaigns. Although the tens of thousands of small and micro-enterprises in British tourism were never ignored by the BTA, it is a fact that traditional NTO marketing methods made it difficult to provide them with facilities for promotion and distribution other than through small classified type adverts in brochures designed to answer overseas enquiries.

The established record of achievement, both for promotion and information, gave the BTA a major strategic advantage in developing and exploiting the opportunities opened up on the Internet when the World Wide Web became generally accessible for the first time via personal computers around 1995. Prior to that, by use of fax-back arrangements and toll-free hotlines the BTA was already extending its reach and provision of convenient accessibility for potential visitors. The overseas offices were linked by e-mail in 1996 and were quick to recognize the possibilities of the World Wide Web. After an initial process of exploration, testing and recruitment the first Web site, *visitbritain.com*, was launched in 1997. It is a hub and spoke network of sites comprising twenty-five individual sites in mid-2000, with a total of forty planned. Each country or market segment site is created and maintained by BTA staff overseas, mainly by local nationals and always in their own language. All editors (with the exception of the USA) use a single central publishing system and core content provided from the UK.

The rationale and objectives for the BTA Web site

At 2000, the rationale can be summarized as:

- Responding to the marketing opportunities being opened up by ICT and the rapidly growing number of people with personal and office Internet access in countries from which the UK draws most of its visitors.
- Providing a user-friendly tourism information database and search tool that would, from the outset, make available to Internet users throughout the world the total knowledge base of the BTA including details of some 40 000 tourism businesses within a total of some 70 000 records.
- Responding to competition from other NTO Web sites. (The WTO reviewed a hundred such sites in 1999 in providing a 'state-of-the-art' assessment.)
- Providing a facility for promotion and distribution (with options for booking via phone, fax, and e-mail) for UK tourism businesses with Web

sites – including virtually all the leading edge small and micro-enterprises.
- Developing a database of actual and prospective visitors to Britain for relationship marketing purposes.
- Connecting to the online booking facilities increasingly operated by the industry and its partners.
- Providing a support service for the network of national and regional tourist boards established in the UK.
- Establishing a leading Internet profile for Britain and for the BTA.
- Increasing the number of enquiries/prospective visitors that the BTA reaches and massively reducing the unit cost per enquiry compared with traditional response methods.

Progress to 2000

In 1998, within little more than a year of its introduction, the site was voted the 'Best NTO Web site' by ENTER (an international tourism technology award) and 'best of twenty-nine OECD countries' official Web sites' and was already handling 1 million site visits (11 million page visits) in its first year to March 1998. This compares, for example, with an estimated 2 million enquiries received at the BTA's overseas offices in the same period via the traditional access methods of mail, telephone, fax and personal visits. Two years later the site registered a twelve-month total of over 5 million site visits and 35 million page visits.

The pace of development has been rapid with details of some 40 000 accommodation properties, attractions and events from the start, and progressively easier and more detailed searching being added, including via street-mapping, by January 2000, when a gazetteer of 30 000 towns and villages was also introduced. It is impossible to estimate with precision, because the number of small tourism businesses in Britain can only be guessed at, but this is probably equivalent to over a third of all the active tourism businesses and events in Britain. To have gained such coverage within two years of launching is a remarkable achievement and it certainly covers at least three-quarters of all the proactive businesses, including many micro-businesses at the turn of the millennium. It is also an indication of the perceived value of the Internet by both customers and businesses alike. The size of the database and the traffic it generates led to major site re-engineering in 1999–2000.

In mid-2000 the site contained around 80 000 Web pages and offers:

- Information on accommodation, events, attractions and tourist areas.
- Information by core activity types, such as walking, cycling, arts and heritage.
- A sophisticated, interactive mapping system – nearly 70 000 records are geo-coded to fourteen digits (better than one metre accuracy).
- Direct links to the sites of individual businesses.
- Promotion of major national events such as millennium festivals (in 2000), sports and cultural events.
- E-mail news facility for surfers that register their interest.

Although technically feasible, to avoid content that needs plug-ins or more bandwidth, video clips were not provided. Bulletin boards and chat rooms were not provided in 2000.

At 2000, tourist use of the Internet was still dominated by e-mail. *Visitbritain* site visitors are asked to register their addressees, which are fed into a database that can be managed as a platform for future relationship marketing. Subsequent promotions targeted as personalized e-mails can be used to draw attention to relevant Web sites of those whose interests are already known. This is one of the new marketing tools that are now available. The database is also an important new source of market research information.

The BTA's personnel manage the Web site (a team of eight in the New Media department, plus the vital resources of the Information Services department who manage the databases). The technical developments are outsourced on a contract basis.

Strategic development plans for the site over the next five years

- Increasing the number of businesses accessible on the Web site.
- Development of the online booking facility, using a secure system for credit cards.
- Development of the relationship marketing possibilities.
- Development of the research information provision that arises from site use.

Summary

The development of Web sites by NTOs/DMOs meets all the criteria established for marketing 'facilitation' in Chapter 20. In terms of *reach* (millions of prospective visitors around the world), *accessibility*, *convenience* and *'instant bookability'* (available twenty-four hours a day, seven days a week in prospective visitors' homes), and meeting *individual needs*, the virtual marketplace is an ideal tool for all DMOs. The unit costs (per visitor enquiry/booking) are substantially lower than those for any other method and there are cost savings in reducing the number of printed items that would otherwise have to be printed and distributed.

Web sites are also an ideal way of developing collaboration with the thousands of small businesses that make up the tourism industry in any developed country. Parallel Web sites at <www.tourismtrade.co.uk> and <www.staruk.org.uk> have been set up to support the supply side of the tourism industry with marketing advice (see below).

Because the advantages are so clear, it is tempting to suppose that the construction and development of national Web sites is a fairly simple process for NTOs. In practice, to operate internationally networked sites successfully, they need first to identify and invest in the likely avenues that the technology will continue to open up (the BTA's New Media, only three years old in 2000, faces a degree of development over the next ten years analogous with that of the motor car over a hundred years). Next, NTOs need to be clear about their business objectives and the relationship between the new media marketing and the traditional communication methods, which continue. Finally, they need to accept that business processes will change – for example, through new linkages and partnerships with portals and other e-commerce operators – and recognize that the new media affects all parts of their marketing operations, with an emphasis on integrated back-end systems that feed the databases on which the customer facing Web site depends. Initially, because of the investment required in hardware, software and personnel, such Web sites are unlikely to make an operating profit in the short run. The longer run possibilities are more encouraging.

The BTA were planning in 2000 to develop commercial partnerships to bring in an integrated e-commerce capability and to acquire a customer relationship marketing system to develop Internet-based CRM activity.

B – Internet facilitation Web sites for the tourism industry

Canadian Tourism Commission's Tourism Exchange

Chapter 20 stressed that an important part of the marketing facilitation role for destination marketing organizations is the provision of research data and other technical information to an industry that mainly comprises small and very small businesses.

The Canadian Tourism Commission (Canada's NTO) designed an industry-focused Internet service in the late 1990s, called CTX, to facilitate the communication of tourism information, news and knowledge to what are mainly private sector partners. The CTX is a B2B Internet-based extranet established in 1999 (that was free) but accessible only by a password and not designed for the general public. As it develops, CTX is planned to support, facilitate and provide leadership for the Canadian tourism industry and its international partner organizations.

Piloted in mid–1997, the system was formally launched in May 1999. The CTC provided the start-up costs estimated at US$5 million with development costs for the subsequent two years at US$1 million. In June that year there were some 4000 CTX members and by mid-2000 membership had expanded to over 15 000 organizations. The CTX has four sections: Information Exchange; Promotions and Marketing Exchange; Resources; and Membership. There were also some twenty discussion groups active at any one time in 2000, which members could join. One of them was for members of the CTC Research Committee and associated working groups. Links could be made to members' individual Web sites.

Depending on the way that members use the exchanges, the CTX has the potential to extend downward to embrace more and more smaller operators.

Two BTA tourism industry professionals sites (TIPS), and Staruk

In 1999 BTA developed a Web site to provide information and support for Britain's inbound tourism industry. It is a form of B2B site although access is not restricted to business users. In 2000 it was available as a free online service with hotlinks to a range of related third party sites. It is supported by another service called Trade Help Desk, which may be accessed by phone, fax or e-mail.

Not nearly as comprehensive as Canada's CTX in 2000, and targeted at those who deal with inbound tourism, it nevertheless is moving in the same direction to facilitate tourism businesses in the UK. Its contents include a comprehensive diary of industry events and access (not online) to library resources containing some 70 000 volumes and seventy journal titles. A password-accessible site links to the BTA's product market fit (PROFIT) analysis of its overseas market segments and the products they use. An open link provides access to basic research data and statistics.

TIPS links with Staruk, which is a Web site for UK tourism statistics, facts, research and publications. Staruk is sponsored by the UK's five national tourist boards and the UK government department responsible for BTA and England. In 2000 the BTA was developing plans to improve industry access to its extensive international market research databank by substantially improving the TIPS Web site with pages of data that can be interrogated to provide specific answers to an individual business's interests, for example analysis by area of the UK, by main markets of origin, by profile of visitors, and so on. There were associated plans to provide analytical synopses of some key research data to boost the value of the site for smaller businesses with only limited competence in undertaking their own interpretation of research material.

Also in 2000, the national boards involved in UK tourism were developing Web sites for specific purposes such as sustainable tourism and advice for small businesses.

Summary

These examples of B2B Web sites designed for the tourism industries in Canada and Britain indicate the way that NTOs around the world will develop their facilitation services over the next decade for the businesses that deliver tourism services at the destination. Many other NTOs are already engaged in the same process for the same reasons. Facilitation is a form of 'internal marketing' (see Chapter 6) and the building of public/private sector relationships that will be particularly valuable for medium and smaller sized companies that lack the resources to undertake such linkages for themselves.

They illustrate the way that businesses can be supported in marketing terms with online connectivity but more importantly illustrate the way that advice and information and up-to-date good practice can be disseminated at low cost and with an immediacy previously impossible. Up to the 1990s, NTOs could only communicate by holding conferences and seminars, direct mail of expensive printed communications and by relying on their regional and local networks. The regional and local networks remain a vital consideration and have their own connectivity upwards to the national level and downward to destination businesses but their access to information and advice is massively improved.

Acknowledgements

Executives in the organizations concerned kindly supplied the material used in these cases. Peter Varlow, Head of Market Access at the BTA, Ian Woodward, Head of Market Intelligence also at the BTA, and Scott Meis, Director of Research at the Canadian Tourism Commission, gave much appreciated help and support in finalizing the text.

Epilogue: Prospects for travel and tourism marketing

Industries don't 'evolve'. Instead, firms eager to over-turn the present industry order challenge 'accepted practice', redraw segment boundaries, set new price-performance expectations and re-invent the product or service concept. (Hamel and Prahalad, 1994: 303)

This book contains many indications of the trends that are driving new approaches to marketing in leading organizations around the world at the start of the new century. The purpose of this concluding chapter is to draw the main implications together within a framework of perceived change. It is also an opportunity for the principal author to indulge his taste for speculation and prediction, and hopefully stimulate discussion.

With the benefit of hindsight it seems fair to claim that most of the marketing trends identified in the epilogues of the first and second editions of this book have developed broadly along the lines indicated. In the 1994 edition, although three of the ten changes dealt with the growing significance of information technology and highlighted the growing importance of distribution issues and direct marketing, the astonishing speed at which the Internet would grow and influence all aspects of marketing in the late 1990s was not anticipated.

Many of the trends discussed in this final chapter under seven broad headings are already fairly clear in their implications but it is the speed of change and the international interaction between the trends that cannot be predicted with any precision. In 2000 the Internet is already available to the majority of the world's international travellers but the speed at which e-mail users and information surfers will turn into e-commerce buyers and make it the main distribution channel for growing numbers of travel and tourism businesses is far from clear.

Similarly, there is growing global awareness that the per capita income and consumption of scarce resources in developed countries, and the associated production of pollution and waste, greatly exceed that of the populations of developing countries. International long-haul tourism for leisure purposes is just one example of such conspicuous high consumption that may be targeted for some restriction in the next decade in the interests of global equity and protecting the environment. If current fears of global warming are justified by improving scientific evidence there are certain to be more fiscal and/or regulatory restrictions to inhibit the hypermobility that characterizes modern societies. The development of new scientific and technological breakthroughs may support the continued expansion of tourism, for example new forms of energy production, but in 2000 it seems likely to be a race against time.

1 The zeitgeist for the *new economy*

This section highlights the post-industrial society trends that are driving the expansion of tourism and determine the way that marketing is practised. The trends underpin the twenty-year projections by the WTO that international tourism could triple in volume by 2020. Those are market *potential* projections, of course, reflecting the tourism development of China in particular, and they do not have regard to the possible environmental impacts and constraints noted later in this epilogue.

During the last three decades, the developed countries that generate the high levels of GDP per capita needed to drive domestic and international tourism and create the 'world's largest industry' emerged from the former industrial era. Their economic, social and political developments reflect a revolutionary shift away from a century or more of primarily national industrial development. Driven by ICT, international trade and increasingly global competition, they are being transformed into what are widely known as the *new economies*. Directly and indirectly all the trends in this Epilogue are influenced by the evolution of the new economy. Led by developments in North America and traced by American authors such as Toffler and Naisbitt, the principal industrial changes are set out in Chapter 1.

With hindsight the zeitgeist or spirit of the industrial era can be seen to be collectivist, nationalist and based on mass production, mass consumption and the development of mass tourism.

As recently as the 1950s and 1960s, although North America was always different in its commitment to the private sector, developed countries generally operated collective mass-production economic systems with nationalized industries including airlines, railways, telecommunications, nationalized broadcasting, nationalized education and health services and nationalized culture for the provision of museums, music and, sometimes, recreation. National trades unions and professional bodies represented the collective bargaining power of 'labour'. By modern standards most people lived in remarkably authoritarian, monocultural nation states that were held together by traditional patterns of family life, collective religion and hierarchical pyramid structures for management and labour that were operated in most large companies and nationalized industries and services.

With access only to mass communications, most consumers were by modern standards uneducated, 'information poor', typically working to regular patterns with limited leisure time and paid holidays. Only a small minority could afford international holiday travel. Personal mobility was limited until car ownership expanded in the last quarter century and pensioners were generally passive consumers; many, especially males, died in their sixties and seventies.

The principal characteristics of the post-industrial era present a remarkable contrast

- Mass production as a standardized process is increasingly superseded by the capability to customize products to meet individual needs. Traditional ideas of mass consumption and mass tourism are irrelevant in the new economy. Hospitality and tourism, once a very minor sector of most urban economies, is increasingly seen as a lead sector in all former industrial towns and cities such as Baltimore in the USA, Bilbao in Spain and Glasgow and Birmingham in the UK.
- The key transport infrastructure is increasingly liberalized and no longer nationalized, while the new communications infrastructure is that of global information technology provided by the private sector including cable, satellite communications, the omnipresent PCs, ISDN and mobile telephones.
- Still developing rapidly, ICT and the Internet have revolutionized the way in which governments, businesses and individuals can communicate online and with 'virtual reality'. National boundaries are increasingly irrelevant to the spread of ideas, while the provision of information and entertainment to which the whole world can gain access – if they have computer and digital television links – has effectively replaced traditional ideas of mass communications. The new generation of digitized, interactive broad bandwidth communications technology that links televisions with the Internet and new forms of mobile telephones, will bring significantly improved connectivity directly into growing numbers of homes in all countries.
- Since the 1960s, national boundaries for trade and the nationalized organization of industry have also been eroded. Nationalized industry monopolies have been split up and sold off to the private sector, while the economic collapse of communist regimes at the end of the 1980s signalled a global shift towards free-market concepts and individualism that are still working their way through. China is developing its own brand of market development and tourism expansion while in Europe the Single Market and the widening of the European Union,

together with political devolution, are further eroding legal and economic concepts of the traditional nation state.

- National trades unions and national collective bargaining have lost much of their former power and from Vietnam protests to Tiananmen Square, World Trade riots in Seattle to protests over green issues, modern society is no longer collectivist and authoritarian in its ethos but individual and 'issue based' in its attitudes. Empowered by online communication and access to litigation, groups of individuals are perfectly capable of organizing themselves when the issues are strong enough to promote action. Single issue actions organized by Internet chat rooms and bulletin boards are where new power lies, as effective campaigns by shareholders, gay rights and anti-nuclear movements have repeatedly demonstrated.

- Divorce, abortion, single-parent families, serial partnerships as distinct from 'marriage for life', immigration and widespread rejection of religion in many countries, the shift to gender equality and multiple income households and the rapid growth of multicultural societies, have all undermined the old norms and the traditional patterns of conformity established in the first half of the twentieth century. While small businesses have always been important, especially in travel and tourism, a combination of the growth of individualism, the break-up of mass production/mass-consumption attitudes, employment flexibility and redundancies, and the availability of low-cost ICT has fuelled the growth of this sector. Small businesses will be increasingly important in travel and tourism in the new millennium.

- The economic pressures that forced the sell-off of previously nationalized industries and services, and the politically acceptable limits to taxation, are also forcing governments to reduce wherever possible the involvement of the state where it is judged that the private sector can undertake the roles more efficiently. Paradoxically, at the same time as governments seek to pull back from direct involvement, the need for regulation in post-industrial societies is increasing, not least for health and safety and environmental reasons. The massive tensions between a simultaneous drive for regulation, market freedoms and a non-interventionist state are part of the political culture of post-industrial society. There is increasing focus on partnerships between private sector and public sector that are certain to become more important in the new millennium – not least in tourism where it is increasingly recognized that neither state regulation nor unlimited free-market competition can achieve sustainable long-run goals.

- Most consumers in post-industrial society are relatively highly educated, have access to infinite amounts of information in any direction they wish to pursue and have relatively long paid holidays. If pressures of work operate to restrict leisure time, many people hope to retire from full-time employment in their fifties and have the income and health to pursue active, mobile lives well into their eighties and beyond.

In post-industrial societies, travel and tourism and mobility generally are no longer a pleasure periphery but an integral and structural part of modern mobile societies that will continue to grow in line with economic progress in all parts of the world. The zeitgeist of the new age, liberated by the 'new economy', is aggressive individualism largely unconstrained by any concepts of collective restraint (other than peer group pressure). It is individualism that is driving the leading-edge companies in the process summarized in the quote at the head of this chapter. It is individualism that underlies the 'new consumer' to which marketing must respond.

2 Information communications technology

No view of the future makes sense without reference to ICT, not least because it both energizes and facilitates the *new economy* outlined above. The issues are discussed throughout this book, especially in Chapters 10, 18 and 19, and were a powerful personal insight for the principal author in revising this book for its third edition is the extent to which the developments of ICT now permeate literally every aspect of tourism marketing. As always, a little history is helpful in setting ICT in context. It is only just over thirty years ago (1967) that the first personal credit cards were issued. If not the dawn of the cashless society, the existence of the cards was a major facilitator in all the ICT processes for tourism that followed. It is only just over five years ago (1995) that the first online access and the dawn of e-commerce were possible for the public using the new Internet portals and Web browsers. Only four points need emphasis here.

First, in terms of evaluating market trends and better understanding visitors, customer databases now contain all the essential details of profile and behaviour in ways previously impossible. They are ripe for data mining as the cornerstone for competition and will improve further in the next decade. Customer knowledge is also a base for strategic business development.

Second, tourism is primarily an information industry in which ICT manipulates multimedia information in every stage of consumer decision-making. Information drives the transactions and booking process, the ticketing process, the paying and invoice process, and the check-in process for transport and accommodation. There are no tangible elements until a customer departs from home and arrives at the destination. Because tourism is an information-based industry it is one of the natural lead industries on the Internet.

Third, ICT has come to dominate the industry's thinking about the role and costs of distributing travel products in the last five years. Although the current levels of e-commerce are still relatively low except for specific sectors such as budget hotels and airlines, the evidence suggests that access or 'place', always last of the classical four Ps of the marketing mix is now becoming the first and most strategically important 'P'. Web sites already embrace two of the Ps for the customers who use them, providing twenty-four hours a day seven days a week (24/7) communication and convenience of access. It is already an essential medium for operating 'fluid' pricing (the third 'P'), and in service industries such as tourism, where advance booking is the norm for many products, it is also the ideal testing ground and monitoring programme for product innovation and development.

As Part Five of this book illustrates, plus or minus one percentage point in the average capacity utilized over as short a period as four weeks can have an immense impact on the annual 'bottom-line' profit/loss contribution of most large corporations in travel and tourism. This is the context in which the role of ICT is commercially evaluated.

Fourth, ICT provides the means whereby global corporations can be managed and developed strategically. The Internet is already fully established in the B2B context for large corporations in travel and tourism. Through destination databases and destination management systems operated by NTOs, the Internet offers the most cost-effective means for communicating with small businesses and providing assistance to them – supporting their marketing and their management needs through dedicated Web sites.

The issues to watch in the next decade are the speed at which consumers will adopt e-commerce in the different sectors of tourism, the speed and competitive edge achieved in connectivity and the speed at which principals will bypass the ambitious dot.com infomediaries of the late 1990s and create their own heavily branded Web sites for marketing direct. A related issue is the speed at which ICT will circumvent and to some extent replace costly traditional retailer distribution systems.

3 The 'new consumer' and market maturity

> As we leave the industrial era behind, we are becoming a more diverse society. The old smokestack economy serviced a mass society . . . [The new economy] services a de-massified society. Everything from lifestyles and products to technologies and the media is growing more heterogeneous. (Toffler, 1990: 167)

The 'new consumers' for tourism are simultaneously both cause and effect of the *new economy*. As every chapter of this book assesses consumer interests and changes, the characteristics set to develop further are simply noted below. They combine to add up to more sophisticated, more experienced, more demanding and often angry and litigious consumers who are unwilling to accept poor standards or poor value for money, and unforgiving of businesses that fail to deliver.

- Greater disposable income.
- Ageing combined with better health and interest in active leisure activities.
- Better-educated leading to greater interest in all forms of activity that fall into the category that Maslow (1954) dubbed 'self-actualization' in his well-known hierarchy of needs.
- More environmentally aware, through a combination of media, education and their own experience. Environment embraces social and community values as well as the physical environment and it is not a separate issue but linked to expectations of product quality.

- More travel experienced with half and more of the population making several visits away from home – for business, leisure and social reasons and for day and staying visits.
- Better informed through access to television and the Internet.
- More individual in their attitudes and approach to products – less responsive to mass product offers.
- Greater personal mobility that promotes and facilitates more active pursuits on day and staying visits to destinations.
- Less time for harassed, stressed-out people in full-time employment, memorably dubbed to be 'time poor and income rich' – a combination that promotes impulse decision-making and last minute 'instant' purchasing.

Of course, although the new consumer described above is now the majority of the population in post-industrial societies, most countries also have significant groups of the old, poor and disadvantaged, and a young so-called underclass that for a variety of reasons drops out of education provision and family life, and has few prospects of employment. Such groups have limited skills for access to the information age and are also identified as below the *digital divide*. Many of the young in this group are likely to turn to drugs and crime and are targeted by governments for support. These exceptions are important and command government attention but their existence does not alter the overall trend and its implications for tourism.

Market maturity

A market can be considered mature when the proportion (*propensity*) of a country's population wishing to participate in tourism activity is close to the maximum attainable. For all practical purposes this means around nine out of ten in a population taking a combination of day visits, short stays for all purposes and longer holidays in any year. When that point is reached the primary focus of marketing switches to:

- Fiercer competition between large branded organizations seeking to grow and fighting for market share. If organizations cannot find sufficient growth in their own markets, they are likely to look for growth through acquisition, mergers and strategic alliances.
- Promoting the year-round frequency with which the same individuals engage in multiple tourism activities in any year to develop the *intensity* of travel experience. Greater intensity generates more revenue and encourages lower-spending visitors to trade up. Greater intensity is, however, associated with shorter lengths of stay (see below) and ever-shorter lead times between booking and travel.
- Competing through improved product quality and 'excellence' targeted at selected customer segments, while holding down or reducing the perceived price to customers. This can only be achieved by a combination of economies of scale, investment in ICT, cutting

out traditional distribution costs and manipulating yield revenue programmes to maximize occupancy rates.

- Developing relationships with 'loyal' customers to sustain repeat purchasing and satisfy as many as possible of their travel interests. Finding ways to bind high-value customers to an organization by rewarding them with incentives, better service and added-value products is, not surprisingly, a primary target for marketing managers in the new century.

An unwelcome side effect of market maturity to many destinations is that more frequent/intense travel experiences often means shorter lengths of stay. An example of maturity is reflected in the international market for visits to the UK, for example, where the number of visits increased by more than 100 per cent between 1977 and 1997 – on the face of it, remarkable growth. But over the same twenty years, as length of stay fell and price competition contained cost to visitors, the actual expenditure increased by under 15 per cent in real terms (after allowing for retail price inflation). Twice as many visitors for little more economic value is a wholly unsustainable trend over the long run because it effectively doubles the use of transport and increases the per capita consumption of other resources and the output of waste.

A welcome side effect of market maturity is that a combination of more experienced and ageing customers in developed countries, comprising those who have many times 'been there and done that' and not enjoyed the stress of flying from congested airports to congested destinations, makes domestic travel look more attractive than at any time since the 1960s. Many businesses dealing mainly with the demanding end of domestic tourism markets, especially if they also target overseas visitors, have invested heavily and greatly improved the quality of their products and their marketing skills. This process will lead to a blending and levelling up of domestic and international in tourism in Europe (as already happens in USA). The new consumers in mature markets will mix and match day visits, weekend visits, short stays and longer stays – in their own countries as well as abroad. Over time, market maturity and multiple travels will close the traditional gaps between domestic and international tourism, which will become indistinguishable.

4 Culture tourism and the environment – 4 'S's to 4 'I's

It follows logically from trends in the *new economy* that more customers are moving up the classic Maslow scale toward the search for self-knowledge and self-fulfilment. Products are increasingly evaluated by the new consumer in terms of the quality of the experiences they offer. High on the list of such products are the more active rather than passive experiences now afforded by heritage, the natural and built environment, the arts and entertainment, hobbies and interests – in other words, culture. The traditional standardized package tour holidays of the 1960s and 1970s, delivering lowest cost beach-based products located in identical high-rise ugly hotels in dozens of identical coastal resorts to a 'mass market', will not die off quickly in the new millennium. Henry Ford style marketing of mass tourism products to mass markets is still to be found in most parts of the world. But its growth phase is over for mature markets in the new economy.

The modern definition of culture is wide. In many ways it reflects the quality of life of residents at a destination. It reflects the heritage and traditions of communities that created the way that places look and feel and the way that local people conduct their lives. It embraces the present as well as the past and includes the characteristics of landscape and townscape, architecture, language, the visual and performing arts, dress and social customs that are particular to places. Culture increasingly means multicultural and reflects all aspects of life, from religion and politics to the theatre and cuisine, representing all that makes places unique and of interest to visitors.

In its broad sense, the evidence reviewed by Middleton and Hawkins (1998) demonstrates that culture and environment already underlies and comprises the most powerful motivations that drives a growing part of modern international tourism.

- Much of the traditional packaged mass tourism to sunshine resorts in the 1960s to 1980s was motivated by the famous four Ss – *sun, sea, sand and sex*.
- Much of the individual independent tourism of *new consumers* will be driven by the four Is – *insights, inspiration, information and involvement*:
  - *Insights* reflect the intellectual curiosity of more educated and self-interested individuals.
  - *Inspiration* is in the mind and may be experienced as a spiritual response, for example to outstanding scenery, music or buildings.
  - *Information* supports the first two Is and its provision is a key part of stimulus to action and understanding
  - *Involvement* is a personal sense of active participation rather than passive observation, for example in sailing, golfing or walking holidays.

Sometimes known as the 'creative industries', the various forms of culture are a core part of the *new economy*. Much of it is subsidized, such as heritage and performing arts, but other parts are commercial as in films, popular music and entertainment. Much of it also serves a wider economic role as a lead sector in economic regeneration. In this context, tourism, culture, economic regeneration, quality of life for residents and environmental goals, can go hand in hand.

5 Globalization and industry polarization

The final decade of the twentieth century witnessed a seemingly inexorable shift towards marketplace dominance in many developed countries whereby a small number of very powerful large firms – usually less than six – often control half or more of the known total sales revenue in each main sector of travel and tourism. This is now characteristic of the main modes of public transport, hotels, tour operation, travel retailing, cruise ships and car rental. Some of the organizations are now global in the scale of their operations. More are likely to be in that category in the next decade.

Certainly until the 1980s there was ample evidence that diseconomies of scale tended to offset the marketing and other economies of scale achievable in operating very large, multi-site businesses. When multi-site combined with multinational, the management problems were compounded. Traditional management hierarchies were too bureaucratic and slow moving and could not exercise efficient management control. Recognition of management failure in large organizations, as well as a wish to inject greater competition and cut costs, led to the world-wide move by governments in the 1980s and 1990s to break up the traditional management structures of large, public sector monopolies.

What changed in the 1990s was the capability to deconstruct traditional bureaucratic management structures, flatten the management pyramid and create newer strategic business entities within an overall corporate structure. It was the ability to process and communicate management information online using the full range of modern ICT that provided the technological breakthrough to facilitate global growth. As noted earlier, ICT also provides the means to market large global corporations effectively. ICT made possible a more entrepreneurial style of management with leaner corporate headquarters. Successful global companies are now able to exploit benefits of scale arising from international branding, customer databases, staff skills and training, access to investment funding, balanced portfolio of businesses and cross-selling opportunities.

While the trend to large scale seems unlikely to diminish in the next decade, those interested in the future should also be aware of the countervailing power of the remarkable number of very small businesses in travel and tourism. The available evidence indicates that there were some 2.7 million SMEs in European tourism, of which the overwhelming bulk (92 per cent) were so called micro-operators with less than ten employees (Middleton, 1998). The micros outweigh the big corporations by at least 1000:1.

Around the world, tourism in the new millennium can be seen to be polarizing around the interests of a few dozen global and large international businesses on the one hand, and millions of micro-businesses on the other hand. As Naisbitt (1994) pointed out, this process contains a fascinating paradox.

On the face of it the large businesses have all the advantages. On the ground, at the destinations visited by tourists, the evidence suggests otherwise. The capability of branded airlines and other transport operators to move millions quickly, efficiently and at low cost is not in question; nor is the ability of branded accommodation chains to cater efficiently for travellers and offer good value. But hardly anyone travels economy class in public transport for the pleasure of it and accommodation is not the motivation for travel for the great majority of visitors. What is provided on the ground – the primary tourism experiences at the destination – is mostly in the hands of small, unbranded local businesses. For most visitors, what they receive of an encounter with the host community and its environment is not provided by local residents but by small businesses, such as pubs, cafés, restaurants, taxis, local attractions, tourist guides, guesthouses, farmhouses and so on. Ultimately and ironically, the long-run future of big businesses in mature markets is heavily dependent on the service delivery capabilities of small businesses over which they have no control.

At their best, small businesses provide all that is excellent and most sustainable in local tourism. They have personality and individuality and are literally unique. Many reflect the local sense of place and culture, identified earlier as of growing importance. At their worst, however, and there are millions of them in total, they represent all that is worst in low-quality visitor experiences and collectively they can destroy an environment by their short-term survival decisions. Looking ahead, systems are needed to support and facilitate SMEs and to connect the interests of the larger global players with the small ones to underpin sustainable tourism at the destination. The systems, for example development of current destination databases, will have to provide quality assurance for the competent and a means of deterring the bad small businesses that undermine a destination's long-run interests.

Traditionally ICT has mainly helped the larger players get larger and compete more aggressively. For the first time ever, ICT is now available to help the smallest of enterprises and begin to even up the balance of competitive advantage between large and small. However hard they try, global corporations and their standardized design and people processes will always be somewhat bland and synthetic and lack meaning except at the very top end of expenditure. The real personality of smaller businesses provides them with an unshakable advantage over the global players that is likely to become more important as they learn to communicate effectively and exploit their potential.

6 More responsible tourism marketing for the twenty-first century

The world's largest industry is not the world's largest polluter. That dubious title probably goes to modern agriculture. But the global scale and growth potential of leisure tourism activity with its particular focus on attractive, usually fragile environments, means that future marketing will have to become far more concerned with sustainable development than hitherto.

Throughout the period of rapid expansion of tourism between the 1960s and 1990s, the great majority of travel and tourism businesses expanded their operations and utilized the environment generally as a 'free resource' for commercial purposes. They were not the only exploiter by any means but most showed little awareness or concern for their impact on destinations. Broadly defined, 'environment' embraces the culture and lifestyle of residents at destinations, as noted earlier. They can no longer be taken for granted.

The results of irresponsible tourism management, ignorance and the failure of destination management in the last quarter of a century are now all too visible. The world has numerous areas of cumulative environmental degradation in which development for tourism played an important, sometimes a leading, part. Examples can be found in the Alpine region of Europe as a result of overintensive skiing, along the Mediterranean littoral as a result of over development of beach resorts, in parts of the Hawaiian Islands, on the Gold Coast in Australia and in parts of Nepal and Indonesia. There is no shortage of examples and it now appears certain that recognition of environmental constraints and the use of marketing methods to achieve sustainable growth will feature much more strongly in tourism marketing decisions in the new millennium (Middleton and Hawkins, 1998).

For travel and tourism, as for all forms of business, the major issues of the next decade and beyond will revolve around defining and attempting to balance the often competing needs of:

Economy, Ecology, Equity – globally.

Economy in this context means a sustainable livelihood and long-term viability of the residents of visited destinations. *Ecology* means the balance involved in sustaining the natural environment that provides the core motivation for much of leisure tourism. *Equity* means a fairer distribution of the use of the Earth's resources between developed and developing countries and consideration for the needs of present and future generations.

In terms of more responsible marketing, travel and tourism has some key advantages. There is no other major global industry that so clearly has a long-run vested interest in maintaining healthy environments and in protecting them from over exploitation. There is no other industry with such widespread influence that covers rural, mountain, coastal and urban areas around the world. No other industry is better placed to communicate with its customers and to influence them at times when they are most likely to be receptive to environment messages – to raise their awareness and modify their behaviour.

The quality expectations of 'new consumers' includes the destination environment and commercial self-interest requires improved management of tourism operations now, in order to safeguard future business and achieve more sustainable development and growth.

7 Destination management issues and developments (limits to growth imposed by environmental concerns)

The second edition of this book noted that 'the major implication of the shift to more responsible tourism is that the visitor-management techniques currently practised at destinations are due for radical overhaul and development' (Middleton, 1994b: 368). Six years on that is still the case although the issues, at least, are better understood and there is some progress at destinations, for example through the International Council for Local Environment Initiatives and locally in several countries. The ineffectiveness of destination management practised at most designated World Heritage Sites is, however, a sad but accurate indicator that management issues are not yet taken seriously in practice. Internationally we are witnessing a massive outpouring of beautifully crafted political sentiments and exhortations to 'wise growth' but overall there still appears to be remarkably little evidence of significant progress in the one area that is vital to the more sustainable future of tourism.

Inevitably, the 'new consumer' interest in outdoor interests such as walking, surfing, golfing, equestrian, water-based activities, nature-watching and so on, will increase the pressure on relatively fragile areas least able to cope with visitor numbers. The interest in cultural activity will have much the same effect. One can safely predict that the need for better destination management techniques will grow.

With hindsight, in a young, rapidly growing, fundamentally rootless tourism industry strongly backed by eager national and local governments, one should not be surprised that mistakes were, and continue to be, made. Tourism has gone through its 'Klondike Gold Rush era' and in the process created hundreds of over-intensively developed sun-belt resorts now losing their attraction to 'new tourism'.

But hindsight reveals also that tourism has contributed massively to the regeneration of towns and cities and created numerous enclosed destinations such as those developed by the Disney Corporation, Center Parcs, most Club Medierannée villages, Sandals in the Caribbean, some ski resorts, many holiday villages and timeshare resorts. The cruise ship industry to all intents and purposes builds floating, mobile self-contained resorts that follow exactly the same destination management principles.

There are, therefore two very different models for visitor management that represent two ends of the effective destination management scale:

- The enclosed destination under single, generally private sector management, usually with defined boundaries and gated points of access. Marketing orientation is normal.
- The traditional 'open' destination in which visitors and residents mingle, ownership and management is in multiple hands and local government controlled by elected politicians and officials is responsible for planning and regulation. A supply-side planning orientation is normal.

The value of the enclosed destination model is the total control of product design, investment and management, organized to deliver the satisfactions that targeted customer segments seek. The model implies fully engineered destinations in which all aspects are under one management control. The notion of engineering is a wholly appropriate approach to minimizing any damage to the surrounding environment, and in many cases to enhance it. The planned use of landscaping can promote biodiversity, the use of new biological waste-water treatments can avoid traditional pollution, energy conservation can be optimized and, through programmes for targeted reduction and recycling of ancillary products, the consumption of resources per capita can be reduced. Most self-contained resorts are designed to be traffic-free and provide an ideal platform for the promotion of appropriate environmental messages.

The management of visitors in successful enclosed resorts is based on an effective co-ordination of supply-side and demand-side controls and influences. It is, by definition, information based. However 'sustainability' for tourism developments is defined in the new millennium, it is most likely to be delivered effectively in controlled environments. In such places the tourism impacts are readily identifiable and *measurable*. Proven techniques, internationally developed and used, make it possible to change the character of existing destinations and the products they provide, and therefore to adapt them to consumer expectations and trends. Planned refurbishment and new product development can avoid the traditional decline phase of destination life cycle analysis, exactly as happens in other product fields. A commitment to marketing principles backed by investment lies at the heart of effective destination management.

Compared with the traditional 'open' visitor destinations model, enclosed resorts have a massive advantage. Fortunately the destination management methods are transferable although co-ordination will never be easy given multiple management responsibility. In particular the critical lack of investment in traditional destinations in the management information systems that enclosed resorts take as the starting point for competition will have to be addressed. In 1999 the principal author undertook a study for the European Environment Agency into the indicators available to measure more sustainable tourism. At that time, across Europe, up-to-date usable management information at destination level just did not exist.

It is an interesting speculation that the Disney parks and Center Parcs of the 1990s were not really new concepts at all but the logical successors of the original purpose-built seaside resorts developed in the USA and Europe over a century earlier. Over the decades the old resorts gradually lost their original integrity of design and product quality, and therefore their appeal to visitors. Their management needs were subsumed within local government structures that took tourism demand for granted. Tourism changed and most old resorts failed to notice until it was too late. Those that can be refurbished should look to their twenty-first century successors to find the visitor management methods essential to accompany redevelopment – a form of technology transfer in reverse.

There are some successful public/private sector hybrid destination management models, such as Las Vegas, which is not an enclosed destination but links a combination of strong-willed and determined local government working with powerful local commercial interests. Another hybrid approach that points the way ahead can be seen in the Balearics case study in Part Six of the book.

Harnessing the global power of marketing

To conclude, in strategic terms there are a number of balancing acts or trade-offs to be undertaken in global tourism in the new millennium.

Seven of them, all related to *new tourism's* role in the *new economy* are noted below:

Economic values	balanced against	Environmental values
Corporate profit	balanced against	Corporate responsibility
Global corporations (thinking local)	balanced against	Small businesses (thinking global)
Quantity/price driven	balanced against	Quality/value driven
Competition driven	balanced against	Collaboration led
Mass production (old economy)	balanced against	Customization for individuals (new economy)
Short-term values (today's business)	balanced against	Strategic long-term positions (tomorrow's business)

Marketing, as it is explained in this book, has a principal management role to play in achieving each of those strategic trade-offs. In one dimension, marketing is a co-ordinated set of levers or tools designed to match the supply of products to current and future demand. In that sense it is the most honed and proven set of skills available in free societies that encourage competition. Marketing has a century of development thinking and practice behind it and one can claim that services marketing came of age in the 1990s.

In a broader management context, marketing contributes the consumer perspective and much of the dynamic energy that makes if possible for successful businesses proactively to innovate and 'overturn the present industry order, challenge "accepted practice", redraw segment boundaries, set new price-performance expectations and re-invent the product or service concept' (see the Hamel and Prahalad quote at the head of this Epilogue).

Strategically, marketing can be identified as the *lingua franca* of the fascinating, volatile and increasingly global business of the *world's largest industry*. Driven increasingly by ICT, which can be harnessed to achieve goals, marketing principles and practice are relevant in all parts of the world. Marketing is *not* a corporate goal. It is an approach to the conduct of business in the public and not-for-profit sectors as well as in the private sector, and a management means to achieve organizational goals.

Tactically, to repeat a quote used in the first edition of this book and still as relevant: *'Excellence is a game of inches, or millimetres. No one act is, per se, clinching. But a thousand things . . . each done a tiny bit better, do add up to memorable responsiveness and distinction . . . and loyalty . . . and slightly higher margins'* (Peters and Austin, 1986: 46).

The quote is a useful reminder that quality of service product delivery is always a combination of multiple actions taken by many people. Whatever skills marketing managers may possess, they will achieve little if the operations and other key divisions of an organization are not performing their part. Marketing is not effective unless it is integrated within the management structure of an organization from the boardroom down. It is implicit that service excellence can be defined, targeted, measured and improved. It is the responsibility of marketing to undertake and communicate those tasks within the organization. By linking memorable responsiveness to profit margins, the quotation stresses that excellence is a customer-orientated approach to business, having particular regard to repeat custom – and the bottom line.

We believe the future lies partly with private sector willingness to recognize its role in sustainable tourism growth and act accordingly in its own long-run self-interest. It lies equally with the political will of governments at all levels to develop and support private/public sector destination partnerships that can achieve better destination management. Neither party is likely to move willingly in directions that compromise their options, but both will in the end be influenced by the demands and expectations of consumers/voters. The trends of the 'new economy' and the demands of 'new consumers', combined with better media coverage and access to information, suggest a more responsible approach to the future of global tourism and destination management in its mature market phase.

It is an optimistic view for the new century, recognizing that marketing knowledge and skills will be at the forefront of developments.

References and select bibliography

Abell, D. F. and Hammond, J. S. (1979). *Strategic Market Planning*. Prentice-Hall.

Adcock, D., Bradfield, R., Halborg, A. and Ross, C. (1997). *Marketing Principles and Practice*. 3rd edn, Financial Times Management.

Alderson, W. (1971). The analytical framework for marketing. In *Modern Marketing Management* (R. J. Lawrence and M. J. Thomas, eds), Penguin.

Allport, G. W. (1935). In *Handbook of Social Psychology* (C. Murchison, ed.), Clark University Press.

Ansoff, H. I. (1987). *Corporate Strategy*. Revd edn, Penguin.

Argenti, J. (1980). *Practical Corporate Planning*. George Allen and Unwin.

Baker, M. J. (1979). *Marketing: An Introductory Text*. 4th edn, Macmillan.

Baker, M. J. (1996). *Marketing: An Introductory Text*. 6th edn, Macmillan.

Baker, M. J. (2000). *Marketing Strategy and Management*. 3rd edn, Macmillan.

Barker, J. A. (1992). *Future Edge: Discovering the New Paradigms of Success*. Morrow.

Bartels, R. (1976). *The History of Marketing Thought*. 2nd edn, Grid.

Bateson, J. E. G. (1995). *Managing Services Marketing: Text and Readings*. Dryden Press

Boyd, H. W. and Larreche, J. C. (1982). The foundations of marketing strategy. In *Strategic Planning Decisions: A Reader* (K. K. Cox and V. J. McGinnis, eds), pp. 3–17, Prentice-Hall.

Bitner, M. J., Booms, B. H. and Tetrealt, M. S. (1995). 'The service encounter', in J. E. G. Bateson (ed.), *Managing Services Marketing: Text and Readings*. 3rd edn, Dryden Press.

Bottomley Renshaw, M. (1992). *The Travel Agent*. Business Education.

Brassington, F. and Pettit, S. (2000). *Principles of Marketing*. 2nd edn, Prentice-Hall.

Brent Ritchie, J. R. and Goeldner, C. R. (eds) (1986). *Travel, Tourism and Hospitality Research: A Handbook for Managers and Researchers*. Wiley.

Broadbent, S. (1984). *Spending Advertising Money*. 4th edn, Business Books.

Burkart, A. J. and Medlik, S. (1981). *Tourism: Past, Present and Future*. 2nd edn, Heinemann.

Buttle, F. (2001). The CRM value chain. *Marketing Business*, **96**, February, 52–55.

Chernatony, L. de and McDonald, M. H. B. (1992). *Creating Powerful Brands*. Butterworth-Heinemann.

Chernatony, L. de and McWilliam, G. (1990). Appreciating brands as assets through using a two-dimensional model. *International Journal of Advertising*, **9**: 111–19.

Chisnall, P. M. (1985). *Marketing: A Behavioural Analysis*. 2nd edn, McGraw-Hill.

Chisnall, P.M. (1994). *Consumer Behaviour*. 3rd edn, McGraw-Hill.

Cooper, C., Fletcher, J., Gilbert, D. and Wanhill, S. (1998). *Tourism Principles and Practice*. 2nd edn, Pitman.

Cossons, N. (1985). Making museums market orientated. In *Museums Are for People* (Scottish Museums Council) HMSO.

Crouch, S. and Housden, M. (1996). *Market Research for Managers*. 2nd edn, Butterworth-Heinemann.

Davidson, J. H. (1975). *Offensive Marketing*. Penguin. (New edn, 1987.)

Davidson, J. H. (1997). *Even More Offensive Marketing*. Penguin.

Davies, A. H. T. (1990). Strategic planning in the Thomas Cook Group. In *The Manager's Casebook of Business Strategy* (B. Taylor and J. Harrison, eds), Heinemann.

Doganis, R. (1991). *Flying Off Course*. 2nd edn, Routledge.

Doyle, P. (1989). Building successful brands: the strategic options. *Journal of Marketing Management*, **5** (1): 77–95.

Economist Intelligence Unit (1992). *The Tourism Industry and the Environment*. Special Report No. 2453, EIU.

Engel, J. F. and Miniard, P. W. (1992). *Consumer Behaviour*. 7th edn, Dryden International.

Financial Times (1998). *Distribution Technology in the Travel Industry*. Financial Times (Retail and Consumer).

Fletcher, K., Wheeler, C. and Wright, J. (1990). The role and status of UK database marketing. *Quarterly Review of Marketing*, **16** (1), October, 7–14.

Gater, C. (1986). Database key to a direct hit. *Marketing,* 2 October: 41–2.

Gee, C. Y., Choy, D. J. L. and Makens, J. C. (1997). *The Travel Industry.* 3rd edn, Van Nostrand Reinhold.

Goeldner, C. R. (2000). *Tourism Principles, Practices, Philosophies.* 8th edn, Wiley.

Greene, M. (1987). *Marketing Hotels and Restaurants into the 90s.* 2nd edn, Heinemann.

Hamel, G. and Prahalad, C. K. (1994). *Competing for the Future.* Harvard Business School Press.

Hanlon, P. (1999). *Global Airlines: Competition in a Transnational Industry.* 2nd edn, Butterworth-Heinemann.

Hart, N. A. (1995). *The Practice of Advertising.* 4th edn, Butterworth-Heinemann.

Hart, N. A. and Stapleton, J. (1996). *The CIM Marketing Dictionary.* 5th edn, Butterworth-Heinemann.

Heath, E. and Wall, G. (1992). *Marketing Tourism Destinations: A Strategic Planning Approach.* Wiley.

Heneghan, P. (1976). *Resource Allocation in Tourism Marketing.* Tourism International Press.

Hoffman, K. D. and Bateson, J. E. G. (1997). *Essentials of Services Marketing.* Dryden Press.

Holloway, J. C. (1985). *The Business of Tourism.* 2nd edn, Macdonald and Evans. (3rd edn, 1992, Pitman.)

Horwath Consulting (2000). *Worldwide Hotel Industry.* Annual report, Horwath Consulting.

Howard, J. A. and Sheth, J. N. A theory of buyer behaviour. (1967), reproduced in *Marketing Classics* (B. M. Enis and K. K. Cox, eds), 3rd edn, 1977, pp. 161–85, Allyn and Bacon.

Hussey, D. E. (1979). *Introducing Corporate Planning.* 2nd edn, Pergamon Press.

International Passenger Survey (IPS) (annual) *Travel Trends.* Reports on the International Passenger Survey – a year-round survey of passengers arriving in and departing from the UK, conducted for the UK government. The Stationery Office.

Jefferson, A. and Lickorish, L. J. (1991). *Marketing Tourism: A Practical Guide.* 2nd edn, Longman.

Jobber, D. (1998). *Principles and Practice of Marketing.* 2nd edn, McGraw-Hill.

Kotler, P. (1976). *Marketing Management: Analysis, Planning, Implementation and Control.* 3rd edn, Prentice-Hall.

Kotler, P. (1991). *Marketing Management: Analysis, Planning, Implementation and Control.* 7th edn, Prentice-Hall.

Kotler, P. and Armstrong, G. (1999). *Principles of Marketing.* 8th edn, Prentice-Hall.

Krippendorf, J. (1971). *Marketing et Tourisme.* Lang and Cie.

Krippendorf, J. (1987). *The Holiday Makers.* Heinemann.

Leppard, J. W. and McDonald, H. B. (1991). Marketing planning and corporate culture. *Journal of Marketing Management,* **7** (3), July, 213–35.

Levitt, T. (1960). Marketing myopia. *Harvard Business Review*, **38**, July/August.

Levitt, T. (1974). Improving sales through product augmentation. In *Analytical Marketing Management* (P. Doyle et al., eds), p. 10, Harper and Row.

Levitt, T. (1981). Marketing intangible products and product intangibles. *Harvard Business Review*, May/June: 37–44.

Lewis, R. C., Chambers, R. E. and Chacko, H. E. (1995). *Marketing Leadership in Hospitality: Foundations and Practices*. 2nd edn, Van Nostrand Reinhold.

Lodge, D. (1991). *Paradise News*. Secker and Warburg.

Lovelock, C. H. and Wright, L. (1998). *Principles of Services Marketing and Management*. Prentice-Hall.

Luck, D. J. et al. (1970). *Marketing Research*. 3rd edn, Prentice-Hall.

Maas, J. (1980). Better brochures for the money. *Cornell Hotel and Restaurant Administration Quarterly*, **20** (4).

Maslow, A. (1954). *Motivation and Personality*. Harper and Row.

McCarthy, E. J. (1981). *Basic Marketing, A Managerial Approach*. 7th edn, Irwin.

McDonald, M. H. B. (1995). *Marketing Plans*. 3rd edn, Butterworth-Heinemann.

McIntosh, R. W. (1972). *Tourism: Principles, Practices, Philosophies*. Wiley.

Medlik, S. (1996). *Dictionary of Travel, Tourism and Hospitality*. 2nd edn, Butterworth-Heinemann.

Medlik, S. (1999). *The Business of Hotels*. 4th edn, Butterworth-Heinemann.

Medlik, S. and Middleton, V. T. C. (1973). Product formulation in tourism. *Tourism and Marketing*, **13**.

Michels, D. (1997). Hotel Marketing Association Annual Lecture (unpublished), delivered in London, 22 May, Chartered Institute of Marketing, Maidenhead.

Middleton, V. T. C. (1979). Tourism marketing: product implications. *International Tourism Quarterly*, (3).

Middleton, V. T. C. (1980). The marketing implications of direct selling. *International Tourism Quarterly*, (2).

Middleton, V. T. C. (1983a). Product marketing: goods and services compared. *Quarterly Review of Marketing*, **8** (4), July.

Middleton, V. T. C. (1989). Marketing the margin. *Quarterly Review of Marketing*, **14** (2), January: 14–17.

Middleton, V. T. C. (1991). Whither the package tour. *Tourism Management*, **12** (3), September: 185–92.

Middleton, V. T. C. (1994a). The tourism product. In *Tourism Marketing and Management Handbook* (S. F. Witt and L. Moutinho, eds), 2nd edn, Prentice-Hall.

Middleton, V. T. C. (1994b). *Marketing in Travel and Tourism*. 2nd edn, Butterworth-Heinemann.

Middleton, V. T. C. (1997). Fouling the nest: environmental impact of small businesses. *Insights*, November, English Tourist Board.

Middleton, V. T. C. (1998a). *New Visions for UK Museums in the 21st Century*. Association of Independent Museums.

Middleton, V. T. C (1998b). SMEs in European tourism: the context and a proposed framework for European action. *Revue de Tourisme*, (4).

Middleton, V. T. C. and Hawkins, R. (1998). *Sustainable Tourism: A Marketing Perspective*. Butterworth-Heinemann.

Millington, K. and Cleverdon, R. (1999). National tourist offices: their budgets and performance. *Insights*, September, English Tourist Council.

Morgan, N. and Pritchard, A. (2000). *Marketing Communications: An Integrated Approach*. Butterworth-Heinemann.

Morrison, A. M. (1989). *Hospitality and Travel Marketing*. Delmar.

Murphy, P. E. (1985). *Tourism: A Community Approach*. Methuen.

O'Connor, P. (1999). *Electronic Distribution in Tourism and Hospitality*. CAB International.

Ogilvy, D. (1983). *Ogilvy on Advertising*. Pan.

Ohmae, K. (1983). *The Mind of the Strategist*. Penguin.

Peters, R. and Austin, N. (1986). *A Passion for Excellence*. Fontana. (Follow-up to R. Peters and R. H. Waterman, 1982, *In Search of Excellence*).

Pine, B. J. and Gilmore, J. H. (1999). *The Experience Economy*. Harvard Business School Press.

Poon, A. (1993). *Tourism Technology and Competitive Strategies*. CAB International.

Porter, M. E. (1998). *Competitive Strategy: Techniques for Analysing Industries and Competitors*. New edn (with new introduction), Free Press.

Porter, M. E. (1995). *Competitive Advantage: Creating and Sustaining Superior Performance*. Free Press.

Rathmell, J. M. (1974). *Marketing in the Service Sector*. Winthrop.

Rooij, N. de (1986). Mature market in Europe. *Travel and Tourism Analyst*, May.

Sasser, W. E., Olsen, P. R. and Wyckoff, D. D. (1978). *Management of Service Operations*. Allyn and Bacon.

Seibert, J. C. (1973). *Concepts of Marketing Management*. Harper and Row.

Shamir, B. (1995). Between service and servility. In *Managing Services Marketing: Text and Readings* (J. E. G. Bateson), Dryden Press.

Shaw, S. (1999). *Air Transport: A Marketing Perspective*. 4th edn, Pitman.

Shaw, S. and Stone, M. (1987). *Database Marketing*. Gower.

Shostack, G. L. (1977). Breaking free from product marketing. *Journal of Marketing*, **41**, April.

Shostack, G. L. (1984). Designing services that deliver. *Harvard Business Review*, January–February.

Smith, P. R. (1998). *Marketing Communications: An Integrated Approach*. 2nd edn, Kogan Page.

Smith, V. (1977). *Hosts and Guests: The Anthropology of Tourism*. University of Pennsylvania Press.

Stanton, W. J. (1981). *Fundamentals of Marketing*. 6th edn, McGraw-Hill.

Swinglehurst, E. (1982). *Cook's Tours: The Study of Popular Travel*. Blandford Press.

Toffler, A. (1990). *Power Shift*. Bantam.

The Tourism Society (1979). *Handbook and Members List*. The Tourism Society.

Wheatcroft, S. (1992). The world airline industry in 2000. *Travel and Tourism Analyst*, (3).

Witt, S. and Moutinho, L. (eds) (1994). *Tourism Marketing and Management Handbook*. 2nd edn, Prentice-Hall.

World Tourism Organization (WTO) (1992). *Presentation on Tourism Trends to 2000 and Beyond*. WTO.

World Tourism Organization (WTO) (1997). *Tourism 20:20 Vision*. Executive summary, WTO.

World Tourism Organization (WTO) (1999a). *Changes in Leisure Time*. WTO.

World Tourism Organization Business Council (1999b). *Marketing Tourism Destinations Online*. WTO.

World Travel and Tourism Council (1992). *Travel and Tourism: The World's Largest Industry*. WTTC.

Wright, L. T. and Crimp, M. (2000). *The Marketing Research Process*. 5th edn, Financial Times/Prentice-Hall.

Zeithaml, V. A., and Bitner, M. J. (1996). *Services Marketing*. McGraw-Hill.

Index